Library of
Davidson College

CHILDREN'S LANGUAGE

CONTRIBUTORS

ELIZABETH BATES
University of California, San Diego, California

INGE BRETHERTON
University of Colorado, Fort Collins, Colorado

BARBARA K. CAPARULO
Yale University, New Haven, Connecticut

DONALD J. COHEN
Yale University, New Haven, Connecticut

CHARLES A. FERGUSON
Stanford University, Stanford, California

INA FITZHENRY-COOR
University of Vermont, Burlington, Vermont

DAVID C. HOWELL
University of Vermont, Burlington, Vermont

NANCY S. JOHNSON
State University of New York, Buffalo, New York

MARCEL KINSBOURNE
University of Toronto, Toronto, Ontario, Canada

HENRIETTA LEMPERT
University of Toronto, Toronto, Ontario, Canada

ELIZABETH A. LEVIN
University of Waterloo, Waterloo, Ontario, Canada

MARLYS A. MACKEN
Stanford University, Stanford, California

MADELINE M. MAXWELL
University of Texas, Austin, Texas

STEPHANIE H. McCONAUGHY
University of Vermont, Burlington, Vermont

SANDRA McNEW
University of Colorado, Boulder, Colorado

ELZA M. STELLA-PROROK
Federal University of Sao Carlos, Sao Carlos, Brasil

KENNETH H. RUBIN
University of Waterloo, Waterloo, Ontario, Canada

JACQUELINE SACHS
University of Connecticut, Storrs, Connecticut

CECILIA SHORE
Miami University, Oxford, Ohio

CATHERINE E. SNOW
Harvard University, Cambridge, Massachusetts

CHILDREN'S LANGUAGE

Volume 4

Edited by
Keith E. Nelson
The Pennsylvania State University

LAWRENCE ERLBAUM ASSOCIATES, PUBLISHERS
1983   Hillsdale, New Jersey   London

Copyright © 1983 by Lawrence Erlbaum Associates, Inc.
 All rights reserved. No part of this book may be reproduced in
 any form, by photostat, microform, retrieval system, or any other
 means, without the prior written permission of the publisher.

Lawrence Erlbaum Associates, Inc., Publishers
365 Broadway
Hillsdale, New Jersey 07642

Library of Congress Catalog Card Number: 78-646625

ISBN: 0-89859-272-0

Printed in the United States of America
10 9 8 7 6 5 4 3 2 1

Contents

Preface   IX

1. **Talking About the There and Then: The Emergence of Displaced Reference in Parent–Child Discourse**
   Jacqueline Sachs   1
   Goals and Methods   3
   Spatial Displacement   4
   Temporal Displacement   12
   Conclusions   20

2. **Saying It Again: The Role of Expanded and Deferred Imitations in Language Acquisition**
   Catherine E. Snow   29
   Expanded Imitations   32
   Deferred Imitations   38
   Deferred Imitations in a Book-Reading Routine   47
   Conclusion   54

3. **Names, Gestures, and Objects: Symbolization in Infancy and Aphasia**
   Elizabeth Bates, Inge Bretherton, Cecilia Shore, and Sandra McNew   59
   The Onset of Vocal Symbols   62
   The Onset of Gestural Symbols   66
   Language Versus Gesture: Some A Priori Differences   75
   Some Empirical Differences Between
         Language and Gesture   79
   Names, Gestures, and Objects in Aphasia   93
   Towards a Model for the Genesis of Names   109

4. **Perceptual Constraints on the Use of Language by Young Children**
   Henrietta Lempert and Marcel Kinsbourne   125
   What Determines Word Choice?   126
   Why Only One Word At A Time?   127
   Representation As Imagery   128
   Semantic Versus Syntactic Approaches To Word Order   129
   Interaction Between Word Order and Animacy Status and Related Factors   131
   "Salience" As Substrate for Early Syntax   132
   Acquisition of Passive Sentences: The Role of Salience   135
   The Role of Action in Passive Sentence Comprehension   138
   The Affect of Action and State Verbs on Noun Recall   140
   How Do Young Children Represent Words?   144
   Why are Action and Function Central?   145
   Young Children's Order Approaches   146
   Changes in Sentence Processing Approaches   149
   Conclusions   150
   Summary   151

5. **Getting Others to Do What You Want Them to Do: Development of Children's Requestive Strategies**
   Elizabeth A. Levin and Kenneth H. Rubin   157
   Piaget and the Concept of Egocentrism   158
   Egocentrism: A Useful Explanatory Construct?   160
   Naturalistic Studies of Communicative Interaction   162
   The Speech Act Approach   164
   Study I: The Development of Requestive Skills   167
   Study II: The Relationship Between Perspective-Taking and Requestive Skills   177
   General Discussion   182

6. **Mother–Child Language in the Natural Environment**
   Elza M. Stella-Prorok   187
   Temporal Patterns in Mother–Child Dialogue: The Predominance of the Alternating Vocalizing Pattern   189
   Developmental Trends in the Interactive Pattern   193
   Age Three: The End of a Developmental Cycle?   195
   The Elocution of Silence: Maternal Sensitivity to the Transitions in the Child's Speech System   197
   Changes in the Temporal Pattern of M-C-M Dialogue As A Compelling Force for Language Development   200

Maternal Approval Versus Maternal Selectiveness   202
Children's Differential Responsiveness   206
Changes in the Interactive Components of the
    Mother–Child Speech System   211
Two-Year-Olds' Differential Responsiveness to Replies
    of Varying Complexity   217
Summary and Conclusions   224

7. **The Role of Play in Phonological Development**
   Charles A. Ferguson and Marlys A. Macken   **231**
   Introduction   231
   Issues   234
   Babbling   235
   Expressive Sound Play   240
   Language Games   246
   Conclusions   250

8. **Cognitive Aspects of Phonological Development:
   Model, Evidence, and Issues**
   Marlys A. Macken and Charles A. Ferguson   **256**
   Introduction   255
   Selectiveness   260
   Creativity   261
   Hypothesis Formation   263
   Discussion: Toward a Cognitive Model   273
   Summary   277

9. **Language Acquisition in a Deaf Child of Deaf Parents:
   Speech, Sign Variations, and Print Variations**
   Madeline M. Maxwell   **283**
   Language Acquisition of the Signing Child   284
   Educators' Concerns With the Variety of
       Deaf Children's Language   285
   Background of the Child   288
   Overview of the Developmental Language Records   289
   ASL Onset Before Emergence of the Other
       Language Varieties   290
   Learning Differentiating Multiple Language Varieties   291
   Strengthening Language Awareness at 49–55 Months   299
   Connecting the Full Range of Language Varieties
       by 65 Months   302
   Separation Achieved: Language At 75 Months   304
   Summary   305

10. **What Do You Do if You Can't Tell the Whole Story?
    The Development of Summarization Skills**
    Nancy S. Johnson — 315
    Models of Story Structure   316
    The Development of Summarization Skills   330
    Children's Summarization: An Exploratory Study   346
    Children's Summarization: General Discussion   372
    Summarization as a Complex Process   377
    Appendix A: Sample Summary of Goldilocks
        and the Three Bears   379

11. **Developmental Differences in Schemata for
    Story Comprehension**
    *Stephanie H. McConaughy, Ina Fitzhenry-Coor, and
    David C. Howell* — 385
    Introduction   385
    Method   396
    Results   398
    Discussion   409

12. **Developmental Language Studies in the Neuropsychiatric
    Disorders of Childhood**
    Barbara K. Caparulo and Donald J. Cohen — 423
    Introduction   423
    Primary Autism: Historical, Theoretical, and
        Clinical Perspectives   428
    Cognitive and Linguistic Performance in High
        Functioning Autistic Persons   436
    The Ontogenesis of Linguistic and Communicative
        Competence   445
    Brain Neuromaturation and Language   452
    Some Conclusions About Autism and Normal
        Language Acquisition   454

Author Index

Subject Index

Preface

I play Haydn after a black day
and feel a simple warmth in my hands.

The keys are willing. Soft hammers strike.
The resonance green, lively and calm.

The music says freedom exists
and someone doesn't pay the emperor tax.

I push down my hands in my Haydn pockets
and imitate a person looking on the world calmly.

I hoist the Haydnflag—it signifies:
"We don't give in. But want peace."

The music is a glass-house on the slope
where the stones fly, the stones roll.

And the stones roll right through
but each pane stays whole.

Tomas Transtömer (Allegro)*

This series, *Children's Language,* reflects the conviction that extensive work on entirely new fronts along with a great deal of reinterpretation of old-front data will be necessary before any persuasive and truly orderly account of language

---

*The poem, *Allegro,* is part of the collection, *Modern Swedish Poetry in Translation,* edited by Gunnar Harding and Anselm Hollo and published by University of Minnesota Press, Minneapolis, 1979.

development can be assembled. For all volumes in the series there is a common scheme of operation with two tactics. First, to give authors sufficient planning time and freedom to arrive at a chapter-length account of their area of thinking which vividly shows both the progress and the problems in that area, with the author of each chapter free to find a workable proportion of new experimental contributions, review, and theory. This flexible approach means that formats vary. It also insures that none of the chapters are simply reviews, and that none of the volumes are "handbooks" or "reviews" or introductory texts. Rather the volumes try to capture the excitement and complexity of thinking and research at the growing, advancing edges of this broad field of children's language. The second tactic concerns the selection of topics for each volume. Again eschewing the general handbook or review approach there is no stress placed on representing all of the facets of children's language in one volume. The chapters placed within one volume are chosen because there are some common themes that tie subsets of them together and because each chapter is "due" in the following sense—the author's theoretical and experimental program has come to a point where a systematic account will be stimulating and perhaps catalytic to the work of other investigators. It is hoped that the present volume will provide a little warmth and excitement for psychologists and linguists. Structures about language and thought and children as employed in certain other fields may well be shaken and stimulated too—particularly in education, sociology, anthropology, literature, and language remediation.

How the child moves from "here and now" reference in speech to talk about objects and people and events "displaced" in various ways is the topic of Chapter 1. Sachs shows that some of the first references to temporarily missing people emerge within familiar conversational routines. For example, at 22 months we see the sequence "Where's Daddy?" (Child), "Daddy is working." (Adult), but by 23 months the child has learned something more about both the routine and displacement—"Where's Daddy? Daddy's in work?" (Child), "Daddy's at work, honey." (Adult). Similar shared routines and meanings are important as the child learns to mark time displacements, future and past. If we compare the expanding scope and complexity of the child's conversations to a developing piece of music, the "glass-house on the slope" in Transtömer's poem may be a valuable point of focus. Thoughts and shared meanings and the conversational "stones" to go with them begin, with the child's development between 1½ and 3½ years, to roll down the slope, to kick off other flying "stones." The adult can and does help trigger an expanded range of elements and the directions they move, in part by the use of "wedges" (Sachs' term). The set of semantic and syntactic stones and their discourse movements becomes richer and richer with the child hitting newly differentiated chords labeled Past ("I had those dancing people" or "Yestermorning I made a tiger"), In-progress ("I'm standinging up"), and Future ("My mom will get up pretty soon"). The child's language becomes both a stable "house," with many parts in an atemporal well-defined whole, and dynamic expression through the particular words and sentences that must fly and roll through time and through the context of any individual conversation.

At another level, language serves to embody theoretical structures concerning the processes the child employs in learning language. Often, however, empirical chunks roll right past or through the theories without any impact whatever. In Snow's view (Chapter 2) this is precisely the case with imitations (broadly defined): "The importance of imitations in children's language has typically been underestimated for theoretical as well as methodological reasons." In the course of discussing fully the possible uses of imitation in discourse and in linguistic progress, Snow rolls out also many new observations on displaced imitation that ought to be housed in some fashion by any developmental account. A room must be found for accurate, delayed imitation of whole songs in foreign languages when no input except the songs has been provided in those languages. Space needs to be alloted for the child's borrowing of both form and content from an earlier reading of a story to provide discourse fuel in a new encounter with the same book. Other examples show the young child reaching back in memory over several months for the bases for utterances such as "No cookies in it." and "Why Jaap doesn't like cucumbers?" What the retrieval system looks like that makes possible such retrieval is not yet clear. But when the language-learning child shoves his retriever-hands into his long-term memory pockets and pulls out a semantic or syntactic plum, the child must feel some simple warmth and satisfaction. To the onlooking theorist true calm should be impossible, but perhaps until imitative processes and long-term memory are better understood for the realm of language growth one approach may be to "imitate a person looking on the world calmly."

Both Chapters 3 and 4 discuss variations on the themes that rules and information known at one level will: (a) come to be known and used in new ways with development; and (b) fail to be used in certain contexts because other information is too compelling. Bates, Bretherton, Shore, and McNew tie in sound and gesture and object relations in aphasia—where all the symbolic keys are *not* willing—to progress in naming by word and gesture during the early stages of first language acquisition. They argue that "both the aphasic, and the infant in transition from first words to syntax, are caught at the level of naming." Decontextualization at successively more complex levels is considered the heart of flexible rather than "stuck" reference. For Transtömer in our initiating poem, playing Haydn on a piano is a metaphor announcing a rich set of meanings. For Carlotta, a child studied from 9 to 13 months by Bates and her colleagues, the word "Bam" moves from within a noise-making script or routine to serve as a reminder or announcement of actions to follow. Thus after weeks of saying "Bam" only during action, Carlotta looks up from a moment of non-play and begins with "Bam," hesitates briefly, and then pounds on her toy piano. Similarly, pointing moves from pointing-for-self through a window to a dog, to use of the point as a clear communication to mother—with a smooth glance to mother for confirmation. The dog is the same, the window remains whole and unchanged, but the situation is transformed by the way the child is learning to use gesture and word for symbolic communication. By around 1½ years of age the child again uses old knowledge when new chords, new relations, are stuck in discourse. "Doggie" now may be used to refer to the dish belonging to the dog and in other more flexible, less context-bound ways. Even after the child has mastered multiple-word sentences and a wide array of syntactic rules, however, the preschool child is very heavily influenced by contextual variables. This is Lempert and Kinsbourne's story in Chapter 4. As the dynamism and salience the child notices undergo shifts, so too does the child's interpretation of particular sentence structures. The younger the preschool child the more their attention can be "entrapped" by contextual factors so that language production (especially word order), comprehension, and recall are distorted away from the strict application of rules necessary to successful linguistic exchange of information. Of course, at still later stages in development a new "freedom exists," the freedom to follow strict rules in some communicative contexts but in others to consciously choose a more open, more divergent route between thought and symbolic expression. These different levels of symbolic use, from the first symbols to the most complex variations, from "Bam" to "Haydnflag," are explored not only in the present volume but throughout the *Children's Language* series.

The use of language draws upon multiple cognitive skills in addition to the child's current language skills. In Chapter 5 Levin and Rubin examine the development of indirect and direct requests with a special eye toward the impact of various perspective-taking skills. They find that preschoolers respond to salient conversational constraints such as social status, but that effective use of more subtle cues requires further cognitive development. In addition, analyzing and correcting non-comprehension and other communication failures requires the refinement of monitoring skills. The direction indicated for further analysis is well chosen: "Examination of *what* children say to one another, and *how* they say it may provide us with a naturalistic index of those cognitive and social-cognitive skills necessary for competent communication." In slightly different terms, we need to identify the Topicflags, what they signify, and how they are responded to, as conversations and conversational development evolve.

Strike, strike. Pause. Strike. Pause, pause. There is a warmth and resonance in the timed patterns of well-built music and conversation. In the analysis of naturalistic mother-child and child-mother patterns across languages and cultures Stella-Prorok scores the changes in timing as the child matures. In speech, as in reading, the "soft hammers" of pausing or spacing are fundamental complements to the central message. Stella-Prorok argues that mother and child are mutually responsive and that at stages (e.g., around age 2 years) when longer pauses are needed by the child to process the linguistic message—rather than relying on contextual information—both child and mother introduce longer pauses before their replies. Experimental work also suggests that developmentally appropriate replies by an adult enhance long chains of adult-child verbal interaction.

Phonology is given a fresh look in Chapters 7 and 8. Ferguson and Macken first explore the ways in which play contributes to phonological development in infancy and beyond. Freedom, joy, no work, no tax, laughter—all are part of productive play with language sounds. "Wake up/hake ut (laugh)/hake ut/bake up/brake ut brake up/wake up week up (laugh) week up." The forms and functions of this play and related phonological play deserve closer examination in relation to other varieties of children's play. In Chapter 8 Macken and Ferguson look at acquisition of phonological rules as a cognitive process involving not only play but hypothesis formation and testing. In their model they allow for individual differences and for shifts across development toward a highly integrated system, with flexible, skillful, conscious variation at a very advanced stage. The mechanisms for learning are basically the same cognitive mechanisms applied to other domains. The flag raised is a Cognitiveflag, signifying the appropriateness of seeing how common mechanisms may be applied by the child to contents that appear very different on their surface. The force of these cognitive mechanisms is frequently seen in the child's creative productions—"Im magic, amn't I?"—along with a tendency, once again, to use salience or focus to highlight the child's own angle on a situation. These phenomena show up in project after project, and I was recently struck by this colorful bit of fore-fronting by a child still a bit green in her syntactic system: "Blue I'm gonna paint the frog."

Play with and mastery of multiple modes of language in a deaf child between 1½ and 6 years is given an interesting analysis by Maxwell in Chapter 9. Play, invention, hypothesis-testing, the use of extralinguistic cues, decontextualization, and metalinguistic awareness all provide parallels to other chapters in this volume. The child under study invented an inappropriate fingerspelled name for a person, N-O-H. She also let compelling pictorial features about Mother by a stove influence her interpretations of the signs GRANDMOTHER and WARM in Little Red Riding Hood. But these "errors," like so many errors by children, represent viable processes at work in language mastery. By age 6 this child had not only learned to deal with (in sequence of emergence) American Sign Language, Spoken English, Fingerspelling and English Print, Sign English, and Sign Print, but also developed considerable monitoring and perspective-taking skills that allowed adjustment to a listener's mode(s) of communication. As in the chapters already reviewed, we therefore see an ability to apply at early ages the same cognitive mechanisms to the encoding and retrieval of widely varying input structures.

Stories rely on sentences but apply their own structural mortar or grammar to give interest and coherence to the sequences that establish Settings and Goals followed by Attempts, Outcomes, Reactions, and Resolutions. In "The Three

Little Pigs," for example, there is little doubt about what the Wolf attempts or about the series of outcomes that end up with the final outcome/event—the wolf ending up as "wolf stew" in the fireplace of the third little pig's brick house. For stories like this, Chapters 10 and 11 establish that considerable developmental change occurs after the preschool in the child's abilities to comprehend and selectively use the structure of narratives. Johnson in Chapter 10 concentrates on story summarization skills and on recall. She argues that children learn to use their own recall as *input* for the well-ordered selection that is needed for a good story summary. First-graders already know a lot about story grammar and will build on this knowledge with development, but the more rapid development across the school years will involve "second-order" operations including selection, monitoring, inference, and flexible co-ordination of component skills. Thus older children will both recall a story well and will choose important statements along with concise, accurate generalizations when asked for limited summaries. By so doing, inappropriate condensations such as "The three little pigs got some bricks and builded houses" are avoided. At the same time, the gist is briefly rendered. When we put Chapter 11 together with Chapter 10, it is clear that adults and older school children place more emphasis than younger children on goals and motivations in their summaries of stories. McConaughy, Fitzhenry-Coor, and Howell further argue, from ratings as well as summaries, that the kinds of inferences drawn change with development. Sequential, external actions give way in importance and salience to goals and to related inferences about motivations and internal responses of characters. Task and contextual variations matter here also. But overall it is a late development that brings in the inference that the dog "Sam," carrying a bone and seeing his own reflection in the water, is "greedy" rather than "hungry" in seeking the reflected bone. If we throw in even a little more perspective-taking and flexibility the child or adult might capture the original story and go beyond it to suggest an alternative ending—where Sam pauses, monitors his reflection, says "We don't give in, but want peace," and rambles contentedly on down the slope to his house.

From the study of autism and other severe language disorders much can be learned about the processes of normal language acquisition. In Caparulo and Cohen's Chapter 12, one lesson is the central importance of others providing clues to and the child's finding of the *social significance* of prelinguistic and linguistic behavior. Another conclusion is that language mastery depends, as we have seen above, on knowing both syntactic rules and social rules on *how* to use indirect and direct expressions to achieve discourse ends. Yet another insight is that when we change the context, even by stress or testing or illness, sometimes the underlying skills are shown to be far beyond any previous estimates for a child. In short, both context and individual variations have been underestimated. A related lesson is that in some instances for children at a particular stage a *small* amount of evidence may trigger a remarkable developmental advance—a green, lively, easy, calm sort of positive change. But this optimistic view, though realistic for most normal children and for a minority of language-deviant children, must be balanced. In many cases we simply do not yet understand why intact abilities and knowledge are not mobilized, are not drawn by the music of human interaction to master the "soft hammers" of verbal interaction in increasingly complex and appropriate exchanges with others. Instead, massive amounts of input may roll past the child without impression—as when an autistic child is trained on a form for 213 sessions without effect. In language as in music there is much more to effective communication than an execution of a series of elements (words, notes). The child must be induced to care about playing as well to learn the rules. Here imitation appears to play a role for autistic children who are bright and make a considerable recovery, but it is far from being the key to the interpersonal matrix that leads to high-level communication success. The latter, to quote Caparulo and Cohen, arises "out of a responsive and fine-tuned interpersonal network in which we must appreciate not just the formal code and the rules upon which it is based, but also the links established and maintained among humans that give the code its meanings." Player and instrument, or child and partner, the beginning is an agreed relationship involving affect as much as cognition, warmth as much as selection of words or strings, with the liveliness and calm beauty of the patterns expanding together in development.

Keith E. Nelson

This book is dedicated to all the children, adults, and places that have periodically given me fresh perspectives. Specifically included are art galleries and studios, sailboats and breezes and anchorages, Kansas and Crete and Scotland and Maine, Boston, Branford, New York, and San Francisco, London, Stockholm, Kyoto, and Vancouver, and some marvelous stopovers in dreamland.

1 Talking about the There and Then: The Emergence of Displaced Reference in Parent-Child Discourse

Jacqueline Sachs
University of Connecticut

Imagine the following scene: A 26-month-old girl is eating a popsicle after dinner. After a brief tantrum because she isn't allowed to eat both halves at once (she shouts "I want the nother one!"), she concentrates on the popsicle, saying "It sticky, It sticky. Sticky." Her mother asks, "What did you do today, Naomi?" and Naomi replies, "Took a nap." What is required to deal with utterances like this one, that bear no relation to a supporting nonlinguistic context? In this paper, I wish to discuss how a little child might come to be able to supply an appropriate response to a question like "What did you do today?"

Such an utterance stands in marked contrast to most speech of the child and to the child at this age. One of the most striking characteristics about young children's speech is its close relationship to a supporting nonlinguistic context. Brown and Bellugi (1964) captured the flavor of children's speech well when they described it as being about the "here and now." The fact that children talk about what they are seeing and doing makes it possible for caregivers to understand many utterances that would otherwise be uninterpretable. Indeed, much of the research on child language rests on the assumption that one can guess something about the child's intended meanings from the combination of the forms uttered and the context (Bloom, 1970; Brown, 1973).

Adults also talk mainly about the here and now when they interact with young children (Brown & Bellugi, 1964; Bloom, 1970). Something of the meaning of the adult's utterance would often be clear even to a listener who did not comprehend the linguistic form at all. The fact that linguistic forms are used in semantically clear contexts makes it possible for the child to begin to break the code of the language and to discover form-meaning correspondence (Clark,

1973; Macnamara, 1972). Thus, it appears that the close correspondence between what is said and a supporting nonlinguistic context is an important characteristic of early speech both from the point of view of the adult and from the point of view of the child.

For conversational partners to communicate about events and objects outside the immediate context, a variety of cognitive, linguistic, and conversational skills are required, and it is not at all surprising that interactions with young children contain few instances of such reference. As a child develops, there is more and more talk about topics that are not in the current context. For example, Moerk (1975) found a sharp increase in speech about past activities and future plans in conversations between mothers and 2- to 5-year-old children. In school-aged children, there has been considerable attention to the increase in the ability to produce and comprehend language in the absence of contextual support. For recent discussions of the large literature on the topic of referential communication, see Glucksberg, Krauss, and Higgins (1975) and Shatz (1978).

However, even from an early point in development, there is some child speech about topics that are not in the here and now. Before the emergence of combinatorial utterances, children request objects that are not in sight (Bruner, Roy, & Ratner, 1982; Greenfield & Smith, 1976), and search for objects named (Huttenlocher, 1974; Zukow, Reilly, & Greenfield, 1982). In conversations between adults and children under 3 years of age, most of the child speech refers to the immediate context, but there is occasional reference to objects or events based on fantasy or prior experience (Bloom, Rocisanno, & Hood, 1976; Keenan & Schieffelin, 1976). The early attempts of children to talk about events that occurred in the past have been documented (e.g., Halliday, 1975; Sachs, 1977; Stoel-Gammon & Cabral, 1977), and the emergence of the syntactic forms for marking temporal distinctions has been studied by a number of researchers (e.g., Antinucci & Miller, 1976; Brown, 1973; Cromer, 1968; Harner, 1975, 1976).

Though we know relatively little as yet about how the child comes to deal with such topics, it is certain that these changes in the child's use of language have profound implications for both interpersonal communication and thinking. The ability to refer to objects or events not in the current context is widely recognized as one of the most important features setting language apart from other forms of communication. Hockett (1960), in his description of the defining features of human language, called this characteristic "displacement." Displacement may involve the spatial domain, with reference to objects that are not in the immediate environment, or the temporal domain, with reference to the past or future. Another term often used to capture the decrease in reliance on support from the immediate situation in speaking and understanding is "decontextualization" (Bates, 1979; Bates, Bretherton, Shore, & McNew, this volume).

As language evolved, it must have taken on an entirely new character once the potential for displaced reference was realized. An ordinary conversation between adult speakers need not have anything to do with the situation they find themselves in. Rather, it is generally the case that the support for interpreting messages comes from the listener's prior experiences and knowledge. We could not expect conversations between adults and children to be like adult-adult conversations in this respect.

The use of displaced reference is also fundamental to the role language plays in thought. In thinking, we re-present objects and events that are not currently at hand. In the evolution of thought, the use of a symbolic system with the capacity for displaced reference would have broadened the possibilities for information storage, problem solving, and planning enormously. It even allows for the possibility of hypothesizing, lying, and fantasizing. As Baron (1977) and Brattacharya and Baron (1979) have argued, the use of language independent of contextual support (what they call "indirect reference") is *the* characteristic that makes possible the complex role language plays in our lives. Clearly, learning more about the child's gradual entry into the world of the there and then should have important implications for our understanding of the complex relationships among cognitive development, social development, and language development.

GOALS AND METHODS

One goal of this study was to describe the emergence of the production and comprehension of certain types of displaced reference, based on data from a longitudinal study of parent-child discourse. As a child develops, we expect not only that displaced reference in the child's speech would become more frequent, but that such reference would become more successful. Furthermore, because this type of reference is difficult for the child to understand, yet very important for successful communication, we expect that various strategies would be used by the adults in order to make comprehension easier for the child.

The second goal was to consider reasons for the child's development, especially in terms of the opportunities for acquisition supplied by parent-child conversation.

We will first consider the development of the ability to refer to objects that are not present. A description of the emergence of reference to past and future events will follow, and the concluding section will contain remarks relating these two semantic domains.

The child observed was my daughter, Naomi, a firstborn child. The data consisted of transcripts of approximately 40 hours of taperecorded interactions between Naomi (ages 17 to 36 months) and her mother or father. Recordings were made every other day in the 22nd and 23rd months, and about twice a month for the rest of the period. These data were supplemented by a diary that began at 11 months. For this project, both child and parental utterances were analyzed for reference to objects that were not in sight and events that were not happening at the moment. At the time the recordings were made (1969–1971), neither parent thought that his or her speech would be the object of study.

SPATIAL DISPLACEMENT

The description of Naomi's development is organized here into periods that reflect similar usage. Examples of successful and unsuccessful communication will illustrate her use and comprehension of speech about absent objects, in order to show when she had the ability to deal with this speech function and how it first emerged. It is important to keep in mind that speech about the here and now always overwhelmingly dominated the conversations throughout the period studied, and the usages described here represent the growing edge of Naomi's abilities at that age, not the established abilities.

The Emergence of Reference to Absent Objects

The observations reported here are based on diary data from the period in which Naomi used only single-word utterances (about 11–20 months).

From 11–16 months of age, Naomi seemed to be truly limited to the "here and now" in her production and comprehension of speech. Around 11 months of age, she started to use some consistent vocalizations, some of which were recognizable as English words, in specific situations. In these "first words," there were no labels for objects; rather, the vocalizations seemed to accompany Naomi's reactions. For example, *bye-bye* was used accompanying waving, a panting sound was used with reaching (seeming to signal desire for an object), *hot* was said when food was placed in front of her, *geah* was used with pointing (seeming to direct the listener's attention rather than to elicit the listener's aid in obtaining the object). A number of studies of early word usage have shown that this type of usage, often called "performatives," is typical before real words are acquired (Bates, Camaioni, & Volterra, 1975; Carter, 1978; Halliday, 1975).

In the 15th and 16th months, Naomi began to imitate adult models, both spontaneously and when asked to do so. During this period, many words referring to objects or persons appeared. There were phonological forms that seemed to be modeled on such adult words as *doggy, kitty, juice, milk, mommy, daddy, jacket, hand, cow, baby,* and *ball.* During this time, however, the words that Naomi knew were never used as requests for objects that were in sight or out of sight. If Naomi wanted something that she could not get herself, she would reach for it and fuss or whimper or make panting sounds to indicate wanting, but she never used the name of the object. This pattern of development is consistent with that in the children studied by Greenfield and Smith (1976), where the function of requesting was not present at the onset of vocabulary acquisition, and the children studied by Bruner, Roy, and Ratner (1982), where nonlinguistic vocalizations appeared in early requests.

At 17 months, Naomi continued to use only single-word utterances, but began to use the names of objects in requesting them, including instances in which the object was not in sight. These requests provide the first clear evidence of the production of a word without a clear eliciting stimulus in the situation. At about the same time, Naomi began to search for objects not in sight if an adult asked her to.[1] This pattern of development in the production and comprehension of words reflects a transition from a period in which words are closely linked to objects or specific situations to a period in which a true symbolic usage emerges (Bates, 1979; Dore, 1978; Nelson, 1974).

When Naomi began to use two-word utterances at 20 months, a means of making reference to absent objects, *where* + *name of object* was among the first combinations she used. As in her earlier use of single words referring to absent objects, these utterances always accompanied searching for the object, as in the following example:

(20 months; child is looking around for something)
Child: [dadi].
Adult: What, honey?
Child: [dadi]. [dadi].
Adult: What's [dadi], honey?
Child: [dadi].
Adult: Dolly? Which dolly do you want?
Child: Want.
Adult: Do you want the bear?
Child: Bear.
Adult: Here's the bear. There, Hug, hug, hug, Naomi.
Child: (rejects bear) [dadi]. Where de [dadi]. [dadi].
Adult: (finds correct doll) There.
Child: There.

Even though Naomi could refer to objects out of sight and understand such reference by the latter part of the period of single-word usage, this aspect of language was still closely tied to her needs and actions. Objects were mentioned when Naomi wanted them. When others said *where's absent object* to her or when she used this form herself, *where* meant "search for" or "get." Displaced reference in its more developed usage functions not only for requests, but as the basis for comment or description. We wished to see how Naomi came to be able to *talk about* objects not in sight.

---

[1]Hearing the name of an absent object did not automatically elicit a search, unless it was said in the context of an instruction such as *where, get,* etc. Furthermore, we often asked Naomi to imitate words, which she would do willingly during this period without interrupting her ongoing activities. In the imitation game, "*say juice*" would not cause Naomi to look for the juice.

The Emergence of Conversations About Absent Objects

In learning to talk about objects that were not present, one of the first types of conversations emerged in the framework of *where's absent object* utterances, as Naomi's understanding of *where* changed from "search for" to "specify location or activity." The word *where* is originally introduced in situations in which the object specified is present and the child's response is "point to." For most children, the pointing response following *where* probably is learned even before the child uses any expressive language. Next, the child accompanies the pointing response with a deictic utterance (e.g., *da* or *dere*). Later, the child broadens the meaning of *where* to "search for" in responding to *where's absent object*. Once the child responds to *where* as "search for," the stage is set for the extension of the meaning of this term. The child can then learn, through discourse, that an exchange of information rather than searching is sometimes an appropriate response to *where* (Miller & Weissenborn, 1978).

At 22 months, some conversational topics appeared in Naomi's speech that did not involve a direct link between naming and searching; that is, she commented on something not in the current context.

The basic problem for both child and parent in using displaced reference is that there is no easy way, such as pointing, to arrive at agreement about the referent. In successful conversations about absent objects, this problem was avoided by references to objects or people in which there was only one possible referent. When conversation about absent objects began, there was a small set of frequently appearing conversational topics that will be referred to as "conversational routines." In these routines, the topic (location of a unique referent) and structure of the conversation was similar from time to time, but the exact content and linguistic forms were variable. One of these conversational routines was the location of the absent parent.[2] Here is one example from the many in the data:

(22 months)
Child: Where's Daddy?
Adult: Daddy is working. Daddy will be home tonight. You'll see him tomorrow morning.

The following example shows that Naomi learned about potential answers to the "where" question through such discourse.

(23 months)
Child: Where's Daddy? Daddy's in work?
Adult: Daddy's at work, honey.

---

[2]*Where* questions are often answered with an utterance specifying an activity that is understood to occur elsewhere. While such answers might misinform the child as to the meaning of *where,* there is no evidence in my data to suggest that they did. Eventually, the child has to learn that only activity descriptions involving habitual locations can serve as specifications of place.

A second frequent conversational routine involved asking about other unique referents: the moon or sun. Sometimes the adult introduced this topic in a situation where a verbal (rather than searching) response was called for. In the following examples, the entire conversation about the absent object is given in order to give a sense of the length of these conversations during this period:

(22 months; looking out window during the day)
Adult: Where's the moon?
Child: Moon.
Adult: Uh huh. Where is it?
Child: Moon sleeping.
Adult: Uh huh. The moon is sleeping. Where is the sun?
Child: Sun. Sun working.[3]
Adult: That's right. The sun is working. Naomi, do you see how the trees are blowing in the wind? Must be windy. Do you remember what wind is?
Child: (makes high pitched "hoooo" sound)

(23 months; just before going to bed at night)
Adult: Tell me about the sun.
Child: Go nite-nite. Bye-bye sun. Bye-bye sun.
Adult: Where's the sun going?
Child: Hey sun. Going nite-nite.
Adult: Uh huh. Think it's going to work?
Child: Bye-Bye sun.
Adult: Can you see it?
Child: All gone.

As in conversations about Daddy, Naomi also introduced the topic:

(22 months; in kitchen, during the day, after eating)
Child: Where's moon?
Adult: Where's the moon? The moon is sleeping. The moon is not out now.
Child: Light.
Adult: Yes, it's light. It's daytime now, honey.
Child: Nighttime.
Adult: No, daytime, not nighttime. Nighttime is dark, honey, and daytime is light.
Child: Night night.
Adult: No, the sun is out now instead of the moon.
Child: Sun hot.
Adult: Sun is hot. That's right. The sun is also light.

(23 months; sitting on Naomi's bed, looking at pictures on her sheet, which included some stars)
Child: Where's sun?

---

[3]These conversations provide nice examples of the learning of the meanings of other words in verbal context, such as *working, windy, daytime,* and *nighttime.* Here, *working* seems to be descriptive of being away.

Adult: Do you want to drink your juice?
Child: Sun gone?
Adult: Sun gone.
Child: All gone sun. Bye-bye sun.

Other conversations during this period about absent objects involved asking about the location and "activities" of a doll not in the room (with no intention of finding the doll), and asking about where her grandmother was (a grandmother who lived in another city). The conversations about grandmother eventually developed into a game in which Naomi would pretend to call her grandmother on a toy telephone.

These conversational routines were initially very primitive as conversations go, but over time the child progressed from a set of learned responses to using appropriate, variable speech content. As other types of displaced reference appeared in the parent-child discourse, they also tended to make their first appearance in conversational routines, as will be shown later in this paper for past reference.

The child's communicative intent can also sometimes be understood by the adult because of shared experiences with the child. Snow (1978) gave an example in which she could not respond appropriately to a child's utterance, but the mother could:

Mother in kitchen. Experimenter (CS) and Meredith (18 months) in living room.
Meredith: Bandaid
CS: Where's your bandaid?
Meredith: Bandaid
CS: Do you have a bandaid?
Meredith: Bandaid
CS: Did you fall down and hurt yourself?
Mother enters.
Meredith: Bandaid
Mother: Who gave you the bandaid?
Meredith: Nurse
Mother: Where did she put it?
Meredith: Arm [p. 254].

In many cases, however, disambiguation of this sort does not occur. With limited linguistic and cognitive abilities, the young child has great difficulty in adding information that would serve to identify an unknown referent for the listener. When Naomi mentioned a referent that belonged to a large set, problems could arise, as the following example shows:

(22 months; Naomi has been pushing a wastebasket around)
Child: I need it.
Adult: What do you need?

Child: I need the book.
Adult: Which one?
Child: I need the book.
Adult: The big one? The Sears catalog?
Child: (growing upset) The book. The book. The book.

Naomi changed "it" to "the book" but then added no more information when the parent did not understand her request.

The problem with reference to absent objects that were not easily identified continued throughout the period discussed here. Even at nearly 3 years, when Naomi had considerable command of linguistic forms (MLU 3.22), she had difficulty in knowing what information to supply for the listener. In the next example, Naomi paraphrased "dancing" with "happy" after the adult's request for more information and indicated that the target referent was "a book" after the adult asked whether the people were on TV; but after that she was able to supply no other clues. Note that the adult attempted to help by supplying "multiple choice" answers and giving explicit directions to "tell us more."

(32 months)
Child: I had those dancing people. (no referent in sight)
Adult: What dancing people, Naomi?
Child: Happy people.
Adult: What happy people, Naomi?
Child: Happy people.
Adult: What happy people? Do you mean puppets?
Child: Uh huh.
Adult: Clowns?
Child: Un huh.
Adult: On television? People on television?
Child: I need that book about dancing people.
Adult: You need the book about dancing people. You mean the Fantasia book? The book about dancing hippopotamuses?
Child: (shouting) I need dancing book. I need it.
Adult: Well, where is it, Naomi? Do you know where it is?
Child: No, I don't know.
Adult: Well, we're trying to figure out which one you want so we can get it. (Naomi has been growing more and more frantic and is now crying).
Adult: Hey, hey, calm down. Tell us more about the book so maybe we'll be able to figure out which one it is.
Child: (crying) I need the dancing people.

Bruner, Roy, and Ratner (1982) have described the adult's strategy in such situations as "successive guidance." Adult queries attempt to pull information from the child that he/she would not know to supply. Such queries can call for information that the adult actually needs in order to understand the child's request, or in cases where the adult knows what the child wants, can encourage the child to use a more complete linguistic message.

When Naomi was close to 3 years old, reference to absent objects occurred fairly frequently, mainly in pretend play or in talking about past events (to be discussed in the next section), but conversations that were not grounded in ongoing activity were brief. After a few turns, Naomi would say something related to her current perceptions and the conversational topic would shift. Thus the talk at this age was still not at all like adult-adult conversation, in which topics are typically not related to the objects and events in the situation. The following example is the longest conversation about an absent object in the data through 36 months. Here the identity of the referent is available to the child on the basis of shared knowledge about family members' possessions.

> (35 months; Naomi sitting with mother; father is getting ready to leave but can't find his shoes)
> Mother: Do you know where Daddy's shoes are?
> Child: No. Maybe they're in the bathroom.
> Father: In the what?
> Child: I don't know where they is.
> Father: I'll find them.
> Child: I know where your shoes are.
> Mother: Where, honey?
> Child: In the bedroom.
> Mother: (calls to father) In the bedroom.
> (Mother comments about Naomi's popsicle; father returns)
> Child: (to father) You found the shoes?
> Father: Yes, thank you.

Conclusions About Reference to Absent Objects

These examples from conversations between parents and a child under 3 years of age show that they did not talk exclusively about objects in sight. However, when displaced reference first appeared, it was limited to a few, highly constrained topics. As the child developed, reference to objects outside the current context became more frequent and the range of topics that was appropriate to discuss broadened systematically.

In the period studied, reference to objects out of sight was difficult and not always successful. The problem that reference to absent objects presents to the young child and his or her listener is that each has to depend purely on the linguistic message to know what the other is referring to. We saw that there were two strategies in early interactions that seemed to make communication easier. In both, the use of shared knowledge provided a basis for success in using displaced reference.

The first strategy was the creation of conversational routines. Initially, these routines functioned as a form of playful interaction between the adult and child. With a routine, the constant structure helps to make the parent-child interaction successful because each knows what to expect of the other. The variability permitted within the routine helps to insure that neither party becomes bored. Furthermore, it would seem that the combination of order and variability in this sort of linguistic play between parent and child can provide a framework for the child's developing linguistic and cognitive abilities. Conversational routines might play a role in the early stages of learning of any aspect of the language,[4] and some examples are already to be found in the literature. Bruner (1975) has argued that play between the mother and prelinguistic child aids the development of early semantic relationships. Sachs and Truswell (1978) found that mothers of children in the one-word stage used linguistic routines with variable words, and suggested that such routines could help the child learn to understand action-object sentences. In the data presented here, there were conversational routines that provided an opportunity for the use of displaced reference, paving the way for productive conversation. In each case, the general topic was set (for example, talking about the moon). However, the exact content and linguistic forms within that conversational topic were variable and became progressively less fixed over time, until there was no longer a routine at all, but simply a possible topic of conversation.

I would not want to suggest that the parents deliberately designed these routines in order to present new linguistic information to the child. In fact, it seems quite clear in my data that it was often the child who controlled the topic of conversation. One important area for future research is to determine those aspects of the child's speech and behavior that signal the parent when various topics are appropriate.

Reference to unique objects was the second strategy that made displaced reference easier during this early period in the child's development. Almost all the successful conversations had to do with referents for which no further specification was required. When Naomi brought up a topic that could not be identified easily, the problem for her seemed to be in knowing what additional information to supply. Since the selection of appropriate features is dependent on an evaluation of the listener's knowledge, we would expect that children even considerably older than 3 years would be limited in their ability to introduce new topics into a conversation.

By the end of the period studied, when Naomi was 3, most of the talk still focused on the here and now, but she could engage in conversations about nonpresent objects with no support from the immediate environmental context. These interactions were short, but had the flavor of real conversations.

---

[4]Routines are also useful, even for adults, in situations in which there is communication difficulty: e.g., beginning and ending conversations, talking with strangers, talking about unpleasant topics (such as condolences). See Ferguson (1976) for a discussion of politeness formulas in languages.

TEMPORAL DISPLACEMENT

The other type of displaced reference to be considered in this paper is temporal displacement: talking about the past or future. Most of the development in the period studied (17 to 36 months) was in the semantic domain making reference to past events. Past reference is a complex part of the language, marked in English both syntactically and lexically. One finds that the child's comprehension and usage of the past changes gradually over a long period of time (Brown, 1973; Cromer, 1968). The child's earliest use of the past markers in English (-ed and irregular past) occurs in descriptions of events in the immediate situation. Often, an end result of the event is still in evidence, as in *I fell down* or *I broke it,* and a number of researchers have pointed out that the past marker in such cases may signal a change in state, or aspect, rather than past time (Antinucci & Miller, 1976; Bloom, Lifter, & Hafitz, in press; Bronkadt & Sinclair, 1973). Aspect is signalled by a syntactic marker that is different from the marker used to indicate past time in many languages other than English, but in English, *-ed* contains both an aspectual and temporal meaning. A number of researchers have studied the acquisition of tense and aspect (e.g., Halliday, 1975; Harner, 1981; Kuczaj, 1977; Smith, 1980). My data are consistent with most of these studies in that there are past references that appear to be temporal rather than aspectual before age 3. It is the emergence of reference to the temporal domain that was the focus in this study; aspect will not be discussed.

A coding system was devised to distinguish between reference to events that had just occurred in the immediate context, called Immediate Past, and events that occurred at an earlier time, called Earlier Past. (See Chafe, 1974, for a discussion of the role of the perception of time in linguistic temporal distinctions.) We did not code for the aspectual usage, and whether or not a verb signalled a change of state was irrelevant for this analysis.

Furthermore, in this study, rather than focusing on the emergence of the syntactic markers for past, we were interested in the emergence of the intention to refer to Earlier Past, and consequently the presence of syntactic markers was irrelevant for the coding. The verbal context and notes about the nonlinguistic context were used in judging semantic intent.

All utterances from the data described above referring to the past were coded by two independent coders[5] into one of three categories: *Immediate Past, Earlier Past,* or *Other.*

1. *Immediate Past* was defined as reference to events that had just occurred, whether or not syntactic marking for past was realized, as in *Closed it* or *I find foot* (said after uncovering her foot).

---

[5]All utterances were initially coded as Nonpast-Past, with an intercoder reliability averaging .87 (range .74 to .96 across different transcripts). Then the Past utterances were subcoded as Immediate Past, Earlier Past, or Other. The mean reliability of this coding was .93, with a range of .91 to .95 across transcripts.

2. *Earlier Past* was defined as reference to events clearly not in the immediate situation, where at least 2 hours had intervened, as in *I play with Todd's toys* (said when talking with mother about what happened that morning).
3. *Other* was defined as reference to past in which neither category described above applied clearly. Such utterances were not analyzed further. Examples would be reference to an event that occurred a few minutes before the utterance (such utterances were rare) or the use of past in narratives and fantasy.

The data were also coded for future reference. A distinction was made between expression of intentions and real future reference:

1. *Intention* was defined as the verbalization of intention to carry out an action in the immediate context, whether or not the intention was realized with words such as *going to* or *will,* as in *Get down* or *Gonna get down* (said just before getting down).
2. *Future* was defined as reference to an event further removed in future time, as in *See Michael today?*

A brief description of some of the features of Naomi's development from several periods will be presented here, and then a more detailed consideration of Time II will follow.

Time I. Reference to Immediate Past and Intentions (17–25 months)

During this period, Naomi referred almost exclusively to ongoing events, Immediate Past, and Intentions. Most Immediate Past references were not marked syntactically, as when *I fall down* was said just after falling. Her first form that included an adult past marker was actually a routine, *I did it,* that was used to indicate successful completion of an action (for example, when she managed to put a book into an opening in a bookshelf). Productive *-ed* endings began to appear around 22 months, but only to signal Immediate Past. The context of her utterances showed that she did not talk about events that had really occurred in the past, but only events that had just occurred, as in:

(22 months)
Child: I throwed it. I throwed it.

(23 months: diary)
Adult: Daddy booed you (= said boo to you).
Child: I booeded Daddy.

At the same time, Naomi began to use *-ing* productively in cases of ongoing activities. The emergence of her *-ing* was quite dramatic because she had learned many of her verbs originally in the progressive form. For a time, she used forms like *I'm lyinging down, I'm sittinging down*, and *I'm standinging up*. The co-occurrence of the emergence of the two morphemes *-ed* and *-ing* suggests that Naomi was acquiring a distinction between *completed events* and *events in progress*.

In this period, Naomi often expressed Intentions (e.g., saying *get down* when she wanted to retrieve a pencil from the floor). Only one utterance is on record that suggests Future reference: At 21 months she spontaneously said *see Daddy* while riding home from the babysitter's with her mother. The diary entry indicated that this was the first future reference that had been observed.

Time II. Reference to the Past Events of the Day and Emergence of Future (26–31 months)

At 26 months, the appropriate topics began to broaden to include activities and events that had occurred within a limited temporal framework: the current day. Naomi's verbs began to be marked with *-ed* endings to signal Earlier Past as well as Immediate Past, and a number of lexical items appeared that reflected her growing awareness of temporal relationships, including *yet, already, still, in a minute*, and *yestermorning* (used to refer to any time in the past).

A frequent conversational routine involved asking about the events of the day. At first, the adult supplied questions and answers and Naomi responded with imitations. These interactions may have helped her learn how to respond appropriately. Eventually, the routines became conversations, as in:

> (27 months; late afternoon after picking up child from sitter)
> Adult: What did you do today with Kimberly? Can you tell me?
> Child: I played toys with Kimberly.
> Adult: You played toys with Kimberly?
> Child: I put the toys away.
> Adult: You put the toys away?
> Child: I put the tinker toys away.
> Adult: Oh, the tinker toys.
> Child: Was messy.
> Adult: It was messy?
> Child: Yep.
> Adult: Oh.
> Child: In Kimberly's room.

These conversations about the events of the day seem to form a bridge between reference to events in the context and reference to past events in general.

To this point in the data, almost all of Naomi's references to future events were expressions of immediate Intentions. In addition, there was little reference to the future by the adults. If we asked questions about the plans for the day, sometimes Naomi became confused, but usually she just seemed disinterested:

(27 months; at breakfast)
Adult: Naomi, where are we going today?
Child: Where are we going today?
Adult: Do you remember?
Child: Julia.
Adult: Yes, to Julia's. What are we going to do at Julia's house?
Child: What are we going to do at Julia's house? I want breakfast.
Adult: Do you want some of this roll?
Child: No.
Adult: Naomi, what are we going to do at Julia's house?
Child: What are we going to do at Julia's house?
Adult: Do you remember? We're going to have a birthday party.
Child: Don't like it. (referring to roll)

During the 29th and 30th months, Naomi began to talk about what was to occur at a later point, as if she had suddenly become interested in the sequencing of events. Here are some examples of child-initiated future references in these months:

Mommy's away. Coming back again.
(at bedtime) We'll have breakfast together.
Gotta put a bandaid on a little later.
I gotta feel better in the morning, when we have dinner in the morning.
We gotta drive pretty soon.
My mom will get up pretty soon.
(at bedtime, pretending) Goodbye, Dr. Melly, we'll see you in the morning when we get up.

Time III. Reference to Past Experience and Future Plans (32–36 months)

During this period, Naomi began to make reference spontaneously to past experiences and future plans and responded readily when these topics were introduced by her parents. By 33 months, she responded appropriately to 76% of the adult questions involving displaced references (as compared to 88% of the questions about the here and now). Although conversations involving displaced references were never very long, they were frequent. For example, in one of the transcripts at 35 months, about 10% of Naomi's utterances referred to the past. She also increasingly related her current perceptions to her more general knowledge. For example, while playing with play dough, she said *Yestermorning I maked a tiger;* when she saw some birds that looked like puffins in a book of hers, she said, *Puffins like in my Magic Carpet book.*

The Role of Parent-Child Discourse in Extending Past Reference

In this section, we will consider the possible role of the parents' speech for Naomi's learning of Earlier Past. To introduce this issue, let us briefly discuss the relationship of input language and language acquisition.

Until recently, controversy about the impact of the input variations on acquisition only considered language in a very global sense. Some researchers argued that the child's pattern of language development was quite resistant to even severe degradations in input; others suggested that even the level of the child's academic performance reflected subtle differences in linguistic background. In the last few years, it has become increasingly clear that the effect of input variations will differ according to the linguistic stage of the child and what aspect of language it is that is being studied (Nelson, 1977). For example, the acquisition of some of the basic semantic relationships may be independent of input variations (Goldin-Meadow & Feldman, 1977). However, the rate of acquisition of linguistic forms by the young child may be affected by the frequency or clarity of opportunities to notice form-meaning correspondences. Children seem to learn faster when adults speak in ways they can best understand: that is, when adults speak simply about simple things (Cross, 1977; Furrow, Nelson, & Benedict, 1979). At the other extreme, exposure to speech from noninteractional sources such as watching TV does not provide the kind of data base that supports language learning at a young age (Sachs & Johnson, 1976).

Zukow, Reilly, and Greenfield (1982) have provided a detailed analysis of the way caregivers use well-understood contexts to facilitate the child's transition from nonlinguistic to linguistic communication. They looked at episodes in which the adult offered an object or activity to children between 9 and 23 months. With the youngest children, offers were primarily nonverbal; then offers consisted of redundant nonlinguistic and linguistic cues; and finally the linguistic message preceded the caregiver's action. The caregivers appeared to be sensitive to the child's growing comprehension abilities in choosing their communicative mode, and by the end of the one-word period, some messages could be understood with no nonlinguistic support.

Once the child has begun to learn to talk, the child must continue to acquire more and more complex aspects of language. Children should benefit if adults do not continue to use the simplest possible speech, but change their input as the child progresses (Gleason, 1977). Relatively little attention has been given, as yet, to the ways in which adults might introduce material that is still outside the child's system, but that the child is ready to acquire. In the following section, we will look at the parents' speech to Naomi as she made the transition from using Immediate Past to Earlier Past. (Some of this material was presented in Sachs, 1979.)

The data consisted of the transcripts of interactions between Naomi and her mother or father during part of the period described above, when Naomi was 20 months (MLU 1.00) to 29 months (MLU 4.00). During this time, there were about 5,700 child utterances recorded, with 253 of them making past reference. There were 319 past references by the parents, and these were classified as Immediate Past, Earlier Past, or Other.

Both adult and child utterances were further coded into Topic Initiations or Responses. Initiations were Comments and Questions that did not follow directly from the partner's utterance. Responses consisted of Answers, Imitations, or Expansion, and Comments or Questions that sustained the topic that had been introduced.

Table 1.1 summarizes Naomi's acquisition of the meaning and syntax of past from 20 to 29 months. From 20 to 25 months in nonimitated utterances she referred only to events in the immediate situation, using the routine *I did it* and other verbs that were occasionally marked for past syntactically. By 22 months, some overgeneralizations appeared, suggesting that the *-ed* morpheme was productive. Reference to earlier events first appeared in the 26th month (at MLU 3.00). Throughout this period, for both regular and irregular verbs, Naomi had not reached the 90% criterion that Brown (1973) used to indicate that the child had acquired a grammatical morpheme, with only 77% of her references to past realized with past markers at 29 months (MLU 4.00).

In the speech of the adults where Naomi was 20–25 months old, over half the references to past were Immediate Past. Furthermore, they were Immediate Past of a special kind. When an adult reports something that just happened to another adult, it would ordinarily be because the listener had not noticed the event, as in *You dropped your scarf*. In talking to a child, on the other hand, Immediate Past usually encoded something that the child had been doing; for example, her father said *You covered your eyes* when Naomi had covered her eyes with her hands.

TABLE 1.1
Some Aspects of Naomi's Acquisition of Past

Age	Semantics	Realizations	%Morpheme Use
20-25 months	Immediate Past	*I did it.* some verbs with -ed some irregular past overgeneralized -ed (e.g., *I booded Gammy*)	72% at 25 months
26-29 months	Immediate Past and Earlier Past	-ed irregular past did (e.g., *I did jump*) was -ing *yestermorning*	77% at 29 months

The parents also used instructional questions about events that had just occurred, attempting to elicit utterances, as in, *What did you do, honey? Did you go nite-nite?* or *Did you boo Gammy?*. Naomi eventually used these instructional question forms in her own speech. For example, at 25 months she would do something and then ask her mother or father *What's Naomi do?*

What about Earlier Past in the adults' speech in the period between Naomi's 20th and 25th months? Did the adults supply some evidence that could help the child learn about this semantic distinction used in English? From some recent literature on child language, we might expect that the adults would *not* use a meaning that is not yet in the child's system. Retherford, Schwartz, and Chapman (1977), Snow (1977), and van der Geest (1977) have suggested that adults limit the content of their speech to match the type of content used by the child while they express this content in syntactic forms that are more complex than the child's. Thus, the child would have an opportunity to learn particular syntactic forms at the time that it was appropriate. Changes in the content the child intends to express presumably result from the child's nonlinguistic cognitive development. The notion that language simply encodes ideas that come about through the child's interaction with his nonlinguistic environment has been very influential in recent years. Although this framework seems reasonable for many aspects of the young child's semantic development, it would seem worthwhile to keep in mind the possibility that *language* may play some role in language development as well.

Within the cognitive development model, parents would introduce new meanings only when the child had given evidence of readiness by trying to express the meaning with still-primitive forms. Snow (1977) gave a hypothetical example involving past to illustrate this:

Child: See Grampa.
Mother: And what did Grampa give you when you saw him [p. 48].

If my data support the cognitive development position, the parents would not use reference to Earlier Past before the child used past in topic initiations to refer to events that occurred earlier. However, in fact, there were some parental comments and questions about Earlier Past from 22 months, as shown in Table 1.2. Some examples:

(22 months; talking about an outing earlier in the day)
Adult: Did you go on the slide?
Child: Go slide.

(24 months; playing with a doll)
Child: What's that?
Adult: That's a handkerchief. You were using it yesterday as a blanket for your baby.

TABLE 1.2
Proportion of Nonimitated References to Past that Referred to Earlier Past

Age	Adults	Child
20-21 months	.00	.00
22-23 months	.21	.00
24-25 months	.17	.00
26-27 months	.88	.68
28-29 months	.72	.32

As further evidence that the child was not always the leader in expressing new semantic content, we find that even after Naomi began to express the meaning Earlier Past, it was not in Topic Initiations but in Responses to parental Initiations. In fact, there were only two instances in the data (of 253 past references) that were similar to Snow's example, where Naomi mentioned events outside the current situation spontaneously, and these both appeared after 26 months:

(26 months; child and mother are eating breakfast; Naomi looks into the living room)
Child: Daddy broke the fireplace.

(29 months; child is objecting to putting on her training pants)
Child: I can't go in my training pants. Yestermorning I wear diapers.

In other cases, it is the parent who introduced Earlier Past, with no stimulus from the child. Some examples before 26 months have already been given. The following examples are from the period after 26 months:

(27 months; talking about what is being cooked for dinner)
Child: I want to cook my chicken.
Adult: It's in the oven. It's cooking in the oven. (pause) What did you do today with Kimberly, honey?

(29 months; child is playing with a doll named Alexandra)
Adult: Who gave Alexandra to you?

In these data, for this semantic domain, the parents did not limit the semantic content of their speech to what the child was already attempting to express.

Not only did Naomi *never* introduce the intent to refer to Earlier Past in the period between 20 and 25 months, but we cannot look to her receptive abilities either as an explanation for the parents' usage. She responded to Earlier Past usage with unrelated responses or with imitations, as in:

(22 months)
Adult: What did we do outside?
Child: Outside.

Then why were there references to Earlier Past by the parents in the child's 20–25 month-old period studied here? Perhaps they were insensitive to Naomi's semantic limitations, or misled by the existence of her emerging past tense forms, which were used for Immediate Past. But the data shown in Table 1.2 do not seem to suggest insensitivity to the content of the child's speech. The more interesting possibility is that these parental references to Earlier Past served to introduce the child to a new idea through linguistic interaction. In suggesting that the parents introduced the child to a new idea, I do not mean to claim that the parents "taught" their child to use past tense in the strongest sense of "teach." Surely certain characteristics of mental functioning that are often discussed under the heading "cognitive development" are necessary for the child to benefit from exposure to this semantic distinction. There is ongoing research in a number of areas that may help refine our understanding of the nonlinguistic substrata for language development. Two areas that seem especially relevant for the acquisition of temporal reference are research on the development of memory in young children and research on the ability (and inability) of nonhuman primates to acquire symbols encoding various conceptual domains.

Given the necessary conceptual underpinnings, the semantic distinctions made in the model language can affect further cognitive development, as has been argued by Vygotsky (1962), Blank and Allen (1975), Bowerman (1978), and others. That is, at a certain point, having *some* language permits the expansion of thinking into new areas. I would suggest that once the step of symbolic reference is attained, conceptual development can never thereafter be separated from language development, because the presence of words makes possible a qualitatively different kind of thought that constantly builds upon itself. Conceptual-linguistic development must be viewed as an everwidening spiral, with each change reflecting what has occurred before.

In this case, the parents' reference to events outside the immediate situation may have functioned to provide support for the child's developing cognitions. The child studied here began to acquire the forms that are used to signal past in English over a limited conceptual domain, commenting on what just happened and answering questions about such events. The emerging abilities to deal with past reference in the "easy" sense seemed to create opportunities for learning to use past in the more abstract sense: reference to earlier time.

CONCLUSIONS

The first goal of this study was to describe the emergence of reference to absent objects and past or future events in the conversations of a child and her parents. These conversations were not *exclusively* about the here and now, although most of the talk focused on current perceptions and events throughout the period studied. When reference to absent objects and reference to Earlier Past and

Future first appeared in the child's or parent's speech, it posed difficulties for communication. Successful reference was typically within the framework of a few, highly constrained topics that I have called "conversational routines." In talking about absent objects, the earliest routines usually involved asking about the location or activities of a unique referent, thus avoiding the problem of establishing agreement on the topic. When Naomi was learning about Earlier Past, the events of that day rather than the more distant past were likely topics of conversation.

As the child developed, reference to objects and events outside the current context became more frequent and the range of topics that was appropriate to discuss broadened systematically. By the end of the period studied, when Naomi was 3 years old, she could engage in conversations about shared past experiences and nonpresent objects with no support from the immediate situation. Both the parents and child related their current perceptions to prior experiences and knowledge, and Naomi began to make spontaneous comments that indicated some interest in the sequencing of events, particularly in what was going to happen later in the day or the next day.

On the other hand, around 3 years of age, interactions about absent objects, past, and future were still relatively rare, with the great bulk of talk about the here and now. Displaced topics were typically initiated by the adult and such conversations were very short; Naomi always returned to comments about the immediate situation after a few turns.

Although considerable development takes place during the 12–36-month period studied here, the child's abilities as a conversational partner continue to change throughout childhood. One example of an area deserving further study is the growth in knowledge about how to specify topics for the listener. Examples given here showed that, at 3 years, Naomi had great difficulty in choosing descriptive information to help her listener understand her meaning. Successful conversation with children often depends more on the skill of the adult in guessing and/or probing than it does on the skill of the child in supplying relevant information.

Deciding *what* to include in talk is complex, involving not only linguistic skills but judgments about relevance for the topic and for the listener. We would expect to find not only developmental changes in such an aspect of language use, but individual differences in the level of ability attained as well. The large literature in the area of "referential communication" represents one way to study this aspect of development, but other methods are currently adding to our knowledge about this important topic. See, for example, Cazden (1979) for a discussion of recent work on the analysis of natural conversation and Olson (1977) for perceptive comments on the relationship between spoken language and the development of writing skills.

The second goal of this study was to explore reasons for the development observed, especially in terms of the parent-child discourse. For both spatial and temporal displacement, there are context-bound language forms that serve as precursors to the development of reference to absent objects and past or future events. The child initially learns to refer to objects or actions by hearing words in the context of those objects or actions, and later uses those words independent of contextual support. Phrases like "Do you want X?" also take on meaning because they are initially combined with nonverbal cues to the semantic intent (Zukow, Reilly, & Greenfield, 1982). Here, we have seen that the word "where," which formed the basis for many of the early conversations about absent objects, first had the limited and concrete meaning, "point to object named," and only later acquired the more abstract meaning "specify location or activity." In acquiring past reference, consistent with results of previous research, the child observed here commented on just-completed events in the immediate situation for some time before she used her language in the more abstract sense, to refer to events that had occurred at an earlier time.

For each form in the language that has an abstract meaning, then, we find a more concrete or limited meaning underlying it. We will call this meaning the "original meaning," suggesting that it provides both the origin of usage of a linguistic form and the basis for further learning.

The aspects of language studied in this paper are both lexical and syntactic. In the case of past tense, the semantic distinction is reflected in terms of syntactic as well as lexical choice in English. Similar suggestions about the development of linguistic forms have been made recently elsewhere. In the acquisition of certain aspects of syntax, de Villiers (1980) argued that a limited prototypical form (Rosch, 1978) provides a core around which syntactic knowledge is structured. Slobin (1982) has described the beginning of syntax as the pairing of a "prototypical event" with a "canonical form." The meaning of the canonical form gradually becomes extended to encompass more than the meaning of the prototypical event.

For the semantic-syntactic domains here, the parents initially used linguistic forms in situations that clarified their original meanings, e.g., the point-elicitation meaning of *where* (asking *Where's baby?* when looking at a picture of a baby in a picture book) and Immediate Past (*You dropped it* right after Naomi dropped something). Anglin (1977) has shown that parents teach object names in the context of good examples of those objects. Similarly, in introducing words that are not object names, certain types of situations may make the underlying concept easier to grasp. It would be consistent with the suggestion made here and by Slobin if there is also some consistency from parent to parent in the situations in which various nonobject words, grammatical morphemes, and syntactic forms tend to be introduced.

As well as using the word or morpheme in a semantically transparent context, the parents used the forms in various types of discourse structures that could help the child acquire the original meaning. Examples of discourse phenomena involving Immediate Past that appeared in these data are Encodings (putting into words something that is noticed in the situation, as if talking for the child, as in *Georgie bumped his head*), Expansions, Clarification Requests, Queries with Supplied Answers (Adult: *What did you do? You bumped your knee*), Queries in which Imitations serve as Answers (Adult: *Did you fall down?* Child: *Fall down*), and Instructional Queries (questions to which the adult knows the answer). Of course, some of these discourse structures place more demands on the child than others, and we would predict that the ones with less child participation would be more frequent at earlier stages in the child's linguistic development. There were too few instances of the various types in my data to be able to test this notion statistically.

Once the original meaning of a word or morpheme is established, then the semantic domain can be extended to include the more abstract meaning. Many of the examples in this paper illustrate the way in which the semantic domain was enlarged for *where* and past tense in Naomi's data. Extending the semantic domain necessitates finding some way of talking about the abstract topic that will be understandable to the child. A metaphor I find useful is that there must be a *wedge* that enlarges the old meaning. The wedge is a form of expression that creates a link between the original meaning and an expanded, more abstract semantic domain. The form used as a wedge need not be identical from child to child, but we might expect that these linking forms would share certain characteristics. They build closely upon shared knowledge and introduce the new meaning in a semantically clear context.[6]

In the acquisition of verbal responses to *where,* the wedge consisted of a few conversational routines about unique objects. Success in learning how to respond in these routines seemed to give Naomi the opportunity to discover that *where* meant "specify location or activity."

In the acquisition of Earlier Past, the initial wedge that opened up the more abstract meaning may have been questions about shared experiences. Here is an example of a conversation, in which Naomi seemed initially to understand little about the adult's intent and at first only responded by imitation.[7] However, eventually she realized something about what was required, responding *Go-go* to *What else?*. The mother was presumably successful in eliciting a relevant response to her Instructional Queries about Earlier Past from Naomi because she provided sufficient cues to lead Naomi to recall the shared experience.

Adult: Did you go on the slide?
Child: Go slide.

---

[6]Just as prototypical situations may be similar across adults talking to children, the choice of wedges may also be predictable to some extent. A number of other researchers have indicated to me that they find early examples of reference to the location of absent individuals, such as *Where's Daddy?*, in their data.

[7]Keenan (1975) has pointed out that, for the child, imitations serve in conversations to take a turn. Here, they sometimes function as appropriate answers as well.

Adult: What else did we do outside?
Child: Outside.
Adult: Did we ride the tricycle?
Child: Tricycle.
Adult: What else?
Child: Go-go.
Adult: Right, we rode the go-go.

Another way to establish context for Earlier Past conversation was to mention a location Naomi had been in earlier, or a person Naomi had been with earlier, as in *What did you do today at Kimberly's?*

We would predict that conversations about shared experiences would be easier than conversations about the child's experiences without the adult. We would also predict that conversations with more clues as to the context in the past would be easier than conversations with few clues. The question that was used in the anecdote at the beginning of this paper, *What did you do today?* should be harder than *What did you do today at Kimberly's?* To the extent that caregivers provide opportunities to engage in these "easy" conversations, acquisition of the more abstract meanings may be facilitated. This does not mean, of course, that children cannot acquire the more complex meanings without such experience. Optimal input may make certain aspects of acquisition easier, but may not be necessary (cf. Nelson, 1980). Clearly, we are just beginning to explore the complex relationship between caregiver-child discourse and language learning.

Furthermore, information about the frequency or even presence of particular discourse strategies is needed before we attach importance to them as influences on the child's language acquisition. The interactions analyzed here were typically those in which "just talking" was on the agenda. The speech used by an adult to a child is obviously influenced by the adult's view of the goal of the communication. The structure of free-time conversations would be different from interactions in which the adult had other goals such as caregiving, explicit instruction, or trying to make the child be quiet. For example, Hall and Cole (1978) showed that adults were much more likely to ask questions, particularly of the instructional type, if they perceived their task as teaching. The adults' goals were to some extent influenced by situational cues (children were less likely to be instructed in a supermarket than in a classroom) but to some extent independent of it (a supermarket could be a situation for instruction). The amount the individual caregivers play with, instruct, control, or ignore children varies, and both the causes and the effects of this variation deserve further study.

Cultural values and beliefs also influence early caregiver-child discourse, and recent work by Schieffelin (1979) on the development of communicative competence in children in a Papua, New Guinea tribe, the Kaluli, shows the importance of comparative studies for our understanding of the role of input in language learning. Discourse among the Kaluli is different from middle-class American discourse in many ways. Schieffelin and Eisenberg (in press) have examined conversations about the past in the Kaluli data and data from middle-class families in Northern California. In the American families, the patterns are similar to those reported in this paper in that the earliest past references were often about shared experiences and the adults used language (especially queries) in an instructional manner. However, such "instructional" conversations never occur among the Kaluli, because talk for its own sake is actively discouraged by the caregivers, and asking children questions about shared information would be viewed as "to no purpose."

With these cautions in mind, I suggest that we look carefully at the child's opportunities to learn other aspects of syntax and semantics in discourse with adults. The following general principles are suggested:

1. We might expect to find original meanings for both words and syntactic forms. These simple, earliest meanings will be closely tied to the child's existing perceptions and knowledge.
2. Various uses of language in discourse, such as Expansions, Clarification Requests, Queries with Supplied Answers, and Instructional Queries, may help the child recognize the mapping between language and meaning.
3. Once the original meaning is established, the meaning of the linguistic form can be enlarged by introducing wedges, where a "wedge" is defined as a use of the linguistic form that relates the old, simple meaning to an expanded, more abstract semantic domain.

The relationship between semantic intention and syntactic realization in the child's developing language has been described as following the principles "New forms express old functions," and "Old forms express new functions" (Bloom, 1970; Slobin, 1973). These same principles can be seen in the relationship between linguistic input and child speech. Once the child knows a form to express a particular function, the input can show the child that the "old form" can be extended to a "new function." In these data, for example, one old form was "use of past markers to refer to Immediate Past" and the new function introduced by the parents was "reference to events that occurred earlier in time."

Thus, the child is exposed to new ideas through interactions with adults. The adults do not deliberately structure their language to teach, but, in the course of quite ordinary everyday talking, they use what the child already knows to provide opportunities for the child to learn something new.

ACKNOWLEDGMENTS

Part of this research was supported by a grant for Basic Research in Education from the U. S. Office of Education and a grant from the University of Connecticut Research Foundation. I am grateful to Diane Brackett and Deborah Pierson for their help in transcription and coding. Some of these data were discussed in papers presented at the Child Language Research Forum, the New York Child Language Group, the Southeastern Conference on Human Development, and Brown University. I appreciate the many useful comments from my colleagues, and wish to particularly thank Bambi Schieffelin, Dan Slobin, and Carlotta Smith for suggestions regarding this manuscript.

REFERENCES

Anglin, J. *Word, object, and conceptual development*. New York: Norton, 1977.
Antinucci, F. & Miller, R. How children talk about what happened. *Journal of Child Language*, 1976, *3*, 167–189.
Baron, N. The acquisition of indirect reference: Functional motivations for continued language learning in children. *Lingua*, 1977, *42*, 349–364.
Bates, E. *The emergence of symbols: Cognition and communication in infancy*. New York, Academic Press, 1979.
Bates, E., Camaioni, L., & Volterra, V. The acquisition of performatives prior to speech. *Merrill-Palmer Quarterly*, 1975, *21*, 205–226.
Bhattacharya, N. & Baron, N. The problem of direct and indirect reference. *Semiotica*, 1979, *26½*, 81–98.
Blank, M. & Allen, D. Understanding "Why:" Its significance in early intelligence. *In* M. Lewis (Ed.), *Infant intelligence*. New York: Plenum, 1975.
Bloom, L. *Language development: Form and function in emerging grammars*. Cambridge, Mass.: M.I.T. Press, 1970.
Bloom, L., Rocissano, L., & Hood, L. Adult-child discourse: Developmental interaction between information processing and linguistic knowledge. *Cognitive Psychology*, 1976, *8*, 521–552.
Bloom, L., Lifter, K., & Hafitz, J. Semantics of verbs and the development of verb inflections in child language. *Language*, in press.
Bowerman, M. The acquisition of word meaning: An investigation of some current conflicts. *In* M. Waterson & C. Snow (Eds.), *The development of communication: Social and pragmatic factors in language acquisition*. London: Wiley, 1978.
Bronkadt, J. P. & Sinclair, H. Time, tense and aspect. *Cognition*, 1973, *2*, 107–130.
Brown, R. *A first language: The early stages*. Cambridge, Mass.: Harvard University Press, 1973.
Brown, R. & Bellugi, U. Three processes in the child's acquisition of syntax. *Harvard Educational Review*, 1964, *34*, 133–151.
Bruner, J. The ontogenesis of speech acts. *Journal of Child Language*, 1975, *2*, 1–20.
Bruner, J., Roy, C., & Ratner, N. The beginnings of request. *In* K. Nelson (Ed.), *Children's language*, (Vol. 3). New York: Lawrence Erlbaum Associates, 1982.
Carter, A. The development of systematic vocalizations prior to words: A case study. *In* N. Waterson & C. Snow (Eds.), *The development of communication: Social and pragmatic factors in language acquisition*. London: Wiley, 1978.
Cazden, C. Peekaboo as an instructional model: Discourse development at home and at school. *Papers and Reports on Child Language Development*, 1979, *17*, 1–29.
Chafe, W. L. Language and consciousness. *Language*, 1974, *50*, 111–133.
Clark, E. V. Non-linguistic strategies and the acquisition of word meanings. *Cognition*, 1973, *2*, 161–182.
Cromer, R. *The development of temporal reference during the acquisition of language*. Unpublished doctoral dissertation, Harvard University, 1968.
Cross, T. G. Mothers' speech adjustment: The contribution of selected child variables. *In* C. E. Snow & C. A. Ferguson (Eds.), *Talking to children: Language input and acquisition*. Cambridge: Cambridge University Press, 1977.

de Villiers, J. The process of rule learning in child speech: A new look. *In* K. E. Nelson (Ed.), *Children's language* (Vol. 2). New York: Gardner Press, 1980.

Dore, J. *Cognition and communication in language acquisition and development.* Paper presented at Boston University Conference on Language Development, 1978.

Ferguson, C. A. The structure and use of politeness formulas. *Language in Society,* 1976, *5,* 137–151.

Furrow, D., Nelson, K., & Benedict, H. Mothers' speech to children and syntactic development: Some simple relationships. *Journal of Child Language,* 1979, *6,* 423–442.

Gleason, J. B. Talking to children: Some notes on feedback. *In* C. E. Snow & C. A. Ferguson (Eds.), *Talking to children: Language input and acquisition.* Cambridge: Cambridge University Press, 1977.

Glucksberg, S., Krauss, R., & Higgins, E. T. The development of referential communication skills. *In* F. D. Horowitz (Ed.), *Review of Child Development Research* (Vol. 4). Chicago: University of Chicago Press, 1975.

Goldin-Meadow, S. & Feldman, H. The development of language-like communication without a language model. *Science,* 1977, *197,* 401–403.

Greenfield, P. M. & Smith, J. H. *The structure of communication in early language development.* New York: Academic Press, 1976.

Hall, W. S. & Cole, M. On participant's shaping of discourse through their understanding of the task. *In* K. E. Nelson (Ed.), *Children's Language,* (Vol. 1). New York: Gardner Press, 1978.

Halliday, M. A. K. *Learning how to mean: Explorations in the development of language.* London: Edward Arnold, 1975.

Harner, L. Yesterday and tomorrow: Development of early understanding of the terms. *Developmental Psychology,* 1975, *11,* 864–865.

Harner, L. Children's understanding of linguistic reference to past and future. *Journal of Psycholinguistic Research,* 1976, *5,* 65–84.

Harner, L. Children talk about the time and aspect of actions. *Child Development,* 1981, *52,* 498–506.

Hockett, C. F. The origin of speech. *Scientific American,* 1960, *203,* 89–96.

Huttenlocher, J. The origins of language comprehension. *In* R. Solso (Ed.), *Theories in cognitive psychology.* Hillsdale, N.J.: Lawrence Erlbaum Associates, 1974.

Keenan, E. O. *Making it last: Repetition in children's discourse.* Papers of the Berkeley Linguistic Society, 1975.

Keenan, E. O. & Schieffelin, B. B. Topic as a discourse notion: A study of topic in the conversation of children and adults. *In* C. Li (Ed.), *Subject and topic.* New York: Academic Press, 1976.

Kuczaj, S. The acquisition of regular and irregular past tense forms. *Journal of Verbal Learning and Verbal Behavior,* 1977, *16,* 589–600.

Macnamara, J. Cognitive basis for language learning in infants. *Psychological Review,* 1972, *79,* 1–13.

Miller, M. & Weissenborn, J. Pragmatic conditions on learning how to refer to localities. *Papers and Reports on Child Language Development,* 1978, *15,* 68–77.

Moerk, E. L. Verbal interactions between children and their mothers during the preschool years. *Developmental Psychology,* 1975, *11,* 788–794.

Nelson, K. Concept, word, and sentence: Interrelations in acquisition and development. *Psychological Review,* 1974, *81,* 269–285.

Nelson, K. E. *Recasts and the introduction of new syntactic forms into the child's language.* Paper presented at the Boston University Conference on Child Language, 1977.

Nelson, K. E. Theories of the child's acquisition of syntax: A look at rare events and at necessary, catalytic, and irrelevant components of mother-child conversation. *Annals of the New York Academy of Sciences,* 1980, *345,* 45–67.

Olson, D. From utterance to text: The bias of language in speech and writing. *Harvard Educational Review,* 1977, *47,* 257–281.

Retherford, K. S., Schwartz, B. C., & Chapman, R. S. *The changing relationship between semantic relations in mother and child speech.* Paper presented at Boston University Conference on Language Development, 1977.
Rosch, E. Principles of categorization. *In* E. Rosch & B. Lloyd (Eds.), *Cognition and categorization.* Hillsdale, N.J.: Lawrence Erlbaum Associates, 1978.
Sachs, J. Talking about the there and then. *Papers and Reports on Child Language Development,* 1977, *13,* 56–63.
Sachs, J. Topic selection in parent-child discourse. *Discourse Processes,* 1979, *2* 145–153.
Sachs, J. & Johnson, M. Language development in a hearing child of deaf parents. *In* W. von Raffler Engel & Y. Lebrun (Eds.), *Baby talk and infant speech.* Lisse, Netherlands: Swets & Zeitlinger, 1976.
Sachs, J. & Truswell, L. Comprehension of two-word instructions by children in the one-word stage. *Journal of Child Language,* 1978, *5,* 17–24.
Schieffelin, B. B. *How Kaluli children learn what to say, what to do, and how to feel: An ethnographic study of the development of communicative competence.* Unpublished doctoral dissertation, Columbia University Teachers College, 1979.
Schieffelin, B. B. & Eisenberg, A. R. Cultural variation in dialogue. *In* R. L. Schiefelbusch (Ed.), *Communicative competence: Acquisition and intervention.* Baltimore, Md.: University Park Press, in press.
Shatz, M. The relationship between cognitive processes and the development of communication skills. *In* B. Keasey (Ed.), *Nebraska Symposium on Motivation,* 1977. Lincoln, Nebr.: University of Nebraska Press, 1978.
Slobin, D. I. Cognitive prerequisites for the development of grammar. *In* C. A. Ferguson & D. I. Slobin (eds.), *Studies of child language development.* New York: Holt, Rinehart & Winston, 1973.
Slobin, D. I. The origins of grammatical encoding of events. *In* W. Deutsch (Ed.), *The child's construction of language.* New York: Academic Press, 1982.
Smith, C. S. The acquisition of time talk: Relations between child and adult grammars. *Journal of Child Language,* 1980, *7,* 263–279.
Snow, C. E. Mothers' speech research: From input to interaction. *In* C. E. Snow and C. A. Ferguson (Eds.), *Talking to children: Language input and acquisition.* Cambridge: Cambridge University Press, 1977.
Snow, C. E. The conversational context of language acquisition. *In* R. N. Campbell & P. T. Smith (Eds.), *Recent advances in the psychology of language: Language development and mother-child interaction.* New York: Plenum, 1978.
Stoel-Gammon, C. & Cabral, L. S. Learning how to tell it like it is: The development of the reportative function in children's speech. *Papers and Reports on Child Language Development,* 1977, *13,* 64–71.
van der Geest, T. Some interactional aspects of language acquisition. *In* C. E. Snow & C. A. Ferguson (Eds.), *Talking to children: Language input and acquisition.* Cambridge: Cambridge University Press, 1977.
Vygotsky, L. S. *Thought and language.* Cambridge, Mass.: M.I.T. Press, 1962.
Zukow, P. G., Reilly, J., & Greenfield, P. M. Making the absent present: Facilitating the transition from sensorimotor to linguistic communication. *In* K. Nelson (Ed.), *Children's language* (Vol. 3). Hillsdale, N.J.: Lawrence Erlbaum Associates, 1982.

2 Saying It Again: The Role of Expanded and Deferred Imitations in Language Acquisition

Catherine E. Snow
Harvard University
Graduate School of Education

Imitation is a factor that has been implicated in the process of language acquisition to a degree dictated more by theoretical orientation than by empirical observation. Learning theorists who could propose no other mechanism to explain the child's production of new utterances assigned imitation a central role in explanations of language acquisition. Transformationally oriented developmental psycholinguists, for whom the essence of language is its creativity and rule-governed character, relegated it to the status of epiphenomenon. Several kinds of demonstrations have been offered that imitation is not important to language acquisition. These include the following arguments:

1. Many mistakes made by children include overgeneralizations, forms that clearly have not been modeled by adults and thus could not have been imitated, such as *catched, buyened, foots,* and *mouthes*. These overgeneralized forms reveal the nature of the child's rule system for marking plurality and past tense.

2. The word order in children's early utterances does not always conform to the (presumed) model. For example, *allgone lettuce* is a frequently observed type of child utterance, for which the adult model must be something like "The lettuce is all gone." Thus, the child must be producing such utterances on the basis of his own word order rules, not by a process of reduced imitation.

3. Children's mistakes are insensitive to correction by modeling of the correct form. This phenomenon has been repeatedly illustrated with various anecdotes, and its existence was confirmed in a study by Berko Gleason (1967), in which children were asked to produce the inflected forms of irregularly pluralized nouns immediately after having heard the correct form. Within a few seconds of having heard 'two mice', children would nonetheless say 'one mouse, two mouses' when asked for the plural.

4. Not all children imitate. Some children imitate as few as 5% of the types they produce; therefore, imitation cannot be a central process in any general explanation of language acquisition (Bloom, Hood, & Lightbown, 1974).

5. Elicited and spontaneous imitations are not progressive. This finding was first reported by Ervin (1964), who found that the MLU, incidence of morphological markers, and use of adultlike forms were all lower in imitated than in spontaneous utterances. Interestingly, subsequent studies, even of children for whom imitation has been demonstrated to be progressive, have replicated this finding for a global comparison of imitated and spontaneous utterances (Moerk, 1977; Snow, unpublished data).

6. To the extent that progressivity has been found in imitated utterances, it is largely restricted to lexical progressivity (Ramer, 1976), i.e., new words are imitated and subsequently learned, but new syntactic constructions are not. (This generalization does not hold for three of the six children studied by Bloom, Hood, & Lighbown, 1974.) Since it is obvious that children learn new words from hearing adult models, the finding that immediate imitation of new lexical items contributes to learning them is not very exciting. The more interesting observation is that many children do not imitate new syntactic constructions or morphological categories.

More recent discussions of imitation have rescued it somewhat from irrelevancy. The potency of imitation as a process supporting lexical acquisition (Ramer, 1976) acquires greater importance within theories that would give lexical acquisition a more central role in syntax (Bresnan, 1978). Furthermore, more recent studies have demonstrated an effect of imitation (at least for some children) on the acquisition of syntax and morphology (Bloom, Hood, & Lightbown, 1974; Clark, 1977, 1978; Moerk, 1977; Moerk & Moerk, 1979), as well as its effectiveness as a device for maintaining conversational exchange (Keenan, 1974, 1977; McTear, 1978). Though it is clear that there are limits placed by the child's own language system and comprehension ability on the sorts of acquisition that imitation can support at any stage of language development, imitation plus reinforcement has been shown in both natural and laboratory experiments to be a more effective method than simple modeling for teaching complex syntactic structures (Whitehurst, 1972, 1980; Whitehurst, Ironsmith, & Goldfein, 1974; Whitehurst & Novak, 1973; Whitehurst, Novak, & Zorn, 1972; Whitehurst & Vasta, 1975). Imitation is a teaching device whose potency is better appreciated when it is seen in the context of a culture that exploits it more fully than the middle-class North American culture does (cf. Schieffelin's 1979 study of the use of ɛlɛma by Kaluli mothers in Papua-New Guinea and Watson-Gegeo & Gegeo's 1982 report of a similar phenomenon in the Solomon Islands).

True appreciation of the role of imitation in language acquisition, however, requires a theory within which the contribution of immediate and reduced imitations, such as those studied by the majority of researchers, is combined with an assessment of the role of expanded and deferred imitations. Expanded imitations are those that include words not present in the modeled utterance; deferred imitation refers to the use of imitated sequences and sentence frames stored in memory for several hours or days before being used. Data on expanded imitations has been presented only by Bloom, Rocissano, and Hood (1976) and by Snow (1981); deferred imitations have been discussed by Clark (1974, 1977) and by Ferrier (1978) as a source of children's language productions. Both expanded and deferred imitations can be seen to have two potential roles in the child's language: a) they increase his performance ability at any given time beyond that available from his own linguistic rule system; this is the function referred to in Clark's (1974) title 'Performing without competence'; and b) they provide the child with a mechanism for learning new constructions by giving him access to information about those constructions in his own output.

The existence of expanded and deferred imitations forces us to reassess the claim that imitation cannot be a crucial process in language learning because immediate, reduced imitation is not a universal feature of early language acquisition. Children who never produce reduced, immediate imitations may, nonetheless, be relying to a very large extent on expanded and/or deferred imitations in their speech.

It is important to assess the role played by children's immediate, expanded, and deferred imitations in their ability to produce multiword utterances, because without estimating the contribution of imitation one can easily overestimate the child's knowledge of rules. To give a simple example, one would not want to credit a 2-year-old with knowledge of the complex rules underlying the formation of yes-no questions in English simply because she had produced the utterances, "Have you any wool?" and "Are you going to Scarborough fair?" The ability to produce such memorized sequences from songs and rhymes is generally recognized to be quite different from the ability to generate such sequences spontaneously. Similarly, the child who produced correct, adultlike English negatives only in utterances that immediately followed parental negations should not be credited with knowledge of the rules underlying negation in English, even if his negative utterances were not *reduced* imitations of the adult utterances (see Table 2.1 for a sample of utterances from this fictional child). This child should be credited, of course, with considerable knowledge about the semantics of negation, and about useful heuristics for communicating complex ideas in linguistically appropriate ways; nonetheless, his knowledge of the syntax of negation remains undemonstrated.

The purpose of the present paper is to assess the available evidence regarding the production of expanded and deferred imitations by children and their potential usefulness to the child in a) expanding his language performance ability beyond the bounds of his syntactic knowledge; and b) serving as a source of syntax acquisition. The first section will deal with expanded imitations, the second with deferred imitations. In each section, relevant data that has been

TABLE 2.1
Adult Negative Utterances and Contingent Child Negations

Adult Utterances	Child Utterances
We don't like peanuts.	I don't like peanuts either.
You didn't finish your dinner.	Roger didn't finish his dinner either
I can't find it.	Daddy can't find it too.
That's not blue.	That's not green.
You're not allowed to walk across the street alone.	Stefan's not allowed to walk across the street alone.
He doesn't like spinach.	I doesn't like spinach.
You haven't brushed your teeth today.	Stefan haven't brushed his teeth today.

presented by others will be reviewed, and data will be presented from a longitudinal study of one child, N, who was observed from 26 through 38 months, with the help of both diary notes and regular tape recordings of natural interaction in the home. The data from N are presented largely as examples of the existence of interesting phenomena and as a way of generating hypotheses about the potential usefulness of expanded and deferred imitations in explanations of the process of language acquisition. Clearly, more extensive studies of many other children must be undertaken before any general conclusion about the role of expanded and deferred imitations in language acquisition can be drawn.

EXPANDED IMITATIONS

Definition

As discussed above, the majority of studies that have focused on children's imitations have used a definition of imitation that excludes any child utterance containing a morpheme not present in the model (see Snow 1981 for a discussion of how different researchers have defined 'imitation'). The exclusion of child utterances that borrow much of their structure and many of their lexical items from adult models can lead to an overestimate of the child's spontaneous production ability, if indeed the utilization of the imitated chunks from the adult model enables the child to produce syntactic structures he would otherwise be incapable of. Furthermore, failure to recognize the existence of expanded imitations has meant that the information available from an analysis of expanded imitations about children's heuristics for reducing processing load while maximizing communicative effectiveness has not been exploited.

There are methodological problems associated with the category expanded imitations, if these are defined too loosely. Inclusion in the child utterance of a word or a phrase from the preceding adult utterance cannot be sufficient criterion for identifying the child utterance as an expanded imitation. Carrying on a conversation related to a single topic places constraints on the things to be talked about and the words to be used. Thus, some repetition of lexical items across speakers is to be expected in any coherent conversation. Calling child utterances that include lexical items from preceding adult utterances 'expanded imitations' is meant, in this paper, explicitly to imply the theoretical claim that such child utterances are produced by the process of imitation, i.e., that the child utterance would have had a different form if the adult utterance had been different in form.

The difficulty of distinguishing between expanded imitations and appropriate conversational responses is made very clear by the results presented by Bloom, Rocissano, and Hood (1976). They found an increase in the incidence of what they term 'contingent speech' with age. Contingent speech was defined as speech that directly followed adult speech and continued the same topic. Older children are better able to continue a topic, and to make topic-relevant remarks, and their utterances tend to be more complete than those of younger children; therefore, it might look like older children are producing more expanded imitations just because of their increasing conversational skill. In fact, of course, one would expect that the incidence of expanded imitations would decrease with development (although perhaps very slowly) to a zero or very low level, if the expanded imitations incorporate incompletely analyzed chunks of the adult model.

In order, then, to exclude from the category of expanded imitations child utterances that are simply appropriate responses to adult utterances, child utterances were classified as expanded imitations only if the imitated portion matched the adult model in content lexical items and in prosody. A child utterance was, thus, not classified as an imitation if it was identical to a preceding adult utterance only in function words, or if the intonation or stress pattern of the adult model had been altered. Analysis of the incidence of expanded imitation in N's speech (Snow, 1981) revealed the following types (X is used to indicate the spontaneous portion of the utterance, I the imitated portion):

> *IX* Mother: What did we crash into last night? N: Crash into living room.
> *XI* Mother: Do you like Cheerios? N: Cheerios? Eat Cheerios?
> *IXI* Mother: You like jingle bells. N: Like other jingle bells.
> *XIX* Mother: Mummy has to do pee-pee now. N: Nathaniel has to do pee-pee now too.
> *IXIX/XIXI* Mother: That's mummy's hair clip. N: That's Nathanial's hair clip too.

It was found that the incidence of the more complex types (IXI, XIX, IXIX, XIXI) increased with age, in proportion to the simpler types, as one would expect, though during the age span studied the total incidence of expanded imitations remained constant (Snow, 1981).

Relationship of Expanded Imitations to Vertical Constructions

Scollon (1979) identified in the speech of the child he was studying the occurrence of sequences of short utterances that expressed different aspects of a particular situation and that looked very much like the separate elements that would, at a slightly later stage, be combined by that child into single, longer utterances. In fact, sometimes the combination into a single utterance occurred directly after the child had uttered the separate elements individually, e.g.:

CHILD	ADULT
Ron	
	OK
Ron talk	

The occurrence of these sequences suggested to Scollon that: a) the sequenced utterances represented a certain structure, which he thus dubbed 'vertical construction'; and (b) the child used the successive production of the elements as a way of decreasing processing load, thus enabling herself to produce the longer utterance that would otherwise have been beyond her capacity.

In some sense, expanded imitations can be seen as two-party vertical constructions. Rather than producing bits of the target construction himself, and then incorporating the already located and outputted bits into one larger utterance, the child borrows bits from the utterance produced by the adult.

Vertical constructions and expanded imitations fulfill highly similar functions in the child's language performance: Both represent discourse support for the process of producing complex utterances. The similarity in function of *vertical* constructions and expanded imitations suggests that they might be either complementary or highly correlated in distribution: If there are some children who require a large amount of discourse support for their complex utterances, they would be expected to use both vertical constructions and expanded imitations, and the frequency of these two phenomena would be highly correlated across children. On the other hand, if all children require approximately the same amount of discourse support for complex utterances, then some might hit upon imitations and others upon self-generated vertical constructions as the best way to provide this. Since no one has looked at vertical constructions and expanded imitations in the same children, the exact relationship between them remains an open question.

Incidence of Expanded Imitations

If a significant proportion of children's utterances consists of expanded imitations, and if expanded imitations are produced even by those children who do not produce large numbers of reduced imitations, then the role of expanded imita-

TABLE 2.2*
N's Production of Reduced and Expanded Imitations

Age	MLU	Number of Utterances	% Reduced + Exact Imitations	% Expanded Imitations
2;2.22	1.97	209	32.5	19.2
2;5.18	2.41	2724	24.8	14.0
2;7.0	2.93	2085	21.7	19.0

*data from Snow (1981)

TABLE 2.3.
Percentage of Child Utterances which are Imitations

Study	Child	# Utterances	% Imitations*
Bloom, Hood & Lightbown (1974)	Alison	1254	4- 6
	Eric	2583	15-17
	Gia	3383	4-14
	Jane	1582	32-42
	Kathryn	2256	11-36
	Peter	6388	27-42
Ervin (1964)	Donnie		6- 8
	Susan		7
	Christy		5
	Lisa		15
	Holly		20
Folger & Chapman (1978)	A	750	12.8
	B	540	14.5
	C	711	18.0
	D	1015	20.0
	E	465	24.5
	F	680	28.1
Ramer (1976)	Greg		1.7
	Danielle		2.0
	Marjorie		5.6
	David N		6.3
	Emily		6.4
	David S		13.2
	Lisa		17.0
Seitz & Stewart (1975)	9 23-month	$\bar{X}$ = 110	$\bar{X}$ = 10.9
	9 56-month	$\bar{X}$ = 108	$\bar{X}$ = 1.2

*The definitions of imitation, and the basis for calculating percentages, varied somewhat from study to study.

tions in supporting acquisition must be further examined. Unfortunately, the incidence of expanded imitations is not available for most of those children whose imitations have been studied. Even some studies that have accepted expanded imitations as imitations do not report incidence of expanded imitations separately from reduced imitations, or do not report incidence at all.

The study of N's imitations revealed that just under 20% of his utterances were expanded imitations, during the period when his MLU developed from 2 to 3 (see Table 2.2). During this same period, his production of reduced immediate imitations declined from 33 to 22%. Compared to other children for whom information about incidence of reduced imitations is available (see Table 2.3), N was a high imitator. Was his production of large numbers of expanded imitations related to his tendency to imitate in general? Examination of the category 'Repeat plus add' in the data from Bloom, Rocissano, and Hood (1976), a category that is closely related if not identical to the category 'expanded imitation' as defined by Snow (1981), indicates that it increases with age from about 12% of contingent speech at MLU 1.2–1.4 to almost 50% at MLU 2.3–2.8. Unfortunately, figures on 'Repeat plus add' are not given for the four children individually, so it is not possible to determine its relationship to imitativeness. But imitation decreases with age, as 'Repeat plus add' increases. The Bloom, Rocissano, and Hood category 'expansion' is also closely related to the category

TABLE 2.4
Relationship between Imitativeness and Production of Recordings and Expansions*

Stage	Child	% Imitation	% Recoding	% Expansion	% Rec + Exp
I	Eric	30	3	38	41
	Gia	42	5	46	51
	Kathryn	50	4	31	35
	Peter	65	9	16	25
II	Eric	15	5	46	51
	Gia	2	3	36	39
	Kathryn	22	7	43	50
	Peter	26	5	22	27
III	Eric	8	4	56	60
	Gia	1	4	51	55
	Kathryn	4	2	54	56
	Peter	6	5	44	49

*Data from Bloom, Rocissano, and Hood, 1976.

'expanded imitation', though it is not clear that an imitated chunk must be a part of an expansion. The data for expansions, which are presented per child, suggest, if anything, a negative correlation with imitativeness (see Table 2.4). It seems, then, to be quite unclear whether the production of expanded imitations is correlated with the production of imitations in general, on the basis of the limited data available.

Contribution of Expanded Imitations to Language Acquisition

The incomplete evidence available suggests that most children, even nonimitators, may produce significant numbers of expanded imitations. These expanded imitations function to keep conversations going and to increase the child's productive, communicative ability beyond his syntactic productive ability. It has not yet been demonstrated that the expanded imitations function to increase the child's own syntactic skill in any lasting way. There are a number of ways in which this demonstration could be made:

1. Showing that the imitated chunks of expanded imitations contain syntactic structures not produced spontaneously at a certain session but produced spontaneously at subsequent sessions.
2. Showing that, at any session, certain syntactic structures of communicative intents are expressed only in (expanded) imitations, and not in spontaneous utterances.
3. Showing that the imitated chunks of expanded imitations decrease in length in some orderly way that reflects the increasing ability of the child to segment them and substitute constituents within them.

Snow (1981) has presented some evidence that N's expanded imitations were concentrated on different syntactic structures at successive stages: a) complex NP constructions at MLU of 1.97; b) responses to wh-questions at MLU of 2.41; and (c) constructions including disiderative markers *enne* and *no* at MLU of 2.93. Snow (1981) did not report any formal analysis of spontaneous utterances for incidence of these constructions or their surrogates, though she reported that these constructions were not frequent in spontaneous speech.

The Potential Usefulness of Expanded Utterances

The expanded utterances a child produces indicate a great deal about his language ability: how he segments adult utterances; how he interprets adult utterances; and what strategies he has developed for producing communicatively effective language in the absence of a complete, adultlike grammar. Furthermore, it seems very likely, though it has not been definitively demonstrated, that many children produce expanded imitations as a way of fulfilling a short-term communicative need while at the same time 'replaying' an adult utterance for analysis and segmentation. Such replaying could contribute in an obvious way to the child's syntactic growth and discovery of grammatical regularities.

DEFERRED IMITATIONS

An assumption underlying language acquisition research has been that long-term memory for utterances plays very little role in contributing to children's language performance. The role of memory in language acquisition has been discussed very little in general, though studies of lexical acquisition have shown (Carey, 1978; Nelson & Bonvillian, 1973) that children can learn and retain lexical items after only very brief exposures. For example, Nelson (1982) demonstrated that relatively brief exposure to exemplars and names enabled 18–60-month-olds to learn the name-concept pairing, and that retention for periods of 2–4 weeks occurred with no further exposure. Given the rapidity of lexical acquisition, brief exposure to words in context must be the mechanism responsible for a large proportion of the words in any child's vocabulary.

For relatively simple items, then, such as a word (which consists of an acoustic/articulatory specification associated with semantic information within the mental lexicon), long-term memory can be established on the basis of a single, brief exposure. Might such establishment of memory traces not also be possible for larger acoustic/articulatory units, equivalent to whole utterances? It has generally been assumed that such is not possible, because units longer than single words or short phrases are too complex to be stored in memory (except, perhaps, for very brief periods) unless analyzed, decoded, and reduced to a representation of the propositional meaning. It has been well demonstrated that even adults, whose encoding and storage capacity is much greater than the child's, do not store linguistic material verbatim. Adults remember linguistic material in such a way that the propositional content is largely retained, but information about syntactic form, sentence boundaries, order of words, and order of sentences is almost completely lost (Sachs, 1967; Bransford & Franks, 1972). Furthermore, it has been demonstrated that, in general, children do this same sort of recoding in memory, losing syntactic but retaining semantic information (Hakuta & Pinker, in prep.; Heras & Nelson, 1972). The normal method of processing linguistic information, both for children and for adults, is to retain information about the specific syntactic form and lexical items present in the material heard only as long as necessary to form a semantic representation of the linguistic material. The semantic content is then stored in long-term memory in a form far removed from its original, linguistic structure.

Furthermore, it has been demonstrated that even short-term memory for sentences depends on comprehension of the sentence. For example, in tasks that require immediate repetition of sentences by children, it has been shown that children significantly reduce, distort, and restructure sentences to cause them to conform to their own understanding of the world and their own grammars (Slobin & Welsh, 1973). Consider, for example, Slobin and Welsh's subject's restructuring of the (admittedly odd) sentence 'Chomsky and veritas are crying' into *Cynthia and Tasha . . . cry*.

The case seems clear, then, that long-term memory, after brief or infrequent exposure, is possible for short, unanalyzable units such as words, but not for longer or more complex units that must be segmented and decoded in order to be understood. Thus, the general tendency in child language acquisition literature to ignore the child's long-term memory capacity as a source of language performance or syntactic acquisition seems well-founded.

A number of observations, however, fail to fit in well with this position. These will be stated briefly here, in order to present a summary of the basic arguments being made, and will then be discussed in more detail in subsequent sections. Evidence that suggests a positive and important role for long-term memory of complex utterances in children's language performance and in their syntactic acquisition comes from:

1. Observations that children do form accurate memories for complex events and retain these memories for long periods of time without support from rehearsal.
2. Observations of children's delayed imitations of whole utterances in communicatively appropriate situations.
3. Observations that children can and do memorize large chunks of obviously unanalyzed material, e.g., songs and verses in a foreign language.
4. Observations of the extensive use of unanalyzed chunks in children's spontaneous productive utterances. This process has been documented for both first and second language learners.

If we accept, then, that children can use long, partially or completely unanalyzed utterances recovered from memory in communicatively appropriate ways, it becomes necessary to assess child utterances in a highly conservative way, considering the possibility that many structures that look spontaneous were produced by stringing unanalyzed chunks together, and to look in a more principled way at adult utterances, even adult utterances far removed in time, as models for child utterances.

In the following sections I will review the evidence available in support of the four observations regarding children's memory listed above. I will then present evidence from a study of the development of N's speech in the context of book-reading routines, where delayed imitation of temporally distant adult utterances will be demonstrated.

Children's Memories for Complex Events

Because of the general assumption among developmental psychologists that young children are incapable of long-term memory for complex events, almost no research has been directed specifically to the question of the limits of children's memories. DeLoache and Brown (1979) reported the first controlled study of children's recall in which retention intervals of longer than 30 seconds were used! They found that children as young as 18 months could retrieve desired toys from hiding places after intervals of several hours, with 77% errorless retrievals. Even when the children observed three different toys being hidden, often in hiding places used for other toys on previous trials, they could retrieve the requested one at first try on 67% of trials, after intervals of three to five minutes. In a sufficiently motivating task, then, children can form and retain memories over relatively long periods of time.

Memory over the retention intervals tested by DeLoache and Brown, however, does not even remotely approach the feats displayed by children in the normal course of daily events. DeLoache and Brown themselves state that "most parents recount numerous instances of their toddler remembering personally experienced events over days or even months [p. 53]." The limits of toddlers' memories will presumably have to be tested by collecting parental anecdotes, by carrying out much more intensive observations, or by systematically testing over retention intervals of several weeks. The usefulness of more intensive observations is demonstrated by findings emerging from use of the 'shadow technique,' in which children's utterances are recorded for several hours at a time. For example, Nelson (1981) observed that one child first produced a tag-question form more than 20 hours after last having heard a tag. It is not clear from the reported data whether the child's tag-question represented memory of an utterance or of a rule for producing tags.

A few anecdotes from the diary maintained of N's early development will demonstrate the existence and the level of complexity of very long-term child memories:

Age 2;4. When N was 2;2, friends of his parents came to stay for four days, bringing along their baby, named Jason. Two months later, the first time since Jason's visit that N's mother had opened up the guest room, N called it 'baby Jason's room'. Jason had not been mentioned in N's presence for at least one month prior to this comment.

Age 2;6. During a play session, N and his mother were building a school. They used an empty tea tin to represent 'the quiet room' and a rattle to represent a tree in the school yard. One week later, N labeled that tea tin (one of many among his toys) 'quiet room'; at 2;8, he labeled that same rattle 'tree.'

Age 2;7. N had at 2;5 visited a Chinese restaurant and received from the waiter a basket with a few fortune cookies in it. The basket was stored in a rarely opened cupboard. At 2;7, N found the basket, said 'no cookies in it.'

Age 2;7. N often played at 'making coffee' and "making tea" (i.e., pouring water from container to container) while in the bath. One evening, his mother suggested he make carrot juice instead. Eight days later, when asked what he was making in the bath, N answered 'carrot juice.'

Age 2;7. Riding in the car to school, N's mother mentioned to him that he couldn't see the stoplight at a particular corner because a beer truck was in the way. Three days later, N saw a truck at the same corner while on his way to school and said 'beer truck.'

Age 3;4. N found a toy car transporter that he had not seen for several months. A similar (though larger) transporter had been on the dresser in the room of his cousin Ian, where N had stayed two nights four months earlier. N immediately took the small transporter to his mother, saying 'have to take this back to Ian.'

Age 3;5. When he was 3;1, a friend of N's parents named Jaap had visited for five days. One evening, Jaap had requested that cucumbers be omitted from the salad because he did not like them. At 3;5, N's mother offered him a piece of cucumber, and he said, 'Why Jaap doesn't like cucumbers? Cause he's Dutch?' Although Jaap had been mentioned occasionally in N's presence, his dislike for cucumbers had been mentioned only once, on the evening they had been omitted from the salad.

Age 3;5. At 2;11, N had been fitted for glasses at an optical shop where two waterfall toys were available. He had played briefly with them. At 3;5, on the next visit to that shop, N played with one of the two toys, then asked where the other one was. He described it in detail when his mother failed to remember it. (Note that N had been wearing glasses since 1;6, and had visited many optical shops on many occasions.)

Several features common to the above anecdotes should be mentioned. First, the memories were not related to events of great personal, emotional importance to N. The events remembered were trivial and incidental. (He also remembered important events, of course.) Second, the memories could persist for very long periods of time with no obvious stimulus to or opportunity for rehearsal during the retention interval. Third, the memories were very specific and often highly complex. Fourth, the memories were in general quite context-bound, i.e., access to a particular memory was triggered by a salient object encountered in a recurrent situation.

Nelson and Ross (in press) report evidence on similar remote memories from 19 children, aged 21 to 27 months. The evidence was collected using structured diary reports from the children's mothers. All the mothers reported at least three such memories, with a mean of six memories reported per child. The demonstration that young children are capable of long-term and complex memories opens up the possibility that such memory capacity is also used in the service of language acquisition.

Another approach to studying the development of young children's memory abilities has been taken by Nelson and Gruendel (1979a, 1979b) in their studies of children's knowledge of scripts. A script can be seen as the synthesis of children's (or adults') acquired and organized knowledge about a particular situation; it is a term borrowed from Schank and Abelson (1977), who have discussed the importance of adults' scripts in language comprehension.

The relevance of the notion 'script' to the study of children's memories is that a script can be seen as the locus of a child's memory about a particular situation. The fact that very young children develop scripts for such events as taking baths, going to bed, going to the store, going for walks, and having lunch at the daycare center indicates that they can and do retain information about these complex events, in generalized forms, over considerable periods of time. Nelson and Gruendel (1979a) have presented evidence from interview studies that children as young as four have realistic scripts for such events as going to birthday parties, planting gardens, and making cookies—events that a given child may have experienced only a few times, and probably not within a few days or weeks prior to being interviewed. The youngest children tested by Nelson and Gruendel were four, but anecdotal evidence of awareness of scripts in much younger children is also presented.

Clearly, the limits of toddlers' memories have not been adequately charted by researchers in the field. Presumption of limitations has substituted for creative research methodology in guiding conclusions. It seems clear, though, that even children as young as two have sufficient memory ability that the proposal that they use delayed imitation of utterances in communicatively appropriate ways to expand their language performance ability cannot be dismissed on the grounds that their long-term memory ability is inadequate.

Delayed Imitation of Complex Utterances

As discussed above, studies of children's imitations of adult utterances have typically been confined to immediate imitations. Although the criteria used in the various studies for 'immediate' differ, attention has been limited in all studies to child utterances that occur within about a minute of the presumed adult model. Attention has been directed specifically to the question of the appropriate interval between model and imitation only by Bloom, Hood, and Lightbown (1974); they had originally used the criterion of five utterances as the maximum interval between model and imitation. For the subjects in their study who were very low imitators, though, they also assessed the incidence of imitation using a 10-utterance interval. They found that the percentage of imitations rose only marginally, and concluded that compensatory use of delayed imitations could not explain the absence of immediate imitation in low imitators. Similarly, in a study of N's imitations, it was found that his incidence of imitation rose only by 3 to 6% when the criterion was expanded from the first utterance after the model to any of the first five after the model. Clearly, the majority of imitations occur immediately, i.e., as the first child utterance following the adult model. Extending the acceptable interval from one to five or ten utterances increases the number of imitations only marginally. It has been argued, however, that this is precisely what might be expected if imitations have a communicative as well as an acquisition function (Snow, in press). A child produces a delayed imitation of an utterance because that utterance expresses a meaning he wants to convey. The occasion for conveying a meaning is not likely to recur within five or ten utterances of the adult's expression of that meaning. Snow (in press) gives the example of N's use of a six-word utterance reduced from the 15-word adult model he heard just after stepping into the bath one evening. The following evening, at the beginning of his next bath N used this utterance to convey the desired meaning—something like 'the bath water will not be too hot.' This was the first occasion after hearing the utterance on which N needed to express that meaning.

Precisely because imitations are used to convey specific meanings in specific communicative situations, no limit can be placed on the time interval between hearing the model and producing the imitations. This means that very strict methodological criteria for identifying child utterances as deferred imitations must be applied, in order to avoid the trivial conclusion that deferred imitation is very important because all child utterances are related to adult utterances heard in the past. In this paper, the criteria that have been adopted for identifying child utterances as deferred imitations include: 1) similarity in form; i.e., in words used and in order of stressed items; 2) prosodic identity; i.e., the same intonation and stress pattern as the adult model; 3) situational identifiability; i.e., some clear (to the adult) source of similarity between the situation in which the model utterance was heard and the situation in which the imitation is produced.

It is very difficult to determine the extent to which children's utterances are deferred imitations, and, understandably, published data on the incidence of deferred imitation is unavailable. Clark (1974, 1977) has claimed extensive use of deferred imitation and memorized chunks in her sons' multiword utterances; other reports of deferred imitation occur in the literature on second language acquisition. It may be that, because the older language learner can produce much longer unanalyzed chunks than young, first language learners, the presence of deferred imitations in their speech repertoire is more likely to be noticed. Huang and Hatch (1978) commented on the coexistence of long, imitated utterances such as 'It's time to go home' and shorter, rule-generated utterances such as 'Cow this' in the speech of Paul, a 5-year-old Chinese boy learning English. Fillmore (1976) has documented much more extensively the use of formulaic utterances in the speech of Chicano elementary school children acquiring English as a second language, and has discussed the role of formulaic utterances in language production in general.

The dichotomy 'rule-learner' and 'data-generator', suggested by Hatch (1974) as a way of distinguishing two observed styles of second language learning, may be the result of some children's tendency to imitate constructions they do not yet fully understand, thus producing a messy grammar. A similar distinction has been reported for phonological aspects of first language acquisition (Macken, 1978). Macken found that children whose phonological systems could be well characterized by fairly simple rules often refused to imitate words that could not be generated by their systems, whereas children who showed messier systems were much more willing to imitate words.

The role of formulaic speech in first language acquisition has been looked at extensively by Berko Gleason and colleagues (e.g., Greif & Gleason, 1980; Gleason, Perlmann, & Greif, 1980), who have analyzed the ways in which parents train children in the production of politeness formulas such as 'hello', 'thank you', 'please may I be excused?', and 'trick or treat.' Such formulas have to be produced, if they are used at all, as unanalyzed chunks; the way they are taught and learned may, furthermore, be relevant to the acquisition of a much wider spectrum of language behaviors, if Fillmore's (1976) hypothesis about the degree to which formulaic speech is used turns out to be correct.

Bolinger (1976) argued that memory for specific combinations of words, rather than rules, may be the source of much of our knowledge of syntax; he proposes a continuum from 'propositional' to 'automatic' speech modes, and places frequently used and conventional expressions toward the 'propositional' end of the continuum. Thomas (1979) has identified a relatively small number of routine utterances used with a particular pragmatic and semantic force in the speech of caretakers to children in the early stages of combining words; these utterances are strikingly frequent in caretakers' speech, and are surprisingly similar across unacquainted families. Such adult formulas are available as a ready source of deferred imitations in early child speech, as can be seen clearly in the utterances N chose as the models for his deferred imitations.

Entries from the diary kept of N's language development reveal considerable use of deferred imitations. Only those child utterances whose source in the adult speech was quite obvious are presented here:

Age 2;9. After dinner, N wanted to go outside to play (a recurrent request that was always refused at this time of day). He said to his father 'Go out in the garden, play with the red car. That's a good idea.' The intonation pattern of 'That's a good idea' mimicked precisely that normally produced by N's mother, who used this expression frequently in attempts to convince him to carry out nondesired behaviors. No exact data are available on when N had last heard his mother use this expression, but she had certainly not used it within the immediately preceding conversation, and probably not for several hours. N used this expression regularly from about 2;7 through 2;10 when trying to get permission from his parents.

Age 2;9. Coming downstairs before breakfast, wearing pajamas with fabric feet in them, N said at the top of the stairs 'The pj's you got on are slippery.' There had been no mention to him of pj's on that day. His mother had said to him 'The pj's you've got on are slippery' as he was walking down the stairs the previous morning. Note that relatives modifying NP's in subject position were not productive in N's speech at this time.

Age 2;9. As he started to climb up on low walls or other objects that required balance to walk on, N would typically say 'Let's see you climb up on this one.' This was the utterance frequently used by his father in encouraging him to walk on such structures. N used this expression regularly from about 2;8 to 2;11. Note the inappropriate pronoun in this (as in the previous) imitation.

Age 3;1. At breakfast, N interrupted his parents' reading of the newspapers to say 'This coffee's not so bad.' Coffee had not been mentioned during the previous ten minutes by anyone at the breakfast table. N's father had produced this utterance at the breakfast table the previous morning, commenting on a new (cheaper) brand of coffee. Note that N did not drink coffee, i.e., the utterance could not have had any real content for him.

Age 3;2. N's mother asked him if he had followed his favorite teacher around all day again at school. He answered, 'Yes, I did actually, not very often.' 'Yes, I did actually' was a relatively frequent utterance in his mother's speech. 'Not very often' is also, of course, an utterance that occurs in adult speech, in isolation, with considerable frequency. The incomplete comprehension of both these imitated chunks is demonstrated by their being used together, despite their noncompatible meanings.

These anecdotes are typical of a much larger number of examples that could be included, documenting N's use of deferred imitations in communicatively appropriate ways.

Once again, such anecdotes cannot be taken as proof of anything more than that complete utterances that have been heard and incompletely analyzed were reproduced by the child after considerable periods of time, in situations similar to those in which he first heard them. The deferred imitations were most likely to be imitations of adult utterances that had been used frequently and in a somewhat routinized fashion by the adult. It is not being suggested that such delayed imitations accounted for N's entire language system; he showed considerable control of syntax and morphology at the time that he was producing these imitations. Nonetheless, he did use deferred imitation to produce utterances that were well beyond his productive syntactic capabilities. Furthermore, he used them in ways that were communicatively effective if, at least, his interlocutors were familiar with his previous experiences and language exposure.

Production of Speech with No Semantic Analysis

Children can and do remember material that has no clear communicative or semantic representation. Examples include songs and verses in foreign language, and phrases and expressions overheard from adult conversations. Children's inability to understand this information does not block their willingness to repeat it. In previous sections, evidence has been presented that children achieve a minimal semantic/communicative representation for utterances heard from their parents, and then use those utterances, as wholes, appropriately. In this section, I will discuss evidence that children are to some extent willing to treat language as sound, i.e., to produce language performances that have no real semantic content for them at all.

The most striking example of this comes in recited performances. N at 3;9 could sing more than 25 Dutch and French songs in their entirety, with no prompting, despite having absolutely no ability to speak or comprehend even the simplest French or Dutch. He had learned these songs simply from listening to records of them, with no parental prompting or help with segmentation. In addition, he could sing tens of songs in English for which he very probably had only an incomplete segmentation and analysis of the texts. It is not chance, of course, that these very long and complex memorized chunks were all songs or verses; it has been frequently noted that rhythm, rhyme, and melody support memorization.

In addition, N's speech after about 3;2 was larded with less striking examples of 'speech as sound.' He picked up phrases and expressions used frequently by his parents, and incorporated these into his own utterances, despite having no real understanding of their meaning. Examples included 'at the moment,' 'actually,' 'I sure do,' 'possibly,' 'probably,' and 'at the fortune' (an attempt at 'unfortunately' somewhat restructured on the model of 'at the moment'). Blank (1974) has suggested that children's frequent production of why-questions during the fourth and fifth years involves their using an expression that has no clear semantic referent. Blank (1974) suggested that children pose why-questions precisely because they are trying to figure out what 'why' means. Answers received to why-questions, and responses that some why-questions are inappropriate, provide children with information about what 'why' means. N's use of imitated phrases may have had a similar motivation.

Incorporation of Unanalyzed Chunks into Spontaneous Utterances

In the first section of this paper it was demonstrated that children can incorporate chunks of speech 'borrowed' from the preceding adult utterances to expand their linguistic performance. It has also been demonstrated, primarily by Ruth Clark (1977, 1978) for first language acquisition, and by Fillmore (1976) and Hakuta (1974) for second language acquisition, that unanalyzed chunks in children's speech can be supplied by memory, from deferred imitations of adult utterances. Stringing together such chunks, or incorporating spontaneously produced strings into utterances that also contain imitated chunks, can enable the child to produce utterances that seem to have a much more complex structure than the child is otherwise capable of producing. At the same time, production of utterances incorporating unanalyzed chunks enables the child to say things he may otherwise have no way of expressing.

DEFERRED IMITATIONS IN A BOOK-READING ROUTINE

The data to be presented here document for one specific situation the way in which N used deferred imitation (see Snow & Goldfield, 1982, in press, for further analyses of these and related data). The situation was reading a particular book, Richard Scarry's Storybook Dictionary (published 1967 by Hamlyn, London) with his mother. Data are available on eight sessions, which occurred on eight different days between the time that N was 2;5,18 and the time that he was 2;6,25. The repeated reading of Richard Scarry's Storybook Dictionary developed for N and his mother into a clearly routinized style of interaction, with a highly predictable form (as was the case for their reading of several other books during the same period). The predictability of the form of the interactions, and the intensified possibilities for joint attention associated with the book-reading situation, had two effects: a) it enabled N to concentrate on the verbal exchange and thus maximized the utility of the language heard during the book-reading sessions to his acquisition process; b) it enables the observer to see the extent to which deferred imitation is being used. The recurrence of very specific and well-defined situations (e.g., looking at a page of the book) reveals the child's use of deferred imitations very clearly; deferred imitations that occur in other, less easily (to the adult, at least) identifiable recurrent situations simply cannot be identified as such.

As argued above, children produce deferred imitations with a communicative purpose and when the communicative situation in which the model was first heard recurs. It is normally very difficult for the adult to assess the degree to which two situations are, from the child's point of view, identical, and it is thus impossible to conclude that a child utterance is a deferred imitation, even if it is a repetition of a previous adult model. The child could have generated an utterance spontaneously that just happened to match an adult utterance he had heard. Evidence that the child is repeating adult models in precisely the situations in which those models were first encountered strengthens considerably the conclusion that such utterances are deferred imitations. The book-reading situation constrains the context sufficiently that it becomes clear what constitutes a recurrence of an event, and therefore what the adult models have been.

The basic data on N's book-reading with his mother are presented in Table 2.5. The Storybook Dictionary consists of 66 two-page displays, including the front cover, back cover, title page, and endpapers. On most of the two-page spreads, 10 to 15 words are presented, in alphabetical order, illustrated by a short narrative text and a narrative picture. Most of the pictures are quite complex,

TABLE 2.5
Picture and Page Selection during Book-Reading

Date of Session	Number of Pages Read (maximum = 65)	Number of Pictures Discussed (maximum = 771)
3 February	35	66
16 February	37	54
17 February	18	30
18 February	39	56
7 March	23	35
8 March	18	30
9 March	17	28
10 March	20	30

representing relationships or activities rather than simply objects; a few of the pictures represent a large class of objects (e.g., different kinds of transport) and lend themselves more to simple labeling.

During the period under consideration, N typically did not want to have books read to him. He preferred to talk with his mother about the pictures in the books. Prior to the initiation of taping, he and his mother had established some ground rules for reading the various Richard Scarry books. The basic procedure was to look at only one or two pictures per two-page spread. As can be seen from Table 2.5, N was almost exclusively responsible for selecting the picture to be discussed, typically by asking a question about it while pointing or looking at it. This pattern, whereby N decided which picture to look at, initiated the discussion by asking a question about that picture, and ended the discussion by selecting another picture or turning the page, constituted a routine for looking at this book.

The routinization that characterized the structure of the picture selection also held to a large extent for the content level. Table 2.6 presents data on the number of times different pictures available for discussion were in fact discussed. It can be seen that: a) the vast majority of pictures in the book were never selected by N to be talked about; b) a significant number were discussed repeatedly during successive sessions. The degree of convergence on a small number of pictures is even more impressive than it appears, because on many readings less than the entire book was perused. Thus, though eight sessions of book-reading are discussed here, many pages of the book were looked at fewer than eight times, so the maximum number of times a picture could be discussed was usually smaller than eight.

A further basis for concluding that the book-reading sessions constituted a routine for N and his mother comes from an analysis of the sequence of conversational events during a typical picture discussion. Both Ninio and Bruner (1978) and Ninio (1980) have described similar kinds of routinization during earlier stages of joint reading, when the focus of the activity was to teach and elicit

TABLE 2.6
Frequency with which Pictures were Selected

	\multicolumn{9}{c}{Number of Mentions of a Given Picture}
	0	1	2	3	4	5	6	7	8
Frequency	564	129	40	23	8	3	4	0	0

labeling of relatively simple pictures. The interactions discussed here are much more complex because the pictures are sufficiently elaborated that many different aspects of them could be (and were) discussed—not just labeling of objects, characters, and parts, but also discussion of the ongoing activity, causation, imminent consequences, locative relationships, comparisons, etc. Accordingly, the conversations have been analyzed using a coding scheme that identifies conversational acts specific to the topics discussed, with reference to each picture. Analysis of contingencies between the conversational acts so identified constitutes the basic data to be discussed here.

The Coding Scheme

Application of the coding scheme is illustrated in Table 2.7, using an idealization of the typical progression of discussion of a single picture. The categories coded included the following:

Wh-question (Wh-Q). An utterance that questions a topic without including the lexical item that encodes the topic.

Specifying question (Sp-Q). An interrogative form that introduces a topic and includes the lexical item used to refer to the topic. Typically a yes-no question (Is Dingo having a crash?) or a where-question (Where's Dingo's car?)

Notice (Not). An utterance that draws attention to a topic without including the lexical item used to encode that topic, e.g., Look at that! Look what he's doing!

Mention (M). First reference to a topic within a sequence that includes the lexical item used to refer to the topic. Subsequent utterances including the lexical item are not coded as *mention,* but as *repetition.*

Repetition (R). Utterance that repeats lexical item from preceding utterance within the sequence by another speaker.

Confirmation (F). Utterance that confirms the correctness of the preceding speaker's use of a lexical item without repetition of the lexical item itself.

Error (E). Use of the wrong lexical item with reference to some topic.

Correction(C). Response to an error, explicitly indicating that it is wrong.

It is important to notice that any single utterance was coded with reference to all the topics it was relevant to, and that *topic* is used here to mean 'information unit.' Thus, an utterance like 'Dingo is eating dinner on his car' was *multiply*

TABLE 2.7
Idealized Example of N's and his Mother's Conversational
Events during Book-reading and the Coding Scheme Used

	Session		
I	II	III	IV
N: Who's that?	Who's that X.		
M: X	X, right.		
	What's X doing?		
N: X	X doing?	X Ying.	
M: X, right.	X is Ying.	That's right.	
N:	X Ying	X have?	
M:		X has a Z.	
N:		a Z.	X Z
M:		right, a Z.	right.
N: Wh-Q (X)*	Mention (X)		
M: Mention (X)	Repeat (X)		
	Wh-Q (Y) / R (X)		
N: Repeat (X)	R (X) Wh-Q (Y)	M (X) / M (Y)	
M: Repeat (X)	R (X) / M (Y)	Confirm (X) / (Y)	
N:	R (X) / R (Y)	R (X) / Wh-Q (Z)	
M:		R (X) / M (Z)	
N:		R (Z)	M (X) / M (Z)
M:		R (Z)	Confirm (X) / (Z)

*Coding category for each of the utterances in the first half of the table are presented, using the abbreviations presented in the text. X, Y, and Z refer to topics. Each conversational event is coded with respect to each of the topics it refers to.

coded for the topics *Dingo, eat, dinner,* and *on car.* The specific coding for each of these topics would, of course, depend on preceding utterances in the sequence.

The Structure of Conversations about Topics

Table 2.8 presents data on the first two nonidentical conversational events relevant to any particular topic during book-reading. A number of points can be made about these data. First, the data present a picture of good turn-taking even at the level of topic. It is, of course, well demonstrated that children the age of N are quite competent to take turns at the level of utterance; the turn-taking demon-

2. EXPANDED AND DEFERRED IMITATIONS   51

strated here is much more subtle. It indicates that both N and his mother tended to pick up on and make a reply relevant to each topic or information unit within the utterances they were exchanging. Only 24 out of 712 pairs of topic-related conversational events violated the principle of speaker-switch, and 9 of those 24 were instances of two adjacent topic-related utterances by the mother.

Secondly, N was responsible for the majority of topic introductions. Of the 712 topic discussions for which data are presented, 487 were initiated by N and only 225 by his mother. Thus, N selected almost all the pictures to be discussed, and 68% of the topics to be discussed as well.

The most frequently occurring pairs of conversational events were:

child mention + maternal repetition	269 times
maternal mention + child repetition	170 times
child error + maternal correction	71 times
child wh-question + maternal mention	59 times

TABLE 2.8
Contingencies between First Two Conversational Events Related to a Given Topic

Second Event	First Event							
	Child					Mother		
	Wh-Q	Sp-Q	Notice	M	E	Wh-Q	Sp-Q	M
Child								
Wh-Q						11		2
Mention (M)	12*		3			20	2	
Error (E)						4		1
Repetition						3	3	170
Mother								
Wh-Q	21			11	3			
Specifying-Q		3		2	1			1
Mention	59	2	9		4		8	
Repetition	1	1		269				
Confirmation		1		13				
Correction		1			71			

*Entries in the table represent frequencies.

N's mother introduced topics by asking questions 43 times, of which 22 were successful in eliciting correct answers from N; four elicited errors. Furthermore, she refused to answer his wh-questions 21 times, instead repeating the question back to him. Evidently, she was quite insistent that he provide the information she felt he knew about the picture, and she was quite accurate in predicting what he did know.

The Relationship Between Successive Conversations

The crucial data for the argument being made here about N's use of deferred imitations come from analyses of contingencies between conversational events at successive discussions of the same pictures, across time intervals of one or more days. Some of the relevant data are presented in Table 2.9. For this analysis the conversational event during the earlier discussion is presented at the top of the table, and the conversational event during later discussions is presented at the left hand side of the table. Entries in the table represent proportions of all topics that were discussed during at least two different sessions. In the picture discussions analyzed here (i.e., all discussions of pictures that were looked at two or more times), 545 discussion topics were identified during the coding. Of these, 391

TABLE 2.9
Contingencies between Conversational Events in Successive Discussions of the Same Topic Across Sessions

Later Discussion of Same Topic	Earlier Discussion of Topic			
	maternal mention, no child repetition	maternal mention + child repetition	child mention	child error
Child				
Wh–Q	20.5*	17.2	0.0	0.0
Sp–Q	0.0	0.0	1.9	0.0
Notice	5.1	0.0	0.0	0.0
Mention	23.1	51.7	79.0	0.0
Error	0.0	5.2	2.9	71.4
Mother				
Wh–Q	0.0	0.0	0.0	0.0
Mention	51.2	25.9	16.2	28.6

*Entries in the table represent percentages of events within each column.

2. EXPANDED AND DEFERRED IMITATIONS 53

TABLE 2.10
Examples of N's Deferred Imitations during Book-reading

1. Acquisition of Referential Lexical Item.

16 February	18 February
N: Who's this the stairs	N: Who's this
M: The stairs	This the *ostrich* again
The *ostrich* walking down the stairs	M: Ostrich again
N: Don't fall off	N: Ostrich again
M: Don't fall off, *ostrich*	

2. Acquisition of Social, Evaluative Lexical Item.

17 February	18 February
N: eh train tracks	N: dere de . . on de train track
M: Train tracks	M: Dingo is driving on the train tracks
N: er de train tracks	Dingo . . . (interrupted)
M: Dingo is drivin' on the train tracks	N: de *silly*
Dingo is a terrible driver	M: Is that silly?
He's *silly*	
N: Dere's a big bump	

3. Acquisition of Syntactic Forms.

9 March	10 March
N: Who's the cake	N: Cake
M: That's the cake	M: um-hmm
N: eh dey're pushing de cake	N: Cake
M: They're pushing it?	M: Cake
N: Pushing eh dit?	N: *To eat cake*
M: They're wishing they could eat it	M: Do you like to eat cake? Do you?
N: Eat it	
M: They want *to eat the cake*	
N. Eat the cake	
M: Cakes are good *to eat*	

topics were discussed only once; this means that N (who, remember, did most of the topic selection) actively chose new features of the pictures to focus on during successive discussions. The data in Table 2.9 are based on the 154 topics discussed two or more times: 91 topics were discussed twice, 45 three times, 9 four times, 7 six times, and 2 seven times.

It is clear from Table 2.9 that N was learning both how to talk about the pictures and what to say about them. N tended to say about a picture what he had heard his mother say about the same picture on previous readings, especially if he had imitated that earlier maternal utterance immediately. An earlier sequence of maternal mention + child repetition was most likely to be followed, in the next discussion of that picture, by child mention (51.7% of the time), whereas maternal mention not followed by child repetition was much less likely to be followed by child mention (23.1%) and was most likely to be followed by maternal mention (51.2%) during subsequent discussions of the same topic. As might be expected, child mention of a topic was most likely to be followed by another child mention (79%) if the topic recurred, though occasionally maternal mention or even a child error followed.

Discussion

The analysis of the data from N and his mother reveal that her utterances about a particular picture in a frequently read book influenced his subsequent choice of topics when looking at that same picture again on subsequent occasions and taught him how to encode reference to those topics lexically. Even more strikingly, there are many instances in the transcripts of the mother's utterances influencing the *form* of N's subsequent utterances about those topics. There are clear examples of his producing referential lexical items (see Table 2.10, example 1), social-evaluative terms (Table 2.10, example 2), and syntactic forms (Table 2.10, example 3) that his mother had produced on previous discussions of the pictures. The specificity of the relationship between N's later utterances about a particular picture and his mother's previous utterances about that same picture strongly support the conclusion from the topic analysis that N was remembering previous discussions and using them as a source of information about what to say in current discussions of particular pictures.

CONCLUSION

Common sense tells us that imitation helps children learn. This insight has been exploited by first grade teachers, speech therapists, second language teachers, and many parents (though not always so extensively as by the Kaluli parents described by Schieffelin, 1979). Nonetheless, it has been very difficult for researchers in child language to demonstrate that imitation helps children learn language in any wide-ranging or general way. The difficulty of demonstrating any effect of imitation on learning derives, I believe, from the fact that imitations have many functions in child language, of which learning something about the lexicon or grammar of the language is only one. It has been demonstrated by many studies that children's imitations function to: a) keep the conversation going when there is no other way to do so (Keenan, 1977, 1978; McTear, 1978); b) continue topics and expand on those topics (Bloom, Rocissano, & Hood, 1976); c) establish social contact and develop games (Garvey, 1977); d) signal noncomprehension (Bohannon & Lotz, 1980). The fact that these other functions are served by imitation does not exclude the possibility that imitation also serves the functions of lexical and syntactic acquisition; it does make it more difficult to identify and demonstrate the contribution to acquisition.

It has been argued in this paper that understanding how children acquire language requires assessing the extent to which their linguistic performance depends on the incorporation of imitations into their productions. The importance of imitations in children's language has typically been underestimated for theoretical as well as methodological reasons. The theoretical reasons are that imitation has been treated as an uninteresting, mechanical process, incapable of contributing to children's mastery of a rule-governed system like language. In addition, children's memory capacity has been systematically underestimated in the literature, leading to an assumption that the models for imitated behavior must be very recent in the child's experience. The methodological reasons have to do with the difficulty of identifying, reliably and objectively, those child utterances that have been influenced in form by memory of adult model utterances, even though those models may be far removed in time, and the imitations may not be exact or reduced versions of the model.

If one can resolve the methodological difficulties associated with identifying expanded and deferred imitations, it becomes clear that such utterances may account for a considerable portion of a child's most sophisticated language performance. Furthermore, the imitated utterances can be seen as a source of information to the language-learning child about the structure of the system he is acquiring—a sort of 'instant or delayed replay' of useful utterances, giving the child a second chance to analyze them, even while he enjoys their communicative effectiveness.

The role of imitations must be assessed in conjunction with other heuristics available to the child, such as the use of formulaic utterances and vertical constructions. The child employs all these heuristics to simplify his tasks of communicating with others, and of learning about how the world works. Learning grammar must have quite a low priority on the agenda of the 2-year-old; it is not surprising that the tricks he has for simplifying the task of acquiring grammar also get used in service of his other, more important obligations.

REFERENCES

Blank, M. Cognitive functions of language in the preschool years. *Developmental Psychology,* 1974, *10,* 229–245.

Bloom, L., Hood, L., & Lightbown, P. Imitation in language development: if, when, and why. *Cognitive Psychology,* 1974, *6,* 380–420.

Bloom, L., Rocissano, L., & Hood, L. Adult-child discourse: Developmental interaction between information processing and linguistic knowledge. *Cognitive Psychology,* 1976, *8,* 521–552.

Bohannon, J. N. & Lotz, E. *Imitations, interactions and acquisition.* Paper presented at the Sixth Biennial Conference on Human Development, Alexandria, Va., 1980.

Bolinger, D. Meaning and memory. *Forum Linguisticum,* 1976, *1,* 1–13.

Bransford, J. & Franks, J. The abstraction of linguistic ideas: A review. *Cognition,* 1972, *1,* 211–250.

Bresnan, J. A realistic transformational grammar. In M. Halle, J. Bresnan & G. Miller (Eds.), *Linguistic theory and psychological reality.* Cambridge: MIT Press, 1978.

Carey, S. The child as word learner. In M. Halle, J. Bresnan & G. Miller (Eds.), *Linguistic theory and psychological reality.* Cambridge: MIT Press, 1978.

Clark, R. Performing without competence. *Journal of Child Language,* 1974, *1,* 1–10.

Clark, R. What's the use of imitation? *Journal of Child Language,* 1977, *4,* 1–10; 341–358.

Clark, R. Some even simpler ways to learn to talk. *In* N. Waterson & C. Snow (Eds.), *The development of communication.* London: Wiley, 1978.

DeLoache, J. & Brown, A. Looking for Big Bird: Studies of memory in very young children. *Quarterly Newsletter of the Laboratory of Comparative Human Cognition,* 1979, *1,* 53–57.

Ervin, S. Imitation and structural change in children's language. In E. Lenneberg (Ed.), *New directions in the study of language.* Cambridge: MIT Press, 1964.

Ferrier, L. Some observations of error in context. In N. Waterson & C. Snow (Eds.), *The development of communication.* London: Wiley, 1978.

Fillmore, L. *The second time around: Cognitive and social strategies in second language acquisition.* Unpublished doctoral dissertation, Stanford University, 1976.

Folger, J. & Chapman, R. A pragmatic analysis of spontaneous imitations. *Journal of Child Language,* 1978, *5,* 25–38.

Garvey, C. *Play.* London: Fontana, 1977.

Gleason, J. Berko. Do children imitate? *Proceedings of the International Conference on Oral Education of the Deaf,* 1967, *2,* 1441–1448. Alexander Graham Bell Association of the Deaf, Washington, D.C.

Gleason, J., Perlmann, R., & Greif, E. *What's the magic word: Learning language through politeness routines.* Paper presented at Sixth Biennial Conference on Human Development, Alexandria, Va., 1980.

Greif, E. & Gleason, J. Berko. Hi, thanks and good-bye: Some more routine information. *Language in Society,* 1980, *9,* 159–166.

Hakuta, K. Prefabricated patterns and the emergence of structure in second language acquisition. *Language Learning,* 1974, *24,* 287–297.

Hakuta, K. & Pinker, S. *Children's memory for forms of sentences.* Book in preparation.

Hatch, E. *Second language learning—Universals?* Working Papers on Bilingualism 3. Ontario Institute for Studies in Education, Toronto, 1974.

Heras, I. & Nelson, K. E. Retention of semantic syntactic and language information by young bilingual children. *Psychonomic Science,* 1972, *29,* 391–393.

Huang, J. & Hatch, E. A Chinese child's acquisition of English. In E. Hatch (Ed.), *Second language acquisition: A book of readings.* Rowley, Mass.: Newbury House, 1978.

Keenan, E. Ochs. Conversational competence in children. *Journal of Child Language,* 1974, *1,* 163–183.

Keenan, E. Ochs. Making it last: Repetition in children's discourse. In S. Ervin-Tripp & C. Mitchell-Kernan (Eds.), *Child discourse.* New York: Academic Press, 1977.

Macken, M. Permitted complexity in phonological development: One child's acquisition of Spanish consonants. *Lingua,* 1978, *44,* 219–253.

McTear, M. Repetition in child language: Imitation or Creation? In R. Campbell & P. Smith (Eds.), *Advances in the psychology of language.* New York: Plenum, 1978.

Moerk, E. Processes and products of imitation: Evidence that imitation is progressive. *Journal of Psycholinguistic Research, 1977, 6,* 187–202.

Moerk, E. & Moerk, C. Quotations, imitations and generalizations. Factual and methodological analyses. *International Journal of Behavioral Development,* 1979, *2,* 43–72.

Nelson, K. E. Experimental gambits in the service of language acquisition theory: From the Fiffin project to Operation Input Swap. In S. Kuczaj (Ed.), *Problems, theories, and controversies in language development: Syntax and semantics.* Hillsdale, N.J.: Lawrence Erlbaum Associates, 1982.

Nelson, K. E. & Bonvillian, J. Concepts and words in the two-year-old: Acquisition of concept names under controlled conditions. *Cognition,* 1973, *2,* 435–350.

Nelson, K. & Gruendel, J. At morning it's lunchtime: A Scriptal view of children's dialogues. *Discourse Processes,* 1979, *2,* 73–94 (a).

Nelson, K. & Gruendel, J. *From personal episode to social script: Two dimensions in the development of event knowledge.* Paper presented at Biennial Meeting of the Society for Research in Child Development, San Francisco, 1979.

Nelson, K. & Ross, G. The general and specifics of long-term memory in infants and young children. In M. Perlmutter (Ed.), *Naturalistic approaches to memory.* Jossey-Bass, in press.

Ninio, A. Picture-book reading in mother-infant dyads belonging to two subgroups in Israel. *Child development,* 1980, *51,* 587–590.

Ninio, A. & Bruner, J. The achievement and antecedents of labelling. *Journal of Child Language,* 1978, *5,* 1–15.

Ramer, A. The function of imitation in child language. *Journal of Speech and Hearing Research,* 1976, *19,* 700–717.

Sachs, J. Recognition memory for syntactic and semantic aspects of connected discourse. *Perception and Psychophysics,* 1967, *2,* 437–442.

Schank, R. & Abelson, R. *Scripts, plans, goals, and understanding.* Hillsdale, N.J.: Lawrence Erlbaum Associates, 1977.

Schieffelin, B. Getting it together: An ethnographic approach to the study of the development of communicative competence. In E. Ochs & B. Schieffelin (Eds.), *Developmental pragmatics.* New York: Academic Press, 1979.

Scollon, R. A real early stage: An unzippered condensation of a dissertation on child language. In E. Ochs & B. Schieffelin (Eds.), *Developmental pragmatics.* New York: Academic Press, 1979.

Seitz, S. & Stewart, C. Imitations and expansions: Some developmental aspects of mother-child communication. *Developmental Psycholgoy,* 1975, *11,* 763–768.

Slobin, D. & Welsh, C. Elicited imitations as a research tool in developmental psycholinguistics. In C. Ferguson & D. Slobin (Eds.), *Studies of child language development.* New York: Wiley, 1973.

Snow, C. The uses of imitation. *Journal of Child Language,* 1981, *8,* 205–212.

Snow, C. Parent-child interaction and the development of communicative ability. In R. Schiefelbusch (Ed.), *Communicative competence: Acquisition and Intervention.* Baltimore: University Park Press, in press. (b)

Snow, C. Unpublished data. 1979.

Snow, C. & Goldfield, B. Building stories: The Emergence of information structures from conversion and narrative. In D. Tannen (Ed.), Georgetown University Roundtable on Language and Linguistics 1981, *Analyzing discourse: Text and talk.* Washington, D.C.: Georgetown University Press, 1982.

Snow, C. & Goldfield, B. Turn the page, please: Situation-specific language learning. *Journal of Child Language,* in press.

Thomas, E. *It's all routine: A redefinition of routines as a central factor in language acquisition.* Paper presented at Fourth Annual Boston University Conference on Language Development, 1979.

Watson-Gegeo, K. & Gegeo, D. *Calling out and repeating: Two key routines in Kwara'ae children's language acquisition.* Paper presented at the American Anthropological Association, Washington, D.C., 1982.

Whitehurst, G. Production of novel and grammatical utterances by young children. *Journal of Experimental Child Psychology,* 1972, *13,* 502–515.

Whitehurst, G. *Imitation, observational learning, and language acquisition.* Paper presented at Sixth Biennial Conference on Human Development, Alexandria, Va., 1980.

Whitehurst, G., Ironsmith, E., & Goldfein, M. Selective imitation of the passive construction by young children. *Journal of Experimental Child Psychology,* 1974, *17,* 288–302.

Whitehurst, G. & Novak, G. Modeling, imitation training and the acquisition of sentence phrases. *Journal of Experimental Child Psychology,* 1973, *16,* 332–345.

Whitehurst, G., Novak, G. & Zorn, G. Delayed speech studied in the home. *Developmental Psychology,* 1972, *2,* 169–177.

Whitehurst, G. & Vasta, R. Is language acquired through imitation? *Journal of Psycholinguistic Research,* 1975, 4, 37–59.

3 Names, Gestures, and Objects: Symbolization in Infancy and Aphasia

Elizabeth Bates
University of California, San Diego

Inge Bretherton
University of Colorado, Fort Collins

Cecilia Shore
Miami University of Ohio

Sandra McNew
University of Colorado

There is a dramatic moment in *The Miracle Worker* (Gibson, 1956) in which young Helen Keller makes the discovery that things have names. The insight is sudden, overwhelming, and creates irrevocable changes in the world of an 8-year-old deaf, blind child. For normal hearing children, the same discovery occurs much earlier and much more gradually. It begins around 9 months of age with a change in the way the child uses communicative signals. By 13 months, some of these signals can properly be called names.

What is it that has changed in between, in the gradual passage from signaling to symbolizing? Is naming a purely linguistic phenomenon, or is it one manifestation of a more general change in cognition? To answer these questions adequately, we need a theory of naming that has eluded some of the best minds in language philosophy, psychology, and linguistics (see Carroll, 1978 for a review). Indeed, there is no universal definition of naming, much less a theory of how and why it happens. In a recent longitudinal study of the emergence of symbols in infancy, we proposed the following definition of symbols (Bates, Benigni, Bretherton, Camaioni, & Volterra, 1979):

> The comprehension or use, inside or outside of communicative situations, of a relationship between a sign and its referent, such that the sign is treated as belonging to and/or substitutable for its referent in a variety of contexts; at the same time the user is aware that the sign is separable from its referent, that is, not the same thing [p. 43].

Within this framework, we offer a further definition of naming:

> The use of a symbol to recognize, categorize, identify, or otherwise label a referent as a member of some known class of entities, or as an instantiation of a known unique individual. This naming act may be carried out for the purpose of identifying that referent for an intended listener, or in a private act of recognition for oneself. When used communicatively, a naming act may be the major point of an utterance or it may be a subsidiary act in the service of making further points about that referent. Similarly, in private cognition a naming act may be carried out in isolation, or as a subsidiary act within a higher relational or predicative construction.[1]

We have adopted these definitions because they provide a reasonably good fit to what we have learned so far about very young children. And because we are interested in the symbolic behavior of 1-year-olds, we have had to use definitions that depart from certain traditions in language philosophy in at least two ways. First, symbols and naming are defined outside of communication, to include aspects of private cognition. Second, symbols and naming are defined outside of the vocal channel, to include gestures of a particular kind.

Though we have broadened the domain of inquiry with these definitions, there are many mental events (signs, associations, patterns of stimulus and response) that are excluded by the unique relationship of "standing for" or "belonging to" that characterizes true symbolic knowing. As discussed by Werner and Kaplan (1963) in *Symbol formation,* a symbol is a state of mind or attitude that is actively constructed by the knower; it is not a "thing" with an independent existence (either mental or physical). Werner and Kaplan describe the "standing for" relationship in terms of "physiognomic knowing," in which a stimulus does not merely remind us of something else, but is fully grasped and known as though it were the thing itself. To illustrate the difference between physiognomic meaning and simple association, they offer the phenomenon of "word satiation." Take a normal English word like "spoon" and repeat it to yourself 20 or 30 times. Something peculiar happens to your experience of the word. Although

---

[1] In the philosophical literature on naming, several taxonomies have been proposed to distinguish names that merely refer or point to individuals (e.g., Walter Scott) vs. names that define or describe their referents (e.g., the author of *Waverley*). Frege (1949) uses the term "reference" to describe the pointing function of a name, whereas the term "sense" includes the full set of meanings that are conveyed when a particular name is used to refer. Frege insists that all names, including proper names like "Walter Scott," have both sense and reference. Our definition of naming is compatible with Frege's view insofar as "reference" corresponds to the entity being named (either a real or an imaginary referent) but "sense corresponds to prior knowledge of a category or unique individual that is connected to that referent via the naming act. However, we are interpreting "sense" and "reference" in mentalistic terms that would presumably be unacceptable to Frege. For further discussion of these issues, see Bates (1976), Chapter 1.

at some level you still know the connection between sound and object, the association becomes empty of feeling. You fail to imbue that sound with a total organismic response, to treat it *as though it were* a spoon. When this physiognomic knowing dissolves, the symbol-referent relationship reduces to mere association between a sound and an object.

The point may be clearer if we take a nonlinguistic example of physiognomized knowing.[2] Envision to yourself a tree stump in the forest. Without allowing that visual image to alter, imagine that you are going to use that stump as a chair. Hold this "chair meaning" briefly, and then change your mind. Keeping the image constant, decide instead to use the same tree stump as a picnic table. As you switch back and forth between chair and table as "meanings" for the same referent, you can actually feel the switch in internal states of readiness, postures, and abbreviated motor commands. This is the kind of full organismic meaning that Werner and Kaplan have in mind in their theory of symbol formation.

Both of these examples involve three-way relationships of *symbol, meaning*[3] and *referent*. In the word satiation example, the sound "spoon" is the symbolic scheme that we select to confer "spoon meaning" (Calling up all the things that we know how to do with spoons) upon some real *or* imaginary referent object. In the tree stump example, we used a nonlinguistic symbol ("readiness-to-sit") to confer "chair meaning" on the imaginary stump as referent. Once we cease to hold these three elements together in a conscious relationship, the symbol dissolves. For example, suppose we actually go over to a tree stump and sit on it, going on with our picnic. Does sitting still confer chair meaning on the stump? According to our definition of symbols, it does not. "Readiness-to-sit" can be a symbol used to identify some referent as a "chair" only for a brief moment in which we *actively* preserve the tension between the signifying act and the knowledge it stands for.

How can we trace the development of such an evanescent state of mind in a child? Only by paying close attention to the contexts and objects associated with conventional sounds and gestures. It is not enough to note *when* a child uses an adult convention; we must also describe *how* that convention is used.

In this paper we will describe some of our own recent studies of the emergence of naming at 13 months, illustrating and defending our use of the above definitions. This is not intended as a review of what is by now an ample literature on the passage from preverbal to verbal communication. For related work by other investigators, the reader is referred to three particularly rich volumes edited by Lewis and Rosenblum (1977), Schaffer (1977), and Lock

---

[2]This is our own example. If it does not work for the reader, Werner and Kaplan should not be blamed.

[3]Analogous to "sense" in Frege's terms.

(1978). Some important theoretical and empirical contributions to this area also include Ninio and Bruner (1976), Sugarman-Bell (1978), Carter (1975), and Dore (1973). Here we will restrict ourselves primarily to our own examples.

An important part of our argument will be that certain gestural conventions used by hearing infants are in fact a kind of naming, insofar as they are used to recognize, categorize, or identify an object as a member of a known class. For example, the 13-month-old infant may execute a brief stirring movement upon seeing a spoon, or place a toy telephone receiver to his ear for one or two seconds as soon as the object is in his hands. The argument that such gestures serve as names is supported not only by our developmental data, but by findings on the breakdown of gesture in certain forms of aphasia. On the other hand, these manual symbols differ in important ways from (a) the vocal symbols of hearing children; and (b) the manual signs acquired by deaf children. These differences have to do with the contexts of symbol use, and the relationship between names and objects.

The rest of the chapter is divided into the following sections:

(1) Some concrete examples are offered from our own research and that of other investigators, illustrating the passage into naming in the vocal channel. Using these examples, we can defend the definition of naming as a process that occurs outside of communication.

(2) Analogous events in the development of gesture will be described, with evidence supporting our claim that something very much like naming takes place outside of the vocal channel.

(3) Some a priori differences between vocal and manual symbols are discussed, factors that could affect the way these two kinds of symbols are acquired and used by children.

(4) Some of our recent research on the similarities and differences between language and gesture is summarized, in relation to the notions of "object dependence" and "script dependence."

(5) Converging evidence for our findings is provided in a brief discussion of naming and gestural symbols in adult aphasics.

(6) Finally, we will try to draw these findings together with some preliminary suggestions for a theory of naming as a psychological process.

THE ONSET OF VOCAL SYMBOLS

It is never entirely clear just when the child understands or produces her "first word." She may begin, like our subject Carlotta (Bates, Camaioni, & Volterra, 1975) with grunts and effort noises (e.g., "MMM-MMM") that become intentional, conventional communications only in a very primitive sense. That these sounds are *intentional* can be inferred from: a) Carlotta's glances back and forth between mother and the desired object; b) the way that she changes her signals—augments, substitutes, recombines—until the goal is reached or abandoned; c) the fact that her signals seem to be contingent on the listener's behavior rather than on the position of the goal itself. Furthermore, we justify the claim that these communications are *conventional* only insofar as: a) they are recognized or agreed upon by a community of at least two individuals; and b) they seem to converge with use onto an increasingly abbreviated and stereotyped form (e.g., a crisp and insistent MMM) that is useful only for the function of clear and unambiguous communication (as opposed to variable grunts and effort sounds that derive naturally out of the child's efforts to grab the object). Despite the fact that these sounds are used in ritualized ways, for clear communicative purposes, most researchers (and parents) would feel uncomfortable calling them "words," much less names for things.

From 9 to 13 months, we find more ambiguous cases in the gradual move toward naming. For example, Carlotta had a clear consonant-vowel combination—"NANA"—which was used for all types of requests. Unlike the "MM" sound, which derived initially from effort noises, this combination seemed quite arbitrary in form. Indeed, it was quite unlike other calls, cries, and babbles in the same period. Another subject, Marta, invented her own peculiar vocal convention "AYI." This was used not for requesting but for exclaiming or commenting on interesting objects—something that we have called a "protodeclarative." These wordlike sounds are conventions, according to the above criteria. But can we call them words?

Sometimes, in the same developmental period, the child may choose an existing adult word to perform exactly the same functions as Carlotta's "NANA" and Marta's "AYI." For example, Piaget's daughter Jacqueline (Piaget, 1962) used the word for grandfather ("PANAMA") as an all-purpose request that bore no apparent relation to the presence or absence of grandfather himself—although her favorite slave must have played some role in the etymology of this sound. In the grownup world, *grandfather* is a name. In Jacqueline's world, however, it seems to be something else entirely.

The problem of locating first words becomes even greater for very specific games like "BYEBYE." Carlotta used the sound "BAM" in a game of knocking over towers, at a regular point in that routine. Similarly, "BRRR" was a sound made while moving vehicles. Shvachkin (in Ferguson & Slobin, 1973) reports on his daughter's first word, "KITTY," used only after throwing her toy cat out of the crib at the point where father was supposed to restore the toy (no doubt having said more than once, "Here's your kitty."). Marta used the Italian word "DA" ("give") while giving or taking objects in a ritual exchange—a routine clearly related to our observation that Italian adults say the word "DA" up to 17 times in a given object exchange. These examples all involve uses of adult words. Some of these words are procedures or routines without clear reference even for the adult (e.g., "Bam!"), whereas others function in the parent language as nouns or verbs, names referring to objects and events. For the child, however, they all seem to be language games, procedures derived from imitating adult behaviors within a narrowly defined situation or script.

Wittgenstein (1958) has argued that all meanings are language games, use of a word in an agreed upon set of verbal and nonverbal contexts. Names do not simply refer or belong to *objects*. Rather, a name is a sound that we use in a variety of *situations*, albeit situations that systematically involve some referent object or class of objects. Put another way, meaning is not a thing that a word "has," but rather a function or activity that a speaker "does" in using that sound (see Bates, 1976, Chapter 1 for further comments). If we adopt Wittgenstein's viewpoint with regard to the above examples, then we must admit that the child's first language games are also words of a sort. But something is clearly missing. The rules of the language game will have to change before we are willing to admit that the 1-year-old has achieved Helen Keller's insight.

To find the missing pieces, let us follow the history of Carlotta's "BAM." Several weeks after the game had become a well-established routine, Carlotta was seated among her toys momentarily silent and empty-handed. She looked up, said the word "BAM," and after a brief hesitation turned to pound on her toy piano. (Note that the sound has become in some sense decontextualized or "unstuck" from the original Bam script, so that it is now being used in advance as a kind of tag, reminder, or perhaps an announcement of the action to follow.) "BAM" begins to function as a sort of primitive verb. At the beginning, BAM *was* a procedure or action, an equal among other related procedures or actions. Now BAM begins to *signify* or *stand for* the rest of the script, or some portion of the script. It had been selected out and elevated to a different status from the other elements in the original routine.

Around the same time that names for actions emerge, other procedures evolve into primitive nouns or names for objects. For example, Carlotta first used the vocal routine WOOWOO exclusively within a book-reading game, in response to the adult signal, "How does the doggy go?" By 13 months, Carlotta began to use WOOWOO to comment on the presence of a whole class of dogs, in books and in real life, including the sound of a dog barking somewhere in the distance. Perhaps because they are so well prepared by preexisting book routines, animal names are frequent in the early noun vocabularies of middle-class children (c.f., Werner & Kaplan, 1963, p. 108). However, names for food and water also appeared quickly in Carlotta's requests, and she soon began to collect names for toys, clothing, and other relevant objects in her world.

In Volterra, Bates, Benigni, Bretherton, & Camaioni (1979), the same passage from preferential routines into acts of reference was traced in the early speech records of 25 infants. By 13 months, both object names and action names were used by most of the children. However, object names tended to predominate at this point (see also Benedict, 1979; Nelson, 1973). Furthermore, words that are not nouns from an adult point of view often seem to serve as object names for the child. For example, a child may use "ahhm" as a term for labeling spoons, "vrrm" to label vehicles, "hello" as a sound regularly used in noticing or recognizing telephones. At the end of this chapter we hope to indicate some interesting processing differences between object names and action names from the child's point of view, in relation to the kinds of feedback provided by the two kinds of referents. For present purposes, however, we want to stress that *all* of the child's first words—whether they are nouns or verbs, predicates or arguments, function terms or substantives from an adult point of view—begin as actions or procedures for the child. The infant does not "have" her first words; she "does" them. The division into form classes or semantic categories is not relevant until the child begins to use words to set up conditions of reference.

Once the child does begin to use names, we immediately find them being used inside *and* outside of a communicative framework. That is, our subjects frequently label things to themselves, without eye contact, without searching for feedback from the adult. We are certainly not the first to notice this behavior. In fact, because solitary naming activity is so striking in normal infants, it is emphasized in almost all major theories of symbol formation (e.g., Piaget, 1962; Werner & Kaplan 1963; Vygotsky, 1962). Although none of these theorists deny the importance of social factors in the acquisition of symbols, they give equal weight to the noncommunicative function of symbols in the child's construction of reality. Indeed, Werner and Kaplan claim that the idea of reference begins prior to symbolization *and* outside communication in the peculiar activity of pointing-for-self. This exploratory gesture supposedly serves as a kind of sensorimotor aid to the establishment of a subject-object distinction: It makes contact with the object, concentrates attention on the object, and yet at the same time literally pushes it away. If this analysis is correct (and, as we shall see later, our own data support it), then even a quintessential communicative gesture like pointing emerges first as an instrument for private thought. In the same vein, solitary naming seems to help the child in categorizing reality.

This developmental view is directly contradicted by certain approaches in language philosophy based on an analysis of symbolization in adults. Speech act theorists like Searle (1975) and Grice (1975) define meaning as the use of social conventions to convey intentions that transcend the private world of the individual. Similarly, for Langer (1962) and Mead (1934) there is no such thing as meaning outside a social framwork. The individual can reason and reflect on his own experience only because he has internalized the shared symbols of social exchange. In short, these philosophers believe that private cognition is created out of interpersonal meanings, not vice versa.

The apparent contradiction between the developmental view and social theories of meaning is resolved by Vygotsky's (1962) description of the socialization of thought by language. For Vygotsky, thought does not actually *originate* in social-symbolic interaction; instead, it is radically *transformed* by it. The 1–2-

year-old infant is capable only of "tool thought." This type of cognition is derived primarily from the child's own transactions with a world of physical objects and events, and is analogous to Piaget's descriptions of late sensorimotor and early representational cognition. However, even though the infant's thought patterns are unsocialized, he is from the very beginning highly motivated to interact, observe, and imitate other human beings. Hence he begins to accompany his private explorations of the world with vocal routines derived from these social interactions. Gradually, this outer speech accompanying action begins to guide or structure action—marking the opening and closing of sequences, ordering behaviors into planned events. At the same time that outer speech starts to guide action, it also becomes increasingly abbreviated until it eventually disappears entirely into what is called "inner speech," which henceforth provides the structure of rational thought. Because inner speech is ultimately derived from the social world, it necessarily results in the imposition of social meaning on private cognition. In this respect, Vygotsky's views accord with those of Mead, Langer, and the speech act philosophers. However, his views on the earliest stages of symbol use agree with those of Piaget and Werner, in stressing the child's use of symbols outside an immediate communicative context to organize and identify a world of objects and events.

To summarize so far, our findings are in line with the prevailing developmental view that naming emerges gradually out of a complex of interactions with objects. Once naming emerges, it serves two major functions: The social function of communication and shared reference; and the private function of categorizing and structuring reality. We do not intend to minimize the role of social factors in the emergence of naming. Our research team has dealt with these factors in some detail in other papers (Bretherton & Bates, 1979; Bretherton, McNew, & Beeghly-Smith, in press). However, in this paper our focus is on the psychological processes that underlie naming inside *and* outside of communication, which brings us to a consideration of communicative and noncommunicative gestures in the same developmental period.

THE ONSET OF GESTURAL SYMBOLS

In the children we have studied so far, there are direct parallels in the domain of gesture to all of the vocal developments described above. Here too the changes are gradual, and it is difficult to determine just when a gesture qualifies as a symbol.

At 9 months, when Carlotta's grunts and effort sounds took on a ritualized "MMM-MMM" form, there were analogous changes in her reaches toward a desired object. Instead of extending her whole upper body toward the goal, she would extend her forearm with the elbow partially flexed and perform an open-shut movement with the hand. This gesture, although it was apparently derived from earlier reaching efforts, was clearly unsuited for actually picking things up.

Instead, it seemed to be an intentional signal to the listener, used interchangeably with "MMM" in the same communicative sequences, with the same criteria for intentionality described above (eye contact to the adult; sequencing and termination of signals contingent on adult response rather than the position of the goal itself).

When Carlotta's vocal repertoire expanded to include more "wordlike" sounds, there were similar expansions in her gestural signaling. These included signals for giving and showing, and eventually pointing to objects out of reach. We do not know whether consonant-vowel sounds like NANA and AYI are deformations of some adult word or inventions by the child. Similarly, we cannot be certain whether the giving, showing, and pointing sequences would have evolved without adult modeling of the same acts. However, the curious history of pointing suggests that these gestures may arise naturally, without modeling. Carlotta began using her index finger to point to objects close at hand in solitary exploration, with no evidence of communicative intent. During this period, we once observed her from around a corner as she extended her forearm toward the window and pointed while exclaiming "Oh" after a dog barked outside. She was unaware that we were watching her, and did not look around for acknowledgment of her pointing act. Indeed, when she finally did begin to point for others, she would first point to the object, then swing around and point to the listener, then turn again to point to the apparent referent. It took several weeks for this chain of acts to smooth into a single action of pointing away while looking for confirmation. If deictic gestures like these were learned through imitation of models, it is certainly not clear when the match-to-model took place.

On the other hand, there is another change in the child's gestural behavior from 9 to 13 months that clearly involves incorporation of new conventions through imitation and repetition for social effects. By 7–8 months, many infants will repeat their own sounds and movements if they are successful in provoking adult laughter and comment. For example, Carlotta had developed a habit of spitting out milk while making a sound commonly called "the raspberries." The effect was comical despite the spillage it involved, and invariably made her parents laugh. By 8 months, she would repeat this sound several times in succession, stopping and smiling toward the parent until each performance was acknowledged. Hence the groundwork had already been laid for "showing off" as a means to a social goal—but with behaviors she had discovered on her own. Between 9–10 months, she began to acquire new gestural routines like peekaboo, waving bye-bye, saluting. These routines differ from giving, showing, requesting, and pointing in two ways: (a) they are much more clearly derived through imitation rather than solitary exploration and play with her own body; and (b) they seem to refer only to themselves, involving no objects or "third parties" outside the social interaction itself.

There is yet another kind of gesture that begins in some children around 10 months but does not become really established until the end of the first year. These are brief imitations of characteristic behaviors with objects, taken from well-known scripts like "lunch" and "bedtime" but executed outside their usual context. For example, the child may see an empty cup on the floor, pick it up and touch it briefly to her lips (perhaps with the head tilted back), then toss it back on the floor. Of course this gesture could have been a mistake, i.e., she didn't know the cup was empty. But as more and more instances accumulate in the observational record, it becomes increasingly clear that such behaviors are in some sense schematizations of the real thing, serving some other purpose. If they were merely mistakes, or clumsy approximations of real acts, we would expect them to get better rather than worse. And yet these gestures continue to occur outside the usual context or script. They are executed only in brief, often caricatured versions of the original act; and if more than one conventional act is produced with a given object (e.g. stirring, sipping, swallowing), the acts are likely to occur out of their original sequence. The associated objects are often only marginally appropriate, e.g. sipping from empty vessels or trying to sit on a 2-inch chair. Indeed, across the next few months the props involved in such enactments tend to bear less and less relationship to the original. For example, by 13 months Carlotta would carry out the gesture associated with telephone receivers (putting it up in the area of her ear but generally oriented badly for listening) with objects as diverse as a spoon and a cigarette package. Like the BAM and WOOWOO examples cited earlier, across the period from 10 to 13 months, these conventional gestures became "unstuck" from their original script, and tended to occur in brief and nonfunctional forms upon the encountering of an object that is associated with (and hence in some sense defined by) stirring, dialing, sipping, etc. Like BAM and WOOWOO, these manual gestures seem to take on a recognitory or labeling function.

The four kinds of gestural schemes that we have described between 9 and 13 months are all *conventions* in a limited sense: They occur in stable and stereotyped form, can be recognized by both the observers and the child himself, and are carried out without any apparent utilitarian payoff beyond their cognitive or communicative function (e.g. the brief recognitory drinking gesture applied to an empty cup doesn't seem to be contingent in any way on liquid in the cup). On the other hand, these gestural developments differ from one another along at least five important dimensions.

First, some of these gestures are obviously derived through imitation of specific cultural acts. These include "showing off" routines like patty-cake, and object-oriented imitations like putting a telephone receiver to the ear. By contrast, other gestures seem to evolve "naturally" out of the child's own self-generated activities. These include giving, pointing, showing, and some of the more idiosyncratic request gestures (although use of these gestures may certainly be enhanced if the adult reciprocates with similar behaviors—see Shotter, 1978).

A second contrast pertains to use inside and outside of communication. Pointing-for-self and most of the object-oriented imitations often occur in solitary play, when the child is apparently oblivious to observers. By contrast, imitative "showing off" as well as the various giving/showing/pointing sequences are all aimed at and contingent upon response by another human being.

A third contrast has to do with the establishment of reference, i.e., with the involvement of some external object, event, or "third party" in the gestural routine. Pointing-for-self and the communicative giving/showing/pointing sequences all serve to orient attention toward external objects or events. Similarly, many of the imitative gestures that emerge by 13 months also involve interaction with and recognition of an associated external object or event. By contrast, such imitative routines as saluting and waving seem to function as "pure performatives" (Austin, 1963; Greenfield & Smith 1976). In other words, they neither point to nor stand for anything beyond the immediate social interaction itself.

Within the set of gestures that do involve external reference, we find a fourth contrast. Imitative enactments like stirring, drinking, and telephoning are all *uniquely* associated with a specific class of referents. But the various giving/showing/pointing gestures can be used with a wide variety of "third parties." This distinction between specific versus general reference in gesture is analogous to a distinction between nouns and pronouns in speech.

Finally, there is a fifth contrast involving the degree to which direct motor contact with the referent is necessarily involved in the scheme. Although children in the early stages of naming do prefer to name objects while touching them (Volterra et al., 1979), they can and will name objects at a distance. In American Sign Language (ASL), children will sometimes violate the conventions of signing space in trying to sign an object name on its referent (Bellugi, personal communication), but this tendency can and must be overcome to use the language correctly. By contrast, the object-associated gestures of hearing children are invariably carried out on the referent object. Although we have heard a few rare anecdotes to the contrary, we have never seen a child in this age range pantomime a gesture empty-handed (e.g. a drinking motion with the head tilted back) except perhaps in direct imitation of an adult. In general, then, this dimension of direct contact with the referent separates vocal names and ASL name signs from the specific, object-referring gestures of hearing infants.

Table 3.1 summarizes gestural developments in infancy, classified according to the above five dimensions: natural vs. imitative derivation, communicative vs. private use, referential vs. nonreferential use, specific vs. general reference, and presence or absence of direct physical contact with the referent. Which of the gestural categories is more "like" vocal naming? Applying the five dimensions, we can argue that the child's first referential words: (1) are imitatively derived; (2) are used in communication at least part of the time; (3) set up (by definition) conditions of reference; (4) refer (by definition) to specific objects, events, routines, states, etc.; and (5) are used at least part of the time while the object is out of direct motor contact. By these criteria, what kinds of gestures are most similar to vocal naming? The manual names of ASL fit these five criteria perfectly. However, none of the gestures we have found in hearing children from 9

TABLE 3.1
Difference among Gestural and Vocal Conventions at 13 months

	Imitative Derivation	Communicative use (at least part-time)	Refers to external objects, events	Points to *specific* referents	Involves direct contact with the referent
1. Pointing-for-self	−	−	+	−	+
2. Giving, showing, pointing for others, ritual request gestures	−	+	+	−	−
3. "Showing off" routines (e.g. pattycake)	+	+	−	−	−
4. Recognitory gestures with objects	+	−	+	+	+
5. Vocal Names	+	+	+	+	−
6. ASL Signs	+	+	+	+	−

to 13 months match vocal names in all these respects. The closest match are the gestures that we have called "manual names": use of an imitative action scheme to recognize or identify a specific set of referents. In our observations, these gestures seem to be used in precisely the same way as solitary vocal naming. But, curiously, we have never seen them used communicatively. Of course they do occur frequently *during* social interactions, for example in videotaped free play with mother. But we have, for example, never seen a hearing infant use one of these imitative gestures in a request, e.g., pantomiming a drinking movement in asking for more juice.[4] Also, such brief recognitory gestures do not seem to meet our criteria for "proto-declaratives" or communicative labeling (Bates, Camaioni, & Volterra, 1975); that is, children do not generally execute one of these gestures and then look directly at the adult for confirmation or approval.

Although none of these gestural categories provide a perfect match to first words on analytic grounds, we now have ample empirical support for our claim that manual and vocal "names" are similar in important ways. In a longitudinal study of 25 infants followed from 9 to 13 months of age, we obtained a large variety of quantitative and qualitative measures of early language comprehension and production, the gestures summarized in Table 3.1 (particularly manual nam-

---

[4]Stern and Stern (1927) do provide an example of a 28-month-old hearing child using a drinking pantomime in a request. We might find analogous examples in younger children if we set appropriate eliciting conditions. Our point here is that, compared with vocal names, communicative use of manual names is rare.

3. SYMBOLIZATION IN INFANCY AND APHASIA 71

ing), plus standardized tests in cognitive development (Uzgiris & Hunt, 1975). The details of this study are published elsewhere (Bates, Benigni, Bretherton, Camaioni, & Volterra, 1977; Bates, Benigni, Bretherton, Camaioni, & Volterra, 1979, see in particular chapters by Bretherton, Bates, Benigni, Camaioni, & Volterra and Volterra et al.). We can, then, restrict ourselves here to a brief summary of the findings.

Starting with the quantitative findings, correlational analyses of the gestures in Table 3.1 and the various language measures do support our claim that manual names are the most "language-like."

(1) "Showing off" routines like saluting and waving were not correlated significantly with any of the language measures. This is the one set of gestures that, according to our analysis, *does not* set up either general or specific reference; therefore, we tentatively conclude that gesture and speech are crucially linked by the processes that underlie "setting up reference by conventional means."

(2) Of the three classes of gesture that do make external reference, the one that shares the fewest features with language in Table 3.1 is "pointing-for-self." And indeed, although this development was correlated significantly with language, the relationships were weak compared with the remaining two categories.

(3) Strong and consistent correlations with the various language measures were obtained with manual names, and with the cluster of communicative gestures comprised of giving, showing, communicative pointing, and ritualized requests. However, much more detailed correlations emerge with manual names. In brief, vocal and manual names emerged around the same time and correlated across the sample in frequency of use, rate of acquisition, number of different schemes reported by the mother, and number of different schemes observed in the video sessions.

(4) Manual and vocal names also showed very similar patterns of correlation with the cognitive measures in the study. Both correlate with aspects of tool use and imitation, but neither correlate with spatial relations and object permanence. This very specific pattern of relations to cognition tells us two things: That manual and vocal names are rooted in similar cognitive processes of some kind; *and* that these correlations probably do not reflect trivial effects of IQ.

Moving beyond the correlational data to more qualitative comparisons, we find still more evidence that manual and vocal symbols are part of the same system. Volterra et al. (1979) compared the vocal and manual repertoires of all 25 children for aspects of *content* and *contextual range of use*. Three interesting conclusions can be drawn from those comparisons.

(1) Both kinds of symbols begin as context-bound routines and go through roughly parallel stages in "decontextualization." Volterra summarizes these gradual changes in four levels (see Table 3.2).

TABLE 3.2
Stages in the Decontextualization of Symbols

1. The child recognizes the appropriate use of an object by briefly carrying out an associated activity.	1. The child uses a word as a procedure or part of a routine or game.
2. The child "pretends" to carry out his own familiar activities (e.g. sleeping) outside of its usual context (i.e. temporal decontextualization).	2. The child uses a word to anticipate or remember the scheme with which it is typically associated (i.e. temporal decontextualization).
3. The child acts out activities usually carried out by others (i.e. decontextualization through role reversal).	3. The child uses words to designate actions carried out by himself or others, or to designate the agents or objects of such actions (i.e. decontextualization through role reversal).
4. The child carries out actions with objects that are inappropriate, or related quite abstractly to the original object (i.e. reference with decreased contextual support).	4. The child uses words to categorize new persons, objects or events (i.e. reference with decreased contextual support).

*From Volterra et al., 1979, p. 175.

(2) With regard to content, Volterra et al. reached the striking conclusion that children use manual and vocal symbols within the very same "scripts," corresponding to the same kinds of objects and events. For example, the corpus of words used by the total sample of 25 children fell into categories corresponding to such situations as dressing, telephoning, eating, exchanging objects. When the corpus of manual names used by the children were classified into types, the very same categories emerged: dressing, telephoning, eating, object exchange, etc. There were a few exceptions. For example, children often had a variety of animal sounds used appropriately to recognize doggies, kitties, etc. We could not discern a comparable range of gestures for animals. The same was true for most proper names. On the other hand, even proper names could be analyzed for corresponding gestures, if we knew enough about the idiosyncratic uses by individual children. For example, one infant had a patty-cake routine that she carried out exclusively with her grandmother. By 13 months, she would briefly execute a segment of this routine when she saw her grandmother for the first time. Because this was done without any follow-through to get the game going, we might infer that the gesture is serving as a kind of recognitory tag for grandmother. Table 3.3 summarizes the classsifications of gesture and sound from Volterra et al. *We conclude from this comparison that vocal and manual names at 13 months involve the same basic stock of meanings.*

(3) Remember that the gesture-sound correspondences of Table 3.3 are based on classifications of words and gestures for the full sample. If we look within the records of individual children, we generally *do not* find corresponding gesture-

TABLE 3.3
A Comparison of Gestural and Vocal Vocabularies (Number of
Subjects with Such Schemes in Parentheses)

Gestural		Vocal	
Waving hello/goodbye	(5)	Hi	(5)
		Bye	
		Byebye Baby	(9)
		Tao (ciao)	
		Ta-Ta	
Placing phone to ear only	(5)	Hello, Hi, Ah	
		Che e (who's there)	
Other phone schemes	(15)	Chi e (who's there)	(9)
Making others phone	(1)	Apo, pronto (speaking)	
		Bye, byebye baby	
Cuddling, hugging, kissing	(19)	Kiss	
Pretending to sleep	(9)	Cara (dear)	
Making others sleep	(4)	Nanna, Ninna (Rockabye)	(2)
Empty containers,		Appa, Acqua, Acca	
utensils, to lips	(3)	Juice	(5)
		Bumba, Ba	
		Ahm, Yum, Mm, Mpa	
		Pappa	(13)
Pretend drinking	(19)		
Pretend eating	(11)	Cookie	
		ToTo (toast)	
Making others eat, drink,			
take child's pacifier	(17)	Cucco (pacifier)	(1)
		Caee (candy)	(1)
		Mm (milk)	(1)
Put on necklace	(9)		
Pretending to dress	(2)	Bee (beads)	(1)
Dressing or undressing doll	(10)	Socks	
		Pappe (shoes)	(1)
Pushing cars or other			
objects in vehicle motion	(5)	Vrmmm	(3)
		Brrr	(3)
		Ga (truck)	(1)
		Aereo (plane)	(1)
Sniffing flowers or other			
objects	(1)	HaHa (sniff noise)	(1)
Pretending to read or			
write	(5)	Ba (book)	(1)
		Write	(1)
		Lalala (reading)	(1)

(*continued*)

TABLE 3.3 (continued)
A Comparison of Gestural and Vocal Vocabularies (Number of Subjects with Such Schemes in Parentheses)

Gestural		Vocal	
Hiding games, peekaboo	(10)		
		Cucutete	
		Tetete	
		Dee (there)	(4)
		Peek	
		Pu (allgone)	(2)
Giving, Taking	(25)		
		Da	
		Ta, te, tie (take)	
		Bah/Dah	
		Grazie (thanks)	(21)
		Please	
		Dadu (thank you)	
		Ga	
		Hey woo (hey you)	
Communicative pointing	(22)		
		Da (there?)	
		See	
		Pe (pretty)	
		Pee (pretty)	(5)
		That	
		Look	

sound pairs for each object or script. Instead, an individual child frequently has *either* a gesture *or* a sound for a given meaning. This tendency seemed puzzling at first, until we related it to findings on very early vocabulary development in bilingual children (Volterra & Taeschner, 1978). In the first stages of lexical development, bilingual children operate with only one lexicon. That is, if they have a German word for "glass" they will not acquire the Italian word for "glass"; on the other hand, they may have the the Italian word for "dog" without acquiring the corresponding word in German. *It is as though, in the first stages, one word per referent is enough.* Prinz & Prinz (1979a, 1979b) report similar findings for the early stages of language development in their daughter, a hearing child who acquired English and ASL at the same time. If the child acquired a word for a given object, she typically did not acquire the corresponding sign, and vice versa (see Wilbur, 1979, for related evidence from ASL). This "reciprocal distribution hypothesis" requires much more study, particularly in comparisons between linguistic and gestural symbols. However, the trend in our longitudinal data is at least compatible with the little that is known about acquisition of dual symbol systems.

In conclusion, on quantitative and qualitative grounds, we can infer that manual and gestural symbols at 13 months are linked by common processes of mechanisms of a very specific sort. However, we still do not know what these processes are.

To investigate the relationship between vocal and gestural symbols in more detail, we must move into a more experimental framework. In our first longitudinal studies, all observations of language and play took place in naturalistic settings, in the child's home, with a standard set of toys and other common objects. Maternal reports of the children's activities were also based on naturally occurring behaviors. By probing extensively for anecdotal information, it is possible to obtain enough information about natural contexts of use to delineate a developmental shift from context-bound to relatively flexible symbol use. For example, at one session the mother might report that her child used the word "ball" only to name his own ball, and seemed confused by any other use of the term if someone asked him for "ball." A month later, according to the mother, the same child might apply this label to his brother's ball as well, and to one that belonged to a neighbor's child. Nevertheless, in collecting such information, we exercised no control whatsoever over the conditions eliciting symbol use. It is difficult to know what *aspects* of the context and the referent object govern the child's use of a gesture or a sound because a variety of cues are typically present at one time. Hence the concept of "decontextualization" is a descriptive term with no explanatory value.

It is possible that the correlations we found between vocal and gestural symbols are created by only a subset of the instances we actually observed. Some aspects of gesture may have nothing in common with language at all, controlled by entirely different mechanisms, whereas others are governed by precisely the same processes.

We have already narrowed our focus of interest to the class of gestures called "manual names." For the remainder of the chapter, we will use the word "gesture" to refer to this kind of behavior. To learn more about the processes linking language and gesture, we have begun to exercise more systematic control over the contexts and objects involved in the comprehension and production of symbols. With this more fine-grained approach to the same developments, interesting differences between vocal and manual symbols have begun to emerge at last.

Before we present findings from our recent experiments, it will be useful to review some of the many a priori differences between sound and gesture that could be responsible for differences in the way these symbols are acquired by children.

LANGUAGE VERSUS GESTURE: SOME A PRIORI DIFFERENCES

One of the most striking differences between the words and gestures used by 13-month-olds is the aforementioned fact that manual symbols are rarely (if ever) used in communication. Obviously this difference in function cannot be due to some general modality difference between vision and hearing, since 13-month-old deaf children use manual names in much the same way that hearing children use words (Bellugi & Klima, 1979; Hoffmeister, 1978). Apparently this is true even for deaf children who have not been exposed to sign language models. For example, Feldman, Goldin-Meadow, and Gleitman (1978) have described the spontaneous use of pantomimes and indexical gestures in communication between deaf children subjected to a strictly oralist training program. Similarly, Volterra (personal communication) has observed deaf Italian children in oral language programs who make considerable symbolic-communicative use of pantomimes as well as caricatured versions of the rich gestural system of normal Italian adults. For example, in one video session, a 4-year-old deaf child used an empty drinking gesture, without an object, to convey to the hearing adult his need for a glass of water. The children studied by Volterra and by Feldman et al. were considerably older than our 13-month-olds. The only reports on communicative gestures in deaf infants come from studies on ASL, where the child does receive gestural symbols as input from adults. Nevertheless, it is clearly *possible* for infants to use signs in exactly the same way that they use words: in private cognition, and in requests and labels addressed to others.

So why don't we see both functions served in our data? Hearing infants acquire manual symbols by observing adults, perhaps even in active play with adults; but we have no evidence that adults address pantomimes and object-related gestures to the child in the communicative sense just outlined. Although ample demonstrations are provided concerning how to eat, dress, etc., we have not observed mothers asking the child to get a cup while making an empty pantomime of drinking. It would be interesting to find out just how the child would react if someone did present such a model—a question that we are now pursuing in some ongoing studies of gestural comprehension. In any case, the difference in function that we have observed between language and gesture is not mysterious, given the different kinds of input associated with each. And these differences may in turn affect the structures and processes that underlie vocal vs. manual naming.

A second major difference has to do with the real world relationships between these symbols and their associated objects. C. S. Peirce (1932) has offered a three-way classification for the kinds of objective relationships that can exist between a potential sign and its referent (see Bates, Benigni, Bretherton, Camaioni, & Volterra, 1979, Chapter 2 for a more detailed discussion):

(1) *Icons* are signs that can be used to stand for their referents by virtue of some literal physical resemblance. For example, a schematic drawing of a flame actually looks like fire to a limited extent.

(2) *Indices* are signs that stand for their referents by virtue of some literal physical participation or association. For example, smoke coincides with and is

produced by fire; for this reason, smoke can serve as a reminder or sign for fire. We can also create mixed, indirect sign relations by combining icons and indices. For example, a schematic drawing of smoke can stand for fire because it is iconically related to smoke and hence indexically related to fire.

(3) "True symbols" (from Peirce's point of view) are signs that bear a purely arbitrary relationship to their referents, assigned by agreement in a community of users. For example, fire is signified in English by the word "fire," in Italian by the word "fuoco," for no other reason than convention.

These three kinds of real world relationships have implications for the way signs are discovered or learned. Icons and indices are "natural" signs that could be discovered independently by individuals or by whole communities. These relationships are insured by objective states of affairs in the world; although these relationships are selected and exploited by knowers, they are not created by knowers. Arbitrary symbols, on the other hand, must be learned from other human beings.

However, there is another respect in which indices and arbitrary symbols differ from icons. The discovery that two actions or objects "look alike" is based on perceptual detection of *similarity* (Tversky, 1977). By contrast, both arbitrary and indexical symbols must be learned by *contiguity,* i.e., by rote memory for repeated associations in space and time.

Let us consider the differences between language and gesture in the light of these Peircian contrasts. Except for a few rare onomatopaeiac words like "boom," words bear an entirely arbitrary relationship to the things they stand for. We cannot expect a child to acquire words by analyzing and/or discovering the similarity between sounds and objects. It has been claimed, however, that gestures do look like their referents, e.g., a pantomime of drinking really looks like drinking. Hence the child has some extra help from the context in discovering relationships between gestural symbols and their referents.

However, if we examine the situation more carefully, it turns out not to be that simple. If we use a drinking movement to mean "drink," we are indeed using an iconic relationship. Suppose, however, our intention was to use a drinking movement to indicate "cup" or perhaps "water." In this case, we are actually constructing a complex, indirect relationship built on both indices and icons. Drinking looks like drinking; but drinking is indexically associated with water and cups. If the 13-month-old already knows about the indexical relationship, then he may be able to use an iconic analysis to work his way toward the meaning of a drinking gesture. But he has to know about the indices first.

To put this another way, if a child uses the act of stirring to "name" or signify stirring, then her gesture functions as a kind of *verb* or *action name* that is iconically related to its referent. On the other hand, if she uses the stirring movement to recognize or identify spoons, then her gesture functions as a kind of *noun* or *object name* based on an indexical relationship. Both of these options are certainly plausible, and to know for certain which one the child intends we would have to read her mind. However, as we shall see later, there is indirect evidence to suggest that most of these gestures at 13 months are used to name objects. For example, they correlate much better with common nouns than with predicates in the children's speech. And their use seems to be governed more by the presence of the associated object than an iconic act by the adult.

In any case, suppose for purposes of argument we assume that the manual gestures of 13-month-olds are based primarily on objective indexical relationships between actions and objects (stirring = spoons, drinking = cups, etc.). How should this fact affect the acquisition of gestures in comparison with words?

An indexical gesture could be acquired either by rote learning (constant observation of stirring in contiguity with spoons) or by an understanding and/or experience with the function of the stirring act. After all, there is a reason why we move spoons round and round: to get the ingredients in a vessel properly mixed. We have already argued that the child's symbolic use of the gesture is apparently detached from its utilitarian "payoff," e.g., it doesn't matter whether there is a bowl. Still, the child's initial interest in and mastery of the symbolic movement might have been based on an understanding of stirring. In Bates, Benigni, Bretherton, Camaioni, and Volterra (1979) we argued that such understanding is most unlikely for the gestures we had observed. Children put phone receivers to their ears regardless of whether they'd ever actually heard a sound from a telephone. And by what stretch of imagination can we infer that the child understands *why* shoes go on feet and hats go on heads? She certainly knows that's where they go, but it is unlikely that she understands the utilitarian motives for clothing (if, indeed, there are any on a 90° summer day). For this reason, we concluded that children must acquire these cultural conventions by the same learning process used to acquire words: perception of contiguity, imitation, and rote learning.

Some additional evidence supporting this interpretation has since been offered by Schwartz (1978), who presented 13-month-old children with a total of 16 nonsense words associated with nonsense objects (hence nouns) or with nonsense actions on objects (hence, supposedly, verbs). The nonsense actions were entirely arbitrary, designed to bear absolutely no functional relationship to their associated objects. There was, in short, no utilitarian payoff of any kind to help the child acquire these gestures. Nevertheless, children had no difficulty imitating and remembering these nonsense actions. And by the end of the study the children had also acquired a mean of 12 words!

If the same kind of learning is involved for indexical gestures and arbitrary sounds—in other words, if they are both equally arbitrary as far as the 1-year-old is concerned—then what kind of difference is there? What is left to distinguish arbitrary actions from arbitrary sounds is the factor of literal physical touch. The manual gestures we have observed in our children, because they are based on indexical acts that adults do with the objects, involve literally holding and moving the object while the action is carried out. Rodgon, Jandowski, and Alenskas (1977) have observed that early vocal naming also tends to occur while the child is touching the object. For example. Rodgon et al. (1977) and Volterra et al. (1979) report that children were manipulating referents in over 66% of the instances of labeling in their records. So in the earliest stages *both* sounds and gestures are carried out in literal physical contact with objects, with consequent kinaesthetic feedback. But the gestures provide a constant, unique, defining kind of feedback; by contrast, the child could be doing any number of things while handling the toy and talking. Simply put, you can do more things to a cup while saying "cup" than you can while drinking from it. As we shall see later, this difference may have an important impact on the acquisition of vocal as opposed to manual names.

SOME EMPIRICAL DIFFERENCES BETWEEN LANGUAGE AND GESTURE

The research we are about to describe comes from a second large-scale longitudinal study, following up on the results of Bates, Benigni, Bretherton, Camaioni, and Volterra (1979). This new study includes a sample of 30 infants studied at 10, 13, 20, and 28 months of age. Although the research includes investigations of several factors in social and cognitive development in this age range, we will concentrate here on comparisons between language and symbolic gesture in the 13–20-month range.

In this study, we have switched from the naturalistic format of earlier work, to a quasi-experimental format in which the eliciting conditions for symbol use are varied much more systematically. We have replicated the general results of earlier work regarding correlations between language and gesture. However, the experimental format has permitted us to draw more precise conclusions about the factors that affect this set of relationships. Perhaps more important is the fact that we have uncovered differences as well as similarities between the two modalities.

Before presenting the language-gesture comparisons, we will begin with a summary of results for the language variables alone at 13 and 20 months. We should stress that extensive use has been made of parental report data at both points in development, as a supplement to short-term observations. In our experience, brief (i.e. 2–3 hour) observations of infants in the second year may yield sparse and unrepresentative samples of many language abilities. It is simply the case that children talk relatively little from 12 to 20 months, compared with the much richer corpora that are traditionally obtained in developmental studies of children beyond 2½ years. In defense of parental report data, we should note that the validity and reliability of a language interview depends on the interview technique that is used.

First of all, parents must be comfortable with the interview format. This usually means that middle-class, well-educated adults are the best source of data. Second, parents should only be asked about current abilities, as opposed to retrospective reports of first words, preverbal gestures, etc. Third, the abilities in question must be at a stage in development where it is reasonable to expect an adult to keep track. Most parents are aware of their children's productive vocabularies early in the second year but are at a loss to assess vocabulary by the second birthday. Similarly, the range of multiword constructions can be assessed around 20 months but have expanded far out of range for most parents by 2½ years. Fourth, we have switched in our research from a "recall format" where parents are asked for items within general categories to "recognition format" in which a detailed item-by-item checklist is provided. For every item checked, we also probe extensively for anecdotal information illustrating how that word or phrase is understood or produced by the child.

Using these procedures, we have obtained reliable assessments of child language at the early stages (i.e., intercorrelations within general categories are high). With regard to validation, the major interview categories do correlate significantly with analogous observational measures at the same session. Finally, our interview measures at 13 and 20 months predict observed language at 28 months (when the observational data base is much richer) as well or better than 13 and 20 month language observations. (For further details on reliability and validation, see Bates, Snyder, Bretherton, & Volterra, 1979, and Bretherton, McNew, Snyder, & Bates, 1982.)

Language at 13 months: The Origins of Reference

The 13-month interview was based on a 100-item word and phrase checklist, drawn from our own research and that of other investigators to reflect typical comprehension and production items at this age. The results of the interview, including the detailed anecdotal data provided by the parents, were analyzed at three levels, for both comprehension and production: rate of development, vocabulary composition, and contextual flexibility (based on a coding scheme rating each item for range and flexibility of use across contexts). The results (presented in detail in Snyder, Bates, & Bretherton, 1981) can be summarized briefly as follows.

Rate. The first finding is the surprising amount of independence between comprehension and production vocabularies at this age. The two were correlated at only $+.29, p < .09$. Although there were children who were high or low on both measures, there was also a good-sized group who understood a great deal more than they said. It was of course the latter group who reduced the correlation. The same independence between comprehension and production also occurred in our observational measures and, as we will see later, was reflected in the different ways that comprehension and production correlate with gesture.

Composition. Nelson (1973) has reported patterns of individual difference around 18 months, with some children ("referential") specializing in production of object names, others ("expressive") have more heterogeneous vocabularies. We found a similar referential-expressive variation as early as 13 months, in both comprehension and production. Furthermore, referential children tended to have larger vocabularies overall—again in both modalities. Finally, even though comprehension and production totals were uncorrelated, it was still the case that proportion of object names in one vocabulary predicted proportion of object names in the other. In short, referential style is an early and pervasive phenomenon, associated with a faster rate of lexical development.

Contextual Flexibility. Each item in the parental report was classified as context-flexible or context-bound; therefore, we were able to correlate the proportion of context-flexible items with rate and composition measures. Within production, results were in the expected direction: For both object names and predicates, a high proportion of flexible usage was associated with a faster rate of development. Furthermore, the referential children tended to have a higher proportion of flexible object names, suggesting that these are the children who really understand the "idea" that things have names. In comprehension, the flexibility codings did not produce analogous results. This could mean that the "unsticking" of items across contexts in comprehension is unrelated to rate or composition; on the other hand, it could also simply mean that we did not uncover the right criteria for coding contextual flexibility in comprehension. *In any case, the one thing we can conclude is that progress in language production is associated with the ability to generalize object names across contexts and referents.*

The Snyder et al. report was limited only to these measures within the 13-month session. In subsequent analyses, we have uncovered some longitudinal relationships that are at least worth mentioning here. There is one 13-month measure that distills the relevant variance from all three of the above levels: the proportion of the child's vocabulary that consists of context-flexible object names. In our view, this ratio captures the transition from simple "word games" to a real grasp of *reference,* or *the idea of naming.* This measure at 13 months is correlated with Mean Length of Utterance at 28 months at the $+.70$ level, $p < .001$. This is some of the strongest evidence for continuity in language development that is currently available in longitudinal studies. Early discovery of naming is associated with progress in the acquisition of grammar more than a year later.

Language at 20 Months: Nominal and Pronominal Style

At 20 months, we used a combination of interview and observational data to test some questions from the literature about the passage into multiword speech (Bretherton, McNew, Snyder, & Bates, 1982). Briefly summarized, a variety of recent studies have emphasized individual differences in multiword speech around the transition from single words to sentences. For example, Bloom, Lightbown, and Hood (1975) have distinguished between "nominal style" and "proniminal style" during Stage I in the acquisition of grammar. Nominal children referred to themselves and their listeners by name, avoiding shifting personal pronouns (e.g. "Mommy drink; Katherine drink"); pronominal children referred to themselves and others with pronouns from the very beginning (e.g., "I drink it; You drink it"). Nominal children typically left out function words and inflections, producing "telegraphic" combinations of content words; pronominal children, by contrast, included inflections and functors in their speech from the earliest stages.

Many other linguistic and nonlinguistic characteristics have been added to this nominal-pronominal division (for reviews, see Bates, Benigni, Bretherton, Carnaioni, & Volterra, 1979; Horgan, 1980; Kempler, 1980). For example, there is evidence to suggest that Nelson's referential style at the one-word stage is associated with nominal style later on; expressive style at the one-word stage is in turn associated with pronominal style in early grammar. It has also been suggested that referential/nominal children are likely to be earlier talkers, firstborn, middle- to upper-class, less prone to imitation, more articulate in their acquisition of phonology, more reflective and analytic in their thinking. In turn, expressive/pronominal children are supposedly more likely to be late talkers, later born, lower-class, more prone to imitation, less precise in their use of phonology (i.e., "mushmouth"), more impulsive, more gregarious, and given to a more "holistic" or "Gestalt" orientation to problem-solving. Nor does this brief list exhaust the set of possibilities that have been proposed.

Perhaps one reason these proposals have proliferated is that the data base for these individual difference studies has been very small—sometimes based on only one or two children. It is not clear, then, whether these different characteristics reflect one or many different and independent dimensions of variation in early language. Although our longitudinal sample of 30 is not large by the standards of psychometric research on individual differences, it is at least large enough to provide a stronger empirical test of how these proposed variables cluster together at 20 months. We also had a number of variables available for the same children at 28 months, which permitted us to test some hypotheses about the nature of the 20-month variations.

In both the interviews and observations at 20 months, the data on single and multiword speech were classified along many of the dimensions described above: type and variety of semantic relations expressed, use of noun and verb inflections, function words, pronominal v. nominal expressions, rates of labeling and imitation, participation in dialogue and question-answering, and several other characteristics (see Bretherton et al., 1982 for details). For the interviews and observations, respectively, we then carried out cluster analyses of these items. In the interview analysis, the following four clusters emerged:

Nominal Constructions. These included the kinds of "telegraphic" utterances described by Bloom et al. (1975) for nominal children, together with several measures of semantic variation (number of different case constructions, and "pivot-open" or "constant-variable" constructions with the words "no," "more," "allgone," and "up/down").

Grammatical Morpheme Constructions. These included utterances with pronominal reference, marked verb morphology, and several kinds of function words (copulas, auxiliaries, prepositions).

Language Participation Items. This cluster was defined by labeling rate, imitation rate, and degree of participation in question-answering and dialogue.

Semantic-Cognitive Flexibility. These included all items reflecting sophisticated use of utterances that might contain only single words, including talking about past events, referring to absent referents, labeling an object with a "pretend" name, and variety of case relations expressed with single words.

In the observational analysis, the first three of these four clusters also emerged. In sum, in both data formats we found support for the nominal-pronominal dimension delineated in small-sample studies. But we also uncovered some surprises. Imitation rate and labeling—supposedly characteristic of different types of children—clustered together and defined *neither* nominal nor pronominal style. Pivot-open constructions were hypothesized to belong to pronominal style, but clustered instead with nominal constructions. Ancillary correlations with additional variables provided some more surprises. Birth order and sex were unrelated to any of the language clusters. Nor did the nominal or pronominal cluster correlate with any of the personality measures we obtained at 28 months, in contrast with the prediction that pronominal/expressive children are somehow more social, gregarious, etc. Neither of the two grammatical style clusters was associated with the 28-month Peabody Picture Vocabulary Test. Insofar as the PPVT can be taken as an early predictor of later verbal intelligence or "IQ", we thus have no support for the view that nominal style is typical of brighter children. In sum, we have no evidence in support of some of the simpler explanations for the nominal/pronominal split: IQ, personality differences, birth order, sex, or general imitative tendencies.

We did, however, find support for the contention that nominal children take a more analytic approach to language, and (perhaps as a result) tend to be more verbally precocious in the long run. First of all, the nominal cluster was a better predictor of 28-month measures than the grammatical morpheme cluster. Second, at 28 months we also administered a test of morphological comprehension. The items in this comprehension test were exactly the same as the items that formed the grammatical morpheme cluster in 20 month production: pronouns, auxiliaries and copulas, verb inflections, prepositions. Hence we might expect strong correlations between the grammatical morpheme cluster and this comprehension test. In fact, we obtained very different results. Nominal constructions (which leave precisely those inflections and functors *out* at 20 months) were positively correlated with comprehension of morphology eight months later; but there was no relation whatsoever between grammatical morpheme cluster scores at 20 months and comprehension of those same items at the later session. Another way of putting this is that pronominal children do not know what they are doing at 20 months! This supports investigators who have argued that pronominal style (and expressive style at the one-word stage) involves a holistic, Gestalt, or formulaic approach to language. Conversely, the fact that nominal style does correlate with later morphological comprehension supports the view that this strategy (and referential style at the one-word stage) involves an analytic approach to language, i.e., don't use a form until you know what it is for.

To summarize the language findings so far, at 13 months we examined lexical development at several levels and found that flexible use of object names is a key predictor of overall lexical development. At 20 months, we examined several aspects of the passage into multiword speech. Here too, the extent to which children used explicit nominal terms proved to be a key predictor of language development. Furthermore, we have also found significant relationships between proportion of object naming at 13 months and nominal style at 20 months, creating a sort of "nominal strand." Finally, this orientation toward nominal reference is associated with more rapid development in comprehension and production of grammar later on. With these patterns in mind, we can now turn to comparisons between language and gesture at the same age levels.

Object Dependence at 13 and 20 Months: A Multiple-Choice Test

One of the experimental techniques adopted in the longitudinal study was a multiple-choice test for infants, described in Bretherton, Bates, McNew, Shore, Williamson, and Beeghly-Smith (in press). Although we had originally designed this test as a measure of comprehension of object names, it also turned out to elicit a large number of spontaneous vocal and gestural productions from the infants—far more than are usually obtained in an equivalent sample of free play. In this task, infants were seated before a transparent plastic box with three wells. Common objects selected for their familiarity in this age range were placed in the wells, and the infant was asked to "Get the _____." The eight objects (car, telephone, teddy bear, doll, cup, bottle, shoe, and spoon) were constructed in two versions: realistic or perceptually detailed, and abstract or schematic, with a minimum of recognizable features (see Figure 3.1). There were 16 trials, 8 realistic and 8 abstract. After selecting an object, the child was permitted to play with it for several seconds so that we could assess spontaneous vocal and gestural conventions with the same realistic or abstract toy (regardless of whether the

3. SYMBOLIZATION IN INFANCY AND APHASIA   85

FIG. 3.1. Abstract objects for comprehension box.

child had chosen correctly or not). The three dependent variables were, then, *object choice* (as an index of comprehension), *gestural production,* and *vocal production.*

These three dependent variables were each analyzed in a 2 (13 × 20 months) × 2 (abstract vs. realistic trials) repeated-measures analysis of variance. The results can be summarized as follows (see Figure 3.2):

Object Choice. This measure increased significantly with age, although 13-month-olds did perform beyond chance; there was no main effect or interaction with abstractness.

Vocal Production. The production of object-associated words also increased significantly with age, and there was a main effect of abstractness favoring realistic toys. There was, however, no interaction between age and abstractness.

Gestural Production. In contrast with the above findings, gestural production actually decreased significantly with age. There was a main effect of abstractness (with more gesturing on realistic toys), and a significant age × abstractness interaction. The interaction, as can be seen from Figure 3.2, reflects the particularly strong effect of realistic vs. abstract toys on gesture at 13 months.

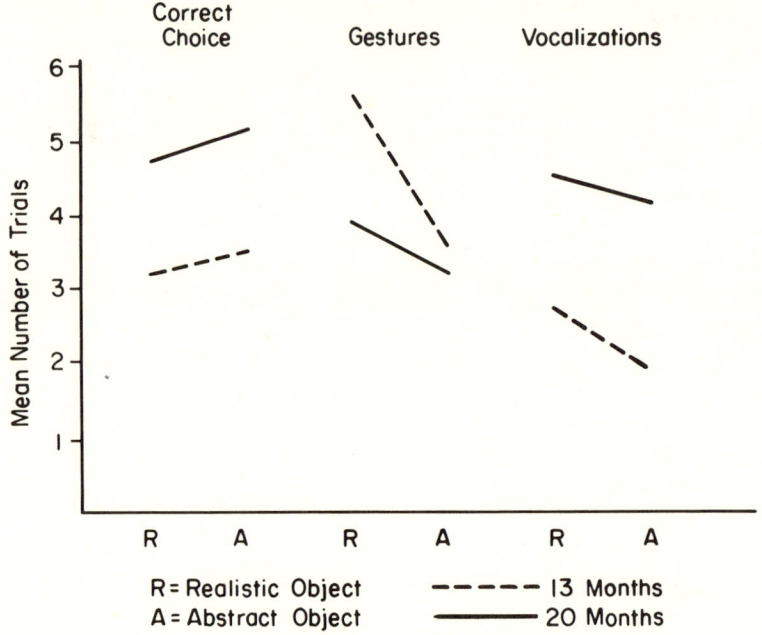

FIG. 3.2. Age and abstractness effects in the multiple choice test.

These results yield several interesting conclusions regarding modality differences in symbolic processing. First of all, the perceptual detail provided by the referent object seems to affect *production* (either vocal or gestural) but not *comprehension*. In other words, to recognize a familiar object it is apparently sufficient to have a handful of characteristic features (as in Figure 3.1), but to recall what to do or say with that object it is helpful to have additional cues.

Another result—particularly important for our purposes here—is that there seems to have been a switchover from 13 to 20 months in the preferred modality for recognizing or "naming" an object. The younger child is more likely to produce a recognitory gesture; the older child is more likely to produce an associated word. This would not be such a surprising finding if we had not already shown in other studies that 13-month-olds have roughly the same *number* of recognitory gestures and words available in their repertoire of conventions. Hence this finding does not just mean that language develops later than gesture, but rather, that the *relative threshold* for eliciting gestures vs. words changes during the second year.

Finally, the age × abstractness interaction on gesture tells us something more about these hypothetical threshold effects. In some poorly understood sense, gestures seem to be more *object-dependent* than words at the early stages. That is, the probability that a gestural symbol will be elicited, seems to be strongly a function of the number and variety of associated cues available in the referent object. The role of kinaesthetic cues should also be stressed here. At either age, the conventional gestures produced by these children were carried out *with the object in hand*. At both ages—but especially at 20 months—vocal symbols were produced with the object at a distance. This provides further empirical support for the analysis presented in Table 3.1, regarding the role of kinaesthetic feedback in the spontaneous gestural conventions of hearing children. We will return to this issue of differential object dependence throughout this chapter (cf. Elder & Pederson, 1978; Fein, 1975).

Of the three dependent variables examined in this study, there is one that is conspicuously missing: a measure of gestural comprehension analogous to word comprehension. At 28 months, we attempted a multiple-choice test like this while pantomiming a familiar gesture empty-handed (e.g., holding back the head and drinking from an invisible cup) and asking the child to "Get the one that goes like this." This procedure proved to be extremely difficult (with performance barely above chance) even for 28-month-olds. This provides an interesting counterpoint to the results reported for 13 and 20 months. Although it seems to be in some sense "easier" to produce gestures at 13 months, it is also very difficult to understand the same gestures produced out of context. This is another example of a comprehension/production split qualifying our comparisons between modalities. As we shall see later, it is analogous to some findings in the adult literature.

Language-Gesture Relations at 13 Months

In a recent paper by Bates, Bretherton, Snyder, Shore, and Volterra (1980), we examined the correlational relations that hold between different kinds of symbolic gesture, and our measures of language development at 13 months. Symbolic gestures were elicited in two situations: with silent modeling, out of context (using a technique adopted from Killen & Uzgiris, 1978); and with gestures presented in sequence, with accompanying language, inside a familiar "script" (a technique adopted from Wolf & Gardner, 1979).

Within both of these elicited imitation tasks, we also manipulated the amount of perceptual support furnished by the target object. This represented our effort to operationalize the elusive notions of "symbolic status" and "object dependence," in keeping with proposals by Piaget (1962), Vygotsky (1962), and Werner and Kaplan (1963) that "true" symbols are representational acts that can be carried out without perceptual/contextual input from their referents. Hence in the Killen-Uzgiris task we modeled familiar acts with an *appropriate object* (e.g., drinking from a cup, brushing with a brush) and with an *inappropriate object* (e.g. drinking from a toy car, brushing the hair with a toy cat). In the Wolf-Gardner scripts, we went through a familiar sequence (e.g. breakfast, or putting baby to bed) with objects at four levels of perceptual support: a *realistic* version (doll, cup, spoon), a *tiny* version of the same objects, a very *abstract* version of each object, and finally, with a plain wooden cylinder or *placeholder* object. (For details on how these procedures interact with order of presentation, and different operational definitions of imitation, as well as sex and content effects, see Shore, 1980.)

As described in Bates et al. (1980), these manipulations of "object support" proved very important in our correlational analyses with language variables. In both elicited gesture situations, the level of gesture that was most strongly related to lexical development was the most abstract or "decontextualized" level: imitation of gestures with inappropriate objects in the Killen-Uzgiris task; imitation of gestures with the placeholder object in the Wolf-Gardner task. Furthermore, these correlational relations tended to be stronger with the common noun or object-name category in our language measures, providing further support for our contention that this reflects some kind of naming dimension (rather than general symbolic fluency, general intelligence, etc.). Finally, there was an interesting comprehension/production split in our data. Even though the abstractness effects were in the same direction in both situations, the Killen-Uzgiris task (gesture elicited out of context) correlated with language production but not with comprehension; the Wolf-Gardner task (gesture elicited within a familiar script) correlated with language comprehension but not with production. We will return to this comprehension/production division later on.

To summarize so far, we showed in the previous study that gestural symbols are the preferred mode for recognizing or naming objects at 13 months, and that gestures tend to be more strongly affected by the amount of perceptual detail in the referent object. However, in this correlational study we have shown that children who can "survive" the removal of such perceptual cues for gesture are also the children who are making the most progress in the development of vocal naming. *Another way of saying this is that "stripped down" or "decontextualized" gestures without perceptual support from the object are the ones most closely linked with language development at 13 months.*

Fiffins at 20 Months

In the 20-month home session, children were taught a nonsense noun ("fiffin," after Nelson & Bonvilliam, 1978) corresponding to a set of slightly varied nonsense objects (plastic pipe fittings with colored fur in the openings). Fiffins were presented to the child with a nonsense gesture (holding it to the center of the forehead and pushing it forward with a downward curve), which was referred to by the nonsense verb "glooping." In the laboratory session several days later, we administered fiffin analogues to several of our usual measures with familiar objects. These included a fiffin multiple-choice test (with realistic and abstract fiffins—the abstract fiffin being a simple T-joint without colored fur), and elicited "glooping" with three kinds of objects: a realistic fiffin, a featureless wooden placeholder, and a counter-conventional object with a meaning of its own (i.e. a toy kitten). Finally, we pushed the child's comprehension of the fiffin complex as far as we could by asking each child to "make the kitty gloop the fiffin."

Results of the various fiffin exercises are reported in Garrison and Bates (1981). Our hypothesis was that decontextualization with familiar concepts at 20 months could either be a product of months of accumulated experience, or it could reflect a true developmental change in the way that symbols are processed. If the novel concept was rapidly acquired and generalized along the same dimensions as the familiar objects, we could conclude that decontextualization at 20 months reflected more than a prolonged experience with the same objects, words, and gestures.

The fiffin results support the view that decontextualization involves a real change in the way symbols are processed. In the multiple-choice test, fiffins were discriminated just as readily as the more familiar objects—including the abstract fiffin. Indeed, one child not only selected the abstract fiffin but told us what was wrong with it: Pointing to the holes in the T-joint without colored fur, he scolded us that "Fiffin got no lights." Children readily glooped fiffins, but were also quite willing to gloop the placeholder (the wooden cylinder) and to gloop the toy kitten. In keeping with our results for more familiar concepts, fiffin comprehension measures were not correlated significantly with fiffin production measures (gestural or vocal, in this case). However, fiffin comprehension did correlate well with the other comprehension tests in our study. Finally, a total of 21 children were able to obey the command to "Make the kitty gloop the fiffin," by placing the fiffin on the kitten's forehead and pulling it forward. In sum, the entire fiffin complex was acquired with alacrity, and generalized to nonfiffins with the same flexibility evidenced in more familiar conceptual systems. The only clear evidence for a difference between fiffins and other concepts was that the glooping gesture seemed to be more readily acquired and accessed than either of the two nonsense words. In this respect, the modality preferences resemble those that we have found at 13 months, suggesting that the visual-gestural modality may then be an easier route into a new symbolic activity at any level of development (more on this point below).

Language and Gesture at the Level of Primitive Grammar

All of the results we have reviewed so far pertain to a link between language and gesture *at the lexical level,* i.e., at the level of individual vocal and gestural schemes for objects. In Shore, O'Connell, and Bates (1981) we have also found evidence for a vocal-gestural link *at the level of primitive grammar,* i.e., shared limitations on combinatorial ability in multiword speech and in multischeme symbolic gesture.

At both 20 and 28 months, we administered an elicited symbolic play task similar to those described earlier for our 13-month session. Three scripts were modeled for each child (having breakfast, putting teddy to bed, giving dolly a bath). Each script was modeled three times, once at each of three levels of abstractness for the "target" object: a realistic doll, bear, and spoon; a plain wooden cylinder for all three scenes; an inappropriate object for each scene (i.e. eating with a comb, putting a toy car to bed, giving a shoe a bath).

The child's imitations on all nine trials were transcribed, and then coded to yield both "lexical" and "grammatical" measures of play. The lexical measure was simply the number of different schemes from the model imitated by each child, at each level of abstractness. To derive the structural measures, we applied a coding scheme that segmented the child's activity into sequences of one or more schemes. For example, take the following pair of sequences: "Pour/drink/ pour/drink . . . eat/wipe the mouth with a napkin." Across these two sequences, the total number of different schemes is four; the absolute number is six. If we calculate sequence length without considering repetitions (in keeping with the standard criteria in language analyses for calculating Mean Length of Utterance—Brown, 1973), then each sequence is two schemes long. If we do allow repetitions, then the first sequence reaches an outer bound of four. Finally, we also derived a measure of the degree to which the child's imitation preserved the order of schemes in the model, across the whole script. In the above imitation of the breakfast scene, three of the scheme transitions (pour/drink, drink . . . eat, eat/wipe) were so ordered.

The lexical and grammatical/structural measures were compared with independent measures of language (described earlier for Bretherton et al., 1982). First we simply examined the descriptive statistics, comparing the "shape" and developmental function of multiword speech vs. multischeme play at 20 and 28 months. Second, we carried out a series of regression analyses to determine the extent to which length limitations were consistent within individual children.

The descriptive statistics for the two modalities were surprisingly close, particularly at 20 months. For example, the 20-month Mean Length of Sequence (MLS), not counting repetitions, was 1.28; the longest sequence ranged from 1 to 4, with a mode of 2. This corresponds to a Mean Length of Utterance (MLU) of 1.13, with a range from 1 to 5 and a mode of 2 in the longest utterance produced. This parallel in length limitations cannot be due simply to some kind of attention span or fatigue effect, since the longest chain of gestures when repetitions were allowed (e.g. pour/drink/pour/drink) ranged as high as 11 schemes. In other words, language and gesture at 20 months seemed to be paced by some kind of shared limit on the number of *different* units that can be executed in a single, uninterrupted sequence.

At 28 months, the two modalities have moved somewhat further apart. MLS was 1.58, with a range from 1 to 5 and a mode of 3 in the longest chain of different schemes produced. Once again, these developmental constraints apply only to the number of different schemes produced; sequence length when repetitions are allowed ranged as high as 15. By comparison, MLU at 28 months was 2.39, with a range from 3 to 12 in the longest utterance produced. In other words, language has moved ahead of gesture by 28 months of age—analogous to the modality switchover we observed from 13 to 20 months in labeling objects. It became clear where this language advantage came from when we examined utterance length in content words instead of morphemes: Mean Length of Utterance in Content Words at 28 months was only 1.13, with a range from 2 to 5 in the longest chain produced. This means that the surge in sequence length in language comes from the grammaticization process, perhaps from the "automatization" of inflections and function words. The strict "one-two-three" constraints that we have observed in the gestural modality may apply only to units that require some level of conscious selection or planning; for many children, grammaticized elements may not require this level of planning by 28 months.

The final comparison involves our measure of the degree to which children preserved the order of elements in the input. Compared with all the other lexical or structural measures in gesture, this variable showed the largest increase from 20 to 28 months—more than a three-fold increase in only 8 months. This provides an intriguing (though very tentative) parallel to the grammaticization process in language, suggesting that the main event in both modalities in this age range involves fine tuning and getting things in the right order.

Our regression analyses complemented these descriptive findings. First, at 28 months we did *not* find significant correlations between language and either the lexical or structural gesture measures. In other words, the two modalities seem to have "unhooked" during the grammaticization process—at least with regard to the measures we have used here.

At 20 months, however, there were significant correlations between the two modalities. In keeping with our earlier findings at the lexical level, these correlations emerged clearly only for the abstract levels of gesture. Using the abstract measures as predictors, we were able to account for 30% to 50% of the variance in several different measures of grammatical development (as described in Bretherton et al.). It is particularly interesting that the 20-month *nominal cluster* showed the strongest relationship with symbolic play: The longest chain of gestures, the total number of different gestures, and the ordering measure all contributed unique variance to the regression equation for this language variable. In short, *language and gesture at 20 months may be linked by not one but several different component processes.* Once again, however, these relationships become clear only when we use a "decontextualized" measure of symbolic gesture.

To summarize the findings from Shore, O'Connell, and Bates, language and gesture seem to be paced by some common upper boundary on the number of different "plans" that can be produced in a single sequence. This relationship is particularly clear at 20 months; by 28 months, the shared constraints apply only at the level of content words, due perhaps to the routinized or automatic status that certain inflections and function words have attained in the meantime. These language-gesture findings at the structural level are analogous to our earlier findings at the lexical level in several respects. First, there is evidence for another modality switchover: In the initial stages of the new combinatorial ability, gesture is ahead of language; at the later stages, the opposite is true. Second, correlational relations emerge only when gesture is assessed with minimal contextual support.

Summary of Results from the Longitudinal Study

All of the conclusions we have reported here must be viewed as interesting but tentative bases for future work. Nevertheless, we have in the interim located some exciting converging evidence for these patterns from an entirely different literature: the breakdown of naming and gesture in adult aphasia. In our child data on language, we have support for the following conclusions:

(1) Comprehension and production are relatively independent, at least at the lexical level.
(2) There is also some dissociation between nominal and pronominal-morphological constructions in the early stages of grammar—a dissociation that may actually involve analyzed vs. unanalyzed use of these grammatical elements.
(3) Contextual flexibility of naming at 13 months and nominal reference at 20 months, are both associated with progress in language acquisition through 28 months of age. In other words, object naming seems to be a kind of central organizer in early language development.

In our child data on language-gesture relations, we have support for the following conclusions:

(4) There is a developmental link between language and gesture at the lexical level at 13 months, although the relationship is strongest with "stripped down" or abstract gestures with minimal contextual support.
(5) There is also a developmental link between language and gesture at the level of primitive grammar at 20 months, although again the relationship is strongest with abstract gestures.
(6) In some poorly understood sense, the "threshold" for gestures seems to be lower at the early stages in the acquisition of a new concept or a new symbolic system. Hence it is "easier" to elicit gestural labels at 13 months, gestural sequences at 20 months. Once the new system is established, language moves ahead.

We will review evidence from adult aphasia relevant to these six points. Before we proceed, however, a note of caution is in order. We want to avoid the overly simple claim that "pathogenesis recapitulates ontogenesis," i.e., that aphasia involves a reversal of developmental sequences (Werner, 1961). In contrast with the fairly orderly sequences observed in the ontogenesis of symbol systems, a mature linguistic-symbolic system can break down in an enormous variety of ways. For example, there are reports on very specific syndromes in which deficits appear primarily in color naming (e.g. Greenblatt, 1973) or in names for body parts (e.g. Yamatori & Albert, 1973). There are individual patients who can write but cannot read, read but cannot write, read and write but cannot understand speech (Brown, 1972). It would be absurd to propose that such diverse patterns are in any interesting sense a simple reversal of normal development. Also, an adult confronted with loss of some aspects of language has at his disposal a variety of mature compensatory devices that are presumably not available to a very young child. In short, adults are smarter than infants, even when considerable damage has been sustained.

Given these difficulties, it is a dangerous enterprise to come into the aphasia literature in search of analogies to our own data. On the other hand, with the proper cautions observed, there are things to be gained from a comparison of language development and language breakdown (Caramazza & Zurif, 1979). In our research with normals we have tried to locate linguistic and nonlinguistic phenomena that "hang together" as units, governed by similar internal and external factors. We view this as a search for the seams and joints of language, the "old parts" that go into the construction of a capacity for symbols (Bates, Benigni, Bretherton, Camaioni, & Volterra, 1979). In this foray into the aphasia literature, we wanted to know if the same units continued to operate in adulthood, with the same seams and joints evidenced in language breakdown.

NAMES, GESTURES, AND OBJECTS IN APHASIA[5]

We will begin by reviewing converging evidence relevant to the above three points on language development: the dissociation of comprehension and production, the dissociation of nominal and pronominal constructions, and the centrality of object naming. Then we will proceed to a discussion of the last three points, discussing the breakdown of gesture in aphasia in relation to our infant data.

Language Comparisons

A discussion (however brief) of dissociable components in aphasia brings us necessarily into the controversy in that field over taxonomies of aphasic syndromes and explanatory models to account for symptom patterns. Reviews of the taxonomic issue are provided by McMahon (1972), Gardner (1975), and Lesser

---

[5]We are grateful to Howard Gardner, Lynn Snyder, and Edgar Zurif for their reading and criticism of an earlier version of this section. Although they have done what they could to relieve our naivete in this area, they are not responsible for what is left.

(1978). McMahon has counted over 113 different types of aphasia that have been proposed in the literature. Lesser restricts her review to some of the more widely cited proposals, varying from one to seven classifications each. Despite disagreements about subtypes, however, most investigators recognize two distinct patterns: Broca's and Wernicke's aphasia, corresponding to lesions in the anterior and posterior areas of the left hemisphere, respectively. These two patterns have been characterized by different researchers in at least three different ways: (1) *Sensory* (comprehension) vs. *Motor* (production); (2) *Fluent* vs. *Non-Fluent;* (3) *Semantic* vs. *Syntactic.*

In Wernicke's syndrome (i.e., symptoms associated with posterior lesions) patients typically produce lengthy and reasonably well-formed utterances from a syntactic point of view. However, depending on the particular subtype, these utterances may involve circumlocution, digressions, jargon and formulaic phrases, semantic anomalies, and a high ratio of pronouns to substantive nouns. In short, they often don't make much sense. In addition, Wernicke's aphasics typically show marked impairment in comprehension. Because of the comprehension problem and the posterior lesions (near the sensory association areas), this syndrome has been historically viewed as "sensory aphasia."

In Broca's syndrome (i.e., symptoms associated with anterior lesions), patients produce either telegraphic speech (restricted to two or three words without functors, inflections, etc.) or indeed single words only. There is a much higher proportion of nouns to pronouns in the speech that they do produce, and even though the utterances are painfully limited, they do typically make sense in context. Finally, Broca's patients may appear to have perfectly intact comprehension of speech. Because of the greater impairment of production compared with comprehension, and because the anterior lesions are adjacent to major motor control areas, Broca's aphasia was historically referred to as "motor aphasia."

This convenient dissociation between sensory and motor aphasia provides a first analogy to our infant findings, i.e., that comprehension and production vocabularies develop relatively independently in the second year. But the analogy is too simple, and misleading as stated. The initial definition of the two aphasic syndromes as "sensory" vs. "motor" has in fact been abandoned by many neurolinguists in recent years, although most recognize that comprehension deficits are proportionally greater in Wernicke's aphasics. For one thing, evidence has accumulated to suggest that Broca's aphasics also show comprehension difficulties if they cannot use information from the nonverbal context, or encyclopedic knowledge of relationships among lexical items (e.g., that dogs bite men, and not vice versa) to disambiguate a grammatically complex utterance. In fact, Broca's aphasics show most difficulty in comprehending the very elements that are missing in their own productions: function words, inflections, pronouns (Caramazza & Zurif, 1976; Caramazza & Berndt, 1978). Wernicke's aphasics are also far from normal in their production. In particular, they tend to have marked difficulty with aspects of production revolving around retrieval of object names. Indeed, this particular production deficit has been held responsible for the high pronoun ratio, and for the "paragrammatism," jargon, circumlocutions, etc. that occur when the Wernicke's aphasic is "stuck" in trying to find a noun.

In abandoning a straightforward sensory/motor division, some aphasiologists have opted for a purely empirical classification system, based entirely on the obvious symptoms (i.e., fluent vs. nonfluent) or on lesions (i.e., posterior vs. anterior). Wepman (1977) have offered yet another classification, arguing that the best single predictor of symptom groupings in aphasia is the ratio of nouns to pronouns in the speech of a brain-damaged patient: Wernicke's aphasics could be called "pronominal types," whereas Broca's aphasics could be classified as "nominal types."

A classification that would incorporate both the comprehension/production differences and the fluency dimension revolving around pronouns can be found in the theory that both Broca's and Wernicke's aphasia involve the dissociation of two major components of language: *lexical semantics* and *syntax*. Caramazza and Zurif have argued that Broca's good comprehension skills are based on an intact lexical system, consisting of "open class" or contentive lexical items that are also spared in the Broca's production. At the same time, in both comprehension and production, Broca's aphasics demonstrate difficulty with "closed class" items: functors, bound and unbound morphemes, items that serve a primarily relational or syntactic function. These closed class items, conversely, are spared in the productions of Wernicke's aphasics; but these patients have enormous difficulty in retrieving open class lexemes. Caramazza and Zurif suggest that such a dissociation between lexical and syntactic processes is compatible with a linguistic theory (e.g. Chomsky, 1965) in which there is an autonomous syntactic component that operates independent of meaning.

But there are problems with this classification as well. It is not at all clear whether the fluent productions of Wernicke's aphasics involve generative, productive syntactic components, i.e., rules ranging over an abstract set of symbols. It is possible, according to some analysts, that the syntactic fluency of Wernicke's aphasics involves the production of frozen forms, semipermeable idioms, or overlearned syntactic routines, rather than truly productive syntactic rules. Indeed, the very rapid nature of Wernicke's aphasics speech (faster and more compressed than that of normals) attests to this possibility. If this is the case, then the division between the two aphasias is not a crisp dissociation of lexical and grammatical processing, but rather a division that has something to do with controlled vs. automatic lexical access, with selective sparing or impairment of just those lexical items that have achieved an overlearned and "routinized" status.

These different proposals remain controversial in the aphasia literature; in any case, we do have further convergence here with the child language data. The respective characteristics of Broca's and Wernicke's aphasia that we have reviewed so far bear a nontrivial resemblance to the nominal/pronominal dimension at 20 months of age. This analogy has also been noted by Horgan (1980) and Kempler (1980). The nominal style involves deletion of inflections and functors, telegraphic constructions made up primarily of open class items, and a rather general association with good comprehension. The pronominal style involves high proportions of pronominal reference, preservation of inflections and functors, but with so little evidence for comprehension that the apparent syntactic well-formedness of these utterances may belie a formulaic and unanalyzed use. It would be a mistake to push these analogies too far, dividing children into Broca's and Wernicke's infants. However, we do have evidence for a dissociation between open and closed class items in both the infant and the aphasic data, a dissociation that has: (a) something to do with comprehension/production differences; and (b) something to do with analyzed vs. formulaic or routinized structures. This does not mean that the infants and aphasics are alike, but rather, that component processes in language seem to divide at the same boundaries in both populations.

A final set of analogies between child and aphasic language have to do with the *central organizing role of object naming*, particularly in regard to *context-dependent* vs. *context-flexible object names*.

We are all familiar with the so-called "tip of the tongue" phenomenon (Brown & McNeill, 1966). This particulate state of mind is the converse of the word satiation phenomenon we discussed earlier with regard to Werner and Kaplan's theory. In word satiation, the relationship between sound and referent is maintained but the sense of meaning is lost. In tip-of-the-tongue states, we have a strong sense of the meaning of a word (like a sneeze coming on) but cannot quite locate the appropriate phonemic representation of that meaning. A common symptom in aphasia is a difficulty in finding names, i.e., "anomia." In fact, anomia is the only symptom that apparently occurs to one degree or another in *all* the major aphasic syndromes (Caramazza & Berndt, 1978; Green, 1969; Lesser, 1978).

There are, however, differences among the aphasias in the relative impairment of naming. The worst cases occur in the Wernicke's syndrome, where both comprehension and production of lexical items is affected. Broca's aphasics, by contrast, are only slightly affected in comprehension and production of names compared with the more serious problem in processing closed class items (prepositions, auxiliaries, etc.). In between these two syndromes is the so-called "anomic" or "amnesic" aphasic, whose primary symptom is a disruption of productive naming; in comparison, comprehension of lexical items seems to be intact. This last syndrome appears to provide still more evidence for the dissociability of comprehension and production—although some researchers have suggested that anomic aphasia is simply a milder form of Wernicke's aphasia that has affected recall (i.e., production) but is not severe enough to affect recognition (i.e., comprehension). This argument is based on the fact that both of these syndromes involve relatively fluent but "empty" speech.

Much stronger evidence for a comprehension/production split comes from the specific category of object naming, in comparison with other kinds of words. Goodglass, Klein, Carey, and Jones (1966) examined comprehension vs. production of several kinds of words including action words, color words, names for objects, names for body parts, in both fluent and nonfluent aphasics. In both populations, objects names were the *hardest* category to produce but the *easiest* category to comprehend. This difference was particularly marked among the fluent patients. Lesser (1978) summarizes several studies like this and comes to the following conclusion:

> Although there is a class of aphasic patients whose major disorder in speech is difficulty in finding the names of objects, it is nevertheless true that when studies are undertaken of large groups of aphasics it is usually found that nouns are easier to recognize, read aloud or repeat than are the other two main categories of substantive words, verbs and adjectives [p. 133].

Although the apparent contradiction between these comprehension and production findings remains unexplained, there is one thing that these studies have in common: objects emerge as the most central category in naming disorders.

Here again we find parallels to the infancy data. As we noted earlier, a high proportion of object names is associated with more rapid vocabulary development at 13 months. Also, multiword nominal constructions at 20 months are associated with greater progress in grammar later on. The predictive value of these two object-naming dimensions seems to cut across comprehension and production lines.

The role of object naming in child language and in adult aphasia becomes more specific when we also consider the contextual conditions that elicit naming in both populations. In this regard, Kogan (cited in Lesser, 1978) has argued that the so-called "confrontation naming" procedure used in testing adult aphasics is pragmatically very odd. In normal discourse, adults rarely name objects that are right in front of them. If we refer to something or someone by name, we are more likely to do so for referents that are not in the room. Kogan suggests that confrontation naming taps an ability to adopt a special attitude toward the object-symbol relationship, an attitude that is in some sense metalinguistic. Naming disorders may involve an inability to adopt that attitude, to reflect upon the naming relationship itself. Like the cliche of asking a centipede how it manages to walk, an automatic procedure may fall apart when it becomes an object of attention.

Caramazza and Berndt have also considered the role of metalinguistic awareness in object naming, and they suggest that factors that facilitate recovery of a name often involve setting up automatic eliciting conditions. In developmental terms, this suggestion is related to the difference between context-dependent word use at the early stages vs. a later stage when the labeling function becomes a focus of attention in its own right. Indeed, it is as though the normal infant practices a confrontation naming procedure, adopting the peculiar attitude of focusing on the symbol-referent link itself, before passing on to complex predications in which naming acts are embedded as subroutines. This is a point of similarity *and* contrast between infants and adult aphasics. Both are in some sense "caught" at the level of conscious naming. However, the 1-year-old has never gone beyond this level to more complex symbolic acts. Prior to injury, the adult aphasic had gone well beyond that level, and as a result completely reorganized his mental world. In the fluent aphasic, the routines for embedding names in phrases still seem to be intact; but the names themselves are difficult to find, so that routines for operating on those names go on in some empty form (with pronouns, circumlocutions, substitutions).

In our longitudinal study, the level of "decontextualization" of lexical items at 13 months (in production, but not in comprehension) was associated with faster vocabulary development overall. Furthermore, "referential" children or children with a high proportion of object names also showed greater contextual flexibility in using those names. Finally, there was a correlation between contextual flexibility at 13 months and the passage into multiword speech later on. In other words, those children who were least bound by the "automatic," stereotypic conditions for eliciting words had the best prognosis for development overall. This result is again complementary to findings in aphasia, where words are more likely to be retrieved at an automatic level while they are lost under the centipede conditions of confrontation naming.

In reviewing the contextual/experiential conditions that facilitate name finding, Caramazza and Berndt include such well-known psycholinguistic variables as word frequency, and concreteness or picturability. However, they also provide some experimental evidence suggesting that word-finding difficulties are qualitatively different in different kinds of aphasia. Whitehouse, Caramazza, and Zurif (1978) and Caramazza, Brownell, and Berndt (1978) have shown that anomic aphasics are disturbed not only in locating the *sound* that goes with a given object meaning, but also in integrating the perceptual and functional parameters that go into forming that object meaning in the first place (e.g. distinguishing cups and bowls on the basis of height and width information, and contextual factors such as the presence of cereal vs. coffee.) By contrast, Broca's aphasics show a normal ability to use this conceptual information, and seem to have difficulty only in locating the way to express that meaning in sound. If they are correct, then anomia is more than a "tip-of-the-tongue" state; it may involve problems in symbol construction at a much more basic level.

In this regard, a study by Gardner (1974) is particularly relevant for comparisons with infant concept formation and lexical development. Gardner presented aphasic patients with two-dimensional pictures of common objects that varied in their literal physical manipulability (i.e., "operativity" in his terms). For example, a picture of a curb or a tree would be low in operativity, but a picture of a flower would be "pickable" and hence higher in operativity. Equating for word frequency, naming was elicited more easily for the manipulable or "high operative" pictures. It is apparently also true that infants tend to acquire words for objects in their environment that they can handle (Nelson, 1973)—shoes, socks, and beads but not jackets; cups and glasses but not tables. At some level, literal kinaesthetic involvement with the object seems to help in "shoring up" object construction and the location of names for objects.

Further evidence for the centrality of object naming, and the role of kinaesthetic experience as an eliciting condition, comes from a disorder that sometimes cooccurs with aphasia: "agnosia" or loss of object meaning, an inability to recognize objects even though perceptual processing is intact. An agnosic patient may be able to detect visual and tactile changes in a particular object (e.g., a cup), and he may be able to match two cups out of a set of other objects by comparing their features. And yet, at the same time, the patient is at a total loss to understand what a cup is. There are frequent reports of agnosia in only one modality. The typical case is visual agnosia, where objects can be recognized only after they are touched. Lesser (1978) describes an even more interesting case in which *imagined* touch was sufficient:

> An alexic patient seen by the author has described her additional visual agnosic difficulties by saying that she did not know what a cup was until she picked it up. Interestingly enough, this happened even with a picture of a cup. Apparently she was able to extract enough information from the picture before she "recognized" it to imagine picking up the object it represented and then at that stage she was able to recognize and name it [p.75].

Cases like this one suggest that visual and kinaesthetic feedback from the object provide dissociable inputs to object recognition, and hence to naming.

To summarize, the severity of an anomic disorder is related to the contextual dependence of word use, the degree to which a patient *must* use or even *can* use object information and script information to retrieve the name of an object. There is evidence to suggest that naming disruptions can take place at different levels in the formation of objects and symbols: sound loss (in many Broca's aphasics); loss of the concept at a visual/contextual level (as in Whitehurst et al.); loss of object meaning at all but the kinaesthetic level. These patterns have direct analogues in the infancy literature on the formation of object concepts and the selection of symbols to stand for those concepts. In particular, the issue of kinaesthetic feedback brings us to a major point of this review: the relationship between vocal and gestural symbols in children and aphasics.

Language/Gesture Relationships in Aphasia

Many of us have had the experience of trying to function in a foreign country where we do not speak or understand the language. To meet our basic needs, we rely as much as possible on context to carry information (e.g., shared knowledge that two people entering a hotel with suitcases probably want a room). What is not already obvious from the context can often be conveyed by gesture: pointing to relevant elements in the situation; or pantomiming to communicate about needed objects, actions, and states. If aphasia were a language-specific disorder in an organism that is otherwise intact, then we should expect the aphasic to circumvent his disorder in the same way that normals do when trying to communicate in the absence of language. Surprisingly, however, aphasics typically *do not* use pantomimic gestures as a substitute or aid for their limited verbal communications.

This fact was first noted in the neurolinguistic literature by Finkelnburg in 1870 (cited by Liepmann, 1905), who argued that aphasia may be one manifestation of a general disorder called "asymbolia," a reduced capacity to produce or comprehend symbols in any modality. This same possibility has been mentioned by Jackson (1878), Brain (1965), Critchley (1939), and Goldstein (1948). Liepmann (1905) was the first to name gestural deficiencies as a separate syndrome, termed "ideokinetic apraxia." An apraxia is an inability to perform voluntary motor activity in a motor system that is otherwise intact. Most of the aphasia literature, insofar as apraxia is discussed at all, stresses the problem of oral apraxia: an inability to perform voluntary acts with the oral musculature (e.g. sticking out the tongue) even though automatic uses such as chewing and swallowing are unimpaired. Clearly an aphasiologist interested in semantic-syntactic disorders would want to eliminate cases in which failures to produce meaningful speech are due to an inability to move the tongue and lips on command. Analogously, many patients also suffer from specific forms of limb apraxia, e.g., inability to organize and execute voluntary acts with a hand or arm. This kind of deficiency would also be of little interest for the study of symbolic disorders. But the ideokinetic apraxias are another matter. *In these cases, the patient is unable to comprehend and/or produce conventional gestures, even though other voluntary movements of the limbs are possible.*

One of the most complete expositions of symbolic apraxia is found in Brown (1972) *Aphasia, apraxia and agnosia*. Brown discusses three distinct types of apraxia: ideomotor, ideational and constructional.

Ideomotor apraxia is defined as difficulty with familiar cultural schemes in the absence of an associated object, i.e., in the "pretend" mode. For example, a patient who is perfectly able to brush his teeth with the proper instrument in hand may be totally unable to carry out the same movement in pantomime, without a toothbrush. This deficit seems to occur both in comprehension and production, although it is not clear whether the two are necessarily correlated in the same patient (i.e., Gainotti & Lemmo, 1976, discussed below). That is, a patient may be unable to imitate the pantomimed gesture and/or he may be unable to match that gesture to its appropriate object in a multiple choice test. There is also a curious in-between level of performance evidenced by many ideomotor apraxics:

At first unable to produce a brushing gesture, the patient may place a body part in the position of the missing object, and then go on to a successful pantomime of the act (e.g., using a finger as a toothbrush). The resulting imitation looks very different from the pantomimes produced by a normal subject (Goodglass & Kaplan, 1963). Overton and Jacklin (1973) have observed that 3- and 4-year-olds will often use body parts as objects in "pretend" gestures, in a form very similar to the behaviors evidenced by aphasics in such tasks. Older children, by contrast, produce gestures that look much more like the object-free pantomimes of normal adult subjects. Overton and Jacklin suggest that the body-part-as-object pattern in some way concretizes the act, perhaps by providing kinaesthetic feedback similar to a real object. This may also be the reason why ideomotor apraxics display this pattern in gestural imitation.

Ideational apraxia is defined as a difficulty with conventional cultural acts even when the relevant object is present. Typically, the patient begins a sequence of appropriate gestural acts but then becomes derailed. For example, he may start the sequence of lighting a pipe but place the pipe upside down in his mouth so that the tobacco falls out; nevertheless, he continues to try to light the top of the pipe. Some researchers (reviewed in Brown) believe that the ideational pattern is simply a more severe form of an ideomotor disorder. Others argue that the perseverations and bizarre associations that characterize cultural acts in these patients comprise a distinct syndrome. Also, some neurologists stress the disruption of sequencing in addition to content.

Constructional apraxia is not a symbolic deficit in the sense intended here. In this syndrome, the patient shows marked difficulty with complex, planned motor sequences such as building a tower. Sometimes these constructional apraxias cooccur with aphasia; in other instances, they seem to be associated with right hemisphere lesions. Brown has argued that such lateralization differences may reflect the kind of analysis required for a particular constructional problem. In some cases, construction may involve pattern-matching and spatial relations of a type generally associated with right hemisphere function; in other cases, the problem may require planning and sequencing of a sort that is frequently impaired with left hemisphere lesions. By contrast, the ideomotor and ideational apraxias are much more strongly associated with left hemisphere damage. For example, Messerli, Tissot, and Rodriguez (1976) carried out correlational analyses of a variety of aphasia measures in relation to apraxia. When the three types of apraxia were combined into a single measure, no correlations were found with any aspect of aphasia. When constructional symptoms were removed from the apraxia measure, almost all of the correlations with aphasia reached significance.

When we first heard about the ideomotor/ideational apraxias, the clear analogies to our infant data struck us immediately, and we went eagerly into the literature to read everything that we could find. This proved to be a frustrating enterprise. A great many works on aphasia do not mention the gestural disorders at all. This is curious, considering that one of the major standardized language tests used in aphasia clinics and in much of the research in clinical aphasiology, the Porch Index of Communicative Ability (Porch, 1967), includes a gestural scale. Hence we can assume that gestural scores have contributed to the diagnoses of aphasic subjects in many studies.

Where investigators do report looking for apraxia in an aphasic population, there are almost uniformly positive results. However, many studies are difficult to interpret because of methodological problems. For example, the standardized test just mentioned (PICA) confounds gestural performance with language comprehension by using verbal instructions. This is also true for some of the studies where investigators constructed their own gestural measures (e.g., Goodglass & Kaplan, 1963; Pickett, 1972). Also, both standardized tests and clinical reports on individual cases often put very different kinds of gestures together in a single category: pointing, symbolic actions associated with objects (i.e., transitive acts), and conventional routines without objects (i.e. intransitive acts like saluting and waving). Our own results with infants suggest that this may be very misleading, since the different categories of gesture may involve different processes (see Table 3.1). Finally, some of the apraxia studies classify patients as "aphasics" without distinguishing different kinds of language symptoms. The results by Whitehouse et al. and Caramazza et al. (1978) on conceptual breakdown in anomic vs. Broca's aphasics suggest that this may be particularly misleading.

Nevertheless, we have located several studies that minimize these interpretation problems, and provide converging evidence for the relationships among names, gestures, and objects that we have found in normal infants. Above all, they suggest that at least some aphasic syndromes involve symbolic processes that are essentially modality-free.

In a naturalistic study, Cicone, Wapner, Foldi, Zurif, and Gardner (1979) investigated gestures that are used spontaneously by Broca's vs. Wernicke's aphasics during clinical interviews. These included meaningful or pantomimic gestures, as well as the kinds of place-marking or rhythmic hand movements that characterize adult cocktail party narratives. They report that the gestural patterns in the two populations parallel their speech in all relevant respects. The fluent aphasics engaged in rapid and fluid gesture but did not use their hands in pantomime, or any other "contentive" meaningful way; the gestures of the Broca's patients were slow, nonfluent, matching the halting rhythm of their speech. Their second major finding confirms clinical observations stretching back to the 19th century that aphasics do not use gesture as a substitute for speech: When patients were unable to retrieve a name, they were also unable to provide gestural substitutes for those names.

The first systematic experimental study of aphasia and apraxia was carried out by Goodglass and Kaplan (1963). Their subjects were 20 aphasics and 19 neurologically damaged control patients. No diagnostic information is given concerning the aphasic symptoms; all analyses were based on a single "severity-of-

3. SYMBOLIZATION IN INFANCY AND APHASIA 103

aphasia" score, a composite of several tests used in their clinic. The aphasics and the controls were matched for age and IQ; however, there was enormous variability within the two groups on both dimensions. Hence a substantial amount of the variance in the sample was necessarily due to differences in intellectual capacity.

Five different tests of gestural ability were administered to the patients. Two of the tests involved what Goodglass and Kaplan call "intransitive acts." One task included so-called "natural gestures," like holding the nose to indicate a bad smell. The other used conventions like saluting and waving. Both of these categories would be classified in our Table 3.1 among conventional schemes that are imitatively derived but do not make reference to a specific associated object. The other three tests involved different kinds of "transitive acts," cultural schemes that are associated with characteristic objects. In one version, the subject was simply told to carry out an action, e.g., "Show me how you brush your teeth." In another, pictures of common objects were presented and the subject was instructed to convey the "idea" of the object to the experimenter through pantomime. Finally, complex pantomimed sequences were presented (e.g., a "Hot Soup" script with pretend eating, burning the mouth, blowing over an imagined spoon, etc.), to be interpreted and imitated by the patient.

As Goodglass and Kaplan admit in their interpretation of the findings, all of these tasks to one degree or another involve a confounding of gestural ability and comprehension of verbal instructions. Nevertheless, the results are analogous to our infant findings in some interesting ways. First of all, there were significant differences between the aphasic and the controls on all five subtests. Second, the difference between the groups was much larger for the "transitive" gestures involving objects. This result fits with our findings in Bates, Benigni, Bretherton, Camaioni, and Volterra (1979) that object-associated gestures correlate with early naming, whereas nonreferential "showing off" routines like waving and peekaboo do not. The significant differences between groups in Goodglass and Kaplan is particularly striking since there was so much within-group variation due to IQ and age. In fact, all of the gestural measures were significantly correlated with these two confounding factors, although the variance due to IQ was smaller in the aphasic group.

Goodglass and Kaplan draw some curious conclusions from what appears to be a study strongly demonstrating a connection between language deficits and symbolic gesture. They make two assumptions. First, they propose that gestural apraxia cannot be called a symbolic disorder if it occurs outside of communication, in simple imitation tasks. Implicit in this statement is a definition of symbols as purely communicative acts, with no role in private cognition. Because noncommunicative gesture did discriminate aphasics from controls, they conclude that apraxia has nothing to do with a general syndrome called "asymbolia." Second, they argue that language and gesture are demonstrably part of the same system only if the *severity* of the gestural deficit within the left-damaged group correlates with *severity* of aphasia. Otherwise, they suggest that co-occuring deficits could simply reflect disruption of pathways that happen to be next to each other but have no functional connection. This seems like an odd assumption, because differences in the size of lesions could also produce a correlation in adjacent but unrelated symptoms. At any rate, to test this second assumption against the data, they looked at the correlation between severity of aphasia and scores on each of the five gestural tests, and found relationships ranging from $-.26$ to $-.66$. Because some of these correlations fall below significance, and the significant relations are small enough to be due to variations in age and IQ, Goodglass and Kaplan conclude: (a) that apraxia is unrelated to severity of aphasia; and hence (b) the differences they observed between the two experimental groups could be due entirely to disruption of adjacent pathways rather than a functional relationship between systems. In examining their findings, we would draw rather different conclusions. A range of correlations from .26 to .66 is probably as high as one could possibly expect in a small sample with enormous within-group differences due to extraneous factors. Nevertheless, Goodglass and Kaplan are cited in the literature as an empirical demonstration that aphasia and apraxia involve separate mechanisms (e.g., Maruszewski, 1975).

A better test of their second assumption is offered by Gainotti and Lemmo (1976). First of all, the sample size in this study was large enough to yield stable, meaningful correlations despite the wide variations in age and IQ that are typical in brain-damaged populations. There were 128 patients in all (53 aphasic, 26 nonaphasics with left hemisphere damage, and 49 with right hemisphere damage, plus 25 normal controls. Although we have little information about initial assignment to diagnostic groups, an advantage of the Gainotti and Lemmo study is that correlations with gesture are based on a single standardized language measure rather than a global score for severity of aphasia. This was a measure of word comprehension (from Gainotti, Caltagirone, & Ibba, 1975), and hence should be comparable in interesting ways to gestural comprehension. Second, Gainotti and Lemmo used a measure of gestural comprehension that was not confounded by verbal instructions. The experimenter silently modeled such cultural conventions as strumming a guitar, and the patient was instructed simply to point to an associated object from an array of three pictures (e.g., a bird, a guitar, a trombone). The gestural production measure had more problems. First, the patient was asked verbally to produce a gesture; if he failed at that point, he was asked to imitate a model of that gesture produced by the experimenter. This task is similar to two used by Goodglass and Kaplan, and is subject to the same methodological problems. Furthermore, Gainotti and Lemmo do not separate scores for gesture produced after verbal command from gestural imitations. Hence their analyses may reflect a confound of two distinct kinds of processing. Finally, in contrast with the gestural comprehension measure, the gestural production task was based entirely on intransitive gestures without associated objects (e.g., saluting). As we have found in our own research with infants, these gestures are the least likely to show associations with other aspects of symbolization (linguistic or gestural). In short, Gainotti and Lemmo's comprehension findings seem to be extremely valuable, but the production findings should be approached with caution.

Two main findings from Gainotti and Lemmo can be summarized as follows:

1. There were significant differences in both production and comprehension of gesture between the aphasics and each of the other three groups. The two nonaphasic patient populations did not differ from normal controls. Although Gainotti and Lemmo do not report correlations between their gestural measures and IQ, the fact that nonaphasics performed as well as controls suggests that the gestural tasks probably do not reflect a general lowering of intellectual capacity regardless of damage site (in contrast with the Goodglass and Kaplan measures). In other words, the results are probably not due to IQ.

2. Within the aphasic group, performance on word comprehension correlated with gestural comprehension at $r_s = .54$ ($p < .001$). Hence the Gainotti and Lemmo results for comprehension meet Goodglass and Kaplan's second assumption concerning correlations in degree of severity between gesture and language. Inexplicably, no information is provided on the correlation between gestural production and language. Gainotti and Lemmo do report that the two gesture measures are not related, in contrast with an earlier study (Gainotti et al., 1975). However, since the production task was based on intransitive items whereas the comprehension task involved transitive items, there is a confound between transitivity and the comprehension/production dimension. In other words, it is probably wise not to interpret the relationship between the gestural tasks.

Duffy, Duffy, and Pearson (1975) have avoided some of the methodological problems of both the above experiments. They examined the relationships among gestural comprehension, vocal production, and vocal comprehension in a sample of 44 aphasics, 30 right hemisphere damaged patients, 26 patients with subcortical (i.e., bilateral) damage, and 30 normal controls; all were matched for class, sex, and age. A unique aspect of this study is that the three kinds of competence were examined with the same stimuli. The comprehension test involved matching 50 pantomimed acts to pictures of associated objects in a multiple-choice format similar to Gainotti and Lemmo (after a carefully documented training procedure that also bypassed difficulties in pointing due to limb apraxia). In separate administrations, subjects were also asked to match vocal names to the same referents, and to produce names for those referents. (The three tasks were administered in a counterbalanced order across subjects.)

The aphasics performed significantly worse than the other groups on all three measures, in keeping with findings by Goodglass and Kaplan and Gainotti and Lemmo. In contrast with the latter study, however, right-damaged patients were also significantly impaired on these measures when compared with normals and subcortically-damaged patients. Furthermore, the right-hemisphere deficits were greatest with the gestural task, leading to the suggestion that comprehension of gesture involves *both* left and right hemisphere processing to a greater extent than vocal naming.

Correlational analyses in the Duffy et al. study indicate significant relationships among all three measures, in all of the experimental groups. This finding is probably due in part to the large item pool (so that there was significant variation even among the normals), and to the fact that the same stimuli were used throughout. If an adult knows an item, then he is likely to know that item in all three testing modes. Interestingly, however, performance was significantly lower on gestural comprehension compared with vocal comprehension for *all* the experimental groups. This fits with our finding with 28-month-old infants that comprehension of empty-handed gestures (e.g., "Get the one that goes like this," making a drinking motion with the hand) is much more difficult than comprehension of names (e.g., "Get the cup.").

In their 1975 study, Duffy, Duffy, and Pearson unfortunately did not include a measure of gestural production with the same items to complete their design. At that point they made the explicit assumption that comprehension and production reflect the same basic competence, and that comprehension is probably a more reliable performance mode for assessing that competence: "We can ask whether there is a single symbolic competence underlying both gestural and verbal performance. Such a view would be consistent with Sapir's view of language as a "system of voluntarily produced symbols" with 'gestural language' and 'auditory vocal language' only incidentally different in their mode or channel of expression [p. 118]." However, Duffy, Watt, and Duffy (1979) have tested this assumption by comparing performance in five tasks: (1) a measure of general language ability (the PICA); (2) a measure of general intelligence (Raven's Progressive Matrices); (3) a non-symbolic test of limb apraxia; (4) a pantomime recognition task (as in Duffy, Duffy, and Pearson); (5) a pantomime production task (devised by Duffy, Duffy, and Alderdice, 1977).

In Duffy, Watt, and Duffy, the discussion centers around multiple regression analyses of these five variables. Prior to regression, all five measures were significantly correlated with one another. When variance due to limb apraxia and general intelligence was removed, however, the relationships between gestural and language measures remained strong. In other words, these relationships were not artifacts of much more global deficits. Interestingly, these regressions did eliminate the correlations between gestural comprehension and gestural production. This second finding disconfirms the "single competence" assumption of Duffy, Duffy, and Pearson. Gestural comprehension and production are dissociable, even though both are related to aspects of language. (Which aspects we are not told.)

There are enormous procedural differences among these three studies: size and heterogeneity of subject populations, instructions, number and level of difficulty of items, comparability of stimuli. Nevertheless, some conclusions can be drawn, all of them analogous to our findings with infants:

1. Deficits in gestural symbols are indeed associated with aphasia, in specific ways that cannot be accounted for by global factors like IQ and limb apraxia.
2. The gestural conventions that bear the closest relationship to language appear to be referential or object-associated gestures ("transitive acts" in Goodglass and Kaplan), carried out in the absence of perceptual support from the object.
3. The aphasia/apraxia relationship appears in comprehension and in production, although comprehension and production in turn appears to be partially dissociable.

These are not the only kinds of nonlinguistic symbols that have been associated with aphasia. For example, Leischner and Fradis (1974) review cases of specific "asymbolias" for Morse code, traffic signs, punctuation marks, national emblems and flags. Lesser summarizes the literature on asymbolia as follows: "From one perspective aphasia can be described as a difficulty in grasping and expressing ideas by means of learned symbols, which permeates through all symbols; and from another, a difficulty with symbols in each individual can be thought of as being very specific to certain symbol systems [p. 99]." Insofar as these syndromes can appear in isolation, there seems to be support for the latter position. However, Gardner (1974) has suggested that many case reports of isolated syndromes may result from the fact that an investigator did not look beyond the phenomenon of interest to measure other, potentially related impairments. For example, Gardner himself investigated a group of patients with alexia—language impairment with written materials. He discovered that these patients were also impaired in their ability to name or recognize eleven other categories of written or two-dimensional schematic signs, including mathematical notations, drawings of well-known faces, swastikas, and dollar signs. Furthermore, performance among the alexics was very similar to performance by aphasic patients with very different diagnoses. Gardner concludes: "The recognition and naming of symbols is impaired across the board in aphasic patients, in the same relative order as in non-aphasic populations [p. 152]."

Although many apparent dissociations among symbol systems can perhaps be attributed to inadequate testing, there are also documented cases of a dissociation between ideomotor apraxia and aphasia. The interesting thing about these dissociations (Goodglass, personal communication) is that they are overwhelmingly in one direction: aphasic patients without detectable gestural impairments. What apparently does not occur (or is at least so rare that most aphasiologists have not seen one) is the converse: a patient with specific ideomotor apraxia, but without aphasia. If the two modalities are truly functionally dissociable, why should the dissociation be so asymmetrical? Here too we can turn to our infant data. In our three longitudinal studies of symbol development, we do occasionally find children who engage in gestural symbolization even though they are not talking. But we have never seen a case of a child making progress in language without any evidence of symbolic play. There are certainly children who are not especially fond of symbolic play, particularly with our toys or in our presence. But there is always some evidence of a basic ability to carry out gestural symbols in a child who has begun to name objects. Hence the same asymmetry that appears in aphasia/apraxia dissociations also appears in normal development. This pattern leads to the following hypothesis: *Perhaps there is indeed a single underlying naming component in both the vocal and the gestural modalities; however, the threshold for eliciting gestures may be lower than the equivalent threshold for language. This means that the two modalities will usually be correlated in symbolic development, but that dissociations favoring gesture may occur.*

Finally, the relationship between language and gesture may not be restricted to symbolic, "lexical" processing. Recall the finding from Cicone et al., that *all* the gestures of Broca's and Wernicke's aphasics paralleled their speech, including nonsymbolic, language-accompanying "cocktail party" gestures (e.g., Duncan and Fiske, 1977). Cicone et al. suggest that these patterns reflect some kind of central planning or organizing center that may be involved in a wide variety of motor sequences (see also McNeill, 1979, on "syntagmas" or motor planning units that unite speech and gesture). A related proposal has been put forth by Kimura and Archibold (1974), who have carried out research on the organization and production of nonsymbolic hand movements in certain types of aphasia. For example, they report on one patient who could produce some syntactically well-formed strings, but could not produce complex syntactic structures (e.g., sentences with center-embedded relative clauses). The same patient had no difficulty imitating a short sequence of novel hand movements. However, he could not imitate gestural movements that paralleled embedded sentences in the number and complexity of movements. Kimura argues very strongly that such difficulties with meaningless hand movements argue against an interpretation of aphasia/apraxia relations in terms of symbolic processing.

At this point, it is worth drawing comparisons to the Shore, O'Connell, and Bates (1981) findings on language-gesture relations at 20 months, at the level of primitive grammar. Before the grammaticization process takes place, language and gesture seem to be paced by a common planning or chunking mechanism limiting sequences to one, two or three schemes at a time. Regression analyses of the different gestural measures against the "nominal cluster" showed that there were unique contributions to this language measure from the number of different gestures (i.e., the lexical or symbolic measure), the outer bound on number of different schemes in a sequence, and the measure of order preservation. In sum, different component processes may underlie correlations between language and gesture, including both lexical and structural processes. This same reasoning may be applied to the findings we have reviewed on language-gesture relations in aphasia. Studies by Duffy, Watt, and Duffy, Gainotti and Lemmo, and Goodglass and Kaplan may pertain to a lexical-conceptual link between modalities. Work by Kimura, and by Cicone et al., may instead involve some kind of a separate structural link. Sign language aphasias and the use of signs with aphasic children also bear on these questions, but observations are scarce (see Bonvillian, Nelson, & Charrow, 1976; Bonvillian & Nelson, 1982).

Despite all the obvious weaknesses in both the infancy and the aphasia literature, we do believe that the analogies are sufficiently powerful to warrant an explanation in terms of common mechanisms. We suggested earlier that both the aphasic and the infant in transition from first words to syntax, are "caught" at the level of naming. How do we escape from that level, rising above it to embed names in predicative operations? In the concluding pages of this paper, we will try to organize the findings on infants and aphasics into a three-stage model for the genesis of names. The model is intended primarily to explain facts about ontogenesis, but may also have implications for the microgenesis and breakdown of naming in adults.

TOWARDS A MODEL FOR THE GENESIS OF NAMES

Three main contrasts have played a role in all of the research reviewed so far: (a) the special status of object names compared with other categories; (b) differences between comprehension and production for both vocal and gestural symbols; (c) similarities and differences between vocal and gestural symbols, particularly with regard to "object" and "script dependence." The model that we are about to present is really an organized collection of speculations about these three contrasts, put together to help us design experiments and make predictions for future work.

More caveats are in order. First, the discussion is organized into "stages" strictly for descriptive convenience. In fact, our own results suggest that the changes involved here are continuous and gradual, albeit with discontinuous results (in particular the passage from one- to two-word speech). Second, we are using the word "object" in its imprecise, ordinary language sense to mean concrete things in the world with properties of mass, weight, color, etc. In practice, the line between objects and perceptually bounded events is not really so clear, and some of the things we have to say about objects must be extended to certain kinds of bounded events in the child's world. The terms "script" and "association" are also intended in an ordinary language sense. "Script" refers to an organized "typical event" comprised of associated objects, gestures, and vocalizations that tend to stand in the same spatial and temporal relations to one another. This is similar to uses of "script" (Schank & Abelson, 1977) and "frame" (Fillmore, 1975; Minsky, 1975) in artificial intelligence and information processing, and to Nelson's (1977) use of the term in describing the organized knowledge preschool children have for such events as "going to MacDonald's for hamburgers." Finally, terms like "association," "connection," and "network" are intentionally left unspecified: We are not aligning ourselves with any particular association model for learning and representation of knowledge.

The constant unit at all three stages in the genesis of naming is the script. Figures 3.3, 3.4, and 3.5 schematize a hypothetical script as a structured network of associations among various objects, sounds, and gestures in an event like "lunch." The number of nodes and links, and their topological representation, are arbitrary here, and we assume that each individual node has further internal structure. The three simplified schemes merely illustrate the idea that symbols, and predications using symbols, do not necessarily involve *addition* of event knowledge. Rather, the three stages are defined by changes in the *usage* of existing information, all of which is present at some level of consciousness while the child is engaged in interactions and thoughts about lunch.

The three stages can be briefly described as follows:

Stage I (Figure 3.3) is the point at which the child has attained some organized expectations, and appropriate actions, within familiar cultural frames or scripts like lunch (10–11 months). Some of that knowledge was acquired through watching only; other aspects (particularly execution of conventional procedures like stirring and wiping) arose through imitation of others or through trial-and-error manipulation of relevant objects. Although the script has structure, it is still not well articulated. As yet, none of the gesture/object/sound links have emerged into a privileged naming status—although some may be more familiar or overlearned than others. When the child participates in a given scenario, all of the links may be activated at once (i.e., "called into readiness"); or a given section may provide input, sequentially, to activate or set up expectation for another. But the child does not yet actively select portions of this knowledge to stand for or remind him of other elements. This is, for example, the point at which a vocal

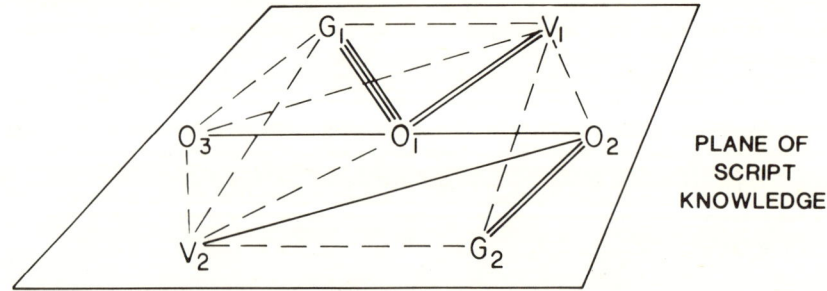

FIG. 3.3 Stage I in the emergence of symbols (10–11 months): pre-referential. O = Objects; G = Conventional Gestures or Actions; V = Verbal Conventions. Width and number of lines represent differential strength of connections.

3. SYMBOLIZATION IN INFANCY AND APHASIA   111

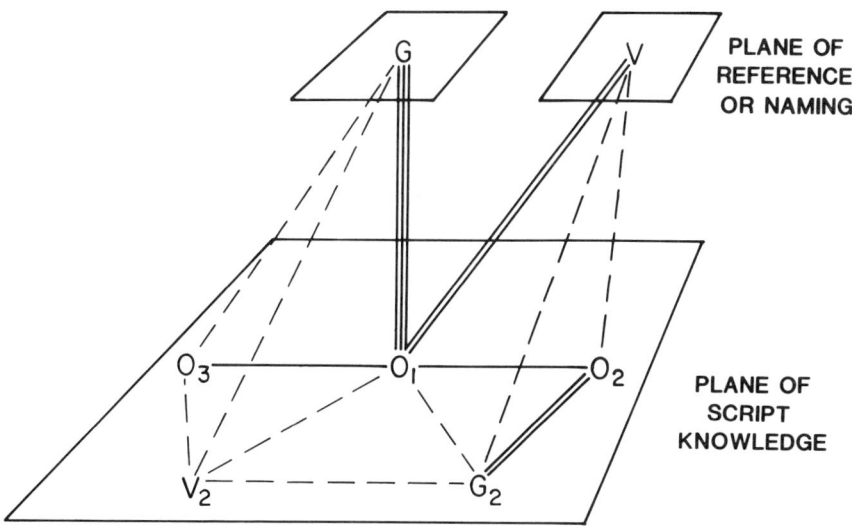

FIG. 3.4. Stage II in the emergence of symbols (13–20 months): reference.

procedure like "Bam" is used to accompany knocking over objects in a well-learned game; "woowoo" is a conventional response at a given point in a book game.

Stage 2 (Figure 3.4) is the point at which the child actively selects some portion of her script knowledge and sets it up in consciousness as a label or mnemonic for the whole, or for some specified segment within the whole script. For example, the vocal procedure "Bam" is now used as a tag or reminder for a banging action that is to follow; "Woowoo" becomes an identifier for the fuzzy four-legged objects that first were named in books alone, now in a wider variety of encounters. Note that the link between object and convention is not formed at Stage 2. Instead, a pre-existing link is used in a new way. The segmentation and tagging process tends to occur first with stable objects rather than events and relationships; and the first tags or identifying procedures tend to be unique, imitatively derived cultural acts.

Stage 3 (Figure 3.5) illustrates a point somewhere between 16 and 22 months in which sequences of individual symbols are used to identify relations among segments of the script. Once again, this passage does not necessarily involve the addition of new links or nodes. Instead, pre-existing knowledge of relationships is analyzed and elevated to a new level. At Stage 2 the child used a vocal or manual symbol to "point to" a referential segment of the script, typically an object. At Stage 3 the same symbol (in a single word utterance) points to the same referent in relation to another salient element in the situation, e.g., "doggie," said while pointing at the dog's dish. Thus a case relationship, already implicit in the child's knowledge, is reconstructed at a symbolic level (e.g., a

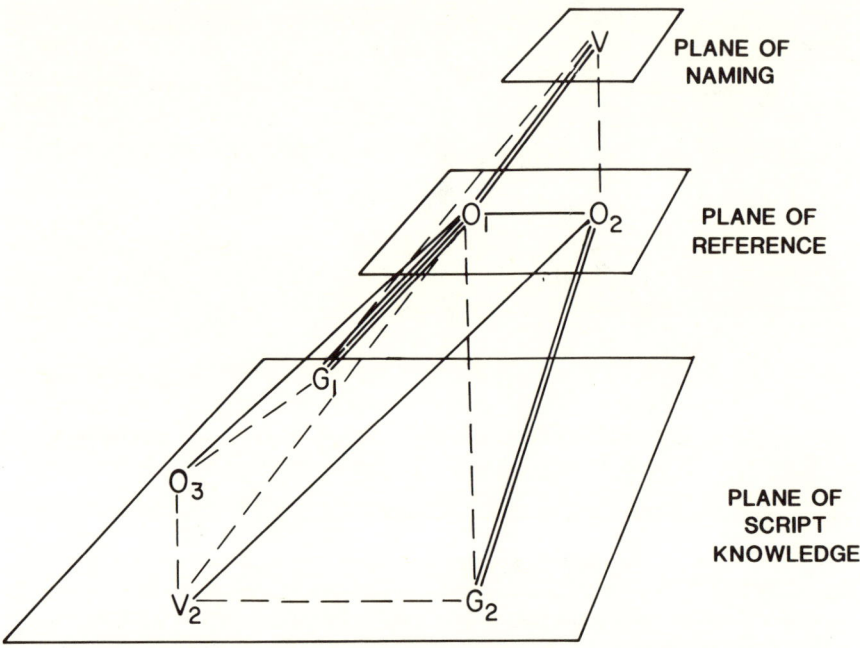

FIG. 3.5. Stage III in the emergence of symbols: predictive or relational speech (example illustrates a single-word predication).

genitive or ownership relation). These acts of indirect reference reflect an increasing "distancing" of the symbolic routine from its script base. Such single scheme acts may soon combine into multischeme acts because they are "free at last." They still belong to their referents at one deeper cognitive level; but they have also been elevated to a higher, "lighter weight" level where there is more room to play with combinations.

What we have said so far is descriptive, but it is not explanatory. There are two hidden explanatory variables: the cognitive weight of objects as key organizers of the system and obstacles to higher levels, and the process of "decontextualizing" or overcoming the cognitive weight of psychological objects. Let us return to these transitions in more detail to see if we can push these descriptions closer to explanation.

We made two points about the transition into Stage 2 that need to be examined further: Objects are central organizers for first acts of reference, and the first symbols tend to be characteristic imitative schemes. We suggest that objects emerge as central organizers because they are by definition stable, invariant sources of feedback to the child's own actions. Nelson (1973) has noted that the first named objects tend to be those that are handled by the child (e.g., socks and shoes rather than dresses and sweaters). However, the "first participation principle" could not in itself explain why nouns preponderate over verbs, since the child could presumably name his own first acts as well. Clark (1974) has pointed out that actions may be less likely referents for early names because they happen briefly, produce their effects on objects, and then disappear. Furthermore, what we call a single type of action (e.g., "drinking") varies enormously in form from one instance to another, so that the invariant properties of the act often have more to do with its results than the actual movements carried out.

Objects also create variations in perceptual input due to spatial factors like occlusion, orientation, and distance from the eye. However, these changes conform to a single transformational system of size and shape constancy in three-dimensional space, which is apparently available to the child by the time objects and events are named (Bower 1974; Haith & Campos, 1977). The transformations in events are more variable and more elusive to eye and hand. Objects sit there much of the time, reliably and predictably.

Gentner (1978) has suggested that differences in stability between objects and actions are mirrored in the representation of nouns and verbs in adult knowledge: "Verbs are different from nouns in ways that go beyond syntax. Verbs are harder to remember, more broadly defined, more prone to alter meaning when conflict of meaning occurs, less stable in translation between languages, and slower to be acquired by children [p. 1]." She goes on to argue that this difference is reflected in the "internal density" of noun representation vs. the "interactive potential" of verbs, adjectives, and other relational terms. Nouns are defined in terms of *what they are,* a rich and internally consistent network of relations within a stable class of objects. Relational terms are defined in terms of *what they go with,* links pointing outward in a multitude of directions instead of inward in a tightly knit structure:

> Simple nouns function in speech as opaque subroutines, simply returning pointers to object concepts. Their associated conceptual structures are largely given by the world, and function in discourse as coherent wholes. Relational terms, in contrast, are meant to be more thoroughly processed during comprehension, more analyzed, more dissected and more altered according to the requirements of the context. In a sense, a verb or other relational term is an institutionalized analogy. It is a set of relationships ready for importing wherever needed [p. 7].

In short, objects "hold still" under mental or perceptual-motor operations and hence take on their central organizing role as the child's operations on the world become more complex. Because they are key organizational points in a representational/presentational world, it becomes increasingly important to set up sensorimotor mnemonics to recognize, label, and remember those objects during play and exploration. That is why, we propose, certain salient cultural acts are selected as the best schemes for recognizing and classifying objects: because they are *uniquely* associated with relevant things in the world.

Take the following concrete example. The child is seated among a set of toys that include an empty cup. She begins a typical sequence of combinatorial play that involves placing objects inside one another, and she plans to use the cup as a gathering point for the game. As she turns around to collect some other toys for this game, she must keep in mind the role of the cup in her plans. If the cup drops out of mind the minute her back is turned, the whole plan might be lost. According to Piaget (and others), memory in a situation like this consists of nothing other than maintaining in activation the "mental file drawer" of possible interactions that comprise cup knowledge. We must assume, however, that the working space of memory is limited and we can keep only so many identifying schemes activated at a given moment (see, for example, Case 1978; Pascual-Leone, 1972). This means that it would be useful to retain only some portion of cup knowledge in this hypothetical activation space, leaving room to put together the rest of the plan. What portion should the child choose, of all the possible kinaesthetic and visual scanning schemes she has in her packet of cup knowledge? Suppose she chooses some reliable old all-purpose scheme like banging, an act that involves not only her cup knowledge but almost all her knowledge packets for small manipulable objects. She holds that scheme in memory, goes off in search of other toys for the Nesting Game, and then returns to the "tag" she left behind with a sensorimotor equivalent of, "Where was I?" Because the banging scheme is shared by so many objects in the child's world, it makes a lousy mnemonic. So the cup is irretrievable in memory from the cluster of toys before her, and the whole plan is lost.

Suppose instead, however, the child had selected a vocal, gestural, or perceptual-exploratory scheme that is unique to cups in her world. The sounds "cup" or "ahmmm" would be pretty good mnemonics, if she has them. So would a lipsmack, or drinking gesture (putting the rim to her lip with her head tilted back). Another good mnemonic might be a combined kinaesthetic-visual image associated with handles, e.g., a finger crook and a visual image associated with handles, or a finger crook and a visual scan pattern for holes. With any of these schemes kept alive in working memory, the child could move away in search of other toys, then return to the original pile of objects and make a successful match between the mnemonic scheme and her renewed perception of the waiting cup. Thus because she has relocated the original object of choice, the game continues as planned.

In sum, culturally derived gestures and vocalizations make good tags or mnemonics because they are uniquely associated with specific cultural objects and confusions among referents are unlikely to occur. In addition, these schemes tend to occur first in active and pleasant social interactions—whether or not the adult is actually trying to teach them. A third motivation for selection of these schemes is less direct, the product of an intrinsic pleasure in imitation that characterizes the young of our species. Our children apparently like to do what others are doing whether they understand it or not. Because of this highly adaptive tendency, routines that will eventually be useful as symbols get into the child's repertoire in the first place.

The idea that symbol-referent relations emerge as mnemonics in Stage 2 can explain some of the differences between manual and vocal symbols associated with objects. We have argued that objects are stable, rich, and dense points of organization in script knowledge; and they are important points to label in cognitive space while constructing and executing plans. The manual symbols of hearing infants (unlike the manual symbols of ASL) participate directly in the manipulation of objects. Hence the feedback between symbol and referent is much richer, involving unique kinaesthetic as well as visual cues. This may be why, when objects are presented to a 13-month-old child in our laboratory situations, recognitory gestures occur much more often than recognitory sounds. The two kinds of symbols do come into the child's repertoire around the same time, at about the same rate, emerging within the same scripts. However, the gestures seem to be more closely tied to presentational feedback from their associated objects. Indeed, it appears from the work with aphasics that definitional gestures (e.g., "You drink from it") are located more quickly and serve in turn as cues eliciting the elusive vocal name. We were initially puzzled when our elicited imitation tasks produced many more gestural than vocal schemes at 13 months. (The opposite is true at 20 months.) This went against reviews of the literature on imitation (Killen & Uzgiris, 1978; Yando, Seitz, & Zigler, 1978) which indicate that infants are much more likely to imitate sounds than actions in the first year of life. However, most of these studies (e.g., Abravanel, Levan-Goldschmidt, & Stevenson, 1976) were carried out with meaningless, object-free sounds and movements. *Indeed, it may be that a greater tendency to imitate sounds had to evolve in our species to balance off the richer eliciting relations between objects and gestures.*

At the next stage, however, the very factors that make object names easier to acquire (and gestural names easier than vocal) can become a disadvantage for: (a) distancing symbol from referent; and (b) constructing flexible combinations of symbols. We have defined symbols as "standing for" but "not the same thing as" their referents, so that to symbolize means to preserve an inherent tension between levels of knowing. It is the quicksilver nature of naming acts that they must be there but not be there at the same time, referring at one level, subsumed at another. If names and their objects fade away from cognitive working space, then we cannot perform higher predicative operations on them. But if they dominate that cognitive space, we cannot hold them in relation to something else. We propose that the "decontextualization" of symbols from their referents is causally related to the passage into predicative use of single words (e.g., Greenfield & Smith, 1976) and the subsequent onset of multiword utterances. As illustrated in Figure 3.5, to produce a predicative or relational symbol we must be able to select and elevate at least one identifying tag for our referents to a higher level of processing (just as we did at Stage 2); but we must also suppress that symbol and its rich associations below, subsuming the name (and in turn, its underlying meaning) to yet another symbolic level of making comments on topics. At this point, those symbols that were the most difficult to construct at the earliest stages may, because of their more tenuous associations with the dense package of underlying meanings, lend themselves more easily to higher order manipulations. Hence action names and relational terms that were more difficult to acquire at the beginning are (once acquired) more easily used when we are trying to activate combinatorial routines. And, for the same reason, vocal names and manual symbols without kinaesthetic feedback from the object (e.g., ASL signs) should be more easily combined.

There is an assumption here about the weight or attraction of underlying meanings, which metaphorically "pull" their symbols down just as surely as they support them in a lone naming act. If we pursue this metaphor a bit further, it may help us to understand some apparently contradictory results concerning differences between comprehension and production. In the metaphoric language of weights and valences, we assume that objects pull their associated symbolic schemes toward them (which is why those schemes make good mnemonics). Furthermore, as central organizing points for script knowledge, objects also pull toward them the associated knowledge of events and neighboring objects that comprise a script. They are the denotative center of the general meanings; just by locating the referents for a given bit of structured symbolic input, we can immediately begin to predict and eliminate the range of possible things that might be said. Because of their dense psychological representation, objects are more easily recognized than actions, and object names are more easily comprehended than other terms. However, when we need to "break into" object meaning, analyzing it and selecting one section for incorporation within a relational meaning, the same dense web of associations may pull us back to a lower level of sensory experience. It is perhaps for this reason that context-flexible use of vocal and manual symbols at 13 months predicts the passage into two-word speech: Children who have overcome the "seduction" of objects relatively early have a head start in exploring the relational properties of symbols.

A number of proposals have been offered for the mysterious shift from one-word speech to primitive grammar. Bloom (1970) has suggested that children at that borderline have all the cognitive structure necessary for relational speech but have not yet acquired the combinatorial rules of their language. However, there are reports in the child language literature of children who combine words without any evidence of adult or adult-like grammatical rules. For example, Bates and MacWhinney (1978) review cases of children whose first word order tendencies reflect a pragmatic process of blurting out interesting, changing, "comment-worthy" information first, followed with related but less novel information. Similarly, Braine (1976) presents a number of cases in which regularities in multiword speech reflect very specific, word-based patterns like "no + X" or

"X + allgone." So this milestone in development need not necessarily follow sensitivity to or acquisition of syntax (although it will certainly help the child notice syntax from that point on). Furthermore, Sachs and Truswell (1978) have presented evidence to suggest that children at the one-word stage can comprehend word combinations that they cannot produce, including unexpected combinations like "Tickle the cup." There is no a priori reason why the same heuristics used to assimilate input like this could not be used by the child to create new expressions. Besides the eventual acquisition and use of conventional rules for combining symbols (i.e., grammar), the production of relational speech seems to involve some additional cognitive work: segmenting meanings at a new level, actively selecting appropriate symbols for those meanings, and inhibiting the myriad bits of additional but irrelevant information that accrue to the symbols that have been selected.

Up to Stage 3 in our model, vocal and manual names develop within the same scripts, associated with the same central objects. There are subtle differences between the two, involving degrees of "object dependence" (primarily in production) and "script dependence" (primarily in comprehension). But both serve the basic identifying or mnemonic function of symbols. However, the manual symbols of hearing children may not continue to develop in lockstep with language for two reasons: (a) they remain too tied to their objects to move into flexible, predicative relations; and (b) they are not used in communication, so that there is less pressure toward conventionalization and extensions of use. Presumably, the same two constraints should not hold for ASL signs, so that basic structural developments in the acquisition of ASL should continue to parallel vocal language for years. Nicolich (1977) has reported pilot data with five children suggesting that the formal properties of "symbolic play" (i.e., manual symbols in hearing children) continue to parallel language at least through two years of age. The findings from Shore, O'Connell, and Bates (1981) show a close relationship between language and gesture at 20 months, when children express primitive predications without benefit of a productive and routinized set of grammatical morphemes. The fact that humans can acquire a complex gestural language like ASL suggests that at least the potential for a gestural syntax is available, whether or not that potential is expressed in normal hearing children who do not acquire sign. By contrast, in hearing children the relationship between language and symbolic play decreases after Stage 3 (Figure 3.5), when the distance between names and objects decreases in the move toward complex predication, with the help of grammaticized elements.

In private thought and in communication, we never completely break the ties between symbols and the sensual world of objects that organized our first steps toward abstract thought. We carry those objects around inside us somewhere, and have to fight to remember that they are no longer real. In *Gulliver's Travels* there is a tale of a group of philosophers at the island Academy of Lagado, who held the theory that language is nothing but pointing at things. Hence they carried around with them in bags tiny replicas of everything they might want to talk about. Maybe, at some level, they were right.

REFERENCES

Abravanel, E., Levan-Goldschmidt, E., & Stevenson, M. B. Action imitation: the early phase of infancy. *Child Development,* 1976, *47,* 1032–1044.

Austin, J. L. *How to do things with words.* Cambridge: Oxford University Press, 1963.

Bates, E. *Language and context: the acquisition of pragmatics.* New York: Academic Press, 1976.

Bates, E. Intentions, conventions, and symbols. In E. Bates, L. Benigni, I. Bretherton, L. Camaioni, & V. Volterra, *The emergence of symbols: Cognition and communication in infancy.* New York: Academic Press, 1979.

Bates, E., Benigni, L., Bretherton, I., Camaioni, L., & Volterra, V. From Gesture to the first word: On cognitive and social prerequisites. In M. Lewis & L. Rosenblum (Eds.), *Interaction, conversation and the development of language.* New York: John Wiley & Sons, 1977.

Bates, E., Benigni, L., Bretherton, I., Camaioni, L., & Volterra, V. *The emergence of symbols: Cognition and communication in infancy.* New York: Academic Press, 1979.

Bates, E., Bretherton, I., Snyder, L., Shore, C., & Volterra, V. The emergence of symbols in language and action: Similarities and differences. *Merrill-Palmer Quarterly,* 1980, *26* (4), 407–423.

Bates, E., Camaioni, L., & Volterra, V. The acquisition of performatives prior to speech. *Merrill-Palmer Quarterly,* 1975, *21,* 205–226.

Bates, E. & MacWhinney, B. A functionalist approach to the acquisition of grammar. In E. Kennan (Ed.), *Developmental pragmatics.* New York: Academic Press, 1978.

Bates, E., Snyder, L., Bretherton, I., & Volterra, V. First words in language and action: similarities and differences. *Papers and Reports in Child Language.* Stanford University Department of Linguistics, Stanford, 1979.

Bellugi, U. Personal communication, 1979.

Bellugi, U. & Klima, E. *The signs of language.* Cambridge, Mass.: Harvard University Press, 1979.

Benedict, N. Early lexical development: Comprehension and production. *Journal of Child Language,* 1979, *6,* 183–200.

Bloom, L. *Language development: Form and function in emerging grammars.* Cambridge, Mass.: M.I.T. Press, 1970.

Bloom, L., Lightbown, P., & Hood, L. Structure and variation in child language. *Monographs for the Society for Research in Child Development,* 1975, *40* (Serial No. 160).

Bonvillian, J. D. & Nelson, K. E. Exceptional cases of language acquisition. In K. E. Nelson (Ed.), *Children's language* (Vol. 3). Hillsdale, N.J.: Lawrence Erlbaum Associates, 1982.

Bonvillian, J. D., Nelson, K. E., & Charrow, V. R. Languages and language-related skills in deaf and hearing children. *Sign Language Studies,* 1976, *12,* 211–250.

Bower, T. G. R. *Development in infancy.* San Francisco: W. H. Freeman, 1974.

Brain, W. R. *Speech disorders: Aphasia, apraxia and agnosia* (2nd ed.). London: Butterworths, 1965.

Braine, M. D. S. Children's first word combinations. *Monographs of the Society for Research in Child Development,* 1976, *41* (Serial No. 164).

Bretherton, I., Bates, E., Benigni, L., Camioini, L., & Volterra, V. Relationships between cognition, communication and quality of attachment. In Bates et al., *The emergence of symbols: Cognition and communication in infancy.* New York: Academic Press (1979).

Bretherton, I. & Bates, E. The emergence of intentional communication. In I. Uzgiris (Ed.), *New Directions for Child Development*, 1979, *4*, 81–100.

Bretherton, I., McNew, S., Snyder, L., & Bates, E. Individual differences at 20 months: semantics and morphology. *Journal of Child Language*, 1982.

Bretherton, I., Bates, E., McNew, S., Shore, C., Williamson, C., & Beeghly-Smith, M. Comprehension and production of symbols in infancy: an experimental study. *Developmental Psychology* 1981, *17* (6), 728–737.

Bretherton, I., McNew, S., & Beeghly-Smith, M. Early person knowledge as expressed in gestural and verbal communication: When do infants acquire "theory of minds"? In M. E. Lamb & L. R. Sherrod (Eds.), *Infant social cognition*. Hillsdale, N.J.: Lawrence Erlbaum Associates, in press.

Brown, J. W. *Aphasia, Apraxia, and Agnosia: Clinical and Theoretical Aspects*. Springfield, Ill.: Charles C. Thomas, 1972.

Brown, R. *A first language: The early stages*. Cambridge, Mass.: Harvard University Press, 1973.

Brown, R. & McNeill, D. The "tip of the tongue" phenomenon. *Journal of Verbal Learning and Verbal Behavior*, 1966, *5*, 325–337.

Bruner, J. Early social interaction and language acquisition. In H. R. Schaffer (Ed.), *Studies in mother-infant interaction*. New York: Academic Press, 1977.

Caramazza, A., Brownell, H. H., & Berndt, R. *Naming and conceptual deficits in aphasia*. Paper presented at the Academy of Aphasia, Chicago, October 1978.

Caramazza, A. & Berndt, R. S. Semantic and syntactic processes in aphasia: a review of the literature. *Psychological Bulletin*, 1978, *85*, 898–918.

Caramazza, A. & Zurif, E. *The acquisition and breakdown of language*. Baltimore: Johns Hopkins University Press, 1979.

Caramazza, A. & Zurif, E. B. Dissociation of algorithmic and heuristic processes in language comprehension: Evidence from aphasia. *Brain and Language*, 1976, *3*, 572–582.

Carroll, J. Names and naming: an interdisciplinary review. *IBM Research Report* (RC 7370). Yorktown Heights, N.Y.: 1978.

Carter, A. The transformation of sensorimotor morphemes into words: A case study of the development of "more" and "mine." *Journal of Child Language*, 1975, *2*, 233–250.

Case, R. Intellectual development from birth to adulthood: A neo-Piagetian interpretation. In R. Siegler (Ed.), *Children's thinking: What develops?* Hillsdale, N.J.: Lawrence Erlbaum Associates, 1978.

Chomsky, N. *Aspects of a theory of syntax*. Cambridge, Mass.: M.I.T. Press, 1965.

Cicone, M., Wapner, W., Foldi, N., Zurif, E., & Gardner, H. *The relationship between gesture and language in aphasia*. Manuscript, Aphasia Research Center, Boston University School of Medicine, 1979.

Clark, E. Some aspects of the conceptual basis of First Language organization. In R. L. Schiefelbusch & L. L. Lloyd (Eds.), *Language prerequisites: Acquisition, retardation, and intervention*. Baltimore: University Park Press, 1974.

Critchley, M. *The language of gesture*. London: Arnold, 1939.

Critchley, M. *Aphasiology*. London: Arnold, 1971.

Dore, J. *On the development of speech acts*. Unpublished doctoral dissertation, City University of New York, 1973.

Duffy, R. J., Duffy, J. R., & Alderdice, M. H. *Limb apraxia and gestural impairment in aphasics*. Paper presented at the ASHA Convention, Chicago, 1977.

Duffy, R. J., Duffy, J. R., & Pearson, K. L. Pantomime recognition in aphasics. *Journal of Speech and Hearing Research*, 1975, *18*, 115–132.

Duffy, J. R., Watt, J., & Duffy, R. J. *Pantomime impairment in aphasia: Path analysis of proposed causes*. Paper presented at the American Speech-Language-Hearing Association Convention, Atlanta, November 1979.

Duncan, S. & Fiske, D. *Face to face interactions: Research, methods and theory.* Hillsdale, N.J.: Lawrence Erlbaum Associates, 1977.

Elder, J., & Pederson, D. Preschool children's use of objects in symbolic play. *Child Development,* 1978, *42,* 500–505.

Fein, G. A transformational analysis of pretending. *Developmental Psychology,* 1975, *11,* 291–296.

Feldman, H., Goldin-Meadow, S., & Gleitman, L. Beyond Herodotus: The creation of a language by linguistically deprived deaf children. In A. Lock (Ed.), *Action, gesture and symbol.* New York: Academic Press, 1978.

Ferguson, C., & Slobin, D. (Eds.) *Studies in child language development.* New York: Holt, Rinehart, & Winston, 1973.

Fillmore, C. An alternative to checklist theories of meaning. *Papers of the Berkeley Linguistics Society (Vol. 1)* 1975.

Finkelnburg, F. C. Niederreinische Gesellschaft Sitzung vom. 21. Marz 1870 in Bonn. *Berlin Klinik Wochenschr,* 1870.

Finkelnburg, F. C. Ueber aphasie und Asymbolie nebst versuch einer theorie der Sprachbildung. *Arch. F. Psychiatr.* 1876, *6.*

Frege, G. On sense and nominatum. In H. Feig., H. Feigl, & W. Sellars, (Eds. and trans.), *Readings in philosophical analysis.* New York: Appleton-Century-Crofts, 1949.

Gainotti, G. The relationship between semantic impairment in comprehension and naming in aphasic patients. *British Journal of Disorders of Communication,* 1976, *11,* 57–61.

Gainotti, G., Caltagirone, C., & Ibba, A. Semantic and phonemic aspects of auditory language comprehension in aphasia. *Linguistics,* 1975, *154,* 15–29.

Gainotti, G. & Lemmo, M. A. Comprehension of symbolic gestures in aphasia. *Brain and Language,* 1976, 451–460.

Gardner, H. The naming and recognition of written symbols in aphasic and alexic patients. *Journal of Communicative Disorders,* 1974, *7,* 141–153.

Gardner, H. *The shattered mind.* New York: Alfred Knopf, 1975.

Garrison, A. & Bates, E. *Object naming at 20 months: novel versus natural categories.* Paper presented to the International Conference on Infant Studies, New Haven, April, 1980.

Gentner, D. *Verbs, nouns, and the topology of mind.* Paper presented at Sloan's Symposium on Cognitive Representation, La Jolla, August 1978.

Gibson, W. *The miracle worker.* New York: Atheneum, 1956.

Goldstein, K. *Language and language disturbances: Aphasic symptom complexes and their significance for medicine and theory of language.* New York: Gruen & Stratton, 1948.

Goodglass, H. Personal communication, 1980.

Goodglass, H. & Geschwind, N. Language disorders (aphasia). In E. Carterette & M. Friedman (Eds.), *Handbook of perception: speech and language* (Vol. 7). New York: Academic Press, 1979.

Goodglass, H. & Kaplan, E. F. Disturbance of gesture and pantomime in aphasia. *Brain,* 1963, *86,* 703–720.

Goodglass, H., Klein, B., Carey, D., & Jones, K. Specific semantic word categories in aphasia. *Cortex,* 1966, *2,* 74–89.

Green, E. Psycholinguistic approaches to aphasia. *Linguistics,* 1969, *53,* 30–50.

Greenblatt, S. Alexia without ographia or hemiagpia: anatomical analysis of an autopsied case. *Brain,* 1973, *96,* 307–316.

Greenfield, P. & Smith, J. *The structure of communication in early development.* New York: Academic Press, 1976.

Grice, P. Logic and conversation. In P. Cole & J. Morgan (Eds.), *Syntax and semantics: Speech acts* (Vol. 3). New York: Academic Press, 1975.

Haith, M. M. & Campos, J. J. Human infancy. In *Annual review of psychology.* Palo Alto, Calif.: Annual Reviews, Inc., 1977.

3. SYMBOLIZATION IN INFANCY AND APHASIA 121

Hoffmeister, R. *Word order in the acquisition of ASL.* Paper presented at the Third Annual Boston University Conference on Language Development, Boston, September 1978.

Horgan, D. Nouns: Love'em or leave'em. *Annals of the New York Academy of Science, 345,* 1980.

Huttenlocher, J. Origins of language comprehension. In R. Solso (Ed.), *Theories in cognitive psychology.* New York: Lawrence Erlbaum Associates, 1974.

Jackson, J. H. Affections of speech from disease of the brain. *Brain,* 1878, *1.*

Jakobson, R. Towards a linguistic typology of aphasic impairments. In A. V. DeReuck & M. O'Connor (Eds.), *Disorders of language.* London: Churchill, 1964.

Jakobson, R. *Child language, aphasia, and phonological universals.* The Hague: Monton, 1968.

Kempler, D. Variation in language acquisition. *Working Papers in Cognitive Linguistics, Vol. 2,* 1980, University of California at Los Angeles.

Killen, M. & Uzgiris, I. *Imitation of actions with objects: The role of social meaning.* Paper presented at the International Conference on Infant Studies, Providence, Rhode Island, March 1978.

Kimura, D. & Archibold, Y. Motor Functions of the left hemisphere. *Brain,* 1974, *97,* 337–350.

Langer, S. *Philosophy in a new key.* Cambridge: Harvard University Press, 1962.

Leischner, A. & Fradis, A. Die Asymbolien. *Fortschritte der neurologie, psychiatrie und Ihrer Grenzgebiete,* 1974, *42,* 264–79.

Lesser, R. *Linguistic investigations of asphasia.* London: Edward Arnold, 1978.

Lewis, M. & Rosenblum, L. A. (Eds.). *Interaction, conversation and the development of language.* New York: Wiley, 1977.

Liepmann, H. Die linke hemisphare und das Handeln. *Munch. Med. Wochensche,* 1905, *2,* 2375–2378.

Lock, A. (Ed.) *Action, Gesture and symbol.* New York: Academic Press, 1978.

MacMahon, R. Modern linguistics and aphasia. *British Journal of Disorders of Communication,* 1972, *7,* 54–63.

Maruszewski, M. *Language, communication, and the brain: A neuropsychological study.* The Hague: Mouton, 1975.

McNeill, D. *The conceptual basis of language.* Hillsdale, N.J.: Lawrence Erlbaum Associates, 1979.

Mead, G. H. *Mind, self and society.* Chicago: University of Chicago Press, 1934.

Messerli, P., Tissot, A., & Rodriguez, J. Recovery from aphasia: Some factors of prognosis. In Y. Lebrun & R. Hoops (Eds.), *Neurolinguistics 4: Recovery in Aphasics.* Amsterdam: Swets & Zeitlinger B. V., 1976.

Minsky, M. A framework for representing knowledge. In P. H. Winston (Ed.), *The psychology of computer vision.* New York: McGraw-Hill, 1975.

Nelson, K. Structure and strategy in learning to talk. *Monographs of the Society for Research in Child development,* 1973, *48* (No. 149).

Nelson, K. *How children represent knowledge of their world in and out of language.* Paper presented to the 13th Annual Carnegie Symposium on Cognition, Carnegie-Mellon University, May 1977.

Nelson, K. E. & Bonvillian, J. Early language development: conceptual growth and related processes between 2 and 4½ years. In K. E. Nelson (Ed.), *Children's language, Volume 1.* New York: Gardner Press, 1978, 467–556.

Nicolich, L. Beyond sensorimotor intelligence: Assessment of symbolic maturity through analysis of pretend play. *Merrill-Palmer Quarterly,* 1977, *23,* 89–99.

Ninio, A. & Bruner, J. *The achievement and antecedents of labelling.* Manuscript, 1976.

Overton, W. F. & Jacklin, J. P. The representation of imagined objects in action sequences: A developmental study. *Child Development,* 1973, *44,* 309–314.

Pascual-Leone, J. *A theory of constructive operators, a neo-Piagetian model of conversation, and*

the problem of horizontal decalages. Paper presented at the meeting of the Canadian Psychological Association, 1972.
Peirce, C. S. *Collected papers*. C. Jartshorne and P. Weiss (Eds.), Cambridge, Mass.: Harvard University Press, 1932.
Piaget, J. *Play, dreams and imitation in childhood*. New York: Norton, 1962.
Pickett, L. *An assessment of gestural and pantomimic deficit in aphasic patients*. Unpublished master's thesis, University of Mexico, 1972.
Porch, B. *Porch index of communicative ability*. Palo Alto, Calif.: Consulting Psychologists' Press, 1967.
Prinz, P. & Prinz, E. *Acquisition of ASL and spoken English in a hearing child of a deaf mother and hearing father, Phase II—Early combinatorial patterns of communication*. Paper presented to the Boston Child Language Forum, Boston University, September 1977.
Prinz, P. M. & Prinz, E. A. *Acquisition of ASL and spoken English in a hearing child of a deaf mother and hearing father: Phase I—early lexical development*. Paper presented at the Annual Child Language Forum, Stanford University, 1979 (Published in Papers and Reports on Child Language Development, Department of Linguistics, Stanford University, August 1979). (a)
Prinz, P. M. & Prinz, E. A. Simultaneous acquisition of ASL and spoken English (in a hearing child of a deaf mother and hearing father). *Sign Language Studies*, 1979, *25*, 283–296. (b)
Rodgon, M. M., Jankowski, W., & Alenskas, L. A multi-functional approach to single-word usage. *Journal of Child Language*, 1977, *4*, 23–44.
Sachs, J., & Truswell, L. Comprehension of two-word instructions by children in the one-word stage. *Journal of Child Language*, 1978, *5*, 17–24.
Schaffer, H. R. (Ed.). *Studies in mother-infant interaction*. London: Academic Press, 1977.
Schank, R., & Abelson, R. *Scripts, Plans, Goals, and Understanding*. Hillsdale, N.J.: Lawrence Erlbaum Associates, 1977.
Schwartz, R. *Words, objects and actions in early lexical acquisition*. Unpublished doctoral dissertation, Memphis State University, 1978.
Searle, J. Speech acts and recent linguistics. In D. Aaronson & R. Rieber (Eds.), *Developmental psycholinguistics and communication disorders*. New York: New York Academy of Sciences, 1975.
Shore, C. *Elicited symbolic play with increasingly abstract objects in 13-month-olds*. Unpublished master's thesis, University of Colorado, 1980.
Shore, C., O'Connell, B., & Bates, E. First sentences in language and play. Submitted for publication, 1982.
Shotter, J. The cultural context of communication studies: Theoretical and methodological issues. In A. Lock (Ed.), *Action, Gesture and Symbol*. New York: Academic Press, 1978.
Shvachkin, N. The development of phonemic speech perception in early childhood. In C. Ferguson & D. Slobin (Eds.), *Studies in child language development*. New York: Holt, Rinehart, & Winston, 1973.
Snyder, L., Bates, E., & Bretherton, I. Context and content in early lexical development. *Journal of Child Language*, 1981, *8*, 565–582.
Stern, C. & Stern, W. *Die kindersprache: Eine psychologische und sprachtheoretische Untersuchung* (4th ed.). Leipzig: Barth, 1927.
Sugarman-Bell, S. Some organizational aspects of preverbal communication. In I. Markova (Ed.), *The social context of language*. London: Wiley, 1978.
Swift, J. *Gulliver's Travels*. London: Penguin Books, 1962.
Tversky, A. Features of similarity. *Psychological Review*, 1977, *84*, 327–352.
Uzgiris, I. & Hunt, J. McV. *Assessment in infancy: Ordinal scales of psychological development*. Urbana, Ill.: University of Illinois Press, 1975.
Volterra, V. Personal communication, 1980.

Volterra, V., Bates, E., Benigni, L., Bretherton, I., & Camaioni, L. First words in language and action: A qualitative look. In E. Bates et al., *The emergence of symbols: Cognition and communication in infancy*. New York: Academic Press, 1979.

Volterra, V. & Taeschner, T. The acquisition and development of language by bilingual children. *Journal of Child Language*, 1978, *5*, 311–326.

Vygotsky, L. S. *Thought and language*. Cambridge, Mass.: M.I.T. Press, 1962.

Wepman, J. M. Aphasia: Language without thought or thought without language? *ASHA*, March 1977, 18, 131–138.

Werner, H. *Comparative psychology of mental development*. New York: Science Books, 1961.

Werner, H. & Kaplan, B. *Symbol formation*. New York: Wiley, 1963.

Whitehouse, P., Caramazza, A., & Zurif, E. Naming in aphasia: Interacting effects of form and function. *Brain and Language*, 1978, *20*, 63–74.

Wilbur, R. *American sign language and sign language systems*. University Park, Pa.: University Park Press, 1979.

Wittgenstein, L. *The blue and the brown books*. New York: Harper & Row, 1958.

Wolf, D., & Gardner, H. Style and sequence in early symbolic play. In M. Franklin & N. Smith (Eds.), *Early Symbolization*. Hillsdale, N.J.: Erlbaum, 1979.

Yamatori, A. & Albert, M. Word category aphasia. *Cortex*, 1973, *9*, 112–115.

Yando, R., Seitz, V., & Zigler, E. *Imitation: A developmental perspective*. Hillsdale, N.J.: Lawrence Erlbaum Associates, 1978.

4 Perceptual Constraints on the Use of Language by Young Children

Henrietta Lempert
Marcel Kinsbourne
University of Toronto
and
Behavioral Neurology Department
Eunice Kennedy Shriver Center
Waltham, Mass.

We shall describe certain changes which occur in sentence processing at about age five and suggest that these indicate fundamental differences in how younger and older children preferentially represent verbal as well as nonverbal information. Until about age five, children's knowledge about the world features information derived from nonverbal rather than from verbal sources: Even 4-year-old children rely on information in visual displays in preference to a verbal source (Blank, 1974; Hayes & Birnbaum, 1980). Also, although preschool children profit from words when storing nonverbal information, they appear to prefer a nonverbal (presumably imagery) code when left free to choose (e.g., Conrad, 1971; Jones, 1973). We describe a phenomenon that goes beyond *preference*. Although nonverbal contextual information influences linguistic processing and retrieval even for adults (Bransford & Johnson, 1972), we shall argue that young children differ from older children (and from adults) in the extent to which context and imagery *control* their comprehension and remembering.

In Piaget's famous demonstrations of failure to conserve, the child, entrapped by a compelling percept, judges accordingly in disregard of a rule that in other contexts he may "know." In the present argument, compelling percepts similarly distort children's understanding or remembering of sentences. Their attention, similarly entrapped, not only guides their "one-word" choice and choice of word order, but even distorts their comprehension and recall of sentences when these relate to or generate salient percepts or images, the impact of which conflicts with the verbal message.

One striking phenomenon is the paradox that, for young children, speech output, which develops later and involves the generally more difficult recall component as opposed to the recognition component in language, may nevertheless embody the rules of word order more accurately than comprehension. This holds for children younger than three years and even as late as age four. Our hypothesis is that young children fail to apply linguistic rules that they know to sentence decoding when the nonverbal context lends itself to a conflicting but for them more immediately compelling interpretation. Failure to use a linguistic rule in the face of salient environmental influences leaves it uncertain whether the child would have been able to use that rule in the absence of these influences.

We hold the same principles to apply to the imposition of linguistic order on experience as apply to the imposition of order on experience in general. The older the child, the better able is he to use a self-selected strategy across situations, with, as Wohlwill (1962) states, "decreasing dependence of behavior on the immediate stimulus field [p. 73]." The younger the child is, the more influential on his behavior are the most salient percepts present. (See Day, 1975, for a cogent discussion of this developmental principle in the context of visual search.) Instances of rule-governed linguistic behavior in young children's speech and comprehension are numerous. They neither add to nor detract from our exposition of the ways in which children interweave words and things.

The environment controls the infant's behavior by capturing his attention. Those stimulus attributes that do so most effectively are termed most "salient." We have elsewhere discussed reasons for regarding attention to salient percepts as determinants of early utterances (Kinsbourne & Lempert, 1979; Lempert & Kinsbourne, submitted for publication). We here begin with a simple instance: the guiding of word choice in the one-word speech stage. The child chooses one word, then another, as his attention shifts to what is most salient from moment to moment. We shall then apply similar principles to learning and using word order.

WHAT DETERMINES WORD CHOICE?

Greenfield and her colleagues (Greenfield, 1978; Greenfield & Smith, 1976; Greenfield & Zukow, 1978) use beginning speakers' choice of words from available alternatives to determine the macrostructure of their perceptual analysis. Also, when toward the end of the one-word speech stage children can encode situations by successive single words, their speech is regarded as a running commentary on their shifting focus of attention. Greenfield regards attention as a determiner of informativeness. We diverge, and treat the capture of the child's attention as itself a sufficient account of Greenfield's illuminating data. (See Greenfield, 1978; Greenfield & Zukow, 1978 for examples.)

Greenfield emphasizes the communicative function of beginning speech. There are two logical steps here. The first point is that the child describes that about which there is least certainty or that which has just undergone change. That by itself is a description of what immature attentional systems are most sensitive to. The selective orienting response is indeed a response to the novel element or the changing element in any circumstance (e.g., Jeffrey, 1968). Young children are known to be selectively sensitive to novelty and therefore uncertainty (as to some extent are adults also). Specifically, the child names what is new in the situation. This act in turn, by establishing this as fact, makes it more "certain." The child next names what now is less certain. For example, establishing the identity of a new object in a scene (e.g., "car") renders that object more "certain," leaving its action relatively less so. Consequently, the next utterance more usually would name the action, not the object.

Greenfield further interprets the child's propensity to orient and comment on the changing element in a situation as having a communicative function. For present purposes we need not take a position on that, or further wonder whether the child is communicating to the mother, to himself, or to the mother as if she were himself. Indeed, we suspect that children first do things in a precommunicative fashion and then adapt the skill for purposes of communication. For our purposes, our more conservative interpretation of Greenfield's data is sufficient. Children in the one-word stage name that single aspect of a scene to which they are attending (regardless of whether extrinsic factors or internal ones account for their interest—Pea, (1979).

WHY ONLY ONE WORD AT A TIME?

Why do children at first say only one word at a time? Bloom (1973) doubts that processes related to information retrieval or to speech production can explain restrictions on speech output. She found that her daughter Allison combined a pivot form ("wide") with another word, for example, "no wide," "more wide." As Allison produced these combinations at the same time that she used mainly single words, she must have had the motor potential to program more than single words. Also, she seemed to have a stereotype about word order, because she almost always used "wide" in final position. Bloom concluded that although Allison knew "something" about word order, this was not enough for multiword constructions. She suggests that the main reason children use single words is that they do not know the linguistic code. They need to learn syntax before they can map their experience onto sentences.

Allison's speech at 16 months (Session 1) revealed that even in the period when her speech mostly consisted of single words or "wide" combinations, she occasionally produced multiword constructions, for example: Mama more wide (p. 155); more cookie (p. 156); car away (p. 163). She also had the basic vocabulary for forming longer phrases, for example: "e down/chair/sit" spoken when turning to sit down in a chair (p. 177). Even at 19 months (Session 3) when multiword utterances were more frequent and Allison clearly knew how to express action relations (e.g., walk school; children rain/walk rain; Mommy [sit on] floor), she usually spoke in single words. So even when Allison seemed to know a rule that could have been used for phrases, she still preferred to use single words. Also, her ability to form phrases indicates that motor immaturity did not restrict her from using more than one word at a time. And, although her vocabulary was limited, when it could have been used for longer utterances, she usually did not do so. So while limitations set by rule acquisition or vocabulary may contribute, they do not fully account for restrictions on Allison's speech output.

A further reason that children say only one word at a time could be that they focus fully on only one aspect of a situation at a time (Jeffrey, 1968), selecting a word in relation to where they attend. If they process component elements of a situation successively, their speech would also be discontinuous. Habituation, intrusion of a novel stimulus, or a successful communication could serve to terminate mental set, resulting in reorienting of attention and setting up the preconditions for a new communication.

Mental set can also change as a result of the child's own actions. Bloom (1973) notes that at an early stage, successive single-word utterances relate to one another only because they coincide with movements that are temporally and schematically related to one another. Inspection of her published data suggests the words are not a running commentary on ongoing activity but reflect the reorienting of the child's attention when changing from one activity to another. For example, Allison utters "cow" while reaching under a chair for her toy cow. When trying to stand the cow on the chair, she says "chair." Turning to her mother for help, she says "Mama."

When children's mental set is directed toward a goal, they still seem to verbalize according to changes in the current situation (in relation to their goal). Guillaume (1927) observed that successive one-word utterances may then be separated by completion of an activity that the child requests someone to perform. He describes the following sequence of utterances by a 14-month-old girl, "richly" interpreting the child's meaning: "Mama/ici" (stopping beside an armchair). "Assis" (sit down). "Oper" (Pick me up). "Dédé" (I want to lie in your lap). "A têter" (I'm going to sleep). The child seemed to speak with a definite goal in mind from the outset, namely, to sleep in her mother's lap. Her speech, however, was tied to the present, occurring in a sequence that conformed to situational changes effected by each action.

REPRESENTATION AS IMAGERY

Guillaume (1927) suggested that the beginning speaker can anticipate a goal by visualizing the successive actions that would be required in order to achieve an outcome. Piaget (1951) contended that very young children plan (represent an intended situation) in terms of actions and later internalize these actions as imagery. As evidence for 'action' planning, he instances a child who opened her mouth, imitating the potential widening of a matchbox opening prior to executing that action. A similar developmental sequence has been proposed by Bruner (1966), who supposes that a child's predominant medium for representing information is imagery until approximately age six or seven.

The notion of imagery representation is attractive. Children's verbalizations about past and intended events would then conform to the same principles as for ongoing situations. We shall later suggest that until about age five, children favor the use of imagery to represent both verbal and nonverbal events. At present, it is sufficient to note that being a nonverbal (iconic) system, we suppose it operates on the basis of principles that reflect the child's perceptual organization and salient experience.

SEMANTIC VERSUS SYNTACTIC APPROACHES TO WORD ORDER

When children are able to describe events in terms of multiword utterances, what accounts for their choice of word order? A related question is: How do children "know" that words expressing diverse semantic functions such as "actor" in relation to an action word (e.g., Gia push) and "experiencer" in relation to an internal state (e.g., Gia want Daddy [doll]) occur in sentence initial position? These issues have been approached both from the syntactic and the semantic perspectives. Bloom (1970, 1973; Bloom, Lightbown, & Hood, 1975) has argued that children learn a grammar which specifies how words can be related in sentences. They acquire a linguistic code that they then use to express semantic relations (what they know about objects, events, and relations in the world). In contrast, Bowerman (1973a, 1975) has proposed that word combinations directly express semantic relations and so are based on how word referents are related to each other. We will now consider these positions in turn.

Bloom et al. (1975) examined speech data from four children who were observed between ages 19 to 26 months. They found that the children used animate nouns as "movers" in relation to intransitive verbs such as "go" and "sit" (where the action resulted in changes in the mover's location), and also as "agent" in relation to transitive verbs such as "put" (where the action changed the location of an affected object). As "movers" and "agents" have different semantic roles, Bloom et al. took their similar usage in preverbal position as evidence that the children had made "higher-order linguistic inductions about superordinate grammatical categories (e.g., sentence-subject) [p. 3]." Also, the fact that two children "developed action, locative-action, and possession relations at the same time was intepreted as evidence that they had learned the superordinate grammatical categories sentence-subject (including agents, actors, movers, and possessors), predicate-object (including objects of actions, locative actions, and possession), and predicate complement (place), so that a number of semantic distinctions could be encoded within the same grammatical system [p. 19]."

Bloom (1970; 1973) also attributes to an actual utterance such as "Mommy book" the fuller underlying structure "Mommy read book" (i.e., subject + predicate). The underlying structure is reduced to its surface manifestation by reduction rules (that delete the verb in this case, but may operate on any sentence constituent). However, as Bowerman (1973a) notes, V + NP_2 ("read book") would be expected on strictly linguistic grounds, as this preserves the integrity of the verb phrase as shown below:

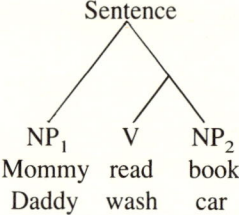

```
           Sentence
          /      \
         /        \
       /          / \
      /          /   \
    NP₁         V    NP₂
   Mommy      read   book
   Daddy      wash   car
```

Bowerman (1973a) used replacement sequences to argue for the psychological unity of a NP_1 + V constituent in early language development. In a replacement sequence, an utterance is followed or preceded by a longer string that incorporates it. She found that the child might produce the subject + verb and then add an object noun, for example: "Daddy . . . daddy wash . . . daddy already wash car." Bowerman also performed a distributional analysis on word combinations in English, Finnish, and Samoan produced by three children whose mean utterance length ranged from 1.10 to 1.83 morphemes at the time. She found that NP_1 + V utterances were almost five times more frequent than predicate V + NP_2 or NP_1 + V + NP_2 strings; the latter occurred with almost equal frequency. She concluded that there was little evidence to support a linguistically based subject-predicate distinction in early child speech.

Bowerman (1975) also pointed out that an adult speaker's ability to use similar words in the same position in diverse sentences is not sufficient evidence that he has acquired abstract syntactical concepts such as sentence-subject. She instanced *John is easy to please* versus *John is eager to please*. In the first, John is the underlying object of *please*. In the second, John is the underlying subject. She concluded that because identity of word order is not enough to establish an equivalence of syntactic form for adults, it could not be a reliable guide to syntactic function for child speech. A child who places words naming agents and possessors in sentence initial position may do so without being aware of any abstract similarity of function among these words.

Bowerman (1973a) instead proposed that children's earliest multiword constructions are produced with simple rules to order words that are understood as performing various semantic functions. Children first acquire an order rule for action verbs which specifies that the name for the agent precedes the name for the action. Later, they learn rules for placing nouns in relation to verbs that take nonagentive noun arguments as subjects (e.g., experiencer in relation to state verb and instrument in relation to action verb). After children realize that words expressing different semantic functions can occur in the same sentence position and have similar transformational possibilities, they might then acquire superordinate grammatical categories such as subject and predicate.

We concur with Bowerman that there is no compelling evidence that very young children employ abstract grammatical categories or even that there is a need to explain their word order in such terms. We also endorse her belief that learning linguistic concepts is based on principles similar to those that underlie concept formation in general. We go further. We will argue that early word order can be explained without postulating specific rule learning for each verb subcategory that appears in children's early word combinations.

INTERACTION BETWEEN WORD ORDER AND ANIMACY STATUS AND RELATED FACTORS

Words that young children use in subject-noun position typically have animate referents (Bloom, 1970; Limber, 1973). Those in object-noun position usually refer to inanimate things that move or change only as a result of external force. According to Bowerman (1973b), these tendencies could be explained if an actual (or an implied, but deleted) verb controls syntactic features such as noun animacy of the pre- and postverbal nouns, banning nouns that are marked (+animate) from object position and those marked (−animate) from the subject-noun position.

Is there any need to assume that very young children code object names in terms of features such as (±animacy)? There is no compelling evidence that they make this distinction at all except indirectly in terms of movement (Laurendeau & Pinard, 1962; Piaget, 1929). Names for vehicles also occur in subject-noun position (Bowerman, 1973a). This implies that movement and not animacy exercises control over early noun order. To postulate an underlying verb that specifies noun animacy is unnecessary if the findings could be explained more simply in terms of perceptual factors.

Movement is a powerful visual stimulus for young children; their attention is captured by it (Tronick & Clanton, 1971; Volkman & Dobson, 1976). Even neonates smoothly track a moving series of vertical stripes (Brazelton, Scholl, & Robey, 1966) and suppress nonnutritive sucking (an attentional index) in response to an intermittent moving stimulus (Haith, 1966). In addition to movement is sound, which can result in attentional response (lateral orienting) even in the neonate (Muir & Field, 1979). The distinction between actor and acted-upon, which children seem to make at a very young age, may actually have a perceptual base. It would actually be a distinction between things that move or are otherwise dynamic and those that are static.

The notion that children allocate nouns to preverbal and postverbal position on the basis of which one is "dynamic" rather than based on which one is animate (French, 1971; Lempert & Kinsbourne, 1979) explains why Bloom et al. (1975) did not note developmental differences between expressing action events in terms of transitive verbs (which take an agent) and intransitive verbs (which take an actor or mover). Although the specific semantic functions of agent, actor, and mover may differ for adults, they all involve movement and may not otherwise be discriminated by young children. But if there is no need to assume that children otherwise differentiate these roles, then there also is no reason to attribute their similar usage in preverbal position to knowledge of superordinate syntactical categories such as sentence-subject.

Similar principles may apply when children talk about experiencer relations. Almost invariably in early use of state verbs, the expressed or implied subject (or "experiencer") is the child (Starr, 1975; see also protocols in Bloom et al., 1975). But even here children seem to be using the verb in an actional manner rather than describing an internal experience as do adults. Leonard (1976) noted that during Stage I speech, children usually produced *want* while reaching for an object and *see* while pointing. Contextual descriptions in Bloom et al. (1975) also reveal that when the children used *see* or *look,* they usually pointed. The verb *want* emerged as a concomitant of reaching and later was used with a second verb, typically when the child was about to perform an action or actually attempting it. For example, Gia is recorded as saying "I want wear it" while picking up a straw hat that she tried to put on.

Although 4-year-old children distinguish between experiencer and actor roles (Braine & Wells, 1978), 2-year-old children may not do so: Their appropriate ordering of subject to verb may be based, not on an order rule specific to the experiencer relation, but on a more general actional one. One such rule may be that the name of the actor precedes the name of the action (Bowerman, 1973a).

Alternatively, early word order might involve a simple "rule" to the effect that the name of the *relatively more salient object* occurs in sentence initial position, preceding the name of the action, whereas the name of the least salient object is placed last in the sentence. When the child omits naming the actor, the name of the relatively less salient referent would still occur in sentence final position (we will consider exceptions in the next section).

"SALIENCE" AS SUBSTRATE FOR EARLY SYNTAX

We turn now to consider how the relative saliencies of different components of a semantic relation might influence semantic-syntactic development. Bloom et al. (1975) noted that all four of the children they observed were able to express action events earlier than stative events. Perhaps this is because action generates situational cues to word order that can guide both the rule acquisition process and its application in speech.

Children's early multiword utterances are mostly descriptions of the "here and now" (Bloom, 1973; Bloom et al., 1975). They talk about action they are currently performing or are about to perform and about ongoing events that involve other people and things. Not only is their speech redundant with respect to the situation in which it occurs, but it actually seems to be supported by nonverbal context. A child who describes an ongoing event may, at some later point, not be able to imitate his earlier utterance (Bloom, 1973). Similarly, ongoing events may serve to guide the young child's noun order. Just as the beginning speaker seems to verbalize discrete components of a situation according to their current salience for him, the child who is beginning to utter phrases may order words according to the relative salience of their referents.

French (1971) has related children's early preference for the agentive (or actor) relation of subject to verb to the perceptual salience of an initiator of action. She suggests that a unit in the perceptual field that moves or causes change is more salient than a unit that is affected by the action. Encoding the situation linguistically then requires a verb that can take as its subject an animate noun, that is, a potentially event-initiating thing. According to French, early utterances can be classified in terms of action as "exhibiting action," "action exhibited," and "receiving action." The thing that exhibits action is encoded first as it is more salient than the thing that receives or is otherwise affected by the action.

The view that actors are perceptually more salient than recipients is supported by outcomes of an investigation by Robertson and Suci (1980). They used a habituation paradigm in which cardiac change was the primary response measure. They showed 9-second filmed agent-action-recipient sequences to 48 infants who were either in the one- or two-word stage. Each sequence contained an actor, a recipient, and a nonparticipant. The actor was still for the first 3 seconds, pushed the recipient down slightly in the next 3 seconds, and again was motionless for the final 3 seconds. On test trials, the actor, the recipient, or the nonparticipant was occluded for 1.5 seconds before, during, or after action. The degree to which infants showed response recovery from habituation when one of the objects was occluded was used to estimate attention to it.

Before action, response recovery to occlusion of actor, recipient, or nonparticipant were comparable. However, during and also after action, occlusion of the actor led to more response recovery than for the recipient or nonparticipant (which did not differ). Children in the one- and two-word speech stages showed the same patterns of behavior. Robertson and Suci concluded that whereas attention was neutrally distributed across the objects in the scene before action, it was focused on the actor during and immediately following action. They also suggested that movement may have been the major determinant of attention. The children were not necessarily processing the events in terms of agent and recipient.

Robertson and Suci also investigated the degree to which naming an object in the scene influenced attention to it. Before action, naming the actor, the recipient, or the nonparticipant comparably increased attention to it. During and after action, however, attention remained on the actor even when the recipient was named. Robertson and Suci concluded that salient, nonlinguistic stimulus information is more powerful than specific language input.

In the Robertson and Suci study, the action had minimal effect on the recipient. This may be the reason why attention remained on the actor even after action. Forceful action that would result in more notable displacement of the recipient or in a more vivid change might be able to shift attention from actor to recipient. This outcome would be anticipated if movement accounted for the salience of actors in the first place.

Pending empirical study, we suggest that although young children's attention may be biased toward a relatively more dynamic object in the visual field, contact that results in a notable change to another object should also be attention-catching. Thus, when children observe an interaction of this kind, their attention would be expected to move from actor to recipient. And, if children were to encode events linguistically in terms of their attentional shifts, their noun order would then correspond to subject + object order.

When young children talk about depicted rather than ongoing events, their expectations about how the event customarily occurs could similarly guide their word order. The same applies when children talk about their intended action. Attentional shifts from self to object could provide a temporal pattern to word order as the intended act can be represented as a sequence that moves from the self to the object. Presumably at some later stage, these early speech patterns become controlled by linguistic rules, but this does not detract from our argument that beginning speakers could arrive at standard subject-object order without linguistic rules.

To this point, we have not discussed the most obvious source of word order information, the linguistic input to the child. Stative relations such as attribution and possession seem based on learned position rules (Braine, 1976). These reflect standard usage in the child's native language, for example, "possessor + object possessed" in English (e.g., "Mommy sock"—Bloom, 1970) and "object possessed + possessor" in French (e.g., "Le popo le papa"—"hat daddy"—Guillaume, 1927).

Were children's word order usage purely a reflection of the most frequent adult usage, then within the limits of a restriction on the number of words uttered, there should be few or no deviations in word order. Any deviations that occur should be randomly distributed across the various semantic-syntactic relations. In fact, this is not so. Children deviate ("reverse") more in expressing action + object than actor + action + object (Braine, 1976). These tendencies are illustrated in the following utterances: "Sofa sit/you sit/you sit couch" (Bloom et al., 1975).

What accounts for a child's ability to use standard word order in one phrase, but not in another? When a thing is animate, or when an inanimate thing moves or undergoes a change in state (e.g., "stick fall," "balloon break"), then its name can occur in preverbal position. But when children say "sofa sit" or "nose blow," their order is regarded as being deviant. Such examples may nonetheless involve the same principle, namely, a bias toward first stating what is currently most salient (or relatively more salient), resulting in standard English word order when the actor is expressed or when a thing is subjected to change but in reversals for "action + static object" phrases. Although the child may know the "rule" for expressing action + object relations, the current salience of the referent may override the rule based on adults' examples.

ACQUISITION OF PASSIVE SENTENCES: THE ROLE OF SALIENCE

In the preceding section, we suggested that action, by directing attention from the situational actor to object, can guide word order. We also argued that when attention is centered on an object, children may 'reverse' verb + object order. In this section, we consider whether factors that in some manner make the object more salient than the actor could help children acquire structures in which the superficial subject and object respectively correspond to recipient and actor, using passive sentences as a prototype.

Mature speakers use passive sentences to indicate their focus on the acted-on entity (Johnson-Laird, 1968a,b). In turn, the listener assumes that sentence is about the acted-on object: Active sentences lead attention to a pictured actor and passives to the recipient (Olson & Filby, 1972; Tannenbaum & Williams, 1968; Hornby, 1972). Strohner and Nelson (1974) demonstrated that focusing young children's attention on the situational actor or object could control their later interpretation of noun order in passives.

Strohner and Nelson first tested the degree to which a group of 4-year-old children understood reversible passive and improbable passive sentences (e.g., *The frog is chased by the fly*). Then they trained the children by showing them pictures that were presented so as to draw their attention first to the actor or first to the object. For example, if the picture illustrated a brown cow chasing a black cow, then for some children, the part of the picture showing the brown cow (actor) was exposed before the black cow (object). For other children, the sequence was reversed. So for one group, the object-actor sequence in viewing the picture matched the object-actor sequence in the passive sentence description that followed the picture. For another group, the sequence actor-object for the illustration was opposite to the object-actor sequence in the sentence. Strohner and

Nelson found that the order in which the children had seen the objects during training determined how they later interpreted word order. Whereas an object-actor training sequence improved children's post-test comprehension of passives, an actor-object sequence actually decreased it.

Passive sentence learning normally proceeds in a much less controlled manner, so that a focus on the situational object at the expense of the actor may largely depend on their relative saliencies. Of course, intonational stress on the surface subject (logical object) in a passive sentence description of an event might also focus a child towards the situational object. Even so, when the stressed word corresponds to the more salient aspect of the scene, a child should be better able to match the two sources of information.

We should expect that when an affected object is in some way more 'dynamic' than the actor, it becomes the more salient thing in the situation. This could occur when action results in a more notable change in the object than the actor, or when the effects on the object are unusually striking, novel, or powerful. As people and animals may show particularly vivid reaction to action, animacy would be expected to have a role in learning the structure of passives. But this would actually involve differences in salience, rather than differences in animacy as such.

Young children who produce full passives usually use animate nouns in surface subject position (Baldie, 1976; Harris, 1978). Horgan (1976) found that full passives elicited from 2- to 4-year-olds mostly had animate things (people and animals) as logical objects (surface subjects). In contrast, inanimate things featured as logical subjects (surface objects). Actually, full passives were uncommon, but truncated passives (which omit reference to the actor or cause of action) were frequent. These were almost always after-the-fact comments on the results of action on inanimate things. Perhaps, when young children attend to change, the cause of that change becomes irrelevant (and thus is not stated).

De Villiers (1980) studied the role of animacy by teaching children ages 2;10 to 4;10 years to produce passive sentences. The sentences described pictured events in which the actor (surface object) was always an animal. For one group, the affected object was also animate, for example, *The sheep is being hit by the pig*. Another group of children were trained to say passives for situations in which the recipient was inanimate, for example, *The book is read by the lion*. Both groups were tested for their generalized use of the passive in situations where the actor was animate, but the affected objects were animate and inanimate things.

De Villiers found that children trained with animate recipients restricted their use of the passive to similar events on generalization trials. Also, these children were strikingly more productive than those who had been trained on inanimate recipient events. Similar outcomes were obtained for inverted cleft sentences such as *It is the girl that the boy is pushing*. In both instances, children seemed better able to learn (and apply) the constructions when the surface subject noun had an animate referent instead of an inanimate referent.

4. PERCEPTUAL CONSTRAINTS ON CHILDREN'S LANGUAGE 137

The studies on passive sentences considered to this point have examined the role of animacy for speech rather than comprehension. But results of a study by Lempert (1978) suggest that young children who are asked to interpret the meaning of passive sentences use dynamism and not animacy to assign actor and object roles.

Lempert asked children ages 3½ to 5½ years to enact the meaning of four types of reversible passive sentences: (1) Animate-Animate (AA), for example, *Goofy is pushed by Mickey Mouse;* (2) Inanimate-Inanimate (II), e.g., *The truck is bumped by the car;* (3) Animate-Inanimate (AI), e.g., *Mickey Mouse is bumped by the car;* and (4) Inanimate-Animate (IA), e.g., *The car is pushed by Goofy.*

Until age five, children gave correct interpretations for AI sentences significantly more often than IA ones. This pattern reflected a tendency to assign object status to the animate rather than inanimate thing. The children had also enacted the meaning of active sentences corresponding in type to the passives (for example, *Mickey Mouse hits the ball* (AI) and *The truck pushes the car* (IA). There was no evidence that animacy affected their interpretation of active sentences; comprehension was 97% for the two younger and 99% for the two older groups. In other words, for the relatively better known active sentence form, both types of objects were regarded as being equiprobable actors (and recipients of action).

How can the animacy pattern for passive sentences be explained? In enactment, the object that the child first reaches out for generally becomes the actor (Bridges, 1979); thus superficial aspects such as differential attractiveness or size might compel a child to choose one object over another. However, the animate toys were attractive to the children as judged by their interest in handling and playing with them; therefore, their preference for assigning the more active role to the inanimate things cannot be explained in these terms. Nor can it be explained in terms of relative size. The Disney dolls were slightly larger than the vehicles, and therefore more probable as actors on this basis.

The sets of animate and inanimate objects did differ in terms of mobility. Although both types of objects were 'dynamic' in some way, this set of inanimate things was more so. Toys such as cars, trains, and balls, once activated, could continue their trajectory and bump, push, and hit other things. The "animate" toys, however, were actually static replicas of animate (or animated) objects. Our interpretation, then, is that the greater *dynamism* of these particular inanimate things accounted for the animacy pattern in passives.

The results could also be interpreted in another way. Performance on the mixed animacy sentences conformed to: *The animate thing is verbed by the inanimate thing.* This accords with the pattern noted by Horgan (1976) when children 2 to 4 years old produced full passives. It may be the case, then, that passive sentence production and comprehension actually involve a similar strategy based on animacy.

The animacy interpretation, however, implies that children younger than five have a relatively mature concept of life. Research by Piaget (1929) and by Laurendeau and Pinard (1962) has instead shown that children in this age range often base their notions of animacy on movement without discriminating between autonomous action and action that is caused by another object. A young child may claim, for example, that although a stone that lies on the ground is not alive, it is alive when thrown into the air.

Evidence that young children use movement as a criterion for their actor concept also argues against the animacy interpretation. Schwartz (1980) elicited judgments of sentence acceptability from children who ranged in age from 4 to 9 years. Even the youngest children thought that sentences with static subject-noun referents such as *The pretty lamp sleeps in the corner* were odd. However, they found nothing unusual about sentences such as *The new car looks at the light* and *The hot sun runs across the sky,* in which the subject-noun referents are objects respectively perceived to move nonautonomously and autonomously.

Finally, Braine and Wells (1978) found that children ages 3 to 4 years conceptualized vehicles as actors and also as objects, so discriminating them from other inanimate things that they regarded only as acted-on objects. Their reasons for allocating actor status to an object stressed action; for example, "the thing that was doing the work" and "person that's doing something." Conversely, the object role was associated with "the thing not doing anything" and the "things that were getting it done to."

The outcomes of these two studies converge towards the conclusion that preschool children base their notion of actor on mobility rather than animacy. We doubt that they actually believe that cars and airplanes, even when moving, are "alive" in the same way as are people and animals. And indeed, whether or not an object is "living" may be irrelevant for children insofar as its semantic status is concerned. Instead, it may be the case that the perceived locus of responsibility for action is the critical factor (e.g., Lakoff, 1977), and that young children confound mobility with intentionality (without otherwise considering an object's animacy status). When children are able to disregard salient perceptual information, they may also become better able to consider whether or not the action is willfully instigated and thus restrict the range of objects they consider as "agents" or animate entities.

THE ROLE OF ACTION IN PASSIVE SENTENCE COMPREHENSION

In the preceding section, we considered the role of referents in relation to their action. Here we focus on action and the results of action. Specifically, we will argue that action that results in more vivid change in the object than in the actor may facilitate passive sentence comprehension. Sinclair, Sinclair, and De Marcellus (1971) found that French, German, and English-speaking children understood the passive voice earlier for verbs such as *break* and *knock down* than for verbs such as *follow* and *push.* They concluded that children learn the passive construction earlier for actions that result in change or displacement of the affected object. They also suggest a role for physical contact between the two entities.

As there was some confounding between sentence reversibility and the order of verb difficulty in the Genevan study, Lempert (1978) studied the effect of verb type using only reversible sentences. Again, passives with *follow* were more difficult to comprehend than those with verbs such as *bump* and *hit*. At age five, comprehension of *bump, hit,* and *follow* were respectively 90%, 80%, and 30%. But although *chase* involves a spatial relationship between the participants similar to *follow*, it was comprehended with 100% accuracy at age five. This can best be explained in terms of how the children understood the meaning of *chase;* that is, as an action that terminated when the actor caught, bumped, or knocked down the object of the chase. Further, whereas comprehension of *push* was 20% at age three in the Genevan study, it was 65% at this same age level in Lempert's study. This is also explicable in terms of how the children interpreted the verb, namely, as an abrupt action similar to *bump* rather than as a slow displacement of both objects.

Results of a study by Maratsos, Kuczaj, and Fox (1980) are also informative. They found that children who understood the passive for action verbs as in *The dog is bitten by the cat* might not understand nonaction passives such as *The boy is remembered by the man*. Whereas *bite* has a notable outcome on an affected object, be it animate or inanimate, *remember* usually does not. The 'vividness' of an outcome (or a potential outcome) may critically influence passive sentence comprehension.

The outcome of an investigation by Fabian-Kraus and Ammon (1980) also points in this direction. They presented cartoon stories depicting two characters engaged in familiar actions to children ages 3;0 to 6;11 years. Then the children were asked several questions. The target question was of the form ''Who was easy/hard/fun to (verb)?'' Fabian-Kraus and Ammon found that most 5- and 6-year-old children could usually answer the target question. For 3- and 4-year-old children, however, the difficulty of the target question varied with the verb, questions with *find* and *catch* being easier (84% correct) than those with *watch* and *hear* (58% and 54% correct respectively). Thus when responding to *find* and *catch,* the young children usually named the recipient, but for *watch* and *hear,* they named either participant almost equally often.

The young children's responses to the target question in Fabian's study may actually have reflected what was most prepotent to them when regarding the illustrations. Both participants in the event were ''animate'' and thus potentially of similar salience. However, by shifting attention to the affected object, events that involved *finding* and *catching* could render the object more salient than the actor when the episode terminated. For this reason, a correct response to the target question may actually have been based in a response bias toward naming the more salient object in the scene rather than in comprehension of the question.

As situations which involve *hearing* and *watching* describe stative events that do not result in change to the affected object, there may in these cases have been a more equitable distribution of salience that resulted in either participant being named with approximately equal frequency.

THE EFFECT OF ACTION AND STATE VERBS ON NOUN RECALL

To this point, we have discussed semantic aspects of verbs in relation to sentence comprehension. We have noted that action and stative elements have differential results on the object and that these differences could in turn lead to earlier comprehension of action than of stative sentences. We turn now to consider verb type further in relation to our work on sentence memory.

On the basis of their work with sentence verification, Olson and Nickerson (1978) concluded that, unlike adults, children do not code sentences as formal representations but instead treat them as if they describe an underlying concrete reality. Olson and Nickerson did not specify how young children might represent sentences, but we believe they might use imagery. We do not intend to imply that they always represent sentences as images, since children usually have acquired a fairly sophisticated linguistic system by age four (see Blank, 1974). We do hold, however, that they use "dual representation" (cf. Paivio, 1970), coding sentences as words and also as images.

We talk about imagery as being young children's "preferred" representational system. It may be the case that preschool children do use linguistic coding to advantage but are better able to retrieve information from imagery than from the linguistic system (or else they prefer to do so). Although we are not able to separate the contributions of representation and retrieval in our discussion of the differential effects of state and action verbs, this does not detract from the position that, when possible, children code sentences as imagery and use these representations when retrieving information about sentences.

If young children imagine the situation that a sentence describes, then they might treat these representations in the same way that they would treat an actual event. Just as action might make a situational object more salient than the actor when the child remembers the event, action verbs might make object nouns more memorable than subject nouns. The actor may be *initially* more salient, but after the event has occurred (or has been imagined), the acted-upon may become the relatively more salient entity.

We examined this idea by asking 52 children ranging in age from 3;8 to 10;3 years to listen to a list of 12 sentences such as *The fireman threw the chair* and *The boy painted the wheel*. An additional three sentences were used as buffer items to guard against recency and primacy effects so that 15 sentences in all were presented. After they had heard all the sentences, the children were asked to recall either the subject or the object noun. To elicit object-noun recall, the child was cued with the subject and verb. When subject-noun recall was required, the verb and object were provided.

Mean subject and object recall is shown in Table 4.1 as a function of age. As age increased, there was a diminishing bias toward better recall of the object than the subject noun. Children aged 3;8 to 5;1 years ("younger") recalled significantly more object than subject nouns (F[1,39)] = 18.54, p. 01), those ranging from 5;5 to 7;3 years ("transitional") showed a nonsignificant trend in this direction (F[1,39)] = 3.46, p. 10), and those aged 8;3 to 10;3 years ("older") showed no difference between subject and object recall (F[1,39] < 1).

As the sentences had been recorded with equal stress on subject and object nouns, intonational pattern cannot account for the better object than subject recall by young children. Also, word familiarity and imagery values of the subject and object nouns were comparable. However, the results could have involved differences in the operations used to retrieve subject and object nouns. Verbs and object as cues for the subject might have required a reversal operation that was not needed for object-noun recall. Although even 3-year-old children seem able to perform "reversal" operations on sentences stored in immediate memory (Lempert & Kinsbourne, 1978), perhaps 4-year-old children cannot do so for sentences coded in a more permanent storage system.

To clarify whether the results are better explained in terms of attentional focus or reversibility, we conducted a further study in which children's attention was biased either toward the subject noun or toward the object noun. In one condition, practice trials were given in which only subject-noun recall was required, again using verb + object as prompts. In the other condition, object-noun recall was required (to subject + verb). It was expected that this procedure would lead children to consider either subject or object as the most important part of the sentence, according to condition.

The subjects were 72 children at three age levels: (1) younger, (3;8 to 5;2 years); (2) transitional (5;7 to 6;9 years); and (3) older (7;1 to 9;1 years). They listened to a list of 16 sentences such as *The monkey broke the drum* recorded with equal stress on subject and object. Afterwards, the child was prompted

TABLE 4.1
Mean Correct Noun Recall (Max = 6) by Children
As a Function of Age and Word Class

Noun Type	Age Group		
	Younger	Transitional	Older
Subject	2.47	3.17	3.39
Object	3.93	3.90	3.85

either for subject- or for object-noun recall according to the procedure observed during practice.

As shown in Table 4.2, even the youngest children could now recall subject and object nouns comparably well ($F[1,66] < 1$). So, the results support not a reversibility, but an attentional explanation. When their attention was directed toward the subject noun, verb + object were as effective as cues for the subject noun as subject + verb cues were for the object noun. It is when young children were left free to choose their own approach that they showed superior object-noun recall.

Before considering what these outcomes imply for sentence representation, we shall describe the results of a third study using action and state verbs (Lempert & Kinsbourne, 1981). In preceding sections, we suggested that stative relationships do not change the distribution of saliencies across objects and that attention is then held by the more interesting object in the scene. Typically, this would be an animate thing, especially if the other object is inanimate. Action events, however, should be able to lead attention from actor to recipient. Thus, by the premise that children construct imagery representation of sentence meaning, the objects of action verbs should (in these representations) be relatively more 'salient' than those of stative verbs, and consequently, better recalled.

In the relevant study, the subjects were preschool children ages 4 to 5½ years and second-grade children 7 to 8½ years. Children in the action verb condition listened to sentences such as *The boy kicked the wheel* and *The monkey threw the cup*. Children in the state verb condition heard sentences such as *The boy kept the wheel* and *The monkey wanted the cup*. A third group of children heard the same nouns presented as unrelated word pairs: *boy-wheel* and *monkey-cup*. After the children had heard all 10 sentences or word pairs, they were cued with the first noun for the object noun.

We found that older children could recall object of state and action verbs comparably well, and that they recalled significantly more nouns from sentences than from unrelated word pairs. In contrast, younger children's recall of object nouns depended on verb type. Children in the action verb condition retrieved

TABLE 4.2
Mean Correct Subject and Object Recall (Max = 16)
By Children as a Function of Age and Noun Type
In Experimental Trials Subsequent to Practice

Noun Type	Age Group		
	Younger	Transitional	Older
Subjects	7.50	9.42	9.79
Objects	7.79	9.75	10.08

TABLE 4.3
Facilitatory and Frequency Rankings of Verbs
Used in the Action-State Experiment

Verb	Facilitation	Frequency	Verb	Facilitation	Frequency
touched	1	19	carried	11	16
painted	2	5	kept	12	10
dropped	3	12	saw	13	2
threw	4	6	wanted	14	4
kicked	5	13	bought	15	11
pushed	6	14	needed	16	18
washed	7	8	heard	17	7
watched	8	12	enjoyed	18	17
had	9	1	sewed	19	9
liked	10	3	remembered	20	20

significantly more nouns than those in the state verb or control conditions who did not differ reliably. We confirmed these results by further studies using a mixed list of action and state sentences. Whereas the 4-year-olds again recalled more objects of action than of state verbs, children older than age six showed no such difference.

When constructing the sentences for the action and state verb studies, we had not been concerned with how specific actional characteristics underlying the verbs might affect noun recall. To determine whether semantic aspects of the verb were playing a role, we took a post hoc look at the data for the younger children in the action and state verb conditions in the experiment we have described. As an estimate of verb facilitatory value for each sentence, we subtracted total correct responses to the corresponding control noun pair (so correcting for possible sources of difference inherent in the noun pairs themselves). For example, correct responses by children who had heard *boy-wheel* were subtracted from correct responses by those who had heard *The boy turned the wheel*. The rank ordering of the relative facilitatory values of the 20 verbs is shown in Table 4.3. As a control for the possible effect of verb familiarity, we rank ordered the verbs in terms of their frequency counts on the Rinsland (1945) norms (also shown in Table 4.3). However, there was no association between verb familiarity and facilitatory value ($r = -0.18$, $t = 0.75$, $p > .10$).

Regarding the verbs in terms of their relative facilitation: Verbs describing events that lead to some change to the object (as in *The girl painted the door*) or action of brief duration (e.g., *The kitten touched the tree*) or else both (e.g., *The baby dropped the cake*) are more facilitative than where these factors are not present (e.g., *The girl saw the door; The kitten watched the tree; The baby wanted the cake*). Also, contact by itself (had, kept, carried) is not very helpful. What seems to be involved here is whether or not attention is led from subject to object noun as it would be if the child actually perceived the scene.

What then accounts for children being comparably well able to retrieve objects of action and state verbs by about age six? Perhaps by then children preferentially use (or retrieve information from) a linguistic code that represents state and action phrases in terms of the same abstract forms, thus allowing children to supercede exigencies imposed by aspectual differences between verbs.

HOW DO YOUNG CHILDREN REPRESENT WORDS?

Given that there are reasons for believing that children's preferred ways of representing sentences begins to change at about age five, is there also evidence for a developmental transition toward age five in how they represent information about words? And if so, does perceptual salience play more of a role for younger than for older children? We will now consider these questions in turn, first examining evidence that between ages three to five, children's word knowledge is organized not in terms of linguistic principles but by superimposition on their experience.

Nelson (1978) studied the relationship between what children know about the world (conceptual information) and what they know about words (lexical information). She investigated lexical knowledge by asking children three to five years to "tell me what X is" (or "what X means"). She studied conceptual information by asking the child to "tell me what you know about X." Nelson found that when the stimuli were basic object terms such as *apple* and *tiger,* the children mostly answered both questions by describing actions or functions associated with the objects (e.g., "they run," "you eat it"). She concluded that young children map language terms directly on an experientially based conceptual network in which objects are related to the child and to other actors through function and action.

Names may actually be attached to static representations of objects (cf. Nelson, 1974), but action and function feature in what children know *about* objects. Using a sentence verification procedure, Prawat and Cancelli (1977) found 5-year-old children better able to verify salient actions of noun referents (e.g., *A horse can run*) than their stative attributes (e.g., *A horse has a mane*). When assessing action/function, the young children actually did as well as third-grade children.

Reference to action and function also predominate in young children's word associations to nouns. Japanese and American children under age six mainly give responses such as "apple-eat" (Moran, 1973). Nelson (1977) described similar findings by Halperin for children ages 3;4 to 4;4 years. Similar outcomes were reported by Heidenheimer (1978) for 4-year-old children. Also, we have found that when young children do give noun responses to nouns, the response term actually is an actor (e.g., hat-person "because a person wears a hat") or an acted-upon in relation to the stimulus word (e.g., hat-head "because you put a hat on your head"). Or else, the nouns are contextually related (e.g., bird-nest "a bird has a nest"). By approximately age eight, children's responses to nouns are usually based on shared categories, for example, "apple-peach," "hat-coat" (Entwisle, 1966; Entwisle, Forsyth, & Muuss, 1964; Ervin, 1961; Palermo, 1963; 1971).

Heidenheimer (1978) suggested that children begin to shift to linguistically based semantic organization at age five. She asked 4- and 5-year-old children to listen to a list of eight basic object category words such as *apple* and *dog*. Four types of distractors were used to test recognition: (1) action (e.g., *eat, bark*); (2) coordinate (e.g., *orange, cat*); (3) superordinate (e.g., *fruit, animal*); and (4) unrelated control (e.g., *shampoo, match*). Whereas action words were the most effective type of distractor at age four, coordinates were more effective than action words at age five. Also, when associating to nouns, 5-year-old children gave more coordinate than action word responses.

To summarize, outcomes of investigations on semantic organization in young children converge toward the conclusion that before age five, children's word knowledge features information derived from their experience with the referents of the word. Data from children's word associations, attribute verification, and word recognition correspond in suggesting that their word knowledge features actions and functions that involve the referent. By about age eight or nine, linguistic principles of organization usually are observed when the structure of children's semantic organization is studied. However, the transition from an experientially based to a linguistically based system seems to begin at about age five.

WHY ARE ACTION AND FUNCTION CENTRAL?

A focus on action and function by young children does not by itself demonstrate an early role for perception in relation to word knowledge. We shall now attempt to do so. Our discussion invokes the notion that dynamic events are contexts that render salience to objects. Young children presumably know a number of different things about an object (or a set of related objects). Yet the information they usually select for utterance corresponds to those aspects of objects that would be expected to have guided their attention to them in the first place. We are concerned here, not with what maintains attention, but with the factors that can orient a child toward a stimulus in the first place. Of course, attention is not always determined by changes in stimulus configurations such as ones caused by movement, sound, or intensity, but action and movement are particularly potent determiners of spontaneous attention.

The centrality of actional information with respect to 'dynamic' objects whether animate or inanimate (such as vehicles, record players, and even mobiles) is due to the perceptual system's bias toward movement and sound. When a young child (or adult) notes an object that moves or produces sound, he usually cannot help but turn and look toward the source of stimulation. Once observing the stimulus, his attention may be captured by other aspects (e.g., shape, pattern, color) but the object's dynamic properties have special relevance in orienting the child toward the stimulus in the first place.

Can similar principles be applied to explain the centrality of functional information in relation to static inanimate objects? Toys and food can become salient in terms of what the child (or another actor) can do with them (and has in the past). Also, of course, adults are likely to stress the uses of objects when conversing with young children. Thus children's functional knowledge about frequently used static objects is multiply determined, and its basis cannot in any obvious way be reconstructed retrospectively from the child's utterances.

To summarize, young children behave as if they retrieve information about relevant situations in the case of object names or by constructing situations in the case of sentences. Situational representation of linguistic information makes children vulnerable to the same sources of stimulus control as those that can influence their reactions to an actual event. How could this constrain children's ability to effectively apply available linguistic knowledge? To illustrate our answer, we use their approaches to word order.

YOUNG CHILDREN'S WORD ORDER APPROACHES

Toward age five, children begin to give more attention to sentence structure when assigning actor and object roles to nouns. However, as children younger than five may correctly interpret a structure in the absence of extrasyntactic cues but still be controlled by such cues when they are present, an increased knowledge of syntactic structure toward age five cannot fully account for the changes that then occur. In the following discussion, we summarize the relevant literature and consider its implications for how younger and older children process sentences.

Bloom (1973) pointed out that children do not need linguistic rules to understand sentences that are redundant with respect to the context in which they occur. However, when meaning resides only in the linguistic message itself, very young children may disregard word order information even when they observe these rules in their speech. Wetstone and Friedlander (1973) found that 2-year-old children who produced two- and three-word utterances with consistent word order seemed to be unaware of deviant word order when processing sentences.

They responded as accurately to phrases such as *Mommy clown to the show* as they did to correctly worded messages such as *Show the clown to mommy*. Also, Chapman and Miller (1975) noted that 2-year-old children used word order correctly to describe enacted events, but when asked to enact the meaning of sentences, they preferred the more probable actor and object relations. Do young children rely on known relations between word referents because they have not acquired the relevant linguistic rules or because they do not use linguistic information even though it is at their disposal in another context?

The décalage between young children's observation of word order relationships in speech as opposed to their apparent disregard of similar information in sentence comprehension has increasingly attracted attention in language development. Bloom (1973), for example, speculated that in early stages of language development, production and comprehension may be based on different but mutually dependent processes. However, even 3-year-old children favor interpretations based on experience rather than word order for simple active sentences (Chapman & Kohn, 1977). Bridges (1980) found that many children aged 2;6 to 3;9 years used extralinguistic solutions when interpreting reversible active sentences such as *The car pushes the lorry*. For example, they might assign the actor role to the nearest toy.

By age 3½, children generally use word order when assigning actor and object roles to nouns in reversible active sentences such as *The kitty bumps the swing* (Chapman & Kohn, 1977), but 4-year-olds may still disregard word order information when the lexical items give cues to a more probable relation. Not until age five do children take full account of word order status in their interpretations of active sentences (Strohner & Nelson, 1974). We find this notable in view of the ease with which correct word order is used by 4-year-olds when they speak.

A similar age progression has been recorded for improbable passive sentences such as *The cat is chased by the mouse*. Strohner and Nelson (1974) found that 3-year-olds invariably produced interpretations based on semantic knowledge alone and 4-year-olds usually did so too. Five-year-olds, however, based their minority of wrong interpretations mainly on event probability.

A second approach to sentence decoding has been noted for reversible passive sentences (where actor and object roles cannot be assigned on a semantic basis). The child may then assign actor and object status to the first and second nouns respectively, thus reversing sentence meaning (Bever, 1970). This approach is thought to represent overuse of the probabilistic generalization that noun-verb-noun sequences often correspond to actor-action-object sequences (e.g., Maratsos, 1974). Strohner and Nelson (1974) found that 3- and 4-year-old children respectively showed 73% and 33% reversal of the meaning of reversible passive sentences. Five-year-olds, however, nearly always interpreted them correctly.

Passive sentence reversal is almost exclusively restricted to children younger than five (Lempert & Kinsbourne, 1978, 1980). However, as most children who reversed passives concomitantly performed correctly on inverted cleft sentences such as *It's the truck that the train pushes,* we suggested that passive sentence reversal actually is based on a semantic approach ("actor + action") rather than on a syntactical overgeneralization. The child assigns the actor role to the noun immediately preceding the verb (the first noun in passives and the second noun in inverted clefts) and then assigns the object role to the "other" noun regardless of whether it is the first or second noun in the sentence.

Perhaps this approach is related to that which Carol Chomsky (1969) described for sentences of the form *The doll is hard to see* in relation to a blindfolded doll. Chomsky found that 5-year-old children assume that the surface subject is also the logical subject. We note in passing that this sentence is particularly difficult for children because it has a stative verb (Fabian-Krause & Ammon, 1980). Also, the children were faced with visual information that conflicted with linguistic input.

The data for age changes in the 'animacy' approach to passives described earlier (Lempert, 1978) also shows changes occurring at about age five. Accuracy of comprehension of AI and IA sentences by 3-year-olds was respectively 90% and 27%. Four-year-olds were less controlled by 'animacy,' showing 78% and 53% comprehension of AI and IA sentences respectively. And 5-year-olds could disregard 'animacy,' interpreting AI, IA, and AA sentences equally well (87%).

One reason that 5-year-olds might use fewer extrasyntactic approaches to passive sentence decoding is that they understand this structure better. Cromer (1976), for example, argues that children resort to extralinguistic strategies when they do not know how to use the grammatical structure in an adult manner. But as we noted earlier, this does not sufficiently explain the change. Maratsos and Abramovitch (1975) found 60% correct comprehension of reversible passives at age three. Lempert (1978) found 63% comprehension of AA and II passives (where animacy could not be used) between ages 3½ and 4½ years and 72% comprehension between ages 4½ and 5 years. These outcomes suggest that children may have some understanding of the passive construction as early as age three, but do not use this information when a perceptual solution can be reached instead.

Of course, group means do not prove that a young child who has structural knowledge subordinates this information to a more obvious solution. To clarify this question, we reexamined the data on passives in the animacy study in terms of individual response patterns. We found that nine children whose interpretations of AA and II sentences were consistently correct, resorted to the 'animacy' approach for the AI and IA sentences. All nine children were younger than five. So at least some young children, who otherwise behave as if they understand the structure of passives, can be controlled by available extralinguistic cues.

Finally, why does experience directly influence children's solutions for improbable active sentences until age five? It is difficult to accept that they do not fully know the structure of active sentences until then. Perhaps they now rely on word order relations because they make more use of a representational system that can by-pass the imagery evoked by the content words and instead treats words as words. Before addressing this possibility, we first need to consider how children's sentence decoding approaches begin to change at about age five.

CHANGES IN SENTENCE PROCESSING APPROACHES

In our work (Lempert, 1978; Lempert & Kinsbourne, 1978; 1980), we have observed a spurt in passive sentence comprehension around age five. Concomitantly, random performance on inverted cleft sentences actually increased. Also, whereas younger children showed an overall better level of performance on inverted clefts than on passives, the reverse pattern occurred toward age five. This is based, not on a better understanding of the structure of inverted clefts relative to passives but on younger children's use of the primitive actor + action rule described in the preceding section. It also reflects older children's relatively better ability to evaluate their knowledge.

When children show a random level of performance for a structure, this need not imply mere guessing but instead, a varied approach to different examples of a structure the child does not as yet understand. Children who show 'random' performance may actually be trying out different solutions. Viewed in this way, 'random' performance implies that the child recognizes that a solution is not immediately available.

Cromer (1970) also found that at about the mental age of six, children vary their approaches when interpreting structures of the form *The wolf is fun to bite*. Previously, the actor role was almost invariably assigned to the named animal. Children continued to show inconsistent solutions until about age nine, when most of them finally resolved this structure.

In their review of syntactical development after age five, Palermo and Molfese (1972) concluded that although there is a general but gradual consolidation of language structures from kindergarten to seventh grade, the period between ages five and seven is especially notable for large increases in grammatical constructions such as the passive and for paradoxical decrements on some forms. For example, noun phrase redundancy, as in *She took it away the hat* increases significantly in use from nursery school to Grade 1 (Menyuk, 1964; 1971). To explain these decrements, Palermo and Molfese suggested that when children acquire new rules for diverse syntactic structures, these rules affect and disrupt other structures that the child has previously been able to handle in a competent manner.

Although significant or abrupt increases in use of structures after age five are explicable in terms of the acquisition and application of productive rules, this does not explain why children become better able to do so at this time. Perhaps, they are then able to restrain their impulses to react to perceptual solutions and instead give more attention to linguistic input. In turn, their attention to linguistic information would lead to major increments in language development. In some instances, this process could result in paradoxical performance decrements as when a strategy that earlier led to correct performance is temporarily replaced by a new but incorrect rule, or when the child tries out different solutions before arriving at the correct one.

CONCLUSIONS

We can now resolve the paradox that children may use information in their own speech that they disregard in comprehension. Young children may fail to use linguistic rules which in other contexts they "know" because the information conveyed by the imagery that the content words or objects themselves evoke is more immediately compelling. If the environment (or its mental representation by the child) does not feature salient stimuli, they may then reveal an ability to apply linguistic information that otherwise is masked. The younger the child is, the less able he is to inhibit his impulse to act in accordance with the more immediately salient perceptual circumstances.

Investigators who test language comprehension inadvertently give children cues to more compelling solutions. They present sentences together with pictures or with toys that the child uses to enact the meaning of the sentence. Because young children prefer visual information to linguistic sources, investigators unintentionally test comprehension precisely in those situations that preclude children from revealing the full extent of their available linguistic knowledge.

The notion that a vivid perceptual experience may override what the child knows from previous learning has rich precedent in child development. Piaget's nonconservation demonstrations may rely on this effect. As Blank (1974) points out, the traditional tasks used by Piaget confront the child with a situation in which the visual elements are dominant. We need not suppose that the child truly believes that moving objects apart can increase their number or that passing liquid from one receptacle to another can change its volume. Rather, in the face of a vividly experienced perceptual change, prior knowledge is overridden and the percept alone determines the response.

It appears that young children are not as well able as older children and adults to inhibit their responses to a compelling experience. We suggest that in order to qualify one's experience on the basis of one's knowledge, one has to be able to detach oneself from stimulus control ("decenter"), and the inhibiting capability that makes this possible becomes available only gradually over the preschool years. During the experience of language, the actual situation and imagery potential of the content words constitutes the stimulus environment; the qualifying influence of linguistic representation only becomes fully usable when children are able to restrain their immediate impulse to act in accordance with the "here and now."

SUMMARY

It is now generally agreed that early language develops on a cognitive base, though the emphasis on a perceptual, rather than manipulatory substrate, is relatively new. As we have discussed, early word choice and word order, though predictable, may be based not on specifically linguistic, but on perceptual rules ("the child tells it as it is—to him").

Visual information provides children with clues to word order status in accompanying linguistic descriptions. However, the rules children derive from an adult's examples may deviate from those used by the adult, even when they lead to the same superficial outcome. The child's early rules are controlled by salient differences between referents; those of the adult, by linguistic principles.

However, beyond that, we attempt to provide a theoretical framework to account for children's syntactic lapses with respect to rules they already "know" (in that in this context they have applied such rules). Rather than judge the child not yet to know the rule very well, or be confused about it, we have pointed to *systematic biases* that could predictably cause children to diverge from "correct" syntactic use in certain situations. The situations prone to generate such divergence are ones that: a) include salient percepts or foster salient imagery; and b) lend meaning to the situation (based on the child's previous experience) that conflicts with the properly construed meaning of the verbal message.

If a young child "knows" a linguistic rule, this does not mean that he will consistently apply it. Such knowledge should be considered as making available one more strategy for dealing with a situation that included a verbal statement. Whether he applies this (linguistic) strategy, or instead is guided by extraverbal "appearances" is determined by how compelling (salient) those appearances are. It is only after several years of maturation that the child is able to "decenter" from the perceptual aspects, and apply to the verbal material, in isolation, the rules he knows, and then interpret accordingly, even if the outcome conflicts with how things seem.

ACKNOWLEDGMENTS

Preparation of this chapter was supported in part by Medical Research Council Grant MA-6461

REFERENCES

Baldie, B. J. The acquisition of the passive voice. *Journal of Child Language,* 1976, 2, 231–248.
Bever, T. G. The cognitive basis for linguistic structure. In J. R. Hayes (Ed.), *Cognition and the development of language.* New York: Wiley, 1970.

Blank, M. Cognitive functions of language in the preschool years. *Developmental Psychology*, 1974, *10*, 229–245.
Bloom, L. *Language development: form and function in emerging grammars*. Cambridge, Mass.: M.I.T. Press, 1970.
Bloom, L. *One word at a time: the use of single word utterances before syntax*. The Hague: Mouton, 1973.
Bloom, L. Talking, understanding, and thinking. In R. L. Schiefelbush & L. L. Lloyd (Eds.) *Language perspectives—acquisition, retardation and intervention*. Baltimore, Md.: University Park Press, 1974.
Bloom, L., Lightbown, P., & Hood, B. Structure and variation in child language. *Monographs of the Society for Research in Child Development*, 1975, *40* (2, Serial No. 160).
Bowerman, M. Structural relations in children's utterances: semantic or syntactic. In T. E. Moore (Ed.) *Cognitive development and the acquisition of language*. New York: Academic Press, 1973. (a)
Bowerman, M. *Early syntactical development: a cross-linguistic study with special reference to Finnish*. Cambridge: Cambridge University Press, 1973. (b)
Bowerman, M. Commentary. In Bloom, L., Lightbown, P., & Hood, L. (Eds.), *Monographs of the Society for Research in Child Development*, 1975, (2, Serial No. 160).
Braine, M. D. S. Children's first word combinations. *Monographs of the Society for Research in Child Development*, 1976, 41 (1, Serial No. 164).
Braine, M. D. S. & Wells, R. S. Case-like categories in children: the actor and some related categories. *Cognitive Psychology*, 1978, *10*, 100–122.
Bransford, J. & Johnson, M. Contextual prerequisites for understanding: Some investigations of comprehension and recall. *Journal of Verbal Learning and Verbal Behavior*, 1972, *37*, 284–290.
Brazelton, T. B., Scholl, M. L., & Robey, J. S. Visual response in the newborn. *Pediatrics*, 1966, *37*, 284–290.
Bridges, A. SVO comprehension strategies reconsidered: The evidence of individual patterns of response. *Journal of Child Language*, 1980, *7*, 89–104.
Bruner, J. S. On cognitive growth: I & II. In J. S. Bruner, R. R. Olver, & P. M. Greenfield, *Studies in cognitive growth*. New York: Wiley, 1966.
Chapman, R. S. & Kohn, L. L. *Comprehension strategies in two- and three-year-olds: Animate agents or probable events?* Paper presented at Stanford Child Language Forum, Stanford, Calif. 1977.
Chapman, R. S. & Miller, J. F. Word order in early two- and three-word utterances: Does production precede comprehension? *Journal of Speech and Hearing Research*, 1975, *18*, 355–371.
Chomsky, C. *The acquisition of syntax in children from 5 to 10*. Cambridge: M.I.T. Press, 1969.
Conrad, R. The chronology of the development of covert speech in children. *Developmental Psychology*, 1971, *5*, 398–405.
Cromer, R. F. "Children are nice to understand." Surface structure clues for the recovery of deep structure. *British Journal of Psychology*, 1970, *61*, 397–408.
Cromer, R. F. Developmental strategies for language. In V. Hamilton & M. D. Vernon (Eds.), *The development of cognitive processes*. New York: Academic Press, 1976.
Day, M. C. Developmental trends in visual scanning. *Advances in Child Development and Behavior*, 1975, *10*, 153–192.
de Villiers, J. G. The process of rule learning in child speech: A new look. In K. E. Nelson (Ed.), *Children's Language* (Vol. 2). New York: Gardner Press, 1980.
Entwisle, D. *Word associations of young children*. Baltimore: John Hopkins Press, 1966.
Entwisle, D., Forsyth, D. F., & Muuss, R. The syntagmatic-paradigmatic shift in children's word associations. *Journal of Verbal Learning and Verbal Behavior*, 1964, *3*, 19–29.
Ervin, S. M. Changes with age in the verbal determinants of word association. *American Journal of Psychology*, 1961, *74*, 361–372.

Fabian-Kraus, V. & Ammon, P. Assessing linguistic competence: when are children hard to understand? *Journal of Child Language,* 1980, *7,* 401–412.
French, P. L. Perception and early semantic learning. *Word,* 1971, *27,* 125–138.
Greenfield, P. M. Informativeness, presupposition, and semantic choice in single-word utterances. In N. Waterson & C. Snow (Eds.), *The development of communication.* New York: John Wiley, 1978.
Greenfield, P. M. & Smith, J. *The structure of communication in early language development.* New York: Academic Press, 1976.
Greenfield, P. M. & Zukow, P. Why do children say what they say when they say it? An experimental approach to the psychogenesis of presupposition. In K. E. Nelson (Ed.), *Children's Language (Vol. 1).* New York: Gardner Press, 1978.
Guillaume, P. Les débuts de la phrase dans la langage de l'enfant. *Journal de psychologie,* 1927, *24,* 1–25.
Haith, M. M. The response of the human newborn to visual movement. *Journal of Experimental Child Psychology,* 1966, *3,* 235–243.
Harris, M. Noun animacy and the passive: A developmental approach. *Journal of Experimental Psychology,* 1978, *39,* 495–50.
Hayes, D. S. & Birnbaum, D. W. Preschoolers' retention of televised events: Is a picture worth a thousand words? *Developmental Psychology,* 1980, *16,* 410–416.
Heidenheimer, P. A comparison of the roles of exemplar, action, coordinate, and superordinate relations in the semantic processing of 4- and 5-year-old children. *Journal of Experimental Child Psychology,* 1978, *25,* 143–159.
Horgan, D. *The development of the full passive.* Paper presented at Boston University Conference on Language Development, Boston, 1976.
Hornby, P. A. The psychological subject and predicate. *Cognitive Psychology,* 1972, *3,* 632–642.
Jeffrey, W. E. The orienting reflex and attention in cognitive development. *Psychological Review,* 1968, *75,* 323–334.
Johnson-Laird, P. N. The interpretation of the passive voice. *Quarterly Journal of Experimental Psychology,* 1968, *20,* 69–73. (a)
Johnson-Laird, P. N. The choice of the passive voice. *Quarterly Journal of Experimental Psychology,* 1968, *59,* 7–15. (b)
Jones, H. R. The use of visual and verbal memory processes by three-year-old children. *Journal of Experimental Child Psychology,* 1973, *15,* 340–351.
Kinsbourne, M. & Lempert, H. Does left brain lateralization of speech arise from right-biased orienting to salient percepts? *Human Development,* 1979, *22,* 270–276.
Lakoff, G. *Linguistic Gestalts.* Papers from the 13th Regional Meeting, 1977, Chicago Linguistic Society.
Laurendeau, M. & Pinard, A. *Causal thinking in the child: a genetic and experimental approach.* Montreal: Institute of Psychological Research, 1962.
Lempert, H. Extrasyntactic factors affecting passive sentence comprehension by young children. *Child Development,* 1978, *49,* 694–699.
Lempert, H. & Kinsbourne, M. Children's comprehension of word order: A developmental investigation. *Child Development,* 1978, *49,* 1235–1238.
Lempert, H. & Kinsbourne, M. Action as substrate for syntax. In P. French (Ed.), *The development of meaning. Series in Child Language, No. 2,* 1979.
Lempert, H. & Kinsbourne, M. Preschool children's sentence comprehension: strategies with respect to word order. *Journal of Child Language,* 1980, *7,* 371–379.
Lempert, H. & Kinsbourne, M. How children represent sentences: Evidence from the superiority of noun recall from action as compared to stative sequences. *Journal of Psycholinguistic Research,* 1981, *10,* 155–166.
Lempert, H. & Kinsbourne, M. Naming and pointing: Does language emerge from orienting? (Submitted for publication, 1980).

Leonard, L. B. *Meaning in child language*. New York: Grune & Stratton, 1976.

Limber, J. The genesis of complex sentences. In T. E. Moore (Ed.), *Cognitive development and the acquisition of language*. New York: Academic Press, 1973.

Maratsos, M. P. Children who get worse at understanding the passive: A replication of Bever. *Journal of Psycholinguistic Research*, 1974, *3*, 65–74.

Maratsos, M. P. & Abramovitch, R. How children understand full, truncated, and anomalous passives. *Journal of Verbal Learning and Verbal Behavior*, 1975, *14*, 145–157.

Maratsos, M. P., Kuczaj, S. A. II, & Fox, D. E. C. Some empirical studies in the acquisition of transformational relations: passives, negatives, and the past tense. In W. A. Collins (Ed.), *Minnesota Symposia in Child Psychology (Vol. 12)*. New York: Thomas Crowell & Associates, 1980.

Menyuk, P. Syntactic rules used by children from preschool through first grade. *Child Development*, 1964, *35*, 533–546.

Menyuk, P. *The acquisition and development of language*. Englewood Cliffs, N.J.: Prentice-Hall, 1971.

Moran, L. J. Comparative growth of Japanese and North American cognitive dictionaries. *Child Development*, 1973, *44*, 862–865.

Muir, D. & Field, J. Newborn infants orient to sound, *Child Development*, 1979, *50*, 431–436.

Nelson, K. Concept, word, and sentence: Interrelations in acquisition and development. *Psychological Review*, 1974, *81*, 267–285.

Nelson, K. The syntagmatic-paradigmatic shift revisited: A review of research and theory. *Psychological Bulletin*, 1977, *84*, 93–116.

Nelson, K. Semantic development and the development of memory. In K. E. Nelson (Ed.), *Children's Language (Vol. 1)*. New York: Gardner Press, 1978.

Olson, D. R. & Filby, N. On the comprehension of active and passive sentences. *Cognitive Psychology*, 1972, *3*, 361–381.

Olson, D. R. & Nickerson, N. Language development through the school years: Learning to confine interpretations to the information in the text. In K. E. Nelson (Ed.), *Children's Language (Vol. 1)*. New York: Gardner Press, 1978.

Paivio, A. On the functional significance of imagery. *Psychological Bulletin*, 1970, *73*, 385–392.

Palermo, D. Word associations and children's verbal behavior. In L. P. Lipsett & C. C. Spiker (Eds.), *Advances in child development and behavior (Vol. 1)*. New York: Academic Press, 1963.

Palermo, D. Characteristics of word association responses obtained from children in Grades One through Four. *Developmental Psychology*, 1971, *5*, 118–123.

Palermo, D. & Molfese, D. L. Language acquisition from age five onward. *Psychological Bulletin*, 1972, *78*, 409–428.

Pea, R. D. Can information theory explain early word choice? *Journal of Child Language*, 1979, *6*, 397–340.

Piaget, J. *The child's conception of the world*. New York: Harcourt & Brace, 1929.

Piaget, J. *Play, dreams and imitation in childhood*. New York: Norton, 1951.

Prawat, R. S. & Cancelli, A. A. Semantic retrieval in young children as a function of type of meaning. *Developmental Psychology*, 1977, *13*, 354–358.

Rinsland, R. H. *A basic vocabulary of elementary school children*. New York: MacMillan, 1945.

Robertson, S. S. & Suci, G. J. Event perception by children in the early stage of language production. *Child Development*, 1980, *51*, 89–96.

Schwartz, R. G. Presuppositions and children's metalinguistic judgements: Concepts of life and the awareness of animacy restrictions. *Child Development*, 1980, *51*, 364–371.

Sinclair, H., Sinclair, A., & De Marcellus, O. Young children's comprehension and production of passive sentences. *Archives de psychologie*, 1971, *61*, 1–20.

Starr, S. The relationship of single words to two-word utterances. *Child Development*, 1975, *46*, 701–708.

Strohner, H. & Nelson, K. E. The young child's development of sentence comprehension: Influence of event probability, nonverbal context, syntactic form, and strategies. *Child Development,* 1974, *45,* 567–576.

Tannenbaum, R. H. & Williams, S. F. Generation of active and passive sentences as a function of subject or object focus. *Journal of Verbal Learning and Verbal Behavior,* 1968, *7,* 246–250.

Tronick, E. & Clanton, C. Infant looking patterns. *Vision Research,* 1971, *11,* 1479–1486.

Volkmann, F. C. & Dobson, M. V. Infant responses of ocular fixation to moving stimuli. *Journal of Experimental Child Psychology,* 1976, *22,* 86–99.

Wetstone, H. S. & Friedlander, B. Z. The effect of word order on young children's responses to simple questions and commands. *Child Development,* 1973, *44,* 734–740.

Wohlwill, J. F. From perception to reference: A dimension of cognitive development. *Monographs of the Society for Research in Child Development,* 1962, *30,* (2-Whole No. 100), 82–101.

5 Getting Others to Do What You Want Them to Do: The Development of Children's Requestive Strategies

Elizabeth A. Levin
Kenneth H. Rubin
University of Waterloo

In recent years, researchers from a wide variety of fields have become increasingly concerned with the study of children's communicative competencies. The extant literature has generally reflected two approaches. The first, which may be labeled the *cognitive developmental* approach, has focused on communicative competence as an index of such intellectual growth markers as egocentrism, sociocentrism, or decentration (e.g., Piaget, 1926). The second approach, *developmental pragmatics,* represents a turn away from the more traditional study of the syntactic and semantic aspects of language and a move toward the more practical consideration of how children use words to communicate.

In the present chapter we will selectively review literature representative of both aforementioned biases. By so doing it will become apparent that many of those who examine developmental pragmatics attempt to account for their findings by employing cognitive or social-cognitive explanations, thereby linking the two approaches. For example, much of the pragmatics literature centers on the seemingly sophisticated nature of preschoolers' discursive skills (Dore, 1978; Garvey, 1975). One common explanation for these data is that preschool-aged children are not nearly as egocentric as Piaget had originally made them out to be. In fact, some researchers suggest that preschoolers are as sociocentered as their older counterparts (Bruner, 1978).

We believe, however, that the story of the development of children's communicative skills is far from fully told. For one, the sociolinguists have not gone beyond the preschool years in describing the course of development. Are we to assume that 4-year-olds have reached asymptote in communicative development? For another, the developmental pragmaticists have not independently related measures of social-cognition (e.g., egocentrism) to naturally occurring indices of communicative development. Thus, to this point, we have little data-based knowledge of the relationship between perspective-taking and communication skills. The studies we describe below examine: (a) the development of discursive skills beyond the preschool years; and (b) the relationships between measures of perspective-taking and these skills.

PIAGET AND THE CONCEPT OF EGOCENTRISM

In the beginning there was Jean Piaget . . . or so it seems to many of us who have been concerned both with the development of communicative and with perspective-taking skills in children. Piaget's classic book, *The Language and Thought of the Child* (1926), has often been cited by developmental psychologists and linguists as the source point from which later research concerning children's social-cognitive and communicative skills emanated.

A major reason for the citation of Piaget's early work on communicative development stems from his unique proposition that much of children's early verbalization is not adapted to the requirements of their listeners. Indeed, Piaget suggested that listeners were not even necessary for children's speech to occur. The explanation for such seemingly strange occurrences was that preoperational youngsters were unable to simultaneously, or for that matter, sequentially, focus on their own and another's point of view. This inability to socially decenter naturally led children to assume that their own viewpoints were shared by all. Thus, the preoperational speaker, when producing abbreviated, grammatically perplexing messages directed to others, was believed to think that his or her speech must necessarily be understood by those others. It was as if the young speaker thought, "If I can understand what I say, so too must everyone else."

Not only did Piaget assume the preoperationally staged child to be unable to take the viewpoints of others into account, he also suggested a lack of social *will* to engage in communicative and social interaction. Take for example, the following quotation: "Thought in the child is egocentric, i.e., . . . the child thinks for himself without troubling to make himself understood nor to place himself at the other person's point of view. . . . The child feels no need to socialize his thought so he is so little concerned with others [p. 9]."

Piaget suggested that mature communicators were those who had learned that individuals have distinct histories and experiences. Such separate histories made the possibility of communicating meaningful information possible. However, immature communicators were egocentric and thus believed that most interpretations of events were identical and shared. As such, early communicative interchanges were predicted to be marked by private utterances thought to be understood by all potential listeners.

The Piagetian position, when buoyed by early supportive data (mainly from Geneva), led many to accept the position that preoperational children, particularly toddlers and preschoolers, spoke mainly in monologues and collective monologues, rarely ever concerning themselves with their potential playmates. Indeed, percentages of 35–40% of all children's speech being "egocentric" was not a rare finding in the early literature (e.g., Adams, 1932). When combined with early observations that the "normative" patterns of social participation were of a solitary and parallel ilk (Parten, 1932), the psychological assumption drawn was that young children could not engage either in successful conversations or in cooperative play because of their inabilities in perspective-taking. Likewise, observations of the relatively many conflicts and few altruistic acts in early peer interactions lent credence to egocentrism as the causal variable.

The concept of egocentrism gained increased North American interest following the publication of Flavell's (1963) monumental text, *The Developmental Psychology of Jean Piaget*. Researchers, including Flavell himself, began to move away from the conservation and classification studies typical of the time and investigated what some have since labeled the "warmer side of cognition" (Cowan, 1978). Much of this work, designed to understand how children come to comprehend their social environments, involved the study of communicative and role-taking skills. In 1968, Flavell published what became the North American stimulus for the onset of serious research concerning social-cognitive development, *The Development of Role-Taking and Communication Skills in Children*. The central position taken by the author was that in early social encounters, the young child confuses his own perspective with those of his playmates. Such confusion could best be demonstrated in studies of communicative and role-taking development.

In a typical Flavell (1968) experiment, children of different ages were required to explain the rules of simple board games to listeners. The games were taught in a nonverbal fashion to each child. The child was then required to verbally explain the rules of the game to both a sighted and blindfolded adult listener. The results of this study indicated that with increasing age children used more different words and provided more useful and less inadequate game information. Moreover, the older children were able to adapt their communications for the blindfolded listeners; the younger children were not. This and other similar studies are representative of those that have suggested that communicative competence is a function of the ability to take perspectives.

A different approach to the study of communicative skills has been taken by Glucksberg and Krauss (1967). Typically, two people are seated opposite one another at a table but are visually separated by a partition of some sort. One of the subjects serves as "speaker," the other acts as "listener." Both subjects receive a set of unusual shapes or other referents. By manipulating (a) the quality of referents to be communicated; (b) the characteristics of the participants; and (c) by placing restrictions on the opportunities to receive feedback from the listener, a great many features of the communicative process can be explored. Usually, however, research has focused on the encoding-decoding process, where only one person speaks. The speaker describes a referent that is discriminable from a group of nonreferents. The task is to provide the listener with enough verbal information so as to allow the correct selection of the referent.

The Glucksberg and Krauss paradigm, as well as other experimental approaches (e.g., Rosenberg & Cohen, 1966), have been used in countless studies, many of which have had a developmental focus. In general, the research has indicated a performance increment with age (cf., Glucksberg, Krauss, & Higgins, 1975; and Dickson, 1981, for reviews of this literature). That is, young children have been found to be less able to describe referents by using *distinctive features* than are older children (e.g., Rubin, 1973; 1978b). Moreover, when called upon to give the listener more information following initial communicative failure, young children are more likely to repeat the original message or to give no further information than are older children. The strategy of older children appears to be to rephrase the original description or to offer an entirely new description of the referent.

As Asher (1978) has recently noted, these age-graded findings have often been interpreted as reflecting a decline in egocentricity. It is, of course, conceivable that other factors play a role in the reported results. Improvement on referential communication tasks may be due to variables such as improved vocabulary, speaker appreciation of task demands, the ability to make fine-line comparisons between referent and nonreferent stimuli (Asher, 1978). Furthermore, the few studies in which the relationship between performance on perspective-taking and referential communication tasks have been examined report only modest correlations (Rubin, 1973; 1978b).

In summary, early research concerning the development of egocentric speech has revealed that communicative competence improves with age. Such findings emanate not only from early naturalistic work using the Piagetian coefficient of egocentrism, but also from later experimental studies of referential communication. Many psychologists and educators have interpreted the results as indicating the egocentric nature of thought in early childhood. However, alternative explanations abound to the extent that we must now ask whether or not egocentrism is a useful construct for the study of communicative development.

EGOCENTRISM: A USEFUL EXPLANATORY CONSTRUCT?

The belief that egocentrism in childhood is an overblown and not terribly useful psychological phenomenon draws sustenance from both naturalistic and paradigmatic data sources. One valuable example of recent efforts designed to reveal the perspective-taking skills of preschool children is the work of Maratsos (1973). Maratsos required children aged three, four, and five to specify which of two toy figures they would like the experimenter to place in a car for a ride down a hill.

For half of the children the experimenter closed his eyes; for the other half, his eyes remained open. The toy arrays were of three types in that one toy could be distinguished from the other by references to either its shape, color, or position. Responses were scored as adequate under both conditions if they were sufficient to specify the desired toy for a blindfolded listener. Out of 12 possible correct solutions, 3-year-olds provided on the average, 8.50, 4-year-olds 9.00, and 5-year-olds 9.25 adequate responses in the blocked vision condition. When the listener was sighted, the average number of adequate responses for the three age groups was, respectively, 1.00, 3.50, and 5.00. At each age level the difference between conditions was significant. In the blocked vision condition, pointing to the desired object was almost nonexistent, whereas in the sighted condition, pointing was the communicative method of choice for the 3-year-olds, occurring on the average 10.50 times. For the 4- and 5-year-olds, pointing occurred 5.00 and 3.75 times respectively. Hence, Maratsos demonstrated that with a simplified task, very young children were able to adapt the form of their messages to take into account their listener's needs.

The Maratsos study was also important in that it highlighted, for those who study communicative development, the significance of nonverbal means of message sending during the early years. Earlier work on communicative development generally denigrated the use of hand gestures during task performance in experimental settings. Thus, although both Flavell (1968) and Glucksberg and Krauss (1967) made cursory notes concerning the presence of children's pointing and tracing movements during verbal communication, in spite of visual barriers, little attention was paid to the possible importance of these gestures. In fact, gesturing was considered to be another index of the young child's egocentric thought rather than as an index of the ability to cope with a lack of verbal repertoire. It is, however, noteworthy that Evans and Rubin (1979) recently revealed that kindergarteners are as capable as Grade Two and Four children in explaining Flavell-type board games (Flavell, 1968) when allowed to use hand gestures to supplement their verbalizations.

Further laboratory evidence for the nonegocentric manner of conversing in early childhood stems from the often cited work of Shatz and Gelman (1973). These researchers gave 4-½-year-old children a toy to play with and then asked them to explain its workings to a 2-year-old, an adult, and an age-mate. Both the average number of utterances and the mean utterance length decreased with decreasing listener age. Furthermore, subordinate and coordinate clauses were produced more often when conversing with adults, whereas visual attention-getters such as "watch," "look," and "see" were more often used with 2-year-olds. Similar findings that preschoolers do modify their communications in response to the perceived differences of their listeners have been reported by Hoy (1975), Meissner and Apthorp, (1976), Menig-Peterson (1975), Sachs and Devin (1976), and Wellman and Lempers (1977). These studies suggest that task demands and other factors may have masked the social communication skills of young children in the earlier described investigations. Suffice it to say that such studies represent a strong challenge to the Piagetian position concerning the egocentric nature of early communication.

NATURALISTIC STUDIES OF COMMUNICATIVE INTERACTION

In recent years there has been a growing interest in studying how communicative competence develops in the natural setting. This interest has evolved out of the burgeoning work on early social interaction that has indicated that infants purposefully initiate much mother-child interaction (Bell, 1974; Brazelton, Koslowski, & Main, 1974). According to Bruner (1978), many early communicative overtures are clearly manipulative in intent. By 12 months, the infant points to toys and shows objects in an effort to initiate interaction or to solicit desired goods (Rheingold, Hay & West, 1976). Recent observational research has also demonstrated the dialogic markers of joint attention, social orientation and turn-taking in early mother-infant interactions (Bruner, 1975; Bruner, Roy, & Ratner, 1982).

During the toddler period, Dore (1975) has demonstrated that holophrases are expressed in prosodically different ways. Dore found that one-word utterances could be used to ask, to label, and to demand. Thus, intonation as a communicative device was part of the naturalistic repertoire of very young speakers.

Some psychologists have found preschoolers to be communicatively facile on "revised" laboratory paradigms, and others have reported that infants and toddlers are socially oriented; still other researchers are observing preschoolers' speech as it occurs in *naturalistic* settings. As in the infant-mother and the toddler studies cited above, the usual procedure in these latter investigations is to videotape the subjects of study in somewhat control-free activity situations.

Mueller (1972) reported the first study that considered both the degree of egocentrism in children's verbal interactions and the factors that facilitated or impeded social communication. Twenty-four same-sex pairs of previously unacquainted children ranging in age from 3-½ to 5-½ years were observed at free play. Mueller found 62% of all utterances resulted in a related response from the listener. Only 15% of all utterances failed to receive any response; the remaining 23% of the utterances elicited visual attention from the listener. The results were consistent over the age range studied, thus indicating that even the youngest children were successful in receiving replies to their messages. Other studies that have demonstrated that approximately 60% of all preschool naturalistic dyadic speech is socially oriented include those of Garvey and Hogan (1973) and Rubin, Hultsch, and Peters (1971). At this point the reader would do well to note that the Piagetian coefficient of egocentrism, which indicated that approximately 35–40% of children's spontaneous utterances were egocentric (Piaget, 1926), represents the "flip side" of the social speech percentage figures reported more recently. That is, the remaining 60–65% of children's speech in the original Piaget studies was found to be socialized—a figure directly supported by the aforementioned recent investigations.

Mueller also found that the two most powerful predictors of success in gaining a related response to a spoken utterance were listener attention to the speaker and the context of the utterance (i.e., whether or not the utterance was related to something the listener had just said). The two major predictors of failing to gain a related response to a spoken utterance were unclear utterances and grammatically poor utterances. Hence communicative failure could be predicted on the basis of the poor technical quality of the message. In a recent follow-up study, Mueller and his colleagues (Mueller, Bleier, Krakow, Hegedus, & Cournoyer, 1977) have extended the earlier analysis to observations of three 2-year-old boys. The authors found that between 22 and 30 months, the mean percentage of utterances receiving a verbal response from a peer rose from 27 to 64%. Consistent with the earlier findings, the strongest predictor of communicative success was listener attention to the speaker.

Taken together, the results of recent naturalistic studies demonstrate that children as young as two years are able to effectively engage in verbal interaction. However, it is clear from these reports that a significant proportion of all speech in social settings (perhaps as much as one-third) is not well received. Why should this be so? For one, Mueller has indicated that utterances must be accompanied by particular situational markers (e.g., listener attention) to guarantee an appropriate response. Whether or not preschool-aged children are capable of explicitly identifying these markers is not yet known (a prospective study for "meta-communication" students). Perhaps by making such markers more salient to the young child, one could decrease the high proportion of speech that does not result in an appropriate ending.

Situational markers aside, there is at least one other potential explanatory source for the consistent finding that one-third of potentially social speech receives inappropriate responses, and that is the *content* of the utterance or speech unit being analyzed. If the content of an utterance is "egocentered" it may well be appropriate for the listener not to respond to it. For example, young speakers may be more likely than their older counterparts to ask their listeners to carry out acts that they are neither able nor willing (for a variety of reasons) to carry out. At any rate, the Mueller (1972; Mueller et al., 1977) and Garvey and Hogan (1973) coding schemes rest on the assumption that all utterances place an equal demand on the listener for a response, regardless of content and manner of presentation. Perhaps a more appropriate way to study the evolution of communicative and social competence would be to examine particular speech forms that place high demands on listeners for a response. Work in this particular areas has centered mainly on the development of children's requestive skills. We will briefly describe this research below.

THE SPEECH ACT APPROACH

An alternative approach to the study of children's communicative competence is drawn from speech act theory. This approach arose out of the language acquisition research and represents a shift in concern from the structure to the function of language. Speech act theorists have suggested that there exists a set of rules governing all verbal interaction (Austin, 1962; Schegloff, 1968; Searle, 1969). The most basic assumption made is that the unit of verbal interaction is the conversation. A conversation requires the active participation and not just the presence of at least two persons (Schegloff, 1968). One person serves as a speaker, the other as a listener. During a conversation, partners alternate roles. Furthermore, there exists a set of conversational conventions used by the participants. These conventions establish certain expectations for the speaker and place certain obligations on the listener. The conventions include codes of conduct that govern the matching of speech rates of the participants, the regulation of turntaking, the allowed points of interruption, and the audibility of the participants (Jaffe & Feldstein, 1970). Such conventions are thought to be common to *all* forms of dialogue.

There also exist other conventions that are more directly related to particular speech forms. A speaker emitting one of the particular forms fully expects the listener to respond with a specific verbal or nonverbal response. Take, for example, the request for action. This particular speech act has the "meaning intended effect" (Grice, 1969) that the speaker expects the listener to carry out an action. In contrast, an indicative has the meaning intended effect of having the listener think that the speaker believes something.

The developmental study of children's speech acts is a fairly recent phenomenon and it borrows heavily from Austin's (1962) three-way classification system of discourse. First, there are *locutionary acts,* in which the speaker performs the action of saying something, i.e., produces an utterance that has a particular meaning (e.g., "There's dog poo on my lawn" says a 4-year-old to an adult experimenter on the way to the lab). Second, there are *illocutionary acts* in which the speaker performs an act in saying something, i.e., expresses some *intention* (apologizes, promises, commands,—e.g., "I promise, I won't tell on you if you won't tell on me" says one 4-year-old to his playmate as they plan to "escape" from the playroom). In performing an illocutionary act the speaker informs the listener how the utterance is meant to be understood. Finally, there are *perlocutionary acts,* in which the speaker performs an act *through* saying something, i.e., the utterance serves to produce an *effect* in the listener (excitement, fear, pleasure, compliance). The characteristics that apply to any particular utterance vary. A *request for action,* for example, has locutionary, illocutionary, and perlocutionary properties. The utterance, "Close the door" has a particular meaning and expresses a particular intent that may produce the effect of compliance.

5. THE DEVELOPMENT OF REQUESTIVE STRATEGIES 165

The relevant linguistic work that has involved children's illocutionary and perlocutionary acts has primarily focused on the preschooler as speaker. The particular speech act that has undergone thorough investigation is the request for action. Garvey's (1975) work, for example, concerns the understanding of the rules and conventions that control the process of making and responding to requests.

We became interested in children's requests for a number of reasons. First, the request places a high demand on the listener for a response. Studying children's requests would thus be one appropriate way of dealing with our earlier criticism of the Mueller (1972) and Garvey and Hogan (1973) coding schemes, which assumed that all utterances placed an equal demand on the listener for a response. Second, being social developmentalists, we were interested in the sociolinguistic interpretation of the request as a socially oriented behavior (Dore, 1978; Garvey, 1975). To these researchers, the request functions as an attempt by the speaker to solicit behavior from the listener (Searle, 1969).

We were further interested in exploring the request literature beyond the preschool years and by employing more fine-grained statistical analyses than has generally been the case in sociolinguistic work. Heretofore, the majority of research has appeared exploratory and has employed the simple use of descriptive statistics. Furthermore, although this research has generally suggested that preschoolers have the "will" to formulate requests, there have been few data that allow inference as to how skilled and successful their requests are. With these particular interests in mind, we shall presently discuss some of the early work on children's requests that led to our own studies.

Children need to learn to discriminate requests from other speech acts. This does not seem to be an easy task to master since there does not appear to be a one-to-one correspondence between form and function in the English language. An imperative cannot be defined or discriminated on the basis of a single invariant feature. A variety of syntactic constructions may be used to convey the illocutionary force of a request as illustrated below:

(a) "Get me my dolly."
(b) "Can you get me my dolly?"
(c) "You have to get me my dolly."

Conversely, a given syntactic construction can express more than one function. Note that "Can you get me my dolly?", although expressed as an interrogative, generally conveys the force of the imperative, request for action.

To reiterate, there exist alternative forms for expressing requests. It follows that these alternative forms are not necessarily equally salient, and that some requests may be expressed more directly than others. What knowledge does the child have of the relationship between the syntactic meaning of an utterance and its intended meaning? Do children know that "Can you give me the crayon?" is a request rather than an inquiry about ability? Is such an indirect request as easily understood as the more direct request "Give me the crayon"?

Recent sociolinguistic work sheds some light on the answers to the above posed questions. Concerning the ability to *comprehend* question directives, Shatz (1974) reported that for a small sample of young children between the ages of 19 and 28 months, mothers' requests issued in the interrogative were as likely to elicit action responses as those used in the imperative. Shatz (1975), however, has suggested that children of this age have a strong action-response strategy to language. Thus, their appropriate behaviors need not necessarily be attributed to a complex understanding of indirectly expressed intentions.

It is interesting to note that the dominant request form produced by mothers for their young children, up to 12 months of age, is the imperative. Thereafter, however, the proportion of indirect requests to all requests increases monotonically with age (Bellinger, 1977). Bellinger has speculated that mothers modify the form of their requests to keep pace with changes in their assumptions about the children's communicative competencies. Unfortunately, Bellinger did not provide any data concerning children's supposed growing comprehension of question directives.

As for the *production* of varying request forms, Ervin-Tripp (1977) has suggested that children first use simple direct requests such as "Pull truck." By the second half of the third year, children use such indirect request forms as interrogatives and declaratives.

Perhaps the most comprehensive description of the production and understanding of requests in children stems from a study by Garvey (1975). She studied the request for action in 36 free play dyads of children ranging in age from 3–6 to 5–7 years. Garvey reported that the children produced approximately nine times as many direct as indirect requests. Younger dyads used fewer indirect requests than older dyads and they produced slightly more direct requests than the older dyads. Fifty-three percent of all the children's direct requests received a compliant response from the speaker's play partner. Twenty-four percent of the requests were acknowledged but not complied with; the remaining 23% were ignored! Seventy-five percent of the indirect requests were successful in achieving their desired effect. The older dyads produced, on the average, twice as many successful indirect requests as the younger dyads. Thus, Garvey's work has been instrumental in demonstrating that preschool children produce and comprehend both directly and indirectly expressed requests. Furthermore, over the age range studied, there was increased success in using the more complex, indirect requests.

More recently, some sociolinguists, who admittedly have studied very small numbers of children, and who have failed to employ statistical analyses of data, have reported that as early as 4 years of age, children are more likely to utter imperatives to younger children and to produce indirect request forms to older children and adults (Lawson, 1967; Gelman & Shatz, 1977). Moreover, by 4 years, imbedded imperatives appear to be common when acquiring goods, whereas direct imperatives are more usual during behavior control. Interestingly, Lawson (1967) noted that in the home, preschoolers were more likely to employ politeness markers and indirect request forms to fathers than to mothers.

Taken together, the naturalistic observations of children's discursive skills have been interpreted as indicating that not only do preschoolers and toddlers have the *will* to engage others in social interaction, but they are also considerably *skilled* at so doing. At times one is left with the impression that those who have studied the communicative competencies of preschoolers infer that asymptote vis-a-vis these skills has been reached. However, there is presently a lack of data to support this inference. It is our impression that preschoolers are quite capable of perceiving the more salient and familiar conversational constraints (e.g., social status within a dominance hierarchy) and, as a result, often appear to be far from egocentric during peer interaction. However, when the constraints are less salient a breakdown in conversational competence may result. Moreover, when a given communicative attempt falls short, preschoolers may be less able than elementary schoolers to monitor the reasons for failure and thus rectify the situation. It is with these thoughts in mind that we carried out the following study.

STUDY I: THE DEVELOPMENT OF REQUESTIVE SKILLS

The general purpose of Study I was to extend recent work on preschoolers' requestive abilities to include those of elementary schoolers as well. There were five specific concerns. First, we sought to examine whether or not preschoolers were as likely to initiate social interaction through the use of requests for action as were older elementary schoolers. If, as Piaget suggested, preschool-aged children are less concerned with their playmates than older children, one might expect the proportion of requestive utterances to all utterances to be lower in the former than in the latter group. To a degree, the request for action was thus viewed as an index of a *"social will."*

Second, we sought to examine whether or not preschoolers were as likely as their older counterparts to produce alternate request forms. Requests may be expressed directly (as in the imperative) or indirectly (as in the interrogative or declarative). Indirect speech acts have been considered to be more sophisticated, polite, and cognitively complex than direct requests. As a result, we predicted that the relative use of indirect requests would increase with the age of the speaker. Thus, one index of *social communicative skill* was the proportion of indirect requests to all requests produced by each age group.

Third, given the longstanding referential communication data that preschoolers are less likely to have their messages understood than older children

(Glucksberg, Krauss & Higgins, 1975), we predicted that preschoolers would be less skilled at gaining listener comprehension than would elementary schoolers.

Fourth, we were concerned with the success rates of children's requests; that is, the degree to which requests were complied with. We expected that the success rate of requests, our third measure of social communicative skill, would increase with age.

Finally, unlike earlier sociolinguistic reports that simply examined the production of various request forms (Dore, 1978; Ervin-Tripp, 1977) or the success rates of preschoolers' requests (Garvey, 1975), we were interested in the sequence of children's behaviors *following* requestive failure. Lubin and Whiting (1977) had earlier studied the behaviors of children following noncompliance with persuasive appeals. These writers reported that rigidity (use of the same persuasive appeals) in "re-manding" behavior decreased, but flexibility (alternative forms of persuasion) increased with age. Thus, as in Lubin and Whiting, we predicted that following request failures, older children would employ more "flexible" re-request strategies, whereas the younger preschoolers would employ more rigid re-request strategies. The flexible strategy involved rephrasing and modification of the original request, whereas the rigid strategy was characterized as a verbatim repetition or very minor modification of the original. Definitions of these categories are more fully described below.

Our prediction concerning the growth, with age, of flexible strategies following requestive failure is also drawn from the earlier work of Spivack and Shure (1974) and Glucksberg and Krauss (1967). Spivack and Shure have noted that the ability to produce alternative solutions to social problems improves as a function of age. Given that situations in which a child attempts to get what he wants done is representative of "social problems," our prediction appears sensible. Moreover, Glucksberg and Krauss (1967) have characterized the responses of *young* children to the question "Can you tell me anything more about the drawing?" (i.e., can the child provide more information concerning the referential stimulus in their paradigm) as being simply repetitive of the original, whereas those of older children contain modifications or complete rephrasings. These data also appear to provide support for our prediction of greater flexibility and less rigidity in the re-requests of older vs. younger children.

Subjects and Procedures

Sixty children, 10 boys and 10 girls in each of grades preschool, one, and three, participated in the study. The children resided in a moderately large urban community in southwestern Ontario. The older children attended a large elementary school located in a predominantly middle-class neighborhood; the younger children attended the University of Waterloo laboratory preschool. The mean ages of the preschool, first- and third-grade children were 53.95 months ($SD = 6.47$), 78.10 months ($SD = 3.82$), and 106.20 months ($SD = 4.19$) respectively.

Within each grade, same sex, familiar children were paired into dyads. The dyads were brought to a playroom by one of two familiar female experimenters. The children were then invited to play with the toys in the room, were told that a camera would be taking pictures of them, and were then left alone.

Each dyad was individually observed in the playroom, which was located either in a mobile trailer at the elementary school or in a similarly sized room in the preschool. The playrooms were furnished with a table and two chairs, a carpet, and curtains at the sides of the one-way mirror. The toys included a bowling game, puppets, crayons, coloring books and paper, activity books and comics, a "lego" set, and puzzles.

The play sessions were recorded on videotape through the observation window. Each session was filmed for 12 minutes and subsequently a verbatim transcript was prepared for each dyad by the two female experimenters. Disagreements were resolved through multiple viewings of the tapes. All analyses were based on the transcripts used in conjunction with the videotapes where necessary.

Coding of Data

Each child's speech was originally coded into utterance units (UUs), defined as "stretches of one person's speech separated by pauses greater than one second or by another person's speech" (Garvey & Hogan, 1973). These UUs were counted for each member of the dyad. The number of words spoken and the mean number of words per UU were determined for each member of the dyad. The individual rate of UU was calculated by dividing the number of seconds in the session by the individual's total number of UUs. The average number of UUs per dyad and the rate of UU for the dyad were also calculated.

The type of utterance of primary interest was the request. Only well-formed requests were considered in this study. Thus requests muttered to the self or addressed to a toy were excluded, as in Garvey (1975). Requests were classified as follows:

Direct requests. This category included requests expressed in the imperative (e.g., "Give me the crayon").

Indirect requests.
(a) *interrogatives*—requests expressed in interrogative form (e.g., "Can you give me the crayon?"; "How about lending me your scissors?").
(b) *declaratives*—requests expressed in the declarative form (e.g., "You have to give me the crayon").
(c) *inferred requests*—Both Garvey (1975) and Ervin-Tripp (1974) have noted that adults, and less often, children, may use subtle means of requesting, in which what the listener has to do is not specified. Here no imperative (e.g.,

"Give me the crayon") is embedded in the larger linguistic context as it is in the above categories of indirect requests. This type of utterance may be considered a request, however, because it fulfills the essential condition that the speaker wants the listener to do something (e.g., "The crayons should be in the box," meaning "Put the crayons in the box").

Once the children's requests were coded as above, their consequences were classified as follows:

Successes. (SV) appropriate response accompanied by verbal behavior; (S) appropriate response unaccompanied by verbal behavior.

Acknowledgments. (A) verbal or nonverbal acknowledgment that a request has been made but not accompanied by the appropriate behavior and/or further query concerning request.

Failures. (FR) refusal to comply with the request; (NR) no response or unrelated response.

The third data preparation stage involved coding the ensuing interaction of those requests that originally met with failure. Only the *first* re-request strategy of the speaker was considered in our coding scheme. Four categories of re-request strategies were coded. A *rigid* strategy consisted either of a verbatim repetition of the original request or of a minor modification (e.g., "Give me a crayon" = verbatim repetition). A *flexible* re-request strategy meant a rephrasing of the original request and may have involved a change from a direct to an indirect form or vice versa (e.g., "Can I have the green crayon now?"). The third category included remarks requesting *clarification* of the listener's reply. The fourth category, which we simply termed *"other alternative responses,"* included performing the requested act by the self, failure to re-request (give up), and changes of topic of conversation.

Reliability. Six full transcripts were given to a second coder in order to assess inter-rater reliability. Percentages of agreement were calculated by dividing the number of rater agreements by the number of rater agreements plus the number of both rater's disagreements. These computations were carried out for the initial classification of requests, the consequences of requests, and the re-request strategies employed following failure. Percentages of agreement for each of these classifications were 84%, 89%, and 92% respectively.

Results: General Linguistic Data

Table 5.1 presents the means and standard deviations for the number of utterances, the rate of utterance, the number of words and the number of words per utterance for each of the grade levels. A series of one-way (grade) ANOVAs

TABLE 5.1
Means and Standard Deviations for the General Linguistic Data

	Grade					
	Preschool		1		3	
	M	SD	M	SD	M	SD
#UU[1]	84.20	24.24	117.85	42.11	132.35	38.13
Sec. per UU	9.11	2.61	7.22	3.75	6.01	2.03
#Words	339.70	128.09	496.65	211.28	525.85	207.12
Words/UU	3.89	0.79	4.16	0.60	3.86	0.65

Note: n = 20 for each group
[1]UU = utterance unit

were carried out for each of the above variables. A significant grade effect was found for the number of utterances, $F(2,57) = 9.60$, $p < .0003$. A follow-up LSD analysis showed that preschoolers produced significantly ($p < .05$) fewer utterances than children in Grades One and Three. A significant grade effect was found for the rate of utterance, $F(2,57) = 5.85$, $p < .005$. A LSD post hoc analysis indicated that the utterance rate was significantly ($p < .05$) lower for the preschoolers than for the elementary schoolers. That is, preschoolers produced, on the average, one utterance every 9.11 seconds whereas Grades One and Three children produced, on the average, one utterance every 7.22 and 6.01 seconds respectively. A significant grade effect was also found for the total number of words spoken, $F(2,57) = 5.79$, $p < .005$, but there was no effect for the number of words per utterance. Again, a post hoc LSD analysis revealed a significantly ($p < .05$) lower number of words for the preschoolers than for the children in Grades One and Three.

Results: Direct and Indirect Requests

Means and standard deviations for all categories of requests are presented in Table 5.2. The number of requests produced by the children was substantial. Preschoolers and Grades One and Three children produced totals of 206, 236, and 378 requests respectively. One-way (grade) ANOVAs were calculated for direct, indirect, and total requests. All indirect request categories were pooled as there were too few data within the cells to make meaningful analyses possible. Although the older children produced a greater number of requests, they also tended to speak more. Thus, analyses were carried out on proportional data. ANOVAs indicated that the proportion of total requests to the total number of UUs did not vary across the age groups. Similar nonsignificant results were found for the proportions of direct and indirect requests to all UUs.

TABLE 5.2
Means and Standard Deviations of the Requests for Action

	Grade					
	Preschool		1		3	
Speech Act	M	SD	M	SD	M	SD
Direct Requests	8.15	5.48	9.50	6.99	15.30	11.24
Indirect Requests	2.15	1.93	2.30	2.52	3.60	2.64
a - interrogatives	0.45	0.58	0.95	0.74	0.95	0.83
b - declaratives	1.25	1.68	0.85	1.35	1.30	1.69
c - inferred	0.45	0.99	0.50	0.89	1.35	1.63
Total Requests	10.30	6.96	11.80	7.37	18.90	12.26

Note: n = 20 for each group

It should be noted that the ANOVAs were calculated for both individual subject and dyadic data for each speech act variable of interest. The results from both sets of analyses were essentially identical.

Results: Success and Failure of Requests

Table 5.3 presents the percentages for the total number of requests of each type that had a given consequence. In order to carry out inferential statistical analyses, the following computations were made. First, percentages of success, acknowledgment, and failure responses to the different request forms were calculated *for each child*. For example, if a child emitted 10 direct requests, 3 of which led to "success" responses, the percentage of such responses was 30%. Second, once these response percentages were calculated for each child, they were summed and divided by the number of children in the grade, thus giving a mean percentage for each group.

Since earlier analyses indicated differences between ANOVA results for individual vs. dyad data to be nonexistent, all subsequent analyses were carried out using individual data. A series of one-way ANOVAs (grade) was computed for direct, indirect, and the total number of requests followed by the success (SV + S) acknowledgment (A), and failure (FR + NR) categories. Significant grade effects were found for the number of direct requests followed by both success, $F(2,57) = 5.37$, $p < .01$, and failure, $F(2,57) = 4.82$, $p < .01$. Post hoc *LSD* comparisons indicated that Grade Three children obtained significantly more success outcomes ($p < .01$) to their requests than did preschoolers. Preschoolers met with significantly more failures than children in both elementary school groups.

Whereas nonsignificant differences were found for the consequences of indirect requests, grade effects were discovered for the *total* number of requests followed by success, $F(2,57) = 4.65$, $p < .01$, and failure, $F(2,57) = 3.69$, $p < .03$. Post hoc *LSD* comparisons ($p < .01$) showed that preschoolers received fewer success responses and more failure responses to their requests than did Grades One and Three children.

Finally, grade differences in showing some awareness that a request had been made (or that the request had achieved its intended illocutionary effect) appeared to be next to nil. Awareness of a request's intended effects was indicated by a listener response in any category other than *NR*. Thus refusals to comply (FR), acknowledgments (A) and compliances (S, SV) were taken as indices that the listener had understood the utterance to be a request. Preschool and Grades One and Three children indicated awareness or understood 67.32, 68.78, and 72.10 percent of the total number of requests respectively.

TABLE 5.3
Percentage of Success, Acknowledgement and Failure Responses to Requests

	Success[1]		Acknowledgement[1]	Failure[1]		Total n[2]
	SV	S	A	FR	NR	
Direct Requests						
Preschool	5.56	39.51	11.11	10.49	33.33	163
Grade 1	11.58	35.79	8.95	9.47	34.21	190
Grade 3	20.62	39.86	7.56	3.78	28.18	306
Indirect Requests						
Preschool	16.28	20.93	16.28	16.28	30.23	43
Grade 1	17.02	19.15	19.15	25.53	19.15	46
Grade 3	23.94	19.72	15.49	14.08	26.76	72
Total Requests						
Preschool	7.80	35.61	12.20	11.71	32.68	206
Grade 1	12.66	32.49	10.97	12.66	31.22	236
Grade 3	21.27	35.91	9.11	5.80	27.90	378

[1]Figures refer to percentage of the total number of a particular speech act which had a given consequence.
[2]Total n = total number of utterances of a given speech act

Strategies Following Noncompliance with Requests

The most meaningful approach in handling the re-request data appeared to be a simple descriptive analysis. Although inferential statistical analyses were initially viewed as preferable, the corpus of data left too many empty cells to have allowed productive interpretation. The numbers of initial requests that met with failure were 64, 76, and 93 for the preschoolers and Grades One and Three children respectively. Of these numbers, the percentages of re-requests which were *rigid* (i.e., those requests that were verbatim repetitions or minor modifications of the original) were 31.3, 18.4, and 8.6 for the three groups respectively. An additional 17.2%, 22.4%, and 29.0% respectively were *flexible* re-requests by the preschoolers and Grades One and Three children. *Clarifications* of listeners' replies occurred for only 1.6%, 0%, and 1.1% of the three age groups' re-requests respectively. The remaining 49.9%, 59.2% and 61.3% of the acts following initial request failure were *other alternative responses* for the preschool and Grades One and Three children respectively.

Discussion

The major purpose of Study I was to investigate the development of children's abilities to convey requests during naturalistic communicative encounters. The production of verbal behavior during the dyadic sessions was substantial and unlike earlier research on discourse processes (e.g., Dore 1977; Garvey 1975), the cross-sectional methodology allowed for the calculation of inferential statistics.

Preliminary analyses generally revealed that the number and rate of Utterance Units (UU) produced by the children increased with age. Concerning the rate of UU, preschoolers produced, on the average, one UU every 9.11 seconds, a figure strikingly similar to that reported by Mueller (1972). The preschool data were also consistent with those of Garvey and Hogan (1973), who found that the overall rate of UU for preschool dyads was one UU per 4.6 seconds. The dyad rate found herein was one UU per 4.56 seconds.

It was initially postulated that the proportion of requests to the total number of utterance units produced would increase with age. Such a finding would have provided support for the traditional assumption that preschoolers are less willing to engage their colleagues in conversation and action than are their older counterparts (Parten, 1932; Piaget, 1926). Although the mean number of requests increased with age, analyses revealed that the proportion of requests to the total number of utterances produced was not significantly different across age groups. Preschoolers were seemingly as socially oriented as their older, elementary school-aged counterparts. These data support the recent work of Goldman and Ross (1978) and Garvey (1977), who suggest that young children are far more socially oriented than previously thought.

Although social orientation, or the *will* to engage another in conversation or action, may not increase with age, an analysis of the *skill* with which directives are produced could conceivably follow a different developmental course. For example, Ervin-Tripp (1977), and Garvey (1975) have found that the use of indirect requests increases with age, at least for preschool and kindergarten-aged samples. Such an increase may be taken to indicate that children become better able to distinguish between the literal and intended meanings of indirect requests with age. Moreover, the increase may be accompanied by the child's greater skill in predicting the behavioral outcome of a request, given its particular form of presentation. For example, with age children may come to predict that listeners will be more likely to comply with polite-indirect ("Can you give me that truck?") rather than with autocratic-direct ("Give me that truck") requests. However, contrary to our prediction, the proportion of indirect requests was invariant across age, accounting for 20% of the total number of requests emitted. In short, preschoolers appeared to be as able as elementary schoolers to produce alternative verbal means by which to initially solicit a listener to perform an act. These data suggest one of two possible interpretations. First, it may be that preschoolers are, to some degree, able to consider or predict their listeners' reactions to the form of requests employed. As such, the use of indirect requests by preschoolers may be a marker of the ability to infer that a listener may think or feel more negatively about being on the receiving end of a command vs. a question-directive.

On the other hand, the use of indirect requests by preschoolers may reflect the degree to which certain conversational or social conventions have become "scripted" (Nelson & Gruendel, 1979). Thus, with experience the young child may come to develop a social rule that "one speaks in certain ways to some people and in other ways to others." Categorization of the listener as an adult or "older kid" may activate scripts or social conventions for appropriate speech styles that differ from those scripts or conventions deemed appropriate when the listener is a younger child (Higgins, 1981). As an example, James (1975) has reported that direct requests are more frequently addressed to younger listeners, whereas indirect forms are more frequently addressed to older playmates. The choice of one speech form over another may have less to do with the ability to infer a listener's needs, thoughts, or emotions and more to do with the simple activation of appropriate social scripts. In Study II, which follows below, the degree to which perspective-taking skills do relate to the production of various request forms is examined.

While the abilities to produce alternative request forms and to distinguish surface from intended meanings may be taken to mean that preschoolers do have fairly sophisticated discursive repertoires, two additional social *skill* markers must be considered in any discussion of communicative *competence*. The first marker is simply the degree to which the request has reached its intended perlocutionary effect. Making requests would certainly not prove profitable unless they were complied with. One criterion necessary to assure a successful outcome requires that the listener be aware that a request has been made. The listener could indicate this awareness not only be responding appropriately but also by acknowledging or by refusing to comply with the directive. Approximately 70% of the requests made by the children in each grade were successful in achieving their intended illocutionary effects. This figure was similar for both direct and indirect request forms. Given that the listeners in each grade appeared to be comprehending their play partners' requests with equal facility, it is noteworthy that the Grade Three children received more compliance with their direct requests than did the preschoolers. Moreover, preschoolers conveyed proportionally more direct requests followed by noncompliance than did the two elementary school-aged groups. Although age differences were not found for indirect requests, results for the sum of direct and indirect requests mirrored those for direct requests with the additional discovery that Grade One children produced more successful directives that preschoolers.

Borrowing from the social-cognitive model of Selman (1976), the above findings may be tentatively interpreted as follows. All age groups were equally oriented toward peer interaction, thereby supporting recent work concerned with the social nature of young children's *behavior*. These data, however, do not speak to the issue of egocentered as opposed to sociocentered *thought*. The age differences found concerning the relative success of requests and the strategies produced following initial requestive failure may, however, reflect varying perspective-taking or social inferential skills.

It is conceivable, for example, that the lesser success of the preschoolers can be attributed to poorer skills at considering the less salient, covert properties of their listeners when issuing directives, thereby reducing the power of their requests. Thus, while ascertaining that their messages could be understood, preschoolers may nevertheless have failed to distinguish what it was *they* wanted done and what their listeners were willing or able to do. As Flavell (1976) puts it, "the younger speaker does not predict what her message will do to the listener's head."

Furthermore, when listener feedback was negative (e.g., a "failed request"), preschool speakers may not have been able to adequately monitor the reasons for failure and thus often came back "rigidly" with the same request as that originally delivered. Again, as Flavell (1976) writes, the young child "does little or no thinking about the message, about the cognitive experiences or interpretations the message may stimulate, or about possible relationships between message and interpretations. As an example, he does not have the metacognition that the message as it stands . . . could be interpreted in more than one way."

The above explanations for the lesser success and greater "rigidity" of the preschoolers vis-a-vis requestive competence may be indicative of what Selman (1976) has labeled the level of "social-informational perspective-taking." Such a level of skill allows the child to consider such salient social information as age, sex, or dominance status of social partners. However, it does not allow the inference that the social partner can make inferences about the child's own thoughts or feelings (or in this case, the content of the speaker's utterances) while he or she is simultaneously engaged in the same inferential process concerning the partner.

By Grade Three, Selman's model would predict that children should begin to anticipate their listeners' reactions to a speaker's own motives or purposes. Moreover, by this age, the ability to monitor messages in order to consider why they have failed should enter the communicative repertoire. Such skills, which have been labeled "self-reflective perspective-taking" (Selman, 1976) may be predictive of re-request flexibility during middle childhood.

In summary, we are suggesting that the ability to perspective-take accounts for a significant proportion of the variance in the development of communicative competency. Given that perspective-taking is not an "all or none" phenomenon (Rubin & Pepler, 1980), we suggest that children must at least be able to consider the salient characteristics of their listeners in order to competently vary their requests when attempting to solicit action from others.

In Study II, the relationships are probed between laboratory indices of social-informational perspective-taking in preschoolers and of self-reflective perspective-taking in Grade Three children and (at both age levels) naturalistic communicative skill. This marks, for the first time, a direct assessment of the relationship between role-taking and naturalistic communicative competence.

STUDY II: THE RELATIONSHIP BETWEEN PERSPECTIVE-TAKING AND REQUESTIVE SKILLS

Although linguists such as Grice (1969) have noted that competent conversationalists must choose messages appropriate to suit their listeners' states of affect and knowledge, there have been few direct empirical studies linking role-taking to conversational competence. Instead, the recent interpretive strategy has been to examine naturalistic child discourse and to infer the presence or absence of perspective-taking skills from the corpus of data. For example, Garvey and Hogan (1973) noted that approximately 60% of preschoolers' utterances emitted during dyadic free play were followed by an appropriate listener response. Shatz and Gelman (1973) and others have indicated that preschoolers are able to adapt their messages to suit the perceived needs of their listeners. These results have been taken by some to indicate the existence of early perspective-taking skills in preschool-aged children. Accordingly, the purpose of the present study was to examine the relationships between children's performances on independent, laboratory measures of role-taking and indices of their discursive competence in a dyadic, free play setting.

It has also been suggested that perspective-taking accounts for some of the variance on laboratory communication tasks. For example Rubin (1978b) has found moderate correlations between performance on a variety of role-taking tasks and on the Glucksberg and Krauss (1967) referential communication paradigm. There are, as yet, no data that link performance on paradigmatic communicative measures to naturalistic communication skills. Thus, a second purpose of this study was to do just that.

A first prediction (1) was that the use of indirect requests by preschool-aged children may reflect an elementary level of perspective-taking skill. Therefore, we predicted that preschool performance on a measure of "social-informational perspective-taking" would positively correlate with the ability to produce indirect requests. Moreover, since a case was made for assuming the significance of perspective-taking in gaining requestive compliance and with modifying initial request strategies following noncompliance, it was predicted that role-taking would positively correlate with preschool requestive success and with the production of flexible re-request strategies. Negative correlations were predicted between the social-cognition measures and the use of rigid re-request strategies and with self-solutions. (2) It was predicted also that performance on a paradigmatic communication task would likewise correlate with the aforementioned discourse variables. (3) For Grade Three children, it was hypothesized that performance in a more difficult task, a measure of "self-reflective perspective-taking," would correlate with the ability to gain requestive success. A positive correlation was predicted between the flexible re-request strategy and perspective-taking. Alternatively, a negative correlation was predicted to exist between the ability to perspective-take and the use of rigid re-request strategies and with self-solutions. (4) Finally, it was hypothesized that performance on a paradigmatic communicative test would likewise correlate with the above naturalistic discourse variables.

Method

The subjects included 18 of the preschoolers and all of the Grade Three children who participated in Study I. Two of the preschoolers were unavailable for testing on the laboratory measures.

The indices of naturalistic discursive skill were those described in Study I. The preschoolers were individually administered the DeVries (1970) "Hide the penny game." The experimenter and child took turns hiding a coin in one of his or her hands. Each child was scored according to the recursive thought, role-taking criteria described at length in DeVries (1970). Note was taken as to whether the children attempted to play the game and whether they did so competitively. The maximum score was 10.

The Grade Three children were administered Chandler's (1973) cognitive perspective-taking task. This measure first required each child to describe a story presented in an eight-picture cartoon sequence and then to retell the story from the perspective of a bystander who enters the sequence late and without knowledge of the preceding events. Four of Chandler's cartoon sequences were employed. These were the snowman, coin, kite, and sandcastle stories. The scoring procedure was taken directly from Chandler (1973). Scores ranged from 4, for which a child would explicitly attribute to the bystander knowledge legitimately available only to himself or herself, to 0, for which a child would clearly distinguish between privileged information known only to the self and facts available to the story characters whose role the child was able to assume.

Finally, the Glucksberg and Krauss (1967) referential communication task was given to all children. This task required the child to communicate descriptive information concerning six novel, low-encodable graphic designs to the experimenter. The listener, who could not be seen by the speaker, had the task of selecting one of the novel figures from the total set on the basis of the verbal message conveyed by the speaker. A recommunicative score, obtained when the experimenter asked the subject for additional information following an initial description, served as the dependent measure. A 0 was accorded a silence, a 1 was given for a repetition of the first description, a 2 was given for a modification of the first description, and a 3 was scored following a completely new, appropriate description.

Results

For preschoolers, the DeVries role-taking measure was significantly related (one-tailed, $df = 17$ for all preschool correlations; all r's are Pearson product-moment correlations) to the proportion of indirect requests to all utterances, $r = .43, p < .03$. This measure was also related to the proportion of successful direct requests accompanied by listener verbal behavior, $r = .47, p < .02$, as well as to the proportion of indirect requests followed by no response, $r = .65, p < .001$. This latter, surprising finding, is discussed below.

The Glucksberg and Krauss task for preschoolers was significantly correlated with the proportion of indirect requests to all utterances, $r = .51, p < .02$. In addition, significant correlations were found for the proportion of requests followed by appropriate responses accompanied by verbal behavior to all requests, $r = .43, p < .03$; the proportion of *direct* requests followed by appropriate responses accompanied by verbal behavior to all direct requests, $r = .42, p < .04$; and for the proportion of indirect requests followed by no response to all indirect requests, $r = .40, p < .05$. Performance on the Glucksberg and Krauss paradigm was also correlated with the use of re-request strategies other than rigid or flexible re-requests, $r = -.43, p < .03$.

For the Grade Three children, performance on the Chandler task was not significantly correlated with any of the measures of interest. The Glucksberg and Krauss measure was related to the proportion of indirect requests followed by appropriate responses accompanied by verbal behavior to all indirect requests, $r = .54, p < .001$ ($df = 19$, one-tailed).

Discussion

The purpose of Study II was to investigate the relationships between commonly used laboratory indices of perspective-taking and communicative skill and measures of communicative competence. Researchers have recently inferred the existence of perspective-taking skills from examinations of discourse. However, empirical support for such inferences has been heretofore nonexistent.

The results of Study II provided limited support for the hypothesized link between role-taking and preschoolers' abilities to produce a variety of request forms. Both the DeVries and Glucksberg and Krauss ($G-K$) tests were positively related to the production of indirect request forms. Because the imperative is generally acquired first (Ervin-Tripp, 1977) it may be suggested that the speaker who employs indirect requests does so purposely. Rationale for such usage may be knowledge that a little kindness, politeness, or tact may go a long way in reaching a desired goal via a listener. Children of preschool age appear able to realize that others may think and feel more positively about indirectly phrased solicitations. Unfortunately, it may also be the case that preschoolers are unable to simultaneously consider both listener affect and their cognitive, comprehensive skills. The former is a more salient, overt phenomenon; the latter are more covert in nature. As such, the speaker's well intended production of indirect requests may not be understood by her or his young listener. This might explain the *positive* relationship between the DeVries role-taking measure (and the $G-K$ measure as well) and the production of *indirect* requests followed by *no response*.

The hypothesis relating role-taking to the production of successful requests was partially supported by the findings that both the role-taking and communication ($G-K$) measures were positively related to the production of successful *direct* requests accompanied by appropriate listener verbalization. The laboratory communication test was also positively related to the production of successful requests of both forms (direct and indirect) accompanied by appropriate listener verbalization.

The only preschool re-request strategy that had sufficient numbers of responses to allow meaningful correlational analysis was the "other alternative responses" category. Communication scores on the $G-K$ task were *negatively* related to the speaker's choice of this strategy. That is, the better laboratory referential communicator appeared less likely to have to resort to self-solutions following request failure than did the poor communicator.

It bears noting, at this point, that in an earlier study, Rubin (1978a) found that preschool performance on the DeVries and Glucksberg-Krauss tasks correlated positively with a number of Garvey and Hogan's (1973) categories of speaker utterance consequence. For example, both measures correlated with speaker skill in producing utterances that were followed by appropriate listener behaviors. The DeVries task also correlated *negatively* with the production of utterances that were followed by unrelated listener speech. Taken together with the present data, the results suggest that the ability of preschoolers to perspective-take does account for some, albeit limited, proportion of the variance in naturalistic communicative endeavors.

The Grade Three data did not turn out quite as orderly as the preschool data. For one, the Chandler measure did not correlate significantly with any of the naturalistic communication variables. The lack of correlations with the ability to produce indirect requests may simply be attributed to a ceiling effect with regard to the production of varying request forms by Grade Three. However, failure to find correlations with re-request flexibility appears much more problematic. Perhaps the results may best be explained by recent findings that have questioned the reliability and validity of the Chandler measure (Kurdek, 1977; Rubin, 1978b). Unfortunately, at the time of data collection, we were unaware of these psychometric problems.

The general absence of correlations (one significant) between the $G-K$ task and naturalistic discourse is a little more difficult to explain. After all, the $G-K$ measure is itself an index of communicative competence. Moreover, the recommunication score that is calculated when a listener asks the speaker for more information about the given referent is similar to the coding of re-request flexibility. In both the paradigmatic and naturalistic data bases, communicative competence is scored by examining whether the speaker: (a) provides no further information; (b) repeats the original statement; or (c) modifies the original statement. Furthermore, both situations appear to place similar demands on the speaker. Thus, for both the laboratory and naturalistic assessments of communicative competence, it would appear as if the speaker who receives negative feedback from his or her listener (e.g., *Glucksberg & Krauss* = "I can't get it. Can you tell me more about the picture?"; *naturalistic* = no response or rejection of request by its recipient) would have to ascertain why it was that the original message/request failed. The child would, for example, have to monitor the original message in an effort to discover whether the description/request was too difficult to comprehend or whether it may have been unreasonable to expect that the listener would provide the anticipated response. Given the monitoring exercise, the speaker, in both the laboratory and natural situation, would have to decide how next to proceed; e.g., "Should I repeat the original statement or should I modify it? Perhaps I should give up." In short, both forms of communicative tasks bore strong similarities vis-a-vis their task demands.

Perhaps it may be that those processes that *account for success* on the laboratory task (e.g., the ability to compare referent vs. nonreferent stimuli; the ability to produce a message for an adult that is dependent upon verbal repertoire alone) are not similar to those that account for communicative success with peers in the natural dyadic setting—at least for Grade Three children. They may, however, be important for preschoolers. At any rate, we are admittedly hard pressed to come up with a satisfactory explanation for the present findings.

GENERAL DISCUSSION

In summary, we have shown that perspective-taking and the ability to communicate referentially (which itself may involve perspective-taking) do, to some extent, predict naturalistic communicative competence in *preschoolers*. We are, as yet, unclear as to the direction of causality. We are, however, quite clear that laboratory indices of perspective-taking, in and of themselves, do not satisfactorily account for a large chunk of the variance in the conversational competence equation for either preschoolers or elementary schoolers. On the face of it, our data are problematic for those who have inferred the ability to role-take from observations of communicative competence in preschoolers (Garvey & Hogan, 1973; Sachs & Devin, 1975).

Perhaps, as Higgins (1981) has suggested, role-taking is not a necessary precondition for effective communication. This hard-line, anti-Piagetian (and anti-sociolinguistic) interpretation has been presented as follows. Consider the Shatz and Gelman (1973) finding that 4-year-olds' descriptions of how to play with a toy are shorter and simpler when their listeners are 2-year-olds than when they are adults. Higgins claims that such speech behavior is learned as appropriate when talking, not only to younger children, but also when talking to dogs, cats, or dolls (e.g., Sachs & Devin, 1976, studied preschoolers' speech to a doll). Because one does not generally infer the thoughts or emotions of animals or inanimate objects during play or interaction, the "role-taking as necessary for communicative competence" argument does not hold water. Instead, Higgins suggests that children categorize their listeners and that these categorizations activate rules (or social-cognitive scripts) for appropriate speech styles without role-taking being required.

There is, of course, the counterargument that role-taking *is* involved in the communicative process and that the lack of strong correlations reported herein is basically the result of faulty laboratory assessment procedures. Rubin and Pepler (1980) have recently suggested that an alternative strategy for the investigation of the development of perspective-taking skills is to search for specific naturalistic behaviors that match, level-by-level, with extant theoretical models (stages) of role-taking. Given this content analysis approach, one may be able to infer perspective-taking skills from naturalistic behaviors. Rubin and Pepler considered various forms of children's play and were able to match these forms to particular levels of Selman's (1976) perspective-taking model. For example, children in the "self-reflective perspective-taking" stage are able to note that others think or feel differently from the self. Moreover, they can take a "second person" perspective by thinking that, e.g., "He is thinking of me in such a way." The child, at this level, cannot, however, make inferences about the self and the other simultaneously or mutually, but only sequentially. Thus, she or he cannot step "outside" the dyadic situation and "view" it from the perspective of a third person. Rubin and Pepler (1980) point out that the simple, competitive game with rules that is typical of children between the ages of six and eight are representative of the "self-reflective" level of role-taking. The competitive games of this age group generally do not have ultimate or fixed winners. The sides or roles chosen for these games are transitory and winning is episodic. Games like hide-and-seek, frozen tag, and dodge ball all necessitate an understanding of reciprocity and role-reversibility, both of which are "self-reflective" skills. However, one need not *simultaneously* consider points of view from the third person perspective (the next highest perspective-taking stage) to engage in such early competitive games. One is only required to keep in mind that "When you are it, I have to flee or hide," and "When I am it, you have to flee or hide." The games played by older children, on the other hand, require strategies based on recursive thought ("If I do this, she or he will do that, so I will . . ."). Such skills appear necessary for games like chess, which is probably reflective of the "simultaneous, mutual role-taking" level (Selman, 1976).

The precise analysis of childhood behaviors may thus allow us to make more reasonable statements concerning the cognitive prerequisites or accompaniments of those behaviors. Instead of simply inferring that the production of various request forms (which may or may not be successful) necessitates perspective-taking skills, it may be preferable to carefully examine the *content* of children's messages. From the examination of request content one may then be able to attribute certain communicative skills to perspective-taking and other skills to other cognitive abilities (cognitive monitoring). As examples, it may be that requestive success is contingent upon factors such as the clarity of the speaker's utterance; the reasonableness of the request from the listener's viewpoint; the use of attention-getting devices; the use of object-oriented ("Give me the ball.") versus person-oriented ("Come here.") requests; the employment of requests that take the form of protests, permissives, suggestions; the perceived beneficiary of the request (speaker, listener, both); and so on. Thus, examination of the interaction between *what* children say to one another, and *how* they say it may provide us with a naturalistic index of those cognitive and social-cognitive skills necessary for competent communication. To this end, we are now in the process of returning to our original transcripts to examine the "hows" and "whats" of children's requests.

REFERENCES

Adams, S. A study of the growth of language between two and four years. *Journal of Juvenile Research,* 1932, *16,* 269–277.

Asher, S. R. Referential communication. In G. J. Whitehurst & B. J. Zimmerman (Eds.), *The function of language and cognition.* New York: Academic Press, 1978.

Austin, J. L. *How to do things with words.* Cambridge: Harvard University Press, 1962.

Bell, R. Q. Contributions of human infants to caregiving and social interaction. In M. Lewis & L. A. Rosenblum (Eds.), *The effect of the infant on its caregiver.* New York: Wiley, 1974.

Bellinger, D. *The pragmatic structure of mothers' directives*. Paper presented at the biennial meeting of the Society for Research in Child Development, New Orleans, March 1977.
Brazelton, T. B., Kowslowski, B., & Main, M. The origins of reciprocity: The early mother-infant interaction. In M. Lewis & L. A. Rosenblum (Eds.), *The effect of the infant on its caregiver*. New York: Wiley, 1974.
Bruner, J. The ontogenesis of speech acts. *Journal of Child Language*, 1975, *2*, 1–19.
Bruner, J. S. Acquiring the uses of language. *Canadian Journal of Psychology*, 1978, *32*, 204–218.
Bruner, J., Roy, C., & Ratner, N. The beginnings of request. In K. E. Nelson (Ed.), *Children's Language, vol. 3*. Hillsdale, N.J.: Lawrence Erlbaum Associates, 1982.
Chandler, M. Egocentrism and anti-social behavior: The assessment and training of social perspective-taking skills. *Developmental Psychology*, 1973, *9*, 326–332.
Cowan, P. A. *Piaget with feeling*. New York: Holt, Rinehart, & Winston, 1978.
DeVries, R. The development of role-taking as reflected by the behavior of bright, average, and retarded children in a social guessing game. *Child Development*, 1970, *41*, 759–770.
Dickson, W. P. Referential communication activities in research and in the curriculum: A meta-analysis. In W. P. Dickson (Ed.), *Children's oral communication skills*. New York: Academic Press, 1981.
Dore, J. Holophrases, speech acts and language universals. *Journal of Child Language*, 1975, *2*, 21–40.
Dore, J. Children's illocutionary acts. In R. O. Freedle (Ed.), *Discourse production and comprehension*. Norwood, N.J.: Ablex, 1977.
Dore, J. Variation in preschool children's conversational performances. In K. E. Nelson (Ed.), *Children's Language*, (Vol. 1). New York: Gardner Press, 1978.
Ervin-Tripp, S. "Wait for me Roller Skate!" In S. Ervin-Tripp and C. Mitchell-Kernan (Eds.), *Child Discourse*. New York: Academic Press, 1977.
Evans, M. A. & Rubin, K. H. Hand gestures as a communicative mode in school-aged children. *Journal of Genetic Psychology*, 1979, *135*, 189–196.
Flavell, J. H. *The developmental psychology of Jean Piaget*. Princeton, N.J. Van Nostrand, 1963.
Flavell, J. H. *The development of role-taking and communication skills in children*. New York: Wiley, 1968.
Flavell, J. H. *The development of metacommunication*. Paper presented at the Symposium on Language and Cognition, Twenty-first International Congress of Psychology, 1976.
Garvey, C. Requests and responses in children's speech. *Journal of Child Language*, 1975, *2*, 41–63.
Garvey, C. *Play*. Cambridge: Harvard University Press, 1977.
Garvey, C. & Hogan, R. Social speech and social interaction: Egocentrism revisited. *Child Development*, 1973, *44*, 562–568.
Gelman, R. & Shatz, M. Appropriate speech adjustments: The operation of conversational constraints on talk to two-year-olds. In M. Lewis & L. A. Rosenblum (Eds.), *Interaction, conversation, and the development of language*. New York: Wiley, 1977.
Glucksberg, S. and Krauss, R. What do people say after they have learned how to talk? Studies of the development of referential communication. *Merrill-Palmer Quarterly*, 1967, *13*, 309–316.
Glucksberg, S., Krauss, R., & Higgins, E. T. The development of referential communication skills. In F. D. Horowitz (Ed.), *Review of child development research* (Vol. 4). Chicago: U. of Chicago Press, 1975.
Goldman, B. D. & Ross, H. S. Social skills in action: an analysis of early peer games. In J. H. Glick and K. A. Clarke-Stewart (Eds.), *Studies in social and cognitive development: The development of social understanding*. New York: Gardner, 1978.
Grice, P. Utterer's meaning and intentions. *Philosophical Review*, 1969, *78*, 147–177.
Higgins, E. T. Role-taking and social judgment: Alternative developmental perspectives and processes. In J. H. Flavell and L. Ross (Eds.), *Social-cognitive development: Frontiers and possible futures*. Cambridge: Cambridge University Press, 1981.

Hoy, E. A. Measurement of egocentrism in children's communication. *Developmental Psychology*, 1975, *11*, 392.

Jaffe, J. & Feldstein, S. *Rhythms of dialogue*. New York: Academic Press, 1970.

James, S. L. *The effect of listener and situation on the politeness of pre-school children's directive speech.* Unpublished doctoral dissertation. University of Wisconsin, 1975.

Kurdek, L. Structural components and intellectual correlates of cognitive perspective taking in first- through fourth-grade children. *Child Development*, 1977, *48*, 1503–1511.

Lawson, C. *Request patterns in a two-year-old.* Unpublished manuscript, University of California at Berkeley, 1967.

Lubin, D. & Whiting, B. *Learning techniques of persuasion. An analysis of sequences of interaction.* Paper presented at the biennial meeting of the Society for Research in Child Development, New Orleans, March 1977.

Maratsos, M. Non-egocentric communication abilities in preschool children. *Child Development*, 1973, *44*, 697–700.

Meissner, J. & Apthorp, H. Nonegocentrism and communication mode switching in black preschool children. *Developmental Psychology*, 1976, *12*, 245–249.

Menig-Peterson, C. The modification of communicative behavior in preschool-aged children as a function of the listener's perspective. *Child Development*, 1975, *46*, 1015–1018.

Mueller, E. The maintenance of verbal exchanges between young children. *Child Development*, 1972, *43*, 930–938.

Mueller, E., Bleier, M., Krakow, J., Hegedus, K., & Cournoyer, P. The development of peer verbal interaction among two-year-old boys. *Child Development*, 1977, *48*, 284–287.

Nelson, K. & Gruendel, J. *From personal episode to social script: Two dimensions in the development of event knowledge.* Paper presented at the biennial meeting of the Society for Research in Child Development, San Francisco, March 1979.

Parten, M. Social participation among preschool children. *Journal of Abnormal and Social Psychology*, 1932, *27*, 243–269.

Piaget, J. *The language and thought of the child.* London: Routledge & Kegan Paul, 1926.

Rheingold, H., Hay, D., & West, M. Sharing in the second year of life. *Child Development*, 1976, *47*, 1148–1158.

Rosenberg, S. & Cohen, B. D. Referential processes of speakers and listeners. *Psychological Review*, 1966, *73*, 208–231.

Rubin, K. H. Egocentrism in childhood: A unitary construct? *Child Development*, 1973, *44*, 102–110.

Rubin, K. H. *The relationship between laboratory and naturalistic indices of role-taking skill in children.* Paper presented at the annual meeting of the Eastern Psychological Association. Washington, D.C., March 1978. (a)

Rubin, K. H. Role-taking in childhood: Some methodological considerations. *Child Development*, 1978, *49*, 428–433. (b)

Rubin, K. H., Hultsch, D. F., & Peters, D. L. Non-social speech in four-year-old children as a function of birth order and interpersonal situation. *Merrill-Palmer Quarterly of Behavior and Development*, 1971, *17*, 41–50.

Rubin, K. H. & Pepler, D. J. The relationship of child's play to social-cognitive development. In H. Foot, T. Chapman, & J. Smith (Eds.), *Friendship and childhood relationships*. London: Wiley, 1980.

Sachs, J. & Devin, J. Young children's use of age-appropriate speech styles in social interaction and role-playing. *Journal of Child Language*, 1976, *3*, 81–98.

Schegloff, E. Sequencing in conversational openings. *American Anthropologist*, 1968, *70*, 1075–1095.

Searle, J. *Speech acts: An essay in the philosophy of language.* London: Cambridge University Press, 1969.

Selman, R. L. Social-cognitive understanding: A guide to educational and clinical practice. In T. Lickona (Ed.), *Moral development and behavior*. New York: Holt, Reinhart, & Winston, 1976.

Shatz, M. *The comprehension of indirect directives: Can two-year-olds shut the door?* Paper presented at the summer meeting of the Linguistic Society of America, Amherst, Mass., 1974.

Shatz, M. *How young children respond to language: Procedures for answering*. Paper presented at the Stanford Language Forum, Stanford, Calif., 1975.

Shatz, M. & Gelman, R. The development of communication skills: Modifications in the speech of young children as a function of listener. *Monographs of the Society for Research in Child Development,* 1973, *38* (5, Serial No. 152).

Spivack, G. & Shure, M. *Social Adjustment of Young Children*. San Francisco: Jossey-Bass, 1974.

Wellman, H. & Lempers, J. The naturalistic communicative abilities of two-year-olds. *Child Development,* 1977, *48*, 1052–1057.

6 Mother-Child Language in the Natural Environment

Elza M. Stella-Prorok
Federal University of Sao Carlos

What are the relationships between the child's linguistic environment and his usage of speech during the course of his development? Recent advances in our knowledge about specific facets of speech addressed to children in the natural environment have turned this into an undeniably relevant question. In contrast to previous work on naturally occurring language development, which has minimized the role of environmental variables (Brown & Bellugi, 1964; Brown, Cazden, & Bellugi, 1969; McNeill, 1966, 1970), recent studies (see reviews by Bowerman, 1978; DePaulo & Bonvillian, 1978; Rees, 1978) have stressed the need for consideration of such variables in order to achieve further understanding of the processes of language acquisition.

Indeed, the successive changes in the basic concerns of investigation have promoted a sound shift of attitudes, opening the field to a new and challenging source of variables. Earlier studies, prompted by the assumptions inherent in the nativist view (Chomsky, 1965; McNeill, 1966), were primarily concerned with the nature of the linguistic input as provided by maternal speech (Broen, 1972; Fraser & Roberts, 1975; Phillips, 1973; Snow, 1972). A more dynamic approach was born with studies focusing on special kinds of interactions observed in mother-child speech (Garvey & Hogan, 1973; Moerk, 1972, 1975; Nelson, 1973; Stella, 1974), and was expanded with studies looking at semantic and formal relations in the mother-child dialogue (Bloom, Rocissano, & Hood, 1976). These advances have brought the consideration of language development into the realm of the communicative event, together with a reassessment of previous theories, and of the suitability of our present methodological tools. This was fairly appreciated by Nelson (in Rees, 1978): ''The new look in language development views the child less as a language learner (worse as a LAD) than as a partner in a two-way communication system with intentions to be expressed and received through whatever means can be managed [p. 234]."

To the extent to which this view enhances the role of environmental variables in language development, it defeats our present methodological strategies for specifying and demonstrating their functional relationships in the same proportion. Indeed it seems that attempts to demonstrate the tutorial effects of some features of maternal speech on language development remain controversial depending on how far the performance measures were isolated from the child's own linguistic and cognitive constraints.

Consistent with the new approach to the mother-child speech system, several methodological and theoretical discussions on the assessment of environmental effects on language development have hastened the need for taking into consideration the child's actual linguistic (and cognitive) repertoire and his own contribution in changing his immediate linguistic environment (Cross, 1978; Furrow, Nelson, & Benedict, 1979; Mahoney, 1975; Nelson, 1980, 1981; Stella-Prorok, 1980a; Snow, 1977). That mother-child speech represents a continuously changing system is generally agreed. Not equally agreed is what to look at and when, in the analysis of language development. In fact, there is a paucity of data documenting the observable transitions in that system during the course of the child's development. Accordingly, it is not well established, as yet, what the relevant dimensions of linguistic input for the child are, as his linguistic and cognitive resources grow.

This is the basic concern to which much of the discussions that follow will be addressed. This chapter reports several analyses of ongoing patterns of mother-child verbal interchanges, and of their concurrent relationships with the child's verbal performance at varying levels of development. Rather than starting with formally generated linguistic dimensions, the basic strategy adopted was the attempt to detect dimensions empirically, relying on the child's differential responsiveness to varying linguistic input. Thus the rationale underlying most of the analyses discussed here is best considered as a functional analysis of mothers' and children's behaviors in the context of the communicative event. In this respect, specifics of the syntactical aspects of the verbal behaviors have not been considered. The implicit assumption made is in agreement with Mahoney (1975) in that the critical facets of the mother-child speech system that might contribute to language development "ought to be explainable in terms of communication efficiency rather than linguistic appropriateness [p. 141]."

For clarity, the discussions on the mothers' and the children's behaviors in the context of dialogue are presented in three sections. The first section examines the temporal organization of the dialogue. The second analyzes the changes in the temporal pattern of mother-child dialogue as a compelling force for language development. The final section discusses some specific issues in the mother-child speech system concerning two maternal categories (models and repetitions) and the child's concurrent performance.

TEMPORAL PATTERNS IN MOTHER-CHILD DIALOGUE: THE PREDOMINANCE OF THE ALTERNATING VOCALIZING PATTERN

The studies that are most relevant to the aspects of mother-child speech considered here are those that have been concerned with the development of the child's skills in conversation, with specific regard to the formal organization of dialogue.

A basic skill required of conversational partners in order that a dialogue can proceed is that of turn-taking between the speaker and listener roles, which indeed characterizes both the temporal sequencing and the interpersonal nature of verbal behavior. The synchrony between any two momentary partners, of two different behaviors—listener attends while speaker talks—is a prerequisite condition for turn-taking to occur effectively. The synchronized interchange of these two complementary roles defines the pattern of interaction underlying the basic structure of dialogue. In fact, it has been suggested as a "language universal" (Miller, 1963), or as a "necessity" for the acquisition of language (Kaye, 1977).

The smoothness of the interactive pattern between the partners at conversation has been attributed to a learned system of "practices, conventions and procedural rules" (Goffman, 1955) concerning the "regularities governing the initiation and termination of conversation, alternation and interruption, pacing and the interspersing of verbal and nonverbal elements [Bateson, 1975, p. 110]." Translated into behavioral cues, some of these regularities refer to the dyadic gazing patterns, gesticulation, and facial expressions (Duncan, 1972; Duncan & Niederehe, 1974; Jaffe and Feldstein, 1970; Jaffe, Stern, & Peery, 1973; Kendon, 1967) which, on the basis of the work by Condon (1970, 1977) and collaborators (Condon and Sander, 1974), can be associated with differentiated patterns in the performance of speech production (Grosjean, Grosjean, & Lane, 1979; Hawkins, 1971). Therefore, in order to engage in an effective pattern of interaction, the partners at conversation must discriminate subtle and varied aspects of communicative behavior.

Although the ontogenesis of the temporal organization of a variety of dyadic behaviors has been receiving increased attention in recent years (Brazelton, Koslowski, & Main, 1974; Condon, 1977; Fogel, 1977; Kaye, 1977; Sander, 1977; Stern, 1971, 1974; Stern, Beebe, Jaffe, & Bennett, 1977; Trevarthen, 1977), studies on the ontogenetic realization of turn-taking performance with specific regard to vocalizations are still scarce. The earliest signs of temporal organization in adult-child vocal interaction, involving children as young as two months, were described by Bateson (1975) as "protoconversations," meaning an alternating pattern of vocalizations between mothers and infants. By examining the nature of the alternation taking place, Bateson showed some evidence for distinguishing between utterances that were "responsive in a sustained sequence and others as trying to renew the exchange when it lagged [p. 104]." The mean time from onset-to-onset of vocalizations was shorter when the vocalizations were separated by a change of speaker than when emitted successively by the same speaker. Bateson characterized the first as "response" time and the latter as "elicitation" time. It is interesting to note Bateson's appreciation of the fact that during the "elicitation" time, which was significantly longer than the "response" time, the mother apparently waits for a response from the infant before renewing her previous vocalizations. Although the intervals for the child were briefer in both cases, Bateson pointed out that in this emergent structure of conversation, infant and mother rarely interrupted each other.

While noting the occurrence of the interactional pattern between mothers and their 3- to 4-month-old infants, Stern, Jaffe, Beebe, and Bennett (1975) have called attention to the predominance of a coactional pattern, in which mother and infant vocalize simultaneously. They suggested that the two modes of vocal communication differ structurally and functionally, and develop as distinct modes: "Co-actional vocalising is not simply an early developmental pattern that later transforms into the alternating pattern of conversational dialogue, but . . . it is also an enduring mode of human communication [p. 90]." Functionally, the two modes serve different communicative purposes. The coactional mode contributes to the formation and strengthening of the mother-infant relationship; the alternate mode serves as a precursor to the conversational interactive dialogue pattern. Therefore, as development proceeds, there would be a shift from a predominantly coactional pattern, seen at 3–4 months of life, to the predominantly interactional pattern observed in adult dialogue. While indicating the lack of data to document this possible developmental course, Stern et al. (1975) advanced the suggestion that one could expect the alternating pattern to be well established as the predominant mode of communication at "some point in the second year of life [p. 96]."

At present, there is a consistent and growing body of developmental data offering evidence that locates the shift suggested by Stern et al. (1975) at an earlier point—by the second half of the first year of life. These data come from several studies that have been concerned with the distributions of mother-child and child-mother speaker-switch pauses (Davis, 1978; Schaffer, Collis, & Parsons, 1975; Stella, 1974; Stella-Prorok, 1978).

By charting the flow-diagrams showing the distribution of mother-child utterances in relation to the actual temporal continuum in which they occurred, the author proceeded to a detailed analysis of mother(M)-child(C) patterns of verbal interchanges for five British middle-class mothers and their firstborn 21-month-old children (Stella, 1974). The results of interest here are the ones concerned with the temporal intervals between M-C and C-M sequences of utterances, referred to as C's or M's pauses, respectively. The pauses were measured down to 0.2-sec and grouped into 1-sec classes for pauses as long as 12 sec. Pauses longer than 12 sec, which very rarely occurred, were grouped in a single class (12+ sec). The distributions obtained showed a striking regularity across mothers and across children, together with a significant difference (p < 0.001) in duration between the pauses of each child with respect to those of his mother. The great majority of M's pauses were smaller than 1 sec, while C's pauses tended to be longer and more variable. The instances of overlapping utterances were null for some dyads and very rare for the others. Therefore the interactional pattern was very well established for children aged 21 months. Moreover, the data indicated that the temporal organization of this pattern differed significantly depending on the sequence of speakers: M-C or C-M. As concluded at the time, it was not possible to decide whether the maternal performance was specific to the child's level or based on more general adult reply strategies or characteristics. Also, it was not clear then, whether the children's longer pauses were related to their level of language development. These points will be considered again further on, with the discussion of more recent data.

Schaffer, Collis, and Parsons (1975), studying a middle-class sample of 16 British mothers and their children aged 12–15 and 23–27 months, reported significant differences between M-C and C-M pauses, supporting the dependence of pause durations on the speaker sequence. In this study, the previous findings were extended by showing that for children as young as 12 months, the alternating pattern was the predominant mode of communication. The occurrence of simultaneous vocalizations was very rare, especially if considered as "turn-taking failures" as distinct from chorusing, laughter, distress occasions, and warning calls.

This evidence was further confirmed and extended by Davis' (1978) data on patterns of vocal interchanges between 10 British working-class mothers and their children aged from 6–16.8 months. Although Davis found considerable variation across mothers and across children in the number of pauses observed, his data showed the same characteristic temporal organization as described in the previous studies. In fact, comparing the distributions he obtained with those of the author (Stella, 1974), he found no significant differences. Davis also reported an extremely rare occurrence of overlapping vocalizations: 1% for the mothers; 0.32% for the children for three of the M-C dyads; and no overlaps at all for the other seven dyads.

Two conclusions are straightforward from this set of evidence: (a) the alternating interactional pattern is the predominant mode of communication for children as young as six months; (b) this pattern is characterized by a differentiated performance within dyads, determined by the children's longer pauses at the speaker-switches. Bearing in mind that Stern et al.'s (1975) subjects were 3–4 months old when the coactional pattern was predominant, and that Davis' youngest subjects were about 6 months old when the interactional pattern was already predominant, then the developmental shift suspected by Stern et al. must occur between the 4th and 6th month of life.

Taking into consideration the differences between the mothers' and the children's linguistic repertoires, one wonders about which behavioral cues could possibly orchestrate the coparticipation of such differing partners in a smooth interactional pattern. Both Schaffer et al. (1975) and Davis (1978) commented on their impression that the mother would take the more active role in regulating the speaker-switches by "following the lead of the child and pacing her own behaviour accordingly" (Davis, 1978, p. 10). Moreover, calling attention to the fact that mothers in the 1-year-old group were not slower in answering than the mothers in the 2-year-old group, Schaffer et al. concluded that the cue that appeared to guide the maternal behavior was the child's silence. That is, "when the child stopped vocalising, the mother would take the floor."

Although this author considers "silence," even of a few seconds duration, to be an operative event in the formal and functional organization of mother-child vocal dialogue (see data by Bloom, 1977; Stella, 1974; Stella-Prorok, 1980a), it does seem that both partners actively contribute to the organization of this dyadic behavior. First, as will be seen further on in this chapter, the maternal pauses that occurred in vocal interaction with 1-year-old children were significantly shorter than the ones that occurred between mothers and their 2-year-old children. Second, when examining the nature of the alternation taking place between the mother's and the baby's vocalizations, Bateson (1975) did not find support for the hypothesis of the mother inserting her vocalizations into a stream of random vocalizations by the baby. As she concluded: "Whatever is happening, it is happening in both directions [p. 104]." In fact, it seems reasonable to suppose that even young children can discriminate the behavioral cues generated in the performance of speech production during conversation and use them in an effective social manner; that is, they avoid concomitant vocalizing and elicit interaction with the mother.

This suggestion is prompted, on the one hand, by a number of descriptions of the ontogenesis of social exchange between infant and caretaker. Various regularities in the temporal patterns of mother-child interactions that predate the onset of the child's usage of speech are similar to those found in adult conversations (Brazelton, Kolowski, & Main, 1974; Condon & Sander, 1974; Freedle & Lewis, 1977; Jaffe, Stern, & Peery, 1973; Sander, 1977). On the other hand, most of the behavioral cues described as operative signals for taking speaking turns in adult conversation (cf. Duncan, 1972; Duncan & Niederehe, 1974; Kendon, 1967), such as intonation, pitch, gaze, gesticulation, and facial expressions, differ from the normal adult pattern, in the degree of exaggeration and slowed tempo when performed in the interaction with the young child. Stern (1974) described maternal variations of three adult interpersonal behaviors in the interactive play with her child: facial expressions, gaze, and vocalizations. He concluded that "the maternal behaviours that are the stimulus events for the infant are a special sub-set of human behaviours [p. 210]." In fact, variations in the temporal phenomena characteristic of adult speech segments have been found in the baby-talk system by a number of investigators concerning higher pitched voices (Ferguson, 1964; Remick, 1976; Weeks, 1971), intonation pattern (Ferguson, 1964; Weeks, 1971), slow rate of speech (Broen, 1972; Phillips, 1973); and they correspond to the cues associated to infants' differential responsiveness to speech signals. For example, Eimas, Siqueland, Jusczyk, and Vigorito (1971), and Morse (1972), reported that 2-month-old infants can discriminate the acoustic cues involved in segmental and intonational patterns. Lieberman (1967) showed that infants tended to produce ("imitated") the frequency levels to which they were exposed. Finally, Condon and Sander's (1974) data from frame analyses of filmed mother-infant interactions indicated an interactional synchrony between the neonate ("listener") movement patterns and the acoustic boundaries in the mother's speech, in which the organization of change in the listener's behavior was isomorphic with the structure of the speaker's speech. Moreover, when vocalizing to her infant, in the first month of life, the mother makes longer pauses between successive (M-M-M) utterances than between interchange (M-C-M) vocalizations (Bateson, 1975), and they are twice as long as those occurring in adult conversation (Jaffe & Feldstein, 1970). Accordingly, it seems that the mothers, when interacting with their children, enhance the cue differences that are operative in the children's discriminations.

By offering such a patterned stimulation in the timing of their behaviors parents are contributing to an important dimension of the infant's environment (Stern et al., 1977) and enhancing temporal phenomena as cues for the sequential organization of human social behavior. Thus it seems that an interpersonal structure of the dialogue, quite well established by the second half of the first year of life, is guaranteed by the ability of prelinguistic children to use the speech discrimination cues in an effective social manner. Of course, this points to the need to investigate the development of intersubjectivity (see Ryan, 1974) and consequently the hierarchical differentiation of the communicative functions associated with turn-taking across development.

DEVELOPMENTAL TRENDS IN THE INTERACTIVE PATTERN

The data presented so far have indicated that the temporal organization of M-C verbal interaction does not substantially change between the ages of 6 and 27 months. A recent study of Brazilian children will be discussed in more detail now, showing some evidence of a developmental trend in that pattern from the age of one to the age of three. Some of the preliminary data were reported by Stella-Prorok (1978) and will be expanded in this chapter.

The same analyses the author used for the British subjects were repeated for 15 Brazilian middle-class mothers and their firstborn children: five aged from 13 to 16 months, referred to as Age Group One; five aged from 20 to 28 months, referred to as Age Group Two; and five aged from 30 to 36 months, referred to as Age Group Three. The basic procedure for data extraction was the same as that used for the British subjects (Stella-Prorok, 1980a), using the recordings of eight sessions for each dyad. Each session was approximately 16 minutes long, with a week's interval between sessions.

The characteristic temporal pattern of the interactional mode of vocal communication was replicated. The proportion of pauses shorter than 1 sec was significantly greater for mothers than for children: means of 0.85, 0.84, 0.92 for mothers and 0.77, 0.66, 0.88 for the children, for age groups One, Two and Three respectively (F [1,28] = 6.22, p < 0.02). That is, mothers were replying in C-M sequences more quickly than their children in M-C sequences. Children in general tended to be slower in taking turns to speak. Moreover there was a clear trend in the durations of C's and M's pauses across the groups. Thus, although the distributions of C's pauses were not significantly different between age groups One and Two (means for pauses < 1 sec of 0.77, 0.66 for 1- and 2-year-olds respectively; < 2 sec of 0.86, 0.81; < 3 sec of 0.91 and 0.88), they were very different between age groups Two and Three: means for pauses < 1 sec of 0.66, 0.88, and 2- and 3-year-olds respectively, (F [1,8] = 16.61, p < 0.004), and for pauses < 2 sec of 0.81, 0.94, (F [1,8] = 10.20, p < 0.01). The 2-year-old children were taking a slightly longer time for exchanging speaking turns than the 1-year-old children, and this difference was significantly increased when compared with the 3-year-olds. The 1-year-old children, when compared with the 3-year-olds, showed a tendency towards longer pauses: for pauses < 1 sec, means of 0.77 and 0.88 for 1- and 3-year-olds respectively, (F [1,8] = 4.59, p < 0.06); for pauses < 2 sec means of 0.86, and 0.94, (F [1,8] = 4.21, p < 0.07). Therefore, the 2-year-old children presented the longest pauses, and the 3-year-olds the shortest ones.

As far as the maternal behavior is concerned, trends were found in the same directions. That is, the mothers of the 2-year-old children showed in general the largest proportions of longer pauses, and the difference was found to be significant between mothers in age groups Two and Three for pauses < 1 sec with means of 0.84 and 0.92 respectively (F [1,8] = 7.03, p < 0.03).

These data extend further the evidence shown in previous studies (Davis, 1978; Schaffer et al., 1975; Stella, 1974) in that they indicate strongly that the pattern of temporal organization of M-C verbal interchanges varies according to the child's verbal development. It should be emphasized that:

1. Both mother and child seem to contribute to the changes in the pattern. This calls attention to the fact that even when the temporal structure of the dialogue is concerned, the mother does not perform simply as a mature speaker (Jaffe & Feldstein, 1970); nor does she merely fill in the pauses between the child's vocalizations (Schaffer et al., 1975). Rather, she shows a kind of adaptation to the child's pace of participation in the dialogue. The case in point shows that M's pauses in the dialogue with children at around two years of age were reliably longer than M's pauses in their dialogue with 3-year-old children.

2. The direction of the change, rather than accommodating a monotonic function with decreasing M-C and C-M pauses according to the increasing linguistic skills of the child, describes a segment of an inverted U-shaped function, in which the pauses increase from age one to age two, and then decrease from two to three. The sharpness of this reversal can be appreciated from the following data.

AGE THREE: THE END OF A DEVELOPMENTAL CYCLE?

The considerable differences between the 2- and 3-year-old children in the temporal pattern of their verbal interchanges with the mother, and the great similarity between the 3-year-olds and their mothers, strongly suggest a positive answer to the question posed in the heading of this section.

The M-C dyads were examined individually, by means of contigency tables, for the proportions of pauses < 1 sec, < 2 sec, and < 3 sec (Stella-Prorok, 1978). Of interest here are the differences between M-C performance in the 2-year-old and 3-year-old groups. In the 2-year-old group, the means of the proportion of children's pauses < 1 sec, < 2 sec, and < 3 sec respectively were 0.66, 0.81, and 0.88, and the means for the mothers were 0.84, 0.91, and 0.94, respectively. In the 3-year-old group, the means for the children's pauses for < 1 sec, < 2 sec, and < 3 sec respectively were 0.88, 0.94, and 0.97; for the mother's the means were 0.92, 0.95, and 0.97. In the 2-year-old group the M-C differences remained significant for each dyad, at $p < 0.001$, for pauses up to 3 sec, indicating longer pauses for the children (except for one pair at < 3 sec), whereas in the 3-year-old group, the difference was significant up to only 2 sec for one M-C pair, and up to only 1 sec for another pair. In these last two M-C pairs, the difference remained in the same direction as described for group Two: that is, the children made the longer pauses. No differences were found in the duration of M's and C's pauses for the other three dyads. These results not only support the developmental trend just described but also indicate that at around age three, temporal aspects of the turn-taking performance in the dialogue seem to reach the characteristics of the adult's, or mature speaker's, behavior.

Indeed the analysis of variance computed for a derived measure that would take into account the performance of both partners of each dyad, that is, the ratio between the children's and the mothers' mean pause durations, strengthens the point mentioned above. The biggest C/M ratios obtained were those for the 2-year-old group: 1.4, 1.27, 1.30, 1.26, and 1.25, indicating the children's longer pauses. The smallest C/M ratios came from the 3-year-old group: 1.19, 0.97, 0.95, 1.06, and 1.06, indicating the closeness of C's and M's performances, although still showing a slight tendency for the child's pauses to be longer. The difference between the C/M ratios for the 2-year-old and 3-year-old groups was highly significant (F [1,8] = 24.13, p < 0.001). Therefore: (a) it does seem as if the children's peculiar participation in the temporal organization of the dialogue contributes to the characteristic pattern previously described; and (b) at age three, the pattern at work is almost, if not totally, the same as for adults.

The evidence presented brings a new contribution to this area concerning the ontogenetic accomplishment of the turn-taking performance in mother-child dialogue. Thus, apart from changes in a number of routines related to children's participation in discourse (Bloom et al., 1976; Garvey, 1975; Garvey & Hogan, 1973; Gelman & Shatz, 1977; Keenan & Klein, 1975), the very structure of the discourse as defined by the temporal pattern changes across development. The sharpness of the change is such that at age three the child is not only performing the turn-taking very well, as suggested by Bloom et al. (1976) and Garvey and Hogan (1973), but is performing just as well as the adult. Therefore, much before the mastery of an endless series of linguistic skills (considering that even in Salzinger's (1970) ironic perspective, the so often called "rapidity of language acquisition" has become an empty jargon), the child around age three performs at turn-taking just like the skilled and mature speaker.

Moreover, the inverted U-shape describing the developmental change occurring from age one to age three suggests an intriguing association between turn-taking performance and the emission of more mature verbal forms. This thought was prompted by the difference in MLU (in morphemes) across ages, and the turn-taking performance described. The average MLU scores for age groups One to Three were 1.96, 3.85, and 4.19, respectively. There was a difference of 2.23 morphemes on average between groups One and Three, but the turn-taking performance of group One was not significantly different from that of group Three. And although the difference in MLU between groups Two and Three was hardly noticeable (0.34 morphemes on average), the difference in turn-taking was highly significant. Finally, one could say that the increase of 1.89 morphemes (on average) from age group One to Two was accompanied by an increase in the length of pauses at turn-taking, though the differences between the two groups were not statistically significant. Thus, roughly speaking, children using one-plus word utterances performed turn-taking almost as well as ones using four-word utterances. This proficiency was disturbed slightly when the children started to put words together frequently, but was then definitely recovered by the time the utterances became four words long. Whatever the process underlying this developmental trend may be, it seems to be tied to the advancement in linguistic, cognitive, and communicative functions.

Indeed, the slightly disturbed proficiency in turn-taking at age two seems associated with a basic transition in the child's communicative strategies. That is, when the primary reliance on deitic gestures combined with one-word utterances gives place to reliance on the linguistic code, albeit limited and often misused, the child makes a slightly longer pause before verbalizing, suggesting that he is making an effort to stretch his resources to achieve the best linguistic fit possible for the ongoing communication. Thus it seems that the sophistication in the usage of the linguistic code at the early development is achieved at the cost of the social function of the dyadic behavior previously mastered.

In the transition from age one to two, the mother's coparticipation appears to be linked to three complementary changes in her interactive verbal behavior with the child. First, there is a noticeable fading out of nonverbal clues offered by mothers enacting or manipulating jointly with her utterances, gradually followed by a fading in of verbal clues to help keep the context clear to the child (Stella-Prorok, 1980b). The same pattern of change in maternal behavior has been found by Zukow, Reilly, and Greenfield (1982) in their investigation on the transition from sensorimotor to linguistic communication, where they focused on mother-initiated offers to their children aged 9–22 months, who were divided into three developmental levels according to their productive use of semantic functions. They reported: (a) a decrease of maternal offer sequences in the sensorimotor modality according to the increased complexity in the children's semantic functions; and (b) an increase of linguistically initiated offer sequences in the same direction.

Secondly, there is a significant change in the emphasis placed by the mother on the child's verbal communicative proficiency. Stella-Prorok (1980b) described it with data showing the increase in WH-questions: means of 18.2% and 25.7% for age one and two respectively, ($F_{[1,8]} = 9.97$, $p < 0.01$); and in "requests" for the child to speak (as exemplified by sentences like "Talk to daddy on the telephone" or "Tell me what you saw in the park this morning," which are then followed by "modeling routines"): means of 1.1% and 3.2%, ($F_{[1,8]} = 6.68$, $p < 0.03$). Moreover, the author reported that this change in maternal verbal behavior is also paired with increased semantic and syntactic complexity. The third change, which is not readily observable and which has not been reported up to now, concerns the change in the maternal pattern of speech production. It is described in detail in the next section.

THE ELOCUTION OF SILENCE: MATERNAL SENSITIVITY TO THE TRANSITIONS IN THE CHILD'S SPEECH SYSTEM

It has already been noted that both partners contribute to the differentiation of the temporal pattern in mother-child dialogue during the first three years of development. The discussion now concerns some specifics of the maternal role as described by the analysis of the mother's pattern of speech production.

The first analysis carried out sought to determine the differences, if any, in maternal performance across the children's three age groups at the emission of successive utterances. Successive utterances, or verbalizations, by the same speaker constitute what has been called in this chapter either M-M or C-C sequences of utterances, in contrast to interchange verbalizations, which constitute the interactive sequences where the speaking turn is exchanged either in the C-M or M-C direction. Pauses recorded between successive verbalizations by the same speaker are referred to here as M-M or C-C pauses, as opposed to the previously described M-C or C-M turn-taking pauses. Thus, for the purposes of the analyses under discussion in this topic, only the M-M pauses were considered and compared across the three age groups. The mean percentages of various maternal pauses between successive verbalizations (M-M) can be seen in the first column of Table 6.1. Once more the results called attention to the 2-year-old group: Here the mother's pauses preceding her own verbalizations were more frequently longer than 1 sec. as compared with age groups One and Three. The differences in such maternal performance were significant in both directions: between M-M pauses at age two and age one ($F [1,8] = 7.61$, $p < 0.02$) and between M-M pauses at age two and age three ($F [1,8] = 5.84$, $p < 0.04$). However, no significant differences were found between M-M pauses in age groups One and Three.

Recalling the previous results of the children's turn-taking performance, the data above indicate that the mother is sensitive to the child's delays in responding verbally to her (that is, in M-C sequences), so much so as to incorporate these delays into her own pattern of speech production. At the age at which the child usually takes longer to reply verbally, the mother also waits longer before uttering the second (or subsequent) consecutive verbalization (that is, in M-M sequences). Taking into consideration the two previous complementary changes in

TABLE 6.1
Mean Percentage of M–M, C–M and M–C Pauses
<1 sec, <2 sec and <3 sec, with F Scores for
M–M vs. C–M and M–M vs. M–C Comparisons.

		M–M	C–M	M–C	M–M vs. C–M		M–M vs. M–C	
					$F (1,8)$	$p<$	$F (1,8)$	$p<$
AGE 1	<1 s	61.8	85.0	76.6	17.01	0.003	5.87	0.042
	<2 s	75.6	89.6	85.6	9.15	0.02	4.34	0.071
	<3 s	85.6	91.4	91.0	3.98	0.08	2.3	0.168
AGE 2	<1 s	48.6	83.6	66.0	59.99	0.00006	8.64	0.019
	<2 s	73.2	91.2	82.0	24.77	0.001	4.13	0.077
	<3 s	83.0	94.2	88.4	19.18	0.002	3.32	0.11
AGE 3	<1 s	60.8	92.4	88.4	58.40	0.00006	34.78	0.003
	<2 s	76.4	95.0	93.6	19.7	0.002	15.23	0.0045
	<3 s	86.4	96.8	96.8	11.76	0.01	11.76	0.01

maternal behavior for exchanging communication with the child, one could susggest that the mother appears to impel the child towards an increasing usage of the linguistic code, while at the same time accommodating her performance to his (or her) efforts in that direction. Considering that by doing that the mother is altering the tempo of her mature performance (Jaffe & Feldstein, 1970), one could indeed suggest that the differentiation in the timing of maternal performance in verbal interchanges with the child across development is associated with different ongoing functions set up by the mother and child in the interaction.

The deeper one goes into the dynamic structure of M-C dialogue, the stronger this possibility appears. Two further analyses were carried out on the same data. The first reports the differences in maternal pauses between M's successive utterances (M-M) when compared with M's speaker-switch (C-M) pauses. As would be expected, the M-M pauses were usually longer, and this pattern can already be seen at work in the earliest interactive sequences between mothers and infants (Bateson, 1975). However, it is worth noting the changes that occur in this maternal behavior across age groups as indicated in Table 6.1: (a) mother's pauses in successive M-M utterances are more frequently longer than mother's pauses in interactive C-M utterances in the two-year-old group (< 3 sec, $p < 0.002$); (b) in the one-year-old group, M-M pauses tend to be less different from C-M pauses (< 3 sec, N.S., and < 2 sec, $p < 0.02$) than the ones observed in age groups two and three.

The second analysis reports comparisons between M-C (i.e., children's) pauses and M-M pauses. Were the mothers incorporating the child's pace of replies into their own rhythm of speech production? If so, then one would expect to find no differences in the distributions of M-C and M-M delays. The results of the analysis using the variance test for the two sets of comparisons are shown in Table 6.1. In fact, no significant differences were found between the proportions of longer M-M and M-C pauses (< 2 sec and < 3 sec) for both age groups One and Two. Recalling that the 2-year-old children took longer to reply verbally, the data in Table 6.1 indicate that in this group, the mother would wait longer for that reply before repeating or changing her next consecutive verbalization (i.e., in M-M-M sequences).

Altogether, these data suggest a fine equilibrium between the mother's and the child's participation in mutual dialogue across the first three years of the child's development. The mother's performance at taking speaking turns, as well as timing her consecutive utterances while she is "holding the floor," deviates from the adult's in the direction of the developmental function described for the children's performance across ages one to three. Bearing in mind the children's developing linguistic repertoire during that period, one would suggest that the changes in the temporal organization of the M-C dialogue serve different functions. In the period when the communicative flow relies heavily on the extralinguistic features of the context, there seems to be no reason for a "slowed tempo of performance," either for exchanging or for holding the speaking turns.

The mastery of an accurate exchange of roles appears to be a primary task to be accomplished in this period of M-C verbal interchanges. Then, by increasing the emphasis on the usage of speech, *the mother sets the occasion for the transition from reliance on the extralinguistic to linguistic features of the context.* That is, the mother strengthens the linguistic function of ongoing interactions with her child. By taking longer to reply when he is stretching his linguistic resources, *the child sets the pace* at which the mother is then "expected" to proceed. In fact, the mother waits longer in sequences of the type M-M; that is, before uttering a second consecutive verbalization, either insisting on her previous utterance or modifying it, or else changing it completely. Moreover, the mother also takes slightly longer at replying to the child, possibly to process the child's utterance with better results.

The slowed tempo of mother's and child's performance at the point when the child begins to put words together suggests that this is the period when the temporal organization of the dialogue subserves the emergence of a new function in M-C verbal interaction, namely, strong reliance on the linguistic code for exchanging communication.

CHANGES IN THE TEMPORAL PATTERN OF M-C-M DIALOGUE AS A COMPELLING FORCE FOR LANGUAGE DEVELOPMENT

For the purposes of the previous discussions, M's and C's short pauses were emphasized. Now, we shall concentrate on those instances in which a sequence of M-C or C-M utterances was characterized by the occurrence of a long pause (for example, > 3 or > 4 sec). Even to the unskilled observer, an ongoing sequence of M-C-M verbalizations having a general pattern of less than 1-sec pauses between speakers does appear to suffer a "break" when an occasional longer pause occurs. This fact should draw attention to the point that in the analysis of mother-child speech, and primarily when the flow of interchanges does not conform to the formal and semantic pattern of mature speakers (see, for example, Bloom et al., 1976), one should consider the possibility that the interchange of successive verbalizations between speakers does not necessarily mean "reply" (or verbal reaction, or "responding"); it might just mean a change of speaker. In other words, on some occasions, the "reply" (or "response") is simply silence. Taken by itself, this might just mean a pause of few seconds. However, when considered in relation to the pattern occurring most of the time, it can be seen as an intriguing disruption in that pattern.

It is suggested here that an appropriate concern with the timing of an ongoing mother-child verbal interaction will direct the attention toward the required level of descriptive analysis of that interaction, together with an acknowledgement of the need for establishing the grounds for defining the boundaries of "social context" and of "communicative event." During an ongoing mother-child verbal interaction, in contrast to a sequence of interchange utterances separated by pauses of about 1 sec, one can have a sequence in which M does not immediately reply to one of C's utterances, creating a gap in the sequence. The gap can then be followed either by a modified utterance (usually a self-repetition), or by M starting a new interchange (usually after a longer pause with change of topic).

Consider the following example in which the vocalizations are presented in the original Portuguese, with an accompanying translation into English. Mother and child are interacting in a free-play situation. The child picks up a book, approaches the mother and starts the sequence:

C1: (unintelligible vocalization)—5-sec pause
M1: "Este aqui é o macaquinho, olha!"—1-sec pause (Look, this is the little monkey.)
M2: "Ah! a bananinha na mãozinha dele."—1-sec pause (Ah! the little banana in his little hand.)
M3: "Ele come banana."—2-sec pause
(He's eating the banana.)
M4: "Come bananinha."—2-sec pause
(Eating the little banana.)
M5: "Aqui a bananinha."—3-sec pause
(Here's the little banana.)
C2: "Bananinha."—1-sec pause
(Little banana.) .
M6: "É, bananinha."—3-sec pause
(Yes, little banana.)
C3: "Bananinha."—1-sec pause
(Little banana.)
M7: "Come bananinha."—2-sec pause
(Eating the little banana.)
C4: (unintelligible) + "Bananinha."—2-sec pause
(Little banana.)
C5: (unintelligible) + "Bananinha."—2-sec pause
(Little banana.)
C6: (unintelligible)—> 12-sec pause
M8: "Vamos brincar de roda?"
(Let's play ring-a-ring-a-roses.)

Note the pauses at M1 and M8, when both of C's previous utterances were unintelligible. Note also that when C4 tries, apparently, to say, "come bananinha" (eating the little banana) and fails: (a) there was no immediate reply like the ones to C2 and C3; (b) C5 tries again, and does not get a reply; (c) C6 tries once more, modifying C5 completely, but failing; and then, (d) M8 does not insist, does not correct, does not provide a new model, but rather just remains silent (> 12 sec in this sequence, but not usually so long) and then changes the topic.

This phenomenon has been overlooked in most of the previous studies of mother-child verbal interaction. If one takes the variations in the M-C interactive pattern, caused by the longer pauses, as indicative of differential responsiveness, it becomes clear that as part of the dynamics of M-C dialogue there is interdependence between turn-taking performance and the kinds of utterances interchanged.

We shall next discuss several analyses based on this kind of phenomenon, and will advance the suggestion that its consideration may prove useful in elucidating mechanisms for the simplification (and/or adaptation) of maternal speech and its contribution to initial language development.

MATERNAL APPROVAL VERSUS MATERNAL SELECTIVENESS

Investigating maternal contingent approval and disapproval, which should theoretically (Skinner, 1957; Staats, 1971) facilitate language development, several authors have in fact documented negative evidence (Brown & Hanlon, 1970; Nelson, 1973). Additional negative results from the search for differential maternal responses to mature vs. primitive constructions in the child's speech led to the conclusion that there was no selective social pressure operating, primarily at home, on children in order to impel them towards mature speech (Brown, 1973; Brown & Hanlon, 1970). However, based upon the data on C-M sequences of utterances in which some pauses fell outside the general pattern, this author suggests that the argument of communication pressure should be considered in a different perspective.

Searching for selection pressures operating in the child's progression from primitive to well-formed constructions, Brown and Hanlon (1970) selected samples representative of the periods when the child was vacillating between the two forms of yes-no questions, tag questions, WH-questions, and negatives, and ascribed the respective maternal replies to two categories: "sequiturs" and "non-sequiturs." The first included "all simple continuations strongly suggesting comprehension of the child's utterance," and the latter, a variety of reactions like: "queries," "irrelevancies," "misunderstandings," "no-responses," and "doubtfuls [p. 43]." They found no significant differences in the maternal replies associated with the child's mature or primitive constructions, and concluded that there was "no support for the notion that there is a communication pressure favouring mature constructions" in the child's usage of speech [p. 45].

On the same rationale, this author proposes the phenomenon to be pursued through a different analysis of M-C verbal interchanges. Taking into consideration the distribution of M's and C's pauses (94% and 68% respectively up to 4 sec long), Stella (1974) defined as a convenient criterion for judging "replies" the preceding occurrence of a pause no longer than 4 sec. (The complete recorded periods of M-C verbal interchanges were also analyzed for two of the pairs, with a 3 sec criterion for maternal replies, and the consequent difference in the results for both mothers corresponded to 2% of the maternal replies.) Then, the differences in the proportion of maternal replies (that is, C-M < 4 sec) and nonreplies (C-M or C-C > 4 sec) were analyzed with regard to the kind of C's previous utterance: intelligible against primitive (i.e., unintelligibles, onomatopoeics, and exclamations). The contingency coefficient ("C") determined for five dyads with 21-month-olds indicated that both the amount of children's verbalizations in each of the two classes and the proportion of maternal replies against nonreplies were significantly associated for two of the M-C pairs (C = 0.14 and 0.20, p < 0.02 and 0.001); C's primitive (vs. intelligible) utterances received more nonreplies. These two among the five children consistently had the higher scores for measures used to describe their speech. Table 6.2 shows the scores of MLU, UT/MIN—(utterances per min), CUT/(CUT +IUT)—(proportion of intelligibles), C's IN/(C's IN + M's IN)—(ratio of interactive chains initiated by C to the total of chains observed), and finally C's EN/(C's EN + M's EN)—(ratio of interactive chains ended by the child to the total of chains observed; note that lower scores here should be associated with "better" performance).

For two other dyads, the contingency coefficient was not significant, but for one it equalled zero. The child in question had the worst scores in each of the measures, as can be seen by looking at the third row in the table. It is also worth mentioning that the association between the rankings of the children according to the various measures is highly significant (coefficient of concordance, $W = 0.96$, $p < 0.001$).

These results indicated that in the cases where the contingency coefficient was significant, the mother was selectively responding to the child, taking into con-

TABLE 6.2
Descriptors of Child's Speech (Ranks)

Ss	MLU	UT/MIN	$\dfrac{CUT}{CUT + IUT}$	$\dfrac{C's\ IN}{C's\ IN + M's\ IN}$	$\dfrac{C's\ EN}{C's\ EN + M's\ EN}$
S1	2.44(1)	5.65(1)	0.90(1)	0.766(2)	0.658(1)
S2	1.95(2)	5.37(2)	0.82(2)	0.768(1)	0.677(2)
S3	1.35(5)	4.33(5)	0.56(5)	0.355(5)	0.798(5)
S4	1.44(3)	5.24(3)	0.73(4)	0.606(4)	0.768(3)
S5	1.42(4)	4.35(4)	0.79(3)	0.618(3)	0.794(4)

sideration those of C's utterances that could be defined as more mature, while ignoring the primitive ones. The maternal performance implied here describes a pattern that could be referred to as mother's silence interspersed with the sequences of interchanges with the child. Given its association with the kinds of C's utterances, it is suggested that in those instances, the mother was promoting a shift of contingencies towards more elaborate verbal forms. The effect of this maternal behavior on facilitating language development is implied by the associated children's performances. In addition, even though the mothers were not responding to all of the child's intelligible utterances, if the unintelligible ones were more consistently ignored, then the child would have information to aid their advances.

It is interesting to consider the implications of this kind of analysis in the light of Brown's (1973) speculations about the role of reinforcement contingencies in the acquisition of syntax. If one were to look at reinforcement contingencies in terms of maternal behavior that makes explicit "approval" or "disapproval," or else explicitly "corrects" C's previous utterance, then one should certainly agree with Brown when he says that parents seem to ignore grammatical errors in their children's speech. The five children mentioned here received a trivial number of maternal corrections, as can be seen from Table 6.3.

By "correction" it is meant that the mother's verbal response to C's previous utterance implied the forms "no" or "that is wrong" (which rarely occurred, if at all), followed by the suitable form. It can easily be agreed that such infrequent maternal correction could not possibly lead to the children's usage of more mature phrases or sentences. As Brown and Hanlon reported: "Explicit approval or disapproval of either syntax or morphology is extremely rare in our records and so seems not to be the force propelling the child from immature to mature forms [p. 48]." Moreover, the two other behaviors usually considered, or applied, as instances of explicit approval ("attention," e.g., "hum-hum"; and "praise," e.g., "that is right," "very good") were not only very rare (mean proportion for five mothers of "attention" was 3.6% and of "praise" was 5.8%)

TABLE 6.3
Number and Kind of Maternal Corrections
of Children's Utterances at 21 Months

Dyads	Total C's UT.	Corrections	Kind
M-C1	339	10	noun(3), adj.(5), plural(1), tense(1)
M-C2	306	8	noun(8)
M-C3	206	13	noun(12), plural(1)
M-C4	262	7	noun(5), plural(1), preposition(1)
M-C5	174	6	noun(6)

but also had either a null (in the case of "attention") or a weak effect in keeping the child talking (see Stella-Prorok, 1980a). Therefore, a contrary effect to the one expected from learning theories was obtained.

On the one hand, it seems unrealistic to expect mothers to correct or provide the child with a specific verbal reply for every immature and/or incorrect form. The children referred to in Table 6.3 produced on average 5 UT/MIN and their mothers 7.5 UT/MIN, and as the number of UT/MIN increases, this maternal behavior becomes still more unlikely. For example, one of the 15 Brazilian subjects, 28 months old, who produced 883 utterances (6.9 UT/MIN) had just one utterance corrected grammatically by the mother, whose rate of speech was 16.05 UT/MIN. On the other hand, focusing on the explicit occurrence of approval, praise, and attention, in the classically explored forms (see Krasner, 1958 and Salzinger, 1959) might not be the best, or most suitable way for analyzing the effects of natural contingencies of "reinforcement" on verbal development, in spite of the great number of operant and social-learning studies (see Whitehurst & Vasta, 1975; Garcia & DeHaven, 1974) having implied so. Not only are those behaviors not representative of natural contingencies (see data by Brown & Hanlon, 1970; Nelson, 1973; Stella, 1974), but also when they occur they seem to be incompatible with the flow of the natural communicative event, especially if they should concern misuse of syntax. Therefore, it is not surprising to find, on the basis of data from the British pairs, and in agreement with Brown and Hanlon (1970), that when contingent approval or disapproval occurred, it was linked to the truth of the child's utterance.

Nonetheless, if one is ready to accept the variation in the temporal pattern of maternal behavior as indicative of mother's selectiveness in replying to the child's utterances, then it becomes clear that there are selective communication pressures operative as dyadic state variables in the C-M-C interactive sequences of utterances. It should be remembered that the present discussion is concerned with the early development of linguistic behavior, or more precisely, with MLU repertoires from 1.42 to 2.44. Assuming an hierarchical organization of behavioral development, different variables and parameters might be operative in the child's progression at more advanced stages. At the point being referred to here, when the child is in the process of expanding the usage of the linguistic code, what seems to be an operative variable to regulate communicative efficacy is expressed in the dyadic interaction through a different modality, i.e., the disruption in the temporal structure of the ongoing verbal interaction. What has been the rule, suddenly gets distorted, and this may be functional for the child's linguistic performance.

Bearing in mind the importance of the temporal phenomena in the organization of different modalities of interpersonal behavior in the M-C dyadic context (Condon, 1977; Condon & Ogston, 1966; Condon & Sander, 1974; Sander, 1977; Stern, 1974; Stern, Beebe, Jaffe, & Bennett, 1977), the author would emphasize the support for her contention concerning the functional effect of the disruption of the temporal pattern as an operative communicative pressure in the child's progressive usage of speech, recalling the consistency of previous data (Davis, 1978; Schaffer et al., 1975; Stella, 1974; Stella-Prorok, 1978) in characterizing the temporal pattern of maternal verbal interaction with the child as a large number of very short ($<$ 1 sec) pauses. The occurrence of longer pauses might indicate, as Segal (1975) speculated, that parents are not so prodigious in interpreting the child's primitive utterances after all. Moreover, considering that: (a) the pattern described is already observable in the first few months of life (Bateson, 1975) and quite well established at the second half of the first year (Davis, 1978); and (b) even infants seem to perceive "a difference between periods in which stimulation was correlated (negatively or positively) with their own vocal responding and periods in which stimulation occurred randomly [Bloom, 1977, p. 367]," it seems safe to assume that an occasional disruption in maternal responding as the child speaks might signal to the child a "communication failure." In other words, it might signal "say it again" or "say it better." On this basis, it is strongly suggested that at the earlier stages, and primarily when the child starts putting words together, the occasional disturbances in the temporal pattern of maternal behavior might be operative as a compelling force for language development. Nevertheless, these assumptions are not intended to imply either that the child is passively subservient to the linguistic environment or that theories of reinforcement can unequivocally explain language development.

Conceiving the child as a functioning and adjusting organism within the M-C system, as the work by Condon, Sander, Stern, and their collaborators has demonstrated, it is clear that the analysis of factors and operations (feedback contingencies) affecting language development has to confront the ontogenetic differentiation of the child's behavioral structures. Although differential reinforcement, in combination with a variety of other operations, in different training procedures, has produced a plethora of morphological, lexical, and syntactical behaviors in delayed language children, the explanatory status of the concept regarding language development has to be faced with Premack's (1970) claim: "A strict training procedure is not an explanation of how, as a result of carrying out the prescribed steps, the organism accomplished the function in question [p. 107]."

CHILDREN'S DIFFERENTIAL RESPONSIVENESS

When one investigates the variations in the child's temporal pattern, the same phenomenon comes to light. The author has found that some categories of maternal speech were consistently followed by longer pauses ($>$ 4 sec) as compared to others that were consistently followed by shorter ones. By defining a verbal chain as an interactive sequence of M-C-M utterances, in which no interval longer than 4 sec has occurred, the author examined the "effects" of maternal speech on "initiating," "maintaining," or "ending" of a chain, or as being "nonreacted" to (verbally) at all. The effects of initiating or maintaining an interactive sequence are self-explanatory. A maternal utterance would "end" an ongoing chain when it was followed by an interval longer than 4 sec before the next utterance, which could be either by M or by C. Nonreacted maternal utterances were those preceded and followed by pauses greater than 4 sec.

The differences in the children's responsiveness were examined with respect to nine categories of maternal speech in relation to the above aspects of verbal chains. (A detailed report is found in Stella-Prorok, 1980a.) The results derived from contingency tables for the nine maternal categories against the four effects were highly significant (Cochran Test for derived "z" scores: $Q = 105.97$, $p < 0.0001$).

Thus, maternal speech in the form of WH-questions was the most effective in initiating a conversation with the child (mean "z": 3.89). In maintaining child response, maternal repetitions of the child's previous utterance had the strongest effect (mean "z" = 2.0), followed by maternal expansions (mean "z" = 1.19) and maternal models (mean "z" = 1.43). Expansions were those immediate maternal replies that would fill the child's previous utterance by adding syntactic items. Expansions occurred only in C-M sequences. Models were defined as the maternal utterances that would provide the "label" (e.g., "this is a car") or "description" ("the car has four wheels"; "the duck is swimming") of any environmental characteristic that was currently focused upon by the child, or presented to him by the mother by pointing or employing attentional and/or deitic utterances (e.g., "look, this is a car"; "here! the monkey is on the tree"). Models would usually happen in M-C (or M-C-M) sequences; on a few occasions models would occur in a C-M sequence, that is, as a "reply" to the child. But these were replies that explicitly corrected the child's utterances, e.g.: C: "Red"; M: "No, it is blue." The kind of maternal utterances most frequently not followed by an immediate reply by the child, therefore, ending an ongoing verbal chain (mean "z" = 4.08) or not being reacted to at all (mean "z" = 3.61) was the one called "comment." This was defined as a complex utterance that would expand the ongoing verbal interaction beyond the "here and now," and/or add too many structural changes in relation to the child's previous utterance. "Comments" could be employed in C-M or M-C sequences. In the first case they would tend to end the ongoing chain, and in the second, they would not be effective in initiating an interaction. For example: C: "Bis lorry"; M: "Maybe you'll see a big lorry before we go home"; or M: "Look, this car is much the same as the one we saw the other day in the car park." Finally, maternal speech implying "attention" or "praise," apart from being rare, was low in impact; there was an almost null effect in the case of attention (mean "z": -0.02), and in the case of praise the effect was much weaker than that of "repetitions" or "expansions" in maintaining the child's responding (mean "z": 0.6).

The implications of these findings for language development are straightforward: Maternal speech differentially affects the child's immediate verbal performance, and the direction of the effect might qualify its influence on the child's development of speech. The maternal utterances more likely to be followed by a child's immediate reply were either the short and simple sentences or the ones structurally close to C's previous utterance. Long and complex sentences had a disruptive effect on the child's responding.

Special aspects of adult (A) speech similar to the above maternal categories positively associated with the child's responsiveness have been documented as facilitative of language development by several investigators. Whitehurst, Novak, and Zorn (1972) reported the acquisition of new words by a 40-month-old child with delayed language as being associated with the maternal provision of models ("labels") plus imitative prompts ("This is corn; say it"). Hursh and Sherman (1973) showed that 15- to 24-month-old children's production of target speech sounds increased with parental modeling plus praise and repetition of the response by the child. Nelson and Bonvillian (1974) reported that maternal modeling of names of toys increased their usage in the speech of 18-month-old children. The category focused upon in all of these studies corresponds to the noncontingent maternal models previously mentioned (in M-C or A-C sequences), and it was studied in a highly structured (or experimental) setting within the basic paradigm of modeling plus imitation, with or without differential reinforcement.

Concerning the effect of contingent replies, one category that has been frequently studied is "expansion." Although the earlier attempts were inconclusive (cf. Cazden, 1965, and Feldman, 1971, as described in Bowerman, 1978), some recent studies carrying more methodological refinement have suggested that expansions might benefit language development. Nelson, Carskaddon, and Bonvillian (1973) demonstrated that 32- to 40-month-old children's linguistic development can be accelerated through the adult provision of replies that supply new syntactic information in relation to the child's preceding utterance. Adult verbal interaction with the child was programmed so that when the child produced a grammatically incomplete sentence, the adult's reply would be an "expansion"; when the child's sentence was complete, the adult's reply would be a "recast" of the child's utterance into a different form, e.g., a child's declarative would be recast into an interrogative reply. Post-test measurements of the children's performance in several linguistic dimensions indicated more advanced developmental levels than the nontreatment control group or than the second treatment group in which the children received replies that specifically introduced new semantic information (cf. also Nelson, 1977). Speed of linguistic development was also found (Cross, 1976) to be associated with the incidence in maternal speech of expansions and related replies "that were semantically similar to the semantic intention of the child's preceding utterance(s)," with correlational data obtained from 19- to 32-month-old children. Another study (Hovell, Schumaker, & Sherman, 1978) focused on the differential effects of parental noncontingent models ("a mother's statement that immediately precedes a child's utterance") and expansion ("a mother's statement following a child's utterance, which includes the child's utterance and other words") in 22- to 24-month-old children's use of adjective-noun combinations. Hovell et al. documented that both parental categories increased the children's usage of the target combinations; moreover, expansions had the strongest effect.

In combination, the above studies strengthen the suggestion that some specific interactional categories of parental or adult's speech can accelerate linguistic development. Be they called noncontingent models, expansions, recasts, or parental immitation, the crucial proviso for their operation in language development seems to be the structural (syntactic and semantic) closeness they share with the child's current linguistic productions (Cross, 1976; Nelson, 1980; Nelson et al., 1973; Snow, 1977; Stella, 1974).

However, how the interactional constraints operative in M-C speech system, in association with the child's linguistic and cognitive functions, relate to language development stands, as yet, as an empirical question. Several strategies have been speculated as being employed by parents and children during verbal interaction. How they are able to change apace with the hierarchical organization of the child's linguistic behavior is yet to be ascertained.

In this section, differential responsiveness has been expanded to the child, and is suggested as an operative event to tune the reciprocity of M's and C's interactive strategies for verbal communication. The descriptor for it, at the beginning of linguistic development, has been suggested as an occasional disturbance in the temporal organization of dialogue. The basic methodological corollary of the above consideration is the haste for a concerted investment in sequential analyses of M-C speech at the microanalytic level (see Schaffer, 1977).

The disruption in the temporal pattern of dialogue as far as the child's performance is concerned is suggested here as a behavioral cue offered by children, primarily when they start putting words together. The mother's ability to use this cue in an effective manner, adjusting her speech and communicative strategies accordingly, will determine the maternal linguistic lead required for development to proceed. A moderate mismatch between the mother's and child's speech has been suggested as eliciting the child's linguistic advancement (Brown & Fraser, 1963; Brown & Bellugi, 1964; Brown & Hanlon, 1970; DePaulo & Bonvillian, 1978; Fraser, Bellugi, & Brown, 1963; Nelson, 1981; Waxler & Yarrow, 1975).

Several authors have documented that the complexity of maternal speech is generally somewhat above that of the child, and that it increases gradually according to the child's developing linguistic skills (Fraser & Roberts, 1975; Moerk, 1974, 1975; Phillips, 1973; Snow, 1972). However, this small difference in complexity, possibly defining an ideal degree of lead between mother and child's speech, is not a stable characteristic of maternal utterances during the mother and child's continuous verbal interaction. Even during a span of time as narrow as 16 min of interactive "free-play," the mother makes a reasonable number of "comments" that are highly complex and five or more times longer than the child's current utterances. These are the maternal utterances that, in most cases, do not establish an interaction with the child, and instead, tend to suppress the child's responding in the ongoing interactive chain. This draws attention to the fact that when broad behavioral episodes are considered, qualitatively different events may be occurring that should be discriminated. In fact, a closer look at the patterns of M-C interchanges allows one to single out continuing M-C-M sequences in which each partner is prompting and/or replying to the other, therefore interacting verbally. These sequences are frequently interspersed with M-M-M and occasionally with C-C-C sequences, giving rise to "peaks" and "troughs" of interactivity in the M-C dialogue. Thus, the ratio of M:C utterances is not 1:1, but varies across development (Stella-Prorok, 1980b). The important implication of this fact is that the potential relational dimensions of input should be considered when the assessment of the role of one component is concerned. That is, the functional efficacy of a single utterance being replied to by C might be determined by M-M-M-C. In other words, what are the definition and boundaries of a "communicative context"?

Recalling the interdependence between C's patterns of responding and maternal speech of varying complexity, the author emphasizes the point that the child's linguistic input, considered in terms of the speech "addressed to him" should not be evaluated as a whole, but should rather be considered in context, discriminating between those segments of the M-C system characterized by M-C-M and M-M-M sequences. One methodological problem arising in such an evaluation concerns the decision on "where" or "when" to cut the stream of interaction. A possible approach is to guide the decision on the basis of the temporal pattern of interaction itself, and therefore, on the child's differential responsiveness. One response by C at the end of a stream of M-M utterances indicates that, at that point, M's utterance met the child's linguistic, cognitive, and attentional constraints in a way that enabled it to be verbally reacted to. The better M takes the child's response as a feedback for her next utterance, the fewer the M-M-M utterances that will follow until the next maternal utterance is reacted to again. Differences in that maternal behavior may qualify some M-M sequences as enhancing the probability of a child's subsequent response (for example, short sequences in which M presents modified self-repetitions) or others as decreasing the probability of a child's response (for example, sequences in which M introduces "background noise" by uttering successive unrelated utterances).

Therefore, roughly speaking, the speech "addressed to" children can be differentiated in terms of dimensions that can be considered as effective for eliciting C's responses (M-C), or as enhancing the eliciting effect (M-M-M-C) or else as noneffective or even disturbing (M-M . . . M). Thus, if the components of the two last sequences are subsumed under a single heading, the possible positive effects of one can be hidden by the null or negative effects of the other. In addition, taking a sequence such as M1-M2-M3-C, what might define the functionality of M3 might not be M3 itself, but the association of M1, M2, and M3. This possibility calls for caution both in the selection of the analytical unit as well as in the conceptualization of the functional relationships between mother's and children's verbal behaviors. Let us take another look at the example of mother-child dialogue presented previously. If one should look at the sequence (on page 201.) just at the point where there was the child's first response—M5: "Aqui a bananinha"; C2: "Bananinha"—then one would probably find a ready theoretical context for the behavior observed. However, if one looks at the beginning of the sequence, then it is clear that the mother's related sentences about the banana and monkey provide a significant context for the child's response, which should be taken into account when considering the processes involved.

CHANGES IN INTERACTIVE COMPONENTS OF THE MOTHER-CHILD SPEECH SYSTEM

For clarity, interactive components are considered here as the segments of M-C speech in which the utterances flow through one exchange: M-C, implying the initiation of the interaction for M in the role of speaker and a response from C as (previously the listener, and now the) speaker; the reverse would apply to a C-M exchange. Special deviations in adult speech to children, encompassed in the above interactive sequences, have been frequently reported as: "occasional questions"; WH-questions; modeling; expatiation or replies like expansions; repetitions; or parental imitations (Brown & Bellugi, 1964; Brown et al., 1969; Cross, 1976, 1977; Ervin, 1964; Moerk, 1972, 1974, 1975, 1976; Nelson, 1973; Nelson, 1981; Rehide, Longhurst, & Stephanik, 1976; Seitz & Stewart, 1975; Snow, 1977; Stella, 1974; Stella-Prorok, 1980b). Though these categories have usually been identified as parental strategies for teaching language, their impact on acquisition is to be ascertained. For detailed discussions the reader is referred to Bowerman (1978), DeVilliers and DeVilliers (1978), Nelson (1980, 1981), Snow (1977), and Rees (1978).

In general, the ontogenetic directions of change in those aspects of dyadic interaction are substantiated (usually on the grounds of MLU) by a fairly good agreement among various studies. Trends have been reported as negative linear for maternal modeling (Moerk, 1975, 1976; Stella-Prorok, 1980b), exact repetitions, modified repetitions or expansions (Bloom et al., 1976; Cross, 1977; Rondal, 1980; Seitz & Stewart, 1975), or positively linear for questions in general (Bloom et al., 1976; Broen, 1972; Reichle et al., 1976; Snow, 1977; Stella-Prorok, 1980b).

Nonetheless, the contribution of each partner towards the developmental functions suggested by several authors are not comprehensively documented.

Beyond the description of changes in the input and its association with varying linguistic levels in the child, the research in this area should allow for the specifics of the input efficacy in eliciting, maintaining, or suppressing the child's participation in the communicative event. Attempts towards that direction have been implemented through contingent-functional or discourse analyses of M-C verbal interactions (e.g., Bloom et al., 1976; Moerk, 1976; Stella-Prorok, 1980b).

In this section, two interactive components of M-C speech, modeling and repetition, will be discussed around some correlational and functional analyses. Further on, the discussion on repetition will be elaborated with some experimental data.

The speech samples used for the present analyses refer to the 15 Brazilian dyads previously mentioned. Seventeen maternal categories were analyzed and reported by Stella-Prorok (1980b). In this section, a closer look will be directed towards the maternal categories called "models" and "repetitions," and to the children's respective "responsiveness."

In the present chapter, the category "maternal model" is being referred to in a much narrower sense than the one usually hinted at under the general assumption of the "model of language" to which the child is exposed. Maternal models (as well as most of the 17 categories descriptive of maternal speech) were defined primarily in terms of communicative functions rather than grammatical structure. They encompassed phrases or sentences that would: (a) provide "labels" of environmental characteristics currently observable and attended to by the child, e.g., "That is a cow"; or to which the child has been asked to attend e.g., "Look, this is a fire engine"; (b) describe any environmental characteristics observable in the current situation, e.g., "The duck is swimming" (similar to what Moerk (1974) calls "modeling from picture books," if the dyad was going through a book) or "the cars have crashed"; (c) start with a corrective feedback, e.g., C: "Look, police car"; M: "No, that is a fire engine"; or (d) start with an explicit instruction followed by the response required from the child e.g., "Say: hello." A basic aspect common to all the maternal utterances ascribed to the category "maternal models" was that they deviated from speech usually directed to adults inasmuch as they implied translations of environmental events into the linguistic code, or some preliminary "lessons" on how to "apply the linguistic code." The above two implications rely on the constant maternal employment of deitic and attentional words in her modeling utterances.

Repetition was defined as a maternal reply that reproduces C's previous verbalization in exact or reduced form, or with modifications (lexical or syntactical), while keeping the same basic referent. Examples: C: "little horse"; M: "little horse"; C: "This one doesn't go here"; M: "It doesn't go"; C: "Little doll is eating"; M: "She is eating." Repetitions were, by definition, utterances occurring in C-M sequences. In a sequence C-M-M-M where all but the first M were similar to C, the maternal utterances would not be considered repetitions.

Thus, "little horse" emitted by M in the sequence C: "little horse"; M: "little horse," would be a repetition, but the same utterance emitted at M2 or M3 in a sequence like C-M1-M2-M3 would probably be a maternal model. Thus, independently of parts of the immediate context, a maternal utterance could be ascribed to different categories. But the momentary position taken by a single M or C utterance in the stream of dyadic behavior was the paramount device for deciding against apparently overlapping instances. The category "maternal expansion" was taken from Brown and Bellugi (1964); therefore, it was discriminated from modified repetitions on the basis of word order and filling-in functors. Reliability scores were computed by scoring the agreements and disagreements between two independent observers in ascribing M's utterances to the 17 categories studied (cf. Stella-Prorok, 1980b). The percentage agreements obtained ranged from 78% to 99% over categories, with a mean of 91%.

The occurrence of maternal models and repetitions was measured in terms of the rate of utterances per min (UT/MIN), obtained by dividing the total number of utterances within a class by the total number of minutes of recorded interchanges for each dyad. The children's responsiveness to the occurrence of these utterances was also determined in terms of the rate of utterances per min, by dividing the total number of replies that followed directly and within 3 sec of a mother's utterances belonging to the class concerned, by the total time of recorded interaction. The data were drawn from M-C speech samples with a mean verbal output per dyad of: 1738, 1613, and 1649 utterances for the mothers, and 626, 1039, and 1345 utterances for the children, for age groups one, two, and three respectively.

The negative correlation shown in Table 6.4 between maternal modeling and the children's MLU, taking the 15 children together, indicates the inverse relationship between this kind of maternal behavior and the child's development, as reported by others (e.g., Moerk, 1975). For maternal repetitions, although the correlation indicates a positive trend with the child's development, it does not reach statistical significance. However, the interesting information lies in the

TABLE 6.4
Correlation Between Rates of Maternal Models and Repetitions with Children's MLU and Rate of Responses to These Categories

	Models		Repetitions	
	C's MLU	UT/MIN	C's MLU	UT/MIN
age 1	0.02	0.74	0.57	0.99
age 2	0.16	0.64	−0.62	0.93
age 3	0.52	0.70	0.11	0.90
all	−0.52	0.48	0.40	0.92

data on the concurrent effects of the maternal categories. In order to better appreciate the relationships between maternal models and repetitions, and the children's performance, Figure 6.1 presents data on C's responsiveness with respect to these two categories. The data were plotted separating the three age groups, and lines were superimposed for each group in each category in order to help show the underlying relationships in the data. These lines were obtained using a "least-squares" curve fitting technique for a linear relation between the mother's rate of utterances in a category and the children's rate of responses to that category. It was also assumed that the rate of responses to a given category could never be greater than the rate of maternal utterances in that category.

The values of the correlation coefficients between the mothers rate of utterances and the rate of the child's responses for "repetition" support the validity of a linear relationship for the data for all three age groups (all better than $p < 0.01$). In the case of "models," the correlation coefficients are only significant at around $p < 0.1$, reflecting weak linear trends in the data.

It can be seen in both graphs that the child's responsiveness, for a given rate of utterances/min by the mother, increases with age. On the other hand, the rate of responses by the child to a class of utterances over a developmental span changes according to the varying complexity of the maternal utterances in that class (Stella-Prorok & Silva, 1980). For example, the 2-year-olds were responding more frequently to maternal models that would "label" objects and events than to those that would "describe" relations between objects and events ($F[1,8] = 7.35$, $p < 0.02$), though the mothers were offering them in well-balanced proportions (48% descriptive). The difficulty posed by the descriptive models was probably related to the increased number of relational items, primarily verbs, included in those maternal utterances. Moreover, particularly in this case, the resulting interactive pattern seems to be different from that described by Moerk (1976) for "mother's encoding of a message" category in which he encompassed several kinds of maternal modeling utterances.

Moerk outlined "kernel and subroutine patterns" of M-C verbal interaction for when mother spontaneously encodes a message (1976). To this category of maternal behavior Moerk ascribes the following "types" of maternal utterances: "models from picture books"; "describes an object on hand"; "models a phrase not from a picture book"; "describes own act"; "labels an object"; "provides information"; or "describes child's act."

Bearing out the emphasis the present author has been giving to the microanalysis of M-C interactive components, it is worth pointing out that though Moerk talks about general patterns of interaction, the kernel and subroutine patterns seem not to make allowance for some smaller changes that do occur in M-C verbal interaction, primarily around age two. Basically, the "nonresponses" are overlooked in Moerk's descriptions and consequently, the relationships between successive utterances by the same speaker. For example, when "mother spontaneously encodes a message" employing a "description" rather than a

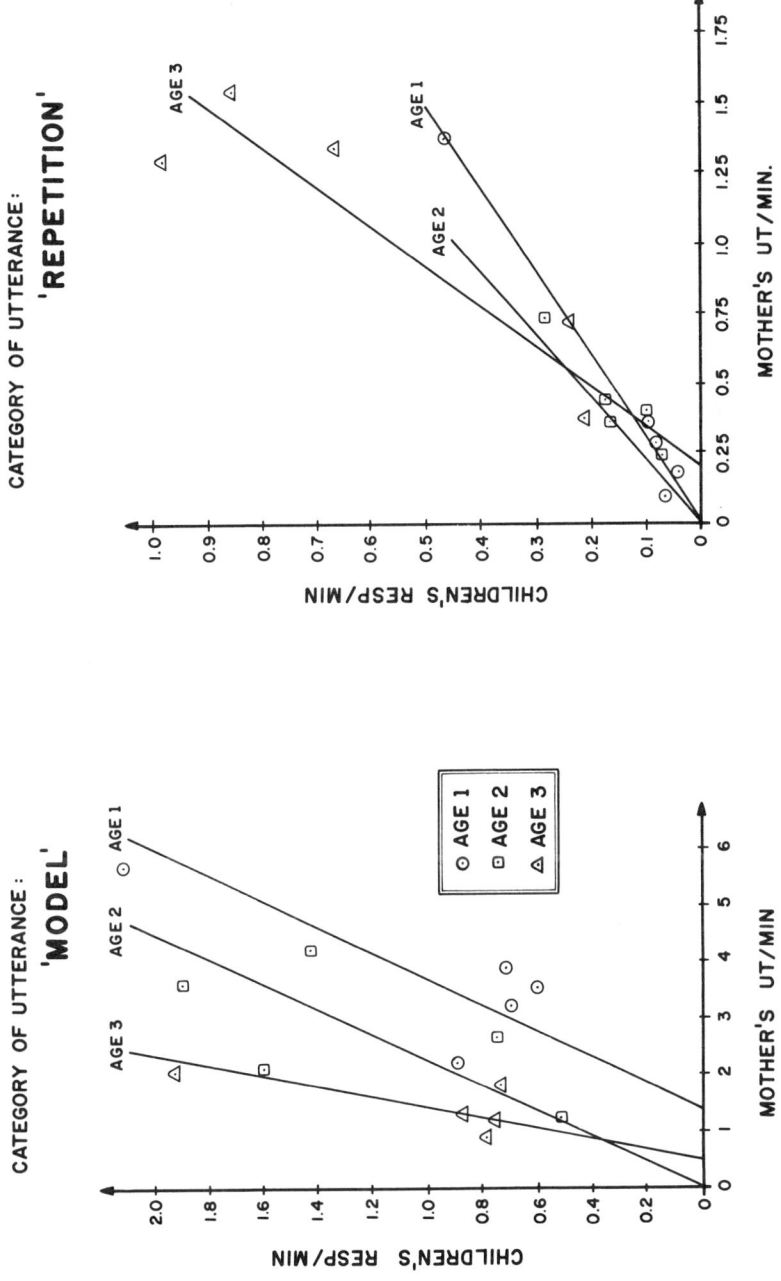

FIG. 6.1. Relationships between mother's rate of utterances for two categories of maternal speech: model and repetition, with the child's rate of responses to those categories.

"label," the present author has quite often found the following pattern for 2-year-olds:

M1 (describes)—no response, i.e., a longer pause
M2 (self-repetition: identical)—no response
M3 (self-repetition: identical or modified)—C3 (exact or partial imitation)
M4 (affirms or not + repeats first description as in M1!)

In fact, in the 2-year-old group, a child's nonreply to a maternal utterance would lead the mother to self-repetitions more frequently expressed in exact than in modified form, and least frequently in reduced form (chi-square = 46.32, $p < 0.001$; Stella-Prorok, 1980b). Thus, it seems that at the same time that she insists on the child's linguistic proficiency, the mother keeps a mismatch between her own and the child's speech, therefore setting a language-learning task some degree ahead of the child's current level. Nonetheless, the mother does not always persist at the child's successful accomplishment of the task; it is frequently observed that after a few trials without an immediate reply by the child, the mother apparently gives up and changes topic. In these instances, one could think of the mother as "testing" the child's repertoire for more advanced linguistic and cognitive functions. But if the modified version of her utterance does not work, the mother does not keep on insisting. She changes the topic or allows for a "break" in the interaction, or follows the lead of the child in whatever direction. Thus, the pattern described by Moerk seems to be more likely to occur in the case of less complex models, when the child does have the repertoire required for the elicited performance, and/or when the primary reliance is on lexical items.

In the case of repetition of C's previous utterance, a general tendency to increase the amount of M's repetition in the course of development, coupled with the increase in C's responsiveness, leads to a definite increase in the rate of C's responses to this category. Considering that a maternal repetition must necessarily occur within a C-M sequence, and that the responsiveness of the child increases with age, it follows that there is also a trend towards an increase of C-M-C clusters associated with M's repetitions. The tutorial benefits of such clustering in M-C verbal interaction are suggested by a noticeable change in the maternal behavior in this class. At age one, most of M's repetitions were exact copies of C's previous utterances. At age two, exact repetitions decreased sharply ($F [1,8] = 13.86$, $p < 0.006$), giving way to reductions that become more frequent ($F [1,8] = 13.22$, $p < 0.007$), and that themselves decrease noticeably at age three ($F [1,8] = 4.76$, $p < 0.06$). At the same time, lexical and/or syntactical modifications increase monotonically from age one to three ($F [1,8] = 7.49$, $p < 0.02$). Thus, when the child starts to say words, M repeats those words; when the child is putting 2 or 3 words together, M repeats some of them, and the observations suggest that the emphasis is placed on the new items; when the child is commonly using four-word utterances, M incorporates some of the items into new sentence frames.

TWO-YEAR-OLDS' DIFFERENTIAL RESPONSIVENESS TO REPLIES OF VARYING COMPLEXITY

Figure 6.1 shows that maternal repetitions of the kinds mentioned above were effective in enhancing C's responsiveness. It has also been shown that when a mother's replies were comments that were quite complex in relation to C's previous utterance, they had a suppressive effect on C's responsiveness. These two kinds of maternal replies bear a close similarity to what Nelson (1980) has defined as "simple" and "complex" recasts. The influence of maternal usage of different recasts on language development was reported by Nelson (1980) with correlational data indicating positive relationships between a high proportion of simple recasts in mothers' replies to 22-month-olds and the children's language growth. Negative relationships were reported when mothers used high proportions of complex recasts. Together, all these data suggest that the direction in which maternal speech affects the child's responsiveness is the direction of its influence on language development.

The next analysis reports the effect of concurrent replies of varying complexity (simple vs. complex recasts) on children's responsiveness in a controlled situation. A portion of the data has been presented by Stella Prorok, dos Santos, Soares, and Casari (1979). The subjects were the five 2-year-olds from the 15 Brazilian M-C pairs.

The study was carried out in the same playroom where the observational sessions for the previous studies had been made. A talking clown located in the playroom was used to provide controlled interaction with the child. The clown was remotely manipulated by the experimenter from the observational chamber. The appearance of the clown was pleasant, and the children apparently enjoyed "interacting" with it. The clown had small lightbulbs in his eyes, and a loudspeaker hidden behind his mouth. The lights would be on when the clown was speaking and off when he was silent. One initial adaptation session was used for free interaction between the child and the clown. After this initial session, the basic procedure was the following: In alternating periods, 4 min long on average, the clown would reply to C's verbalizations with: (a) repetition of most of C's previous verbalization, adding new items, but keeping the basic referent, which would be related to anything observable in the situation; (b) a comment, including some of the words in C's previous verbalization, adding new items and expanding the referent to events not observable in the situation.

Within each period, a variable interval schedule of on average 30 sec (VI 30") was applied to control the timing of new questions used to initiate further verbal interaction with the child, thus avoiding prolonged periods of silence. According to that schedule, the clown would ask the question "What is that?" if the child were holding and/or examining a toy, or "What are you doing?" if the child were engaged in active play. A response by the child would be followed by (a) or (b) according to the experimental period. Any spontaneous verbalization by the child would also be followed by (a) or (b) in the same manner. If the child did not answer the clown's question within 2 sec, the lights would be turned off, and a new question would be asked again at the beginning of the next interval. If the child kept talking to the clown, the clown would continue replying, so that the child's continued performance would diminish the question-asking behavior in the clown. The sessions were carried out at one-week intervals and were 16 min long, therefore allowing for four alternate periods of replies of type (a) and (b). The mother was present at all the sessions, reading a newspaper; she would respond to C's interactions directed towards her, but would avoid initiating interactions with him. Half way through the sixth session, a disruption in the temporal pattern of interaction between C and the clown was introduced. In the new procedure, replies (a) or (b) were presented with an average delay of 3 sec. This was continued for the next one and a half sessions, and then the previous immediacy was resumed for two further sessions.

Example periods for "simple" and "complex" replies are shown below for one subject. The clown (whose name is "Pirilim") is denoted by "P," and the child by "C." English translations are shown below the Portuguese originals. The session starts with a "simple" period, and is presented from the very beginning.

1st. period: 'Simple' replies

    P—"Tudo bem, Fabiana?"
       ("Is everything all right, Fabiana?")
    C—"Tudo bem."
       ("Everything's fine.")
    P—"Tudo bem!"
       ("Everything's fine!")
    C—"Olha aqui Pirilim."
       ("Look here Pirilim.")
    P—"O que é isso Fabiana?"
       ("What's that Fabiana?")
    C—"É coisinha."
       ("It's a little thing.")
    P—"O que é essa coisinha?"
       ("What's that little thing?")
    C—"Aqui, badezinha."
       ("Here, a little tway.")
    P—"Uma bandeijinha."
       ("A little tray.")
    C—"Uma bandeijinha."
       ("A little tray.")
    P—"É uma banbeijinha branca."
       ("It's a little white tray.")

6. MOTHER-CHILD LANGUAGE IN THE NATURAL ENVIRONMENT 219

C—"Uma bandeijinha branca?"
("A little white tray?")
P—É, bandeijinha branca com xicrinhas."
("Yes, a little white tray with little cups.")
C—"Aqui o fosão ó."
("Here's the stove, look.")
P—"Olha o fogãozinho branco Fabiana!"
("Look at the little white stove Fabiana!")
C—"É o bojão."
("And the gas cylinder.")
P—"O bojãozinho é vermelho!"
("The little gas cylinder's red!")
C—"Ihh, ó, quebrou."
("Oh, look, it broke.")
P—"É, essa pecinha quebrou mesmo."
("Yes, that little piece really has broken.")
C—"De onde que é essa pecinha?"
("Where's that little piece from?")
P—"Essa pecinha é do fogãozinho."
("That little piece is from the little stove.")
C—"É?"
("Is it?")
P—"É, é do fogãozinho branco."
("Yes, it's from the little white stove.")
C—"Olha, panelinha do fogão."
("Look the little pan for the stove.")

2nd. period: 'Complex' replies

P—"O que você tá fazendo Fabiana?"
("What're you doing Fabiana?")
C—"Cuando café!"
("Sieving coffee.")
P—"Ah, que café gostoso que a Fabiana tá coando
pra ela tomar!"
("Ah, what delicious coffee Fabiana is
sieving for her to drink!")
C—"Ahm?" (long pauses)
("Ahm?")
C—"Tomar? heim?"
("Drink? ey?")
P—"O que você tá fazendo Fabiana?"
("What're you doing Fabiana?")
C—"Tomando café."
("Drinking coffee.")

P—"Ontem eu tomei um café tão quente que
queimei minha boca!"
("Yesterday I drank a coffee so hot that
I burned my mouth!")
C—". . . ha? . . . ha? . . . ha?"
(". . . ha? . . . ha? . . . ha?")
C—". . . quê?"
(". . . what?")
C—". . . cê queimou?"
(". . . burned yourself?")
P—"Eu queimei minha boca porque eu tomei
um café muito quente."
("I burned my mouth because I drank a
very hot coffee.")
C—". . . ah!"
(". . . ah!")
C—". . . café ruim?"
(". . . bad coffee?")
P—"Nao sei se o café estava ruim porque
consegui tomar muito pouco."
("I don't know if it was bad because I
could drink very little.")
C—". . . ha? . . . eu não sei . . . oi!—ó
você, qué mais?"
(". . . ah? . . . I don't know . . . hey! (to a doll)
. . . hey you (to the doll)
. . . want more?")
C—". . . não?"
(". . . no? (to the doll) ")
C—(intermittent onomatopoeics to indicate drinking)
P—"O que você tá fazendo Fabiana?"
("What're you doing Fabiana?")
C—(long pause)
P—"Oi Fabiana! O que é isso?"
("Hey Fabiana! What's that?")
C—"Um caminhão"
("A truck.")
P—"Eu vi um caminhão igualzinho a esse
na estrada carregado com uma porção
de carros."
("I saw a truck just like that one
on the road, loaded with cars.")
C—(long pause)

P—"O que é isso Fabiana?"
("What's that Fabiana?")

The data in Figure 6.2 show the number of C's verbalizations during each period of the various experimental sessions for one child. For the child shown, the simple replies were given during the first and third periods of each session, and the complex replies in the second and fourth periods.

The sharp contrast in the effects of the two kinds of replies on the child's responsiveness is clear. During the periods of simple replies, long interactive chains occurred, allowing few occasions for a question to be asked by the clown. During the periods of complex replies, not only would the chains frequently end after the clown's replies, thus being only two exchanges long when initiated by the clown with a WH question, or just one exchange long when initiated by the child, but also, during the course of a complex period, the child would actually stop answering the questions as well. Further, in the case of simple replies (i.e., modified repetitions) the data correspond to the positive effects described for naturally occurring maternal repetitions of the sort previously described for the same Brazilian subjects, as well as for the British ones, whereas for the complex replies ("comments"), they correspond to the negative effects as previously described for the British children. In addition a delay in producing a simple reply also had a suppressive effect on the child's performance. The effect was not just to slow down the flow of communication, but to impede the establishment of the communicative event. In fact, the children gave the impression that they simply did not know what to do in the situation. Thus, the delayed simple replies had the same effect as the immediate complex replies, with the child's performance being completely disturbed.

Also, qualitative changes were found in C's performance during the different periods (chi-square = 23.99, $p < 0.001$). Intelligibles related to the clown's replies were more frequent during the "simple" periods (60%) than during the "complex" (49%) periods; partial or modified repetitions also occurred more frequently during the "simple" periods (18% vs. 12%); and finally the frequency of unintelligibles plus onomatopaeics and exclamations was higher during the "complex" periods (39% vs. 22%). Turning to the performance of this child in natural interaction with his mother, the proportion of partial or modified repetitions in his speech samples was doubled during the "simple" periods (18% vs. 9%), whereas a noticeable proportion of unintelligibles, "onomatopaeics, and exclamations was added to his speech during the "complex" periods (39% vs. 28%). This outcome is interesting in that it suggests that if the child's performance is not able to change input that does not accommodate his current repertoire (in this case the clown's "complex" input), he engages in a kind of speech production that is absolutely ineffective for dialogue. It appears that he finds no way in which to participate in the flow of interaction, and so reverts to more primitive speech.

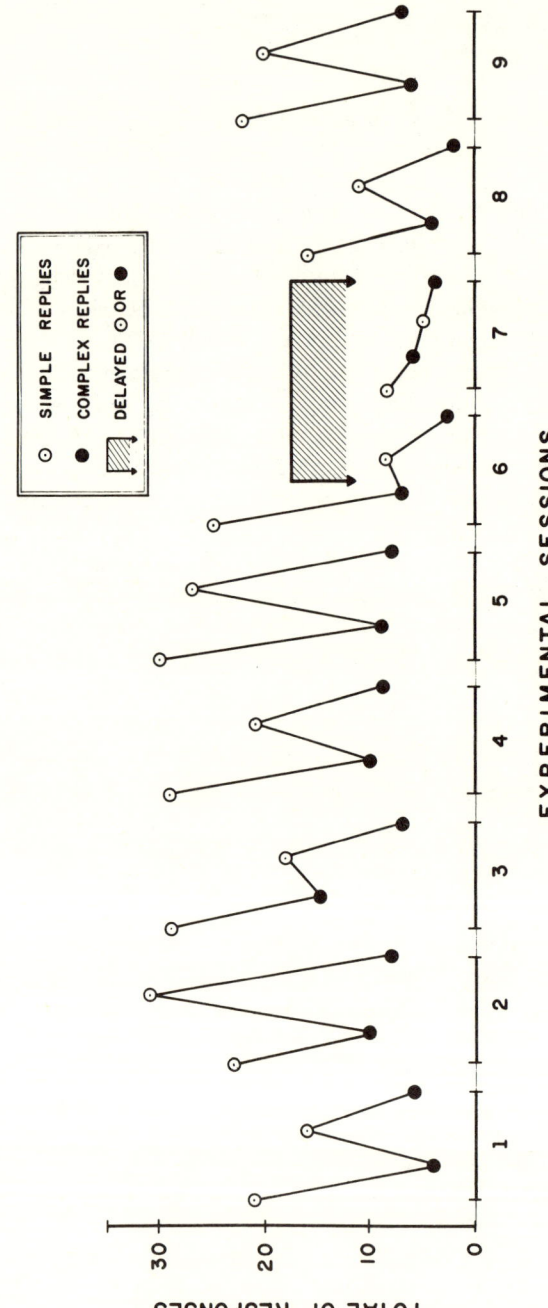

FIG. 6.2. Total of verbal responses emitted by one 2-year-old child during controlled periods of "simple" and "complex" replies throughout the experimental sessions.

6. MOTHER-CHILD LANGUAGE IN THE NATURAL ENVIRONMENT   223

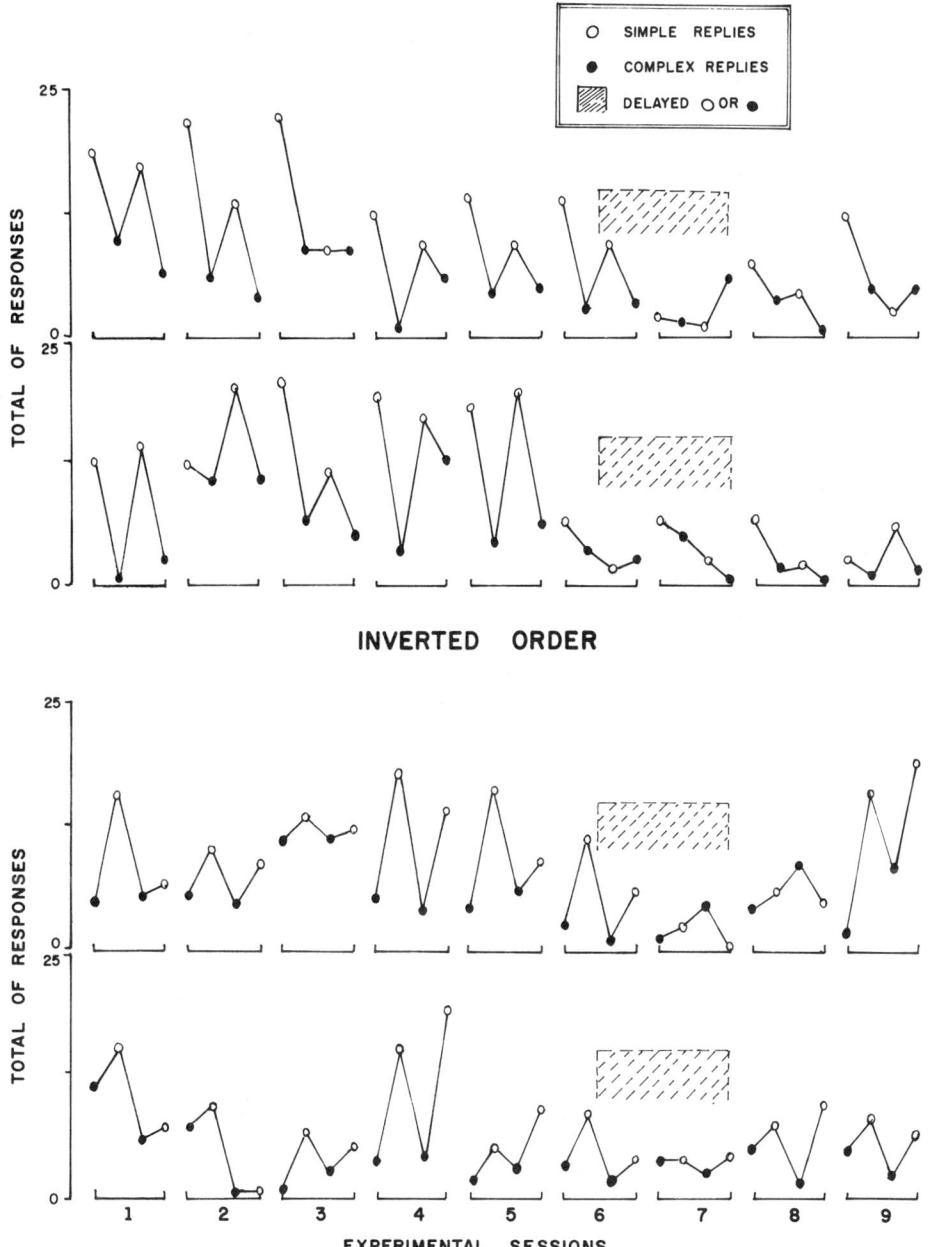

FIG. 6.3. Total of verbal responses by four children in the 2-year-old group during controlled periods of "simple" and "complex" replies throughout the experimental sessions.

In this context, the results allow the speculation that a higher occurrence of "comments" or other complex replies in the input, particularly around the age of two, might change the path of development. The communicative function of the dialogue weakens because the verbal behavior that the child emits does not have a chance to affect the input, which in its turn continues not to "reach" the child. Accordingly, this would produce an ineffective pattern of "interaction" between the child and his linguistic environment that could give rise to problems in his language development. The strength of such speculations is enhanced by the similarity in the performances of the other four children studied, as can be appreciated from Figure 6.3.

The effects of expansions, repetitions, and recasts have been discussed on different grounds according to the emphasis given to different defining dimensions by different investigators (DePaulo & Bonvillian, 1978; Nelson, 1980). The studies discussed here do not represent an exception. In fact, whenever expansion and repetition, or simple and complex replies were considered, the emphasis was placed on the communicative efficacy of such examples of maternal speech as assessed in terms of maintaining or withdrawing the child from the dialogue. The evidence presented for the 2-year-old children was consistent in one direction: When provided with concurrent adult verbalizations of varying complexity, the children responded differentially on the basis of: (a) structural similarity between the adult's and the child's ongoing verbal responses; and (b) correspondence of the adult's verbal responses to semantic events currently accessible to the child in the course of the interchanges. As to the way in which those examples of maternal speech might affect language development, it is argued that this line of evidence fits well with Nelson's (1980) contention that the conversational events "held to be necessary to the child's advances in syntax or discourse are the successful comparisons between input constructions and closely related constructions already in the child's language [p. 7]."

SUMMARY AND CONCLUSIONS

One relevant conclusion to be drawn from the evidence given in this chapter is that there are extrinsic forces in the M-C dialogue propelling the child's language development. Furthermore, any analyses of the effects of input on language development that take into account the functions of linguistic stimuli in sequences of mother and child behaviors will agree with that. The evidence presented in this chapter has indicated a characteristic temporal organization in the pattern of mother-child dialogue that changes with the child's progression in development. Occasional disturbances in the mother's and in the child's patterns of interaction were suggested as extrinsic forces impelling the child towards development. By responding differentially to the child's mature and immature utterances, the mother introduces a communication pressure in the dialogue, and this propels the child towards the usage of more mature linguistic forms. By responding differentially to the mother's speech of varying complexity, the child indicates to the mother the dimensions of input that are operative in his linguistic system, and by doing so, he can generate the conditions that are productive of language development. Associated with the child's pattern of responding, some dimensions of input were suggested as facilitative of language development in contrast to others, which might impose detrimental effects on development. Emphasis was given to repetitions (or simple recasts) in the first case, and comments (or complex recasts) in the second.

As far as the conceptualization of the effects of input is concerned, the need is argued for attention to the relational dimensions implied in input-output components of the mother-child speech system. Because there is every reason to believe in an hierarchical organization of input concerning the child's pattern of responding, more longtitudinal (naturalistic) data are required to guide the implementation of cross-sectional and experimental designs in language development research. Moreover, because the organization of the input interacts with the child's developing behavioral structures, efforts should converge towards sequential analyses of M-C speech changes at microanalytical levels. Consequently this calls for a reconsideration of the analytical unit of most correlational studies. On the same line, it calls for more appropriate selection of what has constituted, in the literature, maternal speech samples. If just being exposed to packages of verbal stimulation does not help language development (Bonvillian & Nelson, 1976; Stella, 1974; Stella-Prorok, 1980b; Whitehurst et al., 1972), then research concerned with determination of the role of input on development should be able to discriminate interactive input from "input by itself." In several sections of this chapter, that point was emphasized and some suggestions about criteria for defining and selecting analytical units were presented within the context of the respective discussions. However, some limitations of the analyses described in this chapter, as well as the paucity of other studies applying similar rationale, pose difficulties for more specific suggestions for further investigations.

Finally, the analysis of phenomena similar to the ones focused upon in the previous discussions might prove useful for the early assessment of delayed language development. Indeed, some current analyses by the author and collaborators (Crnkovic, Monteiro, & Stella-Prorok, 1981; Stella-Prorok, Golfeto, & Brandão, 1981) on the temporal patterns of vocal interchanges between mothers and their Down's Syndrome children are revealing some preliminary data on interactive and/or disruptive patterns quite different from the ones described here for normal young children. The implications of these results, if they should be confirmed at the final stages of analysis, are clear for the well-known delay in the language of those children, in the sense that the deviant patterns may cut short all the interactive experiences that have been suggested as crucial for normal young children's language development.

ACKNOWLEDGMENTS

Some of the research reported here was supported in part by Grant Psicologia—0353/76 from Fundação de Amparo à Pesquisa do Estado de São Paulo, and by the facilities rendered at the Department of Growth and Development, Institute of Child Health, University of London, by courtesy of Dr. N. Blurton Jones, to whom the author is grateful.

Special thanks are extended to: the mothers and children who served as subjects; to my students R. C. O. Santos, V. L. Casari, and V. M. Soares who helped with much of the data collection; and, finally, to Dr. Jacek G. Prorok.

REFERENCES

Bateson, M. C. Mother-infant exchanges: The epigenesis of conversational interaction. In D. Aaronson & R. W. Rieber (Eds.), *Developmental psycholinguistics and communication disorders*. New York: New York Academy of Sciences, 1975.

Bloom, K. Patterning of infant vocal behavior. *Journal of Experimental Child Psychology*, 1977, *23*, 367–377.

Bloom, L., Rocissano, L., & Hood, L. Adult-child discourse: Developmental interaction between information processing and linguistic interaction. *Cognitive Psychology*, 1976, *8*, 521–552.

Bonvillian, J. D., & Nelson, K. E. Sign language acquisition in a mute autistic boy. *Journal of Speech and Hearing Disorders*, 1976, *41*, 339–347.

Bowerman, M. Semantic and syntactic development: A review of what, when and how in language acquisition. In R. L. Schiefelbush (Ed.), *Bases of language intervention*. Baltimore: University Park Press, 1978.

Brazelton, T. B., Koslowski, B., & Main, M. The origins of reciprocity: The early mother-infant interaction. In M. Lewis and L. A. Rosenblum (Eds.), *The effect of the infant on its caregiver*. New York: Wiley, 1974.

Broen, P. A. The verbal environment of the language learning child. *American Speech and Hearing Monographs*, 1972 (No. 17).

Brown, R. *A first language: The early stages*. Cambridge, Mass.: Harvard University Press, 1973.

Brown, R. & Bellugi, U. Three processes in the child's acquisition of syntax. *Harvard Educational Review*, 1964, *34*, 133–151.

Brown, R., Cazden, C., & Bellugi, U. The child's grammar from I to III. In J. P. Hill (Ed.), *Minnesota symposia on child psychology*. Minneapolis: University of Minnesota Press, 1969.

Brown, R. & Fraser, C. The acquisition of syntax. *In* C. N. Cofer & B. S. Musgrave (Eds.), *Verbal behavior and learning*. New York: McGraw-Hill, 1963.

Brown, R. & Hanlon, C. Derivational complexity and order of acquisition in child speech. *In* J. R. Hayes (Ed.), *Cognition and the development of language*. New York: Wiley, 1970.

Chomsky, N. *Aspects of the theory of syntax*. Cambridge, Mass.: MIT Press, 1965.

Condon, W. S. Method of micro-analysis of sound film behavior. *Behavioral Research, Methodology and Instrumentation*, 1970, *2*, 51–54.

Condon, W. S. A primary phase in the organization of infant responding behavior. In H. R. Schaffer (Ed.), *Studies in mother-infant interaction*. New York: Academic Press, 1977.

Condon, W. S. & Ogston, W. D. Sound film analysis of normal and pathological behavior patterns. *Journal of Nervous and Mental Diseases*, 1966, *143*, 338–346.

Condon, W. S. & Sander, L. W. Neonate movement is synchronized with adult speech: Interactional participation and language development. *Science*, 1974, *183*, 99–101.

Cross, T. G. Motherese: Its association with rate of syntactic acquisition in young children. In N. Waterson & C. Snow (Eds.), *The development of communication: Social and pragmatic factors in language acquisition*. New York: Wiley, 1976.

Cross, T. G. Mothers' speech adjustments: The contribution of selected child listener variables. In C. E. Snow & C. A. Ferguson (Eds.), *Talking to children: Language input and acquisition*. Cambridge: Cambridge University Press, 1977.

Cross, T. G. *Mothers' speech adjustments and child language learning: Some methodological considerations*. Paper presented at The First International Congress for the Study of Child Language, Tokyo, August 1978.

Crnkovic, L. M. P., Monteiro, M. I. B., & Stella-Prorok, E. M. *Analises comparativas de mudancas evolutivas no intercambio verbal mae-crianca normal e com Sindrome de Down*. Paper presented at the 33rd. Reuniao Anual da Sociedade Brasileira para o Progresso da Ciencia, Salvador, Bahia, Brazil, July 1981.

Davis, H. *A description of aspects of mother-infant vocal interaction*. Manuscript submitted for publication. City of London Polytechnic, 1978.

DePaulo, B. M. & Bonvillian, J. D. The effect on language development of the special characteristics of speech addressed to children. *Journal of Psycholinguistic Research*, 1978, *7*, 189–211.

de Villiers, J. G. & de Villiers, P. A. Semantics and syntax in the first two years: The output of form and function and the form and function of the input. In F. D. Minifie & L. L. Lloyd (Eds.), *Communicative and cognitive abilities—early behavioral assessment*. University Park Press, Baltimore, 1978.

Duncan, S. D. Some signals and rules for taking speaking turns in conversation. *Journal of Personality and Social Psychology*, 1972, *23*, 283–292.

Duncan, S. D. & Niederehe, G. On signalling that it's your turn to speak. *Journal of Experimental Social Psychology*, 1974, *10*, 234–247.

Eimas, P. D., Siqueland, E. R., Jusczyk, P., & Vigorito, J. Speech perception in early infancy. *Science*, 1971, *171*, 303–306.

Ervin, S. Imitation and structural change in children's language. In E. H. Lenneberg (Ed.), *New directions in the study of language*. MIT Press, Cambridge, Mass., 1964.

Ferguson, C. A. Baby talk in six languages. *American Anthropologist*, 1964, *66*, 103–114.

Fogel, A. Temporal organization in mother-infant face-to-face interaction. In H. R. Schaffer (Ed.), *Studies in mother-infant interaction*. New York: Academic Press, 1977.

Fraser, C., Bellugi, U., & Brown, R. W. Control of grammar in imitation, comprehension, and production. *Journal of Verbal Learning and Verbal Behavior*, 1963, *2*, 121–135.

Fraser, C. & Roberts, A. Mothers' speech to children of different ages. *Journal of Psycholinguistic Research*, 1975, *4*, 9–16.

Freedle, R. & Lewis, M. Prelinguistic conversations. In M. Lewis & L. A. Rosenblum (Eds.), *Interaction, conversation, and the development of language*. New York: Wiley, 1977.

Furrow, D., Nelson, K., & Benedict, H. Mothers' speech to children and syntactic development: Some simple relationships. *Journal of Child Language*, 1979, *6*, 423–442.

Garcia, E. E. & DeHaven, E. D. Use of operant techniques in the establishment and generalization of language: A review and analysis. *American Journal of Mental Deficiency*, 1974, *79*, 169–178.

Garvey, C. Requests and responses in children's speech. *Journal of Child Language*, 1975, *2*, 41–60.

Garvey, C. & Hogan, R. Social speech and social interaction: Egocentrism revisited. *Child Development*, 1973, *44*, 562–568.

Gelman, R. & Shatz, M. Appropriate speech adjustments: The operation of conversational constraints on talk to two-year-olds. In M. Lewis & L. A. Rosenblum (Eds.), *Interaction, conversation, and the development of language*. New York: Wiley, 1977.

Goffman, E. On face-work: An analysis of ritual elements in social interaction. *Psychiatry*, 1955, *18*, 213–231.

Grosjean, F., Grosjean, L., & Lane, H. The patterns of silence: Performance structures in sentence production. *Cognitive Psychology*, 1979, *11*, 58–81.

Hawkins, P. R. The syntactic location of hesitation pauses. *Language and Speech*, 1971, *14*, 277–288.

Hovell, M. F., Schumaker, J. B., & Sherman, J. A. A comparison of parents' models and expansions in promoting children's acquisition of adjectives. *Journal of Experimental Child Psychology*, 1978, *25*, 41–57.

Hursh, D. E. & Sherman, J. A. The effects of parent-presented models and praise on the vocal behavior of their children. *Journal of Experimental Child Psychology*, 1973, *15*, 328–339.

Jaffe, J. & Feldstein, S. *Rhythms of dialogue*. New York: Academic Press, 1970.

Jaffe, J., Stern, D. N., & Peery, J. C. Conversational coupling of gaze behavior in prelinguistic human development. *Journal of Psycholinguistic Research*, 1973, *2*, 321–329.

Kaye, K. Toward the origin of dialogue. In H. R. Schaffer (Ed.), *Studies in mother-infant interaction*. New York: Academic Press, 1977.

Keenan, E. O. & Klein, E. Coherency in children's discourse. *Journal of Psycholinguistic Research*, 1975, *4*, 365–380.

Kendon, A. Some functions of gaze-direction in social interaction. *Acta Psychologica*, 1967, *26*, 22–63.

Krasner, L. Studies of the conditioning of verbal behavior. *Psychological Bulletin*, 1958, *55*, 148–170.

Lieberman, P. *Intonation, perception and language*. Cambridge, Mass.: MIT Press, 1967.

Mahoney, G. J. Ethological approach to delayed language acquisition. *American Journal of Mental Deficiency*, 1975, *80*, 139–148.

McNeill, D. Developmental psycholinguistics. In F. Smith and G. A. Miller (Eds.), *The genesis of language: A psycholinguistic approach*. Cambridge, Mass.: MIT Press, 1966.

McNeill, D. *The acquisition of language: The study of developmental psycholinguistics*. New York: Harper & Row, 1970.

Miller, G. A. Review of J. H. Greenberg (Ed.), Universals of Language. *Contemporary Psychology*, 1963, *8*, 417–418.

Moerk, E. L. Principles of dyadic interaction in language learning. *Merrill-Palmer Quarterly*, 1972, *18*, 229–257.

Moerk, E. L. Changes in verbal child-mother interactions with increasing language skills of the child. *Journal of Psycholinguistic Research*, 1974, *3*, 101–116.

Moerk, E. L. Verbal interactions between children and their mothers during the preschool years. *Developmental Psychology*, 1975, *11*, 788–794.

Moerk, E. L. Processes of language teaching and training in the interactions of mother-child dyads. *Child Development*, 1976, *47*, 1064–1078.

Morse, P. A. The discrimination of speech and non-speech stimuli in early infancy. *Journal of Experimental Child Psychology*, 1972, *14*, 477–492.

Nelson, K. Structure and strategy in learning to talk. *Monographs of the Society for Research in Child Development*, 1973, *38* (Serial No. 149).

Nelson, K. E. Facilitating children's syntax acquisition. *Developmental Psychology*, 1977, *13*, 101–107.

Nelson, K. E. Theories of the child's acquisition of syntax: A look at rare events and at necessary, catalytic, and irrelevant components of mother-child conversation. *Annals of the New York Academy of Sciences*, 1980, *345*, 45–67.

Nelson, K. E. Toward a rare-event cognitive comparison theory of syntax acquisition. In P. S. Dale & D. Ingram (Eds.), *Child language: An international perspective*. Baltimore: University Park Press, 1981.

Nelson, K. E. & Bonvillian, J. D. Concepts and words in the 18-month-old: Acquiring concept names under controlled conditions. *Cognition*, 1974, *4*, 435–450.

Nelson, K. E., Carskaddon, G., & Bonvillian, J. D. Syntax acquisition: Impact of experimental variation in adult verbal interaction with the child. *Child Development,* 1973, *44,* 497–504.

Phillips, J. Syntax and vocabulary of mothers' speech to young children: Age and sex comparisons. *Child Development,* 1973, *44,* 182–185.

Premack, D. A functional analysis of language. *Journal of Experimental Analysis of Behavior,* 1970, *14,* 107–125.

Rees, N. S. Pragmatics of language: Applications to normal and disordered language development. In R. L. Schefelbush (Ed.), *Bases of language intervention.* Baltimore: University Park Press, 1978.

Remick, H. Maternal speech to children during language acquisition. In W. Raffer-Engel & Y. Lebrun (Eds.), *Baby talk and infant speech.* Lisse, Netherlands: Swets & Zeitlinger, 1976.

Rehicle, J. E., Longhurst, T. M., & Stepanich, L. Verbal interaction in mother-child dyads. *Developmental Psychology,* 1976, *12,* 273–277.

Rondal, J. A. Fathers' and mothers' speech in early language development. *Journal of Child Language,* 1980, *7,* 353–369.

Ryan, J. Early language development: Towards a communicational analysis. In P. M. Richards (Ed.), *The integration of the child into a social world.* Cambridge: Cambridge University Press, 1974.

Salzinger, K. Experimental manipulation of verbal behavior: A review. *The Journal of General Psychology,* 1959, *61,* 65–94.

Salzinger, K. Pleasing linguists: A parable. *Journal of Verbal Learning and Verbal Behavior,* 1970, *9,* 725–727.

Sander, L. W. The regulation of exchange in the infant-caretaker system and some aspects of the context-content relationship. In M. Lewis & L. A. Rosenblum (Eds.), *Interaction, conversation, and the development of language.* New York: Wiley, 1977.

Schaffer, H. R. Early interactive development. In H. R. Schaffer (Ed.), *Studies in mother-infant interaction.* New York: Academic Press, 1977.

Schaffer, H. R., Collis, G., & Parsons, G. *Vocal interchanges and visual regard in verbal and preverbal children.* Paper presented at the Loch Lomond Symposium, University of Strathclyde, September 1975.

Segal, E. F. Psycholinguistics discovers the operant: A review of Roger Brown's A First Language: The early stages. *Journal of the Experimental Analysis of Behavior,* 1975, *23,* 149–158.

Seitz, S. & Stewart, C. Imitations and expansions: Some developmental aspects of mother-child communications. *Developmental Psychology,* 1975, *11,* 763–768.

Skinner, B. F. *Verbal behavior.* New York: Appleton-Century-Crofts, 1957.

Snow, C. E. Mothers' speech to children learning language. *Child Development,* 1972, *43,* 549–565.

Snow, C. E. Mothers' speech research: From input to interaction. In C. E. Snow & C. A. Ferguson (Eds.), *Talking to children: Language input and acquisition.* Cambridge: Cambridge University Press, 1977.

Staats, A. W. Linguistic-mentalistic theory versus an explanatory S-R learning theory of language development. In D. I. Slobin (Ed.), *The ontogenesis of grammar.* New York: Academic Press, 1971.

Stella, E. M. *A field-descriptive and experimental study of verbal behaviour in one year old children.* Unpublished doctoral dissertation, University of London, 1974.

Stella-Prorok, E. M. *Mother-child verbal interchanges: A field-descriptive study with Brazilian children aged from one to three.* Paper presented at The First International Congress for the Study of Child Language, Tokyo, August 1978.

Stella-Prorok, E. M. Mother-child verbal interchange: A descriptive study of young children's verbal behavior. *Journal of Psycholinguistic Research,* 1980, *9,* 451–471. (a)

Stella-Prorok, E. M. *Conversando com criancas: Aquisicao da linguagem no contexto do dialogo.* Thesis for Livre Docencia, University of Sao Paulo, 1980. (b)

Stella-Prorok, E. M., dos Santos, R. C., Soares, V. M., & Casari, V. L. *Desempenho verbal de criancas em situacao controlada: Efeitos de consequentes verbais de dois niveis de complexidade.* Paper presented at the IX Reuniao Anual de Psicologia, Ribeirao Preto, October 1979.

Stella-Prorok, E. M., Golfeto, E. M., & Brandao, S. *Caracteristicas comunicativas na interacao entre a mae e seu filho com Sindrome de Down: Analises preliminares.* Paper presented at the 33rd Reunião Anual da Sociendade Brasileira para o Progresso da Ciência, Salvador, Bahia, Brazil, July 1981.

Stella-Prorok, E. M. & Silva, M. A. Influencia da fala materna sobre a responsividade verbal de criancas de dois anos de idade no intercambio natural mae-crianca. *Psicologia*, 1980, *5*, 29–40.

Stern, D. N. A micro-analysis of mother-infant interaction behavior regulating social contact between a mother and her 3½-month-old twins. *Journal of the American Academy of Child Psychiatry*, 1971, *10*, 501–517.

Stern, D. N. Mother and infant at play: The dyadic interaction involving facial, vocal and gaze behaviors. In M. Lewis & L. A. Rosenblum (Eds.), *The effect of the infant on its caregiver.* New York: Wiley, 1974.

Stern, D. N., Beebe, B., Jaffe, J., & Bennett, S. L. The infant's stimulus world during social interaction. In H. R. Schaffer (Ed.), *Studies in mother-infant interaction.* New York: Academic Press, 1977.

Stern, D. N., Jaffe, J., Beebe, B., & Bennett, S. Vocalizing in unison and in alternation: Two modes of communication within the mother-infant dyad. In D. Aaronson & R. W. Rieber (Eds.), *Developmental psycholinguistics and communication disorders.* New York: New York Academy of Sciences, 1975.

Trevarthen, C. Descriptive analyses of infant communication behaviour. In H. R. Schaffer (Ed.), *Studies in mother-infant interaction.* New York: Academic Press, 1977.

Waxler, C. Z. & Yarrow, M. R. An observational study of maternal models. *Developmental Psychology*, 1975, *11*, 485–494.

Weeks, T. Speech registers in children. *Child Development*, 1971, *42*, 1119–1131.

Whitehurst, G. J., Novak, G., & Zorn, G. A. Delayed speech studied in the home. *Developmental Psychology*, 1972, *7*, 169–177.

Whitehurst, G. J. & Vasta, R. Is language acquired through imitation? *Journal of Psycholinguistic Research*, 1975, *4*, 37–59.

Zukow, P. G., Reilly, J., & Greenfield, P. M. Making the absent present: Facilitating the transition from sensorimotor to linguistic communication. In K. E. Nelson (Ed.), *Children's Language* (Vol. 3). Hillsdale, N.J.: Lawrence Erlbaum Associates, 1982.

7 The Role of Play in Phonological Development

Charles A. Ferguson
Marlys A. Macken
*Stanford University
Department of Linguistics*

INTRODUCTION

That children play with vocal sounds, including speech sounds, and that they play with language in terms of sound similarities and differences, are truisms. Several different kinds of phenomena are included in what may be called "sound play." There are problems in providing an adequate definition of "play" in general, but it is clear even without careful study that sound play is a very frequent childhood behavior. Moreover, language play, and more particularly sound play, is of considerable importance to language development in at least three different ways: as contributing to the phonetic substrate, as a factor in phonological development, and as something to be learned as part of the socially accepted use of language. These three aspects of sound play will be discussed here primarily in connection with: (1) babbling, i.e., early vocal play contributing to the mastery of the phonetic substrate; (2) expressive sound play, i.e., the sound-based word play common during the development of phonological organization, ages 2–5; and (3) language games, i.e., socially specified, sound-based ways of altering language, used especially in early adolescence and among special groups.[1]

---

[1]Chapter 3, Language Play and Games, in Weeks, 1979, covers roughly these same three topics in the same order, although the two treatments were prepared independently. Weeks' discussion draws on some of the same data cited here as well as a good deal of her own observations of children. Her additional material and insightful comments offer a valuable complement to this paper.

The role of play in human life has been discussed at least as far back as Heraclitus in Western philosophical and scientific traditions, and it figures in ancient Hindu traditions and doubtless elsewhere in early times. The great burst of modern intellectual concern about play as a fundamental human phenomenon, however, is often traced to the Dutch historian Huizinga, whose 1938 book *Homo ludens* (English translation 1949) seems to have set off a train of major responses that contributes to the recent development of play-centered models, play theory, and game theory in sociology, psychology, anthropology, economics, mathematics, psychiatry, literary analysis, philosophy, and even theology.[2] Recognition of the importance of play in child development, however, preceded Huizinga's lectures and book. For example, two investigators who theorized about play in development in the first decades of the 20th century were the Swiss psychologist Claparède and Sigmund Freud. The former (e.g., Claparède, 1906) held that play is necessary in childhood as a kind of practice at becoming an adult. The latter (e.g., Freud, 1908) held that play is the way the child gets pleasure out of unreality when faced with the reality of adults controlling his world. (Neither was interested in language development as such, and both would probably have been puzzled or bored by the question of how children acquire the phonology and syntax of their mother tongue.)

Similarly, Piaget, when he discussed play in relation to sensorimotor and cognitive development in his book *La Formation du Symbole chez L'Enfant* (1946; translated into English as *Play, Dreams, and Imitation in Childhood* 1951), was only marginally interested in the acquisition of linguistic structure as a part of child development. His three categories (and various corresponding stages) of practice play, symbolic play, and social play are valuable concepts in child development, but he did not relate them directly to language development. More recently, as developmental theorists have focused more on play, they have extended and modified the Piagetian perspective and now include more direct attention to language (cf. e.g., Bowes, 1979; Bruner, Jolly, & Sylva, 1976; Garvey, 1977a; Herron & Sutton-Smith, 1971; McCune-Nicolich, 1981). Most of this work is still concerned, however, with cognitive development and the acquisition of communicative skills, and very little attention is paid to the development of phonology as such in spite of the phonological basis of much language play. Bruner's argument, in agreement with a number of other writers, is that play "draws attention to communication itself" and facilitates the development of segmentation and substitution, joint (caretaker-child) routines, and sequencing rules (Bruner, 1975). His illustrations are at the level of word-in-sentence or

---

[2]For the study of language play and child development the two most important lines of research and theory building have been the psychological and the anthropological. Among the many studies in these fields we found three books the most stimulating: Herron & Sutton-Smith, 1971; Bruner et al., 1976, and Schwartzman, 1979.

component-in-speech-act, but the argument could be applied just as well at the level of sound-in-word.³

A few studies of sound play itself have appeared in recent years in connection with research on language development. Increased sophistication in techniques of recording and instrumental analysis of speech has made it possible to study babbling more systematically than could be done before. For example, Cruttenden (1970) reported on the babbling of a pair of twins, utilizing tape recordings and making comparisons with the phonology of their early speech; Pierce (1974) reported on 750 children recorded during the first year of life; Oller and his associates analyzed the babbling of one child studied intensively and 15 or more other infants (e.g., Oller, Wieman, Doyle, & Ross, 1976); and Stark has done cross-sectional studies of many infants and detailed longitudinal studies of two infant girls (e.g., Stark, Rose, & McLagen, 1975). All these studies attempt to categorize the vocalizations of the babbling infant and compare the categories with those of early speech. Although they occasionally use such expressions as 'vocal play,' the authors make no attempt to define play behavior as such or to specify its relation to language development.

A number of observational studies of child language development, including traditional diary studies as well as highly focused discourse analyses and experimental investigations, have commented on the sound play in children aged 2 to 5 years and provide us with concrete examples of this behavior. The two most frequently cited studies are those of Weir, 1962, and Keenan, 1974. The former reported on the extensive vocal play of her son Anthony (2;10) in his presleep monologues; the latter recorded the joint sound play of her twins (2;10) in early morning interactions when they were by themselves. Garvey's more recent study of dyadic interactions among nursery school children (2;10–5;7) also includes explicit discussion of sound play (Garvey, 1977b). Although some attention is paid in these studies to the role of 'practice play' in language development, the authors are generally more concerned with the child's ability to play as part of communicative competence and with sound play as a major category of child discourse. Garvey (1977b), for example, states: "Different aspects of language and language use become available for play as they are acquired, and . . . a closer look at play may help to reveal what has been learned . . . [p. 47]." Or Keenan (1974): "The systematic nature of [joint] sound-play discourse brings out the degree to which young children attend to the formal features of one another's utterances [p. 183]."

Recent studies in the paradigm of ethnography of communication that focus on language play deal more explicitly with phonology (Sanches & Kirshenblatt-

---

³In the article cited, Bruner mentions phonological phenomena in connection with "puzzling" prosodic place-holders and, more incidentally, in an illustration involving *boo* and *achoo* in parallel episodes.

Gimblett, 1976; Sherzer, 1976), but not with phonological development. Sanches & Kirshenblatt-Gimblett in their article on children's traditional speech play simply assert that "for a young child—and progressively less so for older children—the phonological component of language is much more strongly organized than the syntactic, semantic, or sociolinguistic [p. 77]." In their view, the traditional child rhymes most popular at 5–7 years are evidence for the child's control of phonology, and if they facilitate language development it is not in phonology but in the acquisition of adult verbal art and poetic discourse. Sherzer's article on the more elaborate play languages or "secret languages" characteristic of young adolescents in many societies examines these phenomena in terms of their social functions and linguistic significance, not in relation to development. These studies are of interest to us here because of the evidence they offer of children's ability to operate relatively abstract and complex phonological rules, different from those of normal speech, in the creation of new, meaningful utterances, and also because they show that children acquire and use the socially accepted phonological games of their community as part of the total cultural inventory that is transmitted and adapted from generation to generation.

ISSUES

In any discussion of the role of play in language development we must first face the definitional question of what constitutes play behavior. We assume that the definitional question is substantive, i.e., that play is in some sense a 'natural' category (or set of related categories) of human behavior and we are not simply exploring the semantic value of such words as *play, jeu, Spiel, igra* in a handful of European languages or ethnocentrically imposing our own work : play dichotomy. Many well-reasoned definitions are offered in the current literature. For example, Sutton-Smith favors the characterization of play as "an exercise of voluntary control system with disequilibrial outcomes [Herron & Sutton-Smith, 1971, p. 344]," a descriptive definition that is based on extensive study of the whole field of play and games and distills much wisdom into a few words. Such definitions are, however, not very helpful at our level of wanting to decide what constitutes language play with sounds as opposed to other linguistic behavior. We adopt here the strategem of listing a number of criterial characteristics on which most observers would agree: Play is pleasurable activity; it is voluntary and it has no apparent extrinsic purpose; it involves repetition and variation; it includes patterns of behavior that also occur in nonplay activities; and it has markers to signal that play is going on. (For a similar list, cf. Garvey, 1977a; on the importance of repetition and variation, cf. Sutton-Smith, 1979; on play signals; cf. Aldis, 1975.)

The basic issues regarding the role of play in phonological development are the same as those in other aspects of child development: How and to what extent does language play consolidate or improve the control of the child's (phonological) behavior at a given stage? How and to what extent does language play serve as preparation for or practice in more advanced nonplay (phonological) behavior? To what extent does the emergence of a type of language play indicate a new (phonological) capability on the part of the child? What is the relation between individual and social aspects of play, and between biologically given and culturally prescribed play? Is (sound) play a necessary or a sufficient condition for normal (phonological) development? With these basic issues in mind, let us turn to direct consideration of sound play phenomena as reported by observers of children's language behavior.

BABBLING

The first type of play to consider is babbling, which is a major factor in the development of the phonetic substrate required for phonological organization. The babbling of infants typically begins about the fourth month, reaches a peak between the sixth and tenth months, continues past the appearance of the 'first words' toward the end of the first year or shortly thereafter, and is still engaged in during most of the second year. Observers have noted the very varied, seemingly random kinds of vocalization that take place, without obvious referential meaning, and they often refer to babbling as vocal play, comparable to other motoric play of infants. In general, most babbling meets the criteria customarily set for play: It gives the appearance of voluntary, pleasurable activity with no utilitarian purposes; it has behavioral similarities to the nonplayful speech, which later replaces it as the predominant vocal behavior of the child; and it is marked as fun by smiles and laughter from the child and the mother or other communication partner. There is general agreement from Piaget on, that the vocal play of babbling contributes in important ways to the development of the sensorimotor skills involved in the perception and production of speech sounds. Fry (1966) stated this clearly: "During the babbling stage, therefore, the child is doing two important things: he is trying out mechanisms that will be needed for speech, combining phonation with articulation and no doubt gaining a certain control of the respiratory system, and he is establishing the circuits by which motor activity and auditory impressions are firmly linked together [p. 190]."

On the relation between babbling and the phonological organization of 'true speech,' however, there is less agreement. Two older views still persist in the literature, although both of them have been shown to be wrong in important respects: the gradual approximation, 'behaviorist' view of Mowrer and others and the discontinuous, 'linguistic' view associated with the name of Jakobson (cf. Ferguson & Garnica, 1975). Recent expressions of these views phrase them as follows: "The babbling of infants in all cultures initially shows a random distribution of phonemes but gradually comes to approximate those of the surrounding culture [Aldis, 1975, p. 252]." "Babbling and the beginnings of verbal activities are as a rule clearly separated in children's behavior either as two concurrent yet quite distinct forms of activity or rather as two temporally delimited stages . . . [and] the variety and opulence of the babbled sounds yield to a rigorous sparseness of speech sounds [Jakobson & Waugh, 1979, p. 62]." The approximation view has inherent plausibility from the fact that babbling typically has a wide range of sound types, including some that do not appear in the phonology of the surrounding language; a simple reinforcement or operant conditioning model of learning would appear to account for development. To the best of our knowledge, however, no supporting evidence from either naturalistic observations or experimental studies has ever been adduced for this position. The discontinuity view has been based on the fact that many children may utter sounds quite freely in their babbling that they later acquire only slowly and apparently with great effort in their speech. This kind of reduction in inventory as well as the more structured nature of the sound system of speech, however, do not preclude continuous aspects of development bridging the two.

Recent research on babbling (e.g., Cruttenden, 1970; de Boysson-Bardies, Bacri, Sagart, & Poizat, 1981; de Boysson-Bardies, Sagart, & Bacri, 1980; Oller, 1980; Oller et al., 1976; Stark, 1978, 1980; Stark, Rose, & McLagen, 1975; Zlatin-Laufer & Horii, 1975), has established beyond doubt that there is a gradual development in the phonetic structure of vocalizations during the babbling period. Different types of vocalization tend to emerge or to predominate at different stages in the development of babbling. The appearance of certain types is so regular that they may be considered 'landmark' types, useful for the measurement of language development. The most notable of these are the early emergence of back sounds combining voicing and friction noise, commonly referred to as 'cooing," and the emergence of strings of identical Consonant and Vowel (CV) syllables (e.g., *dadada* . . .), referred to as 'canonical babbling.' The research has further shown that there are systematic relationships between the phonetic characteristics of a child's babbling and those of the child's early speech. These include the development of 'speechiness' in babbling parallel to development in permitted phonetic complexity in speech; similarities in the order of acquisition and relative frequency of particular sound types; the progression in vowel qualities that seems to cut across babbling and speech; and the appearance (or increased frequency) of sound types in a child's babbling that are about to appear or have just appeared in the child's speech.

By the development of speechiness in babbling is meant the movement from internally undifferentiated sound complexes toward increased clarity of segmentation (sequences of consonant-like and vowel-like sounds). The most comprehensive phonetic classification of babbling behavior is that of Oller, 1980, which lists 12 vocalization types, from QRNs (quasi-resonant nuclei) to GIBs (gibberish). Oller is able to identify corresponding characteristics of adult human speech for most of his vocalization types. The appearance of the successive additional characteristics constitutes a developmental line proceeding from a nonsegmental vocalization hardly like adult speech at all to sequences of recognizable syllabic structure and internal phonetic variety quite comparable with adult speech. The significance of play in this development is shown first by the onset of cooing, which is the first appearance of apparently voluntary, pleasurable vocalization, as opposed to crying or other 'distress' vocalizations and so-called 'vegetative' ones. The role of play is even more evident later on as the child is apparently "constantly trying out new combinations and recombinations of soundmaking skills" (Stark, 1980) in his or her vocal play.

A striking parallel to this development in speechiness appears in the gradual increase in the range of syllabic structures and phonetic variety of segments within the same syllable or word, which occurs in phonological development at a later stage. Early in children's phonological development they typically have such severe constraints on syllables or words as: only open syllables of the shape CV; no word of more than two syllables; all words stressed on the first syllable; and so on. They have such severe constraints on phonetic co-occurrence as: All vowels or all consonants in a word must be identical; all two-syllable words must be reduplicated; no stops and fricatives co-occur in the same word; and so on. Gradually, such constraints are relaxed and disappear. Although children seem to vary greatly in the orderliness of this development in "permitted complexity," it is likely to be a universal phenomenon; for general discussion and the detailed analysis of one child, cf. Macken, 1978. The gradual increase in permitted complexity of segmental phonetic structure is thus another example of Piaget's décalage, or Bruner's spiraling, or Sutton-Smith's genetic recursiveness. The child follows a similar path of development first at a simple, more basic level, and then again later at a more complex, hierarchical level of behavior.

The progression in speechiness is of interest also in that it manifests the primacy of prosodic features over segmental ones in phonological development. Although a number of investigators have claimed the very early acquisition of sentence prosodies, especially intonation contours, in comparison with the acquisition of the segmental material (e.g., Bever, Fodor, & Weksel, 1965), this issue remains controversial because of the methodological difficulties in the collection and analysis of the data (Bloom, 1973; Crystal, 1973, 1978, 1979; Menyuk & Bernholtz, 1969; Scollon, 1976).[4] The last several years, however, have seen a succession of studies of the acquisition of word prosodies, especially lexical tone, pointing to early acquisition. Most of these studies are based on varieties of Chinese, and the total number of subjects studied is fairly small, but

---

[4]Our view of the present evidence is that children typically acquire some intonation contours of the adult language during the babbling period, but that children vary greatly in the extent to which they attach to the contours distinctive semantic values matching the adult ones. Differences in opinion among investigators reflect this individual variation in children as well as different theoretical assumptions and research methods. See now the papers of the Symposium on Prosody in Child Language, in *Papers and Reports on Child Language Development* 21 (1982).

the evidence indicates early phonetic accuracy, early mastery of combinatory rules (tone sandhi), and relatively few errors at any stage as compared, for example, to the acquisition of consonant systems (Clumeck, 1977; Jeng, 1979; Li & Thompson, 1977; Tse, 1978. The pioneer study is Chao, 1951 [reprinted 1973]. For a review of the field, cf. Clumeck, 1980). The speechiness development and early acquisition of prosodic aspects of speech are doubtless related to the importance of the word as a total phonetic unit at the early stages of speech (cf. Chiat, 1979; Ferguson & Farwell, 1975; Macken, 1979). It may even be worth speculating that the ontogenetic primacy of prosodic phenomena may reflect a phylogenetic primacy. Certainly one of the unique characteristics of human speech is the use of a small inventory of commutable segments as opposed to the nonsegmentable vocal signals of other animals.[5]

Phonological development in early speech is characterized by certain universal patterns of acquisition. Certain sounds tend to be acquired before others no matter what the language being learned. For example, stops tend to be acquired before fricatives (e.g., *p t k b d g* before *f s sh v z*), labial consonants before alveolars (e.g., *b m* before *d n*), nonglottalized before glottalized (no English examples), low vowels before high (e.g., *a* before *i u*), semivowels before liquids (e.g., *y w* before *l r*). The apparently random vocal play of the infant, when examined carefully, is found to exhibit these same patterns. The child plays more with stops than fricatives, more with low vowels than high, etc. The patterns appear both in the relative frequencies of occurrence overall in babbling and in the order in which they tend to emerge and predominate during the babbling period. Cruttenden (1970) and Oller et al. (1976) address this point directly. This patterning goes counter to the predictions of both the approximations model and the discontinuity model. In opposition to the former, the developmental pattern is repeated at another stage in the phonology, and in opposition to the latter, the underlying principles assumed for phonological organization are prefigured in the babbling period. The same physiological constraints (articulatory and auditory) affect the vocal play in babbling and the development of phonological organization in speech, although the cognitive level of the latter is higher (see Macken & Ferguson, this volume).

The development in vowel production, as reported by recent researchers, shows a phonetic continuity in two respects: the increasing total range of vowel qualities and the increasing separation of different vowel qualities (i.e., reduction in borderline productions and overlapping productions of apparently different vowels). This point was made earlier in studies by Irwin and his colleagues, but without the sophistication of separation of babbling and speech, identifica-

---

[5]This view is not meant to suggest that word prosody phenomena in a given language are older or more primitive in the phonological system of the language. In many cases it is clear that the tonal system has arisen secondarily as a result of diachronic change in the phonology of a language.

tion of non-English sounds, and use of advanced techniques of acoustic phonetic analysis. Recent accounts are given by Gilbert (1979) and Lieberman (1980).

Probably the most striking connection between babbling and speech is the phenomenon of increased vocal play with a particular sound at about the same time that the sound first appears in the phonological repertoire of speech. This phenomenon, which by its very nature occurs only during an overlap period when a child is producing both babbling and speech, is well attested for a few children. The best account in the recent literature is the acquisition of /d/ described in Labov and Labov, 1978. Their child J, a "relatively late talker," produced both babbling and words during her 17th to 20th months. Her principal words were *cat* and *mama,* but she experimented with a half-dozen other words during the period, one of which was *dada.* She had babbled sequences including a [d] sound as early as 9;15, but showed no ability to use it in words until toward the end of the 16th month. At that time there was a great deal of babbling with [dæ] syllables culminating after a few days in *daddy,* which reappeared a month later in a stable form [dæ dæ]. The details of the fluctuation in both babbling and speech give a fairly complicated picture, with several peaks of different kinds, but the Labovs' conclusion is unequivocal: "Phonetic experiments with *dada* originated in babbling and the impulse given by vocal play [p. 838]." On the basis of this kind of evidence, as well as other evidence from semantics and syntax, the Labovs state as a characterization of language development: "Learning language is a game played with great intensity and energy. . . . The child is learning how to control the linguistic mechanism, so that it will eventually go where she wants it to go, and say what she wants it to say [p. 851]." This characterization is not defended in detail, however, nor explicated by careful definition of the terms.

Of greater interest in the Labovs' article is their view that the primary function of vocal play and experimentation during late babbling is not mastery of sensorimotor skills or the prefiguring of the sound types of early speech but the acquisition of certain "generalized abilities" or "operating principles" that are needed for phonological development. The Labovs list the most prominent of such principles as maximal dispersion, arbitrariness of the sign, unnaturalness of canonical forms, and the asymmetry of speaker and hearer in pronunciation. This view of vocal play is reminiscent of Bateson's "deutero-learning" and play theorists such as Vygotsky and Sutton-Smith. By means of play, the child is "learning to learn" rather than simply preparing for or practicing specific skills. This view is attractive, and the data from J are highly supportive of it. During the 5-month period that the Labovs describe, J repeatedly shifted the focus of her play and acquired very few stable words. At the end of the period, she began to lose both her vocabulary and her phonological system, and in about a month and a half they were almost all gone. When she restarted her lexical and phonological development in her 21st month, she apparently brought with her these generalized abilities rather than specific sounds and words, and the new phonology developed along different lines. Unfortunately for the generalizability of the Labovs' view, J's development does not seem to be typical of the transition from babbling to speech, and detailed descriptive studies of other children are needed. Nevertheless, even if J's development is highly idiosyncratic in some respects, this "deutero-learning" function of babbling needs to be investigated in other children's behavior.

The transitional phenomena at the overlap of late babbling and early speech constitute a critical locus for understanding phonological development and in particular the role of vocal play in such development. As is apparent from the literature cited here, the most sophisticated studies of babbling have stopped short of early speech, and the phonological studies of early speech do not reach down to babbling. The most promising line of research on this transition period are the recent studies on the emergence of prewords (variously called "vocables," "phonetically consistent forms," "sensorimotor morphemes," "protowords," etc.) as reported in Carter, 1975, 1978, 1979; Dore, Franklin, Miller, & Ramer, 1976; Menyuk & Menn, 1979; and elsewhere. Most of these investigations are only incidentally concerned with phonology and none of them focus on play. The goal of our current study on "Phonological precursors to early speech" is the analysis of the transitional phenomena.

EXPRESSIVE SOUND PLAY

The second type of sound play to be considered is the language play in which a solitary child or interacting children produce successive utterances with the primary focus on the sounds rather than the meanings. Such sequences may involve juxtaposition of real words or phonetic modifications of them, or may consist in whole or in part of nonsense material. Typically the fact that sound play is taking place is signalled by laughter and other devices. On this last point we quote Keenan's (1974) comments on expressive sound play between her twins: "First, paralinguistic cues indicate that the children themselves realize they are using language in some manner out of the ordinary. Sound play is often engaged in on a relatively high pitch level. Further it is generally accompanied by laughter. An utterance is produced. A burst of laughter follows. The utterance is repeated or modified by the co-present interlocutor, and so on [p. 171]."

The speech of children between 2 and 5 years is full of this kind of sound play, and variants of it continue for the next several years; yet there is very little systematic study of the phenomenon. Perhaps developmental psycholinguists are so much impressed with the seriousness of playing their own professional game that they tend to exclude the child's kind of playing from the purview of their research. Be that as it may, so pervasive a phenomenon during this important period of language development deserves more attention. The behavior has been so poorly described that it is difficult to subcategorize it, but at least three kinds of behavior seem to be involved (not excluding some indeterminacy or overlapping between them). The first, and least well documented, is exploratory behavior, in which the child seems to be seeing whether a particular sound or sequence of sounds is sayable. The second is sound practice, in which the child seems to be deliberately drilling on phonetic or phonological characteristics of the language being acquired. The third is what we might call "pure" sound play in which improvement in the mastery of the sound system—if it is taking place at all—is not obvious: The child is enjoying the sound play for its own sake.

Exploratory activities are sharply differentiated from play activities by many theorists (e.g., Aldis, 1975). Object *exploration,* for example, is a "serious" activity in which the novel object is approached cautiously and the main goal seems to be to acquire information about the object—its physical properties and possible uses—through receptor contact. Object *play,* on the other hand, is nonserious activity in which the object is approached in a direct, relaxed way and the main goal seems to be effector activity. Also, the incidence of exploratory and playful activities in different species varies independently. Yet, exploration may precede play in a natural sequence of behaviors (as in the approach to a new toy), and the boundary is not always easy to draw (cf. Garvey, 1977a; Millar, 1968). Studies that distinguish between the effects of exploration and play and suggest that prior play correlates with level of creativity and problem-solving ability (e.g., Sylva, Bruner, & Genova, 1976) do not usually deal with language play. Hutt (1966), in her careful distinctions between kinds of exploration and play, explicitly excludes human play that has linguistic content.

It is likely that some babbling behavior belongs in the category of exploration and manipulation rather than pure play, but observers have not tried to distinguish between them. Garvey's brief discussion of babbling (1977b) seems to suggest that all babbling is exploratory and that the "verbal play with sound" begins with the first words. This area needs more focused research. Is there a vocal analogue to object exploration and play? Does the child, for example, sometimes react to a novel sound from the mother, or from the environment, with serious exploratory imitations of it, and then shift into playful repetitions with variation?

Weir identifies what she calls "sound practice" as distinguished from "sound play" (Weir, 1962). Sound practice, "a conscious exercise of learning a new phonemic contrast," is not common in her corpus. She reports that it occurs with two phonemes that her subject, Anthony, was still having trouble with: /θ/ and /æ/. The example she discusses is practice in differentiating /ɛ/ and /æ/. Anthony had been given some raspberries at a neighbor's house and had enjoyed eating them. At one point in his evening monologue he seemed to be referring to this episode and ended up practicing the contrast between /ɛ/ and /æ/ in the word *berries*. In the transcript of this episode here the two pronunciations are spelled in ordinary orthography; for full phonetic transcription cf. Weir, 189–190.[6]

thank you (5 ×)	*wicked Alice*	*b_erries*
thank you for the b_erry	*good*	*not b_arries*
go back Mommy	*that's good*	*b_arries* (2 ×)
back for the b_erries	*berries*	*not b_arries*
all gone (2 ×)	*lookin' b_erries*	*b_erries*
for the b_erries	*back please*	*b_a* (2 ×)
ah		

Intentional practicing of a sound is better documented for a somewhat younger child, Brenda, whose linguistic development is described in Scollon, 1976. Brenda did a great deal of repeating when she was still at the one-word sentence stage, age 1;0–1;7, and Scollon discusses the function of repetition at this stage.[7] Some of the repetitions are successive approximations in the sense that Brenda seems to be trying to achieve a better pronunciation of a word for her own satisfaction. For example, at 1;7.2, she says in succession *s, sI, s, sIs, su, su?, sus, si, sI, su?* for *shoe*. Such sequences Scollon calls "phonological repetitions." Others are repetitions of a word in various pronunciations until it is understood and gets a response. For example, at age 1;0.2, the following exchange took place:

Brenda	Mother
fēĭ	
fæǰ	Hm?
fæǰ	Bathroom?
fanī	Fan! Yeah.
fãi	
kʰu	Cool, yeah. Fan makes you cool.

Such sequences Scollon calls "discursive repetitions." The difference between the two types, however, is not always clear cut. For a period of several months, over half of Brenda's uses of words involved repetition, usually once or twice, but sometimes as many as ten or more times. Scollon concludes: "Probably the

---

[6]This sequence includes a number of other instances of Anthony's /æ/, /ɛ/, and [a], and this is probably related to the practice on *berries*. His /æ/ appears in *thank, back,* his /ɛ/ in *that's,* and his /a/ in *Alice;* these pronunciations of the respective words were stable at the time and show the last stages of perfecting the pronunciation and lexical incidence of /æ/.

[7]Scollon notes that most observers edit out the repetitions of the same word along with unintelligible stretches and imitation. One of the merits of the Scollon study is the detailed analysis of the imitations and repetitions in his data.

most plausible explanation of this high number of repetitions is that Brenda is using them to learn phonology [p. 79]." Apparently he means that she is both trying to get the pronunciation just right (as she intends it to be) and also testing the range of acceptable phonetic variation. He sees imitation and repetition as two phases of the same learning process. "Imitation provides the means for the child to practice contrasts that are not yet within her own productive phonological system. Repetition provides the means for elaborating that system from within and testing it against the model system [p. 221]." He also points out that the amount of prior repetition or "rehearsal" seems to be a factor that affects the phonetic shape of utterances.

Another case of sound practice is documented in Weeks' study of Leslie, a bright and highly verbal child whose phonology developed very slowly. During the period 2;10 to 3;0 she repeatedly picked "target words" that gave her difficulty and drilled herself on particular segments (Weeks, 1974).

If we wish to include sound practice in our notion of play, the data and interpretations of Weir, Scollon, and Weeks help us to see it as contributing to phonological development. Weir, however, seems to find sound practice a more serious, extrinsically motivated behavior that may be embedded in playful use of language but is not itself play. Scollon does not attempt to classify Brenda's verbal behavior into play and nonplay,[8] and Weeks does not regard the practice as play.

The category of sound play most often found in the literature is neither exploration nor practice but "pure" sound play, in which the pleasurableness for the child and the apparent lack of developmental function are noted. In Weir's account, which is one of the fullest (it includes 65 pages of Anthony's monologues), the primary function of sound play is said to be the *poetic function* in the Jakobson sense, i.e., the poetic exploitation of the resources of language. Thus the child's sound play is held to be an early manifestation of the function of language that appears in adults in a variety of uses ranging from puns, word play, and advertising slogans, to pure poetry. Anthony's numerous instances of assonance, alliteration, rhyme, and repetition are persuasive evidence for this view, just as his numerous paradigmatic drills are persuasive evidence of the *metalinguistic function* of language. In addition, however, the sound play may very well contribute to phonological development. In connection with grammar Weir comments: "The child finds great joy in practising his discovery that linguistic units can be combined freely up to a point, but subject to rules which he is

---

[8]In spite of recognizing seven Hallidayan functions and identifying seventeen types of speech act in his data, Scollon nowhere treats play as a separate category or set of categories. Once, in discussing grammatical constructions, he characterizes replacement sequences as "apparently a form of play in which the possibilities of systematic construction are explored [p. 201]," but he does not apply the category "play" directly to Brenda's behavior and does not mention play in connection with phonology.

exploring [p. 109]," and Miller, in his forward, comments that Anthony's activities are "a kind of self-imposing drill—a playful drill, admittedly—that must serve to bring what he already knows up to a level of complete automaticity [p. 16]." Such views can be extended to phonology.

One common form of sound play is commutation, i.e., ringing the changes on a particular sound in a particular slot, such as replacing a vowel in a particular word with other vowels. For example, Otto Jespersen reported that his son Frans at 2;3 "amused himself by rounding all his vowels (*o* for *a*, *y* for *i*)" and at 3;1 changed all the words of a line (of verse he had learned) to begin with *d* (Jespersen, 1922). This kind of play is especially pleasurable when the child happens to hit a real word in running through the commutation. Canta, Y. R. Chao's granddaughter, sometimes played with tones by taking a syllable and running it through the four tones of Mandarin Chinese, and Chao reports she was "surprised and amused" when she hit on a real word, in this instance a semantically related one (Chao, 1973). Keenan (1974) reports similar instances in her twins' dialogues, which they greeted with "enormous hilarity."

—ʃa batʃ
—batʃi bitʃi badi bidi babi
—badi [*body*] (laughing) [p. 171]

Although all this play seems to be done for the fun of it, what better way could a child find to explore the phonotactic constraints of the phonological system being acquired?[9]

In various patterns of pure sound play, the word, the syllable, or the phoneme may be the focus of repetition, commutation, or expansion. Some patterns involve mostly or exclusively real words; others have more or less nonsense material. The most frequently cited example from Weir is Anthony's pet phrase *blanket like a lipstick* with its interplay of stops and /l/. The sequence *l* . . . *k* occurs in three words, with a labial stop next to the *l* and an alveolar stop preceding the *k* in the first and last words; the consonantal play is enhanced by the prosodic and vocalic similarities. Examples from Weir and Keenan will illustrate different patterns. (Full phonetic transcriptions for all of them appear in the original sources.)

Weir	Keenan
bink (2 ×)	—doo
let Bobo bink	—(laughing) dooch

---

[9]Play of this kind can be used by experimenters to obtain evidence of phonological competence and awareness, and might even be tried by speech specialists interested in accelerating a child's phonological development or improving a child's deviant phonology, just as many psychologists and recreation specialists have devised kinds of play to assist in the child's physical or emotional development.

Weir	Keenan
bink ben bink	—doo (repeats over and over) (pause)
blue kink	—fuppy doo
no good	—wake up
nong good	—hake ut (laughing)
nong goos (2 ×)	—hake ut
	—bake up
[ɛˈg yo biaˈ m]	—brake ut brake up
[yɛm yə::m]	—wake up week up (laugh) week up
[lam::]	
[li:]	—[gi:nɔg] (3 ×)
[blɛm yi::] (2 ×)	—[gi:nar] (repeats over and over)
[yam]	—(laughs)
[yi::::]	—[ki:tar] (2 ×)

Keenan sees sound play as a part of children's acquisition of conversational competence and as evidence of children's growing ability to "attend to the formal features of one another's utterances [p. 183]." She suggests a partial formalization of discourse procedures for young children that includes provision for nonreferential sound play. Thus, the two best descriptions of sound play (Weir and Keenan) propose somewhat different rationales for it. To be sure, the sound play of the Keenan dialogues differs from that of the Weir monologues in having long stretches of nonsense word exchanges and, as might be expected, in having interruptions and attempts to gain attention, but the kinds of phonological relations between successive utterances are essentially the same in both.

Why do young children engage in expressive sound play? Why is it fun? It seems to us that sound play has the same rationale as other kinds of play. Like the young of other mammals—only more so—human children find pleasure in slightly novel objects and events and enjoy repeating them and varying them within behavioral frames common to the species. Further, they enjoy doing so in interaction with others. Because such behavior seems to improve the ability to cope socially with the needs of normal adult life, the selective advantage of the trait is not hard to imagine, and the increase in play going from nonmammals to mammals to primates to humans is an apparent evolutionary phenomenon. Since control of the phonological system of the language of one's community is necessary for almost any function of language, it is not surprising that phonological play takes place, and it is plausible that it contributes to skill in control of the system itself as well as contributing to other abilities, such as the use of language for poetic and metalinguistic functions and the phonological aspects of the management of conversation.

The immediate relationship of phonological play and phonological development is, however, not unidirectional but circular. As children acquire new vocal skills, they have new resources to play with; as children play with speech sounds they consolidate and extend their control over the phonological system. It is difficult to go beyond this kind of commonsense speculation in the absence of many more descriptions and experimental studies. Our ignorance of the nature, amount, and conditions of occurrence of expressive sound play is great. Weir thought that Anthony's presleep playful monologues were typical child language behavior, only to discover that her younger son did not engage in it. Keenan seemed to think that the playful morning dialogues of her twins was typical of child behavior, but Garvey reported relatively little sound play in the dyadic interactions of her young subjects. Existing diary studies and child discourse texts can undoubtedly be mined more thoroughly, but we really need new studies that directly examine the phenomena of language play.

Of particular importance is the investigation of sound play in communities that are linguistically and culturally different from urban, middle-class, Euro-American settings. Schieffelin's (1979) study of the acquisition of communicative competence among the Kaluli in New Guinea is an instructive example. She observed young children engaging in sound play but found that mothers disapproved of it, called it *obɛi towɔ* 'bird talk,' and stopped it. She reports that the Kaluli see the process of language acquisition as a 'hardening' process, during which mothers encourage their children to speak 'hard' talk. As part of this process, the mothers terminate sound play in order to ensure that 'hard language' develops and explicitly instruct the children to speak 'good talk,' not 'bird talk'. In the same vein, mothers do not allow older children to imitate young children's speech. Once children's speech is sufficiently hardened (about 3½ years) they are free to play with words so long as they do not do so in the presence of younger children.

Finally, if we observe that sound play is common in children's language behavior and if we assume that it assists in the acquisition of phonological competence in their mother tongue (L1), it is reasonable to hypothesize that sound play would occur with a similar function when children acquire a second language (L2). Some supporting evidence comes from a study of two 7-year-old boys: Angel, a Spanish speaker from Mexico, and Joe, an English speaker in Los Angeles (Peck, 1979). "Through sound play in which Joe mocks Angel, and sound play in which both boys enjoy themselves, Angel is practicing and probably learning something about phonology [p. 395]." This interesting and insightful study should stimulate further research along this line, which could confirm the hypothesis and add to our understanding of the role of sound play in L1 and L2 phonological development.

LANGUAGE GAMES

Developmentalists have often noted that as children grow older many of the games they play become more elaborate and the rules of the games become more conscious, explicit, and socially prescribed. Indeed Piaget and his followers see

7. PLAY IN PHONOLOGICAL DEVELOPMENT   247

early, unstructured play as relatively pure "assimilation," showing the limited cognitive development of the child, whereas they regard the social play of older children and adults as evidence of greater cognitive competence and rational behavior.[10] This same sequence may be observed in the development of language play in the child, and in this section we will examine some language games with rules played by older children.

The best described of the various types of sound-based language games is the "secret language" or "play language" (PL), as exemplified by the familiar Pig Latin of American English speakers. A game of this kind typically has a single rule or small set of rules which has as its input a word of ordinary language and as its output the properly altered form of that word in the secret language. Thus, Pig Latin has the rule: Move the initial consonant of the word to the end of the word and add the vowel sound *ay*. The rule when applied to *pig* yields *igpay*.[11] Games of this sort are widely attested, with examples from every continent and in dozens of different languages (Jespersen, 1922; Haas, 1969; Sherzer, 1976).

The range of phonological processes applied in such PLs and the social functions of PLs have been analyzed in some depth. Typical processes are in terms of syllables or consonants and include:

Process	Comment	Example
1. syllable addition	commonest type adds a whole syllable either at one place in the word or after every syllable; next most common adds a syllable consisting of a new consonant and a vowel taken from the base word	English *pig* → *igpay* Spanish *niño* → *nipoñopo* Cuna *pia* → *piriara*
2. syllable permutation	commonest type moves first syllable to the end	Cuna *uwaya* → *wayau*
3. syllable deletion	not so common; usually loss of noninitial syllable(s)	Javenese *arep* → *ar*
4. consonant addition	commonest type = (1)	
5. consonant permutation	commonest type is exchange of first and last consonants in a syllable	French *l'école* → *qu'élole*

---

[10]This view of play development has been sharply criticized on various grounds (e.g., Sutton-Smith, 1966; Schwartzman, 1979) and we are not endorsing it here except as a convenient frame of reference.

[11]Actually the rule is more complicated than this because it must include provision for words with initial consonant clusters, no consonant at all, various stress patterns, inflectional endings, etc. There is considerable fluctuation in the application of the rule by users, i.e., "players" of the game.

Process	Comment	Example
6. consonant substitution	commonest is replacement of initial or final consonant by the PL consonant; most complex is replacement of every consonant by another	Hanunoo *rignuk* → *rignuŋ* Javanese *gawe* → *rade*
7. prosodic changes	includes stress shift, length shift, tone shift, added nasalization	

Some PLs utilize special material or information outside the base language. For example, a number of PLs make some use of the orthography of the language. This is true not only in highly literate societies (e.g., France, U.S.A.) but in communities where the use of writing is very limited, such as the Hanunoo speakers in the Philippines (Conklin, 1959). Also, some PLs make use of special vocabulary taken from another language (Price & Price, 1976). Thus both the base forms and the phonological processes applied to them may go outside the normal structures of the spoken language from which the PL is derived.

Typical social functions of PLs include: Concealing messages from outgroup users of the base language; marking special group membership; exhibiting socially valued verbal skills; serving as socially approved channels for pleasure; and learning vocabulary and orthography. Sometimes a configuration of such functions has such cohesion that it may be identified as a specific social function, as in Hanunoo society where the use of PLs is primarily a feature of courting behavior (Conklin, 1959). Hanunoo PLs are used primarily between pairs of marriageable males and females, and their use by younger children or older married people seems to be either making fun of courting behavior or a nostalgic reenactment of it. Typically, PLs around the world are used by adolescent groups, most often males, as a way of identifying membership in the group and excluding others, such as younger or older siblings, other family members, or other peer groups. Even in Saramaccan society where PLs belong to particular villages and are used by older people to exhibit verbal skills or prevent comprehension by people from other villages, observers have concluded that PLs generally have their origin in small groups of teenagers (Price & Price, 1976).

Play languages have proved to be a productive area of research for linguists primarily because they provide evidence for behavioral units corresponding to abstract elements and relations of phonology such as syllable, segment, underlying representation, phonological rule, rule ordering, cyclical application of rules. For example, 'talking backwards' in Cuna gives independent evidence for syllable boundaries in the phonological system of the language and for the analysis of long medial consonants as geminates. In moving the initial syllable to the end of the word, a single intervocalic consonant goes with the second syllable but a consonant cluster is split, thus *ipya* → *yaip*, not *pyai or *aipy and *ome* → *meo*, not **eom;* in pronouncing *in:a* backwards, two *n*'s appear: *nain*, not **n:ai*

7. PLAY IN PHONOLOGICAL DEVELOPMENT   249

(Sherzer, 1976). (For discussion of PLs in the light of phonological theory, cf. Halle, 1962, and especially Sherzer, 1976.)

PLs are also valuable in showing that at points where linguists have difficulty in agreeing on the "correct" units, representations, or rules, the users of the PL often also show vacillation and alternative options. PLs present a challenge to phonological theory in that some of the typical processes operating in them are rare or nonexistent in ordinary synchronic phonologies and in diachronic change. For example, consonant metathesis occurs under fairly limited conditions in natural languages (Ultan, 1978), but the kind of wholesale permuting of syllables or segments common in PLs seems not to occur in natural languages.

The interest of PLs for developmentalists, and in particular child phonologists, is twofold. As noted above, the rules of PLs offer striking evidence of children's ability to apply very precise phonological rules, sometimes of quite complex character, to the word shapes of a language, and to do so with considerable fluency in actual communication situations. Further, the rules of the game, although precise and socially prescribed, are often neither explicit nor formally taught, but are acquired "naturally" by observation and use in communication. Particularly valuable would be studies of children's acquisition of these games. In the sizable literature on PLs that has come to our attention, we have not found a single study in which children's use of a particular PL is followed developmentally (but cf. Day, 1973, which uses laboratory acquisitions of PLs as a research tool). Some experimental data would also be valuable: At how early an age can children master the use of a PL? Which types of PLs are easiest to acquire? How well do users comprehend the messages in PL exchanges?

The second aspect of interest for the developmentalist lies in the acquisition of social rules in general. The PLs of a speech community or of social groups within the community are part of the total repertoire of language structures and uses that must be acquired by members of the community and/or group. Just as each language presumably has a unique phonology, each speech community has a unique repertoire of conventional sound-based language games, and it is surely of interest to explore the range of possibilities and the nature of the differences among them.

Social play in the sense of conventional games with explicit rules may have its origins (ontogenetically) in mother-child interaction routines in infancy (Garvey, 1977a; cf. the persuasive account of peek-a-boo in Bruner & Sherwood, 1976). The infant is simultaneously learning the particular game and learning how to play games. Infant games of the peek-a-boo sort in which there is a sequence of attracting attention, performing a certain movement, uttering the appropriate vocalization,[12] and expressing pleasure at completion, are very widespread. The

---

[12]The vocalizations or "game cues" that typically serve also as the names of the games are part of the lexicon of baby talk registers in many languages. Ferguson (1977) suggests that the games "may play a helpful role in the child's ability to recognize the . . . connection between vocal signal and referent" and that the cues may "constitute one of the sources of action predicates [p. 222]," but does not mention phonological development as such.

exact details of the movements and the vocalizations, however, differ considerably from one speech community to another, with corresponding differences in these very early sound-meaning pairs being learned.[13] Also, the rules of the games being acquired become part of the child's repertoire, which can be used with others; and finally, when the child is grown up, can be used with infants, thus transmitting the cultural content of the community.

In both of these aspects of language games—as evidence of the operation of phonological rules and as locus for learning social rules—the games and rules are not rigid. They allow for the kind of theme-and-variation behavior typical of play, as well as for individual differences in verbal ability and the emergence and spread of adaptations that constitute linguistic and cultural change.

In this limited discussion of sound-based language games, we have examined play languages and suggested their origin in mother-infant routines, but we have not attempted to discuss the many other kinds of games. For example, in the Middle East, children and adults play a game of quoting proverbs or lines of verse in which the player must produce an item that begins with the same sound (or letter) that the preceding item ended with. Many speech communities around the world have gibberish rhymes in which some, most, or all of the rhyme is composed of phonologically possible nonsense "words" that do not occur in ordinary talk and have no semantic value. Such games and the many others that appear in the literature could also be investigated in reference to phonological development. It is conceivable, for example, that the quoting game, which requires conscious recognition of identical sounds, serves to develop the child's metalinguistic (phonological) awareness (cf. Cazden, 1974; Read, 1978) and that the recitation of gibberish rhymes consolidates the unconscious knowledge of phonotactic constraints (Greenberg & Jenkins, 1964; Messer, 1967). What we need are developmentally focused studies of language games and experiments investigating phonological competence with respect to the games.

CONCLUSIONS

Although the research literature on child phonology almost never touches on play behavior as a relevant topic for investigation or analysis, the bits and pieces of research that involve children's language play, directly or by implication, permit several preliminary conclusions.

First of all, during the babbling period, the time of transition to speech, and the earliest stages of speech development proper, vocal play is probably the fundamental means of acquiring phonetic skills and "learning how to learn" phonological organization. Future research should focus on this early vocal play

---

[13]Games of the peek-a-boo, pat-a-cake type are not, however, universal. Some speech communities seem to make no use of this kind of mother-child interaction; cf. Heath, forthcoming.

as such, drawing on the general literature on play and development and integrating the ludic component into models of phonological development.

Second, the extensive sound play that has been described in 2- to 5-year-olds is important: (a) as a kind of practice or rehearsal of certain aspects of phonology; (b) as an indicator of the child's phonological competence; and (c) as the ontogenetic beginnings of the verbal arts. Current research has acknowledged the third of these areas of importance, but attention should be given to the first two.

Finally, the structure and use of the rule-governed, sound-based language games that are played especially in late childhood and early adolescence in many speech communities are of theoretical interest in showing the potentialities and limits of the learnability of phonological rules and their cultural transmission. These language games offer a fruitful field for contributions to phonological theory and to functional approaches to language analysis.

ACKNOWLEDGMENTS

Some of the research reported on here was done under the auspices of the Child Phonology Project of the Department of Linguistics at Stanford. The CPP has conducted a series of studies since 1967 on various aspects of phonological development, supported by grants from the National Science Foundation, the National Institute of Child Health and Human Development, the National Institute of Education, and the William T. Grant Foundation. This paper has benefitted from discussions with E. V. Clark and B. Sutton-Smith and from comments of the editor and anonymous reviewers. We have, however, perversely ignored advice on some points, and we accept full responsibility for the positions taken. A preliminary version of this paper appeared in *Papers and Reports on Child Language Development,* 18, (1980).

REFERENCES

Aldis, O. *Play fighting.* New York: Academic Press, 1975.
Bever, T. G., Fodor, J. A., & Weksel, W. Theoretical notes on the acquisition of syntax: A critique of "contextual generalization." *Psychological Review,* 1965, 72, 467–482.
Bloom, L. *One word at a time: The use of single word utterances before syntax.* The Hague: Mouton, 1973.
Bowes, J. Children's language play and awareness of language; some possible relationships to reading. *Working Papers in Language and Linguistics* (Tasmanian College of Advanced Education), 1979, 9, 42–61.
Bruner, J. S. The ontogenesis of speech acts. *Journal of Child Language,* 1975, 2, 1–19.
Bruner, J. S., Jolly, A., & Sylva, K. (Eds.). *Play: Its role in development and evolution.* Harmondsworth, England: Penguin Books, 1976.
Bruner, J. S. & Sherwood, V. Peekaboo and the learning of rule structures. In J. S. Bruner et al. (Eds.), *Play.* Harmondsworth, England: Penguin Books, 1976.
Carter, A. L. The transformation of sensorimotor morphemes into words: A case study of the development of 'more' and 'mine'. *Journal of Child Language,* 1975, 2, 251–260.

Carter, A. L. From sensori-motor vocalizations to words: A case study of the evolution of attention-directing communication in the second year. In A. Lock (Ed.), *Action, gesture and symbol*. London: Academic Press, 1978.

Carter, A. L. Prespeech meaning relations: An outline of one infant's sensorimotor morpheme development. In P. Fletcher & M. Garman (Eds.), *Language acquisition*. Cambridge: Cambridge University Press, 1979.

Cazden, C. Play and metalinguistic awareness: One dimension of language experience. *Urban Review*, 1974, *7*, 23-39.

Chao, Y. R. The Cantian idiolect: An analysis of the Chinese spoken by a twenty-eight-month-old child. In C. A. Ferguson & D. I. Slobin (Eds.), *Studies of child language development*. New York: Holt, Rinehart, & Winston, 1973.

Chiat, S. The role of the word in phonological development. *Linguistics*, 1979, *17*, 591-610.

Claparède, E. *Psychologie de l'enfant et pédagogie experimentale*. Neuchâtel: Delachaux & Niestle, 1906.

Clumeck, H. V. *Studies in the acquisition of Mandarin phonology*. Unpublished doctoral dissertation, University of California at Berkeley, 1977.

Clumeck, H. V. The acquisition of tone. In G. Yeni-Komshian, J. Kavanagh, & C. A. Ferguson (Eds.), *Child phonology: Production* (Vol. 1). New York: Academic Press, 1980.

Conklin, H. Linguistic play in its cultural context. *Language*, 1959, *35*, 631-636.

Cruttenden, A. A phonetic study of babbling. *British Journal of Disorders of Communication*, 1970, *5*, 110-118.

Crystal, D. Non-segmental phonology in language acquisition. *Lingua*, 1973, *32*, 1-45.

Crystal, D. The analysis of intonation in young children. In F. D. Minifie & L. L. Lloyd (Eds.), *Communicative and cognitive abilities—early behavioral assessment*. Baltimore: University Park Press, 1978.

Crystal, D. Prosodic development. In P. Fletcher & M. Garmna (Eds.), *Language acquisition*. Cambridge: Cambridge University Press, 1979.

Day, R. S. On learning "secret languages." *Haskins Laboratories Status Report on Speech Research*, 1973, SK-34, 141-150.

de Boysson-Bardies, B., Bacri, N., Sagart, L., & Poizat, M. Timing in late babbling. *Journal of Child Language*, 1981, *8*, 525-539.

de Boysson-Bardies, B., Sagart, L., & Bacri, N. Phonetic analysis of late babbling: A case study of a French child. *Journal of Child Language*, 1981, *8*, 511-524.

Dore, J., Franklin, M. B., Miller, R. T., & Ramer, A. L. H. Transitional phenomena in early language acquisition. *Journal of Child Language*, 1976, *3*, 13-28.

Ferguson, C. A. Baby talk as a simplified register. In C. E. Snow & C. A. Ferguson (Eds.), *Talking to children*. Cambridge: Cambridge University Press, 1977.

Ferguson, C. A. & Farwell, C. B. Words and sounds in early language acquisition. *Language*, 1975, *51*, 419-439.

Ferguson, C. A. & Garnica, O. K. Theories of phonological development. In E. H. Lenneberg & E. Lenneberg (Eds.), *Foundations of language development* (Vol. 2). New York: Academic Press, 1975.

Freud, S. Der Dichter und das Phantasieren. *Neue Revue*, 1908, *1*, 716-724.

Fry, D. B. The development of the phonological system in the normal and the deaf child. In F. Smith & G. A. Miller (Eds.), *The genesis of language*. Cambridge, Mass.: MIT Press, 1966, 187-206.

Garvey, C. *Play*. Cambridge, Mass.: Harvard University Press, 1977. (a)

Garvey, C. Play with language and speech. In S. Ervin-Tripp and C. Mitchell-Kernan (Eds.), *Child discourse*. New York: Academic Press, 1977. (b)

Gilbert, J. On the vowel and its nature, between eighteen months and five years. *Proceedings of the Ninth International Congress of Phonetic Sciences* (Vol. 2), 1979, 134-141.

Greenberg, J. H. & Jenkins, J. J. Studies in the psychological correlates of the sound system of American English I, II. *Word,* 1964, *20,* 157–177.
Haas, M. R. Burmese disguised speech. *Bulletin of the Institute of History and Philology (Academia Sinica* 39, Part 2), 1969, 277–285.
Halle, M. Phonology in generative grammar. *Word,* 1962, *18,* 54–72.
Heath, S. B. *Ways with words: Ethnography of communication—communities and classrooms.* Forthcoming.
Herron, R. & Sutton-Smith, B. (Eds.). *Child's play.* New York: Wiley, 1971.
Huizanga, J. *Homo ludens; proeve eener bepaling van het spil-element der cultuur.* Haarlem: Tjeenk Willink, 1938.
Huizanga, J. *Homo ludens, a study of the play element in culture.* London: Routledge & Kegan, 1949.
Hutt, C. Exploration and play in children. In P. A. Jewell and C. Loizos (Eds.), *Play, exploration and territory in mammals.* London: Academic Press, 1966.
Jakobson, R. & Waugh, L. *The sound shape of language.* Bloomington, Ind.: Indiana University Press, 1979.
Jeng, H-H. The acquisition of Chinese phonology in relation to Jakobson's laws of irreversible solidarity. *Proceedings of the Ninth International Congress of Phonetic Sciences* (Vol. 2), 1979, 155–161.
Jespersen, O. *Language: Its nature, development and origin.* New York: Holt & Co., 1922.
Keenan, E. O. Conversational competence in children. *Journal of Child Language,* 1974, *1,* 163–183.
Labov, W. & Labov, T. The phonetics of cat and mama. *Language,* 1978, *54,* 816–852.
Li, C. N. & Thompson, S. A. The acquisition of tone in Mandarin-speaking children. *Journal of Child Language,* 1977, *4,* 185–199.
Lieberman, P. On the development of vowel production in young children. In G. H. Yeni-Komshian, J. F. Kavanagh, & C. A. Ferguson (Eds.), *Child phonology: Production* (Vol. 1). New York: Academic Press, 1980.
Macken, M. A. Permitted complexity in phonological development: One child's acquisition of Spanish consonants. *Lingua,* 1978, *44,* 219–253.
Macken, M. A. Developmental reorganization of phonology: A hierarchy of basic units of acquisition. *Lingua,* 1979, *49,* 11–49.
McCune-Nicolich, L. Toward symbolic functioning: Structure of early pretend games and potential parallels with language. *Child Development,* 1981, *52,* 785–797.
Menyuk, P. & Bernholtz, N. Prosodic features and children's language production. *MIT Research Lab Electronics Quarterly Progress Report,* 1969, 93.
Menyuk, P. & Menn, L. Early strategies for the perception and production of words and sounds. In P. Fletcher & M. Garman (Eds.), *Language acquisition.* Cambridge: Cambridge University Press, 1979.
Messer, S. Implicit phonology in children. *Journal of Verbal Learning and Verbal Behavior,* 1967, *6,* 609–613.
Millar, S. *The psychology of play.* Harmondsworth, England: Penguin Books, 1978.
Oller, D. K. The emergence of the sounds of speech in infancy. In G. H. Yeni-Komshian, J. F. Kavanagh, & C. A. Ferguson (Eds.), *Child phonology: Production* (Vol. 1). New York: Academic Press, 1980.
Oller, D. K., Wieman, L. A., Doyle, W. J., & Ross, C. Infant babbling and speech. *Journal of Child Language,* 1976, *3,* 1–11.
Peck, S. Child-child discourse in second language acquisition. In E. M. Hatch (Ed.), *Second language acquisition; a book of readings.* Rowley, Mass.: Newbury House, 1979.
Piaget, J. *La formation du symbole chez l'enfant.* Neuchâtel: Delachaux & Niestlé, 1946.

Piaget, J. *Play, dreams and imitation in childhood.* London: Routledge & Kegan Paul, 1951.
Pierce, J. A study of 750 Portland, Oregon children during the first year. *Papers and Reports in Child Language Development,* 1974, *8,* 19–25.
Price, R. & Price, S. Secret play languages in Saramaka: Linguistic disguise in a Caribbean creole. In B. Kirshenblatt-Gimblett (Ed.), *Speech play.* Philadelphia: University of Pennsylvania Press, 1976.
Read, C. Children's awareness of language with emphasis on sound systems. In A. Sinclair, R. J. Jarvella, & W. J. M. Levelt (Eds.), *The child's conception of language.* Berlin: Springer Verlag, 1978.
Sanches, M. & Kirshenblatt-Gimblett, B. Child language and children's traditional speech play. In B. Kirshenblatt-Gimblett (Ed.), *Speech play.* Philadelphia: University of Pennsylvania Press, 1976.
Schieffelin, B. *How Kaluli children learn what to say, what to do, and how to feel: An ethnographic study of the development of communicative competence.* Unpublished Doctoral dissertation, Columbia University. 1979.
Schwartzman, H. *Transformations: The anthropology of children's play.* New York: Plenum, 1979.
Scollon, R. *Conversations with a one-year-old: A case study of the developmental foundations of syntax.* Honolulu: University of Hawaii Press, 1976.
Sherzer, J. Play languages: Implications for (socio) linguistics. In B. Kirshenblatt-Gimblett (Ed.), *Speech play.* Philadelphia: University of Pennsylvania Press, 1976.
Stark, R. E. Features of infant sounds: The emergence of cooing. *Journal of Child Language,* 1978, *5,* 379–390.
Stark, R. E. Stages of speech development in the first year of life. In G. H. Yeni-Komshian, J. F. Kavanagh, & C. A. Ferguson (Eds.), *Child phonology: Production* (Vol. 1). New York: Academic Press, 1980.
Stark, R. E., Rose, S. N., & McLagen, M. Features of infant sounds: The first eight weeks of life. *Journal of Child Language,* 1975, *2,* 205–211.
Sutton-Smith, B. Piaget on play: A critique. *Psychological Review,* 1966, *73,* 104–110.
Sutton-Smith, B. *Play and learning.* New York: Halsted Press, 1979.
Sylva, K., Bruner, J. S., & Genova, P. The role of play in the problem-solving of children 3–5 years old. In J. S. Bruner et al. (Eds.), *Play.* Hammondsworth, England: Penguin Books, 1976.
Tse, J. K-P. Tone acquisition in Cantonese: A longitudinal case study. *Journal of Child Language,* 1978, *5,* 190–204.
Ultan, R. A typological view of metathesis. In J. H. Greenberg et al. (Eds.), *Universals of human language: Phonology* (Vol. 2). Stanford: Stanford University Press, 1978.
Weeks, T. E. *The slow development of a bright child.* Lexington, Mass.: D. C. Heath, 1974.
Weeks, T. E. *Born to talk.* Rowley, Mass.: Newbury House, 1979.
Weir, R. *Language in the crib.* The Hague: Mouton, 1962.
Zlatin-Laufer, M. & Horii, Y. Fundamental frequency characteristics of infant non-distress vocalization during the first twenty-four weeks. *Journal of Child Language,* 1975, *4,* 171–184.

8 Cognitive Aspects of Phonological Development: Model, Evidence, and Issues

Marlys A. Macken
Charles A. Ferguson
*Stanford University
Department of Linguistics*

INTRODUCTION

Linguistic research in child phonology of the past decade or more has been dominated by two central ideas about children: First, that the child is largely a passive organism in which development unfolds; and, second, that the child is simply a scaled-down version of the adult. Both ideas stem largely from the presumption of universals of language and acquisition (e.g., Chomsky 1965, 1980a,b). Because the phonology of a child was assumed to be quantitatively simpler than that of the adult and, at least in the early stages, universally the same across languages, linguists looked to child phonology to answer questions of interest to linguistic theory. Generally, the formalisms of linguistic theory were adopted for the analysis of child data and in large part dictated not only the questions of interest but also the methods of data collection and analysis. In short, the focus of these analyses was on purely linguistic regularities in the child corpus.

During the last 10 to 15 years, three competing theories of acquisition have dominated linguistic research on child phonology, and these three are essentially variants of a universalist theory, each being an extension of a particular phonological theory.[1]

---

[1]Outside the universalist school are Olmsted (1966, 1971), who extended the behaviorist theories of Mowrer, 1952 (see also Murai, 1963; Timm, 1977; Winitz, 1969) and Waterson (1970, 1971), who works within the Firthian prosodic analysis theory (one of the few approaches to emphasize individual differences).

Jakobson (1941). (Translated into English in 1968; most recent version in Jakobson & Waugh, 1979.) This author was the first to put forth a general theory of the acquisition of phonology based on linguistic universals. Jakobson's theory is by far the most influential of the various universalist models, and the data from many children, acquiring a wide variety of languages, have been analyzed as conforming to the general Jakobsonian outline of development (e.g., Jeng, 1979, Chinese; Pačesova, 1968, Czech; and Velten, 1943, English). Although this theory has been criticized on many grounds (e.g., Ferguson & Garnica, 1975; Kiparsky & Menn, 1977; Macken, 1980a; Olmsted, 1966, 1971), it is often quoted as if it were fact (e.g., Mikeš, 1976). Moskowitz (1970, 1973, 1978) includes elements of classical generative phonology, but essentially her work is a revision of Jakobson and thus structuralist in form.

Generative Phonology. The leading figure working within the classic generative phonology paradigm is Smith (1973, 1974, 1975). Smith (1978) presents some revision of the earlier work (partially as a response to criticisms in Macken 1980b), but the general universalist framework remains the same. Dodd (1974) uses the Smith model to characterize the phonological development of normal, retarded, and deaf children. Generative phonology (with its subsequent revisions) has also provided key concepts that have been used to advantage in the child phonology literature: For example, Ingram (1974) applies the notion of ordered rules (cf. also Stampe) and draws on Stanley's (1967) discussion of redundancy rules (cf. also Menn, 1974); Jones' (1967) work was based on that of Halle (and Jakobson), and Menn (1971) attempts to handle the problem of child surface structure constraints within Jones' system; and Branigan (1976) applies the notions of constraints (Ross, 1967) and conspiracies (Kisseberth, 1970) to child phonology.

Natural Phonology. Stampe (1969, 1973) presents a different theory of phonology—"natural phonology"—which emphasizes universal, innate natural processes and includes an explicit acquisition theory based on these processes (cf. also Donegan & Stampe, 1979). Edwards (1971, 1978a, 1978b, and 1979) treats the acquisition of liquids and fricatives in terms of Stampe's model. (Hooper (1977), following the "natural generative phonology" model, is an example of the application of child data to controversial questions in phonological theory (cf. also Venneman, 1971).)

This universalist, linguistic-theory-dominated decade has been highly productive in a number of ways. A great deal of information has been amassed on the sounds and the substitutions that children produce, the order in which segments and rules are acquired, and the acoustic and articulatory principles on which these sound patterns are based. The attention drawn to child phonology by Jakobson, Chomsky-Halle, Stampe, and others, and the impressive contributions of the research of this decade to linguistics, have firmly established child phonology as a legitimate subfield of linguistic inquiry. Increasingly, however, data have been collected that cannot be handled within the universalist-linguistic framework. The anomalous data include evidence of widespread individual differences between children acquiring the same language (and also differences across languages) and evidence (particularly from 'recidivism' or apparent loss of an ability) that the acquisition process is not a linear progression of unfolding abilities.[2] An identifiable shift is in progress toward a more cognitive model of phonology acquisition. The central focus is now on *learning*—not the automatic, mechanistic form of learning advocated by the behaviorist theories of the 1930–1950s, but an *active* form of learning in which the child acts on environmental input to 'create' knowledge (albeit, always within constraints of human structures and processing capabilities). The child is now seen as an active seeker and user of information—an active hypothesis-generator.[3] Child phonologists increasingly look to syntax and semantics acquisition studies and to developmental and cognitive psychology for parallels, analogies, and formalisms, rather than solely to linguistic theories of the organization of adult phonology. This newer research (with its forerunners) constitutes a shift in focus from purely linguistic regularities to linguistic regularities that reveal the processing carried out by the child.

It is misleading, however, to regard a cognitive model as being totally different from a universalist linguistic model. It is misleading in at least three ways. First, it erroneously implies that previous work in child phonology was not concerned with psychologically real units, rules, and stages. Most child phonologists evaluated competing units of analysis (e.g., features vs. segments) at least in part by behavioral evidence that they entered into the child's processing of language (e.g., the discussion as in Moskowitz, 1970, against the feature on the basis of its nongeneralizability; cf. also Smith, 1973 and 1974, which present evidence intended to establish the psychological reality and, hence, validity of the particular rule system proposed for A's speech). Secondly, such a contrast is misleading in its suggestion that the cognitive model of phonology acquisition is not concerned with linguistic universals. Although the shift is toward, for exam-

---

[2]There are also data that would suggest that the child's organization of phonology is qualitatively different from the adult's, but we will not deal directly with this issue here.

[3]Chomsky (1975, particularly Chapter 4) specifically rejects a hypothesis-formation model for language acquisition. The argument crucially depends on the formal identity between such a model and the hypothesis-formation model required for the learning of, say, physics. Even if we were to accept that Chomsky's argument establishes that knowledge of language is not isomorphic to knowledge of physics in either acquisition process or final state, we would not be committed to the position that *no* similarity exists between the two or that nonisomorphism is proof for a biological/growth model (see, particularly Chomsky 1980b). Our claim is that a hypothesis-formation capacity is common to both. Although there may also be special characteristics of this capacity as applied to language, the language-learning child who is 'constructing' and 'testing' hypotheses is not nearly as deliberate, conscious, or systematic as is the adult engaged in rational inquiry who is 'constructing' and 'testing' a scientific theory.

ple, universal constraints on hypothesis-formation and a universally valid developmental model, the search for specifically linguistic universals continues (e.g., Macken, 1980a; Macken & Ferguson, 1981; Vihman, 1978).[4] Furthermore, it is misleading to even label the new trends as a model—cognitive or otherwise—until they give rise to a more explicit, comprehensive, and testable theory. Certainly, many child phonologists have moved away from the strong form of universal acquisition theories such as those of Jakobson and Stampe. Likewise, many researchers have abandoned attempts to analyze the data from very young children in terms of the assumptions and specific constructs of 'classical' Chomskian generative phonology. But those same researchers have varied in the directions of change that they have taken. The trends hardly constitute a fully developed model. The change is not dramatic (certainly not nearly as dramatic as the change that occurred between the structuralist and Chomskian periods) and for the most part must be inferred from the organization and analysis of recent papers. The most explicitly articulated cognitive model is found in a paper by Kiparsky and Menn, and this paper was only published in 1977 (see also Ferguson, 1979a; Fey & Gandour, 1979, 1982; Macken, 1976, 1979; Menn, 1976).

That such a shift is taking place in child phonology is not surprising in that a similar shift has taken place in the field of child language development as a whole. Chomsky's claim of a highly specific 'language acquisition device' was countered at least as early as 1972 by Macnamara, who argued for the existence of general skills that the child applies to language learning as well as to other complex tasks (cf. the even earlier proposals by Slobin, 1966 and Fodor, 1966 of general analysis procedures). The specifically linguistic LAD has been replaced by an impressive 'hypothesis-formation system.' The attribution of such sophisticated reasoning abilities to the child is itself a major departure from the previously widely held Piagetian view of limited intellectual capabilities in the child under seven years; again, it has been largely the research of the 1970s that has led to this shift in the view of the young child's abilities (cf. Donaldson, 1978; Gelman, 1979).

In spite of many similarities, the shift to a more cognitive model of child phonology is surprising at least in part because phonology is frequently thought to be less cognitive than, say, semantics or word use; or, in fact, *not* to be a cognitive domain at all. (There are, however, notable exceptions; see, for example, Sapir 1925; more recently Anderson, 1981.) At its extreme, this assumption translates to a view of acquisition in which learning to pronounce is a lower-level skill more directly constrained by anatomical and physiological characteristics of the human auditory and articulatory tracts. Terminology often reflects the pretheoretical concepts of the practitioners in a field, and the terminology of phonol-

---

[4]It is ironic that it has been data on individual differences that has propelled the shift toward a cognitive model in phonology acquisition, because cognitive models in psychology tend to ignore individual differences.

ogy is a specialized system quite divorced from traditional cognitive terms like categories, concept formation, mental models, understanding, etc. Whether intentional or not, child phonologists create a picture of acquisition that is quite mechanical, simply by the use of their terminology and formalisms. Yet, a "phoneme" can be viewed as a category, a "rule" as a mental representation for the organization of categories, and "the acquisition of phonology" as the way in which the child learns to form categories, recognize patterns, form rules on the basis of those patterns and reformulate hypotheses on the basis of new data and counter examples. It is significant that in many recent child phonology articles, terms like "phoneme" and "phonotactic filter" have been replaced by or subordinated to terms like "final-position focuser," "favorite sounds," "hypotheses," "strategies," and "word-pattern preferences." Although the traditional constructs are not abandoned, the newer terminology reflects changes in the underlying conceptions about children, their capabilities, and the nature of the acquisition process in the following ways: (1) the child, formerly seen as passive is now viewed as active (Selectiveness, below); (2) the child was considered limited in intellectual abilities, but is now seen as 'creative,' with quite flexible reasoning, inferencing, and learning abilities (Creativity, below); and (3) acquisition, previously seen as a set of predetermined stages, is now considered as processes of hypothesis-forming and testing (Hypothesis-formation, below).

Although it is premature to fully extend the analogy of phonology acquisition as a cognitive, categorization process, we discuss here the data suggestive of a cognitive model because we view a shift toward more cognitive considerations as accurately reflecting the empirically valid assertion of cognitively relevant aspects of phonology acquisition. In addition, we hope to refocus attention on some critical aspects of acquisition that were largely ignored in the research generated by the universalist-linguistic model. As is typically the case, no one model handles all the data, and we discuss at the end of this chapter some limitations to a cognitive approach.

The material is organized under three headings: selectiveness, creativity, and hypothesis formation. Selectiveness refers to preferential strategies in the exploitation of input, or the child as a highly selective seeker of phonological information. The child avoids, selects, or makes favorites of particular phonological characteristics of the language as a basis for active use. Creativity refers to the child's creativity, not in the usual linguistic sense of producing novel sequences on the basis of a limited set of rules, but in the sense of creating segments or patterns that do not occur in the adult phonology at all. Finally, hypothesis formation refers to the child's formulating, testing, and revising of hypotheses about the phonological structure of the language. Although an analysis of children's data does suggest that hypothesis-formation is a crucial aspect of the acquisition process, it should not be assumed that the child is systematic or aware of his or her rules and the changes in those rules. The child is not a logician or scientist, carefully seeking out counterexamples or setting up the most parsimonious system. And, although by 2½ years, a child may be able to comment on the difference between his or her pronunciation of a word and that of an adult (e.g., Smith, 1973) or appreciate the humor of an adult's imitation of the child's own pronunciation (see Table 8.2, note 3), very young children give little evidence of such metalinguistic awareness.

SELECTIVENESS

Evidence for active selection and/or avoidance of words with a particular structure was—with the documentation of widespread individual differences in phonology acquisition—one of the earliest findings that indicated the active role of the child during acquisition. Engel (1965), Drachman (1973), and Ferguson and Farwell (1975), and since then several other papers, present data that appear to demonstrate that children can be highly selective in deciding what words to produce and, further, that the choice is at least sometimes made on the basis of how easy or difficult a word is to pronounce. First, these studies have found that there is a close correlation between the types of words children can say and the types of words they attempt. Second, it is argued that the distribution of word types in the child's vocabulary does not reflect that found in the adult vocabulary; nor could the child's distribution have occurred by chance. The conclusion drawn is that children actively choose or avoid words with particular sounds or sound structures. Although some aspects of the avoidance/selection hypothesis have been criticized (see Macken, 1980a), and although not all authors have been able to document it (see Leonard & Newhoff, 1978), supportive evidence for it has been found in the data from a number of children acquiring a variety of languages (e.g., Farwell, 1976, English; Itkonen, 1977, Finnish; Labov & Labov, 1978, English; Macken, 1979, Spanish; Vihman, 1971, Estonian). A particular subtype of selection that has been reported is one in which the formation of a new 'output pattern' (i.e., a new way to combine particular consonants and vowels) is immediately followed by the acquisition of new vocabulary items that, in the adult form, structurally resemble the child's output pattern (e.g., Branigan, 1976; Macken, 1979; Menn, 1976; Vihman, 1976). This correlation is interpreted to mean that once the child figures out a new articulatory routine, the child looks for or is especially receptive to new words that can be handled with the new routine.

Evidence like the above, which suggests that the child selectively attends to input stimuli, draws largely on the differences between the child corpus and that of the adult language. We will cite, below, differences between individual children as the main evidence for the child as a creative user of information and differences in stages within a single child's corpus as the main evidence for the basic constructive—or hypothesis-forming—nature of the acquisition process. However, all three types of evidence overlap. For example, evidence for the child's creativity also is evidence for the child's active role in the learning process, and children's 'created' segments and word patterns also demonstrate the rule formation process. In all the examples, the focus is on novelty, the creation of knowledge, the nonautomatic nature of child responses, and the nonlinear nature of the progression to the adult norm.

CREATIVITY

The most striking evidence for the creativity of the child comes from cases where children produce segments or word patterns for which there is no distinct model in the adult language. In each of these cases, a child has formed an hypothesis about possible segments or permissible sequences that is plausible given the child's existing system or certain properties of the adult system but is incorrect from the adult point of view and is unique or nearly unique to the child in question. An example of the creation of a novel segment is reported in Macken, 1979, where a monolingual Spanish-speaking child, referred to as Si, (at 2;0.7) expanded the class of permissible word-initial velar consonants to include a velar nasal, possibly on analogy to her previously established class of possible word-initial labial consonants, which included both stops and nasals. The velar nasal is not a phoneme in adult Spanish and only occurs under certain assimilation conditions. Si's phonemicization of the velar nasal is incorrect by adult standards and unique among the six Spanish-learning children studied by Macken; however, it is a plausible extension of Si's rules for the formation of possible words. A similar case can be found in Ferguson, Peizer, and Weeks, 1973: A child named Leslie, who was acquiring English, created a word-initial velar nasal that essentially filled a gap in the English distribution of the velar nasal. These examples (and others like them) reveal the children's existing rule system, and they are creative extensions or hypotheses based on the children's (incomplete) knowledge of their respective language's system for word formation (or 'phonotactics'). An analogous case for the acquisition of syntax comes from Brown and Hanlon, 1970. Adam, one of the children studied, produced the novel tag question "I'm magic, amn't I?". 'Amn't I?' should be a possible English tag but actually is not (at least in American English); its use by Adam, however, clearly demonstrates Adam's (incomplete) knowledge of the general rule system for the formation of English tags *and* his creativity.

Sometimes children's errors also provide evidence for nonadult segmentation and categorization. For adult speakers of English, the word *sweet* apparently consists of four segments, the first two being [s] and [w]. However, for a number (but not the majority) of children acquiring English, *sweet* is at some stage apparently only three segments: *sweet* is produced *feet* (e.g., Greenlee, 1973; Barton, Miller, & Macken, 1980). The production of [f] for [sw] is interpreted as a conflation in which features of two adult segments are combined into one child segment (frication from the *s* and labiality from the *w*)—in other words, as a failure by the child to segment the input in an adult-like fashion. There are many examples of such conflated units (or nonadult segmentation) at the morphological level in the lexicons of children: Si, the Spanish-speaking child mentioned above, lexicalized the article *la* 'the' and a noun in one case—[nanina] for *la niña* 'the girl' (Macken, 1979); Tessa, a child who participated in one of our studies, regularly produced [p^{h}It^{h}on] for *pants* (from *pants on,* according to her father);[5] R, another Spanish-speaking child we have studied, had a favorite 'word' [kikeko] derived from the Spanish sentence *¿Qué es ésto?* 'What is that?'; Adam considered *it's* to be one word (Brown, 1973); and three children in Farwell, 1976 all treated *what's that* as a single unit (see Berman, 1977, for examples from a Hebrew-speaking child). Examples like these can either be unique to a particular child (as in the Si, R, and Tessa examples) or may be fairly common (as the *it's* example probably is), but, in any event, they demonstrate—like the [sw] example—that children must *learn* to segment the acoustic input, lexically, morphologically, and phonologically.

Categorization, like segmentation, requires making judgments of phonetic similarity across items. The categorization is difficult to prove if the child's production is quite close to the adult form. For example, children acquiring English often produce /tr/ as [tʃ] (e.g., *tree* as *chee*). This may mean that these children are categorizing adult /tr/ and /tʃ/ as similar or the same, or it may mean that the production of the highly affricated [tʃ] is only the child's attempt to replicate the strong frication that *does* occur in adult production of /tr/. In the latter case, the child's [tʃ] for both /tr/ and [tʃ] does not necessarily imply a category based on a similarity judgment. However, sometimes we do have evidence for categorization based on a similarity judgment: Amahl (Smith, 1973) produced /tr/ correctly but produced initial /tʃ/ as [tr] (so *tree* is all right but *chalk* is [trɔk]). Presumably, there is nothing in the adult production of *chalk* that a child could interpret as [r]; thus, we infer that the anomalous [r] in *chalk* is due to Amahl's categorization of English /tr/ and /tʃ/ as similar.

The data from individual children often provide examples of novel "word patterns," i.e., the strategies that a child devises for the sequencing of particular consonants and vowels. When a child discovers a pronounceable sequence, he or she uses it as a general pattern for many other words. Si's earliest word pattern was C_1VC_2V, where the first consonant was a labial consonant, the second consonant was a dental, and both vowels were the same. She used several rules for achieving this output, one of which was metathesis, i.e., switching the adult order of consonants. Furthermore, when she devised a new pattern, she would add words to her productive vocabulary—words that roughly "fit" her new pattern; and she would occasionally change the pronunciation of some old words

---

[5]Tessa later added [p^{h}ænts] to create her own unique contrast between *pants/trousers* [p^{h}ænts] and *underpants* [p^{h}it^{h}on].

8. COGNITIVE ASPECTS OF PHONOLOGICAL DEVELOPMENT 263

to fit the new pattern (Macken, 1979). J, another child in the same Spanish study, kept the ordering of consonants the same as in the adult model but used consonant harmony, changing the place of articulation of one of the consonants to insure that any two consonants in a word were the same (Macken, 1978). More examples could be cited to demonstrate the diversity of very young children's created rules (see, in particular, Braine, 1974; Ferguson, Peizer, & Weeks, 1973), but two particularly unusual ones are the following: The child in Priestly, 1977, produced adult disyllabic words as [CVjVC] (e.g., *sucker* as [fajak] and *cupboard* as [kajat]); and A in Smith, 1973, went through a stage in which he produced initial unstressed syllables as [ri-] (e.g., *guitar* as [ri 'ta:], *attack* as [ri: 'tæk], etc.).

Also evidence of the very young child's creativity are invented words. Ferguson (1978), who calls these inventions "vocables," finds that at some point in the babbling period, the child typically begins to make active use of sound—meaning correspondences of his/her own, i.e., the child produces a set of vocables which function communicatively much like the later "first words" but are not based on words of the adult language. Ferguson cites an example from a German diary study when a child used a long [m] to mean 'Here comes a wagon' or 'I hear a wagon.' Halliday (1975) reports that his son at 10 months had 11 or 12 expressions in more or less consistent use, and only one ([bø], roughly 'Give me my toy bird,') had an obvious source in the adult language. (See also Menn, 1978 on "proto-words.") Examples can be cited from children acquiring many different languages (e.g., Norwegian—Vanvik, 1971; Hindi—Srivastava, 1974), and the phenomenon is not restricted to oral language: Goldin-Meadow and Felman (1977) report that deaf children spontaneously develop a structured sign system that has many of the properties of natural spoken language, and that this system is "largely the invention of the child himself, rather than of the caretakers." Peters (1974) discusses words invented by children (i.e., words with no apparent adult models) and reports that "most children seem to have invented at least one word." An analogous invention in the area of syntax comes from Kunsman (1976), who reports on a child who used reduplication as a means of expressing negation prior to the use of *no*: Father: "Want to go to bed?" Child: "Betiti" (i.e., *no* bed). Child: "Shoesisi" (i.e., Don't put on my shoes).

HYPOTHESIS FORMATION

Universalist theorists assume the acquisition process to be constrained by innately given principles that effect an orderly progress of improvement toward the adult model. For example, Jakobson (1941/1968) observed a set of stages in the data from children acquiring various languages and explained these stages in terms of a universal hierarchy of structural laws based on feature contrasts; these 'universals' in effect function like a filtering device that automatically sequences acquisition. These general 'universals' stem (in part) from the fact that all children possess roughly the same human auditory and articulatory apparatus. However, Jakobson's model—like universalist models in general—predicts that the child's output at any given time period is systematic and that changes in the output across time will be similarly systematic and progressive.

If we look closely at the corpus from a given child, we find, however, significant variation in addition to systematicity. Some of the variability in a child's corpus is due to performance errors typical of unskilled behavior and will not concern us here (as, for example, the phonetic range [ṣ, s, ç, tʃ . . .] found in a particular child's productions of English /s/). The types of variation that will concern us are those that present clear problems for a universalist model and simultaneously provide support for some kind of more cognitive model. First, evidence of substantial individual differences between children can be in and of itself a convincing argument against a universalist model. Documentation of such differences is now extensive and has been drawn upon in critical evaluations of universalist theories, especially those universalist theories that have made explicit and testable predictions (e.g., the critiques in Kiparsky & Menn, 1977; Macken, 1980a). Second, some variation seems to be due *not* to performance problems but rather to rule-governed changes or interim systems being formulated by the child. Since our goal is to also provide an overview of the kinds of data that are leading researchers to a consideration of a more cognitive model, we will here deal only with within-child variation that excludes performance errors, because it is such variation that appears to reflect most clearly an underlying process of active hypothesis- (or rule-) formation on the part of the child.

Before continuing, we note that there is a possible alternative explanation for some and maybe all such errors, within one of the universalist-linguistic theories. Chomsky's recent government-binding theory (e.g., 1980a, 1981) employs the notion of "parametric variation," partially to account for variation between languages. Crucial to this notion is the distinction between Universal Grammar (UG), which contains the "principles that sharply restrict the class of attainable grammars . . . but with parameters that have to be fixed by experience [Chomsky, 1981, pp. 3-4]," and Core Grammar, which is the particular grammar achieved when "the parameters of UG are fixed in one of the permitted ways [p. 7]." We could attempt to handle both cross-language and individual variation in language acquisition as parametric variation (as in, e.g., Solan, 1981). However, to give content to the claim of "parametric variation," a finite list of parameters must be determined, along with a finite set of values for each parameter; to establish its explanatory power in language acquisition, the variation that is found must be exhaustively accounted for by the parametric model. Such a research program is interesting and would be highly significant if accomplished. Less ambitious but still quite interesting would be a parametric analysis that revealed new generalizations while handling a significant subset of the variation data. Yet even if the parameters and values could be defined (and this has been attempted for only a few syntactic complexes of properties), it appears that the theory renders the construct untestable: "But it is hardly to be expected that what are called 'languages' or 'dialects' or even 'idiolects' will conform precisely or perhaps even very closely to the systems determined by fixing the parameters of UG. . . . Each actual 'language' will incorporate a periphery of borrowings, historical residues, inventions, and so on, which we can hardly expect to . . . incorporate within a principled theory of UG [pp. 7–8]." Even if we exclude borrowings and historical residues (which should be amenable to a principled account in the language from which they are borrowed or a prior historical stage of the language), it would still appear that the theory admits of no counterexamples, but only irrelevant data (that are assigned to the "marked periphery"). This theory is still being developed. Few researchers in language acquisition have adopted it, and no attempts that we know of have been made to apply it to phonology acquisition.

Isolated Accuracy

Occasionally, a child will produce an early word in a quite accurate form. Moskowitz (1973) calls these cases of isolated accuracy "progressive idioms." The prototypic case is Hildegard Leopold's *pretty*. This word was Hildegard's first permanent word (at 0;10), and she pronounced it with near perfect phonetic accuracy for nearly a year. Then, however, it changed to [pɪti] and a month later to [bɪdi]. These latter two changes occurred when rules of consonant cluster reduction and consonant voicing (respectively) appeared elsewhere in her system (Leopold, 1947). In cases like this one, a word (or sound; cf. Itkonen, 1977) is produced accurately and then loses its accuracy at about the time that a rule 'appears' in the child's system (see other cases of 'regression' or loss of accuracy below). The early, accurate pronunciation is taken to be an unanalyzed whole and evidence of a prerule stage (as distinct from regression due to changes in rules, below). A parallel from semantics is the kind of underextension where a child produces a word correctly in an isolated context, but where the concept represented by that word remains outside the child's semantic system, as for example Hildegard's early use of *white* for the color of snow only.

Experimentation

On tapes from four longitudinal studies, we found occasional examples of variation that were interpreted by the adults present at the time of utterance as deliberate effortful attempts by the child to find an acceptable (to the child) way to say a word. Similarly, during the analysis, these examples were interpreted on structural grounds as evidence of experimentation preceding an innovation. That these examples are not common on the tapes is attributable at least partially to the problem of sampling interval. The same explanation may hold for the rarity of such examples in the literature, although it may also be the case that when an author is working within the assumptions of a universalist model, such cases of variation are judged anomalous or as irrelevant surface phenomena. Nevertheless, the relative rarity of such crucial examples is a problem for the cognitive model, a point to which we will return.

Table 8.1 gives two examples of experimentation from children we have studied. With regard to the first example, Tessa's productions in Sessions 1–3 show the final /t/ in *boat* deleted or replaced by [ʔ] (as were all final stop consonants). In Session 4, the first examples of velar consonant harmony appeared (*coat* [kʌk] *goat* [kʌᶦk]), and her productions of *boat* indicate a search for a rule to handle initial labial/final alveolar words. The subsequent sessions were characterized by widespread use of velar and labial harmony. An interpretation of these data is that Tessa was, in Session 4, experimenting with two

TABLE 8.1
EXPERIMENTATION: Tessa's *boat*, session 4 / Si's *elefante*, session 10

	Child[1]	Target	Session	Phonetic transcription[2]	#of productions	Age
A.	Tessa	*boat*	1	[p°ɔ/o]$_{3x}$, [p°ɔʔ]	4	1;4.28
			2	[p°ɔ]$_{4x}$, [p°ʌʔ]	5	
			3	[p°ɔ]$_{3x}$, [p°o/ɔʔ]$_{3x}$	6	
			4	[p°ɔpʰ kʰ]	11	1;5.30
				[p°otʰ]		
				[p°ʌp'pʰu̥k']		
				[p°ʌkʰ]$_{2x}$		
				[p°ɔkʰ]$_{2x}$		
				[p°ɔkʰ kʰ]$_{2x}$		
				[p°apʰ kʰ]		
				[p°ʌkʰ kʰ]		
			5	[p°ɔpʰ]$_{2x}$	2	1;6.15
			6	[p°op'], [p°oʔ]	2	
			7,8	—	—	
			9	[p°ʌp]$_{3x}$	3	
			10	—	—	
			11-16	[p°otʰ], [p°ot']	2-3x/session	1;9.2
B.	Si[3]	*elefante* 'elephant'	10	[¹hwan t°u t°i]	4	1;9.12
				[pf an t°ɪn dɪ]		
				[p°an t°i]		
				[b an t°ɪn di]		
			12/13	[p°a t°e], [p°an t°e]		1;10.2

(1) Both children were subjects in studies conducted by the authors.

(2) Broad segmental transcriptions, simplified from originals. Productions listed under A (session 4) and B were independently transcribed by four and two transcribers, respectively.

(3) Macken 1979, p.33-34

8. COGNITIVE ASPECTS OF PHONOLOGICAL DEVELOPMENT 267

solutions to the problem posed by the structure of *boat:* (a) treat final /t/ as [k] or (b) harmonize final /t/ to initial labial. (Note that one instance of a correct final [t] also occurs.) The subsequent data show that she settled on (b). Also in Table 8.1 are data from another subject—Si. The experimentation shown in these data is associated with the production of a new word in her active lexicon. Three of the variable forms of Session 10 were both longer and more complex than any other words from the same session; these were replaced in Session 11 by a single form [pate], the structure of which was fully consistent with the structure of the rest of her words. (Later, Si produced [pante] during the stage in which she (re-) acquired the *nt* cluster.)

The variation seen in idioms and experimentation precedes the stage in which particular words are produced in a form that is stable and systematic with respect to other words of a similar type. Such variation demonstrates that at least some aspects of acquisition are not automatic. The onset of systematicity is increasingly viewed as evidence that the child has "discovered" or "invented" a rule. Stronger evidence that the child's rule constitutes an hypothesis or theory about the relationship between *several* items in a system comes from the phenomena of overgeneralization and regression—two (partially overlapping) types of variation that are as difficult for the universalist model to explain as the variation seen in idioms and the experimentation data.

Overgeneralization

Overgeneralization is a term applied to cases in which the child extends a rule for a particular set of sounds or words to a set of sounds or words where the extension is inappropriate from the adult's view. Table 8.2 charts development of stop + /r/ clusters in the speech of Jane, a 1976 subject. From 1;6.9 to 1;10.7, Jane reduced initial stop + /r/ clusters by deleting the /r/ (n.b. adult initial singleton /r/ was [w] for her). From 1;11.0 to 1;11.14, initial /tr/ and /dr/ were produced as [f]. Evidently the strong aspiration combined with labiality (in the /r/) in adult pronunciation of /tr/ and /dr/ led to the child's decision to switch from [t] to [f] productions for /tr/ and /dr/ (cf. "Changing hypotheses" below). To this point, Jane's rules operate on classes of segments sufficiently close to the adult classes that the process is "rule formation." However, at the next stage, 1;11.28 to 2;1.16, Jane uses [f] for all initial /pr/, /tr/, /dr/, and /kr/ words. The extension of [f] to /pr/ and /kr/ is overgeneralization.

Overgeneralization is distinct from simple rule formation (or generalization) in the following ways: (1) the extension is to items more clearly inappropriate from an adult point of view;[6] and (2) the newly included sounds were closer to

---

[6]Although the original inclusion of /dr/ with /tr/ is also an 'error' from the adult vantage, /tr/ and /dr/ form a more natural set for the adult language than a set comprised of /pr, tr, dr, kr/.

TABLE 8.2
OVERGENERALIZATION: Jane's *pr* and *kr*, session 13

			Child Forms		
Session Age	1 — 9	10	11-12	13(2)-16	Home Visit(3)
Adult	1;6.9-1;10.7	1;10.14	1;11.0-1;11.14	1;11.28-2;1.16	2;6.1
Clusters					
pr	([p°] >) [pʰ] 1;9.15	[pʰ]	[pʰ]	[f]	[pʰw]
tr	([t°] >) [tʰ] 1;9.15	[hw](4)	[f]	[f]	[f]
dr	[t°]	?	[f]	[f]	[f]
kr	([k°] >) [kʰ] 1;10.7	[kʰ]	[kʰ]	[f]	[f]

Examples *pretty*   (5) *pretty*   *prune*
          [pʰɪtʰi] ─────────────────────────────>| [fɪtʰi] ────────> [pwun]

          trousers   *tree*   *tree*
          [t°auwɪs]   [hwi]   [fi] ──────────────────────────────>|

          drawer   *drink*   *drink*
          [t°ɔ:] ──────────>   [fwɪŋk]   [fɪŋkʰ] ────────────>|

          cracker ─────────────────────────>   *cream* ─────────────>|
          [k°æk°ə]   [fim]
                                                     cradle ────────────>|
                                                     [fedɛl]

Notes: (1) Beginning on session 13, Jane overgeneralized her /tr, dr/ → [f] rule to include adult /pr/ and /kr/. Throughout this period, [f] is never produced in place of adult /br/, /gr/ or /r/ or for stops in any other environment.

(2) On session 13, Jane's mother commented "She's got those stop plus *r* [as] *f*. . . .It's getting very difficult to tell what she's saying. It's just that she's generalized suddenly to everything. *Bread* is *bed/ Pretty* [is] *fitty. Cradle,* you'll get *fatal.* . . . Depends on the word. . . ."

(3) At the home visit, Jane's mother confirmed the patterns reported, again helped elicit relevant words, and also commented: "Within the last few weeks, [Jane] has become aware that she doesn't say words like adults do. If I say to her ''Are you [fɪŋkʰɪŋ] your milk?'', she smiles. She understands."

(4) Only one token.

(5) The arrow indicates a time period during which no change occurred in the example word.

the adult model before than after the extension (e.g., [k] is in a sense more 'correct' for /kr/ than is [f]). Both rule formation and overgeneralization must have a plausible phonetic or phonological base (however distant from the adult language) to qualify as rule-governed behavior. A further restriction, for the present, is that the rule of overgeneralization be fairly uncommon among chil-

8. COGNITIVE ASPECTS OF PHONOLOGICAL DEVELOPMENT 269

dren acquiring the same language; this is to insure that the case for active rule formation draws on only the clearest and strongest examples.[7]

Such phonological overgeneralizations are similar to those found in syntax and semantics as, for example, the use of *wented* at the stage in which the past tense *-ed* is learned (and where the correct *went* was previously used) (Cazden, 1968) or the extension of *more* + noun (*more cookies*) to *more* + verb (*more read*) (Braine, 1963).

Regression

Over fifty years ago, Jespersen (1922) observed that "sometimes a child will acquire a sound or sound combination correctly and then lose it till it reappears a few months later [p. 110]."[8] We will use the term "regression" to describe those cases in which a child, at one stage, produces a sound or sequence of sounds *correctly* (i.e., as an adult would) and then, at a subsequent stage, produces it incorrectly. In one sense, regression is the complement of overgeneralization: the use of the term "overgeneralization" draws attention to the formation of a new rule, while the term "regression" identifies consequences of child's new rule. In this section, we will restrict "regression" to the loss of a correct production. In the following section, "changing hypotheses," we will discuss examples where a change in the child's hypothesis takes the child's production further from the adult model than was the case in an earlier stage.

In the data from J (Macken, 1978), a Spanish-speaking child, the following five stages in the production of *taza* 'cup' were observed:

(1)	[ta]	1;9.15
(2)	[tata]	1;11
(3)	[tasa]	2;0
(4)	[sasa]	2;1
(5)	[tasa]	2;2

(from Macken, 1978: transcriptions simplified)

First, we observe that in Stages 1–3, J produces the initial /t/ of *taza* correctly. Second, in both Stages 3 and 5, J produces the whole word as an adult speaker of Spanish would. The interesting stage is Stage 4. Here, J has applied a rule of

---

[7]Kiparsky and Menn (1977), however, claim that *all* rules, even so called "natural" rules, must be discovered.

[8]Bower (1976) and others have documented somewhat related phenomena in the nonlinguistic, physical development of the child: "As an infant grows, he can acquire certain skills, lose them and ultimately acquire them." Similarly, Meltzoff and Moore (1977) report on the imitation of facial and manual gestures by neonate infants, but Jacobson (1979) challenges the Meltzoff-Moore interpretation.

consonant (i.e., fricative) harmony that results in the loss of the previously correct initial /t/. In discussing data of this type, Macken refers to the phenomenon as one of "permitted complexity" and argues that the limits on complexity seen at each stage of development are frequently limits on the child's production (not perception or storage). In the present context, the important point is that J, at Stage 4, devised a rule that enabled him to add a difficult fricative (intervocalic /s/) to his set of productions and still avoid the problem posed by pronouncing this sound in a word with an initial stop. That Stage 4 represents a step backward from the adult point of view is clear; for the child, however, such a stage is progress.

A different type of regression is discussed in Macken's 1980b paper, which presents a reanalysis of the data found in Smith, 1973. Macken notes the following correspondences:

	puddle	pickle
Stage 23	[p∧gəl]	[pikəl]
Stage 29	[p∧dəl]	[pitəl]

Note that *pickle* and several similar type words are correctly produced from at least Stage 23 on, but that their pronunciation 'regresses' at Stage 29. The interpretation given to these data is that prior to Stage 29, Amah had words like *puddle* mentally stored with an intervocalic *g* (or *k* depending on the voicing of the target sound) and that when the child 'discovered,' at Stage 29, that *puddle* words should have an intervocalic *d* (or *t*), he changed his *g* (*k*) to *d* (*t*)—a change that results in the errors seen in the *pickle*-type words. The data show that the child actively organizes phonologically relevant information, constructs an organizational network (and at times a unique network) for words in his mental lexicon, and formulates rules that then operate on sets of related words.

Changing Hypotheses

Sometimes children replace one systematic rule with another rule that is equally systematic but does not represent a step toward the adult language. We interpret such a rule change as an indication that the child has changed an hypothesis about an acceptable way to pronounce a difficult sound or set of sounds. These "changing hypotheses" often involve overgeneralization. Overgeneralization is itself a type of regression but one in which a production is simply further from the correct adult pronunciation at Time 2 than at Time 1 (rather than regression, which instead represents a loss of a previously *correct* sound). Thus, when Jane overgeneralizes her /tr,dr/ → [f] rule to other stop + *r* clusters (see above, "overgeneralization"), one consequence is that her previous production of [p^h] for /pr/ "regresses" in that [f] for /pr/ is less adult-like than was [p^h]. Note, however, that neither [p^h] nor [f] is correct—the former is simply more like the adult [pr] than is the latter. Further, the regression to [f] seems to be the result of a change in Jane's hypothesis about an acceptable way to pronounce stop + *r* clusters. That this is a change in hypotheses is inferred from the fact that, prior to this point, Jane had an equally systematic rule whereby all such clusters were produced as singleton stops. A similar example of changing hypotheses comes from Smith, 1973:[9]

	A̲	B̲	C̲
side	[ḍait]	[ḍait]	[lait]
light	[ḍait]	[lait]	[lait]
	2;2	2;4	2;5

In stage C, Amahl has regressed in two senses: First, he has lost the contrast between *side* and *light* that he maintained in his speech at Stage B; and, second, in *side* the production of [l] is less close to adult /s/ than was [ḍ] (Stage B). Smith describes this change as a change in Amahl's hypothesis about how to pronounce /s/:

> What appears to be happening is that the child is confronted with a number of perceptually discrete but for him unpronounceable sounds and proceeds to formulate hypotheses as to their nature in terms of the distinctive features already available to him. Having mastered the sonorant continuant [l] he presumably hypothesised that [continuant] rather than [fricative] was the crucial feature characteristic of /s/ . . . as well as of /l/. . . . In fact, there was a very slight tendency to generalize beyond the examples given here, and extend the rule to /θ/—*thank you* appeared briefly as [lɛŋku:]—and to all occurrences of /s/ irrespective of environment [p. 153].

Itkonen, 1977, gives several examples of the overgeneralization type of regression from a corpus based on the speech of a young child acquiring Finnish.

Cases of overgeneralization, regression, and changing hypotheses within a single child's corpus provide the best evidence for the child's active role in the formulation of rules, but evidence can also be found in the differences between the rules of individual children. Farwell (1976) reports on four approaches for the production of fricatives ("favorite sounds," "avoidance," "syllabic fricatives," and "word position") that were used by seven children. Farwell identifies these approaches as "strategies" and observes that they demonstrate the "child's active organization of his language." Of particular present relevance is the syllabic fricative strategy of MF (the only child among the seven to devise this particular rule): "For two months (10 sessions), only four adult fricative words occurred in her production, only one more than once. Then MF began to produce fricative words as mid to back fricatives and affricates without a vowel. . . . She used this method for *sheep, shoe, juice, chip, chicken, zebra, fish,* and *flower* [p. 101]." Farwell comments: "I thought this an idiosyncratic way of learning fricatives until last year when, in another study, I found a child,

---

[9]Smith calls such cases examples of "recidivism."

Amy, who had adopted the same strategy, using it for the words *cheese, juice,* and *shoe* [p. 101]." Another striking example of the novel rules children may invent comes from our 1976 study: at 1;10.7, Tessa—for the first time—contrasted final voiced vs. voiceless stops, and she did so not as adults would but by aspirating the final voiceless stops (e.g., *book* [pʊɪk] and producing final voiced stops as a separate syllable, voiced stop + [ə] (e.g., *pig* [pɪgə]). These two rules—syllabic fricatives and the extra syllable for voiced stops—are unusual, and for this very reason they are also good evidence of the child's 'creation' of phonological rules.

Much more could be said about individual differences in phonology acquisition (cf. Leonard, Newhoff, & Meslama, 1980); however, before leaving this topic, we should point out that there have been many attempts to find patterns in the variation between children. Leont'ev (1965; quoted in Jones, 1967) refers to the possibility of classifying a certain stage in the speech behavior of children into two types: At about one year some children produce speech forms that represent a reduction of adult forms to monosyllable utterances, whereas others tend to produce utterances that have the same syllabic and accentual patterns of the adult forms (but apparently with imprecise phonetic qualities). Peters (1977) discusses two types of speech—analytic and gestalt—that may reflect two language-learning strategies. Vihman (1976) suggests that different phonological styles may correlate with different personalities of children—cautious vs. noncautious; similarly, Leopold (1947) attributes the absence of metathesis in Hildegard's speech to her "generally cautious speech habits [p. 237]" and her "conscientious . . . attempts at reproducing standard words [p. 239]." (Cf. also Ingram, 1979.) Drawing on an information processing model for interpreting individual differences (cf. Zelnicker & Jeffrey, 1976), Macken (1976, 1979) relates two different types of phonological behavior to the difference between global vs. detail processing styles (Macken, 1979): "This analysis of differences in terms of cognitive style is not an unreasonable extension of a cognitive model of phonology, one emphasizing the problem-solving nature of acquisition, and is promising in that it may—if successful—restrict the range of individual phonological differences to several sets or syndromes typical of different styles [p. 47]." The point remains, however, that even children who could be said to be similar in general style or strategy still devise quite different and sometimes unique rules. It is partly because there are widespread individual differences (e.g., nearly every child we have studied produces at least one *unique* but systematic rule) that we suggest that the general acquisition process is one of hypothesis formation.

DISCUSSION: TOWARD A COGNITIVE MODEL

Above, we culled data from a variety of sources and interpreted those data as evidence for cognitively relevant aspects of phonology acquisition. Implicit in the order of presentation was a broad outline of what a cognitive model of acquisition might look like. In this section, we will make the model explicit to the extent possible and attempt to evaluate its strengths and weaknesses. We emphasize that such an attempt is premature: More data must be collected to verify even the phenomena we have identified and more new analyses from a cognitive perspective must be carried out to enrich and/or limit our generalizations. In short, only future work will decide whether such an outline can be replaced with an explicit and testable model.

What, then, is the picture of the acquisition process that emerges from these data? We begin with the observation that the data from a very young child—one just learning to talk—are piecemeal and apparently unintegrated. It seems that the child initially analyzes word shapes on an individual basis. It is not surprising that such a child should produce phonological *idioms,* because idioms are in fact simply isolated cases of accuracy. At some point, the child begins to recognize similarities between classes of sounds and sounds-in-combination, and to construct rules for relating similar sounds and word shapes and to formulate rules that solve the pronunciation difficulties that are encountered. That the process is not automatic can be shown in the variable *experimentation* forms that children sometimes produce as they search for a solution and in the "range and diversity of [different children's] solutions" (Kiparsky & Menn, 1977). A child's experimentation can reveal the conflicting parameters that the child is struggling with. As a result of what appears to be a basic *hypothesis-forming and testing* process, the child decides on a particular rule and then applies it to other, related items— i.e., to sounds or words forming the membership of the child's category. It is generally the case that the child's categories do not correspond directly to those of an adult. The child may then *overgeneralize* the newly discovered rule, as the child integrates the new rule into his or her system. Often, the formation of a rule and/or its overgeneralization results in *regression*—or apparent loss of ability. Such cases of regression demonstrate that the process is not a simple unfolding of abilities or a linear progression toward adult competence. As the child comes to recognize new and relevant information (or, alternatively, the relevant 'counterexamples' to his or her hypotheses—Karmiloff-Smith and Inhelder terminology, below), the child *changes hypotheses* (or 'theories') and creates new rules. Many steps in this process can be seen in the development of Jane's clusters as presented in Table 8.2.

Stated in the above way, the process of acquiring phonology looks very similar to the development of what are more commonly called cognitive abilities and, in particular, to the process of acquiring physical (weight and balance) information as reported in Karmiloff-Smith and Inhelder, 1974/75. Those authors report a study that investigated children's ability to perform a block-balancing task in which the blocks were of different sizes and shapes and had unexpected distributions of weight over their lengths. From the developmental process the authors observed, we can extrapolate the following stages: (a) single item match; (b) gradual recognition of a pattern; (c) period of exploration; (d) construction of a theory, followed by generalization ('overgeneralization' in the sense used in the hypothesis-formation section above) and loss of ability (i.e., loss of successes of Stage a); (e) gradual recognition of regularity of counterexamples; (f) construction of a new theory, distinct from the first theory; and (g) gradual development of a single unifying theory. Clearly this 'model' is similar in important respects to the one we have outlined for the acquisition of phonology.

To evaluate this cognitive model, we first note that it handles well precisely those kinds of data that we have presented here and, further, that such data are difficult to explain with a universalist-linguistic model.[10] Second, as we have tried to show in each section, the phonological phenomena seem to have direct analogues in other areas of language development. Third, if the analogy with, for example, the Karmiloff-Smith and Inhelder model of cognitive development is well-founded, the cognitive-phonology model promises to interact well with a general model of child development.[11] Thus, the model begins to account for the data, is consistent with general aspects of language development and is based on a defensible model of the general conceptual, problem-solving skills of young children.

The model of phonological development sketched here also fits well with aspects of other models of cognitive development. For example, the language and communication-oriented Cognitive Pendulum Theory advanced by Nelson & Nelson (1978) matches our model in at least four ways: (1) The two models show a pattern of stages moving from idiosyncratic first steps through relatively broad rules to a repeatedly revised and integrated rule structure; (2) they both allow for wide individual differences; (3) they both acknowledge that perception/comprehension and production may develop to a considerable extent independently, with the former generally ahead; and (4) they share the view that development is not unilinear but has shifts and apparent regressions. Our model, however, was constructed largely in terms of the development of individual rules and small sets

---

[10] There are, of course, other alternative models, including hybrid varieties. Although in this paper we discuss two sharply contrasted points of view to clarify the cognitive approach, the model we are developing includes elements of both: While we emphasize the point that the same, simple hypothesis-formation process is basic to both phonology and other cognitive acquisitions, we also expect that there exist very broad linguistic and nonlinguistic constraints on the child's possible hypothesis space. Given that such constraints can be argued to be antecedently given, our model can be made compatible with nativist models other than the highly deterministic models of, say, Chomsky, 1980b or Jakobson, 1941, provided that such constraints are sufficiently broad as to allow a very wide range of hypotheses and that the constraints are not limited to strictly linguistic content.

[11] The Karmiloff-Smith and Inhelder model is based on data from children who are several years older than the children for whom morphological overgeneralizations (like *wented*) are reported (e.g., Cazden, 1968), and both these groups of children are older than the children we discuss here. It may be that evidence of general hypothesis-formation processes can be documented for phonology in quite young children because the intense period of phonological learning comes so early in language development.

of rules rather than in terms of overall phonological development, whereas the Cognitive Pendulum Theory addresses the development of whole 'systems.' It would be an instructive exercise from both perspectives to try to fit phonology into the broader framework. Nelson & Nelson examined such different cognitive systems as the development of basic concepts and labels, sentence and discourse systems, and the use of figurative language. They mention phonology only once, but we hope the explanations and focus of the present chapter will facilitate more detailed examination of phonological development in relation to their model.

What problems will a cognitive model of phonology acquisition encounter? We will discuss four: empirical verification; data that the model may not handle well; the absence of distinguishing features of the model as a model of *phonology* acquisition; and the model's generality.

First, internal to the model are the tasks of checking on the apparent relative rarity of some examples (e.g., idioms, experimentation, etc.), and of elaborating the model. One particular problem in this category is the fact that some children produce few forms of the types discussed above in the selectivity, creativity, and hypothesis-formation sections; these children stay fairly close to the adult models (cf., however, the discussion under Hypothesis Formation of the attempts that have been made to reduce individual differences to a set of styles or syndromes). These are essentially empirical problems to be solved by future research.

Second, it could be argued that such a model will have difficulty handling universals: if we assume a thoroughgoing cognitive or problem-solving process as basic, how do we explain the fact that so many children arrive at the same or similar solution? We have already suggested that universals are due to universal characteristics of the human auditory and articulatory apparatus. To this we now add that children presumably share the same or a significantly similar conceptual apparatus. As a result, constraints are imposed on the range of possible variation and broadly similar sequences of phonological development are followed.[12] It is important to note that those universals that do exist are less of a problem to a cognitive model than is the large number of individual differences to a universalist model. Nevertheless, for the cognitive model to represent an advance in the field, it must incorporate the results of previous research. We fully expect there to be an interplay between prewiring (perhaps even of the sort with specifically linguistic consequences), experience, the learner, and the language. The point to be emphasized is that the hallmark of the child's development—in phonology as elsewhere—is the child's flexibility in creatively adapting to new information. The important problem is to specify how all factors interact to produce the

---

[12]It is also possible that universal characteristics of the language input to children are a factor in phonological development (cf. Ferguson, 1964, 1977, 1979b). Recent research (e.g., Heath, forthcoming; Ochs, 1980; Schieffelin, 1979), however, raises serious doubts about some of the proposed input universals.

observable developmental sequence. In phonology studies, the conceptual abilities of the child and the cognitive aspects of the task have been generally ignored.

The third problem, which perhaps is a concomitant of the model's compatibility with a general cognitive model, is the absence of any unique features. As outlined above, there appear to be no particular aspects of the model that relate to any unique features of phonology as the domain of acquisition. On the one hand, it is reasonable to hypothesize that, although there will be differences in conceptual *structures* across domains due to differences in content between those domains, there will be no differences in conceptual *processes,* such as categorization, inferencing, etc. Yet it also seems to be the case that human behavior is highly affected by context—by the structure of particular domains. Specialized strategies are devised to solve certain problems and these strategies are affected by the problems themselves. Thus, we would caution researchers in phonology acquisition not to ignore those unique aspects of phonological learning—if such exist—that derive from the unique properties of phonological systems.

The fourth and most serious problem is the generality of this model. For example, this model is inexplicit on how the phonological categories are formed or what the specific form of the phonological representation is. A more insidious difficulty is that such a model can in theory explain anything and thus is difficult to constrain, test, and disprove. For example, we drew heavily on children's errors and interpreted them as more or less 'clever' solutions. The problem here is one of overinterpretation. Clearly, criteria must be established to distinguish low-level matches (e.g., a=b) from higher level organizational or categorization strategies (e.g., a is like b); both of these result in errors from an adult point of view but only the latter, we would argue, is 'cognitive' in the sense the model intends.[13]

Because the processes and structures are all inferred and the model not formally constrained, it will be difficult to find answers to questions such as the following: What child errors or other data could serve as counterevidence to the model? What child productions or behavior could count as independent corroboration? And—most importantly—what testable predictions does the model make? We began this chapter by noting that a trend toward a more cognitive model of phonology acquisition was emerging. Clearly at such an early stage, firm answers to questions like these cannot be given. We believe that enquiry along lines suggested here (and already being pursued by a few workers in the field) will prove valuable and that future research will result in a full model that is both explanatorily adequate and testable.

---

[13]It may, however, prove to be true that low-level auditory and articulatory processes are relevant for a cognitive theory (cf. Norman, 1979, on the cognitive aspects of the development of skills like typing).

SUMMARY

Linguistically oriented research on phonological development has generally been focused on a proposed universal order of acquisition of phonemes or oppositions, the nature of children's substitutions for adult segments ("realization rules"), changes in rule structure as related to language change over time, or child phonology as evidence for universal constraints on linguistic structure. For the most part, this research has been dominated by three universalist theories of acquisition, each an extension of a particular phonological theory. However, there is a shift emerging in the field of child phonology away from the prevalent universalist-linguistic models of phonological development. This chapter utilized the research literature and the authors' research experience to focus not on segments or universal order of acquisition, but on those aspects of phonological development that have been ignored by universalist theories or that remained crucially unintegrated in such theories. Noting that these aspects show similarities or parallels to cognitive development, we outlined a broadly cognitive model of acquisition—one that, while incorporating specifically linguistic constraints, ascribes central importance to hypothesis formation processes.

Data presented show that very young children attend selectively to language input in terms of sounds, that they create sound sequences in their speech that have no adult models, and that they devise systematic and sometimes unique phonological rules, proceeding non-linearly toward the adult grammar via an active yet constrained process of hypothesis formation and testing. The proposed model holds that children initially analyze whole word shapes (or larger complexes) on an individual basis, then begin to recognize similarities between classes of sounds and sounds-in-combination and to construct rules for relating similar sounds and word shapes and for solving pronunciation difficulties of various kinds. The developmental process is not automatic and it is not a simple unfolding of abilities or linear progression toward adult competence. As they come to recognize new and relevant information, children change hypotheses and create new ones. Evidence for this hypothesis formation process includes the incorporation of "phonological idioms" into larger rule structures, children's experiments with acceptable pronunciations, the creation and overgeneralization of phonological rules, changes in rules that are not steps toward adult models, and substantial individual differences in interim rule systems.

In evaluating the model, we noted that the model is very similar to those proposed for cognitive development (of which two are specifically described), with the important difference that the specified kinds of behavior occur at earlier ages than for other areas of cognitive development. We found that while a model of this sort handles well the various kinds of data brought forward in the chapter and is consistent with more general models of language development, it is less obviously appropriate to account for universal tendencies in language development; to do so, it must shift explanation to presumed universal characteristics of the human auditory, articulatory, and conceptual/cognitive apparatus that significantly restrict the possible variation or limit the possible hypothesis space. Finally, we noted that the model is too general (in that it neither highlights those features of phonological development that are unique within cognitive development nor fills in sufficient detail to account for specific paths of development) and that it is both unconstrained and difficult to test.

In sum, however, we take the position that the cognitive model is superior to previous universalist-linguistic models and that further research along the lines suggested will lead to more elaborated models that are more constrained, more testable, and more explanatory. It is our hope that such models will be valuable to cognitivists as well as phonological theorists, in both cases broadening the theoretical perspectives and tying the theory more closely to the behavioral evidence.

ACKNOWLEDGMENTS

Some of the research reported here came from Stanford Child Phonology Project studies, and we gratefully acknowledge the support of grants from the National Science Foundation, the National Institute of Child Health and Human Development, and the William T. Grant Foundation. We also thank E. V. Clark, W. Leben, L. Menn, N. V. Smith, the editor, and anonymous reviewers for helpful advice and criticism. A preliminary version of this paper appeared in *Papers and Reports on Child Language Development,* 18 (1980).

REFERENCES

Anderson, S. R. Why phonology isn't "natural." *Linguistic Inquiry,* 1981, *12,* 493–539.
Barton, D., Miller, R., & Macken, M. Do children treat clusters as one unit or two? *Papers and Reports on Child Language Development,* 1980, *18,* 105–137.
Berman, R. A. Natural phonological processes at the one-word stage. *Lingua,* 1977, *43,* 1–21.
Bower, T. G. R. Repetitive processes in child development. *Scientific American,* 1976, *235,* 38–47.
Braine, M. D. S. The ontogeny of English phrase structure: The first phase. *Language,* 1963, *39,* 1–13.
Braine, M. D. S. On what might constitute a learnable phonology. *Language,* 1974, *50,* 270–299.
Branigan, G. Syllable structure and the acquisition of consonants: The great conspiracy in word formation. *Journal of Psycholinguistic Research,* 1976, *5,* 117–133.
Brown, R. *A first language: The early stages.* Cambridge, Mass.: Harvard University Press, 1973.
Brown, R. & Hanlon, C. Derivational complexity and order of acquisition. In J. R. Hays (Ed.), *Cognition and the development of language,* New York: Wiley, 1970.
Cazden, C. The acquisition of noun and verb inflections. *Child Development,* 1968, *39,* 433–438.
Chomsky, N. *Aspects of the theory of syntax.* Cambridge, Mass.: The MIT Press, 1965.
Chomsky, N. *Reflections on language.* New York: Pantheon Books, 1975.
Chomsky, N. *Rules and representations.* New York: Columbia University Press, 1980. (a)

8. COGNITIVE ASPECTS OF PHONOLOGICAL DEVELOPMENT 279

Chomsky, N. Rules and representations. *The Brain and Behavioral Sciences, 3,* 1–61, 1980. (b)
Chomsky, N. *Lectures on government and binding.* Dordrecht: Foris Publications, 1981.
Dodd, B. *The acquisition of phonological skills in normal, severely subnormal and deaf children.* Doctoral dissertation. London: University of London, 1974.
Donaldson, M. *Children's minds.* New York: W. W. Norton & Co., 1978.
Donegan, P. J. & Stampe, D. The study of natural phonology. In D. A. Dinnsen (Ed.), *Current approaches to phonological theory.* Bloomington: Indiana University Press, 1979.
Drachman, G. Some strategies in the acquisition of phonology. In M. J. Kenstowicz & C. W. Kisseberth (Eds.), *Issues in phonological theory.* The Hague: Mouton, 1973.
Edwards, M. L. One child's acquisition of English liquids. *Papers and Reports on Child Language Development,* 1971, *3,* 101–109.
Edwards, M. L. *Patterns and processes in fricative acquisition: Longitudinal evidence from six English-learning children.* Doctoral dissertation. Stanford: Stanford University, 1978. (a)
Edwards, M. L. *Word-position in fricative acquisition.* Paper presented at Boston University Conference on Language Development, 1978. (b)
Edwards, M. L. *Phonological processes in fricative acquisition.* Paper presented at Stanford Child Language Research Forum, 1979.
Engel, W. v. R. Un esempio di "linguistic consciousness" nel bambino piccolo. 1965. Translated in C. A. Ferguson & D. I. Slobin (Eds.), *Studies of child language development.* New York: Holt, Rinehart, & Winston, 1973.
Farwell, C. B. Some strategies in the early production of fricatives. *Papers and Reports on Child Language Development,* 1976, *12,* 97–104.
Ferguson, C. A. Baby talk in six languages. *American Anthropologist,* 1964, *66,* 103–114.
Ferguson, C. A. Baby talk as a simplified register. In C. E. Snow & C. A. Ferguson (Eds.), *Talking to Children.* Cambridge: Cambridge University Press, 1977.
Ferguson, C. A. Learning to pronounce: The earliest stages of phonological development in the child. In F. D. Minifie & L. L. Lloyd (Eds.), *Communicative and cognitive abilities—early behavioral assessment.* Baltimore: University Park Press, 1978.
Ferguson, C. A. *Phonological development: Some cognitive aspects.* Lecture given in the series Current Issues in Cognitive Science, Brown University, Providence, R.I., 1979. (a)
Ferguson, C. A. Talking to children: A search for universals. In J. H. Greenberg, C. A. Ferguson, & E. A. Moravcsik (Eds.), *Universals of human language* (Vol. 1). Stanford: Stanford University Press, 1979. (b)
Ferguson, C. A. & Farwell, C. B. Words and sounds in early language acquisition. *Language,* 1975, *51,* 419–439.
Ferguson, C. A. & Garnica, O. K. Theories of phonological development. In E. H. Lenneberg & E. Lenneberg (Eds.), *Foundations of language development* (Vol. 2). New York: Academic Press, 1975.
Ferguson, C. A., Peizer, D. B., & Weeks, T. E. Model-and-replica phonological grammar of a child's first words. *Lingua,* 1973, *31,* 35–65.
Fey, M. & Gandour, J. *Problem-solving in phonology acquisition.* Paper presented at the 54th Annual meeting of the Linguistic Society of America, Los Angeles, Calif., 1979.
Fey, M. & Gandour, J. Rule discovery in phonological acquisition. *Journal of Child Language,* 1982, *9,* 71–81.
Fodor, J. A. How to learn to talk: Some simple ways. In F. Smith & G. A. Miller (Eds.), *The genesis of language.* Cambridge, Mass.: MIT Press, 1966.
Gelman, R. *Human development.* Paper presented at the La Jolla Conference on Cognitive Science, University of California, San Diego, La Jolla, Calif., 1979.
Goldin-Meadow, S. & Felman, H. The development of language-like communication without a language model. *Science,* 1977, *197,* 401–403.

Greenlee, M. Some observations on initial English consonant clusters in a child two to three years old. *Papers and Reports on Child Language Development*, 1973, *6*, 97–106.

Halliday, M. A. K. *Learning how to mean*. London: Edward Arnold, 1975.

Heath, S. B. *Ways with words: Ethnography of communication—communities and classrooms*. Forthcoming.

Hooper, J. B. Substantive evidence for linearity: Vowel length and nasality in English. In W. A. Beach, S. E. Fox, & S. Philosoph (Eds.), *Papers from the 13th regional meeting, Chicago Linguistic Society*. Chicago: CLS, 1977.

Ingram, D. Phonological rules in young children. *Journal of Child Language*, 1974, *1*, 49–64.

Ingram, D. *Cross linguistic evidence on the extent and limit of individual variation in phonological development*. Paper presented at the International Congress of Phonetic Sciences, Copenhagen, 1979.

Itkonen, T. Notes on the acquisition of phonology. English summary of Huomiota lapsen äänteistön kehityksestä. *Virittäjä*, 1977, 279–308. [English summary, 304–308.]

Jacobson, S. W. Matching behavior in the young infant. *Child Development*, 1979, *50*, 425–430.

Jakobson, R. *Kindersprache, Aphasie und allgemeine Lautgesetze*. 1941. [Translated by A. R. Keiler. *Child language, aphasia and phonological universals*. The Hague: Mouton. 1968.]

Jakobson, R. & Waugh, L. R. *The sound shape of language*. Bloomington: Indiana University Press, 1979.

Jeng, H-H. The acquisition of Chinese phonology in relation to Jakobson's laws of irreversible solidarity. *Proceedings of the Ninth International Congress of Phonetic Sciences* (Vol. 2), 1979, 155–161.

Jespersen, O. *Language: Its nature, development and origin*. New York: H. Holt & Co., 1922.

Jones, L. G. English phonotactic structure and first language acquisition. *Lingua*, 1967, *19*, 1–59.

Karmiloff-Smith, A. & Inhelder, B. If you want to get ahead, get a theory. *Cognition*, 1974/75, *3*, 195–212.

Kiparsky, P. & Menn, L. On the acquisition of phonology. In J. Macnamara (Ed.), *Language learning and thought*. New York: Academic Press, 1977.

Kisseberth, C. W. On the functional unity of phonological rules. *Linguistic Inquiry*, 1970, *1*, 291–306.

Kunsmann, P. W. *Reduplication as a strategy for language acquisition*. Paper presented at the summer Linguistic Society of America Meeting, Oswego, N.Y., 1976.

Labov, W. & Labov, T. The phonetics of *cat* and *mama*. *Language*, 1978, *54*, 816–852.

Leonard, L. B. & Newhoff, M. *The nature of early child phonology: Evidence from the speech of twins*. Unpublished manuscript, 1978.

Leonard, B., Newhoff, M., & Meslama, L. Individual differences in early child phonology. *Journal of Applied Psycholinguistics*, 1980, *1*, 7–30.

Leopold, W. F. *Speech development of a bilingual child: A linguist's record. Sound learning in the first two years* (Vol. 2). Chicago: Northwestern University Press, 1947.

Macken, M. A. *Individual differences in phonological acquisition: Strategies versus cognitive styles*. Paper presented at the Child Language Seminar Series, Stanford University, Stanford, Calif., 1976.

Macken, M. A. Permitted complexity in phonological development: One child's acquisition of Spanish consonants. *Lingua*, 1978, *44*, 219–253.

Macken, M. A. Developmental reorganization of phonology: A hierarchy of basic units of acquisition. *Lingua*, 1979, *49*, 11–49.

Macken, M. A. The acquisition of stop systems: A cross-linguistic perspective. In G. H. Yeni-Komshian, J. F. Kavanagh, & C. A. Ferguson (Eds.), *Child phonology: Production* (Vol. 1). New York: Academic Press, 1980. (a)

Macken, M. A. The child's lexical representation: The 'puzzle-puddle-pickle' evidence. *Journal of Linguistics*, 1980, *16*, 1–17. (b)

Macken, M. A. & Ferguson, C. A. Phonological universals of language acquisition. *Annals of the New York Academy of Sciences*, 1981, *379*, 110–129.
Macnamara, J. Cognitive basis of language learning in infants. *Psychological Review*, 1972, *79*, 1–13.
Meltzoff, A. N. & Moore, M. K. Imitation of facial and manual gestures by human neonates. *Science*, 1977, *198*, 75–78.
Menn, L. Phonotactic rules in beginning speech. *Lingua*, 1971, *26*, 225–251.
Menn, L. *A theoretical framework for child phonology*. Paper presented at summer Linguistic Society of America Meeting, Amherst, Mass., 1974.
Menn, L. Evidence for an interactionist-discovery theory of child phonology. *Papers and Reports on Child Language Development*, 1976, *12*, 169–177.
Menn, L. *Pattern, control and contrast in beginning speech, a case study in the development of word form and word function*. Bloomington: Indiana University Linguistics Club, 1978.
Mikeš, M. *Universal and language-restricted rules in the development of the phonological systems in child language*. Paper presented at the International Symposium on Child Language, Mexico City, 1976.
Moskowitz, B. A. The two-year-old stage in the acquisition of English phonology. *Language*, 1970, *46*, 426–441.
Moskowitz, B. A. Acquisition of phonology and syntax. In K. J. J. Hintikka, J. M. E. Moravcsik, & P. Suppes (Eds.), *Approaches to natural language*. Dordrecht, Holland: Reidel Publishing Co., 1973.
Moskowitz, B. A. The acquisition of language. *Scientific American*, 1978, *239*, 92–108.
Mowrer, O. H. Speech development in the young child: The autism theory of speech development and some clinical applications. *Journal of Speech & Hearing Disorders*, 1952, *17*, 263–268.
Murai, J. The sounds of infants, their phonemicization and symbolization. *Studia Phonologica*, 1963, *3*, 18–34.
Nelson, K. E. & Nelson, K. Cognitive pendulums and their linguistic realization. In K. E. Nelson (Ed.), *Children's Language* (Vol. 1). New York: Gardner Press, 1978.
Norman, D. A. *Twelve issues for cognitive science*. Paper presented at the La Jolla Conference on Cognitive Science, University of California, San Diego, La Jolla, Calif., 1979.
Ochs, E. *Talking to children in Western Samoa*. Mimeo., University of Southern California, Department of Linguistics, 1980. (To appear *Language in Society*.)
Olmsted, D. L. A theory of the child's learning of phonology. *Language*, 1966, *42*, 531–535.
Olmsted, D. L. *Out of the mouths of babes*. The Hague: Mouton, 1971.
Pačesová, J. *The development of vocabulary in the child*. Brno: University J. E. Purkyne, 1968.
Peters, A. M. The beginnings of speech. *Papers and Reports on Child Language Development*, 1974, *8*, 26–32.
Peters, A. M. Language learning strategies. *Language*, 1977, *53*, 560–573.
Priestley, T. M. S. One idiosyncratic strategy in the acquisition of phonology. *Journal of Child Language*, 1977, *4*, 45–66.
Ross, J. R. *Constraints on variables in syntax*. Doctoral dissertation. Cambridge, Mass.: MIT, 1967.
Sapir, E. Sound pattern in language, *Language*, 1925, *1*, 37–51.
Schieffelin, B. *How Kaluli children learn what to say, what to do, and how to feel: An ethnographic study of the development of communicative competence*. Unpublished Doctoral dissertation, Columbia University, 1979.
Slobin, D. I. Comments on 'Developmental Psycholinguistics.' In F. Smith & G. Miller (Eds.), *The genesis of language*. Cambridge, Mass.: MIT Press, 1966.
Smith, N. V. *The acquisition of phonology*. Cambridge: University Press, 1973.
Smith, N. V. The acquisition of phonological skills in children. *British Journal of Disorders of Communication*, 1974, *9*, 17–23.

Smith, N. V. Universal tendencies in the child's acquisition of phonology. In N. O'Connor (Ed.), *Language, cognitive deficits and retardation*. London: Butterworths, 1975.

Smith, N. V. Lexical representation and the acquisition of phonology. In B. B. Kachru (Ed.), *Linguistics in the seventies: Directions and prospects.* Special issue of *Studies in the Linguistic Sciences*, 1978, *8*, 259–273.

Solan, L. Fixing parameters: Language acquisition and language variation. *University of Massachusetts Occasional Papers in Linguistics*, U. Mass. Amherst, 1981, *6*, 121–136.

Srivastava, G. P. A child's acquisition of Hindi consonants. *Indian Linguistics*, 1974, *35*, 112–118.

Stampe, D. *The acquisition of phonetic representation*. Paper presented at the 5th Regional Meeting of the Chicago Linguistic Society, Chicago, Ill., 1969.

Stampe, D. *A dissertation on natural phonology*. Doctoral dissertation. Chicago: University of Chicago, 1973.

Stanley, R. Redundancy rules in phonology. *Language*, 1967, *43*, 393–435.

Timm, L. A child's acquisition of Russian phonology. *Journal of Child Language*, 1977, *4*, 329–339.

Vanvik, A. The phonetic-phonemic development of a Norwegian child. In H. Vogt (Ed.), *Norsk tidsskrift for sprogvidenskap*, 1971, *24*, 269–325.

Velten, H. V. The growth of phonemic and lexical patterns in infant language. *Language*, 1943, *19*, 281–292.

Venneman, T. Language acquisition and phonological theory. *Lingua*, 1971, *70*, 71–87.

Vihman, M. M. On the acquisition of Estonian. *Papers and Reports on Child Language Development*, 1971, *3*, 51–94.

Vihman, M. M. *From pre-speech to speech: On early phonology*. Paper presented at the 8th Child Language Research Forum, Stanford University, Stanford, Calif., 1976.

Vihman, M. M. Consonant harmony: Its scope and function in child language. In J. P. Greenberg, C. A. Ferguson, & E. A. Moravcsik (Eds.), *Universals of human language: Phonology* (Vol. 2). Stanford: Stanford University Press, 1978.

Waterson, N. Some speech forms of an English child—a phonological study. *Transactions of the Philological Society*, 1970, 1–24.

Waterson, N. Child phonology: A prosodic view. *Journal of Linguistics*, 1971, *7*, 179–211.

Winitz, H. *Articulatory acquisition and behavior*. New York: Appleton-Century-Croft, 1969.

Zelniker, T. & Jeffrey, W. E. Reflective and impulsive children: Strategies of information processing underlying differences in problem solving. *Society for Research on Child Development Monographs*, 1976, *41*.

9 Language Acquisition in a Deaf Child of Deaf Parents: Speech, Sign Variations, and Print Variations

Madeline M. Maxwell
University of Texas at Austin
Department of Speech Communication

This chapter is about language development in one deaf child of deaf parents. The child, Alice, was exposed to and learned to communicate in language through American Sign Language (ASL), Sign English, fingerspelling, speech/speechreading, sign print, and English orthographic print. The focus of the study reported here was the interaction of all these varieties of language in this child's development.

Before examining Alice's linguistic development, it is worthwhile to examine the background from which this study derives its concerns.

It is well known that prelingual deafness imposes severe limitations on the educational achievement of individuals, limitations that are rarely overcome. Reading achievement rarely advances beyond fifth grade level (Furth, 1966), and linguistic competence in written English usually remains inferior to that of a 10-year-old hearing child (Quigley, Wilbur, Montanelli, & Steinkamp, 1976). In spite of the fact that schooling for deaf children has focused on mastery of the English language, most of them leave school without having attained competence.

The perception of many educators that deaf children whose parents were deaf and who signed performed better academically and socially than deaf children whose parents were hearing has now been documented (Brasel & Quigley, 1975; Meadow, 1966). Interest in signing children has come primarily from two directions: the desire to know the similarities and differences between language acquisition in the visual and auditory modalities; and the desire to know if using signs with young deaf children enables them to progress farther academically and maintain more pleasant relationships with their hearing families.

LANGUAGE ACQUISITION OF THE SIGNING CHILD

The first line of research on signing children has attempted to understand the process of language acquisition in deaf and hearing children who are exposed to sign language in the home (Bellugi & Klima, 1975; Jones, 1976; Prinz & Prinz, 1979a,b; Schlesinger & Meadow, 1972; Stoloff & Dennis, 1978). Recently such studies have focused on the acquisition of particular properties of ASL learned by children whose deaf parents sign ASL (Hoffmeister & Wilbur, 1980). For example, the aspect of ASL that has received most attention from linguists and nonlinguists alike is its high degree of iconicity (Bellugi & Klima, 1972). One might expect iconicity to facilitate language learning, and, in fact, it appears to be helpful for certain language-handicapped nondeaf individuals (Baron, 1981; Bonvillian & Nelson, 1978; Brown, 1977; Konstantereas, Oxman, & Webster, 1978; Wilbur, 1979). The exposure of these individuals to signs, however, has been through deliberate teaching in which the iconicity plays a central part. Of those researchers studying natural sign acquisition, only Prinz has suggested that iconicity was an enabling factor in the sign acquisition of a hearing child raised by a signing (hearing) father (Prinz himself) and a deaf mother. His examples of enabling iconicity, however, are highly suspect. He suggests, for example, that his child learned a baby form of the sign MILK quite early because it is representational of milking a cow. The child, however, had never seen a cow, much less a cow being milked, and we have no evidence that she associated milk with cows at all. Thus the use of iconicity in natural development is unpersuasive at this level. In contrast, several researchers have noted a relative *lack* of iconicity in the signing of young deaf children exposed to fluent ASL. As reported to date this lack is of two types: 1) absence of spatial or directional modulations on sign; and 2) absence of spatial elements either in exploitation of the signing space or in the use of action and noun classifiers or size and shape specifiers (Ellenberger & Steyaert, 1978; Maxwell, 1979; Mow, 1974). For example, a child describing a gymnast used the handshape classifier for a crawling insect instead of the one for a person and was unable to use the signing space to make clear the actions of the gymnast as an adult signer would do.

Only gradually did either of the two children studied longitudinally incorporate spatial or locational modulations. At seven years of age, one child studied (Maxwell, 1979; the child is also the subject of this report) still did not have the structuring of space or the use of either classifiers or specifiers under consistent control. A slightly different report exists for two other deaf children of deaf parents (Hoffmeister, 1978). When these children were 52–53 and 53–56 months, respectively, they "usually modulated properly" all the verbs that allowed modulation, with locative the most common and source the least common modulations in use. Pronominalization and location began in these children as simple pragmatic gestures but also gradually "yielded to the emergence of spatial indicators" as the children learned to structure space linguistically. One of Hoffmeister's subjects is also Ellenberger and Steyaert's child, so the evidence is somewhat contradictory. This child and the child who is the subject of this chapter were both exposed to Sign English as well as to ASL. Both children alternated spatial structuring and English word order after about 60 months.

Bernstein (1979) and Schwam (1979, 1982) both replicated Clark's (1973) experiment to test whether deaf signing children (1½ to 6 years of age) could use the iconicity of the signed spatial relations IN, ON, and UNDER to help them complete a manipulative task. The signs for these relations iconically relate to their meanings. If iconicity were productive for these children, their performance on the task should have been facilitated by the signs. Because it was not, it appears that the children were unaware of (or at least not using) iconicity in their comprehension of even spatial relations. In similar work involving other semantic relations, Schwam shows that only a subset of the potentially useful iconic information in signs is actually of salience and benefit for the deaf child in the process of language acquisition.

EDUCATORS' CONCERNS WITH THE VARIETY OF DEAF CHILDREN'S LANGUAGE

Educators have generally compared groups of deaf children distinguished by the variable of parental or school language variety with the aim of identifying which language environment—an English-like sign system, ASL, oral, or auditory-emphasis/oral—leads to better school achievement (e.g., Moores, Weiss, & Goodwin, 1978). For a description of these, see Moores (1974, 1978), Bonvillian, Charrow, & Nelson (1973), or Wilbur (1976, 1979). In summary, deaf children of deaf parents do better academically than deaf children of hearing parents. Meadow (1966) reported that they also displayed better self-concepts.

A splinter controversy exists over *what kind* of signs to use, with various systems proposed, and their degree of Englishness argued. For a discussion of signs and sign systems, see Wilbur, 1976, 1979. No research has compared the effectiveness of the various systems for developing English competence, although inflectional morphemes have been studied in deaf children for one system in a grammatical judgement format (Gilman & Raffin, 1975; Raffin, 1976) and for another system in spontaneous communication (Bornstein, Saulnier, & Hamilton, 1980; Bornstein & Saulnier, 1981). Another group, Griswold and Commings (1974), has studied early vocabulary in signing children.

The child in the present study was not exposed to one of the strict systems but was exposed to English-like signing with invented signs for such English words as *the* and for bound morphemes like *-ing, -ly,* and *-ed*. In order to avoid strict association with one of the educational sign systems, this language variety will be referred to as Sign English in this report. It differs in detail from Pidgin Sign

English as described by Woodward (1973), but is clearly a pidgin variety in that it shares elements of both ASL and English.[1]

At the heart of the oral/manual controversy in the education of deaf children is a persistent fear that the use of one mode somehow precludes the other. Parents are sometimes told that allowing their deaf child to use *any* gestures will inhibit speech development. Educators who sign are often asked if they do not want deaf children to learn to speak. There exists, however, no direct evidence that the use of manual communication is detrimental to the development of speech (Moores, 1971, 1974, 1978; Power, 1974). It may even be facilitative (Meadow, 1980).

Alice, the child in this study, was exposed to the normal speech of four hearing and hard-of-hearing siblings and to the mostly intelligible speech of her deaf parents. Various other people, including teachers, also spoke to her.

One assumption shared by proponents of English-like signs and those of exclusive speech is that their mode will lead to better competence in English. In a longitudinal study of school programs, Moores (1971) found no significant difference in the speech of deaf children exposed to manual and auditory modes, but he found that the children exposed to manual modes performed significantly better in academic and social skills. In investigating the English of the deaf, researchers regularly test reading and writing (Swisher, 1976). One problem with this approach is apparent in view of the difficulties that many hearing children with normal spoken language have with reading and writing. On the other hand, deaf children are often said to have reading problems when, in fact, they really have problems with the English language. When deaf children who sign are reading English print and signing what they are reading, the Englishness of their signs has an inverse relationship to comprehension; that is, the worse their comprehension, the more English-like their signs (Ewoldt, 1977, 1978). Such deaf children also apparently comprehend better when the English printed words are arranged in an ASL-like word order and some inflections are omitted (Odom & Blanton, 1970). Although some teaching strategies have stressed the need to "go from sound to print," it appears from short-term memory experiments (Conrad & Rush, 1965; Conrad, 1970, 1972, 1973) that some deaf readers store information phonologically and some store it graphically. Some make use of signs (St. Pierre & Maxwell, in preparation).

The child in this study began to read some English print before instruction in school. Like many hearing children, Alice displayed considerable interest in print and in books and considered them a means of interacting socially with her family.

Instructional books for sign language have usually contained illustrations of signs with a gloss provided in English print. This concept has been expanded in a set of storybook materials designed to help parent and child learn one particular

---

[1] Fischer (1978) argues that ASL is itself a creole recreated by each generation of deaf children, and her argument fits my six years of observations of deaf children in schools.

sign system. Parents are to learn the sign system by reading these books to their child and by using the signs to communicate with the child on a regular basis (Bornstein, Saulnier, & Hamilton, 1976). The parent (or teacher) reads each English-print word and makes the sign illustrated above it to read a story to a child, thus learning the system without studying grammar or learning lists of signs. Although the books were not intended for use as reading texts, some children read the signs as a print form. Ewoldt (1977) presented one of these books to a 6-year-old deaf child who signed but was not a native signer. The child was also unfamiliar with the format of the books. The child's treatment of the sign illustrations was only minimally successful. The parents of the child in the present study, who of course knew sign, read some of these storybooks to her. Her father also told her some of the same stories in ASL in the best tradition of father storytelling.

Fingerspelling is used regularly as an adjunct to the sign systems and as a means of borrowing English words into ASL (Battison, 1977, 1978). Fingerspelling differs from ASL and the sign systems for English in that it corresponds directly to the 26 letters of the alphabet. Although it seems cumbersome to most signers, except as a supplement, and is difficult to read in any but the optimum light and distance conditions, deaf children as young as three and a half have used it in school (Quigley, 1969). The cumbersomeness of fingerspelling perceived by deaf signers may be due to limited English abilities more than to the mode itself. For hearing signers the balance may shift the other way: greater knowledge of English but less skill in transmitting or receiving the mode. Or it may be the case that the mode is inherently awkward and slow. More certain is the limitation imposed by level of spelling skill. Some young hearing children begin to write before they have knowledge of standard spelling (Read, 1975), making up their own rules for phoneme-grapheme correspondence. The child in this study was exposed both to productive uses of fingerspelling and to certain frozen or borrowed uses such as name signs and expressions like T-V and O-K.[2]

These are the varieties of language in the data that follow—ASL, Sign English, Fingerspelling, Speech, English Print, and Sign Print. It is a lengthy list. The discussion of the data will focus on three themes. The first theme is that the

---

[2]The conventions for writing the language utterances are rather complicated. I have followed the convention of writing signs in capital letters. Where a sign is glossed with more than one English word, a hyphen connects the words to indicate that they are glossing just one sign. No attempt is made here to indicate modulations on signs because the focus of this paper is the interaction of signs with other varieties of language. Capital letters connected by hyphens indicate fingerspelling. A distinction is made between fluent *fingerspelling* and what I call *spelling out* words, which is not fluent expression. Speech is represented by regular type enclosed in quotation marks. Mouthing (speech without voice) is represented by regular type enclosed in single quotation marks. Occasional translations are printed in regular type and enclosed in parentheses. No distinction is made in print between ASL signs and Sign English signs.

development of each variety of language is marked by alternation between attention to form and attention to meaning. The second theme is one of interaction. The varieties of language Alice learned interacted in both conscious and unconscious ways. The third theme is Alice's active role as a learner. Although there is really nothing new about these themes, especially the first and third, which have been well documented for child language acquisition, they are still being established for deaf children's language acquisition. The second theme, that of the interaction of language varieties in development, has a special importance. First, there is a general feeling among many educators that deafness places such enormous strains on the language acquisition process that input must be rigidly structured and limited to only one language modality and one language variety, and, if that variety is a form of sign, only one sign per English word. There is also some fear of a sensory overload or at least a diffusion of attention if more than one variety or modality is in use. It was even said by some, not so long ago, that learning to read and write should await intelligible speech and speechreading to prevent the deaf child from relying on any nonspeech variety of language for communication. The present data will speak to these issues.

BACKGROUND OF THE CHILD

Alice has deaf parents and deaf maternal grandparents. Her father was deafened at age 2 or 3 and attended a school for the deaf where he learned ASL. The mother is hard of hearing and is a native signer of ASL. The parents report that they use ASL and fingerspelling with deaf friends and with each other, some form of Sign English and/or speech with hearing people. Both parents have speech that is usually intelligible, but has typical prosodic, pitch, and articulation features of hearing impaired speech. Both parents, who have been professional educators of deaf children, are very conscientious parents and are obviously very fond of Alice.

Alice, who has always appeared to be bright and curious, also appears to have above normal intelligence as measured by the Leiter and Merill-Palmer scales. Audiometric testing elicited responses only at 250 Hertz and 500 Hertz. The hearing loss is presumed to be hereditary; however, Alice has four older hearing and hard-of-hearing siblings who required no special education.

Her father discovered Alice's loss when she was eight months old. Until that time, most of the parents' communication to the child was in speech. Although they wanted their presumed hearing child to sign, they felt their first responsibility was to give their hearing children speech models. After long discussion about Alice's best interests, the parents decided to expose her first to ASL and then to gradually introduce fingerspelling and Sign English. In their plan, they did not place any emphasis on the development of oral skills. Nor did they consciously try to teach Alice to read, believing reading was a late developing skill that Alice should learn at school. On the other hand, much of parent/child interaction took place in the context of books or storytelling. The father also kept a notebook of Alice's language development. She literally grew up watching him write down her spoken and signed utterances.

OVERVIEW OF THE DEVELOPMENTAL LANGUAGE RECORDS

There are two sets of data for Alice. The larger set was videorecorded at monthly intervals between the ages of 2 years 3 months and 6 years 3 months, alternating between Alice's home and Ursula Bellugi's Laboratory for Language Studies at the Salk Institute for Biological Studies in California. One taping session took place in Alice's classroom. During these sessions, Alice conversed with a variety of people, including parents, siblings, friends of the family, and researchers. She also addressed language to the family dog, a rabbit, and various toys. The videotapes were transcribed and checked by at least one native signer and another fluent signer. The author transcribed several of the tapes and viewed all the tapes, comparing them with their transcripts.

The second set of data is a collection of home records Alice's father kept from the time she was 18 months old until she was 6 years and 3 months. We anticipate yearly videotapings of Alice at which her father will continue to provide a written record. Under the guidance of Dr. Bellugi, Alice's father wrote down language that was of interest, especially the emergence of some new expressive or receptive ability.

Alice's output during the early taping sessions was discouragingly limited in quantity and quality. She seemed very shy and quiet. The early taped utterances consisted primarily of two signs or a sign with a point, with only an occasional longer, more complex utterance. The home records, in contrast, described a vivacious talker, with more long and complex utterances such as AFTERWHILE POINT (candy), EAT FIRST (the candy must wait until after I eat my dinner). After about three months this discrepancy faded, although the home records continued to note some functions and structures a month or two before they appeared in the videotape sessions. Others, however, appeared in the sessions that were not included in the home records.

The data were classified according to the varieties of language used: oral, ASL, Sign English, fingerspelling, Sign Print, and English Print. Because book and storytelling behavior seemed to be such an important factor in Alice's linguistic development, as revealed in the videotape records, general facets of story behavior beyond attention to print itself were extracted from the data for discussion.

ASL ONSET BEFORE EMERGENCE OF THE OTHER LANGUAGE VARIETIES

There were no data on the emergence of ASL alone, for it was the foundation language, established before the project began. Alice's father recalled that the first sign he was sure of, DADDY, appeared at 12 months of age. ASL is the language on which Alice depends for almost all communication in the early tapes. Such aspects of language as semantic relations, functions of language, grammatical functions, and vocabulary growth paralleled the reports for hearing children (Collins-Ahlgren, 1975).

The parameters of signs appeared to be meaningful to Alice from the beginning of the taping, although certain grammatical processes emerged only gradually. A study was made of all Alice's apparent invented signs (Maxwell, 1977), that is, nonstandard signs that were explainable neither as phonological simplifications nor as other sorts of pronunciation "mistakes." If the sign were still recognizable, it was considered a pronunciation deviation and eliminated from the data. Analysis of the inventions still revealed the use of sign parameters and processes common to standard ASL. A partial list may be illustrative:

Metonymy—Alice referred to Mary Poppins by the sign UMBRELLA.

Puns—Alice shortened the sign LONG instead of signing SHORT to tease her father when he asked for a long kiss.

Novel uses of size and shape specifiers (hereafter called SASSes; see Newport & Bellugi, 1976 or Klima & Bellugi, 1979)—Alice referred to a bathtub as ELLIPSE.

Original compounding of regular signs or of SASSes and signs—Alice compounded LONG, THIN FIRES to mean traffic flares.

Modulations on verbs using classifiers whether or not they are appropriate—Alice signed the "legs" two-finger classifier to refer to persons and some animals appropriately, but used the full-hand classifier to refer to other animals and persons.

Grammatical incorporation in unexpected contexts—Alice appropriately incorporated negative with KNOW to produce DONT-KNOW, but overgeneralized the process to produce a nonstandard DONT-REMEMBER; similarly, she combined the verb feature inchoate and the classifier for ball-shaped objects with the verb LARGE to produce a single sign meaning "the pumpkin grew large."

Of particular difficulty for Alice was control of classifiers and SASSes, which is consistent with previous findings of limited exploitation of iconicity in child signing. Although some SASSes and classifiers appeared to be used appropriately before age 3, full mastery eluded Alice at the end of the project. In sum, Alice clearly was actively learning the rules of ASL when other varieties of language began to emerge, and she continued to learn its rules while learning the other varieties.

LEARNING AND DIFFERENTIATING MULTIPLE LANGUAGE VARIETIES

ASL was, in overwhelming proportions, the language of Alice's communication for the first three years. Although she began to use oral language as early as 18 months, and fingerspelling as early as 25 months, and could even respond to the alphabet in English and Sign print at 26 months, these varieties were more often to be found in parent-child routines than in everyday communication. When Alice entered school at about age 3 years, the other varieties were joined by Sign English and gradually began to assume more communicative importance. During the final videotape session at 75 months, over 50% of Alice's utterances were Sign English and included fluent reading of a story in English print.

Manual Oral Distinction at 18–23 Months

At the time that Alice has a vocabulary of at least 90 lexical signs and the POINT system (Hoffmeister, 1978), she made the first distinction in language varieties between manual and oral language. She resorted to speech for the first time to resolve communication failure. When her sign COOKIE was not immediately understood by her older sister, Alice spoke the words "eat cookie" clearly enough that her sister acted without further delay. Thus from the early age of 18 months, Alice was able to recode a message in an alternate mode to achieve communication.

During this time Alice's father reported in the home records that Alice surprised the family by attending to others' mouth movements though there was no indication that she speechread any specific messages. She also made mouth movements herself that "sometimes came close to what it should look like when a person says 'dog' or 'house'." From early on Alice attended to the oral as well as the manual mode for language, although she clearly relied on signs for almost all communication. Alice's oral language use was quite limited and rare—days went by with no speech at all—but was noticeable.

It is likely that Alice had little knowledge of the specific content of oral language. In her second and third years, she frequently engaged in a behavior that may be called scribble speech. Scribble speech is a sort of talking behavior, with or without vocalization, that cannot be analyzed into words. It is like energetic babbling but is intentionally playful or mocking. Older deaf children and adults scribble speak this way to imitate excessive talking, as when mocking someone who talks on the telephone a lot or chatters incessantly. Hearing people scribble speak in a similar fashion when imitating speech in a foreign language. Children go through a similar stage just before writing (Clay, 1975) when they scribble on paper and think the scribbling says something. One example of Alice's early scribble speech came at 20 months when she scribble spoke without voice in mock anger after watching her father scold the older children in speech.

Alice was imitating the parts of the behavior perceptible to her, the visual parts. Thus Alice gave evidence of attending to the form and function but not the content of oral language.

Alice showed considerable awareness of oral language even at this early stage. Although the quantity of oral language was miniscule, in qualitative terms it had a number of functions in relation to sign: 1) Speech could serve to recode a sign message for a second attempt at communication success; 2) Oral behavior could accompany sign communication; and 3) Oral communication could be used instead of sign communication.

A Second Manual Variety at 25–26 Months

The first fingerspelled sequences to appear were some short words borrowed from English by ASL: N-O, T-V, O-K, B-J (a name), O-F-F. They were uttered as wholes rather than as spelled sequences, with the letters losing their separability and taking on the shape of the cognate sign where there was one (cf. Battison, 1977, 1978). Typically signers produce a gesture that is half sign and half fingerspelling, following (in reduced scale) the principles of sign compounding within ASL (Bellugi, 1975; Klima & Bellugi, 1979). In these early fingerspellings, there was no reason to ascribe to Alice any awareness of individual letters.

Intense Attention to Form at 26–30 Months

Alice's parents used a set of flash cards with English block letters on one side and fingerspelled letters on the other to teach her the alphabet and the spelling of her name. Frequently, they spoke the letter names, giving Alice the opportunity to associate the oral version of the letters with the other varieties. Although Alice went through the alphabet with little excitement but dogged determination, she tackled the spelling of her name with great enthusiasm. She could recognize her name in both English print and fingerspelled form, dependably matching the two varieties of the first and last letters, though not the intermediate ones. The point should be made that Alice's fingerspelling of her name was not fluent *expression* of the name in fingerspelling. It was *spelling* of the name in fingerspelling.

The striking characteristic of Alice's language during this six months was the attention to form, especially with regard to fingerspelling and English print. The forms themselves were quite empty, usually limited to recitation of the alphabet. Alice, nevertheless, was interested enough in the forms to spell out words in the environment using fingerspelling without overtly trying to ascribe or discover any meaning. Once, for example, she saw the word *can* in a public restroom and fingerspelled C-A-N, a word not in her lexicon. Another time she read *all* in a newspaper headline as A–11, mixing a letter and a number.

Her name was the only instance of attention to the meaning of spelled sequences. Alice claimed that the letters of her name, in any order or mixed in among other letters on a book cover, still meant her name. Her parents reinforced this attention to the print form of her name by printing it on most of her belongings. They gave this activity great importance and considerable time in their daily interactions with Alice. She was also learning to appeal to the authority of print, holding up something, signing POSS[1] (mine) and pointing to her printed name as proof of her claim. The name was the only instance of a meaning for which Alice already knew she had a means of expression, that is, a sign.

In oral language Alice was able to identify parts of the body through speechreading and to use a shift from a manual to an oral mode to create emphasis. She simultaneously signed LEAVE, SPANK, and mouthed 'Leave, spank you.' The change in mode had the effect of emphasizing the word 'you,' even though she used no voice, because Alice was talking back to her father, who frequently told her that if she did not leave something alone, he would spank her.

Routines with the alphabet, with Alice's name, and to a lesser extent with identifying parts of the body, dominated the videotape sessions and the home records so much that there was little evidence of other developments.

Analysis of Form and a Search for Meaning at 31–36 Months

When she was 36 months old, Alice entered school, where the variety of sign was Sign English and training in both speech, and speechreading was part of the curriculum. Alice had been exposed to some Sign English at home and a few items had been recorded in the home records. The first expression of Sign English during videotaping was accompanied by the first attention to Sign print at 34 months. Alice's fingerspelled vocabulary grew somewhat, but most fingerspelling activity continued at the level of spelling. Alice resisted spelling practice, but began to spontaneously imitate some fingerspelling. She began also to wave her fingers in the analogue of scribble speech and to engage in imitative writing (purposeful rather than wild scribbling) as a social activity with members of the family.

The dominant concept during this period of development was an apparent metalinguistic effort to analyze form and to connect a form in one variety with a form in another. Alice was most successful in connecting signs with sign print and fingerspelling with English print. She was least successful in connecting fingerspelling with other varieties. Although Alice used more speech and speechreading as a means of interacting more often, she did not appear to attend to the form of oral language or to connect it with other varieties of language.

Alice's earliest utterances of Sign English were at least partially memorized and associated with Sign print. In some cases, the association was quite marginal, as when Alice signed a nursery rhyme she knew was printed on a poster but gave no evidence that she could follow the signs on the poster. In another case she sat down with a familiar book to which she had partially memorized the opening lines and attempted to segment the Sign print in order to match it with the signs she knew were represented on the page.

In the first of these examples, the verse, Alice appeared to make very little meaning, pausing inordinately long between signs as if trying to remember what came next and signing some nonsigns similar in configuration to the target signs. When adults sang the verse, Alice signed BLOW, S . . . THE, POINT AND . . . retaining most of the Sign English elements from the verse and losing the meaning. Alice repeated the new kinds of forms she had learned to make for the recitation, suggesting that they may have seemed special to her.

In the second example, the familiar story of Little Red Riding Hood, Alice performed very differently. Although she again paused inordinately long between signs, she was working with meaning she already knew. Alice made one of the signs before finding it in the Sign print. Hearing children also pause a long time between words or get ahead of the print as they try to match known speech to English print (Clay, 1972; Durkin, 1966). The difference between Alice's treatment of the story and of the poster was that here instead of focusing on the new kinds of signs, Alice ignored them and produced only the content words and root signs. She also skipped some other signs and was confused about two similar signs that both appeared in the sentence, LITTLE and LIVE. In this and a similar confusion on the next page between WARM and GRANDMOTHER, Alice attended to her semantic expectations for the story (Mother was standing in front of a stove handing over a basket of goodies for Grandmother) and to the shapes of the root signs printed on the page. She did not attend to the directions for movement represented on the page by tiny arrows and dotted lines or to English morphology. Thus Alice used familiar meaning and features of the signs represented in print to segment the sign stream and match signs to sign print with some initial success. Alice completely ignored the English print in the book.

There is a formal relation between signs and Sign print and between fingerspelled letters and English print, but there is no such relation between signs and fingerspelling or English print. Alice was given the opportunity through her books to discover the first two formal relations and the arbitrary one between signs and English print. At this point, however, she did not take advantage of the fact that the books matched Sign print with English print. She was presented with the arbitrary relation between signs and fingerspelling when she was taught to spell some signs in fingerspelling.

That she apparently recognized the function of fingerspelling as a mode of communication is indicated by her scribble fingerspelling as a sort of place holder for content she could not produce. Similarly she began imitative writing and progressed to the printing of a few letters. She recognized the function of writing, in the sense that it was a serious behavior, and its form in the sense that it consisted of letters, but not the content or any meaning (except her name). When she asked her father to write something and he asked WHAT?, Alice thought and then fingerspelled A, C, D. After thinking and thinking, she added P. Although Alice had been exposed to fingerspelling and had used some for communication and had been read to from English print since infancy, she apparently did not relate to the varieties in terms of message content.

Another aspect of the treatment of form with no specific content is offered by something Alice did with numbers. Numbers are similar to letters in fingerspelling, as they are in print, and Alice had shown some difficulty in separating numbers and letters in both fingerspelling and print since the previous six months. (Recall her use of A–11.) Alice would spontaneously count objects and not stop at the right number, as if 1,2,3,4,5, meant several instead of a specific number. Perhaps this counting behavior was of a piece with the scribble behavior in fingerspelling, speech, and print. It recognized the function of the linguistic behavior it resembled but was not yet analyzed to produce specific meaning. In other words, Alice understood that people used their voices in various situations, but she did not know what words to speak. She understood that people fingerspelled, but did not know what words to spell. She understood that people wrote but did not know what to write. She understood that people counted but did not yet know how to count things.

Possibly as a means of discovering the basis for fingerspelling, Alice began to imitate some spontaneous fingerspelling. Because much of the available fingerspelling was English function words and bound morphemes at this time, it is questionable how much information about relations between meaning and form this practice gave Alice. It did give her information about structure within form (spelling sequences) and about English syntax and morphology. It may have given her some wrong information as well, as English-bound morphemes are often expressed by just one letter in Sign English, e.g., *ed* is signed D.

Although Alice was spontaneously imitating some fingerspelling, she was beginning to resist prompted word spellings. Thus she did not take advantage of the information provided by the spelling of known signs. Some of the fingerspelled and English print letters apparently had enough meaning of their own at this stage to interfere with letter identification and spelling "lessons." The block letter *A* in English print prompted, for example, Alice to refer to the parental refrain ALICE IS A BAD GIRL. That she had learned the relation between initial letters and name signs was clear from her frequent interruptions of spelling to sign the names of friends. Thus even while the analysis of form was suggested by matching signs and Sign print, there was also an insistence on making meaning in her own ways and a resistance to dwelling on form in the context of a familiar activity.

Progress in Separating the Language Varieties and Play with Form at 37–42 Months

Although Alice's communication was still primarily in ASL, her other language varieties appeared more often outside of routines and unprompted. While the non-ASL varieties together probably constituted less than 10% of her output, they now appeared throughout the day in all sorts of settings. There was a new ease and a fluency in all the varieties of language available to Alice. In English print she began to deal in units of meaning larger than individual letters and beyond the use of her name. The uses of speech became broader and revealed the first evidence of forms specific to speech. Her attention to form changed in character to a sort of metalinguistic play. At this time Alice enjoyed showing off her language or playfully resisted demands to perform.

Separating the Language Varieties

Most of Alice's early spoken utterances were structurally identical to her signed utterances, whether or not the two modes were simultaneous. She simply realized an ASL structure in speech. The beginnings of a concept of separation may have arisen in using speech to express elements that have surface realization in English but not in ASL. In such cases, Alice was not just speaking the same things she was or could be signing; she was expressing distinctions that are not expressed in ASL. The home records noted some common phrases that Alice frequently uttered orally, sometimes with signs and sometimes independently:

"Put it back."
"Come here."
"Hurry up."
"Over there."

When signs did accompany this speech, the signs were:

PUT
COME
HURRY
THERE

It may be of some significance that these multiple word utterances in English have single sign equivalents in ASL. When Alice uttered sign and speech simultaneously, there was meaning correspondence but not item-for-item correspondence, as there would have been if Alice had signed all the elements. Sometimes an utterance emerged as a mixed mode production, with for example, HURRY in sign and "up" in speech. It was common at this time for particles like "up" and for English function words to be spoken, as in "this is" POSS[1] (mine), with the shift in modes sometimes marking emphasis.

Play with Form

Alice seemed to greatly enjoy playing with spelling things out in several ways. She teasingly resisted spelling or saying the alphabet with a semiarticulate form of scribble fingerspelling. When asked to spell C-A-T once, for example, Alice produced C-A-5-W-V-3-V, real configurations instead of wiggling fingers but with no sense to them. When teased for this spelling, Alice laughed and produced C-A-T, proving she knew the sequence. She seemed to greatly enjoy spotting mistakes, whether in herself or others. As a means of showing off, Alice asked for signs to fingerspell or English print to spell out and particularly enjoyed the labels of food containers, although the variations in script were hard for her to decipher. Hearing children also treat script differently from block print early (Clay, 1972; Durkin, 1966; Goodman, personal communication). Although it is doubtful that Alice understood the concept of brand names, she knew what was in these containers, because they were in use, just as she knew the meanings of the signs she spelled. In a sense, then, the issue of meaning was removed and Alice could concentrate on form.

A second sort of play was the antithesis of concentrating on form: The creation of communication failure by refusing to attend to form rather than to meaning. In one incident both parents tried to get Alice to copy their spelling of H-O-L-E. Alice coolly replied: YES POINT YES, where the POINT referred to an air hole in the bread she was munching. Clearly, Alice comprehended the work, knew what was expected of her, and insisted on controlling her own production by making a joke—and by insisting on attending to meaning when her parents were attending to form.

The other two sorts of play both involved storytelling. The first took place as someone read a familiar Sign print story to Alice. With her shining eyes studying both the storyteller and the book with rapt attention, she would follow along, repeating the story almost word for word, sometimes omitting parts, sometimes getting ahead of the teller, and sometimes repeating inaccurately. Parts of the stories would be told to Alice in ASL, summarizing some events, but most of them, and especially the dialogue, would be produced as Sign English and fingerspelling. In her spontaneous language Alice began using the Sign English conjugated forms of BE (ASL has no similar copula) and the Sign English pronoun I (ASL does not distinguish between subject and object forms), forms that were quite frequent in the stories.

Alice also imitated the storytellers' expressions and gestures in these sessions and was reminded of the stories by things that people did. At such times, or in looking at the story pictures, Alice might adopt these gestures and expressions and paraphrase language from the stories.

A final kind of play observed involved Alice's relation to her father's notebooks. She came to enjoy doing or saying something and then telling him to write it down. She also would point to writings in the notebook and ask what they said, sometimes seriously and sometimes in fun, as if testing her father. She showed off by printing her name correctly.

The activities involving the notebook and the storybooks must have had considerable effect on Alice's concept of written language. She was repeatedly exposed in these months to the relation between English print in the notebook and language that she herself had uttered through signing, speech, or fingerspelling. She was repeatedly transferring stories from Sign print to Sign English and fingerspelling and learning about English dialogue and story behavior.

Cazden (1975) suggested that, for hearing children, play with language such as Alice engaged in is a crucial element in developing metalinguistic awareness. Metalinguistic awareness, according to Cazden, and to Baron (1974), is important to the uses of language in schools. Play is also considered by Ferguson and Macken (this volume, Chapter 7) as a fundamental process in hearing children's speech development not only in infancy but throughout the preschool and school years.

Greater Independence of the Non-Print Varieties at 43–46 Months

Fingerspelling, Sign English, and speech were the vehicles of more and more actual communication during this period. A few short dialogues were conducted completely in speech or with an occasional sign for disambiguation. Now an utterance might start in speech and then shift to sign for emphasis, changing the balance from six months earlier. The quantity of the non-ASL varieties remained roughly constant, but the quality changed markedly as Alice extended their contexts beyond the routines dominant to this time.

Fingerspelling was used within sign communication for more and more content words as a means of expression rather than just for spelling out words. Alice still had some difficulty in dealing with a sequence of letters and tended to invest letters with larger units of meaning when she did not immediately understand the spelling. For example, when she was looking at name tags on Christmas gifts, she thought one that started with M must belong to her brother, Mark. When her mother said it was not his, Alice spelled out the tag, M-O-T-H-E-R, and said the R meant it was her sister, Rebecca's.

Alice began to generate a few of her own utterances using the Sign English adjectival Y, the plural S, THE, and A; and she began to use IS and ARE more. The verb affix S was restricted to verbs in present tense but not restricted to third person and was sometimes attached to verbs following modals, producing such structures as ELSIE AND TOM LOVE S and CAN'T WALK S. There were also a few stereotypical English structures, including several contexts for infinitives. The most common one was I WANT N_2, but Alice had difficulty expanding N_2. I WANT I-C-E was appropriate, but Alice began to use TO after WANT and other phrases without a following verb. Alice often used TO inappropriately in other contexts. She may have formed a rule along these lines: When in need of a functor in a Sign English sentence, use TO. Her parents began modeling some sentences for Alice to imitate; for example:

> Alice: I WANT TO IT POP.
> Mother: I WANT TO DRINK SOME POP.
> Alice: I WANT TO SOME DRINK POP.
> Mother: I WANT TO DRINK SOME POP.
> Alice: I WANT TO DRINK SOME POP. . . . FAST, FAST
>   (I am fast in signing this sentence.)

Alice did not always make these corrections as desired, exhibiting the same resistance to correction of grammar that has been described for hearing children (Brown, 1973; McNeill, 1966).

One Sign English bound morpheme that behaved oddly when it first appeared was ING. It was first seen in the song, "Santa Claus is Coming to Town." In its first recorded spontaneous use a month later Alice signed: WRITE THAT NAME ING POINT. WRONG R PRO[1] (Write that name there. I made the R wrong.) Here ING was not only misplaced following a noun, but was also inappropriate for the verb in the sentence, because Alice signed WRITE as an imperative.

Despite many confusions, in these months Alice was actually using fingerspelling and Sign English for communication and was learning that there were right and wrong ways to express meanings in the Sign English variety.

Exploration of the Print Varieties at 47–48 Months

Around Alice's fourth birthday, many strategies for relating language varieties began to appear. At 48 months Alice, without instruction, attended to the forms of four different varieties at once. Laboriously she began signing and vocalizing Sign print items in a book one by one. Then she pointed to the English print below the Sign print, then signed and spoke the words. To figure out some Sign print, she twisted her body to align herself with the figure on the page. She did not treat the material as a story or even as sentences, just as unordered signs. She was concentrating on the forms with no apparent attention to meaning, and she was relating the different varieties to each other. The books containing both Sign print and English print provided Alice with a rich resource for exploring these relationships and she would pore over them for as much as an hour at a time, sometimes alone, sometimes asking a parent for information about a sign configuration or a printed word.

A pattern also emerged quickly for the treatment of English print in text without accompanying Sign print. Alice signed words she recognized and knew signs for, and fingerspelled other words. She paid no attention to word boundaries and transposed, omitted, and substituted many letters. Sometimes she recognized a word after she had fingerspelled it and then made the sign. Alice often spoke as she was signing from English print but seldom when she was fingerspelling large chunks of text, suggesting that she only used speech when she understood the words in the English print.

STRENGTHENING LANGUAGE AWARENESS AT 49–55 MONTHS

Alice greatly increased communication in speech, fingerspelling, and Sign English. She used speech about 75% of the time and with greater clarity, and began to assess her own and other people's abilities to speak and hear. Alice became very proud of her abilities to speechread and to speak but also shy about her limitations, as when she refused to deliver a message to a hearing neighbor, protesting that she could not talk. Alice's awareness of differences in people's abilities to hear and to speak and be understood must be considered a remarkable metalinguistic discovery, which could be expected to strongly affect Alice's perception of her place in the world. She had used this knowledge in various ways at least since 18 months, but between her fourth and fifth birthdays she began to exhibit some insights into the varieties of languages, their uses and users.

All the language varieties increased in use and in structure. Brown's (1973) thirteen morphemes of English were all observed in spontaneous production in Sign English. Fingerspelling increased in density from an occasional word to as many as three words per sentence. There was a sudden increase in mouthing from only an occasional activity through the 60th month to a point where in the 65th month 9% of videotaped utterances contained at least one mouthed word.

Whereas earlier Alice had been willing to shift between speech and sign to resolve communication failure or create emphasis, now she resisted switching and tended to repeat without recoding. In particular, she wanted her speech to be understood, sometimes, as in the following fishing game, leading to everyone's frustration:

Alice: "Butterfly."
Mother: SHRUG. PRO^1 (me) NEG UNDERSTAND, HUH?
Alice: (mouthing without vocalization) 'Butterfly' POINT
Mother: (Looking confused)
Alice: FORGET (forget it)
Mother: PRO^2 (you) SIGN, PRO^2
Alice: NEG
Mother: SIGN . . . PRO^1 TELL PRO^2. PICK-OUT FISH. (In frustration Mother says to go ahead and take another turn if Alice refused to sign what she wants to say.)
Alice: POINT (vaguely to the toys)
Mother: WELL QUESTION. NOW PRO^2 Tell PRO^1. (Well, what is it? Tell me what you want.)
Alice: GIVE-PRO^1 BUTTERFLY.

She gave up, to her mother's great relief.

The most startling development in fingerspelling was the invented name, N-O-H, which had no relation in sound or spelling to the actual name. Combined with the use of fingerspelling scribbling as a general placeholder in spontaneous communication and in response to English print, this invention suggests that Alice had learned that all people if not all concepts have a fingerspelled sequence as one label but that she still had not figured out where the sequences come from or their relation to other labels.

There were many structural and strategic similarities between Alice's emerging English grammar and the grammar of hearing children, but many differences too, as she began to separate spoken and Sign English from ASL grammar. Alice consistently signed Sign English pronouns, and often used regular past tense D and regular plural S. She signed irregular verbs and plurals without the Sign English inflection but often spoke the English past or plural simultaneously. For example, Alice signed EAT but said "ate," signed MAN with ASL plural modulation but said "men." Certain functors that had been expressed through speech only, for example "do," now emerged in Sign English forms also. Subject/verb agreement continued to be unstable, as it is for hearing children well past age five. Question forms resembled those of hearing children at a similar stage. Consider, for example, these WHY questions:

WHY YOU CAN WALK? (asked of a sick person)
WHY WERE YOU GO PAST? (Why did you go out?)
"Why were you went?"

Similar question forms have also been found for children who hear but have deaf signing parents and are learning both ASL and spoken English (Jones, 1976).

The suffix ING provides an illustration of confusion of ASL and Sign English structures. Consider the following sentences:

1) DOG CAT BITE ING (a dog is biting a cat)
2) YOU ARE GOOD GIRL DRIVE ING.
3) MY RED IS MIX ING (My red bedspread is mixed up; i.e., in disarray.)
4) MY TEACHER IS ANGRY ING ING

Sentence 1 is in ASL word order (Fischer, 1975; Liddell, 1977). Sentence 2 is a combination of two English structures. Sentence 3 is a possible English structure applied incorrectly. Sentence 4 is the only one that attaches ING to a nonverb, but it is sometimes difficult to distinguish an adjective from a verb in ASL (Klima & Bellugi, 1979) and the problem may be similar to the one with MIX in Sentence 3. Alice may not have known the restrictions on ANGRY or MIX in the two different languages, ASL and English. MIX, in the sense meant in Sentence 3, is transitive in English and blocks the structure Alice produced. English requires the past participle and the particle *up*, not the present participle, for this passive state. Sentence 2 is, interestingly, similar to sentences of hearing children before they have mastered verb inflections (Cazden, 1968). Thus Alice generated a mixture of ASL and English sentences with ING in both appropriate and inappropriate syntax.

A major vehicle for the learning of English continued to be nursery rhymes and songs. In some cases the structures in these rhymes may have been quite far beyond Alice's level of competence. Apparently Alice was completely overwhelmed by trying to learn the lines:

All the king's horses
And all the king's men
Couldn't put Humpty together again.

The 'S floated all through Alice's rendering of the lines, suggesting incomplete understanding of both its distribution and its semantic function:

'S KING 'S MAN HORSE
ALL 'S KING HORSE 'S MAN, A GREAT ALL 'S KING
COULD PUT 'S KING
CAN'T PUT MAN 'S KING, HUMPTY DUMPTY 'S KING MAN CAN 'T PUT
HUMPTY DUMPTY 'S KING TOGETHER AGAIN

Whether it was the complexity of the relations among king, horses, men, and Humpty Dumpty, or the density of plurals and possessives that caused Alice trouble, the fact that this odd distribution of Sign English affixes occurred more frequently in recitations than in spontaneous language is undoubtedly a result of the greater load on processing entailed by the complexity and unfamiliarity of the language and ideas in the recitations.

This environment for Sign English may have been confusing, but it could still facilitate Alice's learning. She revealed that she not only understood that D indicated past tense but that she could analyze a novel form: HUMPTY DUMPTY HAVE D. D. D PAST, YES . . . HAVE D PAST . . . HAD. At first Alice remembered meaning and used a known form, the regular past, then thought about it and finally came up with the new form she had been taught, HAD.

CONNECTING THE FULL RANGE OF LANGUAGE VARIETIES BY 65 MONTHS

Alice's performance with Sign print books gained in confidence and quantity as she read several pages at a time, but the first real change in character was recorded in the videotaping at 65 months. At that time, unsolicited, Alice read an entire story on videotape. Perhaps because she was familiar with the story, Alice was able to pause and make the relations among specific forms explicit. Several phenomena emerged:

Shaping Out Signs, Analogous to Sounding Out English Print Words in Hearing Children. Alice was able to attend to more than the alignments to the page she followed at 48 months. Some of her signs were similar to the Sign print, as when Alice signed ANSWER as ORDER by changing only one feature, orientation. Other times Alice shaped out the sign correctly but still did not make sense of it, as when she signed OWN and still asked what it meant. Other times Alice produced a similar sign and rejected it because of the context or made placement and handshape but could not reach closure on a sign.

Omitting the Last Parts of Signs. Alice typically omitted the second part of signs that were represented by a second hand in the text. Many Sign English signs have such two part structures, whether or not they are composed of two morphemes; for example THEY and THEIR had identical starting handshapes but THEY ends in a Y and THEIR in an R handshape.

Increasing Fluency and Increasing Intonation. About a fourth of the way into the story, as Alice built up context and confidence, her fluency and use of intonation increased. (A similar phenomenon occurs in hearing children's reading aloud.) Looking up less for feedback as she made her way into the story eliminated the long pauses and losses of place that were characteristic of the first pages.

Vocalizing to Supply Unsigned Meaning. The same phenomenon occurred in Alice's normal conversation, as when she signed GO instead of GO PAST but said "went." Ewoldt (1977) also found this vocal use in her deaf readers.

Omitting Vocalization When Closure Was Not Reached on Signs.

Vocalizing by Sounding Out English Print. Alice did this as a way of asking for meaning from an adult and for deriving meaning herself. For example, when Alice could not shape out the unfamiliar Sign English sign MAY, she sounded out the English print below it to ask her mother and then called up from her own lexicon the sign equivalent for "may" and signed CAN. Her sign was different from the text but it was the semantically appropriate sign known to her.

Spelling Out English Print in Fingerspelling. This was used as a means of asking for help.

Using Another Variety as a Check on Understanding. Alice spelled out H-U-N-G and signed HUNGRY, but then asked for help because the Sign print did not look like HUNGRY.

Fingerspelling as a Means for Expressing Meaning. Alice fingerspelled one entire page slowly, looking up from the English print to the Sign print frequently, as if checking her interpretation by or getting the meaning from the Sign print.

Attending to the English Print When no Communication Failure Had Occurred. Alice paused at the Sign print KNOCK D, spoke the word, held up the picture of the wolf banging on the door, fingerspelled the print K-N-O-C-K-E-D, and signed KNOCK D, as if to say 'see how smart I am!' Another time Alice came to a sign she understood but seemed dissatisfied with, BRICK S. She varied it for her mother several times and then spelled it out from the English print, D-R-I-C-K-S. Her mother outlined a B and a D, showing Alice which side of the line the loop is on for each English print letter, and agreed that they look alike. Alice spelled again: D-B-R-I-C-K-S, correcting herself. Alice looked at the word *bricks* a little longer and then signed STICK. D-B-R-I-C-K-S SAME K STICK. B-R-I-C-K, YES, C-K, C-K, C-K, YES S-C-K-S. YES, C-K-S. Alice was commenting on the spelling relation among words she had read (an earlier house had been made of sticks) though she had not fingerspelled the word *stick* at any time during this reading.

Using Illustrations as Clues to Meaning of Individual Words as Well as of the General Story. In the part of the story where Alice encountered many new words in both Sign print and English print forms, she matched words one by one to an illustration to figure out sentences about hanging a pot of boiling water in a fireplace to catch the wolf.

Perhaps Alice knew this story so well that she could afford the luxury of exploring its form. At the beginning of the book, she attended only to Sign print and Sign production. At other points in the story she attended only to English print and fingerspelling. In between these extremes, she used all her varieties to reproduce the meaning of the story.

Alice also at this same time produced her first sentence entirely in fingerspelling: M-A-Y I K-I-S-S Y-O-U-R N-O-S-E? and used a shift from sign to speech and then to fingerspelling to emphasize an order she was giving her brother, thus adding a third form to this function of shifting-for-emphasis.

SEPARATION ACHIEVED: LANGUAGE AT 75 MONTHS

Although Alice's spontaneous language continued to mix the structures of English and ASL, English was more often the dominant structure than it had been, over 50% in the videotape session. An example is I WATCH T-V LITTLE-BIT, T-H-E-N-I Go Bed, O-K? where the word order and basic structure are English but the lack of a determiner and the unmarked verbs are characteristic of ASL. In sentences like this one, space was not exploited as it is in ASL structures.

Alice revealed an expanded ability to learn language in one variety and transfer it to another to express both appropriate and inappropriate language. She attempted to fingerspell words she had been exposed to through speech, as when "picnic" was rendered as P-E-C-K. Her attempts conformed to English spelling rules and generally reflected the visible parts of the words. P-E-C-K is a possible English sequence (indeed, an actual one), and C-K is the characteristic spelling of /k/ in final word position. Alice had figured out the relation between fingerspelling and speech.

Alice also learned words from print and then transferred them to fingerspelling, speech, or invented signs. One roundabout trip for a word came to Alice by way of advertising. On a visit to Seaworld in San Diego, Alice saw a mermaid swimming in a tank. She did not learn a word for mermaid there, but she did have an association with a word from prior experience and she used that word when trying to tell about the event. She fingerspelled T-A-R. Her mother imitated her blankly, and Alice, aware she was not succeeding, added some clues: T-V, depiction of a mermaid, the explanation that it was GIRL AND FISH and the S-A-T. Her mother, still baffled, guessed S-T-A-R-T-R-E-K, but then Alice provided another important clue: TUNA CAN. PRO^2 (you) SEE T-V POINT (you). Her mother was able to add up the clues to produce S-T-A-R-K-I-S-T. Somehow Alice had associated the brand name of Starkist with the mermaid on the Chicken-of-the-Sea can.

For more than two years Alice had known to sign to some people and speak to others. For the first time, though, she gave evidence that she understood differences in signing as well. In one instance she asked her mother an ASL question without voice, then turned to a hearing researcher who signed and recoded the question in Sign English. When another hearing researcher asked what a certain sign meant, Alice fingerspelled the word very slowly and carefully and then spoke it, trying to enunciate and project. She had learned to switch not only modes but codes and she had learned to take into account the receiver's abilities to receive in a certain language variety.

In this final taping Alice demonstrated that she had made two major breakthroughs—the discovery of the relation between speech and fingerspelling, and the ability to recode in not only another mode but another structural variety, taking into account a receiver's language abilities.

SUMMARY

Six varieties of language emerged for one deaf child of deaf parents. The order of emergence was: ASL, Spoken English, Fingerspelling and English Print, Sign English and Sign Print. The development of productive use for communication of each variety except ASL, the foundation variety that had emerged before the study began, can be characterized by shifts back and forth between attention to meaning and attention to form, including a high degree of metalinguistic awareness for each variety at some point. In some ways this progression is similar to Bloom's (1970) finding that hearing children express structural forms in inappropriate contexts before they express them with adult meanings. Alice had a preanalyzed scribble form for each variety of language except Sign print before she could encode specific content in the varieties. This was the first issue treated in the data, as outlined in Table 9.1.

From the beginning of use of a second variety of language, Alice made a distinction between manual and oral modes for language. Very gradually she

TABLE 9.1
Alice's Major Developments in Non-ASL Varieties and in Mode Interrelations

Age in Months	Oral English	Fingerspelling	Sign English	Sign Print	English Print
18-23	recodes sign to speech; mouths words with sign; scribbles				
25-26		uses standard borrowed words			
26-30	speech reads parts of the body; for emphasis	laboriously imitates spelling; recognizes name			spells out words; recognizes name
31-36		spells signs but resists prompts; scribbles; imitates spontaneous fingerspelling; interprets letters as signs	learns nursery rhymes and stories from books and sign	matches some Sign English to Sign Print	scribbles; instructs father to write letters; interprets letters as words
37-42	speaks some English functors without signs	teases about errors and about spelling when meaning is obvious	follows along with storyteller, imitates gestures and expressions; uses story language when real life is similar		spells labels; tells father to write words and actions in notebook; points to words and asks meaning; prints name

44-46	engages in short dialogues with no sign	uses more content words in discourse	shifts from oral for emphasis; produces a few sentences; uses TO and ING oddly; practices sentences

laboriously vocalizes and signs Sign Print words one by one, points to English Print and signs the words

47-48	may speak with signs or prints but not with large chunks of fingerspelling	fingerspells print when doesn't know sign, paying no attention to words' boundaries	signs words when she knows signs for English print, sometimes signs after fingerspells	when there's no sign print, sign words she knows signs for and fingerspells others
49-65	speaks 75% of the time, with improved clarity; assesses own and others' abilities to speak and hear; mouths 9%	fingerspells as many as 3 words per sentence; invents name	uses Brown's thirteen morphemes, pronouns, regular past D, plural S; signs functors only spoken previously;	reads several pages at a time

(*continued*)

TABLE 9.1 *(continued)*
Alice's Major Developments in Non-ASL Varieties and in Mode Interrelations

Age in Months	Oral English	Fingerspelling	Sign English	Sign Print	English Print
65	says "went" as signs GO, etc. does not vocalize when reaches no closure on sign print or English print; sounds out English print	spells out words to ask for meaning; reads whole page slowly, looking at both prints; fingerspells occasional whole sentences; shifts after speech and after Sign English for three way emphasis		reads entire story; shapes out signs; omits second handshape; she improves ¼ way into story compares Sign print with English print to check understanding; compares both to pictures to get meaning	sounds out words; pauses for apparent interest; notes spelling similarities;
75	uses no voice in ASL utterance to deaf people; enunciates clearly to hearing listener	fingerspells words known only from speech; spells slowly for hearing listener	signs over 50% of a conversation in English structure; recodes from ASL for hearing listener		adds vocabulary from English print (sometimes wrong, as in starkist mermaid)

came to understand that not everyone could understand language in both modes. As she added forms in different language varieties, she at first made no structural distinctions. She slowly added structural elements of English through the oral and fingerspelling varieties and then added more Sign English signs in English word order. Not until 75 months did Alice indicate that she understood that she was dealing with two basic and separate language structures. The mixing of language structures led to some unique rules. On the other hand, the various varieties of language supplement each other and provide Alice with a means of eliciting information and adding up clues to make meaning in the contexts of storybooks. The second theme of the interrelation of the varieties has been established as a major one in Alice's development.

Some of Alice's utterances in English-like varieties are unusual, but many are like those of hearing children developing spoken English and suggest that at least some of the rules children develop as they are acquiring English are not affected by the modality (manual/visual or spoken/oral) through which the language is expressed. The finding of such developmental rules, together with Alice's strategies for relating language varieties to make meaning and her use of context in both interaction with people and with books, establishes that this deaf child has been an active participant in the language acquisition process.

These findings suggest once again that deafness itself is no barrier to language acquisition, though it may indeed be a barrier to acquisition of some aspects of language and to consistent clear speech. The danger associated with generalizing from one child is probably magnified for this study because of the atypical environment of this deaf child. Alice's behavior does, however, suggest several lines of research for both deaf children of deaf parents and deaf children of hearing parents. In what ways are such children similar and dissimilar to Alice? What sorts of instruction might allow children to use their language in some of the ways that Alice does to acquire new language themselves? In what ways are the rules generated by children learning Sign English similar and different from the rules for children learning spoken English? In what ways are the rules generated by deaf children learning only Sign English different from those generated by deaf children learning both ASL and Sign English? How do deaf children who are not specifically taught the relation between fingerspelling and English print come to understand the relation? Does speech intelligibility contribute to a deaf child's ability to relate speech and fingerspelling, and if so, in what ways? Are the generalizations that deaf children make about spelling patterns in their early fingerspelling like those of hearing children who write early? These are a few of the broad questions, the answers to which would help us to understand how communication develops without the ability to hear speech clearly. Moreover, information on these questions would help us to help the children who lack good hearing to exercise their language learning ability and to help them and their parents interact with the interest, joy, and wit that Alice and her parents enjoyed.

ACKNOWLEDGMENTS

This work was supported in part by National Institute of Health Grant #NS-09811 and by National Science Foundation Grant BNS-76-12866 to the Salk Institute for Biological Studies. I wish to express my appreciation to Dr. Ursula Bellugi for her generous assistance and guidance in this research. My thanks to Alice's father for answering all my questions about Alice's environment. Invaluable assistance in analyzing the copious data was provided by Patricia Van Metre, Christine Tanz, Adrienne Lehrer, and Yetta Goodman, who have all read earlier versions of this work in my dissertation. Mistakes are, of course, my own.

An early report of Alice's language development based on the father's records and observations of another researcher was reported by M. Collins-Ahlgren, "Language Development of Two Deaf Children," *American Annals of the Deaf* 120: 524–539. Another report on her development also based on the home records was reported by L. Newman, "When Cherry Blossoms come to Bloom," *The Deaf American*.

REFERENCES

Baron, N. *Metalinguistics and reading readiness*. Paper presented at the Third Linguistics Institute. Providence College, R.I., 1974.

Baron, N. *Speech, Writing, and Sign: A Functional View of Linguistic Representation*. Bloomington, Ind.: Indiana University Press, 1981.

Battison, R. *Borrowing in ASL*. Unpublished doctoral dissertation. University of California at San Diego, 1977.

Battison, R. *Lexical Borrowing in American Sign Language*. Silver Spring, Md.: Linstok Press, 1978.

Bellugi, U. *The process of compounding in American Sign Language*. Salk Working Paper, Salk Institute for Biological Studies, San Diego, Calif., 1975.

Bellugi, U. & Klima, E. S. The roots of language in the sign talk of the deaf. *Psychology Today,* 1972, *76,* 61–64.

Bellugi, U. & Klima, E. S. Two faces of sign: Iconic and abstract. In S. Harnad (Ed.), *Origins and evolution of language and speech*. New York: New York Academy of Sciences, 1975.

Bernstein, M. E. *How iconicity doesn't help in the acquisition of American Sign Language*. Paper presented at the Boston University Conference on Language Development. Boston, Mass., September, 1979.

Bloom, L. *Language development: Form and function in emerging grammars*. Cambridge, Mass.: MIT Press, 1970.

Bonvillian, J. D., Charrow, V. R., & Nelson, K. E. Psycholinguistic and educational implications of deafness. *Human Development,* 1973, *16,* 321–345.

Bonvillian, J. D. & Nelson, K. E. Development of sign language in language-handicapped individuals. In P. Siple (Ed.), *Understanding language through sign language research*. New York: Academic Press, 1978.

Bornstein, H. & Saulnier, K. L. A brief follow-up to the first evaluation. *American Annals of the Deaf,* 1981, *127,* 69–72.

Bornstein, H., Saulnier, K. L., & Hamilton, L. B. *A guide to the selection and use of the teaching aids of the Signed English System*. Washington, D.C.: Gallaudet College Press, 1976.

Bornstein, H., Saulnier, K. L., & Hamilton, L. B. Signed English: A first evaluation. *American Annals of the Deaf,* 1980, *126,* 467–481.

Brasel, L. & Quigley, S. P. *The influence of early language environments on the development of language in deaf children*. University of Illinois, Urbana-Champaign: Institute for Research on Exceptional Children, 1975.

Brown, R. *A first language: The early stages*. Cambridge, Mass.: Harvard University Press, 1973.

Brown, R. *Why are sign languages easier to learn than spoken languages?* Paper presented at the National Symposium on Sign Language Teaching and Research. Chicago, Ill., 1977.

Cazden, C. B. The acquisition of noun and verb inflections. *Child Development*, 1968, *39*, 433–448.

Cazden, C. B. Play with language and metalinguistic awareness: One dimension of language experience. In C. B. Windsor (Ed.), *Dimensions of language experience*. New York: Agathon Press, 1975.

Clark, E. What's in a word? On the child's acquisition of semantics in his first language. In T. E. Moore (Ed.), *Cognitive development and the acquisition of language*. New York: Academic Press, 1973.

Clay, M. M. *Reading: The patterning of complex behaviour*. Auckland, New Zealand: Heinemann Educational Books, 1972.

Clay, M. M. *What did I write?* Auckland, New Zealand: Heinemann Educational Books, 1975.

Collins-Ahlgren, M. Language development of two deaf children. *American Annals of the Deaf*, 1975, *120*, 524–539.

Conrad, R. Short-term memory processes in the deaf. *British Journal of Psychology*, 1970, *61*, 179–195.

Conrad, R. Short-term memory in the deaf: A test for speech coding. *British Journal of Psychology*, 1972, *63*, 173–180.

Conrad, R. Some correlates of speech coding in the short-term memory of the deaf. *Journal of Speech and Hearing Research*, 1973, *16*, 375–384.

Conrad, R. & Rush, M. L. On the nature of short-term memory encoding by the deaf. *Journal of Speech and Hearing Disorders*, 1965, *30*, 336–343.

Durkin, D. *Children who read early*. New York: Teachers College, Columbia Press, 1966.

Ellenberger, R. & Steyaert, M. A child's representation of action in American Sign Language. In P. Siple (Ed.), *Understanding language through sign language research*. New York: Academic Press, 1978.

Ewoldt, C. *A psycholinguistic description of selected deaf children reading in sign language*. Unpublished doctoral dissertation, Wayne State University, Detroit, Mich., 1977.

Ewoldt, C. Reading for the hearing or hearing impaired: A single process. *American Annals of the Deaf*, 1978, *123*, 945–948.

Ferguson, C. A. & Macken, M. A. The role of play in phonological development. In K. E. Nelson (Ed.), *Children's language* (Vol. 4). Hillsdale, N.J.: Lawrence Erlbaum Associates, 1983.

Fischer, S. *Influences on word-order change in American sign language*. Proceedings of the Santa Barbara Symposium on Word Order and Word-Order Change, Santa Barbara, Calif., 1975.

Fischer, S. Sign language as Creole. In P. Siple (Ed.), *Understanding language through sign language research*. New York: Academic Press, 1978.

Furth, H. A comparison of reading test norms of deaf and hearing children. *American Annals of the Deaf*, 1966, *111*, 461–462.

Gilman, L. A. & Raffin, M. J. M. *Acquisition of common morphemes by hearing-impaired children exposed to the Seeing Essential English Sign System*. Paper presented at the Annual Convention of the American Speech and Hearing Association, Washington, D.C., 1975.

Goodman, Y. Personal communication, 1978.

Griswold, L. E. & Commings, J. The expressive vocabulary of preschool deaf children. *American Annals of the Deaf*, 1974, *119*, 16–28.

Hoffmeister, R. *The development of demonstrative pronouns, locatives, and personal pronouns in*

the acquisition of ASL by deaf children of deaf parents. Unpublished doctoral dissertation, University of Minnesota, 1978.
Hoffmeister, R. & Wilbur, R. Developmental: The Acquisition of Sign Language. In H. Lane & F. Grosjean (Eds.), *Recent Perspectives on American Sign Language.* Hillsdale, N.J.: Lawrence Erlbaum Associates, Inc., 1980.
Jones, M. L. *A longitudinal investigation into the acquisition of question formation in English and American Sign Language by three hearing children with deaf parents.* Unpublished doctoral dissertation, University of Illinois, Urbana-Champaign, 1976.
Klima, E. & Bellugi, U. *The signs of language.* Cambridge, Mass.: Harvard University Press, 1979.
Konstantareas, M. M., Oxman, J. Q., & Webster, C. D. Iconicity and sign language in autistic children. In P. Siple (Ed.), *Understanding language through sign language research.* New York: Academic Press, 1978.
Liddell, S. *An investigation into the syntactic structure of American Sign Language.* Unpublished doctoral dissertation, University of California at San Diego, 1977.
Maxwell, M. M. *A child's garden of lexical gaps: Lexical inventions in sign language.* Salk Working Paper, Salk Institute for Biological Studies, 1977. (Also presented at the Stanford Conference on Child Language, April, 1979.)
McNeill, D. Developmental psycholinguistics. In Smith, F. & Miller, G. (Eds.), *The Genesis of language: A psycholinguistic approach.* Cambridge, Mass.: MIT Press, 1966.
Meadow, K. P. *The effect of early manual communication and family climate on the deaf child's development.* Unpublished doctoral dissertation, University of California, Berkeley, 1966.
Meadow, K. P. *Deafness and child development.* Berkeley, Cal.: University of California Press, 1980.
Moores, D. *Recent research on manual communication.* Research and Demonstration Center in the Education of the Handicapped, University of Minnesota, 1971.
Moores, D. Nonvocal systems of verbal behavior. In R. L. Schiefelbusch and L. L. Lloyds (Eds.), *Language perspectives—Acquisition, retardation, and intervention.* Baltimore, Md.: University Park Press, 1974.
Moores, D. F. *Educating the deaf.* Boston, Mass.: Houghton Mifflin, 1978.
Moores, D. F., Weiss, K. L., & Goodwin, M. W. Early education programs for hearing-impaired children: Major findings. *American Annals of the Deaf,* 1978, *123,* 925–936.
Mow, S. *Notes on the acquisition of sign language by deaf children of deaf parents.* Salk Institute for Biological Studies, La Jolla, California, 1974.
Newport, E. & Bellugi, U. *Linguistic expression of category levels in a visual-gestural language: A flower is a flower is a flower.* Social Science Research Council Conference on Nature and Principles of Formation of Categories, Arrowhead, Calif., May, October 1976.
Odom, P. & Blanton, L. Implicit and explicit grammatical factors and reading achievement in the deaf. *Journal of Reading Behavior,* 1970, *2,* 1.
Power, D. Language development in deaf children: The use of manual supplements in oral education. *Australian Teacher of the Deaf,* 1974, 15.
Prinz, P. & Prinz, E. A. *Acquisition of ASL and spoken English in a hearing child of a deaf mother and a hearing father: Phase I—Early lexical development.* Forum on Child Language, Stanford University, Stanford, Calif., 1979. (a)
Prinz, P. M. & Prinz, E. A. Simultaneous acquisition of ASL and spoken English (in a hearing child of a deaf mother and hearing father). *Sign Language Studies,* 1979, *25,* 283–296. (b)
Quigley, S. P. *The influence of fingerspelling on the development of language, communication, and educational achievement in deaf children.* Institute for Research on Exceptional Children, University of Illinois, Urbana-Champaign, 1969.
Quigley, S. P., Wilbur, R. B., Montanelli, D. S., & Steinkamp, M. M. *Syntactic structures in the language of deaf children.* Institute for Child Behavior and Development, University of Illinois, Urbana-Champaign, 1976.

Raffin, M. J. M. *The acquisition of inflectional morphemes by deaf children using Seeing Essential English.* Unpublished doctoral dissertation, University of Iowa, 1976.

Read, C. Lessons to be learned from the preschool orthographer. In E. Lenneberg and E. Lenneberg (Eds.), *Foundations of language development.* New York: Academic Press, 1975.

Schlesinger, H. S. & Meadow, K. P. *Sound and sign: Childhood deafness and mental health.* Berkeley, Calif.: University of California Press, 1972.

Schwam, E. M. *Sign language and the comprehension of relational terms in deaf and hearing children.* Unpublished doctoral dissertation. New School for Social Research, New York, 1979.

Schwam, E. M. Signs and strategies: The interactive processes of sign language learning. In K. E. Nelson (Ed.), *Children's language* (Vol. 3). New York: Gardner Press, 1982.

St. Pierre, R. & Maxwell, M. M. *Short-term memory processes in the deaf: Phonological, graphic, and sign encoding.* In preparation.

Stoloff, L. & Dennis, Z. Matthew. *American Annals of the Deaf,* 1978, *123,* 452–459.

Swisher, L. The language performance of the oral deaf. In H. Whitaker, & H. A. Whitaker, (Eds.). *Studies in Neurolinguistics, Vol. 2.* New York: Academic Press, 1976.

Wilbur, R. B. The linguistics of manual languages and manual systems. In L. L. Lloyd (Ed.), *Communication assessment and intervention strategies.* Baltimore, Md.: University Park Press, 1976.

Wilbur, R. B. *American Sign Language and Sign Systems.* Baltimore, Md.: University Park Press, 1979.

Wilbur, R. B. & Quigley, S. P. Syntactic structures in the written language of deaf students. *Volta Review,* 1975, *77,* 194–203.

Woodward, J. C. Some characteristics of Pidgin Sign English. *Studies in Sign Language,* 1973, *3,* 37–56.

10 What Do You Do if You Can't Tell the Whole Story? The Development of Summarization Skills

Nancy S. Johnson
State University of New York at Buffalo

The ability to comprehend and produce discourse, i.e., sets of spoken or written utterances that are produced by one or more speakers and relate to a particular theme or set of themes, is a critical aspect of language development that has only recently begun to receive widespread theoretical and empirical treatment. Two factors have contributed to the growth of interest in how children process discourse. One is the discovery that an adequate account of language development cannot be formulated without relating children's individual utterances to the context in which they occur, a context that includes both nonlinguistic factors (such as the objects present at the time of an utterance) and, of greater interest here, the preceding and following utterances made by the child or another participant in the discourse (cf. Bates, 1976; Bloom, Miller, & Hood, 1975; Dore, Gearhart, & Newman, 1978; Gleason & Weintraub, 1978; Shatz, 1975). The second factor is the development of more adequate theoretical analyses of discourse. Some of these analyses involve abilities and issues traditionally associated with language, e.g., speech act theory (Austin, 1962; Searle, 1975), analyses of presuppositions (Kempson, 1975; Lakoff, 1971) and conversational postulates (Grice, 1975), and linguistic "text grammars" (cf. Dressler, 1977; van Dijk, 1977b). Others have come from fields such as cognition and memory, which focus on abilities that fall outside the area of linguistic competence as traditionally defined, but have come to play an increasingly important role in analyses of language processing as it occurs in normal communicative contexts. Examples of the latter type of development are provided by analyses of cognitive schemata (e.g., scripts, story grammars, and plans) that are not necessarily restricted to linguistic applications but are thought to provide a basis for predicting and organizing linguistic input and formulating linguistic output (cf. Fillmore, 1979; Johnson & Mandler, 1980; Lichtenstein & Brewer, 1980; Rumelhart, 1977; Rumelhart & Ortony, 1977; Schank & Abelson, 1977).

In the present chapter, I will be concerned primarily with one type of discourse, namely simple stories, and with the problem of how children come to be able to comprehend, remember, and operate on the information in such stories. In particular, I will focus on the development of processes involved in summarization. The first section of the chapter includes a brief review of recent models of the organization of traditional stories and a discussion of the relationship between story structure and the cognitive schemata that a listener or reader might use in processing stories. The second section focuses on abilities involved in summarization and their development. In the last section, I will present a recent developmental investigation of story recall and summarization, in which children and adults were asked to recall and summarize two well-formed stories. The results of this work indicate, somewhat surprisingly, that even children in the first grade can produce reasonable summaries of stories, at least under conditions designed to optimize performance. However, some of the developmental differences indicate that a number of the component processes involved in summarization are not typically fully developed until at least early adolescence. In addition, the results suggest that current models of summarization (Kintsch & van Dijk, 1978; Rumelhart, 1977) may overestimate the extent to which summarization results from automatic processes that occur during comprehension or retrieval.

MODELS OF STORY STRUCTURE

Although models of higher-order text structure that can be applied to any type of text have been proposed (e.g., Frederiksen, 1975; Meyer, 1975), the models to be reviewed here have focused on the structure of stories, especially stories from the oral tradition. These models share an assumption that stories have a specifiable higher order structure that can be used by a reader or listener in deriving an organized representation of the information in a particular story (cf. Johnson & Mandler, 1980; Mandler & Johnson, 1977; Rumelhart, 1977; Stein & Glenn, 1979; Thorndyke, 1977; van Dijk & Kintsch, 1977). In all of these models, the organization of a story is characterized by rules that specify the constituents of a story and the relations among constituents. Although there are some differences in the specific constituents that have been postulated, there is a good deal of overlap, especially in the set of models (Johnson & Mandler, 1980; Mandler & Johnson, 1977; Rumelhart, 1977; Stein & Glenn, 1979; Thorndyke, 1977) based on earlier work by Rumelhart (1975).

The model proposed by Johnson & Mandler (1980), which provides the theoretical background for the developmental study reported later in the chapter, will be used to illustrate this approach. The model, which is sometimes referred to as a "story grammar," characterizes the underlying structure of a well-formed story from the oral tradition in terms of a set of rewrite rules that specify the constituents of a story and the causal and temporal relations among constituents. These rules are presented in Table 10.1.[1] The terminal elements (Setting, Beginning, etc.) are instantiated in a particular story by specific states and events, which are typically expressed as sentences or parts of sentences in the surface structure of a story. A very simple story might consist of a Setting, which identifies the protagonist, followed by a single Episode. An Episode includes a Beginning, in which some initial event happens to the protagonist, a Development that describes the protagonist's internal and external response to the Beginning, and an Ending, which often emphasizes long-range consequences of the Development. The Development is the most complex constituent in a simple Episode. It most frequently takes the form of a Complex Reaction followed by a Goal Path. The Complex Reaction includes both a Simple Reaction, the protagonist's thoughts or feelings about the Beginning, and a Goal. The Goal Path includes an Attempt to achieve the Goal and the Outcome of that Attempt.

The organization of more complex stories is accounted for by rules for concatenating and embedding constituents. Coordinate sequences of temporally connected Episodes can occur (Rule 2). An entire Episode can function as the Beginning, Outcome, or Ending of another Episode Rules (3, 8, and 9). A Development can consist of a series of causally connected, coordinate Developments (Rule 4) in which the protagonist makes a series of Attempts to achieve a single Goal. An Attempt can include an embedded Development in which the protagonist pursues a subordinate Goal (Rule 7).

In addition to the phrase-structure rules that describe the underlying structure of canonical stories, there are transformational rules that account for certain regular deletions and movements of story constituents. For example, if the general nature of the Complex Reaction can be inferred from surrounding constituents, it can be deleted from the surface structure of the story. Under similar circumstances the Goal can be moved to a position following the Attempt.

Most of the rules described above are illustrated in the two stories—the story of the Little Rabbit and the story of the Three Little Pigs—that were used in the present study of children's summarization. The text and underlying structure of the Little Rabbit (a simplified version of one of Aesop's fables) are presented in Table 10.2 and Figure 10.1, respectively. The story, which is about a rabbit's attempts to get away from a fox, has a single Episode with three coordinate Developments. Each Development includes an Attempt by the rabbit to enlist the aid of one of her friends and the Outcome of that Attempt. Within each Attempt

---

[1]The rewrite rule for the Attempt node in Table 10.1 (Rule 7) includes an optional Development that is not included in the corresponding rule in Johnson and Mandler (1980). This modification permits a more detailed representation of the internal structure of Attempts in which the protagonist pursues a subgoal before making a direct attempt to achieve the main goal.

TABLE 10.1
Rewrite Rules for the Underlying Structures of Simple Stories

1. STORY	--------->	Setting And EPISODE
2. EPISODE	--------->	$\left\{ \begin{array}{l} \text{BEGINNING Cause DEVELOPMENT Cause ENDING} \\ \text{EPISODE} \left(\left\{ \begin{array}{l} \text{And} \\ \text{Then} \end{array} \right\} \text{EPISODE} \right)^n \end{array} \right.$
3. BEGINNING	--------->	$\left\{ \begin{array}{l} \text{Beginning Event} \\ \text{EPISODE} \end{array} \right.$
4. DEVELOPMENT	--------->	$\left\{ \begin{array}{l} \text{Simple Reaction Cause Action} \\ \text{COMPLEX REACTION Cause GOAL PATH} \\ \text{DEVELOPMENT (Cause DEVELOPMENT)}^n \end{array} \right.$
5. COMPLEX REACTION	--------->	Simple Reaction Cause Goal
6. GOAL PATH	--------->	ATTEMPT Cause OUTCOME
7. ATTEMPT	--------->	(DEVELOPMENT Enable) Attempt Event
8. OUTCOME	--------->	$\left\{ \begin{array}{l} \text{Outcome Event} \\ \text{EPISODE} \end{array} \right.$
9. ENDING	--------->	$\left\{ \begin{array}{l} \text{Ending Event} \\ \text{EPISODE} \end{array} \right.$

Note: Nodes that are not further rewritten except for their instantiation in terms of specific states and events are written in lower case.

TABLE 10.2
Terminal Nodes and Text of "The Little Rabbit"

Node	#	Proposition(s) representing each node
Setting	1	Once upon a time there was a little rabbit. The rabbit thought she had a lot of friends.
Beginning Event	2	One day the rabbit was being chased by a fox.
Simple Reaction	3	The rabbit was really scared.
Goal	4	And she wanted to get away from the fox.
[Complex Reaction][a]	5	[Goal = Get to horse]
⎡ Attempt Event[b]	⎡ 6	⎡ The rabbit ran to her friend the horse.
⎣ Outcome Event	⎣ 7	
Attempt Event	8	And she said, "Please horse, give me a ride on your back."
Outcome Event	9	But the horse said, "I'm too busy. No, I won't help you."
[Complex Reaction]	10	[Goal = Get away from fox]
[Complex Reaction]	11	[Goal = Get to bull]
⎡ Attempt Event	⎡ 12	⎡ Then the rabbit ran to her friend the bull.
⎣ Outcome Event	⎣ 13	
Attempt Event	14	And she said, "Please bull, protect me with your sharp horns."
Outcome Event	15	But the bull said, "I'm too busy. No, I won't help you."
[Complex Reaction]	16	[Goal = Get away from fox]
[Complex Reaction]	17	[Goal = Get to goat]
⎡ Attempt Event	⎡ 18	⎡ Then the rabbit ran to her friend the goat.
⎣ Outcome Event	⎣ 19	
Attempt Event	20	And she said, "Please goat, hide me in your pen." The goat was really nice.
Outcome Event	21	He hid the rabbit in his pen.
Ending Event	22	And she was saved from the fox at last.

Note: Nodes are numbered in the order that they appear in the underlying structure of the story. (See Figure 1.)

[a]Complex Reactions that have been deleted from the surface structure of the story (see nodes 5, 10, 11, 16, and 17) are represented in brackets; the nature of the Goal within each of these Complex Reactions is also presented in brackets.

[b]Pairs of nodes that are represented by a single statement in the surface structure are indicated by connecting lines (e.g., Attempt Event-6 and Outcome Event-7).

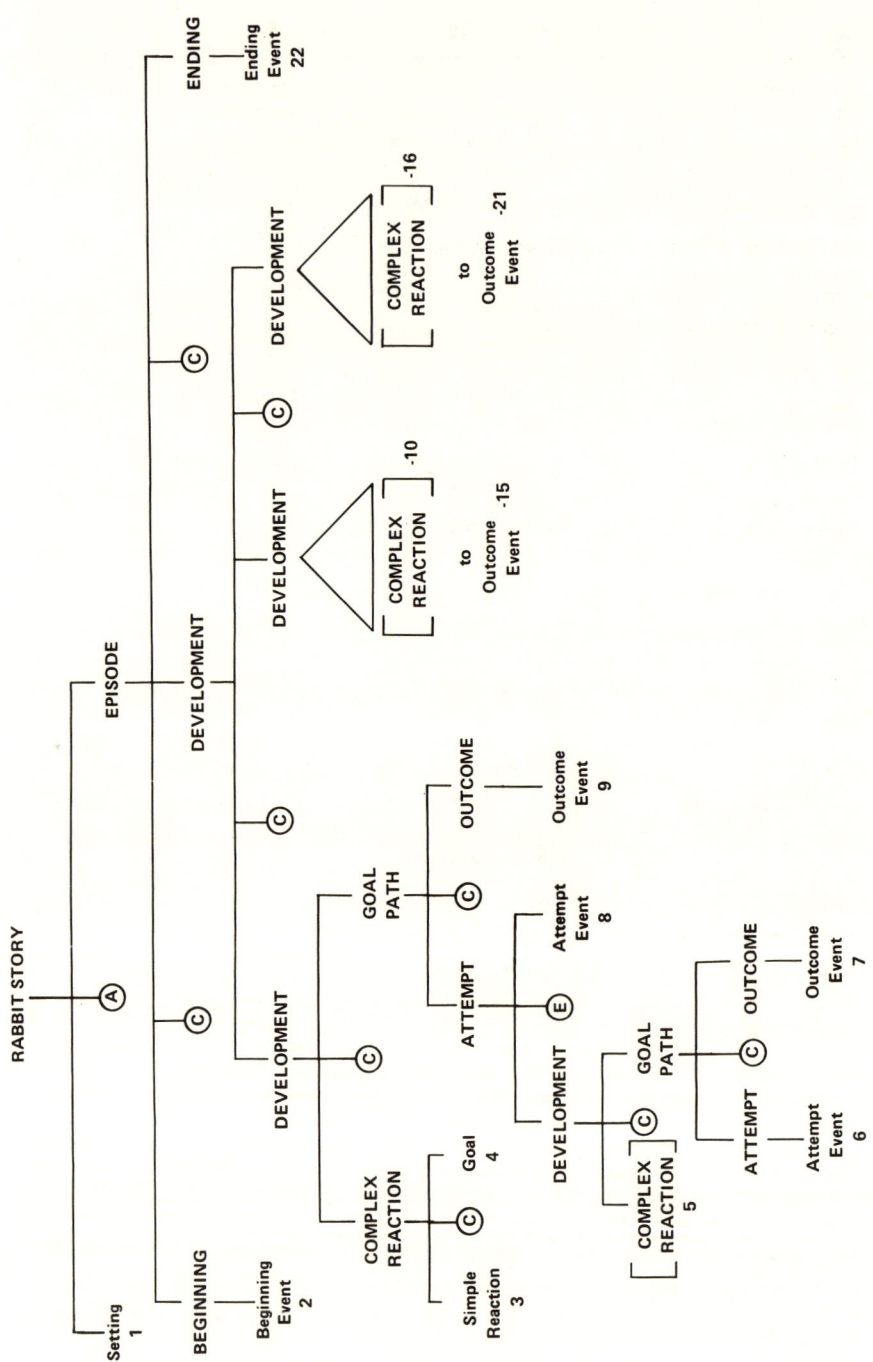

there is a subordinate Development (in which the rabbit pursues the subgoal of getting to each friend) and a higher level Attempt Event (asking for help). The Complex Reactions (nodes, 5, 11, and 17) that motivate each of the lower level Goal Paths have been deleted from the surface structure of the story, as have the Complex Reactions (nodes 10 and 16) motivating the higher level Goal Paths in the second and third coordinate Developments.

The text and structure of the story of the Three Little Pigs are presented in Table 10.3 and Figure 10.2. The story has five Episodes: 1) the three pigs each build a house; 2) the wolf tries to get the first pig; 3) the wolf tries to get the first two pigs; 4) the wolf tries to get all three pigs; and 5) the pigs capture the wolf. The connections between Episodes represent three of the four types permitted by the grammar: Then-connection, Ending-embedding, and Outcome-embedding.

In the first Episode, the pigs act as joint protagonists during the Beginning and Complex Reaction and then follow separate Goal Paths in which each builds a house. According to Johnson and Mandler (1980), this type of sequence is derived transformationally from an underlying structure with three coordinate Episodes, one for each protagonist. The representation of Episode 1 in Figure 10.2 corresponds to the structure that results from the application of transformations that conjoin those parts of an Episode in which protagonists act in concert. (See Johnson & Mandler, 1980, for details.)

The second Episode, in which the wolf tries to get the first pig, is temporally connected to the first. After arriving at the pig's house and deciding to eat the pig, the wolf first pursues a subgoal (getting into the pig's house, the Goal of Complex Reaction-25). The wolf's first Attempt to get into the house fails, so he makes a second Attempt, which succeeds. However, the first pig foils the wolf's plan by running to the second pig's house (Outcome Event-32) before the wolf can catch him (blocked Attempt Event-31).

The wolf's arrival at the second pig's house marks the Beginning of Episode 3, because the wolf changes his plan and decides to have *both* pigs for dinner (Goal-37). Consequently, the highest level Attempt Event and Outcome (nodes 33 and 34) of Episode 2 remain empty. Episode 3 has the same structure as Episode 2. Episode 4, in which the wolf decides to eat all three pigs, has the same initial structure as Episode 3. However, when the wolf fails to blow the third pig's house down, he makes yet another Attempt to get into the house. The Outcome of this Attempt is Episode 5, in which the pigs carry out a successful counterattack. Because the wolf is killed, the higher level Attempt Events and

---

FIG. 10.1 (page 320) A representation of the underlying structure of the Rabbit story. Numbers beneath nodes correspond to the node numbers in Table 10.2. Nodes deleted from the surface structure are enclosed in brackets. The causal and temporal relations *And, Cause, Enable,* and *Then,* are represented by the encircled letters A, C, E, and T, respectively. Hierarchical and temporal relations among nodes in sections of the story represented by triangles are the same as the relations among corresponding nodes in the preceding section of the story.

TABLE 10.3
Terminal Nodes and Text of "The Three Little Pigs"

Node	#	Proposition(s) representing each node
Setting	1	Once upon a time there were three little pigs who lived in a house with their mother.
Beginning Event	2	One day their mother called them together and said, "My dear children, you are all grown up now, and it is time for you to live on your own."
[Simple Reaction]	3	Deleted
Goal	4	And so the three little pigs decided that they would each go off and build a house to live in.
[Complex Reaction]	5	[Goal = Get materials for house]
Attempt Event	6	The first little pig walked along until he met a man who was carrying a bundle of straw. "Please sir, give me that straw
Goal (r, d)	4	so I can build myself a house," said the first little pig.
Outcome Event	7	And so the man gave him the straw.
⎡ Attempt Event	⎡ 8	⎡
⎣ Outcome Event	⎣ 9	⎣ And the first little pig built a house with it.
[Complex Reaction]	10	[Goal = Get materials for house]
Attempt Event	11	The second little pig walked along until he met a man who was carrying a bunch of sticks. "Please sir, give me those sticks
Goal (r, d)	4	so I can build myself a house," said the second little pig.
Outcome Event	12	And so the man gave him the sticks.
⎡ Attempt Event	⎡ 13	⎡
⎣ Outcome Event	⎣ 14	⎣ And the second little pig built a house with them.
[Complex Reaction]	15	[Goal = Get materials for house]
Attempt Event	16	The third little pig walked along until he met a man who was carrying a load of bricks. "Please sir, give me those bricks
Goal (r, d)	4	so I can build myself a house."
Outcome Event	17	And so the man gave him the bricks.
⎡ Attempt Event	⎡ 18	⎡
⎣ Outcome Event	⎣ 19	⎣ And the third little pig built a house with them.
[Ending]	20	Deleted

TABLE 10.3 *(continued)*
Terminal Nodes and Text of "The Three Little Pigs"

Node	#	Proposition(s) representing each node
Beginning Event	21	That night, a wolf came along and saw the straw house with the first little pig inside.
Simple Reaction	22	The wolf thought that the first little pig looked especially plump and juicy
Goal	23	and decided that he would have the pig for his supper.
[Complex Reaction]	24	[Goal = Catch pig]
[Complex Reaction]	25	[Goal = Get into pig's house]
Attempt Event	26	And so, in his nicest voice, the wolf said, "Little pig, little pig, let me come in."
Outcome Event	27	"Not by the hair of my chinny chin chin," said the first little pig.
[Complex Reaction]	28	[Goal = Get into pig's house]
Attempt Event	29	And so the wolf huffed, and he puffed.
⎡ Attempt Event (r)	⎡ 29	
⎣ Outcome Event	⎣ 30	And he blew the house in.
[Attempt Event]	31	[Blocked by Outcome Event 32]
Outcome Event	32	But the first little pig went out the back way and ran to the house of the second little pig.
[Attempt Event]	33	[Unfilled because of change in goal]
[Outcome]	34	[Unfilled because of change in goal]
Beginning Event	35	The wolf followed the pig and came to the house built of sticks with the two little pigs inside.
Simple Reaction	36	The wolf thought that the two little pigs would be even better than one
Goal	37	and decided that he would have the pigs for his supper.
[Complex Reaction]	38	[Goal = Catch pigs]
[Complex Reaction]	39	[Goal = Get into pig's house]
Attempt Event	40	And so, in his nicest voice, the wolf said, "Little pigs, little pigs, let me come in."
Outcome Event	41	"Not by the hair of my chinny chin chin," said the two little pigs.
[Complex Reaction]	42	[Goal = Get into pig's house]
Attempt Event	43	And so the wolf huffed, and he puffed, and he puffed, and he huffed.

(continued)

TABLE 10.3 *(continued)*
Terminal Nodes and Text of "The Three Little Pigs"

Node	#	Proposition(s) representing each node
⎡ Attempt Event (r) ⎣ Outcome Event	⎡ 43 ⎣ 44	And he blew the house in.
[Attempt Event]	45	[Blocked by Outcome Event 46]
Outcome Event	46	But the two little pigs went out the back way and ran to the house of the third little pig.
[Attempt Event]	47	[Unfilled because of change in goal]
[Outcome]	48	[Unfilled because of change in goal]
Beginning Event	49	The wolf followed the pigs and came to the brick house with the three little pigs inside.
Simple Reaction	50	The wolf was even hungrier than before
Goal	51	and decided that he would have all three little pigs for his supper.
[Simple Reaction]	52	Deleted.
[Complex Reaction]	54	[Goal = Get into pig's house]
Attempt Event	55	And so, in his nicest voice, the wolf said, "Little pigs, little pigs, let me come in."
Outcome Event	56	"Not by the hair of my chinny chin chin," said the three little pigs.
[Complex Reaction]	57	[Goal = Get into pig's house]
Attempt Event	58	And so the wolf huffed, and he puffed, and he puffed, and he huffed.
⎡ Attempt Event (r) ⎣ Outcome Event	⎡ 58 ⎣ 59	But he could not blow the house in.
Simple Reaction	60	When the wolf saw that he could not blow the house in,
Goal	61	he decided that he would go down the chimney to
Goal (d)	53	get the little pigs.
[Complex Reaction]	62	[Goal = Get to chimney]
Attempt Event	63	And so he started to climb up to the top of the little brick house.
[Outcome Event]	64	[Wolf got to chimney]
Beginning Event	66	But the three little pigs saw what the wolf was doing

TABLE 10.3 *(continued)*
Terminal Nodes and Text of "The Three Little Pigs"

Node	#	Proposition(s) representing each node
[Complex Reaction]	67	[Goal = Catch Wolf]
Attempt Event	68	and built a fire in the fireplace and put a big pot of water on to boil.
Attempt Event (d)	65	So when the wolf came down the chimney,
Outcome Event	69	he landed in the pot of water.
Ending Event	70	And the three little pigs put the lid on the pot and had wolf stew for supper that night.
[Attempt Event]	71	[Blocked by Ending Event 70]
[Outcome]	72	[Wolf didn't catch pigs]
[Attempt Event]	73	[Blocked by Ending Event 70]
[Outcome]	74	[Wolf didn't eat pigs]
Ending Event	75	And that was the end of the wolf.

Note: Nodes are numbered in the order that they appear in the representation of the structure of the story in Figure 2. The letter *r* after a node label indicates that the content of the node has been repeated; the letter *d* after a node label indicates that the node has been displaced in the surface structure of the story, relative to its position in the underlying structure. See notes *a* and *b* in Table 2 for other notational conventions.

Outcomes of Episode 4 remain empty. The story comes to a close with an emphatic Ending (Ending Event-75).

As noted earlier, proponents of story grammars have suggested that their characterizations of story structure also characterize the set of expectations about the structure of stories, or the "story schema," that people use in processing stories. The hypothesis that such a schema provides a basis for predicting incoming information, organizing the information in memory, and guiding retrieval, has led to a common set of predictions about the relationship between story structure, as described by the grammars, and performance in tasks requiring comprehension and memory. For example, the constituent structure assigned to a story by the grammars should correspond to the organization assigned by readers or listeners, departures from canonical form should make comprehension and retrieval more difficult, and stories that are noncanonical should tend to be recalled in a more canonical form. A number of recent studies, some of which will be considered in more detail below, have provided support for these predictions (e.g., Buschke & Schaier, 1979; Glenn, 1978; Mandler, 1978; Mandler & DeForest, 1979; Pollard-Gott, McCloskey, & Todres, 1979; Stein & Nezworski, 1978; Rumelhart, 1977; Thorndyke, 1977).

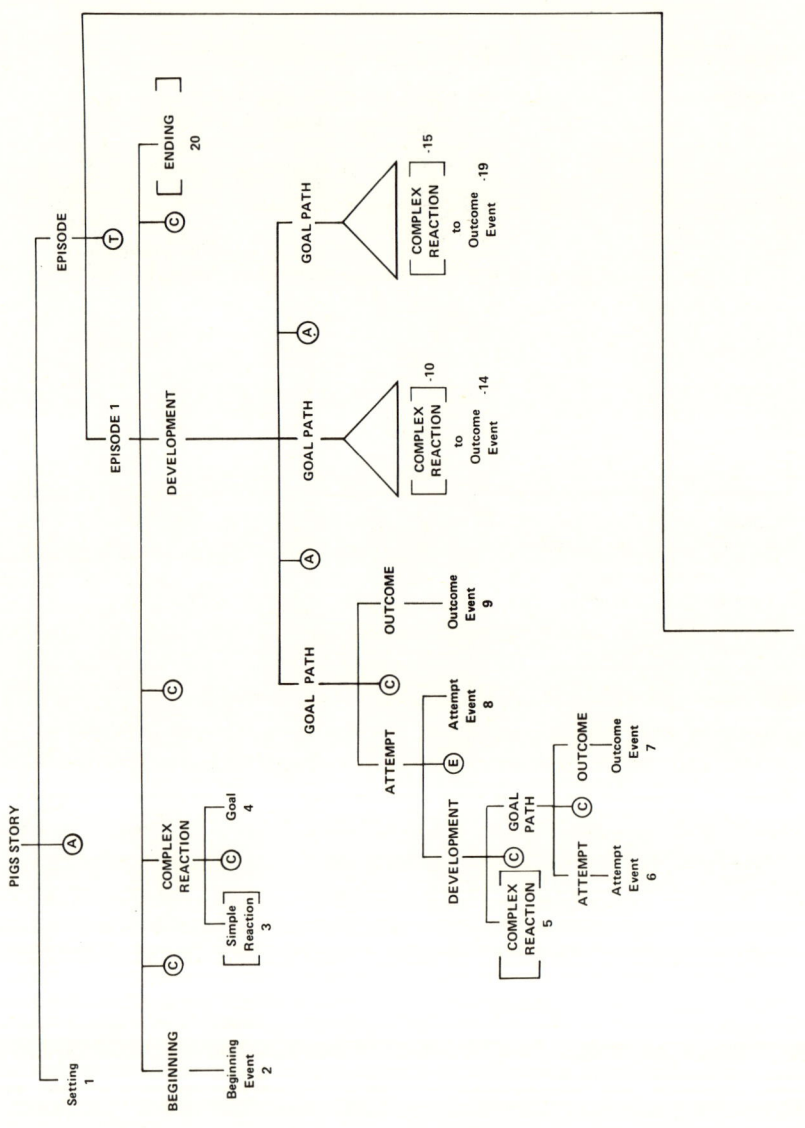

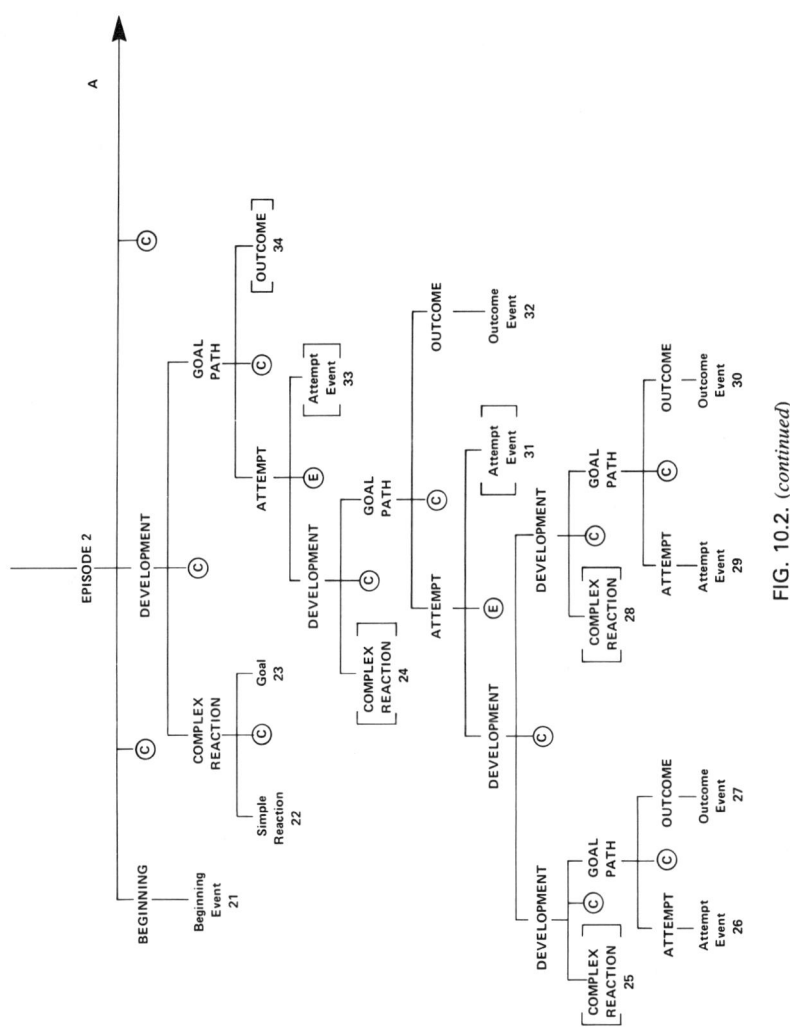

FIG. 10.2. (continued)

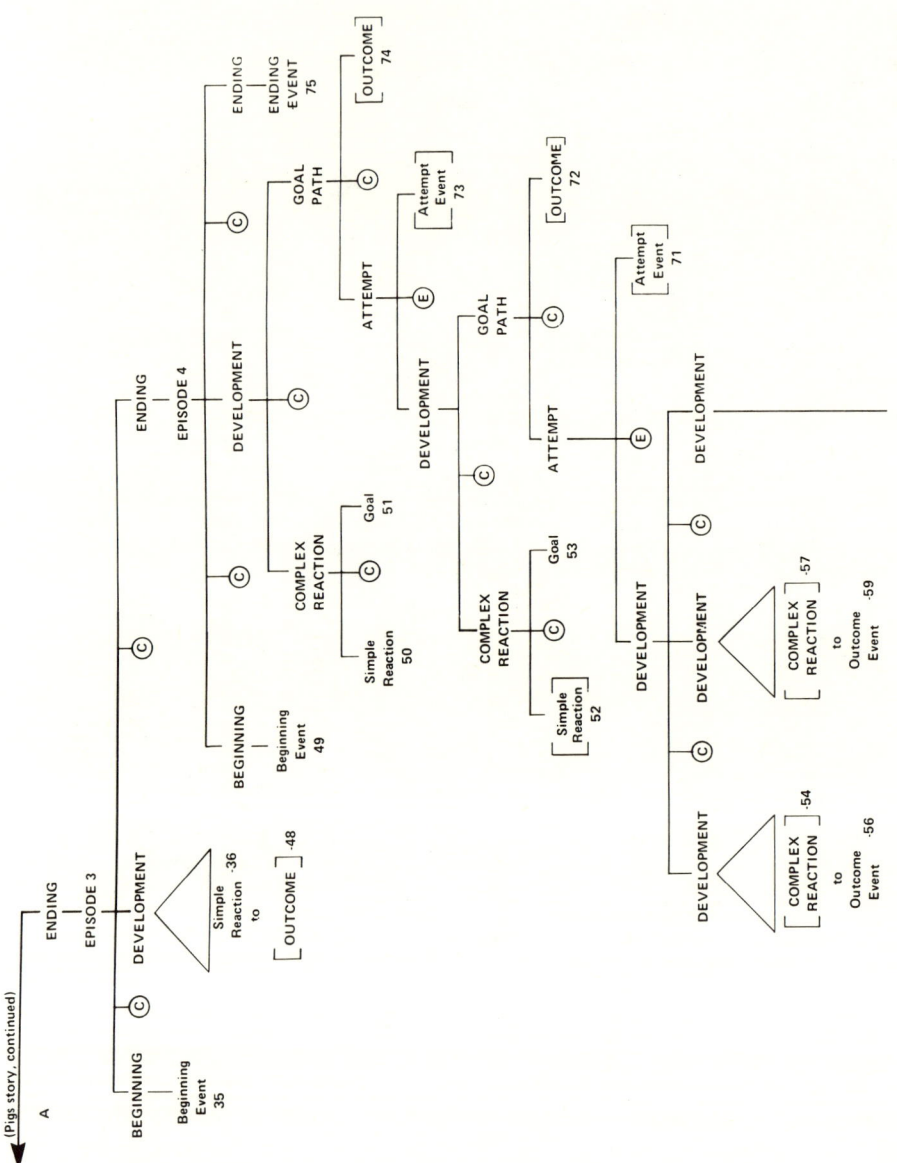

328

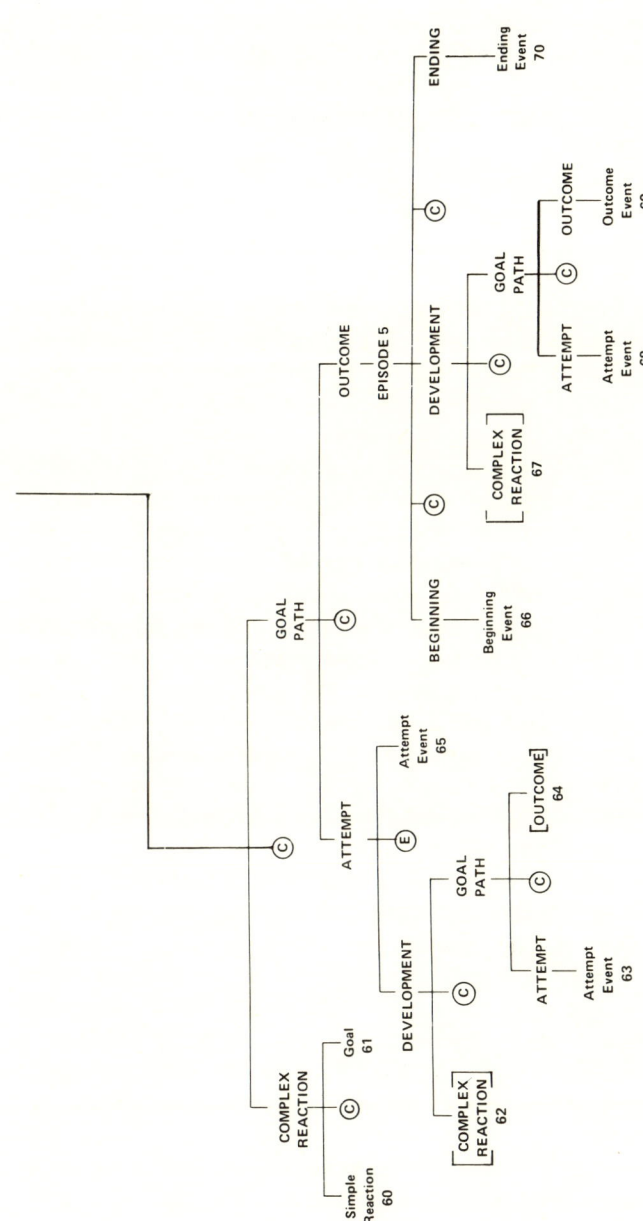

FIG. 10.2. A representation of the structure of the Pigs story. See Table 10.3 for the corresponding text. See Figure 10.1 for an explanation of notational conventions. The intermediate structure assigned to Episode 1 is discussed in the text of the paper.

THE DEVELOPMENT OF SUMMARIZATION SKILLS

In analyzing the development of the ability to summarize, it is necessary to define what will be meant by the term "summary." Although it is generally agreed that a summary should reflect the gist of a story, the term "gist" is itself used in a number of different ways; and extracting different types of gist may require different types of processes.

The first type of "gist" is represented by what subjects are able to recall after reading or listening to a story that they have been asked to comprehend or remember. Although recall protocols are often relatively complete, they almost always involve some reduction of the original information. Because this reduction is most likely to occur in those parts of a story that subjects judge to be less important (Brown & Smiley, 1977, 1978; R. Johnson, 1970), even gist recall could be considered to be a "summary," in the sense that the subject's output represents a condensation of the story as presented.

The second type of "gist" is represented by a plot summary, which can be thought of as a further condensation of gist recall and is probably what is most often meant by the term "summary." That is, when experimenters ask their subjects to summarize, they usually assume that the subjects will engage in more reduction than is involved in gist recall. Because *adults* are able both to recall the gist of a story and to produce plot summaries that involve further reduction, it is difficult to determine whether or not they establish both types of "gist" simultaneously (e.g., as a result of processes occurring during comprehension, as suggested by Kintsch & van Dijk, 1978, and Rumelhart, 1977). However, some of the developmental evidence to be reviewed here suggests that the ability to recall the gist of a story may be distinct from the ability to generate a plot summary (Brown & Smiley, 1977, 1978; Denhière & Le Ny, 1980; Yussen, Mathews, Buss, & Kane, 1980).

The third type of "gist" is the point or essence of a story and is the sense of gist closest to a standard dictionary definition. The American Heritage Dictionary (Morris, 1976), for example, defines *gist* as "The central idea of some matter, such as an argument or speech; essence [p. 558]." To some extent, the ease with which the central idea of a story can be identified will depend on the particular story involved. Although some stories, such as fables, clearly have a central idea, other stories may not. In addition, the ability to extract this type of gist may involve processes that are not typically required in either gist recall or plot summaries.

For present purposes, a "summary" will be defined as a coherent piece of discourse that represents either the second or third type of "gist," i.e., a coherent plot summary or a statement of the point or moral of a story. Thus, a given production will only be considered to be a "summary" if it represents a reduction or condensation of the information accessible to a subject during recall.

In the remainder of this section, processes required for summarization will be considered, along with available evidence about their development. Although additional processes may be involved, the present discussion will focus on the following six: 1) comprehending the individual propositions of a story; 2) establishing connections between propositions; 3) identifying the constituent structure of the story; 4) remembering the information in the story; 5) selecting the information to be represented in the summary; and 6) formulating a concise and coherent verbal representation of that information. The first four processes are of interest here primarily as prerequisites for summarization rather than as processes strongly identified with summarization per se; i.e., they would also be relevant in a more general discussion of the development of discourse comprehension and memory.

Prerequisites for Summarization

Comprehending Individual Propositions

Comprehension of individual propositions is obviously a *sine qua non*. Unless children understand the individual elements of a story, they have no basis for establishing relations between those elements, remembering more than the few items in short-term memory, or assigning sets of propositions to story constituents. Basic syntactic and semantic competence develops early enough that comprehension of propositions per se should not be an major obstacle to summarization for school-age children (cf. Dale, 1976; de Villiers & de Villiers, 1978). It is important, however, to insure that the situations described in a story can be assimilated on the basis of children's existing knowledge and that the syntactic constructions that are used do not require transformations or other structures that are acquired relatively late (see Bowerman, 1979, for a review).

Establishing Connections between Propositions

As with comprehension of individual propositions, it is difficult to imagine how summarization could proceed in the absence of the ability to make causal and temporal connections between elements in a story. Such connections, although they are often omitted from the surface structure of a text, provide the cohesion that distinguishes connected discourse from a string of unrelated sentences. The relevance of this distinction for summarization has been well stated by Rumelhart (1975).

> Connected discourse differs from an unrelated string of sentences (among other ways) in that it is possible to pick out what is important in connected discourse and summarize it without seriously altering the meaning of the discourse. The same is not true of strings of unrelated sentences. Since such strings lack structure and do not make a meaningful whole they cannot be summarized at all [p. 226].

The available evidence concerning the development of inferential abilities suggests that children as young as four may integrate narrative sequences by making inferences about causal and temporal relations. There are, however, indications that young children tend to make fewer inferences. Omanson, Warren, and Trabasso (1978), for example, presented 5- and 8-year-old children with simple stories and assessed both recall and the ability to answer probe questions that required various types of inferences. Their taxonomy included inferences about psychological motivation, physical causation, spatiotemporal relationships, and elaborative details, as well as evaluations of the morality and appropriateness of the actions of characters (Warren, Nicholas, & Trabasso, 1979). Both the 5- and 8-year olds gave answers to some questions in each category that were correctly constrained by the given information. However, the proportion of such inferences was greater for the older children, even when subjects in the two age groups were equated in terms of the overall percentage of premises they were able to recall.

These results are generally congruent with earlier work by Paris and Upton (1976) indicating that older children make more inferences even when memory is controlled. The two studies, however, led to different conclusions about the relationship between inference *type* and age. Paris and Upton found that differences between age groups were greater for "contextual inferences," which required the integration of information across substantial portions of the text, than for inferences that required integration within smaller text units. A related manipulation in Omanson et al.'s (1978) study, in which inferences were based on premises within or across sections of the text, revealed no difference between the two inference types for either age group. Hildyard (1979), using inference probes that were even more similar to those used by Paris and Upton, also found little difference between the two types of inferences.

On the whole, studies such as these do indicate that even relatively young children are capable of making many of the types of inferences that are needed to integrate the information in a story. However, their tendency to make fewer inferences than older children could differentially increase the difficulty of summarization, if the missing inferences are needed to construct a well-integrated representation of a story. At present the factors that lead younger children to make fewer inferences are not well understood. Hildyard (1979) found that differences between age groups could be accounted for largely by differences in memory. However, Omanson et al. (1978) and Paris and Upton (1976) have argued that older children make more inferences than younger ones, even when their memory for premises is comparable.[2] The extent to which younger and older children are equally familiar with the types of event sequences described in stories may also influence the extent to which developmental differences in

---

[2]Although remembering presented information is a precondition for making appropriate inferences, making inferences may also facilitate memory for presented information, by leading to the construction of a better integrated representation of a story. If so, the relationship between remembering presented information and making inferences may be more of a "chicken-and-egg" problem than is apparent in most discussions in the developmental literature.

inference production are found. (See Mandler, in press, for a discussion of the importance of familiarity of materials in tests of reasoning skills.)

Identifying the Constituent Structure of a Story

At present there are two models of story summarization in the psychological literature, one proposed by Rumelhart (1975; 1977) and one proposed by van Dijk and Kintsch (Kintsch & van Dijk, 1978; van Dijk & Kintsch, 1977). Both models, which have been developed to describe adult performance, assume that the summarizer knows about the constituent structure of stories and uses that knowledge to guide the operations required to reduce a complete story to a summary. In Rumelhart's model, the probability of including the information from a given node in a summary increases as a function of the height of the node in the tree structure and as a function of the number of lower level nodes that it subsumes. In van Dijk and Kintsch's model, the information to be included in a summary is determined by macrorules (processes of deletion, generalization, and integration) that operate on the propositions of the input text to produce a macrostructure. The macrostructure consists of macropropositions, each of which represents the gist of a given portion of the original text. Knowledge about the constituent structure of stories influences the formation of the macrostructure in that each terminal constituent in a story is assumed to be represented by at least one macroproposition.

As illustrated by the differences between these two models, there are disagreements about the precise role that a story schema plays in summarization. However, proponents of different story grammars do seem to agree that knowledge about the constituent structure of stories plays either a direct (Bower, 1976; Rumelhart, 1977; Thorndyke, 1977) or indirect (Johnson & Mandler, 1980; Kintsch & van Dijk, 1978; van Dijk & Kintsch, 1977) role in the selection of the information to be represented in a summary. Without a story schema, processes of selection would have to proceed in a "bottom-up" fashion, based entirely on the specific content of a text and whatever cues to relevance are explicitly provided by the author (e.g., headings or underlining in a written text, vocal stress, or phrases such as "most important," or "in summary").

A growing body of evidence suggests that children develop at least a rudimentary story schema by four of five years of age, if not earlier. One major line of evidence contributing to this argument comes from studies that compare younger and older subjects' recall of canonical and noncanonical stories (Glenn, 1978; Mandler, 1978; Mandler & DeForest, 1979; Stein & Glenn, 1977b). The reasoning underlying these studies is that if subjects of different ages use a common schema to guide comprehension and retrieval, departures from canonical form should lead to similar difficulties for both older and younger subjects. The results obtained to date support this argument, and there is even some evidence (cf. Mandler, in press) suggesting that children may actually be more dependent on a canonical schema than adults are. For example, Mandler (1978) asked second-, fourth-, and sixth-grade children, and adults, to recall simple, two-episode stories in which nodes were presented in either canonical or noncanonical orders. When recalling the noncanonical stories, subjects of all ages tended to restore the nodes to the canonical order, rather than maintaining the presented order. Such reorderings were most prevalent in the younger age groups, suggesting that the children were less able to use a retrieval strategy other than the one provided by the story schema. In addition, distortions of content occurred more often in recall of noncanonical stories for all age groups. Similar results have been reported by Glenn (1978) and Mandler and DeForest (1979).

Additional evidence for the role of a story schema in children's recall has been provided by Stein and Glenn (1977b). In their study, children in the first and fifth grades were told either canonical stories, which had no deletions, or stories in which one constituent (Beginning, Complex Reaction, Attempt, Outcome, or Ending) had been deleted.[3] Deletion of the Beginning (for both age groups) or the Outcome (for the first graders) led to significantly poorer recall of the remaining constituents, relative to recall of canonical stories. The children also made more additions in recall after hearing stories with Beginning-, Attempt-, or Outcome-deletions than after hearing canonical stories, and the majority of the additions represented the structural category of the deleted information. Reaction-deletions did not significantly affect performance, a result consistent with the transformational rules proposed by Johnson and Mandler (1980). However, the failure of the children to generate Endings when those were deleted is not consistent with predictions based on any of the current grammars. It is possible that children have yet to develop strong expectations about the occurrence of Endings. An alternative possibility is that Endings are deletable in a wider range of circumstances than has previously been proposed; this interpretation would be consistent with the finding that Endings, like Reactions, are often more poorly recalled than other constituents, even by adults (Mandler & Johnson, 1977; Mandler, 1978; Glenn, 1978).

A second line of evidence for the position that children are influenced by the structure of a story comes from studies indicating that the selection of information in children's recall reflects the organization of a given story, rather than simple primacy or recency effects or an idiosyncratic sample of statements from the story. Both children and adults are most likely to recall the Setting, Beginning, Attempt, and Outcome of a story and are least likely to recall Reactions and Endings (Glenn, 1978; Mandler, 1978; Mandler & Johnson, 1977; Stein & Glenn, 1979).[4] Furthermore, this pattern recurs in successive episodes in stories

---

[3]To facilitate comparisons of studies, the category names from the Stein and Glenn (1979) grammar have been replaced with corresponding category names from the Johnson and Mandler (1980) grammar.

[4]This pattern of recall is not assumed to be invariant across stories. For example, Goals should be better recalled if they are not inferable from the Beginning and Attempt (cf. Johnson & Mandler,

with two or more coordinate episodes (Mandler, 1978), suggesting that episodes are treated as higher level organizational units by both children and adults.

A third type of evidence for children's knowledge of story structure comes from studies of the stories that children generate. Botvin and Sutton-Smith (1977) report that the majority of 3- and 4-year olds generate "stories" with no clear structure. By four years of age, however, at least some children generate stories with "one nuclear dyad" (e.g., villainy + villainy nullified), and by age five, the majority of children add other plot elements. Stein and Glenn (1977a), using a different structural analysis (Stein & Glenn, 1979), report similar results. Although nearly half of the stories generated by the 5-year-olds in their study either lacked structure entirely or were simple descriptive sequences, a number of the children in this age group did generate stories that had the outline of a simple episode. By the fifth grade, descriptive sequences were generated much less frequently than complete episodes; and when they did occur, they were most often used as a constituent (e.g., the Setting) within a larger structure.

The results of generation studies should probably be taken as a conservative estimate of children's knowledge about story structure, given the processing demands of a story generation task (Mandler, in press). Four-year-olds, for example, in spite of what appers to be a limited ability to generate stories, can recall two-episode stories accurately and with few sequencing errors, even when the episodes represent a type of embedded structure that is generated only by considerably older children (Johnson & Mandel, 1980).

Overall, the investigations of children's recall of well- and ill-formed stories suggest that, by the age of four or five, children have a story schema that has developed sufficiently to guide encoding and retrieval of stories with a variety of types of episodic structure. Summarization, however, may require more deliberate use of a story schema than recall; and children's use of a story schema may be more limited when deliberate, rather than automatic, processing is required. As noted above, children have difficulty retrieving stories presented in a noncanonical order (Mandler, 1978; Mandler & DeForest, 1979), a task that may well require conscious and somewhat flexible use of a story schema—perhaps noting that the input order is a particular transformation of the canonical order and then using that knowledge to control the application of subsequent retrieval processes. Similarly, the story generation task may require deliberate use of a story schema, and here, too, children's performance lags behind their performance in story recall. Finally, as will be seen below, identifying a subset of information within a larger representation and then reorganizing that information so that it is expressed concisely may be aspects of summarization that require deliberate rather than automatic use of knowledge about the structure of stories.

1980). The point is simply that, for a *given* set of stories, children and adults are likely to represent the same constituents, a result that would not be expected if their methods of organizing the information in the stories were dissimilar.

Remembering the Information in a Story

The importance of memory in summarization depends, to some extent, on when the information to be included in a summary is identified and organized for retrieval. Van Dijk and Kintsch (Kintsch & van Dkjk 1978; van Dijk & Kintsch 1977) have suggested that summaries are based on macropropositions that are automatically generated during comprehension. If so, children would only need to remember specific story propositions long enough during encoding to generate the appropriate macropropositions; remembering the set of macropropositions would be sufficient for summarization. Similarly, given Rumelhart's (1977) model, children would only need to access the higher level nodes of a story in order to generate a summary. Because the constituent structure of a story is identified during comprehension and higher level nodes are assumed to be the most accessible, memory for the story as a whole would presumably not play a major role in summarization. If, however, the processing assumptions of these models do not apply to children (or adults), the ability to summarize could be influenced by the ability to establish and maintain a well-integrated representation of the specific states and events in a story.

As noted earlier, the literature on children's memory for stories indicates that the *patterns* of recall of younger and older children are qualitatively similar. However, the *amount* recalled from a story increases with age (Glenn, 1978; Mandler, 1978; Mandler & Johnson, 1977; Stein & Glenn, 1977b, 1979), and children's lesser recall could adversely affect summarization in at least two ways. First, to the extent that children remember less of a story, they may simply have fewer options for accomplishing additional reduction when asked to summarize rather than recall. Deletion, for example, may be one of the simplest ways to condense information, but it is only appropriate if one's representation includes nonessential information. Second, children's lesser recall may indicate a less integrated representation of the information in a story. This interpretation would be consistent with the finding that younger children tend to generate fewer inferences when they listen to a story (cf. Omanson et al., 1978), although the qualitative similarities argue that children's representations can hardly be considered to *lack* integration.

Limitations in younger children's short-term, or working, memory could also contribute to the difficulty of summarization. Numerous studies have indicated that the number of items that can be maintained in working memory typically increases with age (cf., Rohwer & Dempster, 1977). Whether the developmental differences are properly conceptualized as reflecting differences in capacity, organizational ability, or familiarity with the type of material to be remembered is a point of current debate (cf. Chi, 1978), but one that does not affect the present argument. All three positions predict that younger children are likely to have more trouble than older children and adults in tasks that require maintaining and transforming information about stories in short-term memory. Such maintenance plays an important role in Kintsch and van Dijk's (1978) model of the generation of macropropositions and is also likely to be important in controlling the retrieval of information in a summary.

Selecting the Information to be Represented in a Summary

Much of the research on the selection of information to be represented in gist recall and summarization is complicated by the lack of a clear distinction between what is important and what needs to be stated explicitly. Information that is not represented explicitly is often assumed to have been relegated to the realm of the unimportant. However, as indicated by some of the research to be considered here, even important information may be omitted from recall or a summary if it can be readily inferred. In the present section, the problems to be considered are how the important parts of a story might be identified and whether or not children and adults make similar judgments of importance. The problem of deciding what needs to be represented explicitly and what can be left for the reader or listener to infer will be deferred until the next section.

Most attempts to characterize the importance of units within a text have been based on the notion that more important units either have more connections with other units or occur at higher levels in a hierarchical representation of the organization of the text. There is, however, no general agreement about the most appropriate criteria for assessing connectivity or hierarchical levels. Connectivity can be based on relatively simple measures, such as argument repetition (Kintsch, 1974), or on more complex measures, such as the number of causal links between units (Graesser, Robertson, Lovelace, & Swinehart, 1980). Similarly, characterizations of hierarchical structure range from the analyses of episodic structure found in story grammars to analyses based on relations among quite general rhetorical predicates such as "attribution," "explanation," "analogy," or "manner" (Meyer, 1975).

Even within the analyses based on story grammars, the role of constituent structure in summarization has, as noted earlier, been construed in rather different ways, although it is generally assumed that a summary of a story should preserve some degree of narrative structure. Kintsch and van Dijk (1978) have suggested that constituent structure serves as a general guide for processes of selection and condensation. In their characterization of an ideal summary, each story constituent is represented by at least one proposition, with the type of constituent constraining the type of information to be represented. For example, propositions that represent the Setting generally include stative information, those representing the Resolution include at least some reference to action, etc. In contrast, Bower (1976), Rumelhart (1977), and Thorndyke (1977) have suggested that the constitutent structure of a story represents importance more directly. In particular, they have argued that the importance of a constituent increases as one moves to higher levels in the hierarchical representation.

The available data on recall and summarization by adults do not discriminate between these two roles for constituent structure. Although preliminary evidence has been provided to support both analyses (e.g., Bower, 1976; Kintsch, Mandel, & Kozminsky, 1977; Rumelhart, 1977; Thorndyke, 1977; Van Dijk & Kintsch, 1977), no attempt to assess their relative merits has been made; and the number of stories to which the models have been applied is still relatively small. Also, as Johnson and Mandler (1980) have noted, decisions about the positioning of episodes in multiepisode stories have not consistently been independent of *intuitions* about their relative importance, thus precluding a clear test of the prediction that constituent height and importance are directly correlated.

There is a need not only for additional empirical data concerning the role of constituent structure in the selection of information in a summary, but also for more explicit theoretical analyses. This is particularly apparent when one examines the claim that higher level constituents are both more accessible *and* more important than lower level constituents. The "level" of a given node has typically been determined by counting the number of nodes that dominate it; i.e., a node dominated by fewer other nodes is considered to be at a higher level. Greater *accessibility* of higher level nodes can be accounted for by postulating that retrieval proceeds in a "top-down" fashion, leading to a higher probability of retrieving nodes closer to the top of the hierarchy. However, there does not seem to be an equally straightforward way to explain a relationship between this measure of constituent height and *importance*.

Within the hierarchical representation of a story, two (or more) nodes that can be grouped together (and thus are subsumed by a higher level constituent) occupy a lower position than nodes that are not grouped. Although one can find branches within which such differences in levels reflect a semantic principle that might be related to importance (e.g., successive subordination of goals within an Attempt node that includes lower level Developments), there does not seem to be a consistent principle that holds throughout the hierarchy (e.g., a principle to explain why a Beginning Event should be more or less important than an Attempt event or to explain why the nodes of an embedded Episode should be less important than the nodes of the matrix Episode that subsumes them). It may turn out to be the case that relationships between "levels" and importance can be accounted for in terms of factors that are often, but not necessarily, associated with differences in hierarchical level. Such factors might include differences between given and new information (Cirilo & Foss, 1980), the number of other nodes to which a given node is connected, and the nature of causal or temporal relationships (e.g., whether a particular node represents a cause or an effect).

Investigations of the extent to which children can identify the important parts of a story have focused on agreement within and between age groups in judgments of importance (Brown & Smiley, 1977; Brown, Smiley, & Lawton, 1978; Stein & Glenn, 1979; Yussen et al., 1980) and on whether or not items that are judged to be important provide an adequate representation of the constituent structure of the story (Denhière & Le Ny, 1980; Yussen et al., 1980). Taken in conjunction with studies showing qualitatively similar patterns in children's and adults' recall, these studies suggest that even young children can identify the important parts of a story when the discrimination between more and less important information is controlled by automatic processes that guide comprehension or retrieval; however, the ability to make deliberate discriminations appears to develop more slowly.

In the study that provided the initial basis for this argument, Brown and Smiley (1977) examined the relationship between selectivity in recall and the development of the ability to make deliberate assessments of the importance of phrases within a story. On the basis of importance ratings provided by college students, they divided the "pause units" (roughly equivalent to verb-based propositions) in each of two multiepisode folktales into four levels of importance. They then examined the relationship between this initial set of ratings and both ratings and recall obtained from third, fifth, and seventh grade children and another group of college students. Their results indicated that only the college students provided ratings that increased significantly across each of the four initially defined levels of importance. The seventh graders' importance ratings separated the top and bottom levels of the original ratings from the middle two levels, which did not differ significantly; the fifth graders rated the most important items from the original set of ratings as being more important than the other three levels but did not discriminate among the lower three; and the third graders' importance ratings simply did not differ as a function of the four original levels of importance. In addition, Brown and Smiley (1977) noted that there seemed to be relatively little agreement *among* the youngest children in their judgments of importance.

In contrast, striking similarities among age groups emerged in recall. For subjects in all four age groups, recall of story units increased across the four levels of importance that were established on the basis of the initial adult ratings, and there was no significant interaction between age and importance level. The same relationship between judgments and recall was observed in a subsequent study with fifth and seventh grade children and adults (Brown et al., 1978).[5]

Similar results have been reported by Yussen et al. (1980). On the basis of work by Brown and Smiley (1977) and Stein and Glenn (1979), Yussen et al. predicted that the tendency to identify the Beginning, Attempt, and Outcome as the three most critical constituents in a story would increase with age. To test their hypothesis, they presented adults and second-, fourth-, and sixth-grade

---

[5]Smiley, Oakley, Worthen, Campione, and Brown (1977) reported that the recall of first graders and of older children who were poor readers was less strongly correlated with adult judgments of importance. Smiley et al. discuss the difference between their results and Brown and Smiley's (1977) results in terms of lesser sensitivity to importance on the part of younger children and poor readers. However, the overall level of recall for these two groups was so low that the diminished relationship between recall and importance may have resulted from floor effects.

children with one-episode stories that were divided into six constituents: Setting, Beginning, Complex Reaction, Attempt, Outcome, and Ending. For half of the stories, the children were asked to pick the three most "important" constituents. For the other half they were asked to pick the three most "critical" constituents, where critical constituents were defined as those that would be needed to communicate a shortened version of the story to someone else.

As expected, the percentage of subjects who chose the Beginning, Attempt, and Outcome as the three most critical constituents increased with age, from 6% for the second graders to 50% for the adults. A similar developmental trend was observed for judgments of importance, although there were indications that the two types of judgment differed; e.g., only 27% of the adults chose the Beginning, Attempt, and Outcome as the three most *important* constituents. Although Yussen et al. do not discuss the choices subjects made when they departed from the Beginning-Attempt-Outcome selection, the results of other studies indicate that Goals are often judged to be important, even though they are less frequently recalled than other constituents (Mandler, Johnson, & DeForest, 1976; Stein & Glenn, 1979).

In a second study, second- and fifth-grade children were asked both to recall stories and to select critical constituents. The selection of critical constituents replicated the results of the first experiment, and the relationship between recall and critical-constituent selections was congruent with the relationship between recall and importance judgments reported by Brown and Smiley (1977). Only the fifth graders exceeded chance in the selection of the Beginning, Attempt, and Outcome as the most critical constituents; but both second and fifth graders were more likely to recall the Beginning, Attempt, and Outcome (taken as a set) than the Setting, Complex Reaction, and Ending.

On the other hand, results obtained by Denhière and Le Ny (1980) and Stein and Glenn (1979) suggest that children between five and eight years of age can make judgments that are not entirely unreasonable. In Denhière and Le Ny's study, 8- and 11-year-old children and adults were presented with one-episode stories. The stories, which were parsed using an analysis similar to that proposed by van Dijk and Kintsch (1977), were longer than the stories used by Yussen et al., but shorter than those used by Brown and Smiley. The children were first asked to pick the eight sentences that were the most important. The instructions were comparable to the "critical-item" instructions used by Yussen et al. but placed greater emphasis on the importance of sampling across the story as a whole. The children were then asked to select the eight *least* important sentences.

Even the 8-year-olds seemed able to differentiate between more and less important information; an analysis of the rank orderings of the 22 sentences in each story in terms of the percentage of subjects who assigned each sentence to the most or least important groupings revealed significant correlations between all pairs of age groups. However, the degree of agreement between the 11-year-olds and the adults was substantially greater than the agreement between the 8-year-olds and either of the two older groups; and the extent to which the "important" sentences adequately represented the constitutent structure of the stories increased with age. Within the set of sentences identified as *most* important by at least half of the subjects in each age group, the adults represented all five of the story constituents (Exposition, Initial Situation, Complication, Resolution, and Evaluation), and the 11-year-olds represented all except Evaluation. In contrast, the 8-year-olds tended to overrepresent the initial portion of the story (Exposition and Initial Situation) and only represented "the most remarkable actions or events of the complication or resolution [Denhière & Le Ny, 1980, p. 157]."

In spite of the younger children's failure to represent the overall organization of the story, the sentences they chose *within* the initial portion seem rather reasonable, at least in the one example provided. In the following text, which contains the first nine sentences of the story, the sentences in italics are those that were selected by at least half of the 8-year-olds.

There was a giant. It was a long time ago. The giant was a good one. *The giant was pleased to help poor people.* One day the giant was walking in the forest. *The giant saw a poor old woman.* The poor old woman was gathering some dead wood. *The giant decided to help the poor old woman* [Denhière & Le Ny, 1980, p. 154, italics added].

It is possible that the younger children's choices would have provided a more adequate representation of the overall structure of the story if the length constraint had been less severe. Given the eight-sentence limit, the children may simply have run out of choices to make, especially if, as appears to be the case, they followed the schematic order and processed the story sequentially rather than moving back and forth within the story.

Stein and Glenn (1979) examined judgments of importance made by first and fifth graders on the basis of remembered information. After hearing stories roughly comparable in length and complexity to those used by Denhière and Le Ny (1980), the children were asked to tell the experimenter "the one thing that happened in the story that was the most important thing to remember [p. 103];" they were then asked to identify the second and third most important things that happened.

If the data from the three judgments are combined, the similarities in the performance of the two age groups are more striking than the differences. In terms of the proportions of judgments falling into each story category, the first graders generated the following order, from most to least important:[6] Outcome >

---

[6]These orderings were obtained by adding the proportion of judgments in each category across the three separate judgments reported by Stein and Glenn (1979); summed proportions that differed by less than 0.05 have been joined by "&," but the order within such pairs has been preserved.

Complex Reaction > Attempt & Beginning > Ending & Minor Setting. The corresponding order for the fifth graders was: Complex Reaction > Outcome > Attempt > Beginning > Ending > Minor Setting. The major difference between the two age groups was the fifth graders' attribution of greater importance to the Complex Reaction than the Outcome, in contrast to the first graders' selection of the Outcome as more important. Also, the occurrence of fewer ties in the judgments made by fifth graders suggests that there may have been somewhat greater agreement among the older children.

As noted earlier, the studies comparing children's ability to recall the gist of a story with their ability to identify important elements when confronted with the story as a whole suggest that the latter ability develops more slowly than the former. At present the most interesting characterization of the difference between the two abilities is that recall of the gist of a story reflects relatively automatic processes that operate during comprehension, retrieval, or both, whereas the identification of important elements when given the entire text of a story requires the deliberate application of the same or similar processes (cf. Brown & DeLoache, 1978; Brown & Smiley, 1977; Denhière & Le Ny, 1980).

To the extent that summarization requires deliberate reduction, the data on importance judgments suggest that younger children may encounter a source of difficulty. However, the discrepancies among the various studies in the quality of performance of children below the age of twelve indicate that such difficulties may be influenced by the choice of stimuli and procedures, a point that has also been made by Brown and her colleagues (cf. Brown & DeLoache, 1978; Brown & Smiley, 1978; Brown et al., 1978). For example, in Stein and Glenn's (1979) study, where relatively good agreement between younger and older children was obtained, judgments were based on memory. Consequently, many of the differentiations between more and less important information may have taken place automatically during encoding, and subsequent differentiations among items in memory may have been facilitated by their differential accessibility. Indeed, Stein and Glenn noted that items in the top one-third of recall (assessed in an earlier experiment in which children of the same ages recalled the same stories) accounted for 75% of the first graders' choices in the importance-judgments task; this figure was reduced to 60% for the fifth graders, suggesting that the younger children may have been influenced by the differential accessibility of items to a greater extent than the older children.

In comparing Brown and Smiley's (1977) study with Denhière and Le Ny's (1980) study, the most obvious difference is that Denhière and Le Ny's stories were considerably shorter and appear to have represented a simpler episodic structure. Current work in my laboratory suggests that judgments of importance are influenced by the nature of the stories that are used. We presented adults and third- and sixth-grade children with two types of stories, one with a simple coordinate structure and one with an embedded structure. Subjects judged the importance of the terminal constituents in each story by ranking them from most to least important. Agreement both within and between age groups was substantially greater for the stories with the coordinate structure, even though the two types of stories were comparable in length and general content (Johnson, Coburn, & Mandel, in preparation).[7]

On the other hand, the poor performance of the second graders in Yussen et al.'s (1980) study is not consistent with explanations based on the difficulty of judging long or complex stories. However, stories that are very short may be as problematic as stories that are very long. In the latter case, children may be overwhelmed by the number of units to be evaluated, whereas in the former case they may be overwhelmed by the difficulty of further reducing a story that already approaches the minimum number of elements needed for well-formedness. In addition, Yussen et al.'s use of an all-or-none measure based on an a priori notion of what should be considered important (percentage of subjects choosing the Beginning, Attempt, and Outcome) may have obscured regularities in the performance of younger subjects.

Being Concise and Coherent

Given stories in which units can be clearly divided into those that are important and those that are unimportant, simply being able to identify and delete unimportant information provides a basis for accomplishing reduction in a summary. However, when a constraint to be particularly concise is imposed or when most or all of the information in a story is important, it becomes essential that the summarizer be able to perform transformations *within* the subset of information that has been identified as important. One general method for accomplishing additional reduction is simply to delete inferable information. Another is to replace an existing unit or units (words, propositions, or nodes) with a new statement that compresses the original information; for example, one can move to a less detailed level of representation (cf. van Dijk, 1977a) or combine related pieces of information by using operations that, at the level of discourse, often correspond to sentence-level transformations such as ellipsis, deletion under identity, and pronominalization. In using either type of transformation, deletion or replacement, the problem for the summarizer is to insure that the resulting representation preserves the essential features of the original text at whatever level of reduction is appropriate for the purpose of the summary.

Deleting inferable information is, in principle, straightforward. Given two (or more) related propositions or other units within a story, A and B, if A can be inferred from B but B cannot be inferred from A, delete A and state B. For

---

[7]The studies by Brown and Smiley (1977) and Denhière and Le Ny (1980) also differed in the procedures used to elicit choices. Brown and Smiley's subjects began by identifying the *least* important units, whereas Denhière and Le Ny's subjects identified the *most* important units first. The latter procedure seems, on intuitive grounds, to be a more natural way to identify the gist of a story. However, Brown et al. (1978) found that fifth graders' judgments were less differentiated than their recall even when the judgment task simply required identification of the *most* important units.

example, given the two propositions, *Once there was a rabbit* and *One day the rabbit was chased by a fox,* one can delete the first because the rabbit's having been chased by the fox entails the rabbit's having once existed. However, complications can arise when *B* is compatible with, but does not strictly imply *A,* a situation considerably more common than the one in which *A* can be unambiguously recovered from *B* (van Dijk, 1977a).

Similar problems arise when replacement transformations are used. Some replacements preserve all of the information in the original text, but most do not. Presumably, decisions about which deletions and replacements are most appropriate in a given summary depend on factors such as the extent to which the summarizer wants the listener to be able to reconstruct various aspects of the story, the summarizer's ability to understand how different transformations might affect the listener's reconstruction, and the difficulty of performing certain transformations, given the nature of the text to be summarized and the summarizer's abilities.

There are a number of reasons to expect that being concise without being incoherent may pose problems for young children. First, they may lack either the general or linguistic knowledge needed to perform appropriate transformations. For example, some summary statements (e.g., certain forms of ellipsis) require syntactic constructions over which younger children may have only marginal control, while others (e.g., generalizations) require specific knowledge about the meanings of words and about ways to categorize objects and events. Second, even when children are capable of making appropriate transformations, they may fail to do so if they lack knowledge about whether and when such transformations ought to be applied. Third, children's use of transformations may be affected by the extent to which other task demands (e.g., keeping track of what has already been said and retrieving additional information) compete for available processing resources (cf. Shatz, 1977). Although these problems are likely to be most pronounced in young children, older children and adults may also have trouble meeting the often conflicting demands of being concise and maintaining the important elements of a story in a coherent form.

The developmental literature provides only indirect evidence about the extent to which children are likely to be able to use the types of transformations described above in generating summaries. Danner (1976), for example, investigated children's identification of subtopics in descriptive paragraphs. He presented second, fourth, and sixth graders with two short paragraphs about animals, each of which included three subtopics: the appearance of the animal (fox or polar bear), its habitat, and its eating habits. For example, in the paragraph about the fox, the following four sentences described its appearance. "The fox looks like a dog. He has a long nose. His tail hangs down. He is red [p. 175]."

As part of a series of tasks, the children were asked to form groups of sentences that "tell about the same thing." The percentage of children who grouped the sentences in each paragraph in terms of the three subtopics increased with age, with the fourth and sixth graders performing substantially better than the second graders. However, when the *experimenter* subsequently grouped the sentences by subtopic and asked the children to identify "the one thing . . . these four sentences tell you about the fox/polar bear [p. 176]," all of the children produced appropriate generalizations (e.g., "They describe him" or "They tell what he looks like") for at least four of the six subtopics.

Less is known about the conditions under which children spontaneously produce generalizations of the type elicited by Danner. The majority of the youngest children in his study failed to group sentences in terms of the taxonomy underlying the descriptions, although they were capable of recognizing and labeling the categories when the relevant groupings had been pointed out. This pattern of results is strikingly similar to that observed when children process categorized word lists. Younger children often fail to utilize taxonomic principles in processing lists of words even when they understand the classification systems. Both sets of results suggest that children may fail to use taxonomic classifications for the purpose of generalization and reduction in a summarization task.

On the other hand, Mandler (1978, 1979, in press) has argued that the type of schematic organization found in stories may be more accessible to young children than taxonomic organizations. Even preschoolers seem to represent "scripts" (e.g., going to McDonald's), which have a schematic organization similar to stories, in terms of what Schank and Abelson (1977) have called "main conceptualizations." When asked to describe the events in a typical school day, for example, preschoolers provide descriptions at the level of "taking a nap" rather than "being told it's time to take a nap, getting my nap rug, putting it on the floor, lying down, and closing my eyes" (Nelson, 1978; Nelson & Gruendel, 1979). Although this tendency to characterize event sequences in terms of major rather than subsidiary actions may be automatic rather than deliberate, it indicates that even very young children are capable of spontaneously generating some types of higher level descriptions.

Perhaps because of the relatively recent emergence of interest in the basic question of whether or not children can *make* various types of inferences (cf. Paris & Lindauer, 1977; Omanson et al., 1978), we know relatively little about their ability to determine whether or not stating a given piece of information will enable *someone else* to make a particular inference. The evidence that is available suggests, not surprisingly, that the ability to make such judgments increases with age. Hildyard and Olson (1978), for example, found that sixth graders were better able than fourth graders to distinguish between inferences that were necessarily true (e.g., transitive inferences) and inferences that were merely plausible.

In addition, much of the work on referential communication (see Glucksberg, Kraus, & Higgins, 1975, for a review) would lead one to predict that when young children summarize, they are likely to make deletions and replacements that would make it difficult for a listener to follow the basic line of a story. Although egocentrism does not seem to be an inevitable characteristic of young children's communications (cf. Nelson & Gruendel, 1979; Shatz, 1977; Shatz & Gelman, 1973), the conditions that facilitate nonegocentric communication may not be present in summarization tasks. Nelson & Gruendel (1979) have argued that children's conversations are less egocentric when the topic is derived from a shared knowledge base, and Shatz (1977) has argued that egocentrism is less likely to be observed when the processing demands of other aspects of a communication task are not excessive. However, in many summarization tasks, the story (or other material to be summarized) cannot be assumed to be familiar to the recipient of the summary, and the processing demands of producing appropriate transformations are likely to be relatively high for young children, even if they understand the material to be summarized.

On the other hand, even unfamiliar stories often have subsections that are based on scripts or other reasonably familiar event sequences, and children may be able to generate appropriate reductions based on their existing characterizations of such sequences. In addition, the overall structure of a story may serve as a guide to selection and reduction in a summary, especially if children summarize on the basis of remembered information and the amount of required reduction is not excessive.

CHILDREN'S SUMMARIZATION: AN EXPLORATORY STUDY

In the preceding section, six abilities that seem essential for summarization were considered: 1) comprehending the individual propositions of a story; 2) establishing connections between propositions; 3) identifying the constituent structure of the story; 4) remembering the information in the story; 5) selecting the information to be represented in the summary; and 6) formulating a concise but coherent representation of that information.

The available evidence suggests that the first four skills have undergone substantial development by the time children enter elementary school. There are, however, quantitative improvements with age, and older subjects are better able to process stories that depart from a canonical format. Both factors may contribute to developmental differences in summarization, because they suggest that young children may be operating closer to the limits of their available processing resources than older children and adults. If summarization requires abilities in addition to those involved in comprehension and recall, younger children may simply have fewer remaining resources to deploy. In addition, the ability to produce noncanonical formats may be important in using summarization techniques that involve deleting, combining, or reordering constituents.

The evidence about developmental differences in the ability to identify the information to be represented in a summary and the ability to state it concisely and coherently is less clear-cut. Although both younger and older subjects are more likely to *recall* important material, the ability to make explicit importance judgments that are not based on memory appears to develop more slowly (Brown & Smiley, 1977, 1978; Denhière & Le Ny, 1980; Yussen, et al., 1980). The relevance of this finding depends on the extent to which the content of a summary reflects automatic processes that occur during comprehension (cf. van Dijk & Kintsch, 1977) or retrieval rather than deliberate judgments of importance. Finally, although the available evidence is indirect, the ability to condense the information in a story while maintaining coherence seems likely to be a relatively late development. Again, however, developmental differences may depend on the extent to which processes of condensation and generalization result from automatic rather than deliberate processes.

In the present study, children in the first, third, and fifth grades, and adults were asked both to recall and to summarize stories. The major goals of the research were: 1) to determine whether or not young children are *able* to summarize; 2) to examine the relationship between the constitutent structure of a story and the selection of information in summaries; and 3) to determine whether or not children and adults use similar methods to accomplish reduction in their summaries. Because total failure by younger subjects could be attributed to factors other than a general inability to summarize (e.g., failure to understand the instructions or difficulty remembering the stories), the stimuli and procedures were intended to maximize the probability that even the youngest children would achieve at least partial success.

Two stories were used, the Little Rabbit and the Three Little Pigs (see Tables 10.2 and 10.3 and Figures 10.1 and 10.2). The Little Rabbit was included as an instance of an unfamiliar story. Pilot work with adults had indicated that it could be summarized in a number of different ways, ranging from simple deletion of nodes, propositions or words, to generalizations and relatively complex combinations of information from different nodes. The Three Little Pigs was included to provide a relatively long story in which a great deal of reduction is possible. A familiar story was used to minimize the possibility that the younger children would have difficulty remembering the material to be summarized. As with the story of the Little Rabbit, the story of the Three Little Pigs can be summarized in a number of different ways.

A practice task was used to explain the difference between recall and summarization. Subjects were presented with a long, familiar story—Goldilocks and the Three Bears—and were then asked to retell the story as completely as possible. Following recall, subjects were given instructions for summarization that stressed the difference between telling the whole story and just telling "about" the story. In addition, an example of a summary of the story was provided. Using an example to clarify the instructions might appear to introduce the risk of teaching an otherwise naive subject *how* to summarize. However, it seemed unlikely that a subject who completely lacked summarization skills prior to the example would possess the analytic skills needed to abstract the summarization principles embodied in the example and then transfer them to other stories. At any rate, such a possibility seemed a lesser and less likely evil than the possibility that the younger children would not understand the difference between recall and summarization instructions without a concrete example.

Method

Subjects. The subjects were 72 children from a predominantly middle-class public school in San Diego and 20 college students from introductory psychology classes at the University of California. Approximately equal numbers of male and female subjects were tested; all subjects were native English speakers. The analyses reported here are based on data obtained from 75 of the 92 subjects, 18 first grade children (mean age = 7;1), 18 third grade children (mean age = 8;11), 19 fifth grade children (mean age = 11;1) and 20 college students (mean age = 19;7).[8]

Stimuli. The story of the Three Little Pigs (Pigs story) and the story of the Little Rabbit (Rabbit story) were used as the experimental stimuli that subjects were to recall and summarize. The version of the Pigs story was one that pilot work had indicated was a close approximation to versions familiar to the subjects. The story of Goldilocks and the Three Bears (Bears story) and a summary of that story were used to explain the recall and summary tasks. The summary of the Bears story (see Appendix A) was based on summaries produced by adult pilot subjects and was designed to represent a variety of summarization techniques (deletion, generalization, combinations of both adjacent and nonadjacent story propositions). All of the stimuli were tape recorded to insure that approximately equal emphasis was given to each proposition during presentation. Subjects were individually tested, and their responses were tape recorded and later transcribed.

Design and procedure. The basic design included factors of age (first, third, and fifth grade, and adult), task (recall, first summary, final summary), task order (whether subjects recalled a story first and then summarized it or summa-

---

[8]The original design called for 20 subjects per age group. Because pilot testing indicated that many of the first graders were having difficulty with summarization, a decision was made to identify and replace first graders who simply recalled one or both stories when asked to summarize. Three first graders were identified as nonsummarizers during the course of the experiment and were replaced. Two additional first graders were dropped because they refused to attempt either the first or second summary of one of the two stories. Three subjects (two first graders and one fifth grader) were replaced for reasons unrelated to the experimental tasks (e.g., mechanical failures). The remaining subject losses are explained in the text.

rized and then recalled), and story order (whether the Rabbit or Pigs story was presented first). Initially, five subjects within each grade level were randomly assigned to each of the task order x story order cells, with the restriction that the number of subjects of each sex be approximately balanced. Because subjects who did not summarize were excluded from the study, the final number of subjects in each of these cells was either four or five for each age group.

The Bears story and the Pigs story were selected because subjects could be expected to be familiar with them prior to the experiment. Consequently, all subjects were asked, prior to the presentation of each story, if they had ever heard it before. Four subjects (three first graders and one third grader) were replaced because they said they had not.

All subjects were told that they would hear stories played on the tape recorder and that they should try to remember them. Subjects were told that they would start with a "practice" story, Goldilocks and the Three Bears. After the story was presented, subjects were given the following recall instructions:

> Ok, pretend that you're on your way home from school with a friend who has never heard the story Goldilocks and the Three Bears. They would like to hear it, and you have plenty of time. So you tell the whole story. Ok? You have lots of time. Be sure to tell your friend everything you remember, the whole story, as much as you can like what you just heard on the tape recorder.

After subjects had recalled the Bears story, the following instructions were given to explain the summary task:

> Ok, that was really good. But now I want you to do something different. Pretend again that you're on your way home from school with a friend who has never heard the story Goldilocks and the Three Bears. They would like to hear it, but you don't have time to tell them the whole story. So you just tell them what the story was about. Ok? You don't have much time. So you'll have to make the story shorter. Don't tell your friend every thing you remember. Just tell them what the story was about.

Following the last line of the instructions, the experimenter offered to provide an example of "how you could tell someone *about* Goldilocks and the Three Bears without telling them the whole story." The sample summary was then presented.

Subjects then heard either the Rabbit or Pigs story and were asked to recall it and then summarize it (in the recall-first condition) or to summarize and then recall (in the summarize-first condition); the instructions for recall and summarization were the same as those used for the Bears story. After both tasks had been completed for the first story, the second story was presented; subjects performed the recall and summary tasks in the same order as for the first story.

After subjects had recalled and summarized the second story, they were asked to produce a shortest possible summary for each story. The following instructions were used:

> Ok, now I want you to think about the story of the Little Rabbit/Three Little Pigs again. What's the shortest possible way to tell about that story? Pretend that you're with a friend who has never heard the story and you have to tell them about the story in the very shortest way that you can think of. What would you say to tell someone about the story of the Little Rabbit/Three Little Pigs in the very shortest way that you can?

Scoring procedures. The text of each recall or summary protocol was initially divided into verb-based statements. A "statement" was defined as a surface structure phrase or clause that contained one main verb and its arguments. (The term "statement" rather than "proposition" will be used to avoid confusion with references to the propositions in the original text of the story.) For a small subclass of verbs (primarily *want, decide, see, need, say, try, think,* and *allow*) that take sentential arguments, both the matrix statement and its argument were considered to be single statement.

The analyses of the structure of each of the two stories (see Figures 10.1 and 10.2) provided the basis for characterizing the content and organization of the protocols. Two judges jointly classified each statement in terms of whether or not it *explicitly* represented information derived from one or more of the terminal nodes of the story. A two-level criterion was used in which a statement was classified as either a "definite" or an "ambiguous" representation of a node. Ambiguous classifications (which accounted for < 10% of all statements) came primarily from two sources: 1) true semantic ambiguities (e.g., saying that the first little pig "got" straw, which may or may not be intended to represent the Attempt in addition to the Outcome); and 2) "unmarked combinations," in which a given statement might have been intended to represent only one node but could also, given the context provided by a subsequent combination of nodes, have been intended to represent more than one node (e.g., saying "The wolf came and blew the first two pigs' houses down," which does not indicate that the wolf came to *both* houses as clearly as the statement "The wolf came to the first two pigs' houses and blew them down"). Preliminary analyses indicated that including the ambiguous classifications did not alter the general pattern of results. Consequently, the analyses reported below include both definite and ambiguous representations.

Each statement was also classified in terms of the method of representation that was used. This classification involved four basic categories: 1) representation of a single node by using propositions from the original story or additions that also referred to specific states and events; 2) representation of a single node by substituting a generalization for the original information; 3) representation of a node or set of nodes by noting that it was the same or similar to a node (or nodes) already represented; and 4) representation of more than one node by combining information from the nodes in a single statement. Examples of each of these categories and further classifications of combinations of nodes are presented in the discussion of the analyses of methods of representation.

Each statement or group of adjacent statements assigned to a given method of representation was then given a quality score to indicate the extent to which the original information in the story was maintained. The categories used in the quality coding are presented in the discussion of the analyses of the specificity and adequacy of representation of nodes.

Results and Discussion

Preliminary Considerations

Before presenting the main body of results, two preliminary aspects of the data need to be discussed. The first involves establishing the occurrence of even minimal summarization by subjects of different ages. The second involves the reclassification of the two summaries produced by each subject as "longer" and "shorter" rather than "first" and "final."

Summarizers and nonsummarizers. A preliminary examination of the recall and summary protocols was conducted to identify subjects who had completed all three of the experimental tasks (recall, first summary, and final summary), but were clearly not summarizing. This screening indicated that 22% of the first graders (5 out of 23), 10% of the third graders (2 out of 20), 5% of the fifth graders (1 out of 20), and none of the adults failed to meet a criterion of producing summaries for *both* stories that were shorter than their recall protocols.[9] This pattern of results provides at least a partial answer to the question of whether or not children can summarize stories. If one accepts the minimal criterion of reduction, relative to recall, as an indication of summarization, it appears that most first grade children are able to summarize. On the other hand, the percentage of subjects who accomplished at least some reduction in both summaries of the two stories increased with age.

Because the major analyses were intended to permit a comparison of recall and summarization across age groups, the "nonsummarizers" were excluded from all of the following analyses. Consequently, the age trends reported below

---

[9]The children who failed to accomplish reduction in at least one of the summary tasks had more trouble with the Rabbit story than with the Pigs story. Only two (both first graders) of the seven children who were excluded as "nonsummarizers" generated summaries of the Pigs story that were as long or longer than their recall protocols. The children's lesser tendency simply to recall the Pigs story when asked to summarize could be due either to its greater familiarity or to its greater length. The reason length may be relevant is that it is hard to recall all of a very long story without making an effort to do so. In contrast, with a comparatively short story, recall may require considerably less effort than summarization.

should be interpreted somewhat cautiously in that the results may tend to overestimate the *average* ability of younger children.

The problem of longer "shortest" summaries. The instructions for the final summaries emphasized telling about the story in the "shortest possible way." Nevertheless, a number of subjects, mostly children, produced final summaries that were actually longer (in terms of number of words) than their first summaries. In some cases, subjects produced a second summary that was essentially identical to their first summary, but with minor changes in wording that slightly increased the length of the second summary. In other cases, subjects seemed to be trying to repair first summaries that had been too short to make sense. Finally, some subjects attempted complex transformations in their final summaries, got into trouble, and then backtracked to repair the damage, ending up with a second summary that was actually longer than the first, even though an effort to comply with the instructions had been made.

The existence of longer "shortest" summaries posed potential interpretative problems, because the final summary task had been intended to provide information about the types of transformations that would occur when subjects condensed the story as much as possible. Consequently, the two summaries were reclassified on the basis of their actual length. A final (ostensibly shorter) summary was considered to be the longer of the two summaries if it exceeded the first summary in both the number of words used and the number of nodes represented. The use of this criterion restricted reassignments primarily to cases in which the first summary was a simple subset of the second. In the Rabbit story, such reassignments were made for four first graders, two third graders, and two fifth graders; the corresponding numbers for the Pigs story were four, one, and one. That none of the adults' final summaries met the reassignment criterion suggests that the adults may have been less likely to produce first summaries that were inappropriately reduced; adults were better able to remember their first summaries; or they were better able to find additional ways to accomplish reduction.

Quantitative and Qualitative Characteristics of Recall and Summarization

In the remainder of this section, the following characteristics of the recall and summary protocols will be considered: 1) their length in number of words; 2) the number and types of nodes explictly represented; 3) the extent to which subjects used methods other than deletion to transform the original text; 4) the extent to which subjects accurately preserved the information in the original text; and 5) the degree of correspondence between input and output order.

Unless otherwise noted, the data were analyzed using unequal-n analyses of variance with unweighted means. To avoid the positive bias introduced by heterogeneity of the covariance matrixes, tests of significance for within-subjects factors were made using the Greenhouse-Geisser adjustment for degrees of free-

TABLE 10.4
Mean Number of Words Used as a Function of Age and Task

	First Grade	Third Grade	Fifth Grade	Adult
Rabbit Story				
Recall	107	119	128	147
Longer Summary	66	76	80	72
Shorter Summary	52	61	64	46
Pigs Story				
Recall	311	372	425	536
Longer Summary	166	187	216	190
Shorter Summary	97	123	140	90

Note: Length of Rabbit Story = 147 words. Length of Pigs Story = 653 words.

dom (Keppel, 1973). The degrees of freedom for all effects that included age as a factor were 3 and 59; the degrees of freedom for all other effects were 1 and 59. Comparisons between pairs of means were done using Newman-Keuls tests with an alpha level of .05.[10]

Length of recall and summary protocols. The mean number of words used by each age group in recalling and summarizing the Rabbit and Pigs stories is shown in Table 10.4. The number of words used decreased as subjects moved from recall to the longer and shorter summaries: $F = 421.29, p < .001$ (Rabbit) and $F = 611.11, p < .001$ (Pigs). Although the difference between recall and the two summaries is partly a result of the exclusion of subjects whose summaries were longer than their recall, the average amount of reduction accomplished by each age group greatly exceeded the minimum criterion for inclusion in the study.

The main effect of age was reliable for both stories: $F = 3.12, p < .05$ (Rabbit) and $F = 6.16, p < .01$ (Pigs), but the differences among age groups changed markedly as a function of the type of task: $F = 10.99, p < .001$

---

[10]Task order and story order were included as factors in all of the analyses of variance. The only effect that emerged for both stories was a tendency for recall to be slightly longer, and for the summaries to be slightly shorter, when subjects recalled first rather than summarizing first. Across all of the analyses, there were only two interactions, both in the Rabbit story, of story or task order with age: 1) an age-by-story order interaction in the analysis of the total number of nodes represented and 2) an age-by-story order-by-quality interaction in the analysis of the quality of representation of nodes. Both interactions were small; neither was readily interpretable.

(Rabbit) and $F = 20.40$, $p < .001$ (Pigs). In recall, the length of protocols increased significantly with age for both stories: $F = 12.97$, $p < .001$ (Rabbit) and $F = 25.07$, $p < .001$ (Pigs). In contrast, the longer summaries produced by the four age groups did not differ significantly for either story, and in the shorter summaries, the adults used slightly fewer words than did the children. In the shorter summaries for the Rabbit story, the main effect of age was small but reliable: $F = 3.61$, $p < .05$. Comparisons between means indicated that the adults' summaries were shorter than those produced by either third or fifth graders but did not differ significantly from the summaries of first graders. In the Pigs story, the same pattern was observed, but the simple main effect of age was only marginally significant: $F = 2.42$, $p < .10$.

Number and types of nodes explicitly represented. Two measures were used to assess representation of the constituent structure of each story: 1) the total number of terminal nodes explicitly represented in each protocol (including nodes not present in the surface structure that were added by subjects); and 2) the pattern of representation within each age group, as indicated by the percentage of subjects who represented each node.

The mean number of nodes explicitly represented in recall and in the two summaries is presented for each age group and story in Table 10.5. Overall, fewer nodes were represented in the summaries than in recall: $F = 110.98$, $p < .001$ (Rabbit) and $F = 303.51$, $p < .001$ (Pigs), indicating that at least some of the reduction in summaries was based on the deletion of entire nodes. The

TABLE 10.5
Mean Number of Nodes Represented as a Function of Age and Task

	First Grade	Third Grade	Fifth Grade	Adult
Rabbit Story				
Recall	14.7	15.2	15.4	16.4
Longer Summary	11.4	12.3	12.8	12.6
Shorter Summary	8.8	11.2	10.7	10.6
Pigs Story				
Recall	34.6	38.9	41.3	46.8
Longer Summary	24.8	27.7	29.8	29.4
Shorter Summary	17.8	23.6	25.3	22.2

Note: Number of terminal nodes expressed in surface structure = 17 and 51 for the Rabbit Story and Pigs Story, respectively.

number of nodes represented also tended to increase with age for both stories: $F = 4.30$, $p < .01$ (Rabbit) and $F = 6.42$, $p < .01$ (Pigs).

In the Pigs story, there was also a significant interaction between age and task: $F = 5.08$, $p < .01$. In recall, the simple main effect of age was highly significant: $F = 21.56$, $p < .001$, with the adults representing more nodes than the fifth and third graders, who, in turn, represented more nodes than the first graders. In the summaries, the number of nodes represented increased from the first to the fifth grades and then decreased slightly for the adults. However, simple main effects tests and comparisons between means indicated that the differences among age groups were not significant in the longer summaries and that only the difference between first and fifth graders was significant in the shorter summaries.

In the Rabbit story, the age x task interaction was not significant: $F = 1.28$, $p > .10$. However, simple main effects tests and comparisons between means indicated that the differences among age groups were significant only in recall: $F = 4.53$, $p < .01$, with the adults representing more nodes than the three groups of children. (It should be noted that the variability in the number of nodes represented increased substantially from recall to the longer and shorter summaries, even though the mean number of nodes represented decreased.)

For both stories, two differences between the patterns of results obtained for the number of words used and the number of nodes represented are of particular interest. First, differences among age groups in the number of nodes represented in recall were less pronounced than differences in the number of words used, suggesting that even the youngest children had an adequate representation of the overall structure of the stories. The first graders, for example, used 27% fewer words than the adults in recall of the Rabbit story but represented only 10% fewer nodes; the corresponding values for the Pigs story were 42% and 26%. Second, although both measures decreased in summaries, relative to recall, reduction in number of words was proportionately greater than reduction in representation of nodes. For example, relative to recall, subjects used 56% and 73% fewer words in the shorter summaries of the Rabbit and Pigs stories, respectively, whereas reduction in the number of nodes represented was only 33% and 45%. This difference was most apparent in the adults' shorter summaries. The adults used fewer words than any other age group in their shorter summaries but did not consistently represent fewer nodes, a result suggesting that the adults found more efficient ways of condensing information than did the children.

To examine the pattern of representation of nodes in each story, the percentage of subjects explicitly representing each node was calculated for each task. The degree of agreement between age groups in the selection of nodes was assessed by determining the correlation (Kendall's tau) between these sets of percentages for each pair of age groups within each task. These correlations are presented in Table 10.6 for each story. All of the correlations were positive and significant, indicating that even the youngest children selected nodes for repre-

TABLE 10.6
Correlations Between Rank-Orderings of Nodes in Terms of Their
Probability of Being Represented by Each Age Group

	Recall			Longer Summary			Shorter Summary		
	Third	Fifth	Adult	Third	Fifth	Adult	Third	Fifth	Adult
Rabbit Story									
First Grade	.62	.65	.66	.50	.63	.56	.91	.79	.62
Third Grade	—	.55	.41	—	.50	.60	—	.84	.64
Fifth Grade	—	—	.63	—	—	.69	—	—	.74
Pigs Story									
First Grade	.71	.71	.70	.80	.70	.59	.75	.70	.56
Third Grade	—	.77	.76	—	.77	.67	—	.76	.61
Fifth Grade	—	—	.76	—	—	.74	—	—	.67

Note: All correlations are significant (Kendall's tau, p < .01).
Rabbit, N = 17. Pigs, N = 51.

sentation in their summaries in a manner similar to that of older children and adults. On the other hand, a developmental trend, similar to that obtained for importance judgments in Denhiere and Le Ny's (1980) study, is apparent in the three tasks where there was sufficient reduction in representation of nodes to permit differences between age groups to emerge. In particular, in the longer summaries of the Pigs story and the shorter summaries of both the Rabbit and Pigs stories, the degree of agreement between age groups decreases as one moves from adjacent groups (e.g., first and third graders) to groups separated by one intermediate age (e.g., first and fifth graders) to groups separated by two intermediate ages (first graders and adults). The specific patterns of representation for each story and task are presented below.

Rabbit story. In recall of the Rabbit story, all nodes except the Simple Reactions, Goals, and Ending were represented by at least 83% of the subjects in each age group. Differences among age groups resulted almost entirely from an increase with age in representation of Goals (both surface and underlying) and the Ending. Although the absolute level of recall is higher than that typically observed, the general pattern is consistent with other studies comparing recall by children and adults (cf. Mandler, 1978; Mandler & Johnson, 1977; Stein & Glenn, 1979).

In the longer summaries, only the Setting and the three main Outcome Events (the horse and bull wouldn't help, but the goat did) remained above 80% for all ages. The Beginning (the fox chased the rabbit) was represented by at least 94% of the subjects in each of the three older groups but only 72% of the first graders. Representation of the Goals and Ending still increased with age, but both were less frequently represented than in recall. Within each of the three Attempts, representation of the embedded Goal Paths (the rabbit went to the horse, bull, and goat) and the higher level Attempt Events (the rabbit asked the horse, bull, and goat for help) was variable, with subjects representing one, the other, or both. The third graders represented the higher level Attempt Events of the first two Developments more frequently than the other three groups did, which was the primary factor contributing to the comparatively low correlations between the third graders and the other groups in the longer summaries of this story.

The omission of both Beginning and Goal by some of the first graders resulted in somewhat peculiar summaries, because the motivation for the rabbit's Attempts was not immediately apparent. The problem is exemplified by the following first grader's summary.[11]

Attempts-8+14+20: He asked all his friends if he could have help. *Attempt-20, repeated:* So he asked his friend the goat. *Outcome-21:* And he helped him. *Ending-22:* And then the fox did not find him (1st Grade, Subject 5, Longer Summary).

The greatest reduction in representation of nodes occurred in the shorter summaries, and differences among age groups increased, although there were still similarities. To facilitate comparisons among age groups, the nine nodes that were represented by at least 70% of the adults will be used as a standard. (The 70% cutoff corresponds to a natural break in the adults' distribution of percentages.) As can be seen in the following adult summary, these nine nodes provide a clear indication of the overall structure of the story.

Setting-1: There was a rabbit who thought she had a lot of friends. *Beginning-2:* But one day when a fox was chasing her, *Attempts-8+14:* she asked the horse and the bull if they could protect her. *Outcomes-9+15:* But they wouldn't. *Attempt-20:* So she asked her friend the goat. *Outcome-21:* But he said he would. So he did. *Ending-22:* And she was saved. (Adult, Subject 13, Shorter Summary)

For all groups, the Beginning and the three main Outcomes were the nodes most likely to be represented. However, the absolute level of representation of the Beginning and the first two Outcomes averaged only 74% for the first graders, compared to 85%, 93%, and 88% for the third graders, fifth graders, and adults, respectively. As was the case in the first graders' longer summaries,

---

[11]To conserve space, the terminal nodes "Attempt Event" and "Outcome Event" will subsequently be abbreviated as "Attempt" and "Outcome" (unless the discussion involves distinctions among Attempt Events within a single higher level Attempt node).

both the first *and* third graders produced some shorter summaries in which the Beginning and Goal were both deleted. Other disagreements among age groups in the selection of nodes resulted primarily from the tendency of the younger children to represent the embedded Goal Paths of the three Attempts more frequently than the higher level Attempt-Events (a pattern that the adults had followed in their *longer* summaries), and from the children's less frequent representation of the Ending.

Pigs story. Characterizing the pattern of representation in recall of the Pigs story is complicated by the larger number of surface structure nodes (51) in the story and the differences among age groups in the total number of nodes represented. The following text provides a condensed representation of the content of the 24 nodes that were represented in recall by at least three-fourths of the subjects in *each* of the four age groups.

> *Setting-1:* Three pigs lived in a house with their mother. *Beginning-2:* Their mother told them they were old enough to live on their own. *Attempt-6:* The first pig asked a man for straw *Attempt/Outcome-8/9:* and built a house with it. *Attempt-11:* The second pig asked a man for sticks. *Attempt-16:* The third pig asked a man for bricks. *Beginning-21:* A wolf came to the first pig's house. *Attempt+Outcome-26+27:* The wolf couldn't get the pig to let him in. *Attempt/Outcome-29/30:* So he blew the house down. *Outcome-32:* But the first pig ran to the second pig's house. *Attempt+Outcome-40+41:* The wolf couldn't get the two pigs to let him in. *Attempt/Outcome-43/44:* So he blew that house down. *Outcome-46:* But the two pigs ran to the third pig's house. *Attempt+Outcome-55+56:* The wolf couldn't get the three pigs to let him in. *Attempt/Outcome-58/59:* And he couldn't blow the house down. *Attempt-68:* The pigs put a pot of water in the fireplace to boil. *Ending-70:* The three little pigs had wolf stew for dinner.

As in recall of the Rabbit story, representation of Goals increased substantially with age.[12] Other differences among age groups resulted primarily from the children's less complete representation of the three Developments in which the pigs build their houses and from the first graders' less complete representation of the attempt/counterattempt sequence in the final two episodes of the story.

To faciliate comparisons among age groups in the summaries of the Pigs story, the adults' pattern of representation will be used as a standard. The following 21 nodes were represented by at least 75% of the adults in their longer summaries. With the exception of Beginning-21, Outcome-32, and Goal-61,

---

[12]It is interesting to note that 85–90% of the adults represented either the Simple Reaction or the Goal in each of the wolf's four stated Complex Reactions, a level of representation considerably higher than that typically observed. One explanation that would be congruent with Johnson and Mandler's (1980) discussion of Reaction-deletions is that the wolf's less than honorable intentions are not readily inferable from his initial Attempts (asking to be let in and climbing to the top of the house).

these are also the nodes that were represented by at least 65% of the adults in their shorter summaries. The two cutoff points formed the first natural breaks in the adults' distributions of percentages.

Setting-1: There were three pigs. *Attempts/Outcomes-8/9+13/14+18/19:* They each built a house. *Beginning-21:* A wolf came to the first pig's house. *Attempt/ Outcome-29/30:* The wolf blew down the first pig's house. *Outcome-32:* The first pig ran to the second pig's house. *Attempt/Outcome-43/44:* The wolf blew down the second pig's house. *Outcome-46:* The two pigs ran to the third pig's house. *Attempt/Outcome-58/59:* The wolf couldn't blow down the third pig's house. *Goal-61:* The wolf decided to go down the chimney. *Attempt-68:* The three pigs put a pot of water in the fireplace to boil. *Attempt-65:* The wolf came down the chimney. *Outcome-69:* The wolf landed in the pot of water. *Ending-70:* The three little pigs had wolf stew for dinner.

Most of these nodes were also among those most frequently represented by the children in their summaries. In the longer summaries, only 3 of the 21 nodes most frequently represented by the adults fell below rank 21 (i.e., did not occur among the 21 nodes most frequently represented) for the first graders; the corresponding numbers for the third and fifth graders were 4 and 1, respectively. Similarly, in the set of 18 nodes most frequently represented by adults in the *shorter* summaries, the number of nodes falling below rank 18 was 3 for the first graders, 3 for the third graders, and 1 for the fifth graders.

Differences among age groups in the summaries came primarily from the following sources. In Episode 1, the children were *more* likely than the adults to represent the Beginning Event (especially in the shorter summaries) and the preliminary Goal Paths (getting straw, sticks, and bricks) and were *less* likely than the adults to represent the higher level Goal Paths (building the houses). In Episodes 2, 3, and 4, the children were more likely than the adults to represent the three unsuccessful Goal Paths in which the wolf *asks* to be let in and were less likely to represent the wolf's Goals. In Episode 5, the children (except for the fifth graders in the longer summaries) were less likely than the adults to represent the Outcome in which the wolf lands in the pot.

In addition, the first graders' *absolute* level of representation of the nodes most likely to be represented by adults was considerably lower than that of the other groups, even if one adjusts for differences in recall. In the shorter summaries, for example, the average level of representation of the 18 nodes most frequently selected by the adults decreased by 29%, relative to recall, for the first graders, compared to 13%, 12%, and 19% for the third graders, fifth graders, and adults, respectively. The first graders' greater reduction within this set of nodes reflected both a greater variability in the selection of nodes across subjects and a greater tendency to accomplish reduction by simply deleting entire nodes, especially in the shorter summaries.

Methods of representation. The extent to which subjects summarized by using methods other than deletion was examined by assigning the statements in each protocol to one of two categories of representation—propositional or transformational. On the basis of these assignments, each terminal node in a protocol was then categorized as having been represented propositionally or transformationally. Propositional representations were statements in which subjects simply reproduced or paraphrased all or part of one or more of the original propositions from a single node in the story (or made an addition that described specific states or events). Transformational representations were statements in which subjects either replaced the content of one or more propositions from a single node with a more general representation, combined information from two or more nodes into a single statement, or represented a set of one or more nodes simply by saying that it was "the same" as a set of earlier nodes. To compensate for differences across age groups and tasks in the total number of nodes represented, the number of nodes within each of these two categories was expressed as a percentage of the total number of nodes represented in each protocol. Nodes that were represented by both propositional and transformational representations contributed to both categories.

The mean percentage (and number) of nodes represented propositionally and transformationally is shown in Table 10.7 for each story, task, and age group. For both stories, propositional representations occurred more frequently than transformational representations: $F = 181.61, p < .001$ (Rabbit) and $F = 188.63, p < .001$ (Pigs). However, this difference decreased as the task shifted from recall to summarization for all four age groups, indicating that subjects of all ages used methods other than deletion to accomplish reduction in their summaries: $F = 38.98, p < .001$ (Rabbit) and $F = 97.34, p < .001$ (Pigs).

The interaction of age with type of representation was significant for both stories: $F = 3.83, p < .05$ (Rabbit) and $F = 4.18, p < .01$ (Pigs): but the major developmental difference occurred in the shorter summaries. In the shorter summaries, the adults used substantially fewer propositional representations and more transformational representations than the three groups of children did. The interaction of age, type of representation, and task was significant for the Pigs story: $F = 3.92, p < .05$, but not for the Rabbit story: $F = 1.99, p < .10$. However, assessments of the interaction of age with type of representation for each task separately indicated that it was significant in the *shorter* summaries for both stories: $F = 5.71, p < .01$ (Rabbit) and $F = 6.44, p < .01$ (Pigs), but did not approach significance in recall or the longer summaries for either story: all F's $< 2.00, p > .10$. Comparisons between means in the shorter summaries for both stories indicated that the differences between the adults and the three groups of children were, indeed, significant for both propositional and transformational representations. Although the third and fifth graders represented a greater percentage and number of nodes transformationally than the first graders did, pairwise comparisons of the three groups of children were not significant.

TABLE 10.7
Mean Percentage (and Number) of Nodes Represented Propositionally
or Transformationally, as a Function of Age and Task

	Recall				Longer Summary				Shorter Summary			
	Prop.		Transf.		Prop.		Transf.		Prop.		Transf.	
	%	(#)	%	(#)	%	(#)	%	(#)	%	(#)	%	(#)
Rabbit Story												
First Grade	97	(14.2)	5	(0.8)	81	(9.6)	22	(2.2)	76	(6.9)	28	(2.2)
Third Grade	96	(14.6)	7	(1.1)	80	(10.3)	25	(2.6)	69	(8.2)	34	(3.4)
Fifth Grade	92	(14.2)	11	(1.7)	76	(9.8)	27	(3.3)	72	(7.6)	33	(3.6)
Adult	92	(15.0)	16	(2.8)	69	(9.0)	34	(4.0)	43	(4.3)	60	(6.5)
Pigs Story												
First Grade	92	(32.0)	14	(4.7)	80	(20.1)	24	(5.7)	68	(12.1)	34	(6.0)
Third Grade	96	(37.3)	9	(3.3)	81	(23.2)	23	(5.7)	58	(14.7)	44	(9.4)
Fifth Grade	96	(39.6)	11	(4.5)	80	(23.8)	27	(8.1)	59	(15.4)	44	(10.8)
Adult	94	(44.0)	15	(6.8)	74	(21.6)	38	(11.2)	33	(7.6)	70	(15.4)

To provide an indication of the types of transformations that were used, transformed representations of nodes were assigned to one of five categories. The definitions of these categories and an example of each type of transformation (in italics) are presented below.

1. *Single-node generalizations.* Representation of a single node by replacing the specific states or events with a more general statement. Ex. *The rabbit asked the horse for help* (Attempt-8).

2. *Same-references.* Representation of a node (or set of nodes) by indicating that it is "the same" as a node (or nodes) already represented. Ex. The wolf came to the first pig's house and asked the pig to let him in. But the pig said no. So the wolf blew the house in, but the first pig ran to the second pig's house. *And the same thing happened there* (Beginning-35 + Attempt-40 + Outcome-41 + Attempt-43/Outcome-44) except those two pigs ran to the third pig's house.

3. *Combinations of nodes from different structural categories.* Representation of two or more nodes from different structural categories (e.g., Attempt and Outcome) by combining information from the nodes in a single statement. Ex. *The horse wouldn't give the rabbit a ride* (Attempt-8 + Outcome-9).

4. *Combinations of nodes from the same structural category.* Representation of two or more nodes from the same structural category (e.g., two Attempts) by combining information from the nodes in a single statement. Ex. *The three pigs asked three men for straw, sticks, and bricks,* or *The three pigs each asked different men for different materials* (Attempt-6 + Attempt-11 + Attempt-16).

5. *Second-order combinations.* Representation of a set of four or more nodes by combining nodes from different structural categories within each of two or more lower-level constituents (e.g., combining the Attempt and Outcome within each of three Goal Paths) and then combining each of those combinations into a single statement. Ex. *The three little pigs each got materials from different men.* (Attempt-6 + Outcome-7 + Attempt-11 + Outcome-12 + Attempt-16 + Outcome-17).

The percentage of subjects in each age group who used a given type of transformation at least once is indicated in Table 10.8 for each story and task.[13] As can be seen by comparing corresponding columns in the top and bottom halves of Table 10.8, the distribution of transformations differed somewhat in

---

[13]The percentage of subjects using a given type of transformation provides a more straightforward indication of similarities and differences in the accessibility of transformations across age groups than measures such as the mean number or percentage of nodes represented by each type of transformation. The latter measures do not distinguish between frequent use of a transformation by a small number of subjects and less frequent use by a greater number of subjects. However, the patterns obtained for the percentage of subjects using different transformations may slightly overestimate the competence of the younger children in that a single occurrence of a transformation may not reflect replicable use of it.

TABLE 10.8
Percentage of Subjects Using Each Type of Transformation as a Function of Age and Task

	Recall							Longer Summary							Shorter Summary						
	Same Cat. Comb.	Diff. Cat. Comb.	Single Node Gen.	Same Ref.	Second Order Comb.			Same Cat. Comb.	Diff. Cat. Comb.	Single Node Gen.	Same Ref.	Second Order Comb.			Same Cat. Comb.	Diff. Cat. Comb.	Single Node Gen.	Same Ref.	Second Order Comb.	
Rabbit Story																				
First Grade	0	17	28	0	0			28	11	28	6	0			28	17	33	6	0	
Third Grade	6	28	6	0	0			28	17	17	11	6			39	33	6	6	0	
Fifth Grade	0	26	26	0	0			37	5	37	11	0			47	5	37	5	5	
Adult	0	60	20	0	5			35	35	30	0	5			60	35	40	5	35	
Pigs Story																				
First Grade	56	61	0	6	6			56	39	6	17	6			56	44	0	17	6	
Third Grade	50	39	6	6	6			44	61	6	17	6			83	56	6	6	28	
Fifth Grade	58	74	11	5	0			53	68	5	32	16			79	74	0	11	16	
Adult	60	65	20	5	20			60	95	45	15	30			85	90	20	0	55	

the two stories, which is not surprising given the differences in content, length, structure, and familiarity. To simplify the presentation, the results for the Rabbit story will be considered first, followed by a discussion of the results for the Pigs story and the similarities and differences between the two stories.

Rabbit story. In the Rabbit story, the most pronounced difference across tasks and age groups involved the use of combinations of nodes from the same structural category (Columns labeled "Same Cat. Comb." in Table 10.8) in the summaries. The following two summaries, produced by a first grader and an adult, illustrate this type of transformation.[14]

> *Setting-1:* Once upon a time there was a little rabbit. He thought that he had a lot of friends. *Beginning-2:* But once a wolf was following him. *Attempts/Outcomes-6/7+12/13+18/19:* And he went to three friends. *Outcomes-9+15:* And two of them said no, that they wouldn't save him. *Outcome-21:* Then one said yes. And the goat hid him in his pen. (1st Grade, Subject 7, Longer Summary)

> *Beginning-2:* This rabbit was being chased by a fox. *Setting-1 (displaced to position of Simple Reaction):* And the rabbit thought she had a whole lot of friends. *Attempts/Outcomes-6/7+12/13+18/19:* So she went to her friends in succession, a horse, a bull, and a goat. *Outcomes-9+15:* And each of first two friends didn't help her. They were too busy. *Outcome-21:* But the goat helped her, *Ending-22:* and saved her from the fox. (Adult, Subject 5, Longer Summary)

Use of same-category combinations in the Rabbit story required that subjects access at least two nonadjacent nodes, n and $n + x$, and construct a single statement to represent them; in addition, when subjects also represented nodes between n and $n + x$ (as was done in the two preceding summaries), the order of output differed from the canonical sequence in the original text. Thus it is not surprising that even among the adults only 35% of the subjects used such transformations in the longer summaries, where there was only a minimal reduction constraint. What is surprising is that 28% of the first graders used them in their longer and shorter summaries, and, in some cases, used them remarkably well. On the other hand, only in the three older groups did the percentage of subjects using same-category combinations increase when maximum reduction was requested; and, as will be seen in the analysis of the quality of representation, children from all three age groups were more likely than adults to make mistakes when generating such combinations.

---

[14]Both stories contained some nodes that were already combined into a single statement in the text presented to the subjects. In the summaries provided as examples, the conjunction of two node labels by a "/" indicates that the combination already existed in the input text. The use of a "+" indicates that the *subject* combined two or more nodes that were not combined in the input text. Both types of notation are used to indicate combinations that include both existing and subject-generated combinations.

The distributions of combinations of nodes from different structural categories (columns labeled "Diff. Cat. Comb.") and of single-node generalizations (columns labeled "Single Node Gen.") did not change systematically across the recall and summarization tasks for all age groups. Different-category combinations actually decreased across tasks for the fifth graders and adults, in part because of the decrease in explicit representation of Goals in summaries. In recall, most of the different-category combinations involved combinations of Attempts and displaced Goals (e.g., "Please, bull, protect me with your horns *from the fox.*"). In contrast, the majority of different-category combinations in the summaries involved adjacent nodes (e.g., Attempt + Outcome or Outcome + Ending). Single-node generalizations were more likely to occur in summaries than in recall, but the difference between tasks was less than that observed for same-category combinations, in part because fewer nodes were represented in isolation in the summaries.

Same-references (columns labeled "Same Ref.") which occurred only in summaries, were used relatively infrequently. This can probably be accounted for by two characteristics of the Rabbit story. First, the rabbit's three requests for help differed in content. Consequently, same-references could only be used appropriately if subjects generalized the antecedent of the same-reference to produce equivalence (e.g., "The rabbit asked the horse *for help,* but he said no. And the same thing happened with the bull"), or explicitly marked the relevant differences at the time the same-reference was made (e.g., "The rabbit went to the horse and said, 'Please horse, give me a ride on your back,' but he said no. And the same thing happened with the bull except that she asked him to protect her with his horns"). Second, the use of same-references in the Rabbit story resulted in little if any increased efficiency of representation.

Second-order combinations (columns labeled "Second Order Comb.") were restricted almost entirely to the adults' shorter summaries. Given that these transformations involve generating sets of combinations and then combining the sets into a single statement, their infrequent use by the children is not surprising.

Pigs story. The most noticeable difference between the Pigs story (Bottom half of Table 10.8) and the Rabbit story was that the percentage of subjects using combinations of nodes from the same structural category was substantially higher in the Pigs story. In recall, the vast majority of such combinations occurred at the beginning of the sequence in which the three pigs strike out on their own; i.e., just after the joint Beginning and Goal, many subjects stated that the three pigs "went out" or "were walking along" *before* they separated the three pigs into their respective Developments. It is possible that such statements should have been classified as additions forming a transition between the Beginning and Attempt rather than as subject-generated combinations of the Attempts from the original story; however, it is also possible that subjects really are more likely to combine subsequent nodes when protagonists act jointly before they undertake separate actions.

As with the Rabbit story, developmental differences in the use of same-category combinations emerged primarily in the shorter summaries; the first graders were less likely to use this transformation than the three older groups. If one considers the percentage or number of *nodes* represented by same-category combinations, differences among the three *tasks* also emerge. The number of nodes represented by this type of transformation increased across tasks for all four age groups; but the increase in the shorter summaries, relative to the longer summaries, was greater for the three older groups (3.6 nodes or 19%) than for the first graders (0.6 nodes or 10%).

Although the use of same-category combinations in the Pigs story did not distinguish the adults from the third and fifth graders, the adults again generated more *second-order* combinations than the children did. The first graders generated almost no second-order combinations. In the three older groups, the use of this transformation increased in the summaries relative to recall.

The percentage of first graders using different-category combinations in the Pigs story decreased across tasks, whereas the percentages for the older groups either remained approximately the same or increased in the summaries, relative to recall. Although different-category combinations were generated by a higher percentage of subjects in the Pigs story than in the Rabbit story, differences in the *types* of nodes combined in recall and in the two summaries were similar in the two stories.

Same-references occurred more frequently in the Pigs story than in the Rabbit story, but their distribution across tasks and ages was similar. The use of same-references reached a peak in the longer summaries (in which many subjects summarized the wolf's episodes using a sequential retrieval pattern) and then decreased in the shorter summaries, as same-category combinations and second-order combinations increased. For example, one of the fifth graders produced the following longer and shorter summaries of the middle three episodes of the story.

Beginning-21: And one night a wolf came along. *Goal-23:* And he wanted to eat the pig. *Attempt+Outcome-29+30:* So he huffed his house down. *Outcome-32:* And then he saw him go out the back way. *Beginning-35:* So he chased him to his brother's house. *Same Reference for Goal+Attempt+Outcome-37+43+44:* And the same thing happened there. *Outcome-46:* And they both went over to their brother that lived in a brick house. *Same Reference for Attempt-55 (lacking a referent):* And he said the same thing. *Attempt/Outcome-58/59:* But only this time he couldn't blow the house down. (5th Grade, Subject 4, Longer Summary)

Beginnings-23+35: And one night a wolf came along. *Attempts-26+40:* And he said to (all the pigs) both of the pigs, the first and second, that he wanted them to let him in. *Outcomes-27+41:* But they didn't. *Attempts/Outcomes-29/30+43/44:* So he blew their houses down. *Outcome-46:* And they both ran over to the third little pig's house. *Goal+Attempt-57+58:* And he tried to blow it down. *Attempt/Outcome-58/59:* But he couldn't. (5th Grade, Subject 4, Shorter Summary)

Single-node generalizations did not change systematically across tasks, largely because most generalizations in the summaries occurred in combinations of nodes. However, *within* each task, the percentage of subjects producing single-node generalizations was greater for the adults than for the three groups of children.

Specificity and adequacy of representation of nodes. Both an overall analysis of the quality of representation and a specific analysis of errors were undertaken to examine the extent to which subjects maintained the original information from the story. The nodes represented in each protocol were initially divided into the following four categories: 1) both main point and most or all details represented; 2) main point represented with few or no details; 3) main point represented by a "reasonable addition" that was congruent with, but not a paraphrase of, the original text (e.g., representing the final Outcome of the Rabbit story by saying "The goat said yes" instead of "The goat hid the rabbit in his pen"); and 4) main point not adequately represented, either because significant distortions were introduced or because only a subordinate aspect of the node was represented. Minor errors, (e.g., calling the fox a wolf or vice versa) that did not affect the overall meaning of the node were not considered in the classification. To control for differences across age grops and tasks in the total number of nodes represented, the number of nodes in each of these four categories was expressed as a percentage of the total number of nodes represented in each protocol.

The mean percentage of nodes at each quality level is presented in Table 10.9 as a function of age and task for each story. Not surprisingly, the distribution of quality scores differed in recall and the two summaries for both stories: $F = 76.65, p < .001$ (Rabbit) and $F = 113.81, p < .001$ (Pigs). In the Rabbit story, both the main point and details of the great majority of nodes were recalled by all age groups: Level 1 (main point plus details) accounted for 88–91% of the nodes. As would be expected, the percentage of nodes at Level 1 decreased in the summaries, and the percentage at Level 2 (main point but missing details) increased. In addition, the percentage of nodes at Level 4 (main point not adequately represented) increased slightly in the summaries, relative to recall. A similar pattern of changes across tasks was observed in the Pigs story.

The interaction of age, quality level, and task indicated that there were some differences in the extent to which the four age groups followed the pattern described above: $F = 3.21, p < .05$ (Rabbit) and $F = 5.51, p < .01$ (Pigs). As in the analysis of transformations, differences among age groups were most pronounced in the shorter summaries. For both stories, the interaction of age with quality level was significant in the shorter summaries: $F = 4.08, p < .05$ (Rabbit) and $F = 4.32, p < .01$ (Pigs). The major developmental difference occurred at Level 2; in their shorter summaries, the adults represented a significantly greater percentage of nodes at a general level than the three groups of children did.

TABLE 10.9
Mean Percentage of Nodes Represented at Each Quality Level as a Function of Age and Task

	Recall				Longer Summary				Shorter Summary			
		Quality Level				Quality Level				Quality Level		
	1	2	3	4	1	2	3	4	1	2	3	4
Rabbit Story												
First Grade	88	9	3	0	60	31	4	5	59	28	1	12
Third Grade	89	8	1	2	63	30	2	5	51	39	3	6
Fifth Grade	88	8	1	2	66	25	2	8	51	39	1	9
Adult	91	9	0	0	67	29	0	4	40	60	0	0
Pigs Story												
First Grade	64	30	2	4	49	37	2	11	43	44	2	11
Third Grade	71	25	1	2	51	44	0	5	35	55	0	9
Fifth Grade	73	24	2	0	51	44	0	5	44	51	0	5
Adult	79	19	1	0	51	43	1	5	28	69	0	3

Both Level 1 and Level 4 representations decreased with age in the shorter summaries. However, the simple main effects of age were only marginally significant for the Rabbit story; comparisons between means indicated that only the difference between the extreme groups (first graders and adults) was significant. In the shorter summaries of the Pigs story, the differences among age groups in representation of nodes at Level 1 were not significant. However, the decrease with age in Level 4 representations was reliable; comparisons between means indicated that the adults again represented proportionately fewer nodes at Level 4 than did the first graders. The interaction of age with quality level was also significant in *recall* of the Pigs story—$F = 5.16$, $p < .01$—primarily as a result of the lower performance of the first graders.

An examination of the inadequately represented nodes (Level 4) indicated that three types of errors were of particular interest, because they seemed to reflect difficulties with summarization per se rather than inadequacies in the children's initial representation of the story: 1) inappropriate deletion; 2) inappropriate substitution of the content of one node for another, similar node; and 3) overextension of the negative Outcomes in the Rabbit story (nodes 9 and 15) to the positive Outcome (Node 21), or, in the Pigs story, overextension of the positive Outcomes (Nodes 30 and 48) of the wolf's first two house-blowing attempts to the negative Outcome (Node 59) of the attempt to blow the third house down.

The following two summaries of the Rabbit story illustrate errors due to inappropriate deletion and overextension, although the second child fixes both types of errors before the end of her summary. Neither child made such errors in recall.

Setting-1: Once upon a time there was a little rabbit. *Beginning-2:* And one day he got chased by a fox. *Attempts/Outcomes-6/7+12/13+18/19:* So he went to all three of his friends' houses. *Outcomes-9+15+21 (overextension error and reply lacking a referent):* And they all said no. They were too busy. *Attempt/Outcome-18-19, repeated:* So when he got to the last house, *Attempt-20:* he said, ''Will you hide me in your shade?'' *Outcome-21, repeated:* And he said yes. So the little goat hid him in the shade. *Ending-22:* And the little rabbit was safe. (1st Grade, Subject 8, Longer Summary)

Setting-1: There was a rabbit. *Beginning-2:* And she was getting chased by a fox. *Attempts-8+14+20 (content of request deleted):* And then she asked all her friends. *Outcomes-9+15+21 (overextension):* But they said no, *Outcomes-9+15, repeated:* two of them said no, the ox and the horse. *Attempt-8, repeated:* because she wanted to ride the horse's back. *Outcome-9, repeated:* But he said no. *Attempt-14, repeated:* And she wanted the bull to protect her by her horns. *Outcome-15, repeated:* But he wouldn't. He was too busy. *Attempt-20, repeated:* But then she asked the goat. *Outcome-21, repeated:* And she said, ''Ok,'' to hide in her pen. *Ending-22:* And so she was safe from the fox. (3rd Grade, Subject 1, Longer Summary)

The problem of inappropriate substitution of similar content is illustrated in the following excerpts from two children's summaries of the Pigs story. Again, neither child made such errors in recall.

> *Attempts+Outcomes-6+7+11+12+16+17:* The three little pigs got some *bricks* *Attempts/Outcomes-8/9+13/14+18/19:* and builded houses. (1st Grade, Subject 1, Longer Summary)

> *Setting-1:* There were three little pigs. *Attempts-6+11+16:* And they were some men with some straw, wood, and bricks. *Attempts/Outcomes-6+ 7+ 11+ 12+ 16+ 17:* And they took the *bricks. Attempts/Outcomes-8/9+13/14+18/19:* And they built houses with them. (3rd Grade, Subject 7, Shorter Summary)

Although some subjects who produced such combinations without error did so by generalizing (e.g., "went out to find stuff to make themselves little houses" or "went out and found different materials to build their own houses"), correct combinations most frequently involved either omitting the acquisition of the materials or listing them separately. The following excerpt from a fifth grader's longer summary neatly illustrates the latter approach.

> *Attempts-6+11+16:* So they were walking. And they all of them meet different men. They asked them for straw and sticks and bricks *Attempts/Outcomes-8/9+ 13/14+ 18/19:* And they all build one house for each. (5th Grade, Subject 7, Longer Summary)

TABLE 10.10
Percentage of Subjects Making at Least One Error Due to Inappropriate Deletion, Overextension, or Inappropriate Substitution, as a Function of Age and Task

	First Grade	Third Grade	Fifth Grade	Adult
Rabbit Story				
Recall	6	6	11	0
Longer Summary	33	28	53	15
Shorter Summary	39	28	42	0
Pigs Story				
Recall	39	6	11	5
Longer Summary	44	6	11	0
Shorter Summary	33	22	21	0

The percentage of subjects in each age group who made at least one error due to inappropriate deletion, overextension, or inappropriate substitution is shown in Table 10.10 for each task and story. Two important trends are apparent. First, the adults were considerably less likely to make errors than the children. Second, except for the discrepancy introduced by the first graders' tendency to confuse the acquisition of straw, sticks, and bricks even in *recall* of the Pigs story, the children were more likely to make errors in their summaries than in recall. The occurrence of fewer errors in summaries of the Pigs story could be a function either of its greater familiarity or of the lesser tendency of subjects to represent the particular nodes that would be most likely to lead to these types of errors

Temporal sequencing in recall and summaries. The present set of analyses examined the correspondence between the order of nodes in the text of each story and the order of nodes in recall and the summaries. For each protocol, the number of displaced nodes (relative to the input order) was tabulated, and a classification of the *types* of displacements was made (e.g., Goal movement, reordering due to clustering of originally nonadjacent nodes from the same structural category).[15]

The percentage of nodes displaced varied as a function of age for both stories: $F = 4.65$, $p < .01$ (Rabbit) and $F = 3.86$, $p < .05$ (Pigs). Collapsed across tasks in the Rabbit story, the mean percentage (and number) of nodes displaced by the first, third and fifth graders and adults was 3.6% (0.5 nodes), 6.4 (0.9), 9.6 (1.3), and 10.7 (1.5), respectively. The corresponding values for the Pigs story were 10.1 (2.9), 8.9 (2.7), 9.6 (3.6), 15.1 (5.2). Comparisons between means for the Rabbit story indicated that the fifth graders and adults displaced a higher percentage of nodes than the first graders. In the Pigs story, the adults made significantly more displacements than the children, but the differences among the three groups of children were not significant. For the most part, the developmental differences in the ordering of nodes reflected the older subjects' greater use of transformational methods of representation (e.g., same-category combinations and second-order combinations).

Differences between recall and the summaries were less pronounced for the analyses of the percentage and number of displacements than for most of the measures previously considered. The only significant effect involving differences between tasks occurred in the Pigs story; there was a small but reliable increase in the percentage of nodes that were displaced in the summaries, relative

---

[15]Decisions about *which* nodes had been displaced in each protocol were made by determining the minimum number of nodes that had to be moved to restore the input order. For example, given the output sequence: Setting, Attempt, Outcome, Beginning, the Beginning (one move) rather than the Attempt and Outcome (two moves) was classified as having been displaced. When more than one node satisfied the minimum-moves criterion, the node that occurred later in the output sequence was considered to have been displaced.

to recall: $F = 4.16, p < .05$. A similar pattern was obtained in the Rabbit story, but the main effect of task was not significant: $F = 2.77, p < .10$.

In spite of the relatively small differences between tasks in the frequency of displacements, there were differences in the *types* of displacements that occurred in recall and in the two summaries. In recall of the Rabbit story, for example, the majority of displaced nodes were Goals, which were displaced either to a position immediately following the Attempts or into a statement combining both Goal and Attempt. In the summaries, this type of displacement occurred less frequently, and there was an increase in displacements involving the clustering of originally nonadjacent nodes from the same structural category. Also, in the summaries, subjects were more likely to output combinations of nodes followed by a restatement of one or more of the nodes in more specific terms. Similar changes across tasks in the distribution of types of displacements occurred in the Pigs story.

CHILDREN'S SUMMARIZATION: GENERAL DISCUSSION

The study reported here addressed several initial questions about the development of summarization skills. The question of whether or not young children would be able to summarize, when doing so required a condensation of what they could remember, was clearly answered affirmatively. The great majority of subjects at all ages accomplished some reduction when asked to summarize rather than recall, although the percentage who failed to do so was greater in the younger groups. A second question was whether or not the representation of the constituent structure of a story in the children's summaries would resemble that found in the adults' summaries. There were clear similarities among the four age groups; but again there was a developmental progression in that as age increased, the children's selection of nodes increasingly resembled that of the adults. Finally, the most interesting question turned out to be whether or not subjects of different ages would use similar methods to condense information when they summarized. Children in all three age groups used some surprisingly sophisticated summarization techniques, but the children clearly relied on deletion to a greater extent that the adults, especially in the shorter summaries.

What Develops?

The generally high level of recall observed in all three groups of children suggests that the skills identified as prerequisites for summarization—comprehending individual propositions, establishing connections between propositions, identifying the constituent structure of the story, and remembering the information well enough to be able to retrieve it—were not the major factors underlying the developmental differences observed here. Most of the differences arose within the two sets of skills that contribute more heavily to summarization than to recall—selecting the information to be represented and formulating a concise and coherent representation of that information.

In the following discussion I will consider a number of component processes involved in selection and condensation that seem like reasonable candidates for an answer to the question of "what develops." It should, however, be noted at the outset that some of the children's limitations may have reflected the difficulty of exercising all of the following abilities simultaneously rather than the total lack of any particular ability.

The Ability To Select a Set of Nodes That Represent the Story Coherently.

The adults' pattern of explicit representation of nodes provided a basis for asking whether or not the children's selection of nodes was sensible. Against this standard, the children's performance, especially in the longer summaries, was considerably better than might have been predicted on the basis of most of the current research involving explicit judgments of importance (e.g., Brown & Smiley, 1977, 1978; Denhière & Le Ny, 1980; Yussen et al., 1980).

The present study, however, was designed to elicit optimum performance from the younger children. For example, no absolute length constraint was imposed in the summary tasks. Consequently, children who "overrepresented" the first part of a story were not automatically consigned to underrepresentation of the latter portions. A second factor that may have been helpful is that both stories included repetitive structures (e.g., the Developments in the Rabbit story) that may have made it easier for the children to use the constituent structure of the story as a guide for selecting information. Also, both stories could be sensibly summarized by deleting nodes or propositions, which meant that a failure to use other transformations did not *necessarily* result in a peculiar summary. Finally, being allowed to summarize from memory may have facilitated the children's selection of nodes, although, as noted below, relying on memory is probably a mixed blessing. The advantage is that less important information is at least partially filtered out as a result of apparently automatic processes that operate during comprehension or retrieval (cf. Brown & Smiley, 1977). It would, however, be difficult to account for either the children's or the adults' selection of nodes entirely in terms of differential accessibility. Although nodes that were poorly recalled were unlikely to be included in the summaries, many nodes that were equally *well*-recalled were not equally likely to be included in the summaries.

In spite of the degree of agreement among age groups in the selection of nodes, there were developmental differences. In the shorter summaries of the Pigs story, some of the children included nodes that the adults clearly found expendable; and in both stories, there were cases where the children deleted nodes that the adults included. The children's omissions had a more deleterious effect than their overinclusions. The adults' shorter summaries included little extraneous information; when the children left out nodes that the adults included, their summaries usually became less coherent.

The children's inclusion of "unnecessary" nodes may have reflected their inexperience as summarizers rather than true developmental differences in judgments of the relative importance of nodes. Given that these nodes were less frequently represented by the children as a whole, it is possible that the children who included them in their shorter summaries would have deleted them if a request for further condensation had been made.

Two explanations for the children's inappropriate deletions seem most likely. First, at least some of the children, especially in the younger groups, may not have know that certain deletions would pose problems for a potential listener. Second, those children who attempted complex transformations may have had fewer remaining resources, relative to the adults, to devote to the problem of simultaneously monitoring the coherence of their output. That some of the deletions (and other types of errors) resulted from factors other than an *inability* to recognize their inappropriateness is supported by the finding that a number of children who made them subsequently repaired their summaries.

The Ability To Replace a Specific Item With a Generalization.

For the most part, when the children deleted information *within* nodes, they did so adequately. However, they were less likely than the adults to *replace* all or part of the specific content of a node with a more general representation.[16] This difference can be accounted for in several ways.

First, some of the adults' generalizations involved words or phrases that were unlikely to have been familiar to all of the children (e.g., "The wolf *attacked* the pigs" or "The three pigs *turned the tables on* the wolf"). A second factor that may have limited the children's use of generalizations is that some generalizations seemed to impose greater processing requirements than others. For example, substituting "animal" for "horse," "bull," or "goat" requires only that one recognize that each of the latter is, indeed, an animal; and it is possible that the semantic components underlying such a generalization are automatically generated when the specific lexical items are processed during comprehension. If so, the basis for the generalization underlying the statement "The rabbit ran to three *animals*" would have been readily available. It is less clear that the semantic configuration underlying "Please horse, give me a ride on your back" would

---

[16]Developmental differences in the use of generalizations tended to be masked in the analyses of methods of representation, because many of the adults' generalizations occurred in statements that combined nodes and the present coding system did not distinguish between generalized and nongeneralized combinations. The analysis of the quality scores, however, did indicate that the adults represented a greater percentage of nodes at a general level (Level 2).

lead straightforwardly to a generalization based on the lexical item "help." Coding the request as a request for "help" (as opposed to a request to be taken on a leisurely Sunday outing) requires both that the Attempt Event be related to the Goal *and* that a relatively extensive and/or complex semantic representation be recognized as one representable by a particular lexical item.

At present our knowledge of the representational format for the information in a story—whether it consists of nonlinguistic cognitive units, semantic primitives, larger semantic units, or some combination of the three—is not sufficiently detailed to permit a clear specification of the differences among generalizations. The relevant factors could include the size or complexity of the configuration to be lexicalized, the frequency with which a given generalization has been produced in the past, or still other considerations. For present purposes, it should simply be noted that such differences exist and that generalizations that require more processing resources are probably less likely to be produced, especially by younger subjects.

Finally, using generalization as a technique for summarization may not have occurred to some of the children, at least in the younger groups. That is, it is possible for subjects to have an appropriate semantic or cognitive representation and to know, in principle, how to encode that representation linguistically without recognizing that they *should* do so when a summary is requested. This suggestion, which assumes that not all generalizations are automatic, is congruent with Danner's (1976) finding, noted earlier, of a discrepancy between children's spontaneous and induced use of generalizations.

The Ability To Operate On Sets Of Nodes Rather Than Single Nodes.

One of the most interesting developmental differences was the increase with age in the use of summary statements that incorporated information from more than one node. In the longer summaries, many subjects from all four age groups relied on a "node-by-node" approach, which appears to be one of the simplest ways to generate a summary. In this approach, as in recall, the terminal nodes of the story were stated separately, and transformations of the presented information were limited to deletions of entire nodes and within-node deletions, condensations, and generalizations. When the node-by-node approach was the only one used in a summary, nodes were also represented in the same *order* as in recall; except for occasional displacements of Goals, the canonical order of the story schema was followed. Given the similarity between recall and node-by-node summarization, the simplest characterization of the latter would be to assume that it involves the same retrieval processes as recall but that subjects are more likely to edit their output in the summaries. In recall, the story schema directs retrieval to each accessible terminal node, and the subject simply states whatever information is accessible within the node. In a node-by-node summary, a "decision stage" intervenes between retrieval of a node and its explicit representation, in which the subject decides whether or not the node should be stated and whether or not some form of within-node condensation is possible. In addition, as Rumelhart (1977) has suggested, some deletions may have been made at the level of intermediate rather than terminal nodes. For example, subjects who deleted the first episode of the Pigs story may have done so by deleting the entire episode as a unit rather than by making individual decisions about each terminal node *within* the episode.

In contrast to the node-by-node approach that predominated in the longer summaries, nearly all of the adults generated statements in their shorter summaries in which information from different nodes was combined (same- and different-category combinations and second-order combinations). Across the three groups of children, the use of such combinations tended to increase with age, but all three groups of children were less likely to generate combinations than the adults. Also, the children's combinations were more likely to involve errors.

Two of the factors that were discussed as possible explanations of the children's lesser use of generalizations may also have influenced their use of combinations. First, deliberately generating combinations as a technique for summarizing may not have occurred to the children. Second, the processing demands of generating combinations may have exceeded the children's available resources. All of the combinations required subjects to access information from more than one node; this seems likely to have increased the amount of information that had to be maintained in working memory, relative to that needed to produce a propositional representation of a single node.

The combinations, like the generalizations, also differed *among* themselves in terms of their processing requirements. Most of the different category combinations observed here involved adjacent pairs of nodes. In contrast, all of the same-category and second-order combinations involved nonadjacent nodes, and many included three or more nodes. Both factors may have differentially increased the difficulty of retrieving and coordinating the information needed to produce same-category and second-order combinations. Combinations also differed in terms of whether they involved "forward" or "backward" regroupings of nodes (e.g., stating Attempts 1, 2, and 3 at the point that Attempt 1 would normally have been stated versus stating both a Goal and its Attempt at the point that the Attempt would normally have occurred). The forward combinations may well have required more "planning" than the backward combinations. Finally, combinations differed in terms of their syntactic and semantic complexity. For example, some combinations included generalizations ("The rabbit asked her friends *for help*"), whereas others were generated by listing or deleting the specific elements that differentiated the propositions to be combined ("The rabbit ran to her friends the horse, bull, and goat" or "The rabbit ran to her friends").

It is interesting to note that same-references were the only nondeletion transformations used more frequently by the children than by the adults. Same-references, however, rarely involved a departure from the canonical order; most occurred at the point where the node(s) that they represented would normally have been stated. In addition, differences between nodes (e.g., asking for sticks rather than straw) were usually dealt with by stating them as exceptions ("the second little pig did the same thing *except* . . . '') rather than by producing a generalization that would have introduced equivalence between a same-reference and its antecedent ("The first pig got some material to build his house with and the second pig did the same thing"). Both factors may have simplified the processing requirements of same-references, relative to some of the other types of transformations.

SUMMARIZATION AS A COMPLEX PROCESS

Both the literature reviewed in the first part of this chapter and the study presented in the previous section indicate that summarization involves a complex set of processes, not all of which develop in synchrony. Furthermore, the processes underlying accurate and well-organized recall appear to develop in advance of those needed for summarization, especially when the summarization task requires maximum condensation.

These results pose some problems for the models of summarization proposed by van Dijk and Kintsch (Kintsch & van Dijk, 1978; van Dijk & Kintsch, 1977) and Rumelhart (1977) because both models incorporate two assumptions that the developmental data do not support: 1) that a summary (or, in Rumelhart's model, the basis for a summary) is an automatic by-product of the processes needed to construct a representation of the constituent structure of a story; and 2) that recall involves accessing a summarized representation and supplementing it with additional detail. In van Dijk and Kintsch's model, a summary is based on a set of macropositions whose derivation is assumed to be an integral part of comprehension. When recall rather than summarization is required, the macrostructure is supplemented with additional detail. In Rumelhart's model, constituents are assumed to be encoded such that more important information is more accessible. In summarization, only higher level nodes need to be accessed; in recall, both higher and lower level nodes are accessed. Given these assumptions, both models would seem to predict that children who can recall a story should not have difficulty summarizing it. In the present study, there were no children who were able to summarize a story but unable to recall it. There were, however, a number of children who recalled successfully but failed to generate a summary. Furthermore, among the children who accomplished reduction in the summarization tasks, there were numerous indications that summarization was considerably more difficult than recall. In fact, several of the *adults* spontaneously commented that they found generating a short summary to be a difficult task, whereas none made similar comments about recall.

This pattern of results suggests that the operations that lead to the *construction* of an organized representation of a story do not automatically result in a summary. Instead, summarization appears to require the use of "second-order" operations, which take such a representation as *input*. If so, the relatively late appearance of flexible, well-coordinated summarization is congruent with the pattern of development found in other domains involving the acquisition and coordination of complex rule systems (cf. Nelson & Nelson, 1978).

It should be noted that I am not arguing that processes of selection, generalization, and condensation are totally absent in comprehension and recall. "Gist" recall obviously reflects such processes. There is, however, little or no evidence to support the claim that simply understanding or recalling a story requires, or even typically involves, the extensive cognitive and linguistic transformations that adults use when they are explicitly *asked* to summarize. Kintsch, Mandel, and Kozminsky (1977), for example, have suggested that macrostructures closely resembling summaries are established during comprehension. Their argument is based on data showing that adults who are given scrambled stories take longer to read them but no longer to summarize them than adults who are given normal stories. Those results, however, simply indicate that the scrambled stories were successfully unscrambled during comprehension; they do not address the question of when the summaries were generated. Indeed, for both normal and scrambled stories, the latencies for producing summaries (which were a maximum of 80 words in length) were long enough—10 minutes—to suggest that subjects were doing more than simply retrieving pre-established macropropositions.

At present we have only begun to study the development of the ability to summarize, and there are a number of profitable directions for further research. One approach involves studying the effects of changes in task requirements or stimuli. To the extent that resource limitations have a negative effect on the summaries of younger subjects, it should be possible to show that reducing one set of processing demands leads to improved functioning in other areas. For example, the role of short-term memory as a constraint on children's ability to retrieve and combine information from nonadjacent nodes could be evaluated by providing external aids to retrieval (pictures or a copy of the story). Similarly, the demands of various types of generalizations and combinations can be investigated by constructing stories that differ from one another in terms of the relationship between the presented text and the set of operations needed to produce a given type of summary statement.

On the other hand, some of the developmental differences may have reflected a lack of awareness that particular processes (e.g., producing generalizations or monitoring for coherence) were relevant to the task. If so, instructions emphasizing the importance of those processes should lead to improvements in performance. Such improvements have been observed in other domains involving the development of strategic processing, including the use of mnemonic strategies (cf. Flavell, 1977) and children's ability to monitor their own level of comprehension (Markman, 1979). It seems unlikely, however, that a simple lack of strategic awareness could account for all of the developmental differences in summarization. In an investigation of a related problem, Brown and Smiley (1978) found that children in the fifth to eighth grades who spontaneously took notes or underlined when studying a passage were considerably more likely to focus on important items and to improve their recall scores than children who only underlined or took notes after being encouraged to do so. Such results suggest that some children may need more explicit forms of instruction in order to employ effective strategies for selecting and condensing information.

What the present research has clearly shown is that many of the component processes needed to produce a coherent summary are available even to first grade children. It is, however, equally clear that there is substantial development beyond the elementary school years in the refinement and coordination of those processes.

ACKNOWLEDGMENTS

I would like to think the following people, who provided many helpful suggestions: Catherine Coburn, Marsha DeForest, Rhonda Gandel, Kathryn Glamm, Jean Mandler, Keith Nelson, Elissa Newport, and Ruth Pitt. I am also grateful to Catherine Coburn for her assistance in coding the recall and summary protocols and to the staff and students of Whitman Elementary School (San Diego Unified School District). The research reported in the second part of the chapter was supported in part by NIMH grant MH–24492 to Jean Mandler. Analyses based on an earlier coding of the protocols from the Rabbit story were reported in my doctoral dissertation and at meetings of the Society for Research in Child Development (March 1979) and the American Educational Research Association (April 1979).

APPENDIX A
SAMPLE SUMMARY OF GOLDILOCKS AND THE THREE BEARS

The story was about three bears and a little girl named Goldilocks. And one morning Goldilocks went inside the bears' house while they were gone. She tasted their porridge and ate the little bear's porridge all up. Then she sat in all of their chairs and broke the little bear's chair. She was tired so she went upstairs and fell asleep in the little bear's bed. When the three bears came home, they saw that somebody had been eating their porridge and that somebody had broken the little bear's chair. The bears thought that there might be a robber in the house, so they went upstairs to look around. They found Goldilocks asleep in the bed, and then Goldilocks woke up and was so scared that she ran out of the house and never went back.

REFERENCES

Austin, J. L. *How to do things with words.* New York: Oxford University Press, 1962.
Bates, E. *Language and context: The acquisition of pragmatics.* New York: Academic Press, 1976.
Bloom, L., Miller, P., & Hood, L. Variation and reduction as aspects of competence in language development. In A. D. Pick (Ed.), *Minnesota Symposia on Child Psychology (Vol. 9).* Minneapolis: University of Minnesota Press, 1975.
Botvin, G. J. & Sutton-Smith, B. The development of structural complexity in children's fantasy narratives. *Developmental Psychology,* 1977, *13,* 377–388.
Bower, G. H. Experiments on story understanding and recall. *Quarterly Journal of Experimental Psychology,* 1976, *28,* 511–534.
Bowerman, M. The acquisition of complex sentences. In P. Fletcher & M. Garman (Eds.), *Language acquisition: Studies in first language development.* Cambridge: Cambridge University Press, 1979.
Brown, A. L. & DeLoache, J. S. Skills, plans, and self-regulation. In R. S. Siegler (Ed.), *Children's thinking: What develops?* Hillsdale, N.J.: Lawrence Erlbaum Associates, 1978.
Brown, A. L. & Smiley, S. S. Rating the importance of structural units of prose passages: A problem of metacognitive development. *Child Development,* 1977, *48,* 1–8.
Brown, A. L. & Smiley, S. S. The development of strategies for studying texts. *Child Development,* 1978, *49,* 1076–1088.
Brown, A. L., Smiley, S. S., & Lawton, S. Q. C. The effects of experience on the selection of suitable retrieval cues for studying texts. *Child Development,* 1978, *49,* 829–835.
Buschke, H. & Schaier, A. H. Memory units, ideas, and propositions in semantic remembering. *Journal of Verbal Learning and Verbal Behavior,* 1979, *18,* 549–563.
Chi, M. T. H. Knowledge structures and memory development. In R. S. Siegler (Ed.), *Children's thinking: What develops?* Hillsdale, N.J.: Lawrence Erlbaum Associates, 1978.
Cirilo, R. K. & Foss, D. J. Text structure and reading time for sentences. *Journal of Verbal Learning and Verbal Behavior,* 1980, *19,* 96–109.
Dale, P. S. *Language development: Structure and function.* New York: Holt, Rinehart & Winston, 1976.
Danner, F. W. Children's understanding of intersentence organization in the recall of short descriptive passages. *Journal of Educational Psychology,* 1976, *68,* 174–183.
Denhière, G. & Le Ny, J. Relative importance of meaningful units in comprehension and recall of narratives by children and adults. *Poetics,* 1980, *9,* 147–161.
de Villiers, J. G. & de Villiers, P. A. *Language acquisition.* Cambridge, Mass.: Harvard University Press, 1978.
Dore, J., Gearhart, M., & Newman, D. The structure of nursery school conversation. In K. E. Nelson (Ed.), *Children's language (Vol. 1).* New York: Gardner Press, 1978.
Dressler, W. U. (Ed.). *Current trends in text-linguistics.* New York: De Gruyter, 1977.
Fillmore, C. J. On fluency. In C. J. Fillmore, D. Kempler, & W. S-Y. Wang (Eds.), *Individual differences in language ability and language behavior.* New York: Academic Press, 1979.
Flavell, J. H. *Cognitive development.* Englewood Cliffs, N.J.: Prentice-Hall, 1977.
Frederiksen, C. H. Representing logical and semantic structure of knowledge acquired from discourse. *Cognitive Psychology,* 1975, *7,* 371–458.
Gleason, J. B. & Weintraub, S. Input language and the acquisition of communicative competence. In K. E. Nelson (Ed.), *Children's language (Vol. 1).* New York: Gardner Press, 1978.
Glenn, C. G. The role of episodic structure and of story length in children's recall of simple stories. *Journal of Verbal Learning and Verbal Behavior,* 1978, *17,* 229–247.
Glucksberg, S., Krauss, R., & Higgins, E. T. The development of referential communication skills. In F. D. Horowitz (Ed.), *Review of child development research (Vol. 4).* Chicago: University of Chicago Press, 1975.

Graesser, A. C., Robertson, S. P., Lovelace, E. R., & Swinehart, D. M. Answers to why-questions expose the organization of story plot and predict recall of actions. *Journal of Verbal Learning and Verbal Behavior,* 1980, *19,* 110–119.

Grice, H. P. Logic and conversation. In P. Cole & J. L. Morgan (Eds.), *Syntax and semantics: Speech acts (Vol. 3).* New York: Academic Press, 1975.

Hildyard, A. Children's production of inferences from oral texts. *Discourse Processes,* 1979, *2,* 33–56.

Hildyard, A. & Olson, D. R. Memory and inference in the comprehension of oral and written discourse. *Discourse Processes,* 1978, *1,* 91–117.

Johnson, N. S., Coburn, C., & Mandel, R. G. *Recall, summarization, and judgments of importance: Developmental changes in operations on higher order structures in stories.* Manuscript in preparation, State University of New York at Buffalo, 1982.

Johnson, N. S. & Mandel, R. G. *Effects of story organization on preschool children's story recall.* Unpublished manuscript, State University of New York at Buffalo, 1980.

Johnson, N. S. & Mandler, J. M. A tale of two structures: Underlying and surface forms in stories. *Poetics,* 1980, *9,* 51–86.

Johnson, R. E. Recall of prose as a function of the structural importance of the linguistic units. *Journal of Verbal Learning and Verbal Behavior,* 1970, *9,* 12–20.

Kempson, R. M. *Presupposition and the delimitation of semantics.* Cambridge: Cambridge University Press, 1975.

Keppel, G. *Design and analysis: A researcher's handbook.* Englewood Cliffs, N.J.: Prentice-Hall, 1973.

Kintsch, W. *The representation of meaning in memory.* Hillsdale, N.J.: Lawrence Erlbaum Associates, 1974.

Kintsch, W. & van Dijk, T. A. Toward a model of text comprehension and production. *Psychological Review,* 1978, *85,* 363–394.

Kintsch, W., Mandel, T. S., & Kozminsky, E. Summarizing scrambled stories. *Memory and Cognition,* 1977, *5,* 547–552.

Lakoff, G. Presupposition and relative well-formedness. In D. D. Steinberg & L. A. Jacobovits (Eds.), *Semantics: An interdisciplinary reader in philosophy, linguistics and psychology.* Cambridge: Cambridge University Press, 1971.

Lichtenstein, E. H. & Brewer, W. F. Memory for goal-directed events. *Cognitive Psychology,* 1980, *12,* 412–445.

Mandler, J. M. A code in the node: The use of a story schema in retrieval. *Discourse Processes,* 1978, *1,* 14–35.

Mandler, J. M. Categorical and schematic organization in memory. In C. R. Puff (Ed.), *Memory, organization, and structure.* New York: Academic Press, 1979.

Mandler, J. M. Representation. In J. H. Flavell & E. M. Markman (Eds.), *Cognitive development.* Volume 2 of P. Mussen (Ed.), *Manual of child psychology.* New York: Wiley, in press.

Mandler, J. M. & DeForest, M. Is there more than one way to recall a story? *Child Development,* 1979, *50,* 886–889.

Mandler, J. M. & Johnson, N. S. Remembrance of things parsed: Story structure and recall. *Cognitive Psychology,* 1977, *9,* 111–151.

Mandler, J. M., Johnson, N. S., & DeForest, M. *A structural analysis of stories and their recall: From "once upon a time" to "happily ever after"* (Tech. Rep. 57). La Jolla: University of California at San Diego, Center for Human Information Processing, March 1976.

Markman, E. M. Realizing that you don't understand: Elementary school children's awareness of inconsistencies. *Child Development,* 1979, *50,* 643–655.

Meyer, B. J. F. Identification of the structure of prose and its implications for the study of reading and memory. *Journal of Reading Behavior,* 1975, *7,* 7–47.

Morris, W. (Ed.). *The American heritage dictionary of the English language.* Boston: Houghton Mifflin, 1976.

Nelson, K. How children represent knowledge in their world in and out of language: A preliminary report. In R. S. Siegler (Ed.), *Children's thinking: What develops?.* Hillsdale, N.J.: Lawrence Erlbaum Associates, 1978.

Nelson, K. & Gruendel, J. M. At morning it's lunchtime: A scriptal view of children's dialogues. *Discourse Processes,* 1979, *2,* 73–94.

Nelson, K. E. & Nelson, K. Cognitive pendulums and their linguistic realization. In K. E. Nelson (Ed.), *Children's language, (Vol. 1).* New York: Gardner Press, 1978.

Omanson, R. C., Warren, W. H., & Trabasso, T. Goals, inferential comprehension, and recall of stories by children. *Discourse Processes,* 1978, *1,* 337–354.

Paris, S. G. & Lindauer, B. K. Constructive aspects of children's comprehension and memory. In R. V. Kail & J. W. Hagen (Eds.), *Perspectives on the development of memory and cognition.* Hillsdale, N.J.: Lawrence Erlbaum Associates, 1977.

Paris, S. G. & Upton, L. R. Children's memory for inferential relationships in prose. *Child Development,* 1976, *47,* 660–668.

Pollard-Gott, L., McCloskey, M., & Todres, A. K. Subjective story structure. *Discourse Processes,* 1979, *2,* 251–281.

Rohwer, W. D. & Dempster, F. N. Memory development and educational processes. In R. V. Kail & J. W. Hagen (Eds.), *Perspectives on the development of memory and cognition.* Hillsdale, N.J.: Lawrence Erlbaum Associates, 1977.

Rumelhart, D. E. Notes on a schema for stories. In D. G. Bobrow & A. Collins (Eds.), *Representation and understanding : Studies in cognitive science.* New York: Academic Press, 1975.

Rumelhart, D. E. Understanding and summarizing brief stories. In D. LaBerge & S. J. Samuels (Eds.), *Basic processes in reading: Perception and comprehension.* Hillsdale, N.J.: Lawrence Erlbaum Associates, 1977.

Rumelhart, D. E. & Ortony, A. The representation of knowledge in memory. In R. C. Anderson, R. J. Spiro, & W. E. Montague (Eds.), *Schooling and the acquisition of knowledge.* Hillsdale, N.J.: Lawrence Erlbaum Associates, 1977.

Schank, R. C. & Abelson, R. P. *Scripts, plans, goals, and understanding.* Hillsdale, N.J.: Lawrence Erlbaum Associates, 1977.

Searle, J. R. Indirect speech acts. In P. Cole & J. L. Morgan (Eds.), *Syntax and semantics: Speech acts (Vol. 3).* New York: Academic Press, 1975.

Shatz, M. How young children respond to language: Procedures for answering. *Papers and Reports on Child Language Development,* 1975, *10,* 97–110.

Shatz, M. The relationship between cognitive processes and the development of communication skills. In C. B. Keasey (Ed.), *Nebraska Symposium on Motivation (Vol. 25).* Lincoln: University of Nebraska Press, 1977.

Shatz, M. & Gelman, R. The development of communication skills: Modifications in the speech of young children as a function of listener. *Monographs of the Society for Research in Child Development,* 1973, *38*(2, Serial No. 152).

Smiley, S. S., Oakley, D. D., Worthen, D., Campione, J. C., & Brown, A. L. Recall of thematically relevant material by adolescent good and poor readers as a function of written versus oral presentation. *Journal of Educational Psychology,* 1977, *69,* 381–387.

Stein, N. L. & Glenn, C. G. *A developmental study of children's construction of stories.* Paper presented at the meeting of the Society for Research in Child Development, New Orleans, March 1977. (a)

Stein, N. L. & Glenn, C. G. *The role of structural variation in children's recall of simple stories.* Paper presented at the meeting of the Society for Research in Child Development, New Orleans, March 1977. (b)

Stein, N. L. & Glenn, C. G. An analysis of story comprehension in elementary school children. In R. O. Freedle (Ed.), *New directions in discourse processing (Vol. 2)*. Norwood, N.J.: Ablex, 1979.

Stein, N. L. & Nezworski, T. The effects of organization and instructional set on story memory. *Discourse Processes*, 1978, *1*, 177–193.

Thorndyke, P. W. Cognitive structures in human story comprehension and memory. *Cognitive Psychology*, 1977, *9*, 77–110.

van Dijk, T. A. Semantic macro-structures and knowledge frames in discourse comprehension. In M. A. Just & P. A. Carpenter (Eds.), *Cognitive processes in comprehension*. Hillsdale, N. J.: Lawrence Erlbaum Associates, 1977. (a)

van Dijk, T. A. *Text and context*. New York: Longman, 1977. (b)

van Dijk, T. A. & Kintsch, W. Cognitive psychology and discourse: Recalling and summarizing stories. In W. U. Dressler (Ed.), *Current trends in text-linguistics*. New York: De Gruyter, 1977.

Warren, W. H., Nicholas, D. W., & Trabasso, T. Event chains and inferences in understanding narratives. In R. O. Freedle (Ed.), *New directions in discourse processing (Vol. 2)*. Norwood, N.J.: Ablex, 1979.

Yussen, S. R., Mathews, S. R. II, Buss, R. R., & Kane, P. T. Developmental change in judging important and critical elements of stories. *Developmental Psychology*, 1980, *16*, 213–219.

11 Developmental Differences in Schemata for Story Comprehension

Stephanie H. McConaughy
Ina Fitzhenry-Coor
David C. Howell
University of Vermont

INTRODUCTION

Psychologists and educators have recently become interested in story comprehension as a way of obtaining clues as to how people organize meaning in text. Stories have been studied in many forms, including films and picture sequences, as well as oral and written narratives. Drawing on Barlettt's (1932) original work on memory, researchers in this area have argued that the underlying organization of narrative stories can be described by a macrostructure, or idealized story "schema" (Kintsch, 1975; Mandler & Johnson, 1977; Rumelhart, 1975, 1977; Stein & Glenn, 1979; Thorndyke, 1977; van Dijk, 1972, 1977). The schema represents people's conceptions of how a typical story is organized from beginning to end. The schema operates as a general framework during the encoding and recall of stories, by allowing information derived directly from the input to be combined with a person's expectations for comprehension. It is argued that people rely on the schema to understand stories as they read or listen to them and when they attempt to recall information from the story. They also use the schema to predict what should take place in other stories of similar nature. The question addressed in this research is whether the internal structure of the schema young children use to interpret and recall a story is qualitatively different from the schema adults use.

The introduction to the paper is organized into two sections. First, a text grammar used to analyze the structure of narrative stories is presented and described briefly. Second, a distinction is made between the ideal structure of a story text as generated by the grammar and the types of story schemata which can be said to represent cognitive structures for comprehension. It is argued that story schemata representing the reader or listener's internal cognitive structures change over development, and therefore can be represented by different generic forms of story schemata. Two generic types of schemata are described. We will demonstrate that these two different types of schemata represent different levels of comprehension of the same story information.

The Choice of a Story Grammar

The internal structure of narrative stories has been described by other researchers in terms of text grammars analogous to Fillmore's (1968) case grammar for sentences. The grammar consists of a set of syntactic rules that generate a deep structure for a story schema and a set of semantic relation rules that interpret the deep structure. The grammar used in the present research is a modification of the grammars developed by Rumelhart (1975, 1977) and Thorndyke (1977). In brief, the grammar defines a story as a system of problem-solving episodes centering on the main character's (or characters') efforts to achieve a major goal. In addition to *episodes,* the major syntactic categories comprising a story schema include the following:

> A *setting,* which introduces the main character(s) and the time and place in the story.
> An *initiating event,* which leads the main character to formulate his major goal and starts the sequence of actions and events.
> A major *goal,* which is the stated or implied overall desire of a main character that leads to the formulation of subgoals or action plans.
> A number of *attempts,* which are the actions of the character.
> A series of *outcomes,* which are events or states produced by a character's actions.
> *Internal responses* which are the subgoals, thoughts and feelings of a character leading to his actions.
> The *resolution,* Which is the final event in the story and reactions to the final event.
> *Reactions,* which are the thoughts or feelings of a character produced in the resolution of the story.

There are also superordinate or "higher order" categories that subsume some of the above components. These include the *theme,* which consists of the initiating event and goal, and the *plot,* which is the organization of the series of episodes. The *resolution* is also considered a higher order component because it is the final result of the individual episodes. All of these components, then, are considered to be the syntactic categories for defining large grammatical units in the structure of a story schema.

Table 11.1 presents a summary of the rewrite rules for generating the syntactic categories in the grammar. A more detailed description is presented elsewhere (McConaughy, 1978, 1980a). The rewrite rules show how the grammar is used to describe the organization of story information in terms of an abstract hierarchical tree. The hierarchical tree can be thought of as representing the deep structure of the schema for a given story. Components of the tree structure are slots or frames (Minsky, 1975) of higher order nodes for different syntactic categories of story information and terminal nodes for single propositions parsed in a particular story.

One of the stories used in the present research is shown in Table 11.2 and its corresponding structure generated by the grammar is illustrated in Figure 11.1. The boxes or nodes in the tree diagram indicate the syntactic categories for the structure of the story. (This particular story did not include an explicit reaction in the resolution.) The numbers in boxes represent the corresponding propositions in the story text. The numbers at the left of the diagram represent hierarchical levels in the tree. These range from most important (level 1) to least important (level 3) propositions for the hierarchical structure of the story.

Semantic relations rules are also defined in the grammar to represent temporal and causal connections between syntactic nodes in the story tree (Rumelhart, 1975; Schank, 1975). The temporal connections consist of AND and THEN relations. Causal connections consist of CAUSE and MOTIVATE relations. As defined in this paper, CAUSE refers specifically to physical causality; while MOTIVATE refers to psychological causality. This distinction in types of causality is an important one and will be elaborated on later in the discussion of different types of story schemata. Semantic relations rules then interpret the

TABLE 11.1
Grammatical Rewrite Rules for Simple Narrative Stories

1.	Story →	[setting + episode system]
2.	Setting →	[character(s)]
3.	Episode system →	[theme + plot + resolution]
4.	Theme →	[initiating event + goal]
5.	Plot →	[episode(s)]
6.	Resolution →	[event/reaction]
7.	Episode →	[internal response + attempt + outcome]
8.	Internal response →	[subgoal/thought/feeling]
9.	Attempt →	[event/episode]
10.	Outcome →	[event]

TABLE 11.2
Text of The Dog and His Shadow[a]

(1) Once there was a big brown dog named Sam.

(2) One day, Sam found a piece of meat

(3) and was carrying it home in his mouth to eat.

(4) Now on his way home, he had to cross a plank lying across a running brook.

(5) As he crossed the brook,

(6) he looked down,

(7) and saw his own shadow reflected in the water beneath.

(8) He thought it was another dog with another piece of meat,

(9) and he made up his mind to have that piece also.

(10) So he made a snap at the shadow,

(11) but as he opened his mouth

(12) the piece of meat fell out.

(13) The meat dropped into the water,

(14) and floated away.

(15) Sam never saw the meat again.

[a]Adapted for use with children from Rumelhart (1977).

hierarchical deep structure of the story schema to generate the correct temporal sequence in the surface structure of the story text.[1] The semantic relations rules have not been shown in Figure 11.1, but will appear in schemata to be described shortly.

The grammar presented here has been drawn from Rumelhart (1975) and Thorndyke (1977) because of the importance of describing the hierarchical organization of the deep structure of stories. The grammar used by Mandler and Johnson (1977), and presented by Johnson in an earlier chapter in this volume, is also modeled after Rumelhart's original version, but with the use of quite different terminology. For example, Mandler and Johnson refer to the "initiating event" and "resolution" as the "beginning event" and "ending event," respectively, and what we have labeled "internal responses" and major "goal," they have included in "simple reactions" and "complex reactions." They have

---

[1]At this point, it is important to note that the organization of the hierarchical deep structure of a story schema will not necessarily be the same as the temporal sequence of propositions in the surface structure of the text. This is because the hierarchy is determined by how important a proposition is to the central theme or general gist of a story. This distinction has not always been clear in previous research on stories, where the emphasis has been on recall of correct sequence.

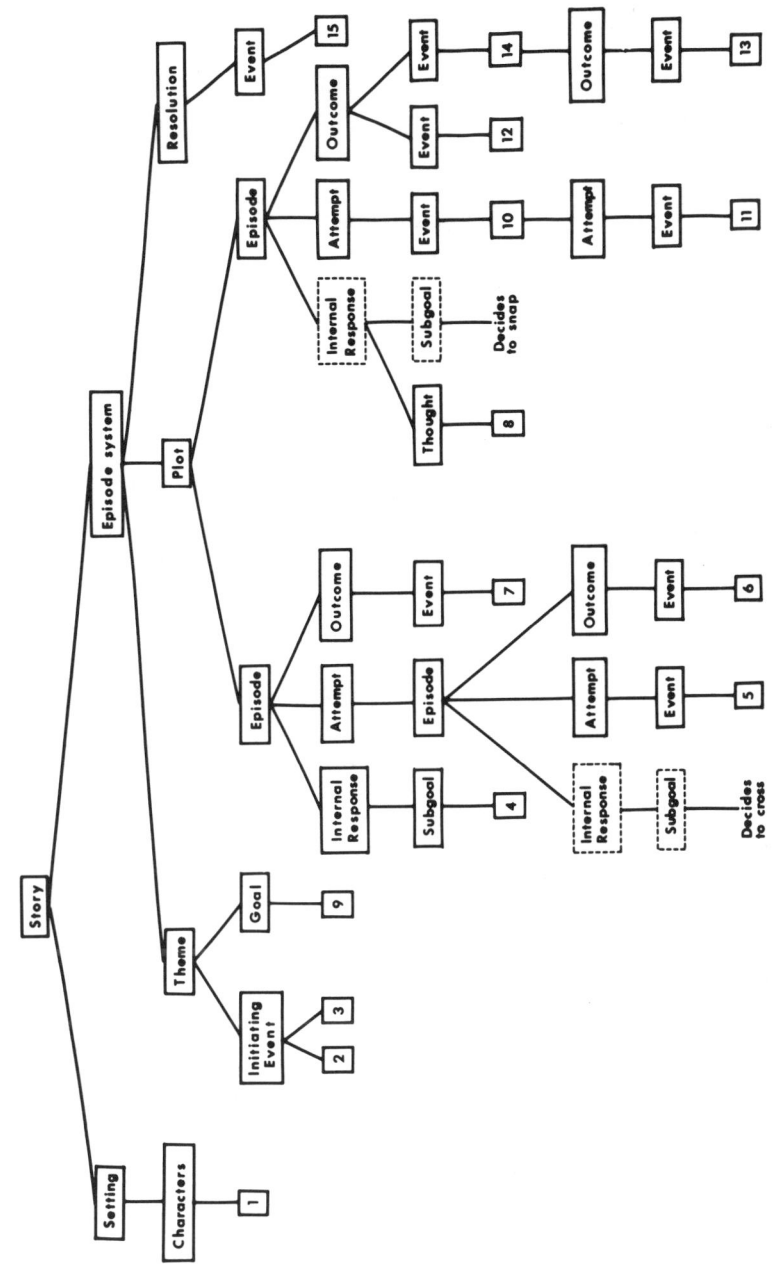

FIG. 11.1. Story structure for *The Dog and His Shadow*

also gone beyond the present grammar and Rumelhart's by adding intermediate nodes for "development" of the plot structure within each episode and nodes for a "goal path" that include attempts and outcomes resulting from thoughts and goals within the development.

In contrast to the present grammar and the one presented by Johnson, Stein and Glenn (1979) have developed a different analysis that places more emphasis on the temporal sequence of events rather than hierarchical organization. As a result, Stein and Glenn's grammar often produces structural tree diagrams for stories that are almost completely sequential in their left-to-right branching. For example, the final resolution of a story is generally pictured by Stein and Glenn as one of the right-ward branching and lowest nodes in a story tree. The major goal usually appears somewhere in the middle branches of the tree, depending on its position in the sequence of the story. Thus, little difference is shown between the deep structure tree and the surface structure of the story text in Stein and Glenn's analysis. The grammar presented here, on the other hand, reflects hierarchical organization in the deep structure by the top-to-bottom branching of the tree diagrams, as shown in Figure 11.1. Thus, the resolution is pictured as one of the highest nodes in the episode system and the major goal is subsumed under the theme at the same level as the final event of the resolution.

The top-to-bottom organization of the story trees is critical because it shows more directly the greater importance of certain syntactic categories for the general gist of a story and the redundant or elaborating aspects of other categories. It can then be argued that recall of a story utilizing a hierarchical schema involves a reconstructive process of memory based on "top-down processing" (Rumelhart & Ortony, 1977). "Top-down processing" occurs when higher level nodes in the logical structure of the story are remembered better and are used to generate lower level nodes in recall. On the other hand, "bottom-up" processing can also occur for encoding stories, for example, in reading or listening, when aspects of the input generate or activate a subschema or lower level nodes that correspond to them, and these, in turn, activate the dominating nodes and overall story schema, setting up expectations for what is coming next in a story. The use of both top-down processing and bottom-up processing then can explain how comprehension of a story may take place through a simultaneous interaction of perceptual input and higher level cognitive processes. This conception of comprehension is compatible with more general theories of information which describe continuous cycles for incorporating salient elements of data input and expectations based on conceptually driven schemata or plans (e.g., Lindsay & Norman, 1977; Neisser, 1976).

The validity of the hierarchical organization of story schemata is supported by several related types of evidence from studies primarily using adult subjects. First, it has been found that recall of stories is best for propositions at higher levels of the hierarchy in a story (Bower, 1976; Rumelhart, 1977; Thorndyke, 1977). No differences in recall occur in story conditions where the hierarchical organization is lacking (Thorndyke, 1977). Similar "levels effects" on recall of propositions have been found for text-base analyses of paragraphs as well (Kintsch, 1975; Kintsch & van Dijk, 1978). Second, propositions rated by subjects as most important are most often those assigned to the top levels of the hierarchy by the story grammar (Bower, 1976). Propositions ranked most important are also recalled best in stories by both children and adults (Brown & Smiley, 1977; Yussen, Mathews, Buss, & Kane, 1980). Finally, the higher the level of a proposition, the more likely it is to be included in a summarization of a story (Kintsch & van Dijk, 1978; Rumelhart, 1977; Thorndyke, 1977).

The differences in the types of structural tree diagrams produced by story grammars is important for examining developmental differences in story schemata. A grammar that is tied closely to the surface structure of stories, such as Stein and Glenn's (1979), precludes, or at least clouds, assessment of qualitative changes that may occur in the hierarchical organization of story schemata over the course of development. We propose here that developmental changes in schemata do occur, particularly in the logical or conceptual importance of different syntactic categories that comprise the nodes in the story schema. Changes also occur in the types of connections between nodes, which are represented by the semantic relations rules. The question to be addressed from this point on is what these changes may look like when comparing adults and children.

Two Types of Story Schemata

The underlying structure of a story schema can be considered from two different perspectives. From one perspective, we can focus on the story text and describe the organization of information inherent in the text itself. This type of analysis produces an ideal schema for a given story, which is generated by the text grammar. This type of schema was shown in Figure 11.1. Taking a different perspective, we can focus on the reader or listener and describe the type of cognitive structure he brings to the text as a mental set for comprehension. This type of schema may or may not match the ideal schema generated by the grammar. It is hypothesized here that a match to the ideal schema will depend on the general age of the story perceiver and the type of comprehension task involved.

The present study was designed specifically to investigate developmental differences in the structure of story schemata used by adults and children for comprehension. Much of the research on story comprehension to date has focused on adults' understanding of ideal story schemata generated by a text grammar without addressing developmental differences (e.g., Rumelhart, 1975, 1977; Thorndyke, 1977), or has interpreted evidence on children's comprehension of stories as showing deficits based on an ideal schema, (e.g. Mandler & Johnson, 1977; Stein & Glenn, 1979). As an alternative approach, we propose that there are different types of story schemata used by adults and by children. The schemata vary in the types of information they emphasize in stories and the way in which this information is organized. A distinction is made between two different types of story schemata: a *causal inference schema,* which emphasizes the causal sequence of actions and outcomes in a story; and a *social inference schema,* which emphasizes internal responses, goals and dispositions of the characters as motivation behind actions and outcomes in a story. Each schema represents a qualitatively different level of comprehension of the same story material.

The *causal inference schema* represents a less mature level of comprehension. A generic form of this type of schema is presented in Figure 11.2 (a), showing an emphasis on the basic information for recalling the sequence of actions and events in the story. In a sense, this schema focuses on the general question, "What happened in the story?" In terms of the syntactic categories described in the story grammar, the causal inference schema includes the beginning components of the story, the *setting* and *initiating event,* and the ending of the story, the final event in the *resoultion.* Details about intervening actions and events are also added in terms of *attempts* and *outcomes* in the individual episodes. This information is then organized into a logical sequence of events by the addition of the superordinate node for *plot.* Thus in addition to including explicit information about events in a story, inferences may also add missing or implicit information about actions and events to explain cause and effect relations. Because the focus is primarily on describing the sequence of events in the terminal nodes, semantic relations between basic nodes are defined only in terms of AND, THEN, or CAUSE connections. These are indicated by arrows in the figure. Comprehension based on this schema, therefore, should show strong effects of temporal sequence, because the deep structure tree is closely tied to the surface structure.

The causal inference schema is so named because it focuses primarily on *physical causality* in stories. In other words, at this level of comprehension, the information that is most important or most salient in a story concerns the character's actions and their outcomes and how these tie into the beginning and end of the story. It is proposed that this type of schema is most characteristic of young children's comprehension of stories up to fifth and sixth grade levels, although the actual age levels will vary depending on the difficulty of the comprehension task (Brown, 1975; Flavell, 1971).

The *social inference schema* represents a qualitatively different type of comprehension at a more mature level. A generic form of this schema is shown in Figure 11.2(b). The schema includes the basic nodes for the sequence of action and events, but adds new nodes for syntactic categories to explain the motivation behind the character's actions. In other words, this type of schema includes not only information about what happened in a story, but also focuses on the question, "Why did X do what he did in the story?" Thus, the social inference schema adds syntactic categories for the major *goal* of the character, his *internal responses,* such as thoughts and subgoals that lead him to perform his actions, and any *reaction* he may have to the final event in the resolution of the story. The

11. DEVELOPMENTAL DIFFERENCES IN STORY SCHEMATA   393

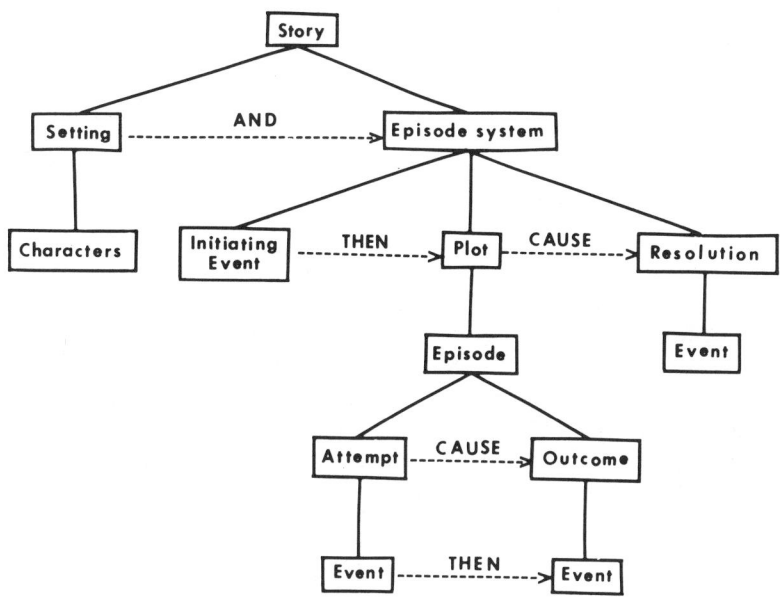

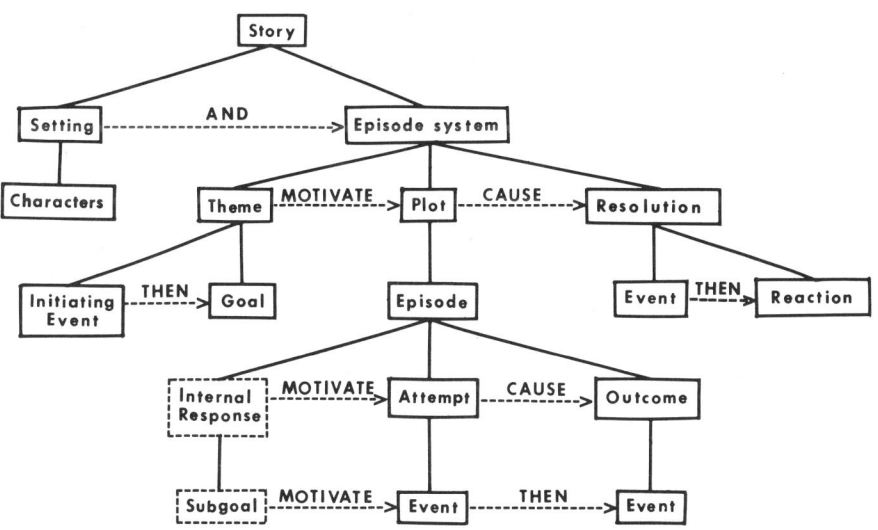

FIG. 11.2. Two types of schemata for story comprehension: The causal inference schema (A) and the social inference schema (B).

broken lines around the boxes for internal responses and subgoal in the figure indicate that these categories are often implicit rather than explict in the story texts, and thus often become the focus for inferences during recall. The nodes for the new syntactic categories are connected to nodes for other syntactic categories by a new semantic relations rule for MOTIVATE, again as indicated by the arrows.

Figure 11.2(b) shows the way in which comprehension based on a social inference schema incorporates both *psychological causality* in terms of motivation as well as *physical causality* to explain the sequence of actions and events in a story. It also shows a more complex hierarchical organization than was seen in the less mature schema, in the way an overall *theme* is incorporated into the tree structure to provide a motivational link between the plot and resolution of the story. The two different types of story schemata taken together then represent a progression through different levels of comprehension of the same story material. The levels of comprehension, in turn, can be related to more general stages of cognitive and social development.

A variety of studies on story comprehension have shown that emphasis on motivational elements in stories occurs later in development. For example, young children (first grade) show almost a complete lack of internal responses or reactions in recall, while retaining initiating events and outcomes (Mandler & Johnson, 1977; Stein & Glenn, 1975, 1979). As age level increases up to fifth grade, significantly more internal responses are recalled, though initiating events and resolutions continue to occur more often in the proportion of categories recalled. Even fifth grade children continue to emphasize actions more than internal psychological causes for actions (Stein & Glenn, 1979).

Research on temporal disorganization of stories and deletion of story information also suggests that motivational elements have a lower saliency in recall for children then do other syntactic categories of information (Stein, 1976; Stein & Glenn, 1977b; Stein & Nezworski, 1977b, 1978). Adults, on the other hand, will restructure recall of stories to emphasize goal statements when this category has been temporally displaced in stories (Thorndyke, 1977). Such evidence suggests that mental events serve a more important function in story comprehension as the age or developmental level of the story perceiver increases. Thus, younger subjects may simply fail to notice deletion or temporal displacement of internal responses, goals and reactions, because these categories of information have not yet become important for their level of comprehension. The present paper proposes that this occurs because young children's story schema is not yet developed to the level of a social inference schema that emphasizes the motivation of characters.

The above interpretation is further supported by a study by Rubin and Gardner (1977) which examined delayed recall of stories. When recalling stories including intentions and dispositional traits of characters, first-grade children in this study included some motivation when the story was retold immediately after hearing it, but not on delayed recall three days later. Third-grade children included an equal amount of motivation on both immediate and delayed recall. Sixth-grade children, on the other hand, included more motivation on the delayed recall than on the immediate recall of the story. This evidence is compatible with Bartlett's (1932) general claim that the story schema becomes more idealized in memory over time delay. What is interesting from a developmental point of view is the move toward a more mature social inference schema by older children over time, and the move back toward a less mature schema without motivation by younger children over time.

The present study is an attempt to provide support for the distinction between the two different types of story schemata by focusing directly on what information children and adults *spontaneously emphasize* in stories. To do this, the study examines differences in summaries of stories and subjects' judgments about the importance of the different propositions in story texts. This is a departure from previous developmental research, which has focused primarily on recall tasks. Such a change in method should more directly assess developmental differences in the internal organization of story schemata than would exact recall of the sequence of events in a story or answers to probe questions. This is due to different task demands for a summary, which require the subject to select out information that is *most important* for the general gist of the story and to delete elaborating details and other less important information. As Rumelhart (1977) and Thorndyke (1977) have shown, summarization involves selecting higher nodes in the hierarchical tree structure, which are more central to the story, and "pruning off" lower nodes to produce a condensed form of story schema. Johnson (this volume) has also argued that summarization for gist involves a more deliberate use of a story schema than does recall, because it requires a condensation of information down to the central idea or "essence of a story." Johnson further described in detail the different processes involved in summarization and showed that children are capable of performing the skills necessary for deleting less important information.

It is expected, therefore, that because of changes in task demands for summarization, developmental differences in the internal structure of story schemata, which are suggested in the variety of recall tasks discussed previously, will become more pronounced in summary protocols. Similarly, judgments by adults and children on the relative importance of propositions for the overall meaning of a story text should also show differences in the organization of story schemata more directly. Previous research on ratings of story propositions has shown that as age span increases, children and adults show less agreement in what they consider to be the most important or most critical elements (Brown & Smiley, 1977; Denhiere & LeNy, 1980; Yussen et al., 1980). The present study carries the earlier work a step further by examining judgments of importance for variation in the specific types of information emphasized by adults and children and relating these judgments to the summarization process.

METHOD

Subjects

Eighty fifth-grade children and 80 college students participated in the study. Fifth-grade children came from four public elementary schools in the Burlington and South Burlington, Vermont school districts. These schools generally contained a mixed population of students from middle to lower socioeconomic status. Teachers in the schools were asked to exclude as participants any students who displayed learning or reading difficulties. College students were volunteers from two large undergraduate psychology courses at the University of Vermont. There were 38 males and 41 females among the fifth-grade subjects (Mean age = 10 years) and 19 males and 61 females among the college students (Mean age = 20 years).

Stories

Four short stories, modified from other research, were used in the study. These were "Melvin the Mouse," "The Dog and His Shadow," The Fox and the Bear," and "The Wolf and the Crane."[2] The modified Dog story was displayed earlier in Table 11.2. Each story was 118 words in length and contained propositions for seven or eight syntactic categories described by the story grammar. One story was missing a reaction: another story excluded the initiating event. The stories varied in the number of propositional units they contained from a minimum of 14 propositions to a maximum of 20 propositions. All of the stories had the same general theme having to do with animal characters eating or acquiring food. Two of the stories had one character and the other two had two characters. No dispositional traits of the characters were explicitly stated in any story. The readability level of all stories was at the fourth grade level as determined by the Dale-Chall (1948) formula. Stories were presented to subjects with each propositional unit numbered as a separate line of type as shown in Table 11.2.

Procedure

Each subject was presented only one of the four stories, for a total of 20 adults and 20 children per story. Subjects were presented a story and the experimental tasks in a booklet form and were tested in groups. All subjects were instructed to read the story once through silently as quickly as they could to get the meaning of the story. After reading, they all completed the experimental tasks in the same order (without looking ahead or back). Instructions were given in written form to adults and in oral form to children.

---

[2]Copies of the modified versions of the stories are available on request, along with their corresponding tree structures as determined by the story grammar used in this study.

Summarization. After reading the story, subjects were asked to write a short summary of their story, telling only what they considered to be "*the most important* parts for the *meaning* of the story." Both adults and children were told to summarize the story in as few words as possible and that they did not have to retell the story exactly as it was written. Children were also instructed not to worry about spelling errors and to try not to write too much, but only what was important. As in Thorndyke's (1977) and Johnson's (this volume) procedures, no specific constraint on length of the summaries was imposed or suggested by the experimenter. Writing time was unlimited for both groups.

Rank Ordering Propositions. After the summarizations, subjects were asked to look again at their stories and to rank order the single propositions numbered in the text according to their importance for the meaning of the story. Each proposition was assigned a consecutive numerical rank without allowing ties. A rank of "1" indicated the most important proposition in the story. For the children, the experimenter gave oral instructions for ranking the first, second, and third most important propositions, and checked to see that each child understood the directions. Children then proceeded to rank order the remaining propositions on their own.

High Potency Words. In addition to the above two tasks, subjects were instructed to list seven single words that they considered most important for the meaning of their story. Two lists were made of important words, one based on memory of the story and then one in which words were selected while viewing the story text. The important words were listed after the summary and before the ranking of the propositions in the text.

Scoring Procedures for Summaries. Each summary protocol was parsed into single statements representing as closely as possible the original propositions in the story. Statements representing possible inferences or other categories of information were parsed into single propositions. Protocols were then typed individually for blind scoring by two raters, with the order of adult and child summaries randomized within each story. Raters scored all summary protocols for one story before scoring protocols for a different story. Each statement in a summary was scored for the closest match to a single proposition in the story text, according to a scoring manual developed by the experimenter.[3] A statement did not have to be an exact repetition of a proposition in the story text, but only give the general gist of the proposition. For example, "It's about a dog named Sam" was scored as an instance of the first proposition in the Dog story, and "he lost his meat" was scored as an instance of the last proposition (cf. Table 11.2). A strict distinction in scoring was made between statements representing actions and outcomes and statements representing motivation such as thoughts or subgoals of a character.

---

[3] A copy of the scoring manual for the summaries is available on request.

If a statement could not be identified as representing an instance of one of the propositions in the story text, it was scored as one of eight additional scoring categories. These additional categories represented a generalized "try" statement, six types of inference, or a distortion. A "try" statement was defined as one that condensed the initiating event and goal of the story into a general statement similar to Rumelhart's (1977) definition. An example for the Dog story would be the statement "a dog tried to get a piece of meat." Inferences were defined as any new information in the summary, which was not explicitly stated as a proposition in the text of the story. These included statements representing implicit *internal responses, attempts, outcomes* and *reactions*, as well as two new categories for *dispositions* or traits of characters, such as "greed" for the Dog story, and any *morals* added to the story. Distortions were defined as incorrect memories of explicit or implicit information in the story. These did not include minor mistakes such as reporting the dog was "black" instead of "brown" or that he found a "bone" instead of a "piece of meat," but did include major distortions of information, such as, "(the dog) jumped into the water."

A high inter-rater reliability was found for the two raters' judgments on scoring, as shown by an 89% agreement across the four stories. This high rate of agreement was comparable for scoring of children's ($\geq$ 88%) and adults' ($\geq$ 90%) summaries. In cases of disagreement, a final score for the statement in question was determined by the experimenter acting as a third rater with no knowledge of the scores assigned by the first two raters. Specific scoring procedures for the ranking task in the study will be described in conjunction with the appropriate data analyses.

RESULTS

Results will be presented primarily from the summarizations and the ranking of propositions. Selection of high potency words will be described only briefly, because this was not of primary concern for the present paper.

Story Summaries

Before examining the specific content of story summaries, it was important to look at the length and accuracy of the summaries, because these are such basic characteristics of recall. In these analyses, length was defined in terms of the number of summary statements parsed in a protocol and accuracy was reflected (inversely) in the number of statements scored as distortions. Table 11.3 presents the mean length of summaries of each story and the mean number of distortions for adults and children. These data can be compared to the number of propositions in the text of each story given as constants in the first column in the table.

Two separate 2 × 4 analyses of variance were used to examine length and the number of distortions. In general, adults produced significantly longer summa-

TABLE 11.3
Mean Number of Propositions in Text, Mean Length and Mean
Number of Distortions of Summaries for Each of Four Stories
for Adults and Children

Story	Number of Propositions in Text	Mean Length of Summaries		Mean Distortions in Summaries	
		Adults	Children	Adults	Children
Melvin	14	7.10	3.80	.45	.37
Dog	15	7.45	4.80	.00	.37
Fox and Bear	20	9.95	4.70	.72	.55
Wolf and Crane	19	8.75	6.15	.00	.22
Mean		8.13	4.86	.09	.15

ries ($\bar{X} = 8.13$) than children ($\bar{X} = 4.86$), $F(1,152) = 77.60$, $p < .001$. This effect was as predicted because, aside from the greater fluency of adults, the more mature social inference schema adds syntactic categories of information that are not included in the less mature causal inference schema, while retaining other information in common with the less mature schema. In addition, longer summaries were obtained for stories that contained more propositions, producing a significant main effect of story: $F(3, 152) = 6.075$, $p < .001$. Since all stories contained an equal number of words, the story effect supports the notion that some stories contained more information than others, based on the number of propositions, and thus provides some validity for the original parsing system.

Overall accuracy of the summaries was quite high. There were generally few distortions introduced into any of the four stories, as shown in the last two columns in Table 11.3. No significant differences were found in the mean number of distortions for adults ($\bar{X} = .09$) and children ($\bar{X} = .15$). This finding suggests that the stories were read with equally good comprehension by both groups, and that the summarization process did not introduce significant distortions for either group.

The specific content of the summaries for the two age groups was then analyzed in three ways: First, by examining the proportion of statements in summaries that represented instances of propositions in eight syntactic categories in the story grammar; second, by examining the number of "try" statements and different types of inferences; and third, by examining the proportion of statements in summaries that represented instances of propositions at three different hierarchical levels in the tree structures diagramed for each story.

Syntactic categories. The single propositions in each story were initially classified by the experimenter and one other rater into one of eight syntactic categories representing the basic nodes in a tree structure defined by the story grammar. The eight syntactic categories included: *setting, initiating event, goal, internal response, attempt, outcome,* the final events of the *resolution,*[4] and a *reaction* to the final events. The number of statements in a summary protocol representing each syntactic category was calculated for each subject. This score was then expressed as a proportion by dividing the number of statements occurring in a given category by the number of propositions in that category in the story text, because the number of propositions in each category varied across stories. The mean proportion of statements for the eight syntactic categories in the summaries of adults and children is shown in Figure 11.3.

As mentioned previously in the Method section, not all stories contained explicit propositions representing instances of all eight syntactic categories. Therefore, the data presented in Figure 11.3 were analyzed by three different mixed analyses of variance. A 2 × 4 × 6 analysis of variance treated six syntactic categories as a repeated measure crossed with four stories for the two age groups. This constituted the major analysis for comparing differences between adults and children on the content of their summaries. Two additional 2 × 3 × 7 analysis of variance treated seven syntactic categories as a repeated measure crossed with three stories for the two age groups. These analyses were used to examine differences between the two age groups in relation to the *initiating event* or the *reaction* of the three appropriate stories. All subsequent multiple comparisons concerning *initiating events* and *reactions* were also based upon the relevant three stories rather than four stories.

As can be seen in the figure, adults produced a significantly greater proportion of statements averaged across all syntactic categories than did children: $F(1,152) = 67.72, p < .001$. This finding is not surprising since adults produced longer summaries in general. A significant main effect was also found for the six syntactic categories across four stories: $F(5,760) = 32.46, p < .001$. The major finding of interest was a significant category by group interaction: $F(5,760) = 4.33, p < .01$. Tests on simple effects showed that there were significant differences among syntactic categories included in the summaries by the two age groups.

For adults, Newman-Keuls comparisons showed that there were significantly greater proportions of summary statements representing *resolutions* (.81), *initiating events* (.64), *goals* (.51), and *outcomes* (.51) as compared to *settings*(.38), *reactions* (.38), *attempts* (.29), and *internal responses* (.20), $p < .05$. These findings are compatible with the description of the social inference schema, which includes the initiating event, goal, and resolution as higher order nodes in the tree structure for the more mature levels of comprehension. The specific finding that adults produced significantly more goal statements than attempts indicates that adults consider the major goal of the character to be more important than specific actions, as predicted by the social inference schema.

---

[4]According to the story grammar, the term "resolution" includes both the final event of the story and the reaction to the final event. For the sake of simplicity in reporting results, the term *resolution,* however, will be used to label the final event only and the *reaction* will be labeled separately.

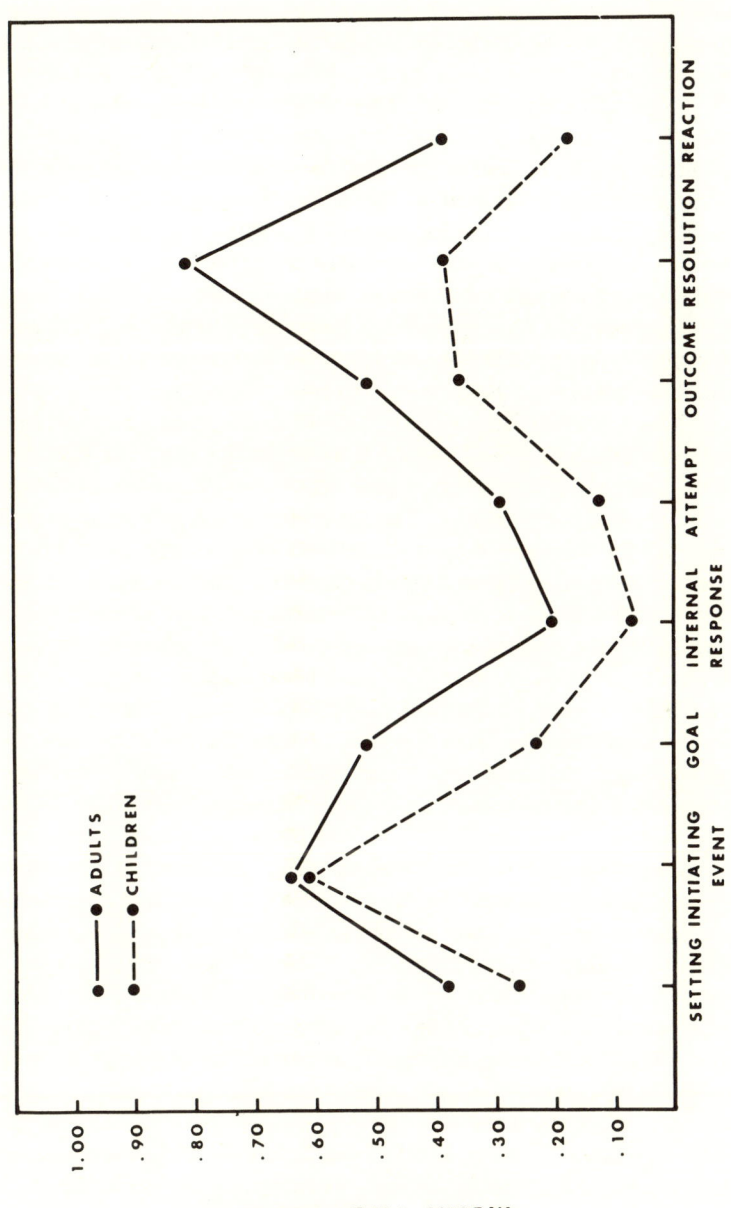

FIG. 11.3. Mean proportion of summary statements for eight syntactic categories for adults and children.

For children, the highest proportion of statements in their summaries represented *initiating events* (.62). Children also had signficantly greater proportions of statements representing *resolutions* (.38), *outcomes* (.35), and *settings* (.26), as compared to *goals* (.23), *reactions* (.14), *attempts* (.12), and *internal responses* (.07), Newman-Keuls, $p < .05$. These findings are compatible with the description of the less mature causal inference schema, which includes only the initiating event and resolution, but not the goal, as higher order nodes in the tree structure. Unlike adults, the proportion of goals for children was equivalent to the proportion of attempts. This finding suggests that fifth-grade children do not yet consider the major goal to be more important than a character's actions in a story, a result predicted by the lower level schema.

Also of interest was the finding that both adults and children had a significantly higher proportion of statements about the events in the *resolutions* than the combined mean proportion of *attempts* and *outcomes*, Dunn's test, $t' = 8.14$ for adults, $t' = 3.10$ for children, $p < .05$. This finding, predicted on a priori grounds, indicates that both groups were able to condense a story in a summary by emphasizing the final resolution more than elaborating details of actions and outcomes leading up to the resolution. The difference in the proportion of goal statements included by the two groups, therefore, indicates that adults placed more emphasis on the goal as a motivational link between the initiating event and the resolution than did children. Thus the differences described in two types of generic schemata fit the observed differences found in the group by category interaction. Finally, it should be noted that the internal response category represented the lowest proportion of summary statements for both groups. This was not predicted by the distinction between the two generic schemata; however, the forthcoming analyses on inferences shed some light on why this effect may have occurred.

Inferences and "try" statements. The number of additional statements in summary protocols was calculated for six types of inferences and generalized "try" statements as defined previously in the discussion of the scoring procedures. The mean number of statements in each of these seven categories produced by adults and children across the four stories is shown in Figure 11.4.

In general, adults made significantly more additions than children: $F(1,152) = 14.37, p < .001$. There was also a significant main effect of type of addition: $F(6,912) = 5.75, p < .001$. As with syntactic categories, the finding of central interest was a significant interaction for the types of additions produced by the two groups: $F(6,912) = 2.20, p < .05$. Tests on simple effects showed that adults inferred significantly more *internal responses* than did children: $F(1,1051) = 22.21, p < .01$. No differences were found between the two groups on any other type of inference or on "try" statements. Comparing the types of additions within each age group showed a significant simple effect of additions for adults: $F(6,912) = 5.92, p < .01$, where the number of inferred *internal*

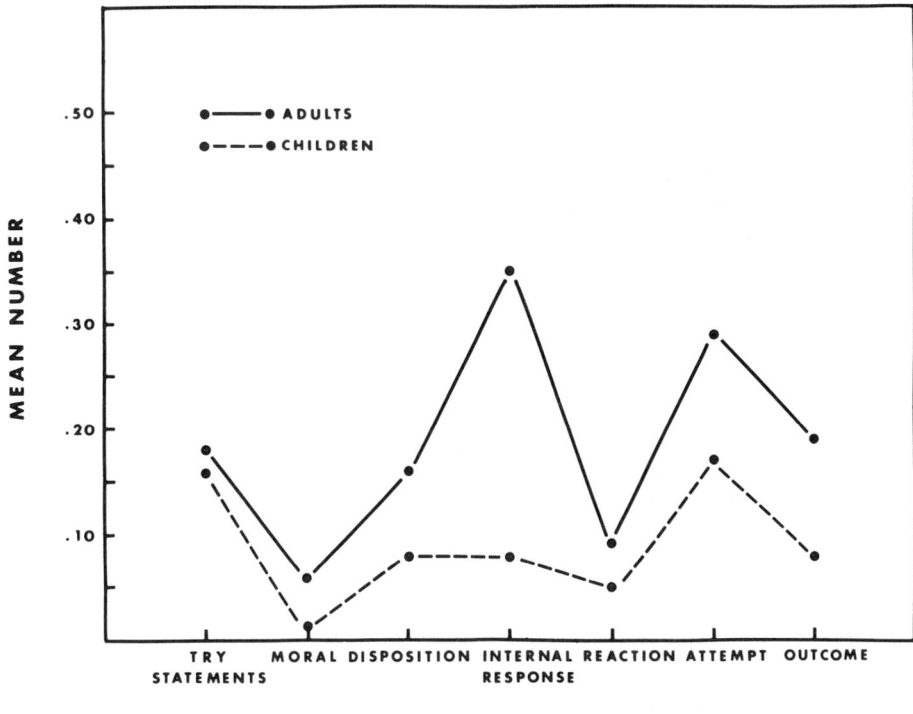

FIG. 11.4. Mean number of "try" statements and six types of inferences in summaries of adults and children.

responses and *attempts* was significantly greater than all other types of inferences or "try" statements, Newman-Keuls, $p < .05$. No differences were found among the types of additions made by children. Thus, it appears that although adults and children had an equally low proportion of explicit internal responses in their summaries, adults were substituting their own *inferred* internal responses, which they may have thought were more important. This supports the hypothesis that an adult's generic story schema includes implicit nodes for internal responses that provide motivation for a character's actions in a story. An additional prediction that more inferred dispositional traits would also be added by adults was not found in the content of the summaries.

Hierarchical levels. The location of propositions at different levels in the hierarchical structure of a story was determined by the organization of tree diagrams constructed for each story based on the grammar. One of these diagrams appears in Figure 11.1, p. 389, with the numbers on the left side of the figure showing the hierarchical levels for propositions. It is important to note, at this point, that the tree diagram constructed for each story text represents a particular instance of a social inference schema, and not the causal inference schema. This is because each story tree is hierarchically organized around a goal or central theme and contains internal responses as well as other syntactic categories. According to the present hypothesis, this type of hierarchical structure should only correspond to the generic schema for more mature levels of comprehension. Thus the summaries of adults should show a closer fit to this hierarchical structure than should the summaries of children.

Each statement in a subject's summary protocol was assigned a hierarchical level matching the level of the proposition it represented in the particular story text. The number of statements within each hierarchical level was calculated for each subject. This score was then expressed as a proportion by dividing the number of statements at a given level by the number of propositions at that level in the story text. The mean proportion of summary statements at three hierarchi-

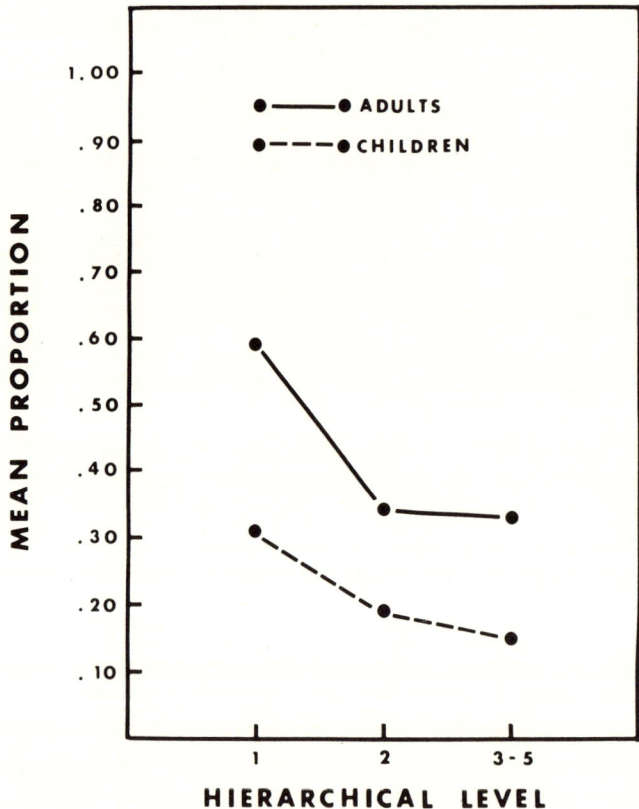

FIG. 11.5. Mean proportion of summary statements at three hierarchical levels for adults and children.

cal levels in the four stories is shown in Figure 11.5 for adults and children. The proportions have been combined for levels 3 to 5 because of the relatively small number of propositions at any one of these lower levels. Statements representing settings were not included in this analysis because setting, according to the present story grammar, is not a node in the episode system. This is a departure from Thorndyke's (1977) analysis of hierarchical level.

The hierarchical level had significant influence on the inclusion of statements in summaries: $F(2,304) = 46.90, p < .001$. Simple effects and Newman-Keuls comparisons indicated that both groups included a greater proportion of statements in their summaries that represented level 1 propositions as compared to the lower hierarchical levels, $p < .05$. A significant main effect of age group was also found, which simply reflected the longer length of summaries produced by adults: $F(1, 152) = 56.18, p < .001$. A significant level by group interaction, however, indicated that the magnitude of the level's effect was larger for adults than for children: $F(2,304) = 4.34, p < .05$, as predicted. This finding is compatible with the earlier finding that adults included a high proportion of goal statements in their summaries along with initiating events and resolutions, whereas children included only the latter two syntactic categories. All three of these syntactic categories represent level 1 propositions in the tree structures. Thus, it appears that both adults and children produced summaries that condensed the story text to central structural elements and deleted elaborating details represented at lower levels in the hierarchy. However, adults' summaries showed a closer fit to the complete hierarchical structure produced by the story grammar than did children's summaries. As argued above, the hierarchical structure produced by the grammar represents an instance of a social inference schema.

Ranks of Propositions

The ranks for importance assigned to propositions in story texts were also analyzed according to syntactic categories and hierarchical levels in the tree structures. These analyses allowed comparisons with the results found for the summaries.

Syntactic categories. The mean ranks of importance were calculated for propositions in each of the eight syntactic categories as those used in the content analysis of the summaries. The mean rank for each syntactic category was determined by averaging the ranks assigned by adults and children to propositions within a given category in each story, dividing by the number of propositions in that category, and then averaging across stories. Figure 11.6 shows the mean ranks assigned to propositions in the eight syntactic categories by adults and children. The Y-axis on the figure has been inverted to show an upward progression in ranks from the least important to the most important propositions.

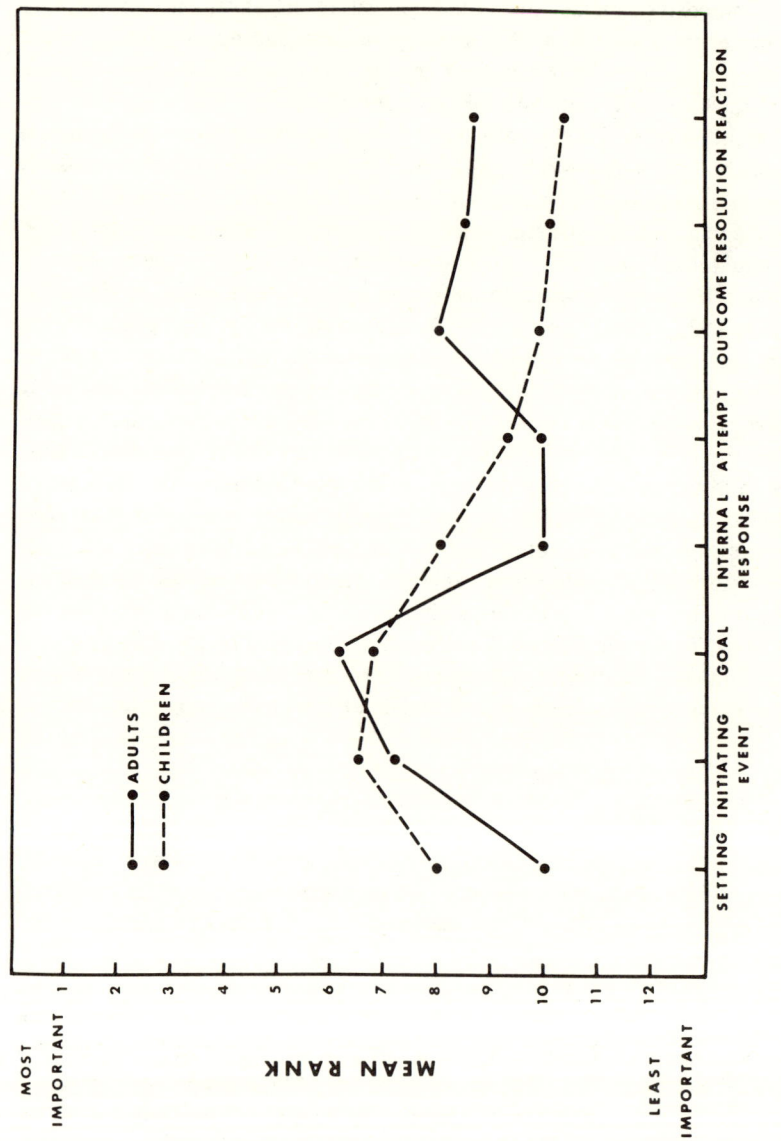

FIG. 11.6. Mean ranks of propositions in stories for eight syntactic categories for adults and children.

The data presented in Figure 11.6 were analyzed by three different analyses of variance in the same fashion as were syntactic categories in the summary data. In general, adults and children differed in the ranks they assigned to propositions in six syntactic categories, producing a significant interaction of category by group: $F(5,760) = 8.08, p < .001$. Tests on simple effects and Newman-Keuls comparisons showed that the differences among categories were significant for both age groups. Adults ranked the *initiating events* and *goals* of the stories as significantly more important than any of the other syntactic categories. The next most important categories for adults were *outcomes, resolutions,* and *reactions. Settings, internal responses,* and *attempts* as a set were ranked least important by adults, $p < .05$.

Children ranked the *initiating event* and *goal* as the most important categories, in line with adults, but in this case, the mean rank for *goal* was also equivalent to the mean rank for *settings* and *internal responses,* Newman-Keuls, $p < .05$. The least important categories for children were *resolutions, reactions, outcomes,* and *attempts*.

The ranks for relative importance given by the adults were generally compatible with the hierarchical organization shown in the social inference schema, though resolutions were ranked at a second level rather than primary level of importance. Because the initiating event, goal, and resolution occur as higher order nodes in the social inference schema, they should be considered more important for the general gist or overall meaning of the story than lower level nodes. The ranks for importance given by the children also suggest that the goal and initiating event are higher order nodes in their story schema, but *not the resolution*. However, the generally decreasing trend evident from initiating event to resolution and reaction in the curve for children's rankings suggests that children's judgments of importance may have been based more on temporal sequence than on the importance of propositions in the hierarchical structure of a story. A sequence effect can be seen because the syntactic categories are laid out in Figure 11.6 by their general order of occurrence from beginning to end in a typical story. In all stories, the setting included the first and sometimes the second propositions, and the resolution included one or more of the last propositions in the stories. The goal propositions appeared in different sequential positions in the four stories, but always occurred at least before the middle of the story. Thus, it appears that children were in part simply ranking nodes at the beginning of the story as more important than those at the end of the story.

In order to examine the differential effect of sequence more directly, a polynomial trend analysis was performed on the rank data for the six syntactic categories contained in all four stories. This analysis showed a significantly different linear trend pattern for the two groups: $F(1,158) = 12.51, p < .001$, as well as significantly different quartic trend: $F(1,158) = 17.25, p < .001$. These interaction effects support the conclusion that a sequential pattern was present in children's judgments of importance of propositions; whereas a nonsequential pattern was present in adults' judgments of the importance, again suggesting the influence of hierarchical structure only for the adults.

Hierarchical levels. Ranks assigned to propositions in stories were then examined directly for their relationship to the hierarchical structure of the episode system of each story. The same hierarchical levels were used in this analysis as in the analysis of the summary data. The mean ranks for propositions at three hierarchical levels in the four stories is shown in Figure 11.7 for adults and children. The ranks have been combined for levels 3 to 5, and no propositions representing settings were included at any hierarchical level.

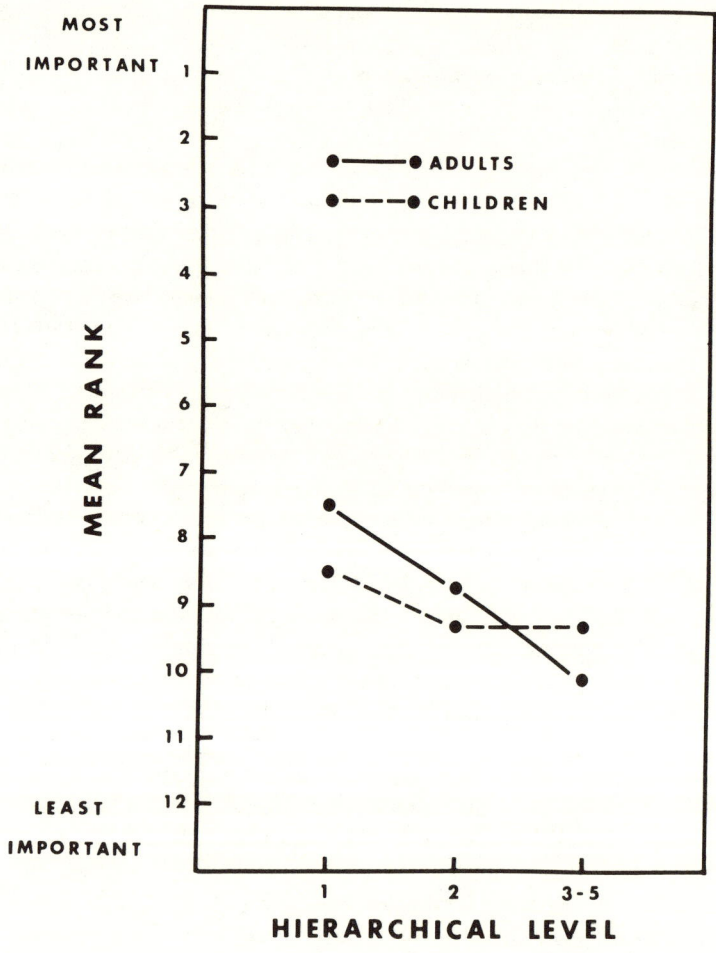

FIG. 11.7. Mean ranks of propositions at three hierarchical levels for adults and children.

As can be seen in Figure 11.7, the ranks for importance decreased significantly for propositions at lower levels in the story hierarchy across the age groups: $F(2,304) = 17.78$, $p < .001$: and there was a significant interaction of hierarchical level with age group: $F(2,304) = 5.53$, $p < .01$.

Tests on simple effects and Newman-Kuels comparisons showed that ranks assigned to propositions by adults were signficantly different for all three hierarchical levels, $p < .05$. Propositions at higher levels were considered more important than propositions at lower levels in the story hierarchy. Children, on the other hand, showed no significant differences in the ranks they assigned to propositions at different hierarchical levels. These findings add further support to the conclusion that the underlying hierarchical structure of each story influenced judgments of the importance of propositions for adults but not for children.

High Potency Words

The lists of important words given by the subjects were examined to determine content categories for words chosen and the relationship of the words to the summaries and propositions ranked most important in stories. These findings relate more directly to the encoding and recall processes involved in reading comprehension in general, and are presented more fully elsewhere (McConaughy, 1980a; McConaughy & Tomlinson, 1980). Here it is important only to point out that although adults and children tended to form similar lists of important words, adults were much more likely to add words for inferred dispositional traits of story characters. This difference was significant when high potency words were selected from memory of a story: $\chi^2 = 5.49$, $p < .05$. An example was the word "greedy" for the Dog story shown earlier. This tendency to infer disposition was so strong in some adults that they also included dispositional traits in their lists of words selected while viewing the story texts, even though they were instructed to select their words directly from the texts, which contained no such disposition terms.

DISCUSSION

The results of this study provide support for the distinction between the causal inference schema and the social inference schema as representing different developmental levels of story comprehension. Both the content of the summaries and the rank order judgments on propositions showed differences between adults and fifth-grade children in the types of information they considered to be most important in stories. As predicted, children seemed to place more emphasis on what happened in the sequence of actions and events in stories. Adults more strongly emphasized motivation in terms of the major goal and inferred internal responses of characters; at the same time, they included information about what happened in a story.

Differences of Emphasis in Summaries

The findings that both adults and children included high proportions of initiating events, resolutions, and outcomes in their summaries indicated that both groups were focusing on what happened in the plot structure of the stories. However, adults' summaries also included a high proportion of statements representing the major goals of the stories. This suggests that adults use the goal to provide an overall theme as a motivational link between the initiating event and resolution of the story, as shown in higher order nodes in the social inference schema. In addition to including the major goal of the story in their summaries, adults also added significantly more inferred internal responses than did children. This further supports the conclusion that adults' internal schema for stories includes mental events that provide motivation for a character's actions in a story.

The motivational elements represented by goals and internal responses were found to be less frequent or absent in children's summaries for stories. Children's summaries included a high proportion of statements for the initiating events, outcomes, and resolutions, but significantly fewer goals. This reflects the organization of the causal inference schema, which organizes the plot structure of a story but excludes the higher order nodes for the major goal. Children also made significantly fewer inferences than did adults, and showed no preference for inferring internal responses over any other types of information as adults did.

It was interesting that adults did not also include in their summaries a high proportion of internal responses that were explicitly stated in the texts of the stories. Perhaps this was because the adults were able to infer more general internal responses and dispositions, for which the majority of subgoals, thoughts, and feelings stated in the story texts provided elaborating details. Therefore, if the inferred elements are included in the summaries, the elaborations need not to be stated, as Johnson (this volume) and Kintsch and van Dijk (1978) have suggested. An example of this was the inference made by many adult subjects that the dog in the story presented in Table 11.1 was "greedy," and that animal characters in other stories were "hungry," "tricky," or were "fooled" in some way (all of which were inferred states or dispositional traits). The fact that inferred dispositions did not show up as a significant category of inference for adults may have been an artifact of the scoring system, since temporary states, such as "hunger," were scored as internal responses and more permanent character traits such as "greed" were scored as dispositions.

The existence in adult summaries of inferences about character traits and mental states suggests that the present story grammar might be expanded to include a new syntactic category for *disposition* in the social inference schema in order to account more fully for this level of comprehension. This is further supported by the finding that, when selecting important words from memory, adults added significantly more high potency words for implicit dispositional traits of characters than did children. It is possible that adults may have added words for inferred dispositions to their lists of important words in order to account for intentions and actions of characters previously described in the summaries. This interpretation is compatible with arguments presented in attribution theory by other authors who suggest that social inference in general involves a chain of inferences, moving from observed actions or behavior to intentions and then to dispositions or character traits that account for intentions (Jones & Davis, 1965; Reeder & Brewer, 1979; Shaver, 1975). It has also been argued that attribution of disposition is a highly efficient method of chunking information about intentions and actions of story characters in terms of personal causality (Bruce, 1975; 1980). We suggest that such dispositional attribution may represent a more condensed form of comprehension at the level of the social inference schema and as such should be more characteristic of adult's summarization process than of children's. This possibility warrants further research, perhaps by restricting the length of story summaries to determine whether such a restriction encourages dispositional attribution in adults, but not in children, as we would predict.

The present findings on developmental differences in the summaries are compatible with earlier evidence from recall tasks (e.g., Mandler & Johnson, 1977; Stein & Glenn, 1979) and evidence presented by Johnson in her chapter in this volume. Johnson's data are of particular interest because she examined developmental differences in both recall and summarization of stories. The major focus of her work was to describe the prerequisite skills and operations involved in summarization and to detail the acquisition of these processes. She argued that first-, third-, and fifth-grade children, as well as adults, had the prerequisite skills for summarizing, such as comprehending individual propositions, establishing connections between propositions, identifying the structure of stories and remembering enough information to make deletions in summaries. This was evident in the high quality of recall of stories, since the recall statements of all age groups represented a high percentage of nodes for the basic constituents of the stories. These included at least 68% of the nodes in a long familiar story and at least 86% of the nodes in a shorter unfamiliar story. The summaries of the two stories differed from the recall protocols by generally including less detail within statements while still retaining the main point for individual nodes, as well as by deleting entire nodes. In addition to use of these general processes for summarization, adults differed from children in their greater tendency to produce transformations of the original text, such as replacing specific content with generalizations and incorporating information from several nodes into one combined statement. Children more often than adults summarized by restating or paraphrasing original propositions and deleting other propositions, though they also were able to perform more sophisticated operations to a lesser extent. These findings by Johnson described developmental differences in the cognitive *processes* involved in summarization, as contrasted with developmental differences in the *content* of summary protocols described in the present study.

In terms of content, it was particularly interesting that Johnson also found evidence for selectivity in the types of information represented in recall and summaries for adults and children that is supportive of the interpretations of findings presented here. In the recall protocols, Johnson found that there was a substantial increase with age in the number of statements representing goals of both the familiar and unfamiliar stories, again suggesting a developmental increase in emphasis on motivation. There was also a greater tendency to include resolutions, or final endings, as age increased, suggesting a developmental decrease in sequence effects in memory. In the summaries, she found a high percentage of all age groups (70% or more) included statements representing settings, initiating events, and major outcomes in stories, which is compatible with our description of a causal inference schema. At the same time, representation of implicit and explicit goals, as well as resolutions, in the summaries, again increased substantially with age. This is compatible with our description of the social inference schema as a more mature level of development.

Differences in Judgments of Important Information

The judgments on the importance of single propositions in stories reflected differences in emphasis on motivational elements similar to those found in the summaries. Adults' judgments on the relative importance of explicit information in stories generally corresponded to the types of information they included in their summaries. Adults ranked the initiating event, goal, and resolution as the most important information in stories. Again, these syntactic categories reflect the organization of information in the social inference schema. Children's judgments on important propositions seemed to reflect a different type of organization of story information. Although like adults, children ranked the initiating event and goal as most important, they ranked the resolution as significantly lower in importance. It was suggested that the lower rank for resolution may reflect a sequence effect in the judgments of children, rather than judgments based on the relative importance of propositions in a hierarchical structure organized around a theme or goal. These findings are similar to Denhiere and LeNy's (1980), which showed that younger children (8 years or less) tend to assign more importance to the initial portions of a story and that the degree of agreement on the importance of propositions which represent the underlying story structure increases with age. We maintain that judgments based on sequence of information rather than hierarchical organization are characteristic of the less mature causal inference schema.

The above conclusions were further supported by findings that adults consistently ranked propositions at higher levels of a story hierarchy as more important than propositions at lower levels, but that children showed no differences in their judgments of importance based on hierarchical levels. Thus it appears that the developmental differences in story schemata shown in the summaries were further highlighted by judgments on important propositions. Brown and Smiley (1977) have shown that such "metacognitive" judgments on the importance of propositions in stories are directly related to recall for both children and adults. They also showed that the ability to make consistent judgments of propositional importance increases significantly with age, with fifth grade seeming to be a transitional age level for acquiring such ability. The findings of the present study show how adults' and children's judgments of importance are related to different syntactic categories of information described by a story grammar.

Yussen et al. (1980) also examined children's judgments of important and critical elements in stories in relation to specific syntactic categories in a story grammar. They found, first, that children's judgments of importance were not necessarily the same as their judgments of critical elements for communicating story information to another person. This may help to explain why children's judgments of importance in the present study did not match the content of important information in their summaries, because our instructions for summarization were closer to Yussen et al.'s definition of critical elements. The rank order task may also have been more difficult than summarizing for children, and, thereby, resulted in the greater sequence effect in their rankings. Yussen et al. also found that older children in their study (fourth, fifth, and sixth grade) were no different from adults in choosing critical elements. The target elements, in this case, however, were only those that the experimenters had identified as key elements for communicating the *action sequence* of the story. These critical elements fit what we have described in our causal inference schema, namely, what precipitated the action (the initiating event), what the character did (the major attempt or our plot), and what resulted from the action (the consequence or our resolution). Thus Yussen et al.'s findings are consistent with our findings on summaries for fifth grade children, but *not* for adults. The reason for the difference regarding adults is most likely because Yussen et al. did not evaluate (or at least did not report) any differences between the groups on the importance of the major goals of the stories because the goal was not included as a critical element. They also made no distinction between major goals and subgoals or other forms of internal responses, and there was no opportunity for the subjects to add inferred information in their judgments of critical elements. Thus the present findings add to the previous research by showing how adults differ from children in the way they go beyond reporting the basic action sequence of story and focus on the motivation for the actions as critical for communicating story information.

Qualitative vs. Quantitative Changes in Schemata

The evidence presented here supports the view that there are differences in the internal generic forms of story schemata used by adults and children as described. Whether these differences represent a qualitative or quantitative shift in story schemata is not clear at this point. The data seem to represent both quantitative and qualitative changes in story comprehension. Quantitative differences are reflected in the findings that: (1) adults included more information on average in their summaries than did children; (2) adults made more inferences in general than did children; and (3) the differences between adults and children were represented by greater proportions of summary statements within certain syntactic categories as compared to other categories. These differences suggest an additive phenomenon based on better memory or retention skills for adults.

Qualitative differences, on the other hand, are suggested by the evidence on ranks of important propositions and their relationships to hierarchical levels in story schemata. The assignment of ranks cannot be interpreted as a function of better retention, because both adults and children had access to the same amount of information in the texts of stories and they were not required to rank from memory. As pointed out above, the rankings of adults suggested a hierarchical ordering of story information, whereas the rankings of children seemed to be based more on sequence. This represents a qualitative difference in the underlying structural organization of story schemata for the two groups. Qualitative differences also seem to be reflected in the data on summaries in a more subtle way by the differential proportions of goals and inferred internal responses. Both groups of subjects were instructed to summarize the stories in as few words as possible and to include only what they considered to be the most important information. Because each story text contained only one goal proposition, both adults and children, in a sense, had equal chances to select goals as important information regardless of the lengths of their summaries. Similarly, both groups had equal chances to infer internal responses over other types of information. The finding that adults included a significantly higher number of goals and inferred internal responses under the above conditions suggests that these categories were more salient or more important in the level of comprehension for adults than they were for children. This again seems to be more of a qualitative difference than a quantitative one. Further research placing a time limit or, better yet, a length limit, on the summaries, would help to clarify this issue by decreasing the quantitative differences in the amount of information given by the two groups.

Task Demands

It is important to qualify the preceding discussion by pointing out that comprehension of a story at the level of the social inference schema should vary with the experimental task demands as well as with the general age of the story perceiver (Brown, 1975; Flavell, 1971). There is evidence to suggest that when the experimental methodology makes it easier for the subject to focus on motivation, such as the use of probe questions, the saliency of internal responses and goals in a story seems to increase for both fifth-grade and younger children. For example, when Stein and Glenn (1979) asked subjects directly what information was most important after recall of a story, they found children placed more emphasis on motives, feelings, and thoughts of characters. Fifth graders, in particular, gave internal responses as the most important categories. Fifth-grade children also seemed less restricted to temporal sequence than younger children, by stressing higher order goals and making inferences about psychological causality when responding to these questions. On the other hand, such emphasis on motivation by children has not been found under conditions of free recall (Johnson, this volume: Mandler & Johnson, 1977; Stein & Glenn, 1979). Shifting the method from verbatim recall to probe questions, then, may show the beginnings of social inference at earlier ages because the task demands under probe make motivational elements more obvious to children. Along similar lines, fifth-grade children may have found it easier to make attributions about intentionality when special attention was called to internal responses by moving them and linguistically marking them in stories (Stein & Nezworski, 1977a), but not when internal responses were moved and left unmarked (Stein & Nezworski, 1977b).

Further evidence on attribution of intentionality under different task demands has been produced by the use of probe questions to assess understanding of psychological causality in stories and manipulation of the story itself to produce ambiguity or discrepancy between characters' intentions and the consequences of their actions. When children are asked questions specifically about psychological causality in stories, developmental differences regarding social inferences become less distinct. It seems that both first- and fifth-grade children were able to give internal responses and goals as the locus of causality for the direct consequences or resolution of a story when responding to such probe questions (Berndt & Berndt, 1975; Fitzhenry-Coor, 1977). Again, however, in both of these studies attribution of intentionality increased significantly with age.

On the other hand, when ambiguity is introduced into stories by making characters' intentions conflict with consequences of their actions, differences reappear in the way older and younger children process the discrepant information. First-grade children either deleted intentions and recalled only actions (Stein & Glenn, 1977a) or showed distortion in recall due to recency effects of later described consequences on earlier stated intentions (Austin, Ruble & Trabasso, 1977). Fifth-grade children were able to retell discrepant stories accurately but inferred reasons for the contradictions between intentions and consequences (Stein and Glenn, 1977a; Trabasso, Nicholas, Omanson, & Johnson, 1977). Similarly, when motives and character traits were deleted from moral judgment stories, older children (9 and 12 years old) supplied their own intentions and dispositions for characters through inference. Younger children (6 years old) seemed content to reiterate the story literally without inferring intentions (Flapan, 1968; Fitzhenry-Coor, & Thompson, 1982).

When a subject retrieves intentions or disposition with the help of probe questions or linguistic markers, this cannot be considered to represent the same level of competence as focusing on motivation *spontaneously* and making inferences to explain psychological causality under conditions where motivational elements are less obvious. The above evidence under different task demands, therefore, suggests that although young children may recognize intentions or other mental events or states with the help of external aids to comprehension, it appears that they do not fully integrate such information into their internal story schema until later ages. What is of interest is not the exact age at which these effects occur, but rather the developmental progression from causal to social inference across ages and tasks in general.

The findings of the present study suggest further that even fifth-grade children do not seem to have fully incorporated motivational elements into their internal story schemata and that fifth grade may represent a transitional age level moving toward social inference. We argued earlier that the way a subject summarizes a story should more closely reflect the hierarchical organization of the internal schema than would attempts at exact recall of a story, responses to probe questions, or manipulation of story organization. This is due to different task demands for a summary, which require the subject to select out information that is most important for the general gist of the story and to delete elaborating details and other less important information. It is important to point out at this point that both the adults and children in the present study were able to meet to the cognitive demands for the summarization task. This was evident in the finding that both groups included significantly more propositions in their summaries from the highest hierarchical levels in the story structures generated by the grammar and excluded propositions from lower hierarchical levels. This finding is compatible with Rumelhart's (1977) rules describing the summarization process in general and the "levels effects" found by other researchers (e.g., Kintsch, 1975; Kintsch & van Dijk, 1978; Thorndyke, 1977). Thus, it can be legitimately concluded that the differences found in the content of the summaries of the adults and children in the present study reflect real differences in what they considered to be most important for the meaning of the stories, rather than a difference in their general abilities to meet the task demands. This conclusion is further supported by Day and Brown's (1980) and Johnson's (this volume) findings, which showed that children, of fifth grade level and younger, are capable of summarizing texts and stories by deleting less important or redundant information. What is most interesting developmentally are the different types of information children and adults choose to delete.

Implications

The present evidence suggests that what adults think is most important in stories is not always the same as what children think is most important, particularly where motivation of characters is concerned. This does not mean that children up to fifth grade level are not capable of comprehending motivation in stories under any circumstances, but rather that they do not seem to focus on it *spontaneously* and emphasize it the way adults do. This difference in emphasis has important implications in several areas of concern. First, the evidence from story summaries and ranking of propositions suggests that the internal generic representations of story schemata used by children will not necessarily match the organization of ideal schemata generated by adult text grammars. Mosenthal (1979) has recently made similar arguments about children's schemata for paragraph organization. He found that children's recall of paragraphs improved when the text was thematically reorganized to match the particular internal schemata demonstrated by children on a pretest task, rather than when the paragraph matched the structure created by a text grammar. As pointed out earlier, much of the story research to date has relied on adult grammars to describe story structure, and tested children's comprehension against these structures.

Second, if it is concluded that there may be different types of internal schemata for stories, this may shed new light on our understanding of the processing difficulties of disabled subpopulations, such as children with reading disabilities. Perhaps disabled readers possess a less mature form of a story schema than do normal children of the same age, and this in part affects their level of comprehension. There is a small body of recent literature that suggests that good and poor readers differ in their ability to organize story information according to its importance in some overall structure (Weaver, 1978). For example, in a study of story organization abilities of kindergarten children, deHirsch, Jansky and Langford (1966) found that one of the best predictors of second grade reading achievement was an early ability to organize and integrate stories into a meaningful whole. In addition, deHirsch's clinical descriptions of older poor readers (11 to 15 years) indicated they had difficulties in telling a coherent story. Fry, Johnson, and Muehl (1970) also showed poor second grade readers characteristically told stories based on picture sequences as a series of descriptive sentences that were not integrated into a cohesive story structure. In a more recent study, Smiley, Oakley, Worthen, Campione, and Brown (1977) compared good and poor seventh grade readers on their ability to recall information according to levels of importance to the central theme of a story. They found that poor readers were significantly less sensitive to gradients of importance than were good readers, and that they performed no better than first grade readers in a second study.

Subsequent to the Smiley et al. study, Weaver and Dickinson (in press) examined the story recall abilities of reading disabled boys ranging from 9 to 15 years of age and compared them to Stein and Glenn's (1979) sample of normal fifth grade readers. They found that the poor readers seem to have the same general knowledge of the underlying story schema as good readers as described by the Stein and Glenn grammar. However, a more in-depth analysis of the protocols showed poor readers used a strategy of trying to recall the stories verbatim, and as a result, they made fewer inferences and produced less coherent stories in terms of causal and temporal organization of plot structure. Weaver and Dickinson concluded that the recall of poor readers showed a "flattening" of differences between centrally important and less important categories, similar to the findings of Smiley et al. (1977).[5]

Taken together, the results of the above studies suggest that poor readers' comprehension problems may be related to an insensitivity to the relative importance of different information to the central theme and hierarchical organization of the underlying story schema. Perhaps this is because disabled readers operate under an "impoverished" form of internal story schema, which may not be developed even to the level of the causal inference schema, much less the social inference schema described here. McConaughy (1978, 1980a,b) has argued elsewhere that there may be a lower level form of story schema that represents simple description of story events in an "and-then" type of temporal sequence rather than focusing on physical or psychological causality. Descriptions of preschool children's storytelling in play examined by Wolf, Grollman, and Scarlett (1982) as well as young children's construction of their own stories (Applebee, 1978; Miller, 1976; Stein & Glenn, 1977a), seem to fit this picture of a schema consisting of loosely strung together sequences of events. Yussen et al.'s (1980) findings that young children (second grade) showed significantly less ability than older children to select critical elements in the action sequence of a story lends further support to this notion of a simple description schema. Such a simpler form of story schema may also be characteristic of certain disabled readers' level of comprehension and is the focus of McConaughy's (1982b) present research efforts.

Finally, differences in internal story schemata have important implications for educational teaching practices as well as future research. McConaughy (1980b, 1982a) has argued that children's level of comprehension in school might be addressed more effectively if teaching methods were tailored to differences in internal schemata for stories. In other words, there may be a natural gap between what the teacher thinks is most important and what the children focus on spontaneously. Strategies for assessing and bridging this potential gap might include direct use of diagrams of story structure (Cunningham & Foster, 1978), use of pre-questions to focus initial attention on important information, and design of post-questions to focus recall on different categories of information outlined by a story grammar (Guthrie, 1977, McConaughy, 1982a). Use of summarization to supplement exact recall would also be a useful technique for gaining a more direct picture of what students think is most important, rather than assuming that children's judgments are the same as adults' judgments.

---

[5]Weaver and Dickinson also concluded that Stein and Glenn's (1979) story grammar was not sensitive to such problems of poor readers because their grammar did not focus on the organization of information according to its importance in the overall story structure. The present authors chose not to adopt Stein and Glenn's grammar for similar reasons, as explained earlier.

ACKNOWLEDGMENTS

This research was supported in part by an Institutional Grants Award from the University of Vermont, and is part of an unpublished doctoral dissertation by Stephanie H. McConaughy for a Ph.D. in Psychology at the University of Vermont, 1980. Initial data from the study were presented by Dr. McConaughy at the fourth annual Boston University Conference on Language Development, Boston, Massachusetts, September 14–15, 1979. We are grateful to Kim Tomlinson and Janet Shoskes for their help in the data analyses and to Teri Gelineau for her endless patience in construction of the figures. We also wish to thank Keith Nelson for his helpful comments on the manuscript and Nancy Johnson for advance copies of her chapter for this series. Requests for reprints should be sent to Dr. Stephanie H. McConaughy, Psychiatry Department, University of Vermont, Burlington, Vermont 05405.

REFERENCES

Applebee, A. N. *A child's concept of story*. Chicago, Ill: University of Chicago Press, 1978.
Austin, V., Ruble, D. N., & Trabasso, T. Recall and order effects in children's moral judgments. *Child Development*, 1977, *48*, 470–474.
Bartlett, F. C. *Remembering: A study in experimental and social psychology*. Cambridge, England: Cambridge University Press, 1932.
Berndt, T. J. & Berndt, E. Children's use of motives and intentionality in person perception and moral judgment. *Child Development*, 1975, *46*, 904–912.
Bower, G. H. Experiments on story understanding and recall. *Quarterly Journal of Experimental Psychology*, 1976, *28*, 511–534.
Brown, A. L. Recognition, reconstruction and recall of innovative sequence by pre-operational children. *Child Development*, 1975, *46*, 156–166.
Brown, A. L. & Smiley, S. S. Rating the importance of structural units of prose passages: A problem of meta cognitive development. *Child Development*, 1977, *48*, 1–8.
Bruce, B. C. Belief systems and language understanding. (Report No. 2973). Bolt, Beranek & Newman, Inc., January, 1975.
Bruce, B. C. Analysis of interacting plans as a guide to the understanding of story structure. *Poetics*, 1980, *9*, 295–311.
Cunningham, J. W. & Foster, E. O. The ivory tower connection: A case study. *The Reading Teacher*, 1978, *31*, 365–69.
Dale, E. & Chall, J. A formula for predicting readability. *Educational Research Bulletin*, Ohio State University, 1948, *27*, 37–54.
Day, Jeanne D. & Brown, A. L. *Developmental trends in the use of summarization rules*. Paper presented at the American Educational Research Association Conference, Boston, April 1980.
de Hirsch, K., Jansky, J. J. & Langford, W. S. *Predicting reading failure*. New York: Harper & Row, 1966.
Denhiere, G. & LeNy, J. Relative importance of meaningful units in comprehension and recall of narratives by children and adults. *Poetics*, 1980, *9*, 147–161.
Fillmore, C. The case for case. In E. Bach and R. G. Harms (Eds.), *Universals in linguistic theory*. New York: Holt, Rinehart, & Winston, 1968.
Fitzhenry-Coor, I. *Children's comprehension and inference in stories of intentionality*. Paper presented at the Society for Research in Child Development, New Orleans, La., March 1977.

Fitzhenry-Coor, I. and Thompson, D. *The role of class inclusion in children's story recall and comprehension.* Unpublished manuscript, University of Vermont, 1982.

Flapan, D. *Children's understanding of social interaction.* New York: Teacher's College Press, 1968.

Flavell, J. H. Stage-related properties of cognitive development. *Cognitive Psychology,* 1971, *2,* 421–453.

Fry, M. A., Johnson, C. S., & Muehl, S. Oral language production in relation to reading achievement among select second graders. In D. J. Bakker and P. Satz (Eds.), *Specific reading disability: Advances in theory and method.* Amsterdam: Rotterdam University Press, 1970.

Guthrie, J. T. Research views: story comprehension. *The Reading Teacher,* 1977, *30,* 5, 574–577.

Johnson, N. What do you do if you can't tell the whole story? The development of summarization skills. In K. E. Nelson (Ed.) *Children's language, (Vol. 4).* Hillsdale, N.J.: Lawrence Erlbaum Associates, 1983.

Jones, E. E. & Davis, K. E. From acts to dispositions: The attribution process in person perception. In L. Berkowitz (Ed.), *Advances in experimental social psychology (Vol. 2).* New York: Academic Press, 1965.

Kintsch, W. Memory for prose. In C. N. Cofer. *The structure of human memory.* San Francisco: W. H. Freeman and Co., 1975.

Kintsch, W. & van Dijk, T. A. Toward a model of text comprehension and production. *Psychological Review,* 1978, *85,* 363–394.

Lindsay, P. H. & Norman, D. A. *Human information processing.* New York: Academic Press, 1977.

Mandler, J. M. & Johnson, N. S. Remembrance of things parsed: Story structure and recall. *Cognitive Psychology,* 1977, *9,* 111–151.

McConaughy, S. H. *A developmental model for story comprehension in reading or listening.* Paper presented at the third annual Boston University Conference on Language Development, Boston, September 1978.

McConaughy, S. H. *Cognitive structures for reading comprehension: Judging the relative importance of ideas in short stories.* Unpublished doctoral dissertation, University of Vermont, 1980. (a)

McConaughy, S. H. Using story structure in the classroom. *Language Arts,* 1980, *57,* 157–165. (b)

McConaughy, S. H. Developmental changes in story comprehension and levels of questioning. *Language Arts,* 1982, *59,* 580–589, 600. (a)

McConaughy, S. H. *Using story structure to diagnose reading problems.* Paper presented at the twenty-seventh annual Convention of the International Reading Association, Chicago, Il., April 1982. (b)

McConaughy, S. H. & Tomlinson, K. P. *Judging the relative importance of words and concepts in text: A foundation of skilled reading.* Paper presented at the twenty-fifth annual convention of the International Reading Association, St. Louis, Mo., May 1980.

Miller, M. *The construction and symbolization of make-believe stories from childhood to adolescence.* Unpublished doctoral dissertation, University of California at Berkeley, 1976.

Minsky, M. A framework for representing knowledge. In P. Winston (Ed.), *The psychology of computer vision.* New York: McGraw-Hill, 1975.

Mosenthal, P. Three types of schemata in children's recall of cohesive and uncohesive text. *Journal of Experimental Child Psychology,* 1979, *27,* 129–142.

Neisser, U. *Cognition and reality.* San Francisco: W. H. Freeman & Co., 1976.

Reeder, G. D. & Brewer, M. B. A schematic model of dispositional attribution in interpersonal perception. *Psychological Review,* 1979, *86,* 1, 61–79.

Rubin, S. & Gardner, H. *Once upon a time: The development of sensitivity to story structure.* Paper presented at the Conference on Researching Response to Literature and the Teaching of Literature, Buffalo, N.Y., October 1977.

Rumelhart, D. E. Notes on schema for stories. In D. G. Bobrow & A. Collins (Eds.), *Representations and understandings*. New York: Academic Press, Inc., 1975.

Rumelhart, D. E. Understanding and summarizing brief stories. In D. LaBerge & S. J. Samuels (Eds.), *Basic processes in reading: Perception and comprehension*. Hillsdale, N.J.: Lawrence Erlbaum Associates, 1977.

Rumelhart, D. E. and Ortony, A. The representation of knowledge in memory. In R. C. Anderson, R. J. Spiro, and W. E. Montague (Eds.) *Schooling and the acquisition of knowledge*. Hillsdale, N.J.: Lawrence Erlbaum Associates, 1977.

Schank, R. The structure of episodes in memory. In D. G. Bobrow & A. Collins (Eds.), *Representation and understanding: Studies in cognitive science*. New York: Academic Press, 1975.

Shaver, K. G. *An Introduction to Attribution Processes*. Cambridge: Winthrop Publishers, Inc., 1975.

Smiley, S. S., Oakley, D. D., Worthen, D., Campione, J. C., & Brown, A. L. Recall of thematically relevant material by adolescent good and poor readers as a function of written versus oral presentation. *Journal of Educational Psychology*, 1977, *69*, 4, 381–387.

Stein, N. L. *The effects of increasing temporal disorganization on children's recall of stories*. Paper presented at the Psychonomic Society meetings, St. Louis, Mo., November 1976.

Stein, N. L. & Glenn, C. G. *A developmental study of children's recall of story material*. Paper presented at the Society for Research in Child Development, Denver, Colo., April 1975.

Stein, N. L. & Glenn, C. G. *A developmental study of children's construction of stories*. Paper presented at the Society for Research in Child Development, New Orleans, La., March 1977. (a)

Stein, N. L., and Glenn, C. G. *The role of structural variation in children's recall of simple stories*. Paper presented at Society for Research in Child Development, New Orleans, La. 1977. (b)

Stein, N. L. & Glenn, C. G. An analysis of story comprehension in elementary school children. In R. O. Freedle (Ed.), *New directions in discourse processing (Vol. 2)*. Norwood, N.J.: Ablex, 1979.

Stein, N. L. & Nezworski, M. T. *The effects of linguistic markers on children's recall of stories: A developmental study*. Unpublished manuscript, Washington University, 1977. (a)

Stein, N. L. & Nezworski, M.T. *The role of organization and instructions in recall and reconstruction of stories*. Unpublished manuscript, Washington University, 1977. (b)

Stein, N. L. & Nezworski, M. T. The effects of organization and instructional set on story memory. *Discourse Processes*, 1978, *1*, 177–193.

Thorndyke, P. W. Cognitive structures in comprehension and memory of narrative discourse. *Cognitive Psychology*, 1977, *9*, 77–110.

Trabasso, T., Nicholas, D. A., Omanson, R., & Johnson, L. *Inferences and story comprehension*. Paper presented at the Society for Research in Child Development, New Orleans, La., March 1977.

van Dijk, T. A. *Some aspects of text grammars*. The Hague, The Netherlands: Mouton, 1972.

van Dijk, T. A. Semantic macro-structures and knowledge frames in discourse comprehension. In M. A. Just & P. A. Carpenter (Eds.), *Cognitive processes in comprehension*. Hillsdale, N.J.: Lawrence Erlbaum Associates, 1977.

Weaver, P. A. Comprehension, recall and dyslexia: A proposal for the application of schema theory. *Bulletin of the Orton Society*, 1978, *28*, 92–113.

Weaver, P. A. & Dickinson, D. Scratching below the surface structure: Exploring the usefulness of story grammars. *Discourse Processes*, in press.

Wolf, D., Grollman, S. and Scarlett, W. G. The development of fictional narrative. In D. Wolf and E. Gardner (Eds.) *Early symbols: A longitudinal study of early representational development*. Unpublished manuscript, Harvard University, 1982.

Yussen, S. R. Mathews, II, S. R., Buss, R. R., & Kane, P. T. Developmental change in judging important and critical elements in stories. *Developmental Psychology*, 1980, *16*, 213–219.

12 Developmental Language Studies in the Neuropsychiatric Disorders of Childhood

Barbara K. Caparulo
Donald J. Cohen
Yale Univeristy

INTRODUCTION

Current interest in Victor, the wild boy from the forests of Aveyron (Lane, 1976; Shattuck, 1980), and Genie, a modern case of forced social isolation (Fromkin, Krashen, Curtiss, Rigler, & Rigler, 1974) suggests how much we still are involved in trying to understand the shaping of human psychological processes, especially language, by social forces. Such cases of failure in the development of uniquely human attributes are equally relevant, however, to several fundamental questions about the nature of human maturation and critical periods of growth, the biological bases of language, and the relationship among pragmatic, social, and meaning systems in the developing child. Those whose work is concerned with human language have come to benefit, more or less routinely, from studies of second language learning, primate and mammalian communication, and the language of music and sign. Only occasionally, however, have children who serve as natural experiments to theories of language and speech acquisition been minded with as much care and perseverance as Itard showed in his study of Victor.

Until quite recently it was assumed that children who never developed the ability to speak, or who were severely delayed in manipulating the symbols of their native language, were extremely rare. Now more readily available child development centers, finer diagnostic tools, and improved societal attitudes about child handicaps have combined with dramatic advances in normal child language studies to allow early identification of such children. Although only four children in every 1000 suffer from severe language disability (American Psychiatric Association, 1980), significant delays in language and speech development are the most common reasons for referral to child development centers and have been found to be associated with increased risk of psychiatric disorder (Baker & Cantwell, 1982; Cantwell, Baker, & Mattison, 1979). Thus, although the child is "set" to learn language, any language, so long as good enough environmental provisions are available, the language system appears to be more susceptible than others to both environmental and biological influences. The obvious fact that a child living in Britain learns to speak English, and one living in Portugal learns to speak Portuguese, speaks to the malleability of the system. Clinically, children with normal developmental histories are found to falter in their ongoing growth during stressful transitional periods, and their language when focused on particular topics or used in certain situations becomes conflicted, charged, or otherwise inhibited. More lasting disruptions in language acquisition and performance illustrate the complexity of the process. Youngsters with dyslexia and other specific learning disorders that affect the ability to manipulate written and mathematical symbols show how these disturbances can exist in the midst of intact general intelligence and overall social competence. There are children who develop receptive and expressive language at an abnormally slow rate, demonstrating a greater asynchrony than usual between these two strands of development, but eventually acquire a normal linguistic system. In atypical childhood psychosis, whose onset follows a relatively smooth early developmental period, acquisition of complex linguistic structures becomes impaired, and items in the lexical system take on peculiar, ideosyncratically determined meanings and associations. Major difficulties in the rapid processing of speech sounds, or in decoding or encoding syntactic structures, as in childhood dysphasia, are often associated with the emergence of a natural sign system used to establish communication when other channels fail; the array of dysphasic disorders are a testimony to the intricacy of the psychological processes upon which language is based and the strength of the human need to maintain contact with others. Finally, there are youngsters with profound and usually lifelong difficulties in the mastery of all aspects of language, as in primary autism. This chapter addresses this last group of children and what we may learn from them about normal language development.

The work we have conducted with language-impaired children and young adults is carried out within the context of short-term and longitudinal studies emphasizing the biological correlates of abnormal child development. After referral, parents and children are seen in several initial research interviews, and may be observed at home and in school. Play sessions in which the child chooses his own activities and is then engaged in structured interactional games and play are videotaped and used as the data base for periodic language sampling. Formal psychological testing is adapted to the child's developmental level, linguistic skills, and attentional control; the McCarthy Scales of Children's Abilities (1972), the revised Wechsler Intelligence Scales for Children, or the Wechsler Preschool and Primary Scales of Intelligence (Wechsler, 1967, 1974) may be presented over a period of three or four testing sessions and supplemented by the results from the Arthur Adaptation of the Leiter International Performance Scale (Arthur, 1952), for younger children, or the Leiter International Performance Scale (1948), which do not require language for administration or test response. The Progressive Matrices (Raven, 1962) test general intelligence but are most useful in assessing spatial aptitude, inductive reasoning, and perceptual accuracy.

Each child receives thorough linguistic and communicative assessment. Young children are tested on the Reynell Developmental Language Scales (Reynell, 1969), and on the Sequenced Inventory of Communication Development (Hedrick, Prather, & Tobin, 1975), which allows analysis of both receptive and expressive communicative behaviors. Many of the children are able to undergo testing on selected subtests of the Illinois Test of Psycholinguistic Abilities (Kirk, McCarthy, & Kirk, 1968); scores on these tests are evaluated for the information they provide about specific strengths and deficits, and the behavior of the child during administration of each subtest often serves as an indicator of his relative comfort in processing information presented in various modalities.

Throughout the course of each child's evaluation, additional information about his developmental history and current behavior at home and school is usually provided by parents and teachers, and detailed clinical records are kept of his social relatedness, overall level of activity, ability to modulate anxiety and attention, and behavioral responses to the clinicians and to his parents. Behavior rating instruments such as the modified Childhood Personality Scale (Cohen, Dibble, & Grawe, 1977) and the Behavior Rating Instrument for Autistic and Atypical Children (Ruttenberg, Kalish, Wenar, & Wolf, 1974), are completed by several clinicians at each point of the child's evaluation (see Cohen, Caparulo, Gold, Waldo, Shaywitz, Ruttenberg, & Rimland, 1978). Although the information provided about the life histories of children with atypical development by these assessments is important in its own right, the child's intellectual and behavioral status at any one point in time is the most reliable correlate of his biological functioning. Just as children may be described and understood in terms of their overall intelligence, linguistic skills, communicative behavior, and behavioral modulation, they may be studied in terms of their biochemistry, brain structure and functioning, and psychophysiology. The major set of questions that have been investigated in our work concerns the etiologies of the pervasive developmental disturbances of childhood, and how changes in biological functioning and structure influence behavior. We have thus studied the neurochemical functioning of children in various diagnostic groups (Cohen, Caparulo, & Shaywitz, 1978, Young & Cohen, 1979), brain structure through computed tomogparaphic scanning (Caparulo, Cohen, Young, Rothman, Katz, Shaywitz, & Shaywitz, 1981), and brain electrophysiology through detailed analysis of EEGs (Waldo, Cohen, Caparulo, Young, Prichard, & Shaywitz, 1978). Children's ability to modulate their attention appropriately and consistently to both internal and external sensory stimulation has been assessed through repeated measurement of cardiovascular autonomic functioning (Kootz & Cohen, 1981).

Over two hundred children with autism, nonautistic psychosis of early onset, severe language delay, developmental language disorders, severe learning disabilities, and Tourette's syndrome of chronic multiple tics have been evaluated since 1972. Many of these children and their parents have formed research collaborations with the evaluation team, and thus have been followed in considerable detail. This collaborative relationship benefits both the child and his family and the progress of scientific research. Children receive the benefits of ongoing evaluation, using the most contemporary medical and psychiatric tools, and families establish a well-informed partnership with clinicians who are able to assist in educational planning and advocacy, decisions about drug therapy, evaluation of the success of various treatments offered by public and private agencies, and lifetime planning or residential living arrangements. In turn, we as research clinicians observe the changes over several years in symptomatology that represent the natural histories of developmental disorders, the ways in which families adjust to the requirements of their child, and shifts in performance and competence among the various intellectual and behavioral domains. Thus, our clinical research with youngsters having pervasive developmental disabilities combines the emphasis on careful control of as many variables as possible with interest in the individual. The research perspectives followed in the work reported here are designed to capture the complexities rather than the purities of development, and use a variety of investigation strategies, data collection techniques, and contexts. Rarely can specific questions about language and cognitive functioning in developmentally disabled children be answered quickly and easily. Instead, patterns that emerge over the course of many clinical interviews and observation sessions, with various assessment tools and in multiple contexts, must be studied to reveal a reliable description of an individual child's development.

Diagnostic and Methodological Issues

It is obviously desirable to study relatively large groups of children whose impairments in linguistic development can be contrasted with those of other children having different clinical presentations, and with normally developing children. Unless diagnostic groups can be clearly differentiated, and unless the children within these groups are relatively homogeneous, even the most sophisticated methods of scientific study are unlikely to show patterns of underlying dysfunction whose identification will lead to prevention and treatment. Two recurrent dilemmas in clinical developmental research make the problem of differential diagnoses extremely complex. First, the children who are the subjects of study have not read the books that have been written about them, and thus do not obey all of the rules child psychiatry has dictated. They tend to populate more heavily the boundaries between, rather than the central territories within, specific clinical syndromes (Caparulo & Cohen, 1977; Cohen, 1976). Leo Kanner, recognized as the founder of child psychiatry, has noted this in a series of theoretical and research papers published over the three decades following his identification of the syndrome he called early infantile autism (Kanner, 1943, 1973). The vast majority of children currently diagnosed by clinicians as autistic are very unlike the attractive, highly intelligent but socially odd and linguistically deviant child portrayed on television and in the popular literature. Most have cognitive impairments whose severity is startling and whose persistence into adulthood may dwarf the social handicaps by comparison. The term autism, and the condition it denotes, thus carries a range of meanings that may be differentially highlighted by various clinicians, child development centers, and researchers. The gulf between the actual dysfunctions demonstrated by some children and the interpretations given measurements of these dysfunctions can thus be deepened by a failure in the formulation of differential diagnoses. We will return to this issue later when we define the children whom we will be discussing here.

The changing nature of the pervasive developmental disorders of childhood further complicates an understanding of the etiology and significance of various functional deficits. A child with a relatively clear-cut "central language disorder" or dysphasia at age 4 years, for example, may more closely resemble a thought-disordered, schizophrenic-like preadolescent 10 years later, and a globally retarded, psychotic patient by the time he has reached young adulthood. How should these shifting clinical pictures, and the overlapping symptoms among syndromic clusters, be reflected in the work of the clinical researcher? By emphasizing the gradual changes in a child's level of competence, especially the way specific abilities and deficits alter relative to one another, one gains the opportunity of appreciating the nature of the disorder—its own natural history—and one gains the advantage of understanding how coping mechanisms may arise by which the child adapts to his environment and to his disabilities. On the other hand, reclassification of a child's disorder according to current symptomatology, regardless of early natural history, may be useful in directing educators and therapists to particular types of treatment that are matched with the child's individual behavioral needs rather than with his diagnostic label. In the research reported here, these two strategies have been integrated by using a multi-axial classification approach (see Cohen, Granger, Provence, & Solnit, 1975; Rutter, 1978). Children are classified on the basis of early natural history as well as current behavioral status and medical condition. This approach allows differences between diagnostic groups to be studied in the same way as differences within diagnostic groups.

In this paper we will diverge from the customary route of decribing early child language development and then hypothesizing about what makes it possible. Instead, we will present the findings of linguistic and cognitive studies on children with autism, and review in considerable detail the natural history of a small subgroup who represent the disorder in its purist form. After consideration of the steps in normal language acquisition, a model for understanding the delayed emergence of language in autism will be presented.

PRIMARY AUTISM: HISTORICAL, THEORETICAL, AND CLINICAL PERSPECTIVES

Child language specialists have been particularly interested in children with autism because of the peculiar constellation of symptoms involving early speech and linguistic development displayed by all children having the disorder. Leo Kanner, who first described 11 children whose unique histories and patterns of social, conceptual, and linguistic development had been previously unrecognized, highlighted the prominent inability to convey meaning to others through language; pronominal reversal, echolalia, and the absence of normal suprasegmental characteristics in the spontaneous expressive language of the children he studied had all followed upon earlier delays in syntactic and semantic development, and appeared to be related to social detachment, aloofness, and failure to display bonding behaviors that Kanner felt were pathognomonic to the disorder (Kanner, 1943). What marked this syndrome as separate from mental retardation, progressive disintegration and retardation associated with neurological and metabolic diseases, deafness, and other disorders then known to exist were the presence of the social and communicative abnormalities from the very first years of life and the emergence of relatively stable areas of normal functioning, or even above average skills; rote memory, for example, visuospatial perception, and motor dexterity were typically preserved intact while receptive language, abstract skills, and imaginative use of play materials were severely restricted. The histories of the children Kanner studied did not include any neurological or medical condition that could explain the development of the disorder.

Various theories about the cause of primary autism have been put forward in the years since Kanner first described the condition. Many children and their parents have spent long, exhaustive years with psychotherapists hoping to uncover the seeds of resentment, communicated by parents to their autistic children, that caused the condition. What has been revealed is that the parents of autistic children possess the usual range of conflicts and defenses found among all parents, as well as an extraordinary degree of devotion and ability to withstand the rigors imposed on them by the demands of their child. Well over 100 studies have been conducted to explore the psychopathology within families hypothesized as contributing to the development of autism (see Cantwell, Baker, & Rutter, 1978, for a thorough review). No evidence exists that autistic children suffer from emotional trauma during the first months of life, from cold, "refrigerator" mothers, or from intrusive, smothering mothers. Most contemporary clinicians and researchers have become convinced that autism is a disorder that develops independently of environmental factors of this sort, although clearly the child's failure to relate to his mother, because of congenital disruptions in the systems allowing for social attachment, may affect her ability to remain available to him (Koupernik, 1971; Cohen, Caparulo, & Wetstone, 1981). Because of the inability to identify autism at birth, there are no systematic studies of autistic newborns and infants, and much about the vicissitudes of mother-infant interactions remain speculative. We have observed several children with autism during the period from 2 to 3 years of age, and have been struck by the discrepancy between what mothers attribute to their children's behavior and what the behavior actually represents. That is, it appears that the mother attempts to "read into" the child's behavior purposefulness and meaning, much like mothers of normal children do (Shotter & Gregory, 1976), but in the case of autism, these attempts to teach meaning to the child, during the very early preschool years, often fail. The autistic child's major difficulties in focusing his attention and in receptive language prevent him from making use of what his mother offers. We will return to this subject later when we discuss the emergence of communicative competence. It is mentioned here because of its relevance to theories that suggest maternal maladaptive styles of parenting contribute to the development of autism; when the effects on his mother of the child's failure in bonding and establishing a shared network of focused attention and action are appreciated, such theories become less interesting.

Because primary autism is perhaps the most enigmatic of the neuropsychiatric disorders of childhood, present in children who, in the early years, are often attractive physically and seem intellectually alert, it draws the attention of a wide variety of proponents of hypotheses that raise a single symptom to the level of causation. Tinbergen and Tinbergen (1972), for example, became fascinated by the autistic child's dramatic avoidance of eye contact and postulated an etiological model that linked this avoidance with earlier overwhelming of the child by too direct or forceful stimulation. Similarly limited understanding of the range of abnormalities in primary autism can be seen in other theories, which are often difficult to disprove but seem to draw to them vehement adherents eager to institute rigorous treatment regimens. Autistic children and their families, of course, are vulnerable to fads in treatment approaches that do not have bases in fact; mysticism, relearning to experience the fetal state, physical punishment to remove "mislearned" social responses, repatterning of basic neural connections supposedly bypassed or underdeveloped during the first years, and multi-megavitamin therapy remain avenues of treatment that often exhaust parents' energies and financial resources. Because scientific investigation using systematic diagnostic criteria and rigidly controlled conditions has not been conducted on these treatment approaches, promises of sure cures or dramatic improvements in the autistic child's motor, social, and linguistic behavior only capitalize unfairly on parental confusion and despair; attention becomes diverted from educational interventions that are known to be useful (c.f., Bartak & Rutter, 1973; Des-

Lauriers, 1978), and, when failure of the unproven treatment results, the abilities of families to remain engaged with their handicapped child are severely jeopardized.

Linguistic and Cognitive Impairments in Autism

There is ample evidence from the studies done by us and many others of pervasive deficits in all areas of language development during the first four to five years in childhood autism. Several researchers have discussed the idea that these deficits, in fact, represent the underlying cause of childhood autism (see Caparulo & Cohen, 1977; Cohen, Caparulo, & Shaywitz, 1976, for a thorough review), and Churchill (1972, 1978a,b) has hypothesized that pervasive language deficits are the necessary and sufficient proximate causes of childhood autism, and can explain the autistic child's impairments in social development, object use, and speech behaviors. Churchill's theory suggests that nonlinguistic deficits, in memory, perceptual, and motor integration, and the effects of differences in psychosocial histories, may combine to make some autistic children more intellectually impaired than others (Churchill, 1978a,b). Thus, he has hypothesized that a single disability—in language—underlies the symptoms common to all autistic children; additional impairments may accompany the primary language impairment but cannot account for the development of the syndrome. Churchill's theory stands alone in being formulated as the result of careful, systematic investigation of 16 children, 13 of whom were autistic, using an experimental language composed of simple nouns, verbs, and adjectives. The children, having an average age of 74 months, were conditioned to associate consistently spoken words and hand signs with three objects, three actions, and size or color attributes of the objects. They were then tested to see if they could make cross-modal associations and could move from one- to two-word, and then three-word, "sentences," following teaching sessions over several months that lasted up to 45 minutes each and contained as many as 75 trials on each linguistic "item." These sessions were conducted to establish what Churchill refers to as "basic conditionability" in symbol-referent associations. The children were then tested on a series of higher order language functions, such as generalization beyond the original stimuli to novel stimuli, and cross-referencing using the nine-word language to test, for example, the child's ability to respond selectively to only color or shape. Prepositions such as *in, on, under,* and *beside,* and then pronouns, were introduced when appropriate, and, finally, the child's ability to generate and comprehend simple sentences using the three parts of speech in the nine-word language was assessed.

The results of Churchill's work with these children, recently made available in detail (Churchill, 1978a), document as never before the degree to which all of the young autistic children experienced major and sometimes insurmountable obstacles in the generation of language. Children who were very severely impaired (i.e., showed marked aloofness, no expressive language, and no indication of internalized language) reached impasses at the most basic levels of the nine-word language. Some, for example, were able to respond correctly to visual, one-word signs only after hundreds of conditioning trials but were unable to reach criterion on auditory, one-word reception. On the other hand, two autistic boys of about 7½ years of age were able to master quickly the nine-word language conditioning tasks (e.g., respond correctly to signed and spoken single words, two-word and three-word sentences such as "Give red block," and "Tap yellow ring"), but had major problems during training on the cross-referencing tasks or when introduced to prepositions and pronouns. The manipulation of simple syntactic structures, such as the possessive ending *s*, remained unachievable despite arduous and what must have been totally frustrating attempts by the instructors (213 sessions, for one child, lasting over a 3½ month period). One child was unable to understand sentences using pronouns ("What am I doing?" and "What color is your shirt?") even though the actions and objects, and the color attributes, were within the child's receptive and expressive vocabulary. Another child could not correctly respond to simple sentences involving prepositions, such as "Put block in ring."

Churchill's results are important because they document the basic competencies in linguistic development that are achieved by some children with more intact intellectual abilities while at the same time demonstrating the degree to which higher order linguistic rules remain inaccessible despite extraordinary training. In our work and that of others (Bartak, Rutter, & Cox, 1975, 1977; Boucher, 1976; Caparulo & Cohen, 1977; Cohen et al., 1976; Pierce & Bartolucci, 1977), similar deficits in semantic and syntactic development in young autistic children have been demonstrated on detailed standardized testing. This set of findings offers a clarification to what was originally described as early language delays in autism, and clearly indicates the futility of a treatment approach based on assumptions that the autistic child can speak if only he wished to. Yet, we are brought up short when the results of careful observation of young autistic children under stress, or in social situations in which true communication becomes essential for the transmission of needs and wants, are added to the results described above. That is, changes in linguistic performance across contexts and involving various communicative forces suggest a level of underlying linguistic competence that resists measurement. For example, parents of autistic children commonly report that their children show greatly improved performance in speech and social relatedness during periods of illness (Foy, 1970; Sullivan, 1975, 1980). Similar periods of dramatic improvement that are, unfortunately, short-lived, occur in the midst of venipuncture for blood testing or during an electroencephalogram (Caparulo & Cohen, 1980). What can account for the picture of a child who has been virtually mute for years, with what seems to be a total inability to understand even three-word sentences, who, at moments of stress, becomes socially aware and is able to shout things such as "Go home now, Mommy."

The brief and transient periods of improved language, purposeful action, and social contact occurring during periods of altered physiological and environmental circumstances may be thought of as parallels to the larger picture of changes in profiles of abilities over the course of development from infancy to early adulthood. Most autistic children remain intellectually retarded as they grow up; their understanding of socially related behaviors and their ability to establish affectionate or meaningful relationships with others persist in being impaired. However, approximately 7 to 10 percent of persons with autism do dramatically better in most areas of development as they reach adulthood (Lotter, 1978). Adult autistic persons who may be described as "improved" or "recovered" are fascinating to study, because of what they teach us about the essential nature of the autistic syndrome, and because of the renewed respect one gains for individual variation.

A Case Study

Dale was the middle child of a professional family, born following a normal pregnancy and delivery. He was healthy at birth, and ate voraciously during the first several days of life. His mother noted that she knew he was "different" at about 10 days; he arched his back when being held, stared at lights, and failed to mold himself into her arms while being fed. During the first half-year of life, he became more resistent to change, and panicked when faced with disruptions in his feeding or sleeping routine, expressed through motor agitation and screaming. He was not cuddly, failed to prepare for being being picked up, and was fascinated with looking out his living room window. The only way in which his mother could comfort him was by propping him up in front of this window. By age 10 to 12 months, Dale showed keen interest in objects but no awareness of or interest in people. He began walking at 12 months, although he never went through a crawling stage. By age 15 months he was running with agility. He only occasionally showed an awareness of sounds, did not respond to his name, did not babble or engage in vocal play. By the end of the second year, Dale began to show an association between single words such as *bed* and *milk* and their referents, but only when they were embedded within familiar bedtime and eating routines. Up until this time, he had shown only fleeting eye contact, had never responded to games such as peekaboo or waving bye-bye, and showed no understanding of the social significance of a telephone's ring or anticipation of his father's arrival home from work. Around age two years, Dale began to develop a range of stereotypic body movements such as hand flapping and moving his fingers in front of his eyes; his mother reported that it was almost impossible for her to interrupt these behaviors wihout causing a temper tantrum. At the age of

24 months, then, Dale was an active, socially aloof, and motorically agile child with no communicative behavior, catastrophic panic reactions to change in routine or in the household environment, comprehension of a few single words, and quite a wide range of unusual and stereotypic hand and body movements.

Over the next two years, Dale's behavioral symptoms grew more unmanageable because of his increased mobility and agility in climbing. Although he had no creative spontaneous speech, he began to echo the last parts of sentences just heard. He communicated his basic needs through screaming, which his mother would try to interpret through trial and error, first giving him juice, then something to eat, then checking to see if he was ill, and so forth. She felt that this period of Dale's life was the most difficult for the family, because it was almost impossible to predict Dale's behavior or to understand the meaning of his temper tantrums and cries. By age 4 years, however, Dale had begun to show evidence that he understood simple subject-verb constructions, and his receptive vocabulary of common household objects increased. At age 5 years 1 month, Dale said his first word; over the next 8 months, he incorporated original words into his echoed responses or remarks, and his vocabulary increased dramatically. Most typically, however, Dale used his expressive language to talk to himself or to objects, which he repetitively manipulated in an unimaginative way. His mother noted that between ages 5 and 6 years, Dale showed keen interest in books and in the letters of the alphabet, and learned to ask his mother to sit with him to look at picture books by saying "Read book." Dale's mother marked this period as the beginning of his improvement in behavior and language, and described it as being much like her first son's development when he was about two years old. Through books, Dale began to use short, three- and four-word phrases to describe pictures, and then to comment on what he saw during car rides and in stores. During his seventh year, Dale became fascinated with manipulation of plastic numbers and letters, and could sit for hours stacking similar letters on top of each other. At six years, nine months, Dale began spelling short words with his toy letters, and developed a written sight vocabulary of approximately 20 words over the next month. He was then enrolled in a nursery school with normal children, where he showed no interest in his classmates and instead spent long periods of time tracing the printing in books and slowly turning the pages of the teachers' record sheets. His mother spent a few months working with him on reading readiness skills, and, by the age of 7¼ years, records from his nursery school show that his expressive or oral reading was at the third grade, first month level. By his eighth year, he was reading encyclopedias with fluency and relatively good comprehension, but his oral reading of story books and his conversations showed none of the changes in intonation and stress that normally accompany recognition of the social significance of the passages or of interpersonal communication. Unlike other children whom we have reported (Caparulo & Cohen, 1977; Cohen et al., 1976), Dale's spontaneous langauge continued to remain slow and labored, as if he were choosing each word one by one. His writing skills resembled his speaking skills. Papers that he had written while attending a class for mildly retarded children, during his eighth and ninth years, show sentences of four and five words in neatly written script that express simple factual thoughts.

Dale's social skills remained poor; he failed to join other children in play, and, while able to establish eye contact, more often looked away or slightly to the left or right of his listener's eyes. The topic of discussion with his parents revolved around what he had read in his encyclopedias, and what maps he had studied that day in school. His parents spent a great deal of time "teaching" Dale about human relationships, what friends are, what family memberships means, and so on. Dale's father remarked that Dale could not understand other people's moods or the fact that members of the household did not know exactly what Dale was talking about when he referred to school events as if his family were active participants in these events. This failure to appreciate the perspectives of others often brought on temper tantrums, because Dale's listeners would demand that he start his stories at the beginning and express clearly exactly what happened.

Over the next four years, Dale's language development showed gradual improvement. In addition to the lexical development begun years earlier, his syntactic and semantic skills followed a generally even, if somewhat slow, progression. No detailed records have been kept in his language development by his teachers, but his mother noted that at 12 years Dale was beginning to use conditional sentences like this one: "If it doesn't rain tomorrow, will we be going into the city?" He began using *because* to introduce statements of cause and effect as part of one-sentence constructions at age 12½ years, replacing his previous style in which he had explained causation for a particular event by constructing another complete sentence: "We had to come home from the beach early. There were too many flies at the beach." Evaluation at age 15 by a child psychiatrist noted that Dale's expressive language appeared "within normal limits, except for some flatness and affective dullness." By this time, Dale had become extremely knowledgeable about many esoteric word meanings as a result of his systematic study of the dictionary and thesaurus, a preoccupation noted in all of the records from evaluations during this period of time. Socially, he was an extremely eccentric, manneristic youngster who took an odd, sometimes surprisingly perceptive view of the people around him. He told his mother, for example, that she was more strict in making him talk about his daily activities at the supper table than she was with his older brother, and he "guessed it was because of the autism."

Over the next few years, Dale underwent some dramatic changes. During his sixteenth year, he became increasingly argumentative and irritable, often provoked battles within his family, and then withdrew to his room where he threw objects at the door. He became quite sad, self-conscious, and worried that he was never going to grow up. Dale later told us about things that had upset him during this period of adolescence. He remembered that on one occasion, when he was about 18 years old, he became panicked and ran out of a theater because he could not follow the actors' lines. On another occasion when he was alone in New York City walking to his father's office, he was approached by someone asking for directions, and recognized how he "drew a blank and stared" at the man, even though he himself could easily navigate through the city using a guide book.

When we first met Dale at the age of 20, he had gone through a series of residential educational programs and had had psychotherapy for depression. He was a good-looking, well-dressed young man who was extremely anxious and intense. He showed no embarrassment over talking with us about his personal life history and all of its recent difficulties, and treated his intimate revelations to us about his wishes to be normal, "to get rid of the autism," as if they were topics of study in a textbook rather than as important, personal issues in his life. He rarely established eye contact, but smiled often while looking down at the floor or at the walls behind us. He seemed to think, periodically, that he should inquire politely about our interests and personal lives, and would do so while looking directly at us but without showing any real interest or pleasure in the answers. If he became anxious, he asked to go for a walk, or would begin to perseverate in speaking about some situation in which he felt similar anxiety, providing for us the most excruciatingly detailed responses to simple and direct questions. His thoughts seemed to drift from one detail to another and he was forced to follow this line of thinking; if we tried to interrupt the flow of his remarks, he became anxious, would try to provide answers relevant to the new topic, but would then switch back to the old topic at the first opportunity. Dale's language possessed strikingly odd intonational qualities; when he told us about a funny situation, for example, one got the impression of a very poor actor trying to match his affect with the lines being spoken, as if he intrinsically could not understand the humor of the situation but knew others would recognize it.

Dale told us that he didn't know "there were people" until he was seven years old, when he was made to play a circle game with the other children in his class; he said he still had to remind himself of this constantly. He very poignantly summed up his feelings about other people by saying, "I could never have a friend. I really don't know, just don't know, what to do with people, really." He decided his inability to plan for the next few years, and to set goals for his life, was caused by the "remnants of the autism. . . . A little bit is still left there."

During other discussions, our impressions of a young man with superior intelligence and quite striking, sophisticated linguistic skills were confirmed. Equally clear, however, were the deficits that remained despite many years of good special education, nurturing and sympathetic parenting, and psychotherapy. These were within the domain usually referred to as social competence; they included avoidance of eye contact, inability to understand the social significance of others' behavior, superficial ability to engage in the give-and-take of playful personal exchanges, failures in self-motivation, and, most painful to him and sympathetic observers, an inability to obtain gratification from social interaction.

COGNITIVE AND LINGUISTIC PERFORMANCE IN HIGH FUNCTIONING AUTISTIC PERSONS

We have studied three other bright young men whose early histories are much like Dale's, and have completed psychological and language assessments on two. The results of Dale's testing and language analysis appear to be respresentative of a small subgroup of persons with primary autism whose natural histories demonstrate the paradoxes that so intrigued earlier clinicians.

Dale was administered the Progressive Matrices, and approached the task willingly, telling us he was pleased to be able to help us in our research. The Matrices consist of 60 designs from each of which a part has been removed. The five series of 12 matrices each require accuracy of discrimination, appreciation of figure-ground relationships, and the ability to educe relations among abstract representations; the more difficult series appearing later in the test involve analogies, and permutation and alternation of patterns, as well as other logical relations. Dale was able to move well into the 5th and final series before encountering problems, and received a ratio IQ of over 160 on this test.

On the Leiter International Performance Scale, Dale successfully completed every item, with one notable exception. An item at the 12-year level requires the subject to match 5 photographs of women's faces, showing extreme emotional states such as joy, horror, and shock, to 5 photos of men's faces showing similar emotions. In contrast to Dale's test-taking strategies on the other items of the Leiter and on the Progressive Matrices, he puzzled long and hard over this one, placing first one and then another of the men's pictures next to the women's pictures. After about 4 minutes, he became quite agitated, and remarked that he was sure there'd been an error because all of the stimulus cards did not match the test cards. He pointed out that he couldn't decide on what basis the photos could be matched. When questioned, he explained: "I was sure they went together according to where they are looking, to the right or the left, but if I do it that way I still have two pictures left over." We suggested that the photos matched each other for a different reason. Dale again studied and manipulated the blocks, and told us that another hypothesis—that the photos matched each other according to the heights of each person's forehead—did not work. After about 10 mintues, we suggested that Dale consider how the people felt. He responded, slowly and with great thoughtfulness, "They probably feel soft." Dale only gradually understood our explanation of the emotions represented on the test, and managed to match three of the five photos successfully. Later, disturbed by his failure on this item, he told us that emotions "were one of the most difficult parts of life" for him to master, and that he had been working on learning how to convey emotions in his tone of voice by joining a local church's acting club.

One of the other older autistic persons studied had similar problems on this item of the Leiter International Performance Scale, but told us his teachers at school had taught him about what emotions were and "how they look on people." He successfully matched three of the five photos, and said he could have done the other two if they had looked more like the ones he had seen in school.

The samples of spontaneous language from these older patients with autism show high levels of competence in structural aspects of linguistic functioning. In fact, we have been impressed by the exact, stilted execution of speech and language, as though the speaker were giving a lecture. Sentences are perfectly enunciated, formal, and even donnish, and very much unlike a sample of conversation with a normal young adult in both content and communicative style. Phrases are typically well coordinated, and transformations are often exactly worded, as if a recipe were being followed in their formulation; to questions such as "What will you be doing this summer?" Dale was apt to answer "I will be doing some reading, but I will not be doing any camping as I had planned." Dale seldom used contractions so that his speech seemed to be taken from an 18th century diction text.

Functional analysis of the spontaneous language samples revealed consistent and important abnormalities in all three young men. In addition to the marked formality and donnishness, each sample contained marked and peculiar hesitations, repetitions and redundancies. The hesitations occurred between utterances, as if at times the speaker lost his bearing, as well as in the middle of phrases. When the latter occurred, the strategy adopted was to begin the sentence over again. More unusual, however, were the degrees to which each of the young men overused synonyms and verbal explications. Examples tell the story better than clinical description. Dale, when anxious, said, "I really need to leave, to exit, to remove myself from this office, really." Another young man told us that he would be unable to realize his dreams of independence and foreign travel because "I simply could not drive. Even the littlest things make me too anxious, too panicked. Unquestionably, unmistakably, if I tried to drive, I would just fall apart. Delays in the airplane departures would make me very anxious, quite nervous." All of this was said with meticulous articulation and clarity, but without the variations in tone, pitch, and stress any of us would use in convincing others of the emotions this young man was trying to describe. Dale's changes of pitch were often unrelated to meaning of the utterances, so that, at the end of a sentence, for example, the final word was not as completely marked with falling pitch as one would expect. Similarly, within a phrase, volume seemed to be unrelated to the meaning; in the phrase "I'm going off to Hartford to the group home," greater loudness was placed on "to the group" than on "Hartford" or "group home." Intonational patterns tended to be flatter and less animated than normal, especially considering the intent of the speaker and the nature of the thoughts being expressed. When the abnormal features of pitch, intonation, and volume are viewed in relation to the repeated use of verbal explications, it appears that the latter are used *in the place of* the former, as substitutes that were somehow more easily evoked than the emotive aspects of language.

At a National Society for Autistic Citizens conference in 1970, a young man whose development had shown improvements similar to Dale's was speaking to a group of people about his current interests, and was posed the indirect request for information, "Do you have a hobby?", to which he responded simply "Yes." He provided more information only when more direct, explicit questions were asked. Another young adult, living on his own as a musician, called his parents to ask them how he should go about cleaning the keys of his piano. His mother told him to use Ivory Soap and a damp cloth. Later he called her back and told her he had searched through every piano supply catalogue and had found no special soap for ivory (Dewey & Everard, 1974). These anecdotal examples of literalness in the use of language among very high functioning autistic adults point to the presence of a deep and pervasive inability to grasp the social nuances of human behavior that persist long after language, as a cognitive facility, emerges. The analyses of spontaneous language samples of the older, improved patients such as Dale whom we have studied are important additions to the studies Churchill conducted with much younger children. According to parental diaries, medical and educational records, the very early linguistic histories of the three adults we have studied were very much like those of Churchill's higher functioning, more intelligent youngsters. How can the superior linguistic competence of these young men coexist with major deficits in emotive and phatic communicative functions? How does this competence evolve out of the severe deficits in basic language skills that mark the early childhood years?

On Autistic Echolalia

Of the wide range of "deficits" in linguistic development among children with autism, echolalia has been the most intensively studied. Kanner's original description highlights what he thought was the noncommunicative parroting of words or phrases just heard (immediate echolalia) or heard days or even weeks before (delayed echolalia). Since Kanner's description in 1943, a great deal more has been learned about both the structure and the function of autistic echoing. The history of this research illustrates the unique impact of the disorder on the people who study it, and the way in which theory can misdirect attempts at understanding.

Echolalia, along with metaphorical speech and the use of neologisms, has been typically classified as a speech abnormality and thus assumed, in the autistic child, to be yet another symptom indicating poor prognosis. The emergence of echolalia has received "bad press" because it was a feature of language development that further separated the autistic child from his normal agemates.

To the listener, echolalia appeared inappropriate and socially unconventional, and seemed to increase the social gap between the listener and the child. Warren Fay's broad-based and intensive investigations of normal echolalia (Fay, 1967), autistic echolalia (Fay, 1969, 1971; Fay & Schuler, 1981), and the echolalia of the blind child (Fay, 1973), established the validity of studying this abnormality in view of the function it serves for the child rather than the effect it has on the listener, and in view of the sociocognitive processes upon which it is based. Fay (1969) first suggested that echolalia in autism, like that in normally developing children, normal adults, and in nonpsychotic disorders, had as its basis verbal comprehension deficits "coupled with an urge to sustain rather than to reject social contact [p. 45]." He eschewed the interpretations reserved for psychotic echoing (see Bettelheim, 1967, and Ruttenberg & Wolf, 1967) that emphasized the willful or hostile turning back onto the interlocutor his own words as a means of retaliation or an expression of anger. Aside from the importance of Fay's focus on comprehension deficits in directing therapists away from clinical management of the autistic child on the basis of social rejection theory (see Lenneberg, 1962), he provided the key impetus for analyzing the behavior of autistic children in terms of its functional significance to the child rather than the reactions it produces in his therapist, teacher, or parent. Following this strategy has proven useful and productive; Shapiro and his colleagues developed a method, based on the speech act, that enabled them to explore the relationship between the specific communicative setting, the autistic child's cognitive abilities, and the demands placed on him by his interlocutor. In two studies, one with a single autistic child (Shapiro, 1977) and a second with five autistic children (Shapiro & Lucy, 1978), the period of latency between the adult's comments and the child's comments was shorter for echoes than for nonechoed, spontaneous responses, and overall, the mean length of echoes was longer than the mean length of nonechoed utterances. Echoing occurred when a question was too complex to be fully understood by the child, and usually tended to cluster into what Shapiro (1977) called a "sticky set [p. 614];" that is, once an echo appeared, it tended to be followed by a long string of echoed utterances. Thus echoes did not undergo the type of linguistic processing that the spontaneous utterances required (as reflected in their longer reaction times), and appeared to serve a phatic function of discontinuing the conversation or at least "filling in the slot." As we have phrased it (Caparulo & Cohen, 1977), "Immediate echolalia . . . may be [the autistic child's] statement that 'I know you're talking and that I should respond in some way, but I don't know what to say, so I'll just say what you did and hope you'll stop asking so much of me [p. 641.' " Seen from this perspective, echolalia is among the very first signs of social awareness, and of dialogic rules. Our longitudinal studies (not including the three young men seen only as adults), based on 31 children with primary autism, indicate that echolalia is positively associated with eventual use of language for social and communicative purposes. Of the 31 children, now ages 5 to 23 years, 24 used echolalic language, and, of these, 18 later or concurrently developed spontaneous language. Two more youngsters developed communicative language that was severely reduced in linguistic complexity. Of the seven children with no history of echolalia, only 1 has developed simple communicative vocal language, and he also, at the age of 14 years, has begun to use simple manual signs to communicate needs and wants and to respond to questions. We have thus found a strong but not perfect relationship between echolalic language and the emergence of social communication through verbal language. Other reports have noted that the presence of "useful" or communicative language (which, by definition, excludes echolalia) is positively associated with outcome, as indicated by at least semi-independent living (Lotter, 1978); yet, among both retarded and normal IQ autistic children, echolalia is not a reliable predictor of outcome (Bartak & Rutter, 1976). It appears then that the development of echolalic behavior is related to the emergence of communicative speech, but it has little significance in the acquisition of skills needed for independent living. Perhaps some of the variance in these relationships is due to the fate of the autistic echo, to whether the child who uses echoing as a predominant linguistic behavior for a period of time is able to continue engaging his teachers and parents in dialogic exchanges or tries their patience to such an extent that they either ignore the echoes or attempt to eliminate them from the child's behavior (see Risley & Wolf, 1967). Naturally occurring conversations between the autistic echoer and his parents or teachers have not been studied, but our clinical experience suggests that the pattern of expansions and recastings used by many parents with their normal young children (Brown & Bellugi, 1964; Brown, Cazden, & Bellugi-Klima, 1969; Nelson, 1980) follows an age-related course with autistic children. Parents of older autistic echoers seem less willing to use the echo as a stimulus for expansion when the echo is the only linguistic behavior demonstrated by the child. With younger children, however, echoing appears to provide the first indication to parents that language is about to emerge, and many take great steps to respond to the assumed meaning of the echo through recastings and expansions. There is wide variability, though, in whether, to what degree, and how parents respond to and initiate language exchanges with their autistic child who echoes (Cohen, Caparulo, & Wetstone, 1981). In addition to the child's age, it appears that the adult's attitudes toward language expression and its mode, and the adult's goals in using language, play especially prominent roles in determining how this abnormal linguistic behavior of echoing is to be treated. This issue is one that deserves research consideration because for the autistic child, what we hypothesize as being *most* influenced by adult responses is not syntactic or semantic development but rather the child's sense of efficacy as a speaker, and his knowledge of the role he plays in social exchanges. In this sense, it would seem that the echo should not be viewed by therapists and parents as a symptom to be eradicated, but as a reason for cautious optimism. We will return to this issue shortly.

Development from Infancy to Adulthood in High Functioning Autistic Persons: A Review

A brief synthesis of the natural history of normally intelligent autistic persons, and of the place of language development in this history, will now be drawn, using the cases we have studied and reports by Kanner (1973), Prior (1977), Ricks and Wing (1975), and others.

We have seen that during infancy there occurs an abnormal sensitivity to sound, reduced responses to the human voice, failure to discriminate among environmental sounds in a meaningful way, and failure to engage in socially based baby games. Anticipatory postures for being picked up and held are not made, nor does the infant show through facial expression the emotions tied to reunion with important caregivers after brief separation (Kanner, 1943). Babbling is typically delayed and diminished.

From ages one to two years, there occur few, if any, indications of comprehension of gestures, single words, or short ritualized phrases, or the ability to use the vocal apparatus in a communicative way (Bartak & Rutter, 1976; Caparulo & Cohen, 1977). A few children, however, do develop immediate echolalia during the end of this period (Kanner, 1943). Gestural language remains absent, and the child does not develop even the basic rules of the dialogue. Play is limited to stereotypic manipulation of objects that demonstrates a fascination with particular patterns of movement. The usual interest in peers and siblings that typically emerges during this period fails to develop.

During the next two years, single words come to be understood, especially when embedded in familiar routines; during the end of this period, short phrases such as direct commands are understood. Echolalia becomes prominent; the child often echoes his own remarks or those of others, and also repeats key phrases from radio or TV commercials. Echoes preserve the prosodic features of the utterances upon which they are modeled; articulation of echoed words is intact (Boucher, 1976). Nonechoed spontaneous language appears for the first time at about 2½ to 3 years of age (Bartak & Rutter, 1976; Caparulo & Cohen, 1977). Awareness of and response to environmental sounds remain sporadic and unpredictable; frequently the child develops a panic reaction to certain sounds such as the washing machine and hair dryer, and demonstrates this by putting his hands over his ears and screaming, but the child appears to be deaf to other sounds, such as his own name, the closing of a door or the ring of the telephone (Bartak & Rutter, 1976). Toward the end of this period, relatively more intact but isolated skill areas emerge, usually involving memory, manipulation of objects, and visuo-perceptual processing.

From years four to six, echolalia declines as spontaneous language increases; short phrases typically appear around 4½ to 5 years. Patterns of lexical development appear to follow the typical route, despite the delay in onset and the fact that the child becomes interested in and learns the names of objects that may preoccupy him (e.g., *cornucopia, extension ladder,* and *Westinghouse dryer* marked the unusual vocabulary of one 5-year-old we have studied). A few children skip the one-word stage of language development and move quickly into short phrase production, much like those 1-year-olds who begin walking without first crawling. Expressive syntactic development is much like that of a normally developing two-year-old child. Competence in understanding is markedly better than in production, but is limited to relatively simple grammatical constructions; locatives, personal pronouns, and other terms of deixis, and language-encoded temporal and spatial concepts are not understood. Very often a fascination with written numbers and letters of the alphabet appears. Social use of language remains impaired to a much greater extent than does language used for instrumental or informational purposes. The development of inner language follows a similarly delayed course (Rutter, 1972).

Over the next two years, all aspects of structural linguistic skills begin to show improvement. This period is described by most parents as similar to what normal youngsters experience from ages 15 months to about 3½ years. Echolalia continues to decline but is revived as a communicative tool during stress, or during periods when the child is alone, playing. When engaged in conversation, there is generally a lack of spontaneous communicative language about the self; questions about the interlocutor, however, may be carried to great extremes, as the child asks about his age, his anniversary, his birthdate, and so forth. The child seems to be talking *at* rather than *with* his listener, using the opportunity of conversation as a way of fulfilling his intense interest in unusual objects, events, or concepts. Quite often one has the sense that the child has his own internal script fully developed before engaging in conversation, and follows the lines regardless of what is said to him. The child may ask his questions and then not wait for the answers, not show any interest in the answers, or fail to incorporate the information conveyed in the responses into the conversation. When an adult prods the child about himself and his feelings, his daily activities, or his family, responses are often perseverative and become quickly diverted from the topic. When speaking about favorite interests, the child speaks in a rushed way, "ejaculating" words (Kanner, 1943) so that his sentences often become unintelligible. Spontaneous language sounds generally flat, affectless, and without normal stress and intonation.

Over the next four years, between 8 to 12 years, the gradual improvement in syntactic and semantic development continues, but these competencies remain noticeably immature. Difficulties in learning multiple meanings for single words parallel problems in understanding idioms and other expressions whose meaning is not determined by the literal interpretation of their lexical items (e.g., a black eye, to give one a piece of one's mind). Major delays in syntactic development evident in the expressive language of these children involve complex aspects of grammar such as relative clauses, verbal modality and voice, and complex transformations. Thematic play and inner language remain remarkably impoverished, and imaginative play is often totally absent; testing on the Rorschach Inkblots, for example, yields two or three simple themes that are perseverated upon across all of the stimulus cards (Bemporad, 1979).

Growth in linguistic competence continues through early and mid-adolescence, despite major difficulties in the acquisition of the social conventions surrounding use in interpersonal situations. Education appears to be absolutely critical to the youngster's eventual attainment of useful communicative language, but it is not clear that the focus of educational intervention must be specifically on linguistic development. Although none of the older improved autistic patients we have studied were enrolled in language therapy to teach complex syntactic or semantic rules, each had spent years in special education programs in which language for communication, and as a means of self-expression, was emphasized. Similar stress was made on interpersonal communication at home.

Our clinical studies and the work of Hermelin and O'Connor (1970), Pierce and Bartolucci (1977), Ricks and Wing (1975), and others indicate that the verbal autistic child and adolescent possesses the basic rule system of language but fails to apply these rules in spontaneous language (see Blank, Gessner, and Esposito, 1979, for a detailed case description). As a young child, the discovery of, or the acquisition of, this rule system is accomplished at a much later time than occurs in normally developing youngsters, so that a 6-year-old normally intelligent autistic child possesses the syntactic skills of a 2-year-old. Once the basic rules of the syntactic system have been discovered, however, the development of proficiency in their use proceeds within a generally normal pattern but at a greatly decelerated rate. The notion that autistic language is, overall, marked by major deviations in syntax has gained general acceptance because children with below average or even retarded intellectual abilities have been studied most often, and because experimental studies have typically failed to control for developmental level, as Prior (1979) has recently noted. When investigations center on what may be called "pure" autism, rather than on autism complicated by mental retardation, serious doubts are cast on the hypothesis that autism stems from or is caused by a pure or even general central language disorder as in developmental dysphasia. Furthermore, comprehension and semantic skills throughout the first two decades of life in primary autism have rarely been investigated, but there is now tentative evidence from experimental studies indicating that relatively high functioning school-age autistic children show comparatively less attention to real world probabilities than to the order of words within phrases in order to comprehend the meaning of sentences (Tager-Flusberg, 1981). These intitial findings suggest that much meaningful information can be derived about the linguistic development of autistic children and the underlying nature of the disorder through careful experimental analysis.

When language competence is defined broadly in terms of communicative skills, we do find major deficits among all autistic children. Youngsters with normal or above average intellectual abilities show in the clearest way possible the pervasiveness of these disturbances in understanding the culturally transmitted and social basis of language. Consistent with the patients studied by others (Bemporad, 1979; Campbell, Hardesty, Breuer, & Polevoy, 1978; DeMyer, Barton, DeMyer, Norton, Allen, & Steele, 1973; Lockyer & Rutter, 1970), the autistic young adults and adolescents we have investigated display their most marked impairments in prosodic competence, in the interpretation of non-portrayable linguistic terms such as idioms, in appropriateness of conversational topics, and in knowledge of the ritualized formulas used to open, continue, or discontinue social communication. These deficits are manifested not only within the sphere of expressive behaviors but also pervade comprehension. The establishment of communicative contact, and the use of the expressive functions of language, are the first developing signs of the healthy infant's entry into his language community (Hebb, Lambert, & Tucker, 1971; Jakobson, 1968, 1972), and have received increasing attention over the past decade (Bates, 1976; Dore, 1974, 1975; Greenfield & Smith, 1976; Halliday, 1975; Ingram, 1974). We have seen in the case history of Dale, and in the synthesis of the natural course of the disorder above, that it is exactly this set of communicative functions whose absence in early development and whose abnormalities in later behavior separates the autistic person from his peers.

A Brief Recapitulation

The questions that led us into this disucssion—of the life histories of a small subgroup of autistic persons who we believe portray clearly the essential nature of the autistic disorder, the evolution of echolalia and other language behaviors—concerned the relationship between competence and performance. Even for autistic children with near normal IQ, both clinical observation and Churchill's experiments in teaching basic language rudiments reveal profound early delays in the acquisition of words, sentences, and communicative exchange. Yet the seemingly impassable obstacle that originally prevented them from attaining the fluent use of basic syntactic structures, of locatives and words such as *I, me, my,* and *mine,* and *you* and *your,* is somehow overcome during the protracted language learning process that appears to continue well into adolescence. These histories are best understood as reflecting the degree to which both deviations and delays affect, in a domino-like fashion, each other and the final outcome; delays in the language acquisition timetable, although notable in and of themselves, seem to alter the overall pattern of acquisition as well, perhaps because in part the system becomes desynchronized with the environmental input from which it must draw meaning. The autistic child, in his expressive language, draws on atypical strategies to convey lack of comprehension, as in echolalia, and affective force, as in the overuse of synonyms and verbal explications. Our clinical work indicates that similarly unusual strategies are employed in order to understand language and object relations. Sroufe, Steucher, and Stutzer (1973) have discovered similar functional significance of the abnormal self-stimulatory, conflictual, and negativistic behaviors of a single autistic child, studied almost daily over a 17–week treatment period, using physiological and time-sampling behavioral measures. Given the evidence for developing at least the foundations of a psychology of autism, in which abnormal behaviors have meaning that can direct us toward underlying causes, we can now apply what has been learned by others about normal language development in order to contrast the development of the autistic child with his healthy peer.

THE ONTOGENESIS OF LINGUISTIC AND COMMUNICATIVE COMPETENCE

Among the significant accomplishments of the normally developing infant, once thought of as a relatively passive recipient of environmental stimuli, several testify to the infant's role in actively stimulating the interest and altering the behavior of others around him, and in establishing interpersonal attachments. These behaviors take on special significance in light of the early development of children with autism.

Biological Predisposition toward Language Learning

The infant of 1 to 4 months of age possesses categorical perception and discrimination of speech sounds (Eimas, Siqueland, Jusczyk, & Vigorito, 1971; Lasky, Syrdal-Lasky, & Klein, 1975; Streeter, 1976). Eimas et al. (1971) concluded from their groundbreaking studies that infants are able to:

> sort acoustic variations of adult phonemes into categories with relatively limited exposure to speech, as well as with virtually no experience in producing these same sounds and certainly little, if any, differential reinforcement for this form of behavior [p. 306].

Studies of evoked potentials to speech and nonspeech sounds (Molfese, 1977; Molfese, Freeman, & Palermo, 1975), and of dichotic listening (Entus, 1977), show clear hemispheric differences in speech and nonspeech sound responsivity at even one week of age. These data on brain specialization, as well as those showing perceptual discrimination of both intonational (Morse, 1972) and phonetic features (Eimas, 1974; Lasky et al., 1975; Streeter, 1976; Trehub, 1973; Trehub & Rabinovitch, 1972), indicate that the infant is biologically equipped with feature detectors that enable him to impose at least a rudimentary structure on his world, and that even early experiences of short duration may sharpen the boundaries between perceptual categories (Bornstein, 1979).

The infant's abilities in feature discrimination appear to be not limited to auditory stimuli. Bornstein's work (1975) shows that the visual spectrum is organized by infants into the adult categories of blue, green, yellow, and red. Furthermore, such discrimination or categorization appears to be resilient to experience; that is, deprivation during early development (caused by congenital cataracts, for example) appears not to eradicate these features, or the ability to detect them: distinctions among hue are one of the first sets of functions to emerge when the source of the light deprivation (i.e., cataracts) is removed (Gregory & Wallace, 1963; von Sendon, 1923/1960). Similarly, limited but suggestive evidence indicates that the ability to detect speech features is resistant to acoustic deprivation (Bennett & Ling, 1973; see Bornstein, 1979, for a detailed discussion).

Because perceptual features assist in the process of contextualizing specific kinds of information, their early existence is an aspect of development with the most far-reaching impacts on learning. The world can be organized into categories which, despite fluctuations both within and outside the child, maintain perceptual stability. Categorization enhances the manageable expenditure of information-processing energy, imposes a clear structure on perceptions, and invokes attention (Bornstein, 1979). In many ways, a great deal of the mental energy expended during the first months of life seems to be devoted to the formation of increasingly well-defined categories that stand against various backgrounds. The emotional state of the child while engaged in mental-perceptual activity is one such background, as is his level of arousal and attention. These "personal backgrounds," so to speak, are one type of context in which the infant's early experiences in listening and seeing occur; other contexts are comprised of the spatial and temporal background and the physical world in which the child's activity occurs. Katherine Nelson's (1974) hypothesis, that early word meanings are comprised of a functional core, emphasizes this relationship between foreground—an object, for example—and background—the child's motor actions on the object, among other things.

Social Transactions during Infancy

It would seem that a similar figure-ground relationship exists between the infant and his social environment. At birth, the human infant is a social creature (Ainsworth, Bell, & Stayton, 1974), or, at least, is predisposed to becoming social (Berger & Luckman, 1967; Richards, 1974). The characteristic behaviors such as smiling and vocalizing are complemented by maternal or paternal interactional behaviors. Freedman (1974) argues that social attachment represents one of the evolved characteristics upon which survival is based; infant behaviors "are intended to facilitate this human mutuality . . . in the sense that they strengthen the social bonds and elicit caretaking on the part of the parents [p. 45]." Korner and Grobstein (1966), Korner and Thoman (1972), Sander (1977), and Stern, Jaffe, Beebe, and Bennett (1975) present particularly interesting treatments of mother-infant negotiations during early development. Rather than trace the molecular development of parent-child interaction, the themes that will be pursued here concern context, meaning, and the emergence of the self-nonself, especially in relationship to the caretaker's role in parcelling out bits of the world for the child by engaging his selective attention on objects, people, events, and on his own actions.

We have discussed the infant's skill in discriminating speech sounds, and this, combined with preferences for human faces over other available visual stimuli (Fantz, 1961, 1963, 1966; Kagan & Lewis, 1965) and the tendency to smile on hearing the human voice (Wolff, 1963), indicates the emergence of attention to humans somewhat selectively, given the range of all things in the world the infant might attend to. Indeed, there is evidence that the neonate not only attends to the human face but actually imitates its movements at about 2 to 3 weeks of age (Meltzoff & Moore, 1977). But what of the periods when the infant is not engaged in looking and attending outword, when he is instead experiencing increased internal excitations from hunger, or discomfort? Freud (1915/1959) suggested that these internal stimuli serve as a means by which the infant learns of or discovers inner and outer reality; that is, the infant's own muscular activity and primary process thinking do not reduce these inner excitations and thus his attention must be directed outward. Although Freud failed to specify the exact mechanisms by which this discovery occurred, the work of contemporary researchers such as Brazelton (1974) indicates that mothers, by their movements, assist their infants in focusing on their faces and in regulating action. The reciprocity established has, as one outcome, the child's growing awareness of his movements in space and in relation to another, and increased self-directed attentional deployment. It is also likely that the mother, by focusing first on one action and then on another (movement toward and away from each other during play, for example) assists the infant in dividing up his own kinesthetic experiences through the capturing of his attention, and provides the background against which the infant can categorize his experiences. This interpretation highlights the role of the context the mother provides, both as a shade against which the infant's movements can be silhouetted (perhaps forming the core of spatial concepts), and as a feature to which the child becomes increasingly attentive.

Aside from the hypothesized significance of these motor routines in the infant's development of spatial and causal concepts (see Bower, 1974), and in self-and-other-concept development, the reciprocal actions of mother and infant are of interest to us for another reason, that of their role in solidifying the earliest "communication network" (Lewis & Freedle, 1973) in which the infant becomes engaged. Lewis and Rosenblum (1974) organized the origins of this network in terms that emphasized both the infant's effect on his caretaker and the caretaker's effect on the infant; the neonate organizes the mother by crying, vocalizing, and by eye-to-eye contact. When the baby moves, mother speaks.

When the infant opens its mouth to feed, mother automatically opens hers. When the infant smiles, she automatically smiles back (Condon & Sander, 1974; Sander, 1975; Stern, 1977). The specific behaviors change over the next several months in relationship to the child's neuromaturational development and his mother's perceptions of his needs and her interpretations of his behavior, but the basic strategies remain essentially the same, and may be seen as revolving around "adaptive issues" (Sander, 1975) such as basic caretaking and regulation that mark the course of human infant development. Throughout, both infant and mother establish what may be described best as a "structure of intersubjectivity" (Habermas, 1970), that may be specific to individual tasks or games, such as peekaboo and diaper-changing, or that may be a general framework such as the one surrounding the dyad's negotiation of whether it is time to play or not. Jerome Bruner's approach to the child's development of language and communication is one that gives fundamental importance to the successful establishment of this "structure of intersubjectivity," and places heavy emphasis on the sociocognitive nature of linguistic competence. Bruner and his colleagues (Bruner, 1975a, 1975b; Ninio & Bruner, 1978; Ratner & Bruner, 1978; Bruner, Roy, & Ratner, 1982), John Dore (1973, 1975), Michael Halliday (1975), and more recently Phillip Dale (1980) have shown that communicative functions preceed the emergence of lexico-grammatical speech. Bruner's (1975a) theory, in particular, seems compelling, even though the basic premise upon which it rests is simple: language is "a specialized and conventionalized extension of cooperative action [p. 2]." According to Bruner (1975a), the structure and order of all natural languages are embedded in or reflect the structure and the order of action. Bruner's major thesis is that what is innate about language is not linguistic but rather special features of human action and attention that permit language to be understood or decoded by the uses to which it is put. Thus, Bruner (1975a) states that the structure of language corresponds directly with the "nature of the cognitive processes whose output it encodes [p. 4]." The argument put forward is that there exists an isomorphism, first, between the universal topic-comment structure of all natural languages and the perceptual phenomena involved in human attention, and, second, an isomorphism between the presence in all natural languages of such categories as agent, action, object (e.g., as described by Fillmore, 1968), and the way in which human activity is organized. The infant's innate capacity to construct schemata for interpreting the intersubjective phenomena is realized with the assistance of significant others who we might say are sympathetic to the child's intentions and who, of course, are similarly equipped in terms of action and attention schemata.

Does the infant come equipped with an innate, if primitive, understanding of the significance of people, objects, and events? According to Bruner (1975a), once the mother and the infant have established joint attention, the mother comments on that which is being attended to, in what he calls the "attend to → act upon routine [p. 9]." The infant, himself, of course, can also play the role of drawing the mother's attention to an object, such that he "hosts" the episode while mother is audience. Brazelton (1974) and Stern (1977) have demonstrated such routines in the microanalysis of mother-infant interactions. It appears that from the child's distinguishing between the roles of host and hosted, substitution rules and reversals may be learned in a way similar to that proposed by so many as underlying the educational nature of baby games such as So Big. Thus, one of the sets of meanings deriving from these games and from the "attend to → act upon" routines is that of deixis, and a second involves signal-system mechanisms and responses.

There is still another way in which meaning is communicated to the child by the caretaker. Both Elkonin (1971) and Bruner (1972) have highlighted the important role that play takes in the life of the child. Elkonin (1971) states:

> Just as the mastery of objective reality is not possible without formation of activity with objects, exactly in the same manner is language mastery not possible without formation of activity with language as the material object [p. 141].

We are reminded again of the significance of attention, directed toward something, but this time toward language itself. Shotter and Gregory (1976) described the action of a mother, routinely sitting with her 8-month old son while he fingered the pieces of a puzzle. When he accidentally placed a piece correctly, the mother suddenly exaggerated her actions, exclaiming to the child how clever he was, all the while drawing his attention to her own excitement and to the puzzle. The child looked at her, at the puzzle, and back at her, and then attempted to reduplicate his "accomplishment." The mother's behavior and utterance had called the infant's attention to the social significance of his act, to his competence as a puzzle-builder, thus bringing him closer to a realization of his identity and its relation to the larger cultural group—that he could do something that others found important. These "instructive social exchanges" are more or greater than simply a translation or interpretation by an adult of the child's actions; they are one of the ways by which the child is taught about the *meaning* of his behavior, and how he may use his feelings and actions to know himself (Shotter & Gregory, 1976). As Vygotsky (1962) noted, the infant's biography is thus given to him by others, words that are reminiscent of those written by James Mark Baldwin in 1895: that the child's personality development could not go on without the continuous modification of his sense of himself by suggestions of others.

Intonation is similarly learned by the child at a very early age, but, given his propensity for attention to speech stimuli during the first weeks of life, it is likely that the child meets his language instructor considerably more than half way. Clearly the ritualized games serve as a fertile field upon which the meaning of the caretaker's intonations can be extracted, and the child's expression of the intonations can be practiced. It is not surprising that the child's first performatives of gestures and simple phonological placeholders such as "eh" appear side by side with the mother's lexical comment on the attended-to object (Bates, Benigni, Bretherton, Camaioni, & Volterra, 1977; Bates et al., this volume). Then, as Dore (1973) has described, rudimentary one-word references take the place of the protolinguistic utterances, and, given intoned "primitive force indicating devices," yield an "intention + word act [Dore, 1975]." Thus, by 16 months of age, the child has merged the intention-signaling, culturally defined intonational system with the lexical system, and, as Nelson (1979) suggests, probably spends the next several months gaining greater control and coordination of these two systems.

It remains to be seen how closely the child of about 20 months follows the pathway Bruner's theory predicts, both during the early stage of entry into grammar and later. The possession of knowledge about topic-comment structures, dialogic rules, and, generally, about the order of elements within utterances, may be quite far from the ability to coordinate tense, or to transform simple declaratives into passive questions. One of the common criticisms about theories that look to infant cognitive strategies and socioemotional foundations of language acquisition is that a gap remains between what are described as nonlinguistic systems and the "true" linguistic system. It is clear, however, that recent developments in knowledge about child communication have come much farther in describing how the child makes his initial entry into his linguistic culture than models emphasizing only the reinforcing environment or the presence of innate linguistic structures. Bruner's theory, among others, incorporates both the significance of the linguistic and socioaffective environment, as well as intrinsic motivation and that provided by sympathetic listeners, with a system of innately determined action and attention patterns that are triggered through appropriate interaction with the world.

The infant's acquisition of communicative intent, protolinguistic structures, and social or culturally-defined meaning outlined above is in stark contrast to some of the impaired communicative abilities of young adult, normally intelligent persons with autism. We have been led to believe that the failure of the autistic infant to form with his primary caretaker the structure of intersubjectivity is an especially useful way to capture the major origin of the deficits we have described, and to emphasize the major difficulties that remain long after less pervasive symptoms have disappeared. As we have seen, it is the development of meaning and intention that is so markedly disturbed, and these are the essence of what defines human and social interaction. It is also fascinating that although certain cognitive and linguistic relationships may be found to be attained more independently of this structure of intersubjectivity, there are subtle pragmatic and conversational rules whose meaning can only derive out of this social matrix. (See Dore, Gearhart, & Newman, 1978, for discussion of an example of this relationship.) Our work with autistic children has given some indication of this. Nuances of meaning seem to be socially transmitted and contain the nonportrayable significance of objects as opposed to the functional significance of objects (see Blank, 1976). Thus, for the healthy 12-month old, the object *ball* and its linguistic counterpart "ball" mean bounceable, squeezable, throwable, round, and so forth (Nelson, 1974), and would be categorized in these ways. But surely the concept *ball* also means to the child something like "having fun," or "pleasurable." Although the sense of mastery gained in playing with this ball may give rise to feelings of pleasure, it seems likely that the shared experiences in which the ball is the object of joint attention and action assist the child in adding an affect meaning and a social meaning to his concept of ball. Anglin (1977), Cassirer (1923/1953), and K. Nelson (1974) have emphasized the importance of recognizing this distinction between a thing's attributes or elements and its meaning, which is greater than the sum of the attributes. The way in which the attributes, including affective perspective toward the thing, or its personal (and interpersonal) significance, mesh together, is a critical factor in the evolution of concepts and categories.

For the young autistic child, and even for the "recovered" autistic adult, we have seen that even basic objects are inadequately defined; in adulthood, it is almost as if an object's elements do, in fact, equal meaning, thus resulting in the literalness with which terms are understood and used productively. An example lying outside the realm of linguistics was documented recently of how pervasive this deficit in establishing meaning is. In contrast to normal children, an autistic child can quite easily recognize the faces of his classmates from both isolated features and from inverted photographs. With age, he does not come to rely on the upper regions of the face, especially the eyes, as clues to recognition (Langdell, 1978). One of the autistic subjects in Langdell's study told the experimenter, "I know people talk with their eyes, but I don't know what they are saying."

Regarding what has been called by others in the primary linguistic disturbance causing autism, the distinction between linguistic and communicative competence assists us in understanding the nature of the disorder (Caparulo & Cohen, 1977). Clearly the autistic child is seriously impaired in the acquisition of knowledge about others, their intentions, and their feelings; sense of self is fragmented, incomplete. For the young autistic child, when attention and arousal are modified in response to stress (Caparulo & Cohen, 1980), the experience of self-awareness appears to occur and become linked with motivation to communicate. Only at these moments does the one system become meshed with the other—that is, the intention-meaning system merges with the lexical-syntactic system for a brief time. However, the fact that a small group of autistic youngsters without the additional burden of intellectual retardation eventually acquire linguistic competence is important; we agree with Churchill that the autistic child's failures in early acquisition of linguistic structures are unique aspects of the syndrome, but we argue that one must concentrate on the forerunners of these structures, on the meanings of events, people and objects that cannot be represented in the physical world and that must emerge from earlier foundations. The failures in learning that others have intentions and that these are communicated, for example, through changes in pitch, intensity, and loudness are just as interesting as the major delays in the acquisition of words. In our view, the disturbances in understanding prepositions and other spatial relationship terms, and in understanding personal pronouns, are epiphenomenal to more basic disruptions, involving the formation of intentions, the recognition of significance of human action and states of feeling. In the healthy child, intentions are the reasons for communicating, and awareness of the meanings of human acts and feelings are the glue that creates interpersonal cohesiveness and cultural membership. The analysis of the development of specific linguistic forms, such as that on the offer by Zukow, Reilly, and Greenfield (1982), and on requesting by Bruner, Roy, and Ratner (1982), suggests that the normal child's conception of the intentional bases of human interactions is the core around which lexicon and grammar is layered. The autistic child early on lacks this basic prerequisite.

BRAIN NEUROMATURATION AND LANGUAGE

We have yet to address the question of how some autistic children are able to arrive at early adulthood with good linguistic abilities, given the disturbances in early development. Our laboratory work involving the specification of how behavior is associated with basic neurochemical processes and functions provides a useful context in which we can discuss the language-brain interaction.

Roman Jakobson, in an address entitled "Brain and Language," recently argued that to understand the development of linguistic competence we must look toward the brain and especially to clinical populations whose facility with language has been interrupted by disease or trauma (Jakobson, 1980). Research of this type must be complemented, however, by an understanding of how normal human brain development proceeds, and how basic neurochemical and physiological processes are involved in the unfolding of psychological processes. The foundations of human developmental neurochemistry are gradually being laid, and have received significant support from the work of research neuropsychiatrists studying disorders such as autism. In addition to the specification of central nervous system neurochemistry and the signal systems that control its operation, major inroads in identifying the areas of human behavior and functions associated with specific chemical substances and processes have been made (Young & Cohen, 1979). One of the most suggestive lines of evidence resulting from these studies concerns the developmental course, from infancy to old age, of the major neurotransmitters, their derivatives, and precursors. With the explication of relationships among various hormonal/endocrinological substances and the neurotransmitters, various patterns of behavior, both normal (e.g., different patterns between boys and girls in the development of behavioral modulation) and abnormal (e.g., stereotypic motor clusters as in Parkinson's disease, chronic multiple tics of Gilles de la Tourette syndrome, and autism) can be understood (Young, Cohen, Anderson, & Shaywitz, 1981). Current understanding of how these networks in the central nervous system become activated, how they affect other systems, and how they become manifested in behavioral change, must be combined with knowledge of environmental impact on biological structures and processes. For the youngsters about whom we have been speaking, the clinical symptomatology and natural history provide clues that direct the search toward biological answers.[1] A developmental neurochemical model offers a useful scheme for organizing the major features of the autistic disorder that we have described, and for explaining the delayed appearance of various linguistic competencies, the brief periods of relatively better performance, and the asynchronous patterns of attainment of other skills (Cohen, Caparulo, & Shaywitz, 1978).

We have found evidence that implicates two brain neurotransmitter systems in primary autism (Cohen, Caparulo, Shaywitz, & Bowers, 1977; Cohen, Caparulo, & Shaywitz, 1978; Young et al., 1981). One of these, the serotonergic system, generally plays an inhibitory role in central metabolism by modulating the activity of brain catecholamines in relation to environmental stimuli. Other studies of central nervous system metabolites measured in the urine of autistic children suggest that a specific site in the brain, the locus coeruleus, which plays a central role in selective attention and the regulation of arousal and anxiety (Mason & Fibiger, 1979; Redmond & Huang, 1979), may be involved, perhaps in relation to norepinephrine, another central neurotransmitter (Young et al., 1981). These studies are being undertaken only as quickly as basic scientific and laboratory procedures become available, and are complicated by major methodological and practical issues, but find verification in complementary investigations of psychophysiological functions in autistic children that link attentional and arousal disturbances with abnormal autonomic indices. Autistic children have been found to have chronically increased pulse rates and blood pressure (Cohen & Johnson, 1977; Kootz & Cohen, 1981; Lake, Zeigler, & Murphy, 1977). These states of higher than average autonomic functioning appear to be associated with chronically heightened sensory rejection that may be a coping mechanism adapted by the body to control what is initially an abnormal overreactivity to external stimulation (Kootz & Cohen, 1981).

We have hypothesized that in autism, periods of heightened stress and anxiety trigger an increase in overall arousal and an improvement in the efficiency of those systems that permit focused attention (i.e., the autonomic system and the

---

[1]It must be reiterated that the processes that eventually appear intact in this small subgroup of autistic youngsters may fail to gain integrity in some autistic children with severe intellectual deficits; in other youngsters, including some with good cognitive potential, these processes may take longer to develop. Even for these youngster, however, a developmental neurochemical model offers one of the most useful explanations currently available.

norepinephrine, dopamine, and serotonin neurotransmitter subsystems—Caparulo & Cohen, 1980). Just as the normal adult may, at times of tremendous stress as in an emergency, act with speed and strength to rescue others in distress, so too does the mute autistic child mobilize his latent linguistic competence to ask to go home, for example, when stressed by a medical procedure. Complex feedback and homeostatic mechanisms, however, return the interconnected systems to their baseline levels, resulting in a return to "typical" behavior as well.

Interpretation of the relationships among behavior, environmental events, autonomic functioning, and central nervous system neurotransmitter levels is clouded by the fact that these systems do not work in a unidirectional way. Experiences that are related to stress exert many effects on brain chemistry; and altered brain chemistry, or brain functioning, alters the way the organism responds to the environment. In addition, the neurochemical systems of the brain act in concert with one another and with endocrinological substances as well, so that a congenital abnormality in one neurochemical system, for instance, must necessarily alter other systems, and perhaps alter the structures involved in all aspects of functioning (Cohen & Young, 1977). In autism, for example, it is now well known that medication such as methylphenidate that normally allows improved attentional deployment and activity modulation results in dramatic disorganization, decreased self-control, and increased stereotypic movements.

SOME CONCLUSIONS ABOUT AUTISM AND NORMAL LANGUAGE ACQUISITION

Many of the symptoms of autism are explained by a model that gives CNS neurotransmitter functioning and perhaps specific brain sites a central place in the unfolding of the disorder. Fascination with stereotyped repetitive manipulation of objects; rigid movements of the body, hands, and fingers, or rhythmic flicking of the fingers in front of the eyes, in which the child seems to "get lost" and which prove resistant to interruption; the need to preserve sameness in the environment and to adhere to strict routines; even the use of nonprocessed echoed responses during stress, seem to be strategies whose functional significance for the child is to impose order and stability on the world and to regulate the flow of sensory input (Caparulo & Cohen, 1977; Cohen, Caparulo, & Shaywitz, 1978; Sroufe et al., 1973). In comparison to the physical environment, however, people and social situations, and language with these as referents, are constantly shifting, not only in physical space but also in time and in appearance. It may be that the rule abstraction deficits we and others (e.g., Hermelin & O'Connor, 1970; Prior, 1979) have described are clues to how the human must process various types of stimuli in order to understand them (Caparulo & Cohen, 1977). That is, the infant and young child can come to know physical objects, their dimensions and relations to one another, in a way that is independent of experience with humans, through manipulation and exploration, as Piaget has described. But something may be sacrificed by using this strategy, something that gives rise to flexible interpretation and comprehension of meaning nuances, particularly evident in semantic development and in communication with others. The syntactic system may be more easily acquired than these two latter systems when such a developmental strategy is taken, as Blank and her colleagues (1979) have suggested, and as Rees (1978) implied in arguing that the structural and communicative systems in language acquisition may stem from two different sources. In comparison to retarded autistic children, perhaps the brighter, generally less impaired autistic children are able to apply, with some success, the strategies developed to understand the physical world to the task of comprehending people and social situations. We suspect that the overall integrity of the neuromaturational system and the degree to which the environment can remain empathic to the child account for much of the variance in achievement made by these young people. We must also be aware of the even more intimate connection between the child's competence, at any point in time, and the degree to which persons providing care and education can adjust themselves in order to establish expectations that combine a knowledge of underlying competencies with an understanding of learning and coping strategies. It appears that the timing of specific behaviors plays an important role also; *when* certain skills emerge may be just as crucial as what set of skills develop. Echolalia, for example, at age 4 or 5 years may serve as a beacon of hope for the parents of a previously nonverbal child, but as a final indication of deviance and poor prognosis if it appears at age 8 or 9.

While the young healthy child moves from preverbal to linguistic competence during the preschool years, he is gaining relative mastery or the integration of various cognitive and social components. As Bates (1979) noted, language as a symbol system involves an analytic component, a gestalt component, and a communicative intentional component. By the time the normal child reaches school, he is well on his way toward attainment of this coordination. But for the autistic child with good intelligence, the integration of the three systems remains incomplete over the entire stretch of childhood and into adolescence. What does this reveal about the process of language acquisition? A place for autistic children within a theory of language acquisition was recently opened by K. Nelson's (1981) review of the evidence on individual differences in language learning. The data she discussed suggest that the child brings with him personal, and in part constitutionally influenced, characteristics (i.e., neurological, motivational, cognitive, and personality) that interact with his language environment (i.e., why and how his parents use language, what kind of language they use) to tilt the scale toward one type of language acquisition "style" or another. Thus some children focus on the wholes or language gestalts, and use these instrumentally to regulate another's actions ("I do it!"), whereas others focus on the parts and use these to talk about the physical world. As Nelson points out, however, styles may change over time and in different contexts. The autistic child may be seen as representing the extreme example of stylistic inflexibility; he is a language learner who uses the object world, as opposed to the social world, as the basis of his language content, and who takes in (and gives back out again, unanalyzed) the whole message, rather than its constituents. Our studies indicate that it is only at the very greatest of costs that the parts of the language system can remain independent of each other. We have argued that the youngsters discussed in this chapter took so long to develop the basics of linguistic rules because of the severe deficiencies in the meaning-intention system that ordinarily serves as a springboard into the language and cultural community. It may be that the development of echolalia should be heralded as a signal that the primitive pragmatic and social meanings are evolving. If this is the case, we have even more reason to suspect that the autistic echoers possess an underlying competence in terms of having a strategy such as imitation or joining with another in establishing shared reference that serves them well. At this point in our understanding, a reasonable conclusion is to suggest that the echolalic strategy works in a "behind the scenes" way, assisting the child in the very first steps of meaning acquisition, recognition of intention, communication of basic state, and attentional focusing on the linguistic code. To Shapiro's and Fay's model of echolalia as a social facilitator we would add its role as a bridge with meaning, as a link with another person in constructing a primitive structure of intersubjectivity. For many of the brighter children with autism whom we have discussed, the period of echolalia is progressive in the sense that it shifts attention from the external world of objects to language, and then to the persons using the language. However, the meaning system never appears to reach a level of sophistication and flexibility achieved by normal youngsters. Perhaps this is the strongest argument for viewing the normal emergence of communicative competence as arising out of a responsive and fine-tuned interpersonal network in which we must appreciate not just the formal code and the rules upon which it is based, but also the links established and maintained among humans that give the code its meanings.

This conception of the origins of language competence—and of the intrinsic relations among this competence, the child's ties to his parents, and the intentions that give rise to discourse—undermines the shopworn distinction between affect and cognition that has burdened the theoretical discussion of disorders of childhood. The goal of clinical research today is to integrate the discoveries of various biological and psychological disciplines and to avoid the theoretical and investigatory fragmentation of disabled individuals into isolated functions. Similarly, the conception of communicative competence to which we have been led by clinical inquiry and the work of others suggest essential ties between the type of research reviewed here and the rich understanding of mother-child interactions and the growth of the self that is rooted in clinical, and particularly psychoanalytic, observation (Loewald, 1980; Winnicott, 1975). Finally, studies such as these with persons having profound difficulties in development raise our awareness of what it means to know, to learn, and to speak.

ACKNOWLEDGMENTS

This research was supported in part by MHCRC grant MH30929, CCRC grant RR00125, NICHD grant HD-03008, Mr. Leonard Berger, The Solomon R. & Rebecca D. Baker Foundation, Inc., the William T. Grant Foundation, and PHS traineeship #MH16127. We are also very appreciative of the encouragement of Dr. Albert J. Solnit, Dirctor of the Yale Child Study Center.

REFERENCES

Ainsworth, M. D., Bell, S. M., & Stayton, D. J. Infant-mother attachment and social development: Socialization as a product of reciprocal responsiveness to signals. In M. P. M. Richards (Ed.), *The introduction of a child into a social world*. Cambridge, England: Cambridge University Press, 1974.

American Psychiatric Association. *Diagnostic and statistical manual of mental disorders (DSM-III)*. Washington, D.C.: APA Task Force on Nomenclature and Statistics, 1980.

Anglin, J. M. *Words, objects and conceptual development*. New York: Norton Press, 1977.

Arthur, G. *Arthur Adaptation of the Leiter International Performance Scale*. Washington, D.C.: Psychological Services Center, 1952.

Baker, L. & Cantwell, D. Language acquisition, cognitive development, and emotional disorder in childhood. In K. E. Nelson (Ed.), *Children's language (Vol. 3)*. Hillsdale, N.J.: Lawrence Erlbaum Associates, 1982.

Baldwin, J. M. *Mental development in the child and in the race*. New York: MacMillan Press, 1895.

Bartak, L., Rutter, M., & Cox, A. A comparative study of infantile autism and specific developmental receptive language disorder. I. The Children. *British Journal of Psychiatry*, 1975, *126*, 127-145.

Bartak, L. & Rutter, M. Special educational treatment of autistic children. *Journal of Child Psychiatry and Psychology*, 1973, *14*, 161-179.

Bartak, L. & Rutter, M. Differences between mentally retarded and normally intelligent autistic children. *Journal of Autism and Childhood Schizophrenia*, 1976, *6*, 109-120.

Bartak, L., Rutter, M., & Cox, A. A comparative study of infantile autism and specific developmental receptive language disorder. III. Discriminant function analysis. *Journal of Autism and Childhood Schizophrenia*, 1977, *7*, 383-396.

Bates, E. *Language and context: Studies in the acquisition of pragmatics*. New York: Academic Press, 1976.

Bates, E. *The emergence of symbols*. New York: Academic Press, 1979.

Bates, E., Benigni, L., Bretherton, I., Camaioni, L., & Volterra, V. From gestures to the first word: On cognitive and social prerequisites. In M. Lewis & L. Rosenblum (Eds.), *Origins of behavior: Interaction, conversation, and the development of language*. New York: Wiley, 1977.

Bemporad, J. R. Adult recollections of a formerly autistic child. *Journal of Autism and Developmental Disorders*, 1979, *9*, 179-197.

Bennett, C. W. & Ling, D. Discrimination of the voiced-voiceless distinction by severely hearing-impaired children. *Journal of Auditory Research*, 1973, *13*, 271-279.

Berger, P. L. & Luckman, L. *The social construction of reality*. London: Allen Lane, 1967.

Bettelheim, B. *The empty fortress: Infantile autism and the birth of the self*. London: Collier-MacMillan, 1967.

Blank, M. Mastering the intangible through language. *Annals of the New York Academy of Sciences*, 1976, *26*, 44-58.

Blank, M., Gessner, M., & Esposito, A. Language without communication: A case study. *Journal of Child Language*, 1979, *6*, 329-352.

Bornstein, M. H. Qualities of color vision in infancy. *Journal of Experimental Child Psychology*, 1975, *19*, 401–419.
Bornstein, M. H. Stability and change in feature perception. In M. H. Bornstein & W. Kessen (Eds.), *Psychological development from infancy: Image to intention*. Hillsdale, N.J.: Lawrence Erlbaum Associates, 1979.
Boucher, J. Articulation in early childhood autism. *Journal of Autism and Childhood Schizophrenia*, 1976, *6*, 297–302.
Bower, T. G. R. *Development in infancy*. San Fransisco: W. H. Freeman, 1974.
Brazelton, T. B. The origins of reciprocity: The early mother-infant interaction. In M. Lewis & L. Rosenblum (Eds.), *The effect of the infant on its caregiver*. New York: Wiley, 1974.
Brown, R. & Bellugi, U. Three processes in the child's acquisition of syntax. *Harvard Educational Review*, 1964, *34*, 133–151.
Brown, R., Cazden, C., & Bellugi-Klima, U. The child's grammar from I to III. In J. P. Hill (Ed.), *Minnesota symposia on child psychology*. Minneapolis: University of Minnesota Press, 1969.
Bruner, J. Nature and uses of immaturity. *American Psychologist*, 1972, *27*, 687–708.
Bruner, J. The ontogenesis of speech acts. *Journal of Child Language*, 1975, *2*, 1–19. (a)
Bruner, J. From communication to language—a psychological perspective. *Cognition*, 1975, *3*, 255–287. (b)
Bruner, J., Roy, C., & Ratner, N. The beginnings of request. In K. E. Nelson (Ed.), *Children's language (Vol. 3)*. Hillsdale, N.J.: Lawrence Erlbaum Associates, 1982.
Campbell, M., Hardesty, A. S., Breuer, H., & Polevoy, N. Childhood psychosis in perspective. *Journal of the American Academy of Child Psychiatry*, 1978, *17*, 14–28.
Cantwell, D., Baker, L., & Mattison, T. The prevalence of psychiatric disorder in children with speech and language disorders: An epidemiological study. *Journal of the American Academy of Child Psychiatry*, 1979, *18*, 450–461.
Cantwell, D., Baker, L., & Rutter, M. Family factors. In M. Rutter & E. Schopler (Eds.), *Autism: A reappraisal of concepts and treatment*. New York: Plenum Press, 1978.
Caparulo, B. K. & Cohen, D. J. Cognitive structures, language, and emerging social competence in autistic and aphasic children. *Journal of the American Academy of Child Psychiatry*, 1977, *17*, 620–645.
Caparulo, B. K. & Cohen, D. J. Improved performance in stressful situations. *Journal of Autism and Developmental Disorders*, 1980, *10*, 239–240.
Caparulo, B. K., Cohen, D. J., Young, J. G., Rothman, S. L. G., Katz, J. D., Shaywitz, B. A., & Shaywitz, S. E. Computed tomographic brain scanning of children with developmental neuropsychiatric disorders. *Journal of the American Academy of Child Psychiatry*, 1981, *20*, 338–357.
Cassirer, E. *Structure and function and Einstein's theory of relativity* (Trans. by W. C. Swaby & M. C. Swaby). New York: Dover Publications, 1953. (Originally published, Chicago: Open Court Publications, 1923.)
Churchill, D. W. The relation of infantile autism and early childhood schizophrenia to developmental language disorders of childhood. *Journal of Autism and Childhood Schizophrenia*, 1972, *2*, 182–197.
Churchill, D. W. *Language of autistic children*. Washington, D.C.: Winston and Sons, 1978. (a)
Churchill, D. W. Language of autistic children: The problem beyond conditioning. In M. Rutter & E. Schopler (Eds.), *Autism: Reappraisal of concepts and treatment*. New York: Plenum Press, 1978. (b)
Cohen, D. J. The diagnostic process in child psychiatry. *Psychiatric Annals*, 1976, *6*, 404–416.
Cohen, D. J., Caparulo, B. K., Gold, J. R., Waldo, M. C., Shaywitz, B. A., Ruttenberg, B. A., & Rimland, B. Agreement in diagnosis: Clinical assessment and behavior rating scales for pervasively disturbed children. *Journal of the American Academy of Child Psychiatry*, 1978, *17*, 589–603.

Cohen, D. J., Caparulo, B. K., & Shaywitz, B. A. Primary childhood aphasia and childhood autism: Clinical, biological, and conceptual observations. *Journal of the American Academy of Child Psychiatry,* 1976, *15,* 606–645.

Cohen, D. J., Caparulo, B. K., & Shaywitz, B. A. Neurochemical and developmental models of childhood autism. In G. Serban (Ed.), *Cognitive defects in the development of mental illness.* New York: Brunner/Mazel, 1978.

Cohen, D. J., Caparulo, B. K., Shaywitz, B. A., & Bowers, M. B. Jr. Dopamine and serotonin metabolism in neuropsychiatrically disturbed children: Cerebrospinal fluid homovanillic acid and 5-hydroxyindoleacetic acid. *Archives of General Psychiatry,* 1977, *34,* 545–550.

Cohen, D. J., Caparulo, B. K., & Wetstone, H. The emergence of meanings and intentions. *Psychiatric Clinics of North America,* 1981, *4,* 489–508.

Cohen, D. J., Dibble, E., & Grawe, J. Fathers' and mothers' perceptions of children's personalities. *Archives of General Psychiatry,* 1977, *34,* 480–487.

Cohen, D. J., Granger, R. H., Provence, S. A., & Solnit, A. J. Mental health services. In N. Hobbs (Ed.), *Issues in the classification of children (Vol. 2).* San Fransisco: Jossey-Bass, 1975.

Cohen, D. J., & Johnson, W. T. Cardiovascular correlates of attention in normal and psychiatrically disturbed children. *Archives of General Psychiatry,* 1977, *34,* 561–567.

Cohen, D. J. & Young, J. G. Neurochemistry and child psychiatry. *Journal of the American Academy of Child Psychiatry,* 1977, *16,* 353–411.

Condon, W. S. & Sander, L. W. Synchrony demonstrated between movements of the neonate and adult speech. *Child Development,* 1974, *43,* 456–462.

Dale, P. S. Is early pragmatic development measurable? *Journal of Child Language,* 1980, *7,* 1–12.

DeMyer, M. K., Barton, S., DeMyer, W. E., Norton, J. A., Allen, J., & Steele, R. Prognosis in autism: A follow-up study. *Journal of Autism and Childhood Schizophrenia,* 1973, *3,* 199–246.

DesLauriers, A. M. Play, symbols, and the development of language. In M. Rutter & E. Schopler, (Eds.), *Autism: A reappraisal of concepts and treatment.* New York: Plenum Press, 1978.

Dewey, M. A. & Everard, M. P. The near-normal autistic adolescent. *Journal of Autism and Childhood Schizophrenia,* 1974, *4,* 17–29.

Dore, J. A developmental theory of speech act production. *Annals of the New York Academy of Sciences,* 1973, *35,* 623–630.

Dore, J. A pragmatic description of early language development. *Journal of Psycholinguistic Research,* 1974, *3,* 343–350.

Dore, J. Holophrases, speech acts, and language universals. *Journal of Child Language,* 1975, *2,* 21–40.

Dore, J., Gearhart, M., & Newman, D. The structure of nursery school conversation. In K. E. Nelson (Ed.), *Children's language (Vol. 1).* New York: Gardner Press (Wiley), 1978.

Eimas, P. D. Auditory and linguistic processing of cues for place of articulation by infants. *Perception and Psychophysics,* 1974, *16,* 513–521.

Eimas, P. D., Siqueland, E. R., Jusczyk, P., & Vigorito, J. Speech perception by infants. *Science,* 1971, *171,* 303–306.

Elkonin, D. B. Development of speech. In V. Zaporozhets & D. B. Elkonin (Eds.), *The psychology of preschool children.* Cambridge, Mass.: MIT Press, 1971.

Entus, A. K. Hemisphere asymmetry in processing of dichotically presented speech and nonspeech stimuli by infants. In S. J. Segalowitz & F. A Gruber (Eds.), *Language development and neurological theory.* New York: Academic Press, 1977.

Fantz, R. L. The origin of form perception. *Scientific American,* 1961, *204,* 66–78.

Fantz, R. L. Pattern vision in newborn infants. *Science,* 1963, *140,* 296–297.

Fantz, R. L. Pattern discrimination and selective attention as determinants of perceptual development from birth. In A. H. Kidd & J. L. Rivione (Eds.), *Perceptual development in children.* New York: International Universities Press, 1966.

Fay, W. H. Childhood echolalia. *Folia Phoniatrica*, 1967, *19*, 297–306.
Fay, W. H. On normal and autistic pronouns. *Journal of Speech and Hearing Disorders*, 1971, *36*, 242–249.
Fay, W. H. On the basis of autistic echolalia. *Journal of Communication Disorders*, 1969, *2*, 38–47.
Fay, W. H. On the echolalia of the blind and of the autistic child. *Journal of Speech and Hearing Disorders*, 1973, *38*, 478–489.
Fay, W. H. & Schuler, A. L. *Emerging language in autistic children.* Baltimore: University Park Press, 1981.
Fillmore, C. J. The case for case. In E. Bach & R. T. Harms (Eds.), *Universals in linguistic theory.* New York: Holt, Rinehart, & Winston, 1968.
Foy, J. *Gone is shadow's child.* San Francisco: Logos International, 1970.
Freedman, D. G. *Human infancy: An evolutionary perspective.* Hillsdale, N.J.: Lawrence Erlbaum Associates, 1974.
Freud, S. Instincts and their vicissitudes. *The international psycho-analytic library, No. 10. Collected papers* ((Vol. *4*). New York: Basic Books, 1959. (Originally published, 1915).
Fromkin, V., Krashen, S., Curtiss, S., Rigler, D., & Rigler, M. The development of language in Genie: A case of language acquisition beyond "the critical period." *Brain and Language*, 1974, *1*, 81–107.
Greenfield, P. & Smith, P. *The structure of communication in early language development.* New York: Academic Press, 1976.
Gregory, R. L. & Wallace, J. G. Recovery from early blindness: A case study. *Experimental Psychology Society Monographs*, 1963, Whole Number 2.
Habermas, J. Introductory remarks to a theory of communicative competence. Reprinted in H. P. Dreitzel (Ed.), *Recent sociology, No. 2.* London: MacMillan Press, 1970.
Halliday, M. A. K. *Learning how to mean: Explorations in the development of language.* London: Edward Arnold, 1975.
Hebb, D. O., Lambert, W. E., & Tucker, G. R. Language, thought, and experience. *Modern Languages Journal*, 1971, *15*, 212–222.
Hedrick, D. L., Prather, E. M., & Tobin, A. R. *Sequenced Inventory of Communication Development.* Seattle: University of Washington Press, 1975.
Hermelin, B. & O'Connor, N. *Psychological experiments with autistic children.* Oxford: Pergamon Press, 1970.
Ingram, D. *Stages in the development of one-word speech utterances.* Paper presented at the Stanford Child Language Research Forum, Stanford, Calif., 1974.
Jakobson, R. *Child language, aphasia, and phonological universals.* The Hague: Mouton, 1968.
Jakobson, R. Linguistics and poetics. In R. DeGeorge & F. DeGeorge (Eds.), *The structuralists from Marx to Levi-Strauss.* Garden City, N.Y.: Doubleday, 1972.
Jakobson, R. *Brain and language.* Paper presented at Yale University, the Department of Linguistics, New Haven, Conn., April 1980.
Kagan, J. & Lewis, M. Studies of attention in the human infant. *Merrill-Palmer Quarterly*, 1965, *11*, 95–127.
Kanner, L. Autistic disturbances of affective contact. *Nervous Child*, 1943, *2*, 217–250. Reprinted in L. Kanner (Ed.), *Childhood psychosis: Initial studies and new insights.* Washington, D.C.: Winston, 1973.
Kanner, L. (Ed.). *Childhood psychosis: Initial studies and new insights.* Washington, D.C.: Winston, 1973.
Kirk, S. A., McCarthy, J. J., & Kirk, W. D. *Illinois Test of Psycholinguistic Abilities.* Urbana, Ill.: University of Illinois Press, 1968.
Kootz, J. P. & Cohen, D. J. Modulation of sensory intake in autistic children: Cardiovascular and behavioral indices. *Journal of the American Academy of Child Psychiatry*, 1981, *20*, 692–701.

Korner, A. F., & Grobstein, R. Visual alertness as related to soothing in neonates: Implications for maternal stimulation and early deprivation. *Child Development*, 1966, *37*, 867–876.

Korner, A. F. & Thoman, E. B. Visual alertness in the neonate as evoked by maternal care. *Journal of Experimental Psychology*, 1972, *10*, 67–78.

Koupernik, C. A pathogenic approach to infantile autism. In M. Rutter (Ed.), *Infantile autism: Concepts, characteristics, and treatment*. Edinburgh and London: Churchill Livingstone, 1971.

Lake, C. R., Zeigler, M. G., & Murphy, D. L. Increased norepinephrine levels and decreased dopamine-beta-hydroxylase activity in primary autism. *Archives of General Psychiatry*, 1977, *34*, 553–556.

Lane, H. *The wild boy of Aveyron*. Cambridge, Mass.: Harvard University Press, 1976.

Langdell, T. Recognition of faces: An approach to the study of autism. *Journal of Child Psychology and Psychiatry*, 1978, *19*, 255–268.

Lasky, R. E., Syrdal-Lasky, A., & Klein, R. E. VOT discrimination by four to six and a half month old infants from Spanish environments. *Journal of Experimental Child Psychology*, 1975, *20*, 215–225.

Leiter International Performance Scale. Chicago: Stoelting, 1948.

Lenneberg, E. H. Understanding language without ability to speak. *Journal of Abnormal and Social Psychology*, 1962, *65*, 419–425.

Lenneberg, E. H. *Biological foundations of language*. New York: Wiley, 1967.

Lewis, M. & Freedle, R. Mother-infant dyads: The cradle of meaning. In P. Pliner, L., Kramer, & T. Alloway (Eds.), *Communication and affect: Language and thought*. New York: Academic Press, 1973.

Lewis, M. & Rosenblum, L. (Eds.). *The origins of behavior: The effect of the infant on its caregiver*. New York: John Wiley, 1974.

Lockyer, L. & Rutter, M. A five-to-fifteen year follow-up of infantile psychosis. IV. Patterns of cognitive ability. *British Journal of Social and Clinical Psychology*, 1970, *9*, 152–163.

Loewald, H. W. On motivation and instinct theory: Instinct theory, object relations, and psychic structure formation. In H. W. Loewald, *Papers on psychoanalysis*. New Haven, Conn.: Yale University Press, 1980.

Lotter, V. Follow-up studies. In M. Rutter & E. Schopler (Eds.), *Autism: A reappraisal of concepts and treatment*. New York: Plenum Press, 1978.

Mason, S. T. & Fibiger, N. C. Anxiety: The locus coeruleus disconnection. *Life Sciences*, 1979, *25*, 2141–2147.

McCarthy Scales of Children's Development. New York: Psychological Corporation, 1972.

Meltzoff, A. N. & Moore, M. K. Imitation of facial and manual gestures by human neonates. *Science*, 1977, *198*, 75–78.

Molfese, D. L. Infant cerebral asymmetry. In S. J. Segalowitz & J. S. Gruber (Eds.), *Language development and neurological theory*. New York: Academic Press, 1977.

Molfese, D. L., Freeman, R. B. Jr., & Palermo, D. S. The ontogeny of brain lateralization for speech and nonspeech stimuli. *Brain and Language*, 1975, *2*, 356–368.

Morse, P. A. The discrimination of speech and nonspeech stimuli in early infancy. *Journal of Experimental Child Psychology*, 1972, *14*, 477–492.

Nelson, K. Concept, word, and sentence. Interrelationships in acquisition and development. *Psychological Review*, 1974, *81*, 267–285.

Nelson, K. The role of language in infant development. In M. H. Bornstein & W. Kessen (Eds.), *Psychological development from infancy: Image to intention*. Hillsdale, N.J.: Lawrence Erlbaum Associates, 1979.

Nelson, K. Individual differences in language development: Implications for development and language. *Developmental Psychology*, 1981, *17*, 170–187.

Nelson, K. E. Toward a rare event cognitive comparison theory of syntax acquisition: Insights from work with recasts. In D. Ingram & P. S. Dale (Eds.), *Child language: An international perspective*. Baltimore: University Park Press, 1980.

Ninio A., & Bruner, J. The achievement and antecedents of labeling. *Journal of Child Language*, 1978, *5*, 1-15.

Pierce, S. & Bartolucci, G. A syntactic investigation of verbal autisitic, mentally retarded, and normal children. *Journal of Autism and Childhood Schizophrenia*, 1977, *7*, 121-134.

Prior, M. Psycholinguistic disabilities of autistic and retarded children. *Journal of Mental Deficiency Research*, 1977, *21*, 37-45.

Prior, M. Cognitive abilities and disabilities in infantile autism. *Journal of Abnormal Child Psychology*, 1979, *7*, 357-380.

Ratner, N. & Bruner, J. Games, social exchange and the acquisition of language. *Journal of Child Language*, 1978, *5*, 391-401.

Raven, J. C. *Progressive Matrices*. London: H. K. Lewis, Ltd., 1962.

Redmond, D. E. & Huang, Y. H. New evidence for a locus coeruleus-norepinephrine connection with anxiety. *Life Sciences*, 1979, *25*, 2149-2162.

Rees, N. S. Pragmatics of language: Applications to normal and disordered language development. In R. L. Schiefelbusch (Ed.), *Bases of language intervention*. Baltimore: University Park Press, 1978.

Reynell, J. K. *Reynell Developmental Language Scales, Experimental Edition*. Windsor, Eng.: N. F. E. R. Publishing, 1969.

Richards, M. P. *The integration of a child into a social world*. Cambridge, England: Cambridge University Press, 1974.

Ricks, D. M. & Wing, L. Language, communication and the use of symbols in normal and autistic children. *Journal of Autism and Childhood Schizophrenia*, 1975, *5*, 191-221.

Risley, T. R. & Wolf, M. Establishing functional speech in echolalic children. *Behavior Research and Therapy*, 1967, *5*, 73-88.

Ruttenberg, B. A., Kalish, B. I., Wenar, C., & Wolf, E. G. *Behavior Rating Instrument for Autistic and Other Atypical Children*. Philadelphia: Developmental Center for Autistic Children, 1974.

Ruttenberg, B. A. & Wolf, E. G. Evaluating the communication of autistic children. *Journal of Speech and Hearing Disorders*, 1967, *32*, 314-324.

Rutter, M. The effects of language delay on development. In M. Rutter & J. A. Martin (Eds.), *The child with delayed speech*. London: SIMP/Heinemann Medical, 1972.

Rutter, M. Diagnosis and definition. In M. Rutter & E. Schopler (Eds.), *Autism: A reappraisal of concepts and treatment*. New York: Plenum, 1978.

Sander, L. W. Infant and caretaking environment: Investigation and conceptualization of adaptive behavior in a system of increasing complexity. In E. J. Anthony (Ed.), *Explorations in child psychiatry*. New York: Plenum Press, 1975.

Sander, L. W. The regulation of exchange in the infant-caretaker system and some aspects of the context-content relationship. In M. Lewis & L. Rosenblum (Eds.), *Origins of behavior: Interactions, conversations, and the development of language*. New York: Wiley, 1977.

Shapiro, T. The quest for a linguistic model to study the speech of autistic children: Studies in echoing. *Journal of the American Academy of Child Psychiatry*, 1977, *16*, 608-619.

Shapiro, T. & Lucy, P. Echoing in autistic children: A chronometric study of semantic processing. *Journal of Child Psychology and Psychiatry*, 1978, *19*, 373-378.

Shattuck, R. *The forbidden experiment: The story of the wild boy of Aveyron*. New York: Farrar, Straus, & Giroux, 1980.

Shotter, J., & Gregory, S. On first gaining the idea of oneself as a person. In R. Harre (Ed.), *Life sentences: Aspects of the social role of language*. New York: Wiley, 1976.

Sroufe, L. A., Stuecher, H. U., & Stutzer, W. The functional significance of autistic behaviors for the psychotic child. *Journal of Abnormal Child Psychology*, 1973, *1*, 225-240.

Stern, D. N. *The first relationship: Infant and mother*. Cambridge: Harvard University Press, 1977.

Stern, D. N., Jaffe, J., Beebe, B., & Bennett, S. L. Vocalizing in unison and in alternation. *Annals of the New York Academy of Sciences*, 1975, *263*, 89-100.

Streeter, L. A. Language perception of 2-month-old infants shows effects of both innate mechanisms and experience. *Nature,* 1976, *259,* 39–41.

Sullivan, R. Hunches on some biological factors in autism. *Journal of Autism and Childhood Schizophrenia,* 1975, *5,* 177–186.

Sullivan, R. Parents speak: Why do autistic children . . . ? *Journal of Autism and Developmental Disorders,* 1980, *10,* 231–241.

Tager-Flusberg, H. Sentence comprehension in autistic children. *Applied Psycholinguistics,* 1981, *2,* 5–24.

Tinbergen, E. A. & Tinbergen, N. *Early childhood autism: An ethological approach.* Berlin: Paul Parry, 1972.

Trehub, S. C. Infants' sensitivity to vowel and tonal contrasts. *Developmental Psychology,* 1973, *9,* 91–96.

Trehub, S. C., & Rabinovitch, M. S. Auditory-linguistic sensitivity in early infancy. *Developmental Psychology,* 1972, *6,* 74–77.

M. von Senden, *Space and sight: The perception of space and shape in the congenitally blind before and after operation.* (Trans. by P. Heath.) London: Methuen, 1960. (Originally published, 1932.)

Vygotsky, L *Thought and language.* Cambridge, Mass.: MIT Press, 1962.

Waldo, M. C., Cohen, D. J., Caparulo, B. K., Young, J. G., Prichard, J. W., & Shaywitz, B. A. EEG profiles of neuropsychiatrically disturbed children. *Journal of the American Academy of Child Psychiatry,* 1978, *17,* 656–670.

Wechsler, D. *Wechsler Preschool and Primary Scales of Intelligence.* New York: Psychological Corporation, 1967.

Wechsler, D. *Wechsler Intelligence Scales for Children-Revised.* New York: Psychological Corporation, 1974.

Winnicott, D. W. Primitive emotional development: Transitional objects and transitional phenomena. In D. W. Winnicott, *Through P to P.* New York: Basic Books, 1975.

Wolff, P. H. Observations in the early development of smiling. In B. H. Foss (Ed.), *Determinants of infantile behavior II.* New York: Wiley, 1963.

Young, J. G. & Cohen, D. J. The molecular biology of development. In J. Noshpitz (Ed.), *Basic handbook of child psychiatry (Vol. 1).* New York: Basic Books, 1979.

Young, J. G., Cohen, D. J., Anderson, G. A., & Shaywitz, B. A. Neurotransmitter ontogeny as a perspective for studies of child development and pathology. In B. Shopsin & L. Greenhill (Eds.), *The psychobiology of childhood: A profile of current issues.* New York: Spectrum, 1981.

Zukow, P. R., Reilly, J., & Greenfield, P. M. Making the absent present: Facilitating the transition from the sensorimotor to linguistic communication. In K. E. Nelson (Ed.), *Children's language (Vol. 3).* Hillsdale, N.J.: Lawrence Erlbaum Associates, 1982.

Author Index

Numbers in *italics* denote pages with bibliographic information.

A

Abelson, R., 42, *57*, 109, *122*, 316, 345, *382*
Abramovitch, R., 148, *154*
Abravanel, E., 115, *118*
Adams, S., 159, *183*
Ainsworth, M. D., 446, *457*
Albert, M., 93, *123*
Alderdice, M. H., 106, *119*
Aldis, O., 234, 236, 241, *251*
Alenskas, L., 79, *122*
Allen, D., 20, *26*
Allen, J., 444, *459*
American Psychaitric Association, 423, *457*
Ammon, P., 139, 148, *153*
Anderson, G. A., 453, *463*
Anderson, S. R., 258, *278*
Anglin, J., 22, *26*
Anglin, J. M., 451, *457*
Arthur, G., 425, *457*
Antinucci, F., 2, 12, *26*
Archibold, Y., 108, *121*
Applebee, A. N., 418, *419*
Apthorp, H., 161, *185*
Asher, S. R., 160, *183*
Austin, J. L., 69, *118*, 164, *183*, 315, *380*, 415, *419*

B

Bacri, N., 236, *252*
Baker, L., 424, 428, *457, 458*
Baldie, B. J., 136, *151*
Baldwin, J. M., 449, *457*
Baron, N., 3, *26*, 284, 298, *310*
Bartak, L., 429, 431, 440, 441, *457*
Bartlett, F. C., 385, 395, *419*
Bartolucci, G., 431, 443, *462*
Barton, D., 261, *278*
Barton, S., 444, *459*
Bates, E., 2, 4, 5, *26*, 59, 60, 62, 64, 66, 69, 70, 71, 72, 76, 78, 79, 80, 81, 82, 84, 87, 88, 89, 90, 93, 103, 108, 116, 117, *118, 119, 120, 123*, 315, *380*, 444, 450, 455, *457*
Bateson, M. C., 189, 192, 193, 199, 206, *226*
Battison, R., 287, 292, *310*
Beebe, B., 189, 190, 191, 193, 205, *230*, 447, *462*
Beeghly-Smith, M., 66, 84, *119*
Bell, R. Q., 162, *183*
Bell, S. M., 446, *457*
Bellinger, D., 166, *184*
Bellugi, U., 1, *26*, 76, *118*, 187, 209, 211, *226, 227*, 284, 290, 289, 301, *310, 312*, 440, *458*

465

Bellugi-Klima, U., 440, *458*
Bemporad, J. R., 443, 444, *457*
Benedict, H., 16, *27*, 188, 227
Benedict, N., 64, *118*
Benigni, L., 59, 64, 69, 71, 72, 76, 78, 79, 82, 93, 103, *118, 119, 123*, 450, *457*
Bennett, C. W., 446, *457*
Bennett, S. L., 189, 190, 191, 193, 205, *230*, 447, *462*
Berger, P. L., 446, *457*
Berman, R. A., 262, *278*
Berndt, E., 415, *419*
Berndt, R., 98, *119*
Berndt, R. S., 94, 96, 102, *119*
Berndt, T. J., 415, *419*
Bernholtz, N., 237, *253*
Bernstein, M. E., 285, *310*
Bettelheim, B., 439, *457*
Bever, T. G., 147, *151*, 237, *251*
Bhattacharya, N., 3, *26*
Birnbaum, D. W., 125, *153*
Blank, M., 20, *26*, 46, *56*, 125, 140, 150, *152*, 443, 451, 455, *457*
Blanton, L., 286, *312*
Bleier, M., 163, *185*
Bloom, K., 192, 206, *226*
Bloom, L., 1, 2, 12, 25, *26*, 30, 31, 33, 35, 36, 42, 55, *56*, 82, 83, 116, *118*, 127, 128, 129, 130, 131, 132, 133, 134, 135, 146, 147, *152*, 187, 196, 200, 211, 212, *226*, 237, *251*, 305, *310*, 315, *380*
Bohannon, J. N., 55, *56*
Bolinger, D., 44, *56*
Bonvillian, J., 38, *57*, 88, 109, *118, 122*, 187, 208, 209, 224, 225, *226, 227, 228*, 229, 284, 285, *310*
Bornstein, H., 285, 287, *310*
Bornstein, M. H., 445, 446, *458*
Botvin, G. J., 335, *380*
Boucher, J., 431, 441, *458*
Bower, G. H., 333, 337, 338, *380*, 390, 391, *419*
Bower, T. G. R., 113, *118*, 268, *278*, 447, *458*
Bowerman, M., 20, *26*, 129, 130, 131, 132, *152*, 187, 208, *211*, *226*, 331, *380*
Bowers, M. B. Jr., 453, *459*
Bowes, J., 232, *251*
Brain, W. R., 100, *118*
Braine, M. D. S., 116, *118*, 132, 134, 138, *152*, 263, 268, *278*

Brandao, S., 225, *230*
Branigan, G., 256, 260, *278*
Bransford, J., 38, *56*, 125, *152*
Brasel, L., 283, *311*
Brazelton, T. B., 131, *152*, 162, *184*, 189, 192, *226*, 447, 449, *458*
Bresnan, J., 30, *56*
Bretherton, I., 59, 64, 66, 71, 72, 76, 78, 79, 80, 81, 82, 84, 87, 88, 90, 93, 103, *118, 119, 123*, 450, *457*
Brever, H., 444, *458*
Brewer, M. B., 411, *420*
Brewer, W. F., 316, *381*
Bridges, J. S., 137, 147, *152*
Broen, P. A., 87, 193, 211, *226*
Bronkadt, J. P., 121, *26*
Brown, A., 40, *56*
Brown, A. L., 330, 338, 339, 340, 342, 343, 347, 373, 379, *380, 382*, 391, 392, 395, 413, 414, 416, 417, 418, *419, 421*
Brown, J. W., 93, 100, *119*
Brown, R., 1, 2, 12, *26*, 90, 96, *119*, 187, 202, 204, 205, 209, 211, *226, 227*, 261, 262, *278*, 284, 299, 300, *311*, 440, *458*
Brownell, H. H., 98, 102, *119*
Bruce, B. C., 411, *419*
Bruner, J., 2, 5, 9, 11, *256* 48, *57*, 62, *119*, 129, *152*, 157, 162, *184* 232, 241, 249, *251*, 448, 449, 452, *458, 462*
Buschke, H., 325, *382*
Buss, R. R., 330, 338, 339, 343, 347, 373, *383*, 391, 395, 413, 418, *421*

C

Cabral, L. S., 2, *28*
Caltagirone, C., 104, 105, *120*
Camaioni, L., 4, *26*, 59, 62, 64, 69, 70, 71, 72, 76, 78, 79, 82, 93, 103, *118, 119, 123*, 450, *457*
Campbell, M., 444, *458*
Campione, J. C., 339, *382*, 417, 418, *421*
Campos, J. J., 113, *121*
Cancelli, A. A., 144, *154*
Cantwell, D., 424, 428, *457, 458*
Caparulo, B. K., 425, 427, 429, 430, 431, 433, 439, 440, 441, 451, 452, 453, 454, *458, 459, 463*
Caramazza, A., 93, 94, 96, 98, 102, *119*
Carey, D., 97, *120*
Carey, S., 38, *56*

AUTHOR INDEX

Carroll, J., 59, *119*
Carskaddon, G., 208, 209, *229*
Carter, A., 4, *26*, 62, *119*
Carter, A. L., 240, *251*
Casari, V. L., 217, *230*
Case, R., 114, *119*
Cassirer, E., 451, *458*
Cazden, C., 21, *26*, 187, 211, *226*, 250, *252*, 268, 274, *278*, 440, *458*
Cazden, C. B., 298, 301, *311*
Chafe, W. L., 12, *26*
Chall, J., 396, *419*
Chandler, M., 178, 179, *184*
Chao, Y. R., 238, 244, *252*
Chapman, R., 35, *56*
Chapman, R. S., 18, *28*, 147, *152*
Charrow, V. R., 109, *118*, 285, *310*
Chi, M. T. H., 336, *380*
Chiat, S., 238, *252*
Chomsky, C., 148, *152*
Chomsky, N., 95, *119*, 187, *226*, 255, 257, 258, 264, 274, *278*, 279
Churchill, D. W., 430, *458*
Cicone, M., 102, *119*
Cirilo, R. K., 338, *380*
Clanton, C., 131, *155*
Claparède, E., 232, *252*
Clark, E., 113, *119*, 285, *311*
Clark, E. V., 1, *26*
Clark, R., 30, 31, 43, 46, *56*
Clay, M. M., 291, 294, 297, *311*
Clumeck, H. U., 238, *252*
Coburn, C., 343, *381*
Cohen, B. D., 160, *185*
Cohen, D. J., 425, 426, 427, 429, 430, 431, 433, 439, 440, 441, 451, 452, 453, 454, *458, 459, 460, 463*
Cole, M., 24, *27*
Collins-Ahlgren, M., 290, *311*
Collis, G., 190, 191, 192, 194, 206, *229*
Commings, J., 285, *311*
Condon, W. S., 189, 192, 193, 205, *226*, 448, *459*
Conklin, H., 248, *252*
Conrad, R., 125, *152*, 286, *311*
Cournoyer, P., 163, *185*
Cowan, P. A., 159, *184*
Cox, A., 431, *457*
Critchley, M., 100, *119*
Crnkovic, L. M. P., 225, *227*
Cromer, R., 2, 12, *26*

Cromer, R. F., 148, 149, *152*
Cross, T. G., 16, *26*, 189, 208, 209, 211, *227*
Cruttendan, A., 233, 236, 238, *252*
Crystal, D., 237, *252*
Cunningham, J. W., 418, *419*
Curtiss, S., 423, *460*

D

Dale, E., 396, *419*
Dale, P. S., 331, *380*, 448, *459*
Danner, F. W., 344, 375, *380*
Davis, H., 190, 191, 192, 194, 206, *227*
Davis, K. E., 411, *420*
Day, Jeanne D., 416, *419*
Day, M. C., 126, *152*
Day, R. S., 249, *252*
deBoysson-Bardies, B., 236, *252*
DeForest, M., 325, 333, 334, 335, 340, *381*
DeHaven, E. D., 205, *227*
deHirsch, K., 417, *419*
DeLoache, J., 40, *56*
DeLoache, J. S., 339, 342, *380*
DeMarcellus, O., 138, *155*
Dempster, F. N., 336, *382*
DeMyer, M. K., 444, *453*
DeMyer, W. E., 444, *459*
Denhière, G., 330, 339, 340, 341, 342, 343, 347, 356, 373, *380*, 395, 412, *419*
Dennis, Z., 284, *313*
DePaulo, B. M., 187, 209, 224, 225, *227*
Deslauriers, A. M., 430, *459*
de Villiers, J., 22, *27*
de Villiers, J. G., 136, *152*, 211, *227*, 331, *380*
de Villiers, P. A., 211, *227*, 331, *380*
Devin, J., 161, 182, *185*
DeVries, R., 178, *184*
Dewey, M. A., 438, *459*
Dibble, E., 425, *459*
Dickinson, D., 417, *421*
Dickson, W. P., 160, *184*
Dobson, M. V., 131, *155*
Dodd, B., 256, *279*
Donaldson, M., 258, *279*
Donegan, P. J., 256, *279*
Dore, J., 5, *27*, 67, *119*, 157, 162, 165, 168, 174, *184*, 240, *252*, 315, *380*, 444, 448, 450, *459*
dos Santos, R. C., 217, *230*
Doyle, W. J., 233, 236, 238, *253*

Drachman, G., 260, *279*
Dressler, W. U., 315, *380*
Duffy, J. R., 105, 106, *119*, *120*
Duffy, R. J., 105, 106, *119*, *120*
Duncan, S., 108, *120*
Duncan, S. D., 189, 192, *227*
Durkin, D., 294, 297, *311*

E

Edwards, M. L., 256, *279*
Eimas, P. D., 193, *227*, 445, *459*
Eisenberg, A. R., 24, *28*
Elder, J., 87, *120*
Elkonin, D. B., 449, *459*
Ellenberger, R., 284, *311*
Engel, W. V. R., 260, *229*
Entus, A. K., 445, *459*
Entwisle, D., 145, *152*
Ervin, S., 30, 35, *56*, 211, *227*
Ervin, S. M., 145, *152*
Ervin-tripp, S., 166, 168, 169, 175, 180, *184*
Esposito, A., 443, 455, *457*
Evans, M. A., 161, *184*
Everard, M. P., 438, *459*
Ewoldt, C., 286, 287, 303, *311*

F

Fabian-Kraus, V., 139, 148, *153*
Fantz, R. L., 447, *459*
Farwell, C. B., 238, *252*, 260, 262, 270, *279*
Fay, W. H., 439, *460*
Fein, G., 87, *120*
Feldman, H., 16, *27*, 76, *120*
Feldstein, S., 164, *185*, 189, 193, 194, 199, *228*
Felman, H., 263, *279*
Ferguson, C., 63, *120*
Ferguson, C. A., 11, *27*, 192, 193, *227*, 235, 238, 249, *252*, 256, 258, 260, 261, 263, 274, *279*, *281*, 298, *311*
Ferrier, L., 31, *56*
Fey, M., 258, *279*
Fibiger, N. C., 453, *461*
Field, N. C., 131, *154*
Filby, N., 135, *154*
Fillmore, C., 109, *120*, 386, *419*
Fillmore, C. J., 316, *380*, *460*
Fillmore, L., 43, 44, 46, *56*
Finkelnburg, F., 100, *120*

Fischer, S., 286, 301, *311*
Fiske, D., 108, *120*
Fitzhenry-Coor, I., 415, *419*, *420*
Flapan, D., 415, *420*
Flavell, J. H., 159, 161, 176, *184*, 378, *380*, 392, 414, *420*
Fodor, J. A., 237, *251*, 258, *279*
Fogel, A., 189, *227*
Foldi, N., 102, *119*
Folger, J., 35, *56*
Forsyth, D. F., 145, *152*
Foss, D. J., 338, *380*
Foster, E. O., 418, *419*
Fox, D. E. C., 139, *154*
Foy, J., 431, *460*
Fradis, A., 107, *121*
Franklin, M. B., 240, *252*
Franks, J., 38, *56*
Fraser, C., 187, 209, *226*, *227*
Frederiksen, C. H., 316, *380*
Freedle, R., 192, *227*, 447, *461*
Freedman, D. G., 446, *460*
Freeman, R. B., Jr., 445, *461*
Frege, G., 60, *120*
French, P. L., 132, 133, *153*
Freud, S., 232, *252*, 447, *460*
Friedlander, B. Z., 146, *155*
Fromkin, V., 423, *460*
Fry, D. B., 235, *252*
Fry, M. A., 417, *420*
Furrow, D., 16, *27*, 188, *227*
Furth, H. A., 283, *311*

G

Gainotti, G., 100, 104, 105, 109, *120*
Gandour, J., 258, *279*
Garcia, E. E., 205, *227*
Gardner, H., 94, 98, 102, 107, *119*, *120*, 394, *420*
Garnica, O. K., 235, *252*, 256, *279*
Garrison, A., 89, *120*
Garvey, C., 55, *56*, 157, 162, 163, 165, 166, 168, 169, 174, 177, 180, 182, *184*, 187, 196, *227*, 232, 233, 234, 241, 249, *253*
Gearhart, M., 315, *380*, 450, *459*
Gegeo, D., 30, *58*
Gelman, R., 161, 166, 177, 182, *184*, *186*, 196, *227*, 258, *279*, 346, 392
Genova, P., 241, *254*
Gentner, D., 113, *120*

AUTHOR INDEX 469

Gessner, M., 443, 455, *457*
Gibson, W., 59, *120*
Gilbert, J., 239, *252*
Gilman, L. A., 285, *311*
Gleason, J., 44, *56*
Gleason, J. B., 16, *27*, 315, *380*
Gleason, J. Berko, 29, 44, *56*
Gleitman, L., 76, *120*
Glenn, C. G., 316, 325, 333, 334, 336, 338, 339, 340, 341, 342, 356, *380, 382, 383, 385*, 390, 391, 394, 411, 414, 415, 417, 418, *421*
Glucksberg, S., 2, *27*, 159, 160, 161, 168, 178, 179, *184*, 345, *380*
Goffman, E., 189, *227*
Gold, J. R., 425, *458*
Goldfein, M., 30, *58*
Goldfield, B., 47, *57, 58*
Goldin-Meadow, S., 16, *27*, 76, *120*, 263, *279*
Goldman, B. D., 174, *184*
Goldstein, K., 100, *120*
Golfeto, E. M., 225, *230*
Goodglass, H., 97, 101, 102, *120*
Goodman, Y., 297, *311*
Goodwin, M. W., 285, *312*
Graesser, A. C., 337, *381*
Granger, R. H., 427, *459*
Grawe, J., 425, *459*
Green, E., 96, *120*
Greenberg, J. H., 250, *253*
Greenblatt, S., 93, *120*
Greenfield, P., 69, 115, *121*, 444, 452, *460, 463*
Greenfield, P. M., 2, 4, 16, 22, *27, 28*, 126, *153*, 197, *230*
Greenlee, M., 261, *280*
Gregory, R. L., 446, *460*
Gregory, S., 429, 449, *462*
Greif, E., 44, *56*
Grice, H. P., 315, *381*
Grice, P., 65, *120*, 164, 177, *184*
Griswold, L. E., 285, *311*
Grobstein, R., 446, *461*
Grollman, S., 418, *421*
Grosjean, F., 189, *228*
Grosjean, L., 189, *228*
Gruendel, J., 41, 42, *57*, 175, *185*, 345, 346, *382*
Guillaume, P., 128, 134, *153*
Guthrie, J. T., 418, *420*

H

Haas, M. R., 247, *253*
Habermas, J., 448, *460*
Hafitz, J., 12, *26*
Haith, M. M., 113, *121*, 131, *153*
Hakuta, K., 38, 46, *56*
Hall, W. S., 24, *27*
Halle, M., 249, *253*
Halliday, M. A. K., 2, 4, 12, *27*, 263, *280*, 444, 448, *460*
Hamilton, L. B., 285, 287, *310*
Hanlon, C., 202, 205, 209, *226*, 261, *278*
Hardesty, A. S., 444, *458*
Harner, L., 2, 12, *27*
Harris, M., 136, *153*
Hatch, I., 43, *56*
Hawkins, P. R., 189, *228*
Hay, D., 162, *185*
Hayes, D. S., 125, *153*
Heath, S. B., 250, *253*, 275, *280*
Hebb, D. O., 444, *460*
Hedrick, D. L., 425, *460*
Hegedus, K., 163, *184*
Heidenheimer, P., 145, *153*
Heras, I., 38, *56*
Hermelin, B., 443, 454, *460*
Herron, R., 232, 234, *253*
Higgins, E. T., 2, *27*, 160, 168, 175, 182, *184*, 345, *380*
Hildyard, A., 332, 345, *381*
Hockett, C. F., 2, *27*
Hoffmeister, R., 76, *121*, 284, 291, *312*
Hogan, R., 162, 163, 165, 169, 174, 177, 180, 182, *184*, 187, 196, *227*
Hood, L., 2, *26*, 30, 31, 33, 35, 36, 42, 55, *56*, 82, 83, *118*, 129, 132, 133, 135, *152*, 187, 196, 200, 211, 212, *226*, 315, *380*
Hooper, J. B., 256, *280*
Horgan, D., 82, 96, *121*, 136, 137, *153*
Horii, Y., 236, *254*
Hornby, P. A., 135, *153*
Hovell, M. F., 208, *228*
Hoy, E. A., 161, *185*
Huang, J., 43, *56*
Huang, Y. H., 453, *462*
Huizanga, J., 232, *253*
Hultsch, D. F., 162, *185*
Hunt, J. McV., 71, *123*
Hursh, D. E., 208, *228*
Hutt, C., 241, *253*
Huttenlocher, J., 2, *27*

I, J

Ibba, A., 104, 105, *120*
Ingram, D., 256, 271, *280*, 444, *460*
Inhelder, B., 272, *280*
Ironsmith, E., 30, *58*
Itkonen, T., 260, 265, 270, *280*
Jacklin, J. P., 101, *122*
Jackson, J. H., 100, *121*
Jacobson, S. W., 268, *280*
Jaffe, J., 164, *185*, 189, 190, 191, 192, 193, 194, 199, 205, *228*, *230*, 447, *462*
Jakobson, R., *121*, 236, *253*, 256, 263, 274, *280*, 444, 452, *460*
James, S. L., 175, *185*
Jankowski, W., 79, *122*
Jansky, J. J., 417, *419*
Jeffrey, W. E., 127, 128, *153*, 271, *282*
Jeng, H. H., 238, *253*, 256, *280*
Jenkins, J. J., 250, *253*
Jespersen, O., 244, 247, *253*, 268, 280
Johnson, C. S., 417, *420*
Johnson, L., 415, *421*
Johnson, M., 16, *28*, 125, *152*
Johnson, N. S., 316, 317, 321, 333, 334, 335, 336, 338, 340, 356, 358, *381*, 385, 388, 391, 394, 395, 397, 410, 411, 415, 416, *420*
Johnson, R. E., 330, *381*
Johnson, W. T., 453, *458*
Johnson-Laird, P. N., 135, *153*
Jolly, A., 232, *251*
Jones, E. E., 411, *420*
Jones, H. R., 125, *153*
Jones, K., 97, *120*
Jones, L. G., 256, 271, *280*
Jones, M. L., 284, 301, *312*
Jusczyk, P., 193, *227*, 445, *459*

K

Kagan, J., 447, *460*
Kalish, B. I., 425, *462*
Kane, P. T., 330, 338, 339, 343, 347, 373, *383*, 391, 395, 413, 418, *421*
Kanner, L., 427, 428, 441, 442, *460*
Kaplan, B., 60, 64, 65, 87, *123*
Kaplan, E. F., 101, 102, *120*
Karmiloff-Smith, A., 272, *280*
Katz, J. D., 425, *458*
Kaye, K., 189, *228*

Keenan, E. O., 2, 23, *27*, 196, *228*, 233, 240, 244, *253*
Keenan, E. Ochs, 30, 55, *56*, *57*
Kempler, D., 82, 96, *121*
Kempson, R. M., 315, *381*
Kendon, A., 189, 192, *228*
Keppel, G., 353, *381*
Killen, M., 87, 115, *121*
Kimura, D., 108, *121*
Kinsbourne, M., 126, 132, 141, 142, 147, 149, *153*, *154*
Kintsch, W., 316, 330, 333, 336, 337, 338, 340, 347, 377, 378, *381*, *383*, 385, 391, 410, 416, *420*
Kiparsky, P., 256, 258, 264, 268, 272, *280*
Kirk, S. A., 425, *460*
Kirk, W. D., 425, *460*
Kirschenblatt-Gimblett, B., 233, *254*
Kisseberth, C. W., 256, *280*
Klein, B., 97, *120*
Klein, E., 196, *228*
Klein, R. E., 445, *461*
Klima, E. S., 76, *118*, 284, 290, 292, 301, 310, 312
Kohn, L. L., 147, *152*
Konstanteras, M. M., 284, *312*
Kootz, J. P., 426, 453, *460*
Korner, A. F., 446, *461*
Koupernik, C., 429, *461*
Kowslowski, B., 162, *184*, 189, 192, *226*
Kozminsky, E., 338, 378, *381*
Krakow, J., 163, *185*
Krashen, S., 423, *460*
Krasner, L., 205, *228*
Krauss, R., 2, *27*, 159, 160, 161, 168, 178, 179, *184*, 345, *380*
Kuczaj, S., 12, *27*, 139, *154*
Kunsmann, P. W., 263, *280*
Kurdek, L., 181, *185*

L

Labov, W., 239, *253*, 260, *280*
Labov, T., 239, *253*, 260, *280*
Lake, C. R., 453, *461*
Lakoff, G., 138, *153*, 315, *381*
Lambert, W. E., 444, *460*
Lane, H., 189, *228*, 423, *461*
Langdell, T., 451, *461*
Langer, S., 65, *121*
Langford, W. S., 417, *419*

Lasky, R. W., 445, *461*
Laurendeau, M., 131, 137, *153*
Lawson, C., 166, 167, *185*
Lawton, S. Q. C., 338, 342, *380*
Leischner, A., 107, *121*
Leiter International Performance Scale 425, *461*
Lemmo, M. A., 100, 104, 109, *120*
Lempers, J., 161, *186*
Lempert, H., 126, 132, 137, 139, 141, 142, 147, 148, 149, *153*, *154*
Lenneberg, E. H., 439, *461*
Le Ny, J., 330, 339, 340, 341, 342, 343, 347, 356, 373, *380*, 395, 412, *419*
Leonard, L. B., 132, *154*, 260, 271, *280*
Leopold, W. F., 264, 271, *280*
Lesser, R., 94, 96, 97, 99, *121*
Levan-Goldschmidt, E., 115, *118*
Lewis, M., 61, *121*, 205, *227*, 447, *460*, *461*
Li, C. N., 238, *253*
Lichtenstein, E. H., 316, *381*
Liddell, S., 301, *312*
Lieberman, P., 193, *228*, 239, *253*
Liepmann, H., 100, *121*
Lifter, K., 12, *26*
Lightbown, P., 30, 35, 42, *56*, 82, 83, *118*, 129, 132, 133, 135, *152*
Limber, J., 131, *154*
Lindaver, B. K., 345, *382*
Lindsay, P. H., 390, *420*
Ling, D., 446, *457*
Lock, A., 61, *121*
Lockyer, L., 444, *461*
Loewald, H. W., 456, *461*
Longhurst, T. M., 211, *229*
Lotter, V., 432, 440, *461*
Lotz, E., 55, *56*
Lovelace, E. R., 337, *381*
Lubin, D., 168, *185*
Luckman, L., 446, *457*
Lucy, P., 439, *462*

M

Macken, M., 44, *57*, 261, *279*
MacKen, M. A., 237, 238, *253*, 256, 258, 260, 261, 262, 263, 264, 266, 268, 269, 271, *280*, *281*, 298, *311*
MacMahon, R., 94, *121*
Macnamara, J., 1, *27*, 258, *281*

MacWhinney, B., 116, *118*
Mahoney, G. J., 188, *228*
Main, M., 162, *184*, 189, 192, *226*
Mandel, R. G., 335, 343, *381*
Mandel, T. S., 338, 378, *381*
Mandler, J. M., 316, 317, 321, 325, 333, 334, 335, 336, 338, 340, 345, 356, 358, *381*, 385, 388, 391, 394, 411, 415, *420*
Maratsos, M. P., 139, 147, 148, *154*, 160, *185*
Markman, E. M., 378, *381*
Maruszewski, M., 104, *121*
Mason, S. T., 453, *461*
Mathews, S. R., II, 330, 338, 339, 343, 347, 373, *383* 391, 395, 413, 418, *421*
Mattison, T., 424, *458*
Maxwell, M. M., 284, 286, 290, *312*
McCarthy Scales of Children's Development, 424, *461*
McCarthy, J. J., 425, *460*
McCloskey, M., 325, *382*
McConaughy, S. H., 387, 409, 418, *420*
McCune-Nicolich, L., 232, *253*
McLagen, M., 233, 236, *254*
McNeill, D., 96, 108, *119*, 187, *228*, 299, *312*
McNew, S., 66, 80, 81, 82, 84, 90, *119*
Mctear, M., 30, 55, *57*
Mead, G. H., 65, *121*
Meadow, K. P., 283, 284, 285, *312*, *313*
Meissner, J., 161, *185*
Meltzoff, A. N., 268, *281*, 447, *461*
Menig-Peterson, C., 161, *185*
Menn, L., 240, *253*, 256, 258, 260, 263, 264, 268, 272, *280*, *281*
Menyuk, P., 149, *154*, 237, 240, *253*
Meslama, L., 271, *280*
Messer, S., 250, *253*
Messerli, P., 101, *121*
Meyer, B. J. F., 316, 337, *381*
Mikes, M., 256, *281*
Millar, S., 241, *253*
Miller, G. A., 189, *228*
Miller, J. F., 147, *152*
Miller, M., 6, *27*, 418, *420*
Miller, P., 315, *380*
Miller, R., 2, 12, *26*, 261, 278
Miller, R. T., 240, *252*
Minsky, M., 109, *122*, 387, *420*
Moerk, C., 30, *57*
Moerk, E., 30, *57*

Moerk, E. L., 2, *27,* 187, 209, 211, 212, 213, 214, *228*
Molfese, D. L., 149, *154,* 445, *461*
Montanelli, D. S., 283, *312*
Monteiro, M. I. B., 225, 227
Moore, M. K., 268 *281,* 447, *461*
Moores, D., 285, 286, *312*
Moores, D. F., 285, 286, *312*
Moran, L. J., 144, *154*
Morris, W., 330, *382*
Morse, P. A., 193, *228,* 445, *461*
Mosenthal, P., 417, *420*
Moskowitz, B. A., 256, 257, 265, *281*
Mow, S., 284, *312*
Mowrer, O. H., 255, *281*
Muehl, S., 417, *420*
Mueller, E., 162, 163, 165, 174, *185*
Muir, D., 131, *154*
Murai, J., 255, *281*
Murphy, D. L., 453, *461*
Muuss, R., 145, *152*

N, O

Neisser, U., 390, *420*
Nelson, K., 5, 16, *27,* 41, 42, *57,* 64, 81, 99, 109, 112, *122,* 144, *154,* 175, *185,* 187, 188, 202, 205, 227, 228, 274, *281,* 345, 346, 378, *382,* 446, 450, 451, 455, *461*
Nelson, K. E., 16, 24, *27,* 38, 40, *56, 57,* 88, 109, *118, 122,* 135, 147, *155,* 188, 208, 209, 211, 217, 224, 225, *226,* 228, *229,* 274, *281,* 284, 285, *310,* 378, *382,* 440, *461*
Newhoff, M., 260, 271, *280*
Newman, D., 315, *380,* 450, *459*
Newport, E., 290, *312*
Nezworski, T., 325, *383,* 394, 415, *421*
Nicholas, D. W., 332, *383,* 415, *421*
Nickerson, N., 140, *154*
Nicolich, L., 117, *122*
Niederehe, G., 189, 192, 227
Ninio, A., 48, *57,* 62, *122,* 448, *462*
Norman, D. A., 276, *281,* 390, *420*
Norton, J. A., 444, *459*
Novak, G., 30, *58,* 208, 225, *230*
Oakley, D. D., 339, *382,* 417, 418, *421*
Ochs, E., 275, *281*
O'Connell, B., 89, 108, 117, *123*
O'Conner, N., 443, 454, *460*
Odom, P., 286, *312*

Ogston, W. D., 205, *226*
Oller, D. K., 233, 236, 238, *253*
Olmsted, D. L., 255, 256, *281*
Olson, D., 21, *27*
Olson, D. R., 135, 140, *154,* 345, *381*
Omanson, R. C., 332, 336, 345, *382,* 415, *421*
Ortony, A., 316, *382,* 390, *421*
Overton, W. F., 101, *122*
Oxman, J. Q., 284, *312*

P, Q

Pačesová, J., 256, *281*
Paivio, A., 140, *154*
Palermo, D., 145, 149, *154,* 445, *461*
Paris, S. G., 332, 345, *382*
Parsons, G., 190, 191, 192, 194, 206, *229*
Parten, M., 159, 174, *185*
Pascual-Leone, J., 114, *122*
Pea, R. D., 127, *154*
Pearson, K. L., 105, *119*
Peck, S., 246, *253*
Pederson, D., 87, *120*
Peery, J. C., 189, 192, *228*
Peirce, C. S., 76, *122*
Peizer, D. B., 261, 263, *279*
Pepler, D. J., 177, 182, *185*
Perlman, R., 44, *56*
Peters, A. M., 263, 271, *281*
Peters, D. L., 162, *185*
Phillips, J., 187, 193, 209, *229*
Piaget, J., 63, 65, 87, *122,* 128, 131, 137, *154,* 157, 158, 162, 175, *185,* 232, *253, 254*
Pickett, L., 102, *122*
Pierce, J., 233, *254*
Pierce, S., 431, 443, *462*
Pinard, A., 131, 137, *153*
Pinker, S., 38, *56*
Poizat, M., 236, *252*
Polevoy, N., 444, *458*
Pollard-Gott, L., 325, *382*
Porch, B., 102, *122*
Power, D., 286, *312*
Prather, E. M., 425, *460*
Prawat, R. S., 144, *154*
Premack, D., 206, *229*
Price, R., 248, *254*
Price, S., 248, *254*
Prichard, J. W., 425, *463*

Priestley, T. M. S., 263, *281*
Prinz, E. A., 74, *122*, 284, 312
Prinz, P. M., 74, *122*, 284, *312*
Prior, M., 441, 443, 454, *462*
Provence, S., 427, *459*
Quigley, S. P., 283, 287, *311, 312, 313*

R

Rabinovitch, M. S., 445, *463*
Raffin, M. J. M., 285, *311, 313*
Ramer, A., 30, 35, *57*
Ramer, A. L. H., 240, *252*
Ratner, N., 2, 5, 9, *26*, 162, *184*, 448, 452, *458, 462*
Raven, J. C., 425, *462*
Read, C., 250, *254*, 287, *313*
Redmond, D. E., 453, *462*
Reeder, G. D., 411, *420*
Rees, N. S., 187, 211, *229*, 455, *462*
Rehicle, J. E., 211, *229*
Reilly, J., 2, 16, 22, *28*, 197, *230*, 452, 463
Remick, H., 192, *229*
Retherford, K. S., 18, *28*
Reynell, J. K., 425, *462*
Rheingold, H., 162, *185*
Richards, M. P., 446, *462*
Ricks, D. M., 441, 443, *462*
Rigler, D., 423, *460*
Rigler, M., 423, *460*
Rimland, B., 425, *458*
Rinsland, R. H., 143, *154*
Risley, T. R., 440, *462*
Roberts, A., 187, 209, *227*
Robertson, S. P., 337, *381*
Robertson, S. S., 133, *154*
Robey, J. S., 131, *152*
Rocissano, L., 2, *26*, 31, 33, 36, 55, *56*, 187, 196, 200, 211, 212, *226*
Rodgon, M. M., 79, *122*
Rodriguez, J., 101, *121*
Rohwer, W. D., 336, *382*
Rondal, J. A., 211, *229*
Rosch, E., 22, *28*
Rose, S. N., 233, 236, *254*
Rosenberg, S., 160, *185*
Rosenblum, L., 447, *461*
Rosenblum, L. A., 61, *121*
Ross, C., 233, 236, 238, *253*
Ross, G., 41, *57*
Ross, H. S., 174, *184*

Ross, J. R., 256, *281*
Rothman, S. L. G., 425, *458*
Roy, C., 2, 5, 9, *26*, 162, *184*, 448, 452, *458*
Rubin, K. H., 160, 161, 162, 177, 180, 181, 182, *184, 185*
Rubin, S., 394, *420*
Ruble, D. N., 415, *419*
Rumelhart, D. E., 316, 325, 330, 331, 333, 336, 337, 338, 376, 377, *382*, 385, 386, 387, 388, 390, 391, 395, 398, 416, *421*
Rush, M. L., 286, *311*
Ruttenberg, B. A., 425, 439, *458, 462*
Rutter, M., 427, 428, 429, 431, 440, 441, 442, 444, *457, 458, 461, 462*
Ryan, J., 193, *229*

S

Sachs, J., 2, 11, 16, *28*, 38, *57*, 117, *122*, 161, 182, *185*
Sagart, L., 236, *252*
St. Pierre, R., 286, *313*
Salzinger, K., 196, 205, *229*
Sanches, M., 233, *254*
Sander, L. W., 189, 192, 193, 205, *226*, 446, 448, *459*
Sapir, E., 258, *281*
Saulnier, K. L., 285, 287, *310*
Scarlett, W. G., 418, *421*
Schaffer, H. R., 61, *122*, 190, 191, 192, 194, 206, 209, *229*
Schaier, A. H., 325, *380*
Schank, R., 42, *57*, 109, *122*, 316, 345, *382*, 387, *421*
Schegloff, E., 164, *185*
Schieffelin, B., 30, 54, *57*, 246, *254*, 275, *281*
Schieffelin, B. B., 2, 24, *27*, *28*
Schlesinger, H. S., 284, *313*
Scholl, 131, *152*
Schuler, A. L., 439, *460*
Schumaker, J. B., 208, *228*
Schwam, E. M., 285, *313*
Schwartz, B. C., 18, *28*
Schwartz, R., 78, *122*
Schwartz, R. G., 138, *154*
Schwartzman, H., 232, 247, *254*
Scollon, R., 34, *57*, 237, 242, *254*
Searle, J., 65, *122*, 163, 165, *185*
Searle, J. R., 315, *382*
Segal, E. F., 206, *229*

Seitz, S., 35, *57*, 211, *229*
Seitz, V., 115, *123*
Selman, R. L., 176, 177, 182, 183, *186*
Senden, M. von, 446, *463*
Shapiro, T., 439, *462*
Shatluck, R., 423, *462*
Shatz, M., 2, *28*, 161, 166, 177, 182, *184, 186*, 196, 227, 315, 344, 346, *382*
Shaver, K. G., 411, *421*
Shaywitz, B. A., 425, 430, 431, 433, 453, 454, *458, 459, 463*
Shaywitz, S. E., 425, *458*
Sherman, J. A., 208, 208, *228*
Sherwood, V., 249, *251*
Sherzer, J., 234, 247, 249, *254*
Shore, C., 84, 87, 88, 89, 108, 117, *118, 119, 122, 123*
Shotten, J., 68, *123*, 429, 449, *462*
Shure, M., 168, *186*
Shvachkin, N., 63, *123*
Silva, M., 214, *230*
Sinclair, A., 138, *155*
Sinclair, H., 12, *26*, 138, *155*
Siqueland, E. R., 193, *227*, 445, *459*
Slobin, D., 39, *57*, 63, *120*
Slobin, D. I., 22, 25, *28*, 258, *281*
Skinner, B. F., 202, *229*
Smiley, S. S., 330, 338, 339, 340, 342, 343, 347, 373, 379, *380, 382*, 391, 395, 413, 417, 418, *419, 421*
Smith, C. S., 12, *28*
Smith, J., 69, 115, *121*, 126, *153*
Smith, J. H., 2, 4, *27*
Smith, N. V., 256, 257, 260, 262, 263, 269, 270, *281, 282*
Smith, P., 444, *460*
Snow, C., 30, 31, 32, 33, 35, 36, 37, 43, 47, *57, 58*
Snow, C. E., 8, 18, *28*, 187, 188, 209, 211, *229*
Snyder, L., 80, 81, 82, 87, 88, 90, *118, 123*
Soares, V. M., 217, *230*
Solan, L., 264, *282*
Solnit, A. J., 427, *459*
Spivack, G., 168, *186*
Srivastava, G. P., 263, *282*
Sroufe, L. A., 445, 454, *462*
Staats, A. W., 202, *229*
Stampe, D., 256, *279*
Stanley, R., 256, *282*
Stark, R. E., 233, 236, 237, *254*
Starr, S., 132, *155*

Stayton, D. J., 446, *457*
Steele, R., 444, *453*
Stein, N. L., 316, 325, 333, 334, 336, 338, 339, 340, 341, 342, 356, *382, 383*, 385, 390, 391, 394, 411, 414, 415, 417, 418, *421*
Steinkamp, M. M., 283, *312*
Stella, E. M., 187, 190, 191, 192, 194, 203, 205, 206, 209, 211, 212, 225, *229*
Stella-Prorok, E. M., 198, 190, 192, 193, 194, 195, 197, 205, 206, 209, 211, 212, 214, 216, 217, 225, *226, 229, 230*
Stepanich, L., 211, *229*
Stern, C., 70, *123*
Stern, D. N., 189, 190, 191, 192, 193, 205, *228*, 230, 447, 448, 449, *462*
Stern, W., 70, *123*
Stevenson, M. B., 115, *118*
Stewart, C., 35, *57*, 211, *229*
Steyaert, M., 284, *311*
Stoel-Gammon, C., 2, *28*
Stoloff, L., 284, *313*
Streeter, L. A., 445, *463*
Strohner, H., 135, 147, *155*
Stuecher, H. U., 445, 454, *462*
Stutzer, W., 445, 454, *462*
Suci, G. J., 133, *154*
Sugarman-Bell, S., 62, *123*
Sullivan, R., 431, *463*
Sutton-Smith, B., 232, 234, 247, 335, *253, 380*
Swift, J., 117, *123*
Swinehart, D. M., 337, *381*
Swisher, L., 286, *313*
Sylva, K., 232, 241, *251*
Syrdal-Lasky, A., 445, *461*

T

Taeschner, T., 74, *123*
Tager-Flusberg, H., 443, *463*
Tannenbaum, R. H., 135, *155*
Thomas, E., 44, *58*
Thoman, E. B., 446, *461*
Thompson, D., 415, *420*
Thompson, S. A., 238, *253*
Thorndyke, P. W., 316, 325, 333, 337, 338, *383*, 385, 386, 388, 390, 391, 394, 395, 397, 405, 416, *421*
Timm, L., 255, *282*
Tinbergen, E. A., 429, *463*
Tinbergen, N., 429, *463*

AUTHOR INDEX **475**

Tissot, A., 101, *121*
Tobin, A. R., 425, *460*
Todres, A. K., 324, *382*
Tomlinson, K. P., 409, *420*
Trabasso, T., 332, 336, 345, *382, 383,* 415, *419, 421*
Trehub, S. C., 445, *463*
Trevarthen, C., 189, *230*
Tronick, E., 131, *155*
Truswell, L., 11, *28,* 117, *122*
Tse, J. K -P., 238, *254*
Tucker, G. R., 444, *460*
Tversky, A., 77, *123*

U, V

Ultan, R., 249, *254*
Upton, L. R., 332, *382*
Uzgiris, I., 71, 87, 115, *121, 123*
van der Geest, T., 18, *28*
van Dijk, T. A., 315, 316, 330, 333, 336, 337, 338, 340, 343, 344, 347, 377, *381, 383,* 385, 391, 410, 416, *420, 421*
Vanvik, A., 263, *282*
Vasta, R., 30, *58,* 205, *230*
Velten, H. V., 256, *282*
Venneman, T., 256, *282*
Vigorito, J., 193, *227, 459*
Vihman, M. M., 258, 260, 271, *282*
Volkmann, F. C., 131, *155*
Volterra, V., 4, *26,* 59, 62, 64, 69, 70, 71, 72, 74, 76, 78, 79, 80, 82, 87, 88, 93, 103, *118, 119, 123,* 450, *457*
Vygotsky, L. S., 20, *28,* 65, 87, *123,* 449, *463*

W

Waldo, M. C., 425, *458, 463*
Wallace, J. G., 446, *460*
Wapner, W., 102, *119*
Warren, W. H., 332, 336, 345, *382, 383*
Waterson, N., 255, *282*
Watson-Gegeo, K., 30, *58*
Watt, J., 106, *120*
Waugh, L. R., 236, *253,* 256, *280*
Waxler, C. Z., 209, *230*
Weaver, P. A., 417, *421*
Webster, C. D., 284, *312*
Wechsler, D., 424, *463*
Weeks, T., 192, 193, *230*
Weeks, T. E., 231, 243, *254,* 261, 263, *279*
Weintraub, S., 315, *380*

Weir, R., 233, 241, *254*
Weiss, K. L., 285, *312*
Weissenborn, J., 6, *27*
Weksel, W., 237, *251*
Wellman, H., 161, *186*
Wells, R. S., 132, 138, *152*
Welsh, C., 39, *57*
Wenar, C., 425, *462*
Wepman, J. M., 95, *123*
Werner, H., 60, 64, 65, 87, 93, *123*
West, M., 162, *185*
Wetstone, H., 429, 440, *459*
Wetstone, H. S., 146, *155*
Whitehouse, P., 98, 102, *123*
Whitehurst, G., 30, *58,* 205, 208, 225, *230*
Whiting, B., 168, *185*
Wieman, L. A., 233, 236, 238, *253*
Wilbur, R., 74, *123,* 284, *312*
Wilbur, R. B., 283, 284, 285, *312, 313*
Williams, S. F., 135, *155*
Williamson, C., 84, *119*
Wing, L., 441, 443, *462*
Winitz, H., 255, *282*
Winnicott, D. W., 456, *463*
Wittgenstein, L., 64, *123*
Wohlwill, J. F., 126, *155*
Wolf, D., 418, *421*
Wolf, E. G., 425, 439, *462*
Wolf, M., 440, *462*
Wolff, P. H., 447, *463*
Woodward, J. C., 286, *313*
Worthen, D., 339, *382,* 412, 418, *421*

Y, Z

Yamatori, A., 93, *123*
Yando, R., 115, *123*
Yarrow, M. R., 209, *230*
Young, J. G., 425, 452, 453, 454, *458, 459, 463*
Yussen, S. R., 330, 338, 339, 343, 347, 373, *383,* 391, 395, 413, 418, *421*
Zeigler, M. G., 453, *461*
Zelniker, T., 271, *282*
Zigler, E., 115, *123*
Zlatin-Laufer, M., 236, *254*
Zorn, G., 30, *58,* 208, 225, *230*
Zukow, P. G., 2, 16, 22, *28,* 126, *153,* 197, *230,* 452, *463*
Zunif, E., 102, *119*
Zurif, E. B., 93, 94, 98, 102, *119*
Zurif, E., *118, 119*

Subject Index

A

Aphasia, *see* Autism, Symbols
Autism, 423–456
  background perspectives, 428–430
  brain neuromaturation, 452–456
  case study, 432–436
  diagnostic issues, 426
  high functioning persons
    cognition and language, 436–438
    developmental course, 441–445
    echolalia, 438–440
  language and cognition deficits, 430–432
  language-learning styles, 444, 455–456
  other severe language disorders, 423–428, 443
  social intentions and exchanges, 429, 446–452, 454–456
  theoretical integration of normal and disordered communicative development, 445–456

C

Cognition-language relations, *see also* Salience
  in autism, 430–432, 436–456
  cognitive monitoring, 183, 344, 378
  displaced language references, 18–25
  long-term memory and language, 38, 40
  metalinguistic awareness, 97, 259, 298–305, 446–452, 454–456
  modeled for phonological development, 255–282
  perspective-taking, 157–163, 177–183
  play and autism, 449
  play, cognition, and phonology, 231–254
  for stories, 331–346, 372–379, 391–396, 416–418
  theories compared across domains, 273–282, 378, 390
  ties between concepts, gestures, scripts, and names, 59–123
Comprehension-production differences, 5, 80, 86, 92–98, 105, 109, 147–151, 442

D

Deaf children's language varieties, 283–313
  acquisition summary for case, 305–309
  background for case study, 288
  differentiations at 12–48 months
    American sign language, 290
    fingerspelling, 292
    form analyses, 292–296
    manual-oral, 291
    play role in, 296–298
    reading, 292, 294, 297, 299
    sign English, 293
    speech and speech reading, 291, 293, 296
    early American sign language onset, 290
    educational approaches, 285–288

Deaf children's language varieties (*cont.*)
  language awareness at 49–55 months, 299–302
  methods, 289
  sign language acquisition reviewed, 284
  transfer and switching at 75 months, 304–305
  variety connections at 65 months, 302–304
Decontextualization, *see* Mother-child dialogue, Perceptual and contextual constraints, Symbols
Discourse, *see* Autism, Displaced reference, Imitation, Mother-child dialogue, Requests, Story comprehension and summarization
Displaced reference, 1–28, *see also* Imitation
  absent objects, 4
  discourse influence, 6, 10, 16, 21, 25
  original meanings, 22–25
  past and future, 12–28
    immediate past, 13
    future, 14
  spatial displacement, 4
  wedges, role in, 23

G

Gestures and signing, *see* Autism, Deaf children's language varieties, Symbols

I

Imitation, 29–58, 211–216
  all forms, 29, 55
  autistic echolalia, 438–440, 456
  deferred, 38
    book-reading routines, 47
    complex utterances, 42
  expanded, 32
  long-term memory, 38, 40
  models and repetitions compared, 211–216
  relation to topic continuation, 33
  vertical constructions and, 34, 55
Individual differences, *see also* Deaf children's language varieties extrasyntactic strategies, 148
  imitation, 30, 34–37
  language and symbols, 82, 98, 116
  mother-child exchanges, 203–204
  phonology learning, 262–264, 270–271
  severe language disorders, 423–436, 441, 455
  stories, 351

L,M

Language disorders, *see* Autism, Symbols
Memory and language, *see* Displaced reference, Imitation, Story comprehension and summarization
Mother-child dialogue, 187–230, *see also* Imitation, Displaced reference
  alternating patterns, 189–193
  children's sensitivity, 206–211, 224–226
  decontextualization, 10, 22, 200
  developmental changes in timing, 193–202
  experimental recast variations, 217–224
  maternal sensitivity, 197–206, 224–226
  models and lessons, 197, 212
  origin of play languages, 249–250
  rare corrections, 204–206
  relevance for autism, 446–451, 454–456
  repetitions and recasts, 211–216

N,P

Naming, *see* Deaf children's language varieties, Symbols
Perceptual and contextual constraints, 125–155, *see also* Autism, Symbols
  actions' influence, 138, 145
  animacy, 131–132, 148–151
  egocentrism limits, 160–162
  imagery role, 128, 140, 150–151
  object and subject recall, 140–144
  passive sentences, 135–140, 149
Play and phonology, 231–254
  babbling, 235–240
  expressive sound play, 240–246
  issues, 234
  language games, 246
  learning to learn, 239, 250
  play languages, 247–250
  shifts in accepted play, 246
  signing play, 296–298
Phonology and cognition, 255–282, *see also* Play and phonology
  cognitive model of acquisition, 257, 272–278

creativity, 261–263
hypothesis use, 263–272
  experimentation, 265
  hypothesis change, 269
  overgeneralization, 267
  regression, 268
idioms, 265, 272
selectiveness, 260
stages compared to other models, 273–282
universalist theory variations, 255

R

Requests, 157–186
  direct and indirect defined, 169
  egocentrism and nonegocentrism, 158–164
  methods of study, 168–178
  and other speech acts, 162–167
  re-request strategies, 168, 170, 174
  perspective-taking, role in, 157–163, 177–183
  scripts, 175, 182
  success, 172

S

Salience, role in message choice and interpretation, 61, 111, 113, 126–128, 132–140, 150–151, 167, 446–452, 456
Story comprehension and summarization, 315–383, 385–421
  causal and social inference schemata, 391–396, 409–418
  models, 316–329, 330–346, 377–379, 385–396, 409–414
  ranking (importance) methods, 397
  results
    proposition rankings, 405–409
    summaries, 351–372, 398–405
  summarization methods, 330, 348–351, 397
  summarization prerequisites and abilities, 330–346
    coherence and concision, 343, 373
    connections between propositions, 331, 375
    disposition inference and use, 410
    identifying the constituent structure, 333
    operating on node sets, 375
    proposition comprehension, 331
    replacing specifics with generalizations, 374
    selecting summary information, 337, 373
    social and causal inferences, 391, 409
  task demands, 330, 414
Symbols, 59–123
  aphasics' gestural and vocal symbols, 93–109
  defined, 59
  gestural, in children, 66–93, 109–118
    onset, 66–69
    performance on production test, 84–87
  made-up concepts (fiffins, gloop), 88
  social scripts, relation to, 41, 47, 109–113, 175, 182
  vocal symbols, in children, 67–93, 109–118
    compared to gestural, 70, 75–79, 87–92, 109–118
    onset, 62–66
    performance on production and comprehension test, 84–87

ISRAELI PACIFIST

Syracuse Studies on Peace and Conflict Resolution
HARRIET HYMAN ALONSO, CHARLES CHATFIELD, AND LOUIS KRIESBERG
Series Editors

Joseph Abileah in his study.

ISRAELI PACIFIST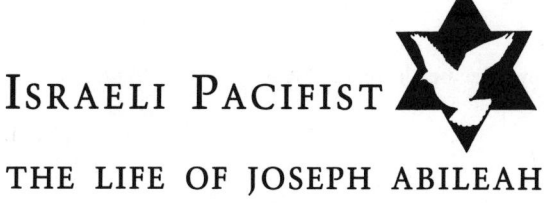

THE LIFE OF JOSEPH ABILEAH

Anthony G. Bing
Foreword by Yehudi Menuhin

SYRACUSE UNIVERSITY PRESS

Copyright © 1990 by Syracuse University Press
Syracuse, New York 13244-5160

All Rights Reserved

First Edition 1990
99 98 97 96 95 94 93 92 91 90   6 5 4 3 2 1

Except where otherwise noted, photographs are from the collection of Joseph Abileah.

The paper used in this publication meets the minimum requirements of American National Standard for Information Sciences—Permanence of Paper for Printed Library Materials, ANSI Z39.48-1984. ∞™

Library of Congress Cataloging-in-Publication Data

Bing, Anthony G., 1935–
    Israeli pacifist : the life of Joseph Abileah / Anthony G. Bing.
       p. cm.
    ISBN 0-8156-2488-3 (alk. paper)
    1. Abileah, Joseph. 2. Pacifists—Israel—Haifa—Biography.
    3. Jewish-Arab relations. 4. Violinists—Israel—Haifa—Biography.
    5. Haifa (Israel)—Biography. I. Title.
JX1962.A35B56   1990
327.1′7′092—dc20
[B]   89-78278
                                                            CIP

Manufactured in the United States of America

Contents

	Illustrations	vii
	Foreword	ix
	Acknowledgments	xi
1.	Introduction	1
2.	A Return to the Roots, 1915–1936	5
3.	Not in the Joshua Way, 1936–1947	27
4.	Fanatic for Truth, 1947–1950	49
5.	A Task Worthy of Jews, 1950–1967	89
6.	Isaiah's Teaching, 1967–1972	123
7.	Society for Middle East Confederation, 1972–1987	153
8.	The True Victories	193

Illustrations

Joseph William Abileah	*frontispiece*
Ephraim Abileah	7
Miriam Abileah	7
Joseph (Willi) Abileah and Avshalom (Rudi) Abileah	12
Abileah music business	15
Walking tour of the Dead Sea	20
Joseph Abileah and Dinah Yarmus Abileah	38
The paralytic of Mount Carmel	44
Altered identity card	48
International work camp in Israel	105
Abileah scooter	111
Lecture tour	136
Conversation with a Palestinian	144
Joseph and the occupation	145
Joseph and Dinah	189
Joseph Abileah	191

ANTHONY G. BING has spent considerable periods of time living and working in the Middle East for the past twenty years. He has set up academic programs in Lebanon and Israel. An active member of the Society of Friends, he has worked with the American Friends Service Committee and other Quaker organizations and serves on the executive committee of the Peace Studies Association. Professor of English and Director of Peace Studies at Earlham College, he is currently working on a book concerning the role of the Middle East and the American peace movement.

Foreword

❧ As ONE WHO HAS repeatedly nominated Joseph Abileah, musician of Haifa, for various peace awards, I am particularly grateful to Professor Anthony Bing for having singled out this unique, committed character. Professor Bing's timely biography conveys the very ancient struggle between the real and practical imperative of moral conduct—as deeply understanding of others as it is determined in its fierce espousal of truth—and the mirage of worldly power and materialistic ambition that have caused man's overwhelming urge to dominate and humiliate distinguishable and competitive brethren.

It is a deadly and tragic struggle that has marked for thousands of years the rich history of the Holy Land. Although this severe and obstinate land has seen the emergence of monotheistic faith from the pluralistic pagan idols and gods, ironically the acceptance of the one binding universal truth by different tribes has led to the renewed betrayal in human hands of the one to the many. Each tribe has seized on the exclusive nature of its own unitary truth and has become intransigent in its opposition to the truths of others. This intransigence argues that the "one and only truth" cannot be whole unless all believers are unanimous.

Today we witness the intolerable consequences; a war between peoples, religions, and states played out on a very small strategic and hallowed site—the "Holy Land"—and carrying disastrous, worldwide implications.

Joseph Abileah stands modest and unassuming in a long and revered tradition of spiritual Zionism, as opposed to the national and political Zionism of Israel today, as every reader can learn from Professor Bing's admirable and sensitive book. He is a frail figure, unarmed and vulnerable, yet spiritually and intellectually strong, standing, as already quite a number of our coreligionists have stood, against tanks, poison gas, and gas ovens.

Can the example of men and women like Joseph Abileah confront and transform the violent forces at work in our world? Though I cannot answer that question, I am humbly content to be a colleague of Joseph Abileah, a fellow violinist.

Yehudi Menuhin

Acknowledgments

✺ IN GATHERING INFORMATION for this book, I have spent many hours at Joseph Abileah's dining room table, listening to his stories, meeting his friends, and eating his food. Whatever the activity, I learned to expect the interruption of the telephone. To whomever called, Joseph offered the same greeting — "Abileah, shalom" — before conversing in whatever language — Hebrew, Arabic, English, German, French — the caller preferred. It was at these times, when "shalom" as a greeting came also to signify an invitation to a way of life, that Joseph's network was opened up to me. I would like to take this occasion to thank the members of that network for helping me to understand Joseph's life and its significance.

To Adi and Dani, his sons, to Benjamin and Rudi, his brothers, to Wajdi-Farid Tabari, Hannah Rubinstein, Ibrahim Sima'an, Aaron Kamis, Elias Jabbour, Cathy Bergen, Elias Chacour, Mary Bergman, Adnan Beidoun, and Landrum Bolling, his friends, I owe thanks for their time and insight. To other frequent visitors at 55A Rehov Hillel I owe different kinds of thanks — to Mrs. Gamzu for fixing our lunches when our interviews ran on too long; to Yossi Yarmus for his photographs of his uncle; and to the hundreds of Joseph's friends I met only through their letters to him.

Above all, I want to thank Joseph himself for opening himself up to me in so honest and straightforward a manner and with a respect for truth about himself that is consistent with his dedication to truth in general. This remarkable man has deserved a better biographer, but I could not have asked for a better subject.

I began this work to understand better what it takes to be

a peacemaker and to see what chance for peace there is in the Middle East today, when voices of reconciliation are either unheard or ignored. Among the many things I learned is that no one can succeed who stands alone. For this reason, my book is dedicated to two women, Dinah Yarmus Abileah and June Woodward Bing, the wives who made our work possible and who have helped to give it whatever value it may possess. Dinah Abileah passed away in May 1986, but her spirit continues to shape Joseph's life now as it did in the past. The gratitude he feels to her for having sacrificed so much in order that he could pursue his dream has informed all of our conversations about his life. He deeply feels that whatever he may have achieved in his life owes its success to their partnership.

ISRAELI PACIFIST

1
Introduction

"JOSEPH ABILEAH IS PERHAPS the most famous pacifist in the Middle East," I recently said to a friend who had asked about the subject of the book I was writing. He replied, "I shouldn't wonder. He must be the *only* one."

To some extent, such cynicism is understandable. The history of Arab and Jewish relations in the twentieth century is a depressing one, and peace between Arabs and Jews seems farther away now than it did seventy years ago when the Balfour Declaration (1917) established some sort of international basis for a national home for the Jewish people in the Arab land called Palestine. Seventy years of distrust and betrayal have deepened into hatred on both sides. The fears generated by threats to the very survival of both peoples have created high barriers to communication, despite a longing on both sides for an end to the conflict. A period marked by wars and interludes between wars has never known a time of genuine peace. Many dreams of coexistence in a moral and just society have been shattered by events that someday may even lead to mutual destruction.

Many dreams, but not all dreams. The life of Joseph Abileah reveals a commitment to a dream of reconciliation that shines with a clear and steady flame through all these years of darkness. There are elements in his life that have led many who have known him to consider him a sort of prophet and saint. This indeed characterizes his standing in the international peace community, where for more than thirty years he has been in demand as a speaker, bringing his optimistic message that peace is possible to groups who hunger for some sort of hope to hang on to as they feel more and more impotent and depressed about what can be done in the Middle East. The peace community, like the rest of the world, loves its saints, and to many people in Europe and America, Joseph is known as the "Jewish Gandhi" or the "Israeli Schweitzer."

It is sad that, in his own country, Joseph Abileah is much less well known than he is abroad. Although he has worked for reconciliation for more than fifty years and has persisted when many others gave up the struggle or moved abroad, many more people have listened to him play the viola than have heard his views on peace. Although he has been involved in almost every group that has worked for peace, groups like the War Resisters International, the Israeli League for Human and Civil Rights, Shutafut (Partnership), the Ihud, the Service Civil International, and the International Fellowship of Reconciliation, and has lectured about his activities at Oxford, Cambridge, Harvard, and Columbia, the University of Haifa, located in the city in which he has lived for sixty years, has never invited him to give a lecture. Since he has most often appeared in the public eye on occasions of protest against his government's attitude, policies, or actions, he has not been publicly revered as either prophet or saint, but criticized or, more often, ignored by the government and the press.

While these comparisons to saints and prophets are not inappropriate, they are not the focus of this book. Some may feel that the world needs saints, but many more would regard sainthood as a handicap, if what we would learn from a reading of another's life is how we might be able to transform our own. The problem with saints is that they set some pretty high standards. Sometimes these standards are so conveniently high that we can take comfort in the inertia caused by our own imperfections rather than be aroused to meaningful action. The excuse we give ourselves is that only saints can perform saintly deeds. A world already skeptical about human beings' ability to live in peace as members of the same human family is likely to say, "Well, if we were all Gandhis, Sister Teresas, Albert Schweitzers, and Martin Luther King, Jrs., then what you propose might work. But we aren't saints, so be realistic—there will always be people and nations to take advantage of the naïve goodwill of peacemakers."

Joseph Abileah, musician of Haifa and Secretary for the Society for Middle East Confederation, is not a saint. He is an ordinary man who has been made extraordinary by his steadfast fidelity to a vision of peace. While the attainment of this peace has proved elusive, the vision itself is not that of a latter-day Don Quixote, out of touch with a world in which gas ovens have replaced windmills. This vision, which has its roots deep in a tradition of Jewish universalism and messianic humanism, has shaped Joseph's life and given it unity; and this wholeness has had a deep effect on those who have come in contact with it. What this vision is, how it evolved, and what it has cost and meant to him and to those near to him lie at the center of this biography.

I believe that his life and vision are of interest in themselves and deserve to be better known than they are. However, I also chose to write about him because I believe that his ideals and the actions inspired by these ideals are not beyond ordinary men and women. It will be ordinary men and women who will create real peace. Perhaps the great statesmen of the world can come up with quinine tablets to stave off the malaria of war, but can they keep up with new strains of the carriers of this disease? As Joseph says, perhaps there ought to be masses of ordinary people working to dry up the swamps where the mosquitos are bred. If we cannot get at the reasons for the fear and hatred that exist between people, then no arms buildup, no defense strategy, no border fences will ever provide real security. When proponents of security systems tell us to be realistic, it may be that they are the ones who have a limited view of reality. Their view is limited to the "what is," revealed to us in history and politics. Martin Buber, who was fully aware of the "what is," called people to a higher reality—"what could be." Joseph Abileah's vision calls us to this same higher reality, and his ability to *embody* this vision gives us some reason to believe that what "could be" already "is." That is, because peace and reconciliation have substance in his life, they can also have substance for the rest of us.

Actually, my friend who dismissed Joseph as the only pacifist in the Middle East was mistaken. There are and have been many peacemakers in the Middle East. The history of Joseph's life is also an encounter with these individuals and with the groups they formed. Often far from the public eye, these groups have been working for reconciliation between Arab and Jew. Joseph's struggles, his hopes, and his disappointments have been theirs as well. Therefore, his personal history is in some respect a window through which can be viewed an alternative to the accepted histories of Israel and Palestine, one which is not very well known and seldom described. Yehudi Menuhin, in his autobiography, *Unfinished Journey*, writes of Joseph, "Were the Nobel Peace Prize mine to give it would be his: once in a while it should go to those in obscurity who devote their lives to reconciliation." In a letter to Menuhin, Joseph replied, "You are right to say that the Nobel Peace Prize should go to those in obscurity working for peace. I myself know hundreds of such people who should receive the prize before me."

I would like the reader of this biography to come away from it feeling that what is true of Joseph could become true of many more of us. He may have been unduly modest in stating that hundreds of people are more deserving than he, but unless he is fundamentally right, true peace, the positive peace that does not mean just the absence of war but the creation and preservation of harmony and cooperation between human beings, will never come to the Middle East, or anywhere else for that matter.

Joseph believes in harmony. As a musician, he creates it all the time. As a peacemaker, who has tried to bring music to the lives of those in conflict, this harmony has been much more difficult to achieve than that found within the score of a Beethoven quartet. But Joseph is convinced that this harmony will come—that if one is attentive to the means, if one strives to be harmonious in all human relationships, the end will be assured. Perhaps those who hear and remember the music of Joseph Abileah's life will come to believe that the harmony he has sought his whole life will one day indeed be possible.

2
A Return to the Roots
1915–1936

> The Jew has remained an Oriental. He was driven out of his land and dispersed throughout the lands of the Occident; he was forced to dwell under a sky he did not know and on a soil he did not till; he suffered martyrdom, and worse than martyrdom, a life of degradation; the ways of the nations among which he has lived have affected him, and he has spoken their languages; yet despite all this, he has remained an Oriental.... The Jew can truly fulfill his vocation among the nations only when he begins anew, and, with his whole, undiminished, purified original strength, translates into reality what his religion taught him in antiquity: rootedness in his native land; leading the good life within narrow confines; and building a model community on the scanty Canaanite soil.
> —Martin Buber, 1916

❧ FIRST THERE WAS MUSIC, and with music came dreams. As the harmonies expanded, the dreams became visions. Because the visions contained the harmonies, they were of peace.

There is a stream that runs by the little town of Mödling, Austria. Beside this stream, Beethoven is said in 1808 to have received inspiration for the "Brook" section of his Sixth Symphony (*Pastoral*). Beethoven had very early turned his back on the organized religion in which he had been raised, but the religious longing and sensibility remained; and he discovered in nature then expressed in the magnificent Sixth Symphony his belief in the immanence of God in all living things, a belief that sustains the symphony through periods of storm until the last movement, the coming of the sun, when the shepherds sing a song of thanksgiving, not only that the good has reasserted itself in the face of evil, but that the good is confirmation that God exists within the human heart. Beethoven the man was never at ease in the world in which he lived, but his works of art are prophesies that evil need not prevail and that one day human beings will live according to their hearts.

The same faith that good will triumph, even in the midst of terrible evil, has sustained Joseph Abileah, a musician from Haifa, Israel. He has found corroboration for this faith in his study of Beethoven's music and life. But the faith itself has come from his direct experiences with life, a life that began on April 25, 1915, in Mödling, Austria, and that, like the structure of Beethoven's symphonies, has gained strength in its final movement, the period since 1967 when he has devoted himself to working for peace in the Middle East. Though he has been neither a member of the Haifa Symphony Orchestra nor a music teacher since 1972, he has not given up music but has extended its meaning. Beethoven drew inspiration for his music from life. Joseph has drawn inspiration for his life from music. His quest for harmony is the focus of this biography. The value of his life is not to be measured by whether the goal has been attained. It is the way to that goal that holds our interest. The architects of the great cathedrals of the Middle Ages never lived to see the finished, concrete embodiments of their dreams. As Joseph himself says, he will never see the fruits of his labors, or perhaps he will never even sit in the shade of the trees whose seeds he has planted. Nevertheless, he has clung to the belief that if the way is right, the goal is assured; and he has made hard life choices based upon the obverse of this maxim: that is, that a just goal demands just means and that compromise on the means must inevitably compromise the goal itself.

Music was in his blood. Joseph's grandfather, Eliezer Niswizski (1840–1906), was a famous cantor in Russia and was among the first to collect and transcribe traditional cantor mu-

Joseph's father, Ephraim Abileah, né Niswizski, and mother, Miriam Abileah, née Mosabowski.

sic. He added to this tradition by composing music of his own. After a long career, his voice began to give out and he became a *shochet*, one who in Jewish communities supervised the ritual killing of animals. It is thought among his family that the combination of watching so much death and losing his song caused him to lose the will to live. Eliezer's son, Ephraim (1881–1953), became a prolific composer of over seven hundred works, half of them religious and half secular. In 1898, Ephraim left Russia for Warsaw where he became band master in the Russian Army Band and a teacher of theory and composition at the Warsaw Conservatory. In Warsaw, one of his piano students was Miriam Mosabowski (1886–1960), daughter of Sadek (1859–1929) and Nehama Helena (1863–1943) Mosabowski, whom he married just before he left Warsaw in 1905. Ephraim's reasons for leaving Poland involved Russia's war with Japan. As a pacifist who would not cooperate in any way with the war, he fled to Vienna where he had to begin a new life with a new language and with new credentials from the Austrian authorities. The pacifist beliefs that brought Ephraim Niswizski to Vienna were not changed by World War I. He was exempted from Austrian army duty because he was not a citizen, but even if he had been one, he would not have served. During the war years, Ephraim would spend what little free time he had from a busy music career walking in the woods above his home in Mödling. In these woods, he sketched out a utopian romance, *Die Macht der Liebe* (The Power of Love), a blueprint for a society ruled by universal love and justice. He felt no deep roots in any of the three societies in which he had lived, but did find a harmony between his dreams and those of Zionism. The kind of Zionism that appealed to him was a sort of messianism that had strong links with the spiritual Zionism of Ahad Ha'am (Asher Ginzberg 1856–1927). Like Ahad Ha'am, Ephraim was not religious in a traditional sense and had trouble with the rituals of Judaism, even though he celebrated its spirit in his music and in his life; but like many members of the Hibbat Zion (Lovers of Zion) movement, he deeply believed in the spiritual renaissance of the Jewish people. Thus, while none of his three sons who were born in Austria received religious training or had a bar mitzvah, all three were exposed from their earliest memories to the idea that Jewish roots were, in Buber's words, sunk deep in the "scanty Canaanite soil."

The Niswizski family settled in Mödling, a small township from which it was possible for Ephraim to commute to his job as choirmaster in several of the large synagogues in Vienna. Mödling was a cosmopolitan sort of life, with only two hundred Jewish families in the town, but the family, which grew rapidly, was very self-contained. Julia, the oldest child, was born in 1906; two children followed who died in their infancy. Then Hans Aaron was born in 1912, Joseph William in 1915, and Avshalom Rudolph (Rudi) in 1916. In keeping with most Jewish families of the time, each male child was given a national name and a Hebrew one. Also in keeping with the times, the sons were called by their national names, and so it is as Willi that most of Joseph's family have known him throughout the years.

The household was made fuller by three grandparents who lived near them and were partially supported by Ephraim and by two nieces, the daughters of Ephraim's younger brother Leo.

Leo's wife, Fée Helles, was as free a spirit as her first name implied and could not be tied down to educating her children, nor, fairly soon, even to her husband, with whom she stayed on friendly but distant terms, preferring to run her famous dancing school on the Champs-Élysées soon after her husband and she had emigrated to Palestine after World War I. A seventh child, an Italian girl named Gisette Vadash, stayed with the Niswizskis in pension. Keeping her helped relieve some of the strain on the family budget, which like that of most families in postwar Austria was severely strained. Miriam's parents had come to Austria from Poland but were unsuccessful in finding work. Ephraim, exhibiting a financial resourcefulness that was to be the hallmark of his whole life, had been reduced during the war to selling pianos in Budapest in exchange for meat and was constantly having to find additional work to meet his financial responsibilities.

When the spiraling inflation fully hit Austria, Ephraim found himself reduced to selling property he had acquired by skillful management of a burgeoning music business simply to pay his taxes. By 1923, the financial situation was so desperate that Ephraim, after weighing the possibilities of emigrating to Italy or to the United States (where five of his siblings had gone), decided to explore the possibilities of making a life for himself in Palestine. Miriam was reluctant to leave Austria, especially when it was unknown how they would survive in Palestine, and so in 1923 Ephraim went to Haifa by himself. Leo, his brother, who had preceded him to Palestine, had changed his name to Abileah, a name that signified he was the father (abi) of Leah, his youngest daughter. Leo, who also changed his first name to Arie, asked his older brother to accept the same family name, so when the Niswizski family landed in Jaffa in 1926, it was as the Abileah family.

Since Ephraim, like other members of Hibbat Zion, was committed to a spiritual and cultural Zionism and not to the political Zionism espoused by the followers of Theodor Herzl, he thought it important to build a nation side by side with the indigenous Arab population. Martin Buber had not been quite accurate in his 1916 article because what he in Europe thought to be the "scanty Canaanite soil" was in fact home to more than six hundred thousand Arabs. Ephraim thought it was quite natural to live with Arabs as brothers, and after living for a while in a cave in the Arab district of Mount Carmel, he established himself in a music school in the house of an Arab family, the Domets. Aziz Domet was to become a famous poet, and he and his German wife visited Mödling while the rest of the Abileah family still lived there. It is a measure of the strong Arab-Jewish ties among large segments of the Haifa population that Aziz Domet wrote a play about Joseph Trumpeldor, one of the early Zionist martyrs killed in Tel Chai in 1920, a play for which Ephraim composed the music.

Not only were the Domets his business partners and many of his students children of wealthy Palestinians, but from the outset Ephraim worked for Arab-Jewish cooperation and, when needed, reconciliation. In 1925, for example, he played at the concert inaugurating the Railway Workers Trade Union, which up to 1948 was the only integrated Arab-Jewish union in all of Palestine. When he became a Freemason in 1929, it was in an integrated lodge that was under the jurisdiction of Egypt. Cosmopolitan in outlook, and already having lived in Russia, Poland, and Austria, Ephraim never thought that the Jewish home promised by the British in their Balfour Declaration of 1917 had to evolve into an exclusively Jewish state. His views were shared by many Jewish immigrants to Palestine at this time, though his views, like theirs, were to be modified through time and by historical circumstances.* Still, in the three years he was separated from his family and in the following years when they were all together, Ephraim was caught up in trying to turn into reality the ideals of universal brotherhood he had dreamt of in the woods above Mödling. Joseph, of all his sons, most fully shared the dream.

*Jewish views were not the only ones to change through time. Aziz Domet, author of the play about Trumpeldor, was later accused of being a German collaborator during the war and of having made broadcasts for the Nazis. Joseph believes he was forced to do so.

For Ephraim his sons' musical education received the first priority. In addition to being a choirboy, Joseph began violin at the age of six. His brother Rudi took up the cello, while Hans, who had suffered the loss of parts of his fingers because of an early childhood illness, was a reluctant pupil of the trumpet. Hans had a great deal of trouble accepting the arbitrary decisions of his iron-willed father and left home soon after the family moved to Palestine. Joseph himself was, initially, a reluctant music student and feels that he really only came to be truly interested in the violin when he was ten. As is often the case with a child whose father is absent for important years in his or her development, Joseph and his brothers were not easy to raise, especially when their care was largely in the hands of their older sister Julia, who ran the household when their mother made an extended trip in 1924 to visit their father in Palestine. Julia married in 1925, a year before the family moved to Palestine, and she stayed behind with her husband, Rudolph Seiden, until they emigrated from Austria to the United States in the thirties, barely escaping the horrors brought on by Nazism.

Joseph's memories of his years in Austria are all happy ones. He loved the crowded household and constant activity. At the same time, he developed a taste for adventure and solitude. His brother Rudi remembers him taking long trips on his tricycle, which in one case led to him disappearing altogether for an alarming period of time. The comfortable boughs of the fruit trees at 7 Spechtgasse were good places to read, to plan, to dream. When his mother told him they were moving to Palestine, Joseph looked upon the trip more as an adventure than as a fulfillment of some Zionist dream. He, at the age of eleven, would have been just as excited about moving to Australia. This does not mean, however, that he was unhappy where he was. In 1926, when the family made their move, he had been studying the violin with the concertmaster of the Tonkünstler-Orchester in Vienna, and it was clear that if he fulfilled his early promise, his career as an Austrian musician would be assured. At the age of eleven, it did not occur to him that he would not get equal instruction in Palestine; and while it was hard

Joseph (Willi) and Avshalom (Rudi) on violin and cello.

to say good-bye to Julia, he loved helping his mother pack and move the family belongings to the boat in Trieste, Italy, and from there, traveling fourth class on deck and feeling a bit isolated as the only Jewish immigrants on board, making their way to Alexandria, Port Said, and finally to Jaffa, the major port of Palestine.

When the Abileah family landed, they were part of eighty thousand Jews who came to Palestine between 1924 and 1929, making up what is called the Fourth Aliyah (Ascent). While they did not face the hardships endured by the visionaries of the Second Aliyah (of the fourteen thousand who came between 1903 and 1914, in 1909 there were only 165 left), life was still very hard, and perhaps 40 percent of the immigrants soon left Palestine. Life had been hard for Ephraim in the three years he was separated from his family. Many times he carried his harmonium on a four-hour walk to give concerts and lessons, and few people in the little port town of Haifa had money to spend buying musical instruments or providing their children with lessons.

Perhaps because Haifa had not been transformed by the British into a major port, it had the atmosphere of a small town. Unlike in Mödling, where the Jewish families kept pretty much to themselves, Haifa was a center where members of all faiths freely mixed. There had for a long time been a strong Christian community among the Arabs, and on Mount Carmel, overlooking the town and port, were to be found strong concentrations of Druze. The Baha'is, whose gardens and buildings are still the city's most notable architectural achievements, revered Haifa as the center of their faith. There was a strong German colony, connected with the Knights Templars, and the new Jewish immigrants from Europe found it easy to mix and settle. Many Jewish immigrants, especially those of a secular frame of mind, found the physical beauty and integrative atmosphere appealing, especially because they were fleeing restrictive ghettos in Europe.

Linguistically the town was as varied as its religions. It would have been possible for families like Joseph's to continue to speak nothing but German (as did many Jewish immigrants just up the Palestinian coast in Nahariya), but the cosmopolitan atmosphere seemed to encourage all Haifa citizens to speak two to four languages with great ease. The interaction of cultures and openness of neighborhoods had an important influence on Joseph, and this interaction seemed to be strengthened by the habit of changing apartments every year. In his first three years in Haifa, Joseph moved three times—once into a flat vacated by the deposed Shah of Iran, which had a living room so large that the intrepid tricyclist learned to ride a two-wheeled bicycle in it! While increased Jewish immigration had caused problems in Jaffa and Hebron, Haifa appeared to be a spot where Arabs and Jews accommodated each other easily. Joseph's belief that Arabs and Jews can live together now is based on his experience of this having been true sixty years ago. Even today, the least amount of friction among the two bitterly divided communities is to be found in Haifa. Joseph has had many opportunities to move from Haifa, such as when he was offered a place in the Israeli Philharmonic Orchestra in Tel Aviv, but he has always felt that there was something special about Haifa and its people.

Because of their straitened circumstances, the family music business was almost always in their flat. But to Joseph, used to the bursting house in Mödling, there was a great joy in being surrounded by music. He has a vivid memory of watching piano movers taking a piano up the two hundred steps to the Stanton Street flat, one person doing all the lifting while two others sang on each side of him to encourage him in his effort. For Joseph, all Haifa and indeed all Palestine were full of song, and at least in the neighborhoods in which he lived, the many songs were in harmony. His own musical training proceeded well, thanks to a gifted teacher, Mrs. Velikovsky, who guided his development from 1927 to 1934. He also had the opportunity of studying with the famous teacher Henri Marteau; for four months Joseph commuted to Tel Aviv for eight-hour master classes. Mrs. Velikovsky inspired him to progress rapidly, and her concern for his talent caused her to waive tuition for him in 1929, when his family was having severe financial problems.

Willi and Rudi at work in Ephraim's music business.

These financial problems forced Ephraim to accept work in Tel Aviv as choirmaster in the Great Synagogue that had recently been built. Since he had received shipments of pianos from Vienna to enlarge his music business, he hoped the move to Tel Aviv would be temporary, but in the end, the family spent the better part of five years there.*

Although Ephraim was a man of immense energies, sleeping no more than four hours a night and composing and working on his Hebrew long after others had gone to bed, it was all he could do to keep the family fed. When a member of his choir

---

*These five years included an important interlude in 1933–34, when Ephraim moved the family to Safad. Sarah Levy had constructed an artist colony on Mount Kena'an, and Ephraim was offered one of the houses. In this mountain retreat, he dreamed of curing wood for fashioning musical instruments, but he returned to Tel Aviv after a time. The houses in this artist colony were pretty much destroyed during the 1936 disturbances, but the family continued to go to Safad for vacations and eventually put up a small house to which they could retreat.

discovered that Miriam cooked on the Sabbath, Ephraim was asked to resign his job in the synagogue. For a while, Miriam took in boarders at lunchtime and in the evening joined her husband to play in the silent cinemas around the city. Ephraim had been comfortable working in the synagogue, although his own family was not observant, because he had always regarded his own commitment to music a religious one. It was with regret and out of some desperation that he began to put together bits of work that would allow him to continue to compose and his family to live. The family itself had been increased with the birth of Benjamin in 1930 and with the arrival of Miriam's mother, Nehama Mosabowski, in 1930. Nehama's husband Sadek, who had never really found work in Austria, became despondent when it was discovered that his son Heinrich (Hirsch) had a terminal illness. In 1929, no longer able to bear the pain of watching his son die, he committed suicide. When her son died soon after, Nehama had nowhere to go except to her daughter in Tel Aviv.

Joseph and Rudi often accompanied their parents to the films. One evening Joseph saw *Les Misérables*. Forgetting his parents' musical accompaniment, transported almost beyond himself, he became engrossed in the story of Jean Valjean, the repentant thief. At the point in the story when the priest gave the remaining silver to the thief, the camera focused on the priest's eyes, filled with sadness and compassion, and then on a broken flower in his garden. The image of the eyes and the flower haunted the young Joseph and remains with him still. What he witnessed was not just the conversion of the thief but the source of the conversion, the expression of compassion in the eyes of one who, while suffering, established contact with the suffering of another and aroused in him hitherto hidden feelings of goodness. From that moment on, human eyes became windows to the soul for Joseph, and this image from a silent film, where his parents played to eat, has assumed more and more importance over the years as it has been reinforced by other eyes made incandescent in their longing for hope in the midst of suffering.

One of the jobs Ephraim obtained was as a teacher of music in the Collège des Frères, a Christian school in Jaffa where Muslims, Christians, and Jews all shared the same school bench. Because he was a teacher there, he could send Joseph and Rudi there for greatly reduced fees. Joseph was aware of the sacrifices made to secure his place in this famous school and so applied himself diligently in the three years he spent there. Unlike his robust father, Joseph had a rather delicate constitution, and it was difficult for him to be up at six, walk the three kilometers from Tel Aviv to Jaffa, then return home on foot and work as a musician at parties until midnight.

At the Collège des Frères, Joseph's education was not only in the academic subjects at which he excelled. There was a great separation between the Jewish community of Tel Aviv and the Arab community of Jaffa. Jaffa, like Hebron, had been the scene of riots in 1929, when Arabs began to resist Jewish immigration as a threat to their own dreams of national sovereignty. Thus, it was somewhat unusual for Jewish children to be educated alongside Arab children. For Joseph it seemed natural, and forever after he referred to Arabs as his brothers. It was also at the school that he developed his amazing facility for languages. He had missed a half year of school when he arrived in Haifa in order to learn Hebrew, and he had a similar half year to make up in order to learn French, the language of instruction at the Collège des Frères, and English, the secondary language taught. Thus by fifteen, he was speaking German, Hebrew, French, English, and rudimentary Arabic. While it was understood that he would be a professional musician, his father wanted him to find work and so urged him to take the course in commerce to develop accounting, bookkeeping, and typing skills. Joseph showed a real aptitude for this work, and it has been the foundation for many nonmusical jobs he has had in his life.

One of the reasons his Arabic was only rudimentary was that he and other Jewish students were excused from the daily two hours of Arabic instruction at the school. During this time, he continued his work with the violin. He also was not forced to have religious instruction, but he was not immune from the religious atmosphere of the school and participated in numerous musical performances of requiems and masses. For Joseph and Rudi the Collège des Frères was an altogether happy time, and through their school contacts they moved freely in both the Jewish and the Arab communities, especially in musical circles. Joseph is particularly proud of his membership in the Jaffa Music Club and of the many friendships he established there.

When Joseph finished school in 1933, he received a special award in typing and languages and decided to look for work in commerce that would also allow him to continue his promising musical career. He often practiced up to six hours a day, but when he moved up to seven and one-half hours, he strained a muscle in his arm so severely that he was advised to ease back to four hours. At the age of eighteen, he was already assisting Mrs. Velikovsky in her lessons and playing in many musical groups, including the family quartet—his father on the harmonium, Rudi on the cello, and his mother on the piano. The family was in demand, and when his first job, with I. G. Farbenindustrie Pharmaceuticals, did not allow enough time for music, he used a contact with an Arab friend from school to get a job in the British Mandate Survey Department, where he finished work by two o'clock and then continued with his music.

At first the work in the survey department was just a job, though the exactness appealed to Joseph's orderly mind. His concern for order and delight in figures became a lifelong preoccupation. Anyone working through Joseph's files today is convinced that he has never thrown anything away, from ticket stubs to dinner menus to letters from an active file of fifteen hundred correspondents. Not only that, he knows where everything is. In Israel, such a person is called a *yeke*, and Joseph, even at an early age, was a *yeke* par excellence. It became clear, however, that he could not keep up with his music and with his clerical work without great danger to his health. His already-delicate physical constitution was worn down to the point that he failed the medical examination that would have made his job in the survey department permanent after the first year's probationary period. His supervisor did not want to lose him and so suggested that he take a leave of absence from the office to rest and build up his strength in a field camp. This decision to go into the field was one of the most important, in retrospect, in Joseph's life and explains a great deal about his later development.

In the camp, Joseph discovered two things: his affinity with his Arab coworkers and his affinity with the land. In some sense, 1934, not 1926, was his real "return" to Israel (in the sense of return mentioned by Martin Buber in the epigraph to this chapter). Joseph was the only Jewish member of his crew and so learned colloquial Arabic quickly. He came more and more to believe that he was being transported back to biblical times as he moved about Palestine. Amidst the Arabs and especially the Bedouin of the Jordan Valley, Joseph, not unlike many spiritual Zionists, experienced a profound discovery of his oriental roots. In Buber's essay "The Spirit of the Orient and Judaism," note is taken that "the Jew is not the same person he once was; he has passed through every heaven and hell in the Occident, and his soul has come to grief. But his original strength has remained unimpaired; once it comes into contact with its maternal soil, it will once more become creative."

"The Jew is not the same person he once was." Joseph came more and more to feel that his time in the camp, and especially in the desert, was a time of discovering his true origins. In this discovery, he became physically and spiritually strong. The Bedouin he spoke with, their values and way of life, were to him an encounter with his own early ancestors. The fundamental brotherhood of Arab and Jew appeared to him as an almost mystical union, and his experiences with the land on both sides of the Jordan River convinced the young Abileah that the land should be as undivided as the kinship.

Joseph's sense of freedom, wonder, and strength led him to spend every free moment from the survey camps hiking and exploring the Jordan Valley and the hills beyond. Twice he went on walking tours around the Dead Sea. He saw the beauty of

Joseph's walking tour of the Dead Sea. Joseph third row at left.

the sun bringing to sparkling life the great salt mountain at Sodom and saw the changing landscapes of the Jordan Mountains as the setting sun revealed their hidden colors and life. Though at first one sees no life, hears no birds, and feels no flies, there is the throbbing presence of life. When learning of the vast chemical riches of the sea itself, Joseph came to feel that the sea, like his own past, was far from dead but was endowed with continuous, if hidden, life. In caves in the Jordan Mountains, he was thrilled to find, as at the Cave of Tuvia, traces of Hebrew written two thousand years ago, tracings that were a confirmation of Buber's claim for common roots. The quietness of the desert made him think, especially when he made his trips alone. At these moments, he heard what was really important in the silence. Beethoven had moved beyond the words of the choral part of the Ninth Symphony to the profundity of his string quartets. Joseph, the master now of many languages, began to sense a reality that lay beyond the scope of words and almost communication.

As important as his contact with the land was, it was even

more important for him to encounter the souls of its inhabitants. In these people, he found traces of his past and a foundation for his hopes for Arab and Jewish reconciliation in the future. Near the end of 1935, on a seven-day trip around the Dead Sea, Joseph and thirty companions came to the police outpost at Ghor es-Safia in the Wadi Hasa. At the outpost were two Circassian policemen who welcomed their guests by cooking for them their entire stock of provisions. When it became clear that there would not be enough food for thirty guests, one of the men made an hour's trip on horseback to bring back some more eggs. Such an example of spontaneous generosity and welcome made a profound impact on Joseph, though he had experienced many similar acts among his Arab coworkers in the survey camp.

He also witnessed the darker side of this humanity. At Es Salt he found people imprisoned like wild animals in outdoor cages. He was told that such cruelty was necessary to provide example to others and that people learned through fear. His experiences in the desert, however, led him to the conviction that fear and hostility could be overcome. Once, when approaching a Bedouin tent, he saw a fierce watchdog running towards him. Overcoming his initial reaction of fear, Joseph sat down in the path, his face level with that of the snarling dog. When the dog sensed that Joseph was not afraid and was not going to try to harm him or his master, the snarling stopped. During this time, the dog's Bedouin owner had been quietly watching from the threshold of his tent. When the dog accepted Joseph, the master received him also. While desert life could be cruel and violent, it was clear that all danger had its basis in fear and that, when fear was absent, danger was absent as well. Joseph also sensed that fear might have something to do with hatred.

In 1936, at a time when the waves of Jewish immigrants escaping from Europe were causing real tensions in Palestine, Joseph decided to go on a four-day holiday to the country of Gil'ad (Jebel Ajlun). Though the times were tense, travel was easy and cheap. No passports were required to cross the Jordan River; and in a matter of a few hours, Joseph and a friend he had met in the survey camp, Hussein Khalaf of Kfar Aboush, were in Amman. These four days commemorated an important Islamic feast, and at its height, Emir Abdullah received guests from many nations. Young Joseph and his friend were dazzled by the pageantry as embassy after embassy sent its cars up the road to the palace, following the emir's car when he left the mosque after his prayers. As he watched the cars pass by, Joseph noticed there was not one from Palestine representing the Jewish Agency. Overcome by a desire to be a part of the celebration and feeling the need to express the best wishes of the Jewish people to the emir, Joseph rather impulsively went up to the royal palace, forgetting that his shorts and hiking boots offered a strange contrast to the formal attire of the other dignitaries. Not surprisingly, he was stopped at the doors of the palace and asked his purpose. Although Joseph's Arabic had improved immensely in his year in the survey camp, he realized that his grasp of colloquial Arabic was not suitable for the occasion and so asked his friend to translate. No less a person than First Vizir Ibrahim Pasha Hashim asked him who he was. "Are you a Jew?" he asked. When Joseph replied affirmatively, the vizir said, "You are a hundred times welcome, please come in." This welcome has stayed in Joseph's memory for more than fifty years. To him, it is remarkable that a young hiker should encounter such a courteous reception. More importantly, when he revealed his Jewish identity, there was not a trace of animosity in the vizir's response. On the eve of an Arab revolt that was to last for three bloody years, a high Jordanian official stood ready to welcome a Jewish youth into the presence of Emir Abdullah. Years later (1944), in a report he sent to the British high commissioner, Joseph still marveled at what he thought was a real promise of Jewish and Arab coexistence. "I could not accept his invitation because I was not well dressed, but asked him to pass His Highness our best wishes in the name of the Palestine nation. So His Highness has never seen me but my heart was beating for him since in love and gratefulness, and I always felt that a day would come when I would be able to show myself grateful in action. I pray God that He will let me live so that I can say one day to His Highness: 'Welcome in Palestine, a hundred thousand times, please accept me as your faithful subject.'"

It is an interesting sidelight on history that Joseph was the only Jew to offer greetings that day. Emir Abdullah had been one of the Arab leaders most open to coexistence with the Jews. In 1926, almost precisely when Joseph landed in Palestine, Abdullah had stated to Dr. Saul Mizan, head of the Jewish Unions for the League of Nations, "Palestine is one unit. The division between Palestine and Transjordan is artificial and wasteful. We, the Arabs and the Jews, can come to terms and live together in peace in the whole country, but you will have difficulty in reaching an understanding with Palestinian Arabs. You must make an alliance with us, the Arabs of Iraq, Transjordan and Arabia. We are poor and you are rich. Please come to Transjordan. I guarantee you safety. Together we will work for the benefit of the country." In 1933, Abdullah said, "The Jews of the whole world will find me to be a new Lord Balfour, and even more than this: Balfour gave the Jews a country that was not his: I promise a country that is mine."

To be sure, there were Jewish hands that reached out to Abdullah, but they worked in secret, and those like Chaim Arlosoroff, who attempted at a secret April 1933 meeting at the King David Hotel in Jerusalem to lay the groundwork for future cooperation in throwing off the British yoke, often paid the price for it. In June 1933, Arlosoroff was killed while walking on the beach at Tel Aviv. By 1936, despite efforts of such Jewish groups as Brit Shalom and Kedma Mizracha, few Jews, even those theoretically interested in Jewish and Arab rapprochement, ventured into Arab territory.

Joseph's parents were convinced that he was foolish to take such risks, and in an effort to ease their minds about his safety, he wrote them the day after his experience at the palace. "The whole atmosphere is wonderful. In Amman people kiss each other in the streets and despite my glasses and my Jewish nose, I have not seen one hateful eye." In this letter, he begged his fellow Jews to experience for themselves the hospitality offered to those who come not as conquerors but as friends. It is often claimed that during this period Zionist leaders did all they could to establish friendly ties, but Joseph's experience in Amman confirms the words of H. M. Kalvarisky who, when chronicling the 1930s, wrote: "It turned out that though we stretched out our hand in peace, we withdrew it immediately when the other party expressed a willingness to take it. This dangerous game did not help to raise us in their estimation as honest people, and their charge, that we are pursuing a two-faced policy,—on the one hand pretending to seek an accord and on the other merely biding time—is not groundless." Joseph approached Transjordan with both hands out, and he did not return empty-handed.

It was not only from the palace that Joseph received this spirit of welcome, generosity, and brotherhood. On the evening before the ceremony, excited about the prospect of seeing Emir Abdullah, Joseph decided he wanted to visit the famous Crusaders' fortress high on one of Amman's hills. Since he had made many moonlight excursions during his year at the survey camp, he did not hesitate to strike off at night to make his visit. On the way, he asked directions of a well-dressed man who advised against going alone at night to the fortress because of the danger of robbers and wild animals. When he saw Joseph was determined to go, he stopped at a nearby shop, purchased bullets for his revolver, and insisted on accompanying Joseph to the fortress. By moonlight, he explained the Roman origins of the site, as well as the Crusaders' additions to the fortress, and then guided Joseph back to town through the cemetery. Joseph never even learned his name, but the memory of his kindness is sharper than the impressive outlines of the fortress silhouetted against the clear moon. The whole four days' journey was full of similar actions on behalf of the solitary traveler, and many times Joseph wondered if such actions would be reciprocated should an Arab be a wanderer in the Jewish sector of Palestine.

After the ceremony, Joseph said good-bye to Hussein Khalaf, giving him a letter of introduction to his family in Haifa. Joseph set out for Jerash, to visit the family of the cook from his survey camp. In Jerash, he was passed from family to family and had to eat many times and drink innumerable cups of coffee. At one of the families' homes, he heard a story that touched him greatly and caused him to be optimistic once again that the growing hostility between Jew and Arab in Palestine might one day be amicably settled. It seems that two families in the village had sons who were inseparable. One of them received the opportunity to study in Damascus. When he returned, he was anxious to show his friend what he had learned in school. One of the physical skills he had picked up was boxing, and while demonstrating how it was done, he delivered a blow to his friend's stomach that killed him. One can imagine his grief, but his friend's father was able to rise above his own sorrow to go immediately to the house of the accidental murderer. There, he offered the family forgiveness and consolation. By doing so, the villagers claimed that the father of the dead boy discovered consolation himself. Such an example of goodness residing in the human heart made Joseph sense even more deeply the falsity of the stereotype of the bloodthirsty, vengeful Arab and filled him with a reservoir of hope from which he was able to draw time and time again in the years ahead.

When he left Jerash, Joseph made his way through the mountain forests to the Crusader castle of Ajlun, stopping by small villages that showered him with hospitality. By his reckoning, he ate five lunches that day and drank fifteen cups of coffee. When he reached the castle, he climbed its ramparts to gaze westward over the Jordan Valley. The oneness of all Palestine came home to him once again, and he looked down on the Jordan River not as a border, but as a vein running down the heart of the country. While he was dreaming about perhaps one day settling in these hills, establishing ties with ancestors who had lived in Gil'ad, he was approached by soldiers and asked to accompany them to their headquarters. Once there, he was interrogated by an officer who seemed to know every one of his movements since he had left the royal palace. There had been a recent Druze uprising in Syria, and Jordan feared spies and agents provocateurs. In a way, the police were like the Bedouin man and his dog. When they were convinced by Joseph's openness and candor that he meant them no harm, they entertained him, found him a comfortable bed, and the next morning, gave him two escorts in civilian dress to accompany him until he could reach the other side of the Jordan.

His adventures were not yet over. As they left Ajlun, Joseph's escorts suddenly broke from him and began running toward an approaching shepherd. When Joseph caught up with them, they said that they had disarmed the shepherd, who had come up from the direction of the Jordan. After the escort explained that they feared the shepherd might shoot Joseph, Joseph took the rifle, returned it to the shepherd, and said to him, "I hope the day will come when you can go back to the Jordan, and throw your rifle in the river." The shepherd sighed, held on to his rifle, and said, "*Inshallah*" (if God wills).

The trip to the Damiya Bridge in the Jordan Valley was extremely exhausting. Once down from the mountains and the protection of the forest, the party was exposed to the severe desert sun. The policemen, one of whom had served with T. E. Lawrence, kept up an unrelenting pace. Jospeh, despite being in much better physical shape than he had been two years earlier, when he joined the survey office, was no match for his companions and, by mid afternoon, was dehydrated and exhausted. The three providentially came upon a Bedouin family who took one look at Joseph and gave him all the water and coffee they had in the tent. Then they forced him to rest until evening. This act was especially meaningful since Joseph learned they had to walk four hours each way to replenish their water supply. Once again he wondered if he would be able to reciprocate if he were in the other's position. His moral education was continuing. As he crossed the Damiya Bridge, he was reminded that Joshua had crossed at that very point. As he crossed into the Promised Land, Joseph promised to redeem the land, but not in the way of Joshua, that is, not through conquest but through cooperation.

3

Not in the Joshua Way
1936–1947

> You know, too, that in my opinion, if we cannot find ways of peace and understanding, if the only way of establishing the Jewish National Home is upon the bayonets of some Empire, our whole enterprise is not worthwhile, and it is better that the eternal people that has outlived many a mighty Empire should possess its soul in patience, and plan and wait. It is one of the great civilizing tasks before the Jewish people to try and enter the Promised Land, not in the Joshua way, but bringing peace and culture, hard work and sacrifice, and a determination to do nothing that cannot be justified before the conscience of the world.
>
> —Judah Magnes, 1929

❧ AFTER HIS RETURN FROM AMMAN, Joseph decided that music could never be the sole focus of his life. He had experienced an almost mystical union with the land of the Jordan Valley and with its inhabitants. In a manner reminiscent of Aaron David Gordon, one of the founders of labor Zionism who saw the attainment of personal redemption through redemption of the land, Joseph determined to work the soil. He was also in agreement with Gordon's belief that there was a connection between redeeming the land and cooperating with the Arabs, the Jews' fellow inhabitants. Gordon, writing in a Tolstoyan vein, had said, "Our road leads to nature through the median of physical labor. The return to nature through labor will enable man to rediscover religion and to regain a sense of cosmic unity and holiness." Gordon saw that the treatment of the indigenous Arab population would become one way to test how pervasive this unity really was. "Our attitude towards them must be one of humanity, or moral courage which remains on the highest plane, even if the behaviour of the other side is not all that is desired. Indeed, their hostility is all the more a reason for our humanity."

Joseph resigned from the survey department and attempted to join a kibbutz, Giv'at Brenner, but was told there was no room for him. He then obtained a job picking oranges in Rehovot and on May 2, 1936, wrote his parents, who were desperate to hear from him. His mother wrote back immediately, begging him to come to Haifa and telling him that he was not made to be a farmer. Her letter was reinforced by one from Rudi, who gently upbraided him for not informing the family of his whereabouts. Exhibiting a stubborn streak that has always characterized his commitment to what he believes, he turned a deaf ear to their appeals and, through the offices of musician friends, gained admittance to the agricultural school at Ben Shemen. It was there that he had an experience that changed his life. Having in his first years in Palestine come to believe in Arab and Jewish rapprochement by experiencing it in all phases of his daily life, he could now, as a result of this experience, see that the basis for that rapprochement lay in goodness and compassion on both sides, which could be awakened only through nonviolence and love. Fourteen years before he read a word about Quakerism, he experienced the reality of the Quaker doctrine of the Inner Light, what he calls the "divine sparkle of God in the human heart."

Joseph's three weeks in Ben Shemen coincided with the outbreak of what is known as the Arab Revolt. For almost three years, the Arab and Jewish communities withdrew into themselves, and only the foolhardy ventured out alone and without weapons. But at twenty-one, it is difficult to suppress love of adventure, and after the experience in Jordan, Joseph saw no need to curtail his activities. While at Ben Shemen, he decided to visit the tombs of the Maccabees, some two and one-half hours' walk to the east. The night before his walk, he slept very soundly and was surprised when he awoke to find that the trees and grass were all burned around the agricultural settlement. He was told that he had slept through an Arab attack. With the rest of the settlement preoccupied with cleaning up after the night battle, no one seemed to take any notice of Joseph as he slipped outside the gates to begin his hike. He had not gone a hundred yards before he met an old Arab on a donkey. After an exchange of greetings and comments about the burned grass and trees, the old man asked Joseph why he was alone and where he was going. Joseph replied that he was on his way to Modi'in, and the man told him to turn back. Joseph thanked him for his warning but continued on his way. The man became highly agitated and followed him and, when Joseph refused again, threw him on his donkey to take him back to Ben Shemen. Joseph, once again displaying the stubbornness that is as much of his temperament as his gentleness and patience, demanded to be set free. After a further exchange, the man let him go but not without a last warning about the hostile reception Joseph was likely to receive.

In some ways, it was difficult to take the warning too seriously: it came from a man who in 1936 was supposed to be his enemy. If he were so anxious for his safety, why would he not receive the same treatment from other Arabs he met on the way? When he visited the graves of the ancient Hebrew warriors without incident, Joseph was beginning to feel he had made the right decision. All along the way, he had greeted Arabs working in their fields, and when he stopped in a village, he was given breakfast. At the village, he was warned not to go farther by himself, and they prevailed upon him to join a passing camel caravan that could escort him to safety. The leader of the caravan was reluctant to take Joseph, but could not, with honor, turn down the villagers' request. As soon as the caravan left the village, however, he pointed to a fork in the road and told Joseph to take the way not used by the camels. He assured Joseph that he was not abandoning him but showing him a shorter way back to the settlement.

As he walked towards the west, Joseph came upon about thirty men at work in the fields. The gap narrowed between them, and Joseph called out in Arabic, "*Salaam aleikum*" (peace be with you). The men paused in their work to ask who he was. He replied, "A man like you." After a brief but friendly conversation covering several topics, one of the men asked, "Are you a Jew?" When Joseph said, "Yes," the atmosphere became charged with tension, and the men gathered round him, their tools now being handled as weapons. He was told that, at the Friday prayers, their imam (religious leader) had laid upon all his listeners the duty of killing every Jew they met. To the amazement of his listeners and to some extent to himself as well, Joseph heard himself saying, "Very well, if it is your duty, perform it." The men drew aside, and Joseph could hear them debating how they should kill him. When he heard them talk about taking him to a nearby well, where they could dump his body and cover it with stones, he interrupted them to ask where the well was and how he should get there. He walked towards it, believing his life was lost but also experiencing a strange sort of calm. Upon reaching the edge of the well, he turned to those following and asked, "Who wants to throw me in?" The men surrounded him, but as he looked into the eyes of each man, he became aware that no one, individually, had the desire to kill him. The men stood as still as statues, not knowing what to do next. Joseph knew that their duty was a matter of honor to them and that they were now caught between the dictates of their heads and those of their hearts. At that moment, a voice Joseph felt must have been God inspired said, "Our commandment was to kill Jews. Are you willing to become a Muslim? If so, you can go free." Joseph asked what that conversion entailed, knowing that the offer was made in an attempt to resolve the matter honorably. He was told that, if he repeated the formula "There are no gods but God and Mohammed is his prophet," he would be set free. As Joseph puts it, he had no trouble accepting the formula, and after repeating the words in Arabic, he was released.

This incident, in which the power of nonviolence awakened

the good instincts of the oppressor, proved incontestably to Joseph the ability of the human heart to overcome hatred. The silent strength of the heart in stilling the voices of hostility set the course of Joseph's life. Whatever else happened to him, he remained loyal to the truth he met on the road to Ben Shemen. Many times his nonviolent response to threatened violence has saved his life, but what remains important is not so much that his life has been saved as that, even in the most tense situations, the power of love could assert itself.

When Joseph's parents heard of his narrow escape at Ben Shemen, they were alarmed both for his safety and for his sanity. When they finally enticed him back to Haifa and saw his highly agitated state, they put him under psychiatric observation for two weeks and extracted a promise from him that he give up thoughts of farming and of surveying. While he was frustrated that his family showed so little interest in what he had learned, Joseph nevertheless agreed to change his profession. His brush with agriculture actually had convinced him that he could not be both a farmer and a musician. To give up music entirely seemed not only to betray his talent but also to take away a vital source of life's meaning. But what to do? His dreams of an undivided Palestine and Transjordan were still vivid, and his lust for travel and adventure made him contemplate a lone journey to Iraq. He spent the late summer of 1936 in Haifa, wondering what he should do next.

His parents' hopes for a return to normalcy seemed to be fulfilled when Joseph took a job in October 1936 with the Holland Bank Union in Haifa. His skill in languages opened up for him a responsible job handling the bank's foreign correspondence. Most of the bank's employees spoke French, so Joseph's school skills were sharpened even further. Working at the bank left him time for music, and the man who was by day a simple clerk could be seen playing chamber music with the wife of the bank's director at night. Just as he felt he became a good musician because of his dedicated practice, so did he become respected in the bank for his thoroughness and methodical approach to all things. He had won the typing prize in school, not because he could type the most words per minute, but because he made the fewest mistakes. It is curious to reflect that these were qualities in the same person who a few months earlier had excitedly ventured on solitary romantic journeys to Jordan, but this combination of vision and exactitude is a key to understanding his character. Like his father, he is a dreamer, but also like his father he is a practical person, whose clerical cast of mind seeks to translate dreams into reality. It was as if he had read Henry David Thoreau's dictum that there is nothing wrong with building castles in the air—the task of those who dream of them must be to build foundations under them. The same combination of the ideal and the practical was the hallmark of the man who was to become Joseph's spiritual hero: Dr. Albert Schweitzer.

At this time, however, Joseph had few spiritual mentors and heroes. One of the remarkable things about his life is how isolated he was in his spiritual and political growth. He knew of few groups like Brit Shalom or other organizations working for Arab-Jewish cooperation. Nor was he aware of the philosophical controversies raging in world Zionist circles. While he was struck by the geophysical indivisibility of Mandated Palestine and Transjordan, he knew nothing of Zionist arguments on the issue of pushing for a Jewish state on some or all of the land. His dedication to his music left him very little time to read books about persons with whom he later felt great fellowship: Gandhi, Schweitzer, Buber, Gordon, Ha'am, and Magnes. At age twenty-one, he formed his remarkable philosophy of life by drawing almost exclusively on his own experiences. While it is undoubtedly true that his father's pacifist and universalist ideas had an important influence on him, his family seemed more concerned with his economic stability than with his spiritual growth. Outside the family, there were few with whom he could discuss the significance of what was happening. His mother, with whom he felt great temperamental affinity, never understood his wanderings and naturally enough seemed solely concerned for his safety and for his future as a musician. One might have thought that his parents could have understood what he was going through, but for some reason, they appeared to have misunderstood him. Despite being idealists in their own right, they preferred to think of Joseph at twenty-one as one who would outgrow his foolishness. Even his brother Rudi, who was so close to him in so many ways, appears to have been unsympathetic to Joseph's burgeoning pacifism. As we shall see, this isolation continued for Joseph, even in the context of his own wife and children. It seems to have had both good and bad effects. On the positive side, by living his ideas as opposed to receiving them uncontested from others, he became unshakeable in his commitment to them. On the negative side, he failed to receive, on the deepest level, confirmation by others at a time (1936–41) when he was struggling into adulthood. How he might have changed under the early tutelage of people like Martin Buber and Judah Magnes will never be known, but his pursuit of his solitary way undoubtedly affected his relative lack of success later in winning over Israeli public opinion to his ideas. Against his own profoundest wishes, he has been regarded as a one-man movement. Even those who have respected his courage and integrity have failed to be challenged by his ideas because they could tell themselves that he was the only one who held such ideas.

So the man who appeared to pass such an uneventful existence at the Holland Bank Union continued to meditate in private on the significance of the royal palace visit and the Ben Shemen encounter. There was, moreover, no real chance for the normalcy his parents had hoped for in a city that was about to explode. In 1936–39 Arabs and Jews who had been friends for years were being pitted against each other. This was a time when Joseph had to go to work in an armored bus, when he had, at times, to crawl across streets to avoid sniper fire. Dreams of a united Palestine and of hikes to the mountains east of the Jordan had to be put on hold. Joseph did not interest himself in politics, though it gradually dawned on him that the British were not playing a very constructive role in the civil strife. It seemed as if the British were deliberately keeping Arabs and Jews from realizing what they might have in common, using their division to pursue their own imperialist objectives. The hostility fostered in the 1936–39 disturbances had certainly not been inherent in Arab-Jewish relations in Haifa before that period, when Joseph and his family had lived with Arab families, rented flats from them, played music with and taught music to most of the well-known Arab families of Haifa. Joseph firmly believed that the separation need not be permanent and that the hostility was to some degree artificial. When the British put an end to the disturbances in 1939 and the Arab boycott was ended, Jews and Arabs mixed as before. One Jewish shopkeeper told Joseph that Arab customers, who had come into his shop on a daily basis up until 1936 and who had then passed the shop without a single greeting for more than three years, suddenly reappeared as if nothing had happened. It may be argued that Joseph's view of the British was not fully appreciative of the difficulties they faced, but his reaction was of one who saw the evil of politics in destroying in a moment relationships that had taken years to develop. Joseph's anger increasingly came to be directed at Jewish and Arab nationalists as well, but in the years 1936–39 it was difficult for him to watch the British helping both the Arab Defense Force and the Jewish Defense Force while claiming to support neither.

Because he was convinced of the threat to the Jewish community, Joseph briefly served in 1936 in the special police, composed solely of Jewish civilians, but he discovered that it was being organized like an army preparing for a war to claim its own national state. Like Judah Magnes, he was convinced that Jewish life should not be established on the basis of violence. Magnes in 1933 had written that Jews should establish their life "not on the basis of force and power, but upon that of human solidarity and understanding. . . . Is our nationality like that of all the nations, pagan and based upon force and violence, or is it a spiritual nationality?" His brief stint with the police force, which purported to be defensive but was planning for offensive activity, convinced Joseph that pacifism was the only legitimate stand for him to take. By 1941, when he was pressured to join the Jewish Brigade to fight alongside the British army in World War II, his convictions were secure. He knew then that all wars were basically civil wars because all men were brothers. The memory of all his earlier experiences allowed him to overcome the fear that gripped both Arabs and Jews during this period, a fear that often led to hatred.

Having explored the early stages of his reaction to hatred, it is now time for us to turn to love. All through school, both Rudi and Joseph had had very little romantic involvement with the young women they met, most often in musical settings. Joseph's colleagues at the Holland Bank Union used to kid him about his lack of a girlfriend and were quick to point this out when he blushed in the presence of an attractive client. If he lacked much real contact with young women, he nonetheless had many dreams. Most of the time, he found himself falling in love with the same girl fancied by Rudi, and he laughingly recalls how their same tastes in women often led to three-person dating. Most of Joseph's social contacts were in musical circles; one in particular deserves mention. Rudi and Joseph were fond of playing trios with Therèse Jaber, a talented pianist from one of the leading Arab Christian families of Haifa. Therèse had received her musical training in North Africa. Both Rudi and Joseph were attracted by her talent and beauty. When Rudi spoke to Joseph about having a romantic interest in "Rezi," Joseph discovered that he, too, was falling in love with her. She was unaware of it and had given him little encouragement. Therèse was darkly handsome and advanced in her outlook and dress. For Joseph there was no problem in their different family backgrounds but a very real obstacle in her modern views, especially in her use of makeup. Joseph, who liked all things natural, had never become accustomed to lipstick. On a 1937 trip to Alexandria, Egypt, and Athens, Greece, he had seen many young women wearing considerable amounts of makeup. In a letter home, he said that perhaps he was getting used to lipstick but that it still offended him. One evening in 1939, Joseph asked Therèse to walk with him on Mount Carmel. It was the first time they had ever been together without playing duets or trios. They walked in silence along the Panorama Road overlooking Haifa Bay. His heart beat quickly as he watched her lovely dark hair catch and reflect the light of the moon. He was just about to ask her to marry him when she turned and smiled, revealing lips whose makeup shone in the moonlight as well. As he stared at her lips, he could not bring himself to ask the question that was on the tip of his own. It was probably a good thing that he did not, because she said to him, "I'm tired and want to go home." Therèse Jaber left Haifa in 1948 and has not been permitted to resettle there. Joseph remained loyal to her family and was present at the bedside first of her dying father and later of her dying mother, who spent her last years in Haifa cut off from her sons and daughters.

It was just at this time that Joseph was getting to know Dinah Yarmus, the daughter of a man who had been a Hebrew teacher in Poland and a farmer after arriving in 1926 in 'Afula, the first Jewish development town in the Galilee. After she had received her secondary education in Haifa, Dinah had gone to work at the Manufacturers' Association, located on the fourth floor of the same building in which Joseph worked. In the disturbances of 1936–39, employees who worked in downtown Haifa had to meet at a certain bus stop to board the armored bus that would take them to work. When groups arrived late for the bus, they would walk together for protection. Dinah and Joseph met in these groups and often walked together. He discovered that she loved music but had never been able to afford music lessons. Her father had never made the transition from teacher to farmer and had died prematurely, leaving the family rather poor. Dinah sang and played the mandolin, and Joseph made arrangements for her to take piano lessons from his mother. As she had no piano, she came daily to their studio to practice. Mrs. Abileah liked this gentle and unassuming young woman, who was clever in her work as a secretary and who would provide stability to her wandering son. But, while Mrs. Abileah had her eye on Dinah, Dinah herself had many suitors. Though Joseph pursued her relentlessly, she was not anxious to commit herself. In the end, he won her through music.

Because of his reputation as a musician, many doors of Haifa high society were open to him. The Moller family in Kfar Ata, for example, had many musical evenings. Alice Moller, the mother of the famous textile manufacturer, was an accomplished pianist and loved to arrange chamber-music concerts. Dinah was impressed that Joseph knew such people. She also liked his playing and his singing of Schubert songs. It is interesting that Schubert composed many of these songs while sitting by the same stream at Mödling from which Beethoven drew his inspiration. When Joseph became the conductor of the student orchestra at the Haifa Technion in 1939, Dinah attended rehearsals and concerts. Before each concert, Joseph often gave some introductory remarks to explain the music he was about to conduct, involving a great amount of research on his part since he had received no real training as a musicologist. In preparing a lecture on Bach, he began reading Dr. Albert Schweitzer's famous study. This reading was to be his first contact with the man whose philosophy of life was a parallel and at the same time an extension of his own. In what is a recurring motif in Joseph's life, music opened up large vistas of humanity, religion, and philosophy as it had for Dr. Schweitzer.

Charles-Marie Widor, Schweitzer's famous organ teacher, wrote the introduction to Schweitzer's work on Bach. In his remarks, Widor acknowledged that the teacher had learned from the pupil when Schweitzer showed him the connection between the German words and the music of the Bach chorales. Schweitzer was as keen as Joseph on connections and parallels, and it was out of gratitude for being shown a new dimension to Bach that Widor ended his preface by saying, "What we enjoy together unites us." Joseph later used these words to introduce a Bach concert when Dinah was in the audience. This concert took place in 1947, just before the War of Independence, and Joseph hoped to alert his audience to the fact that the orchestra was composed of Arab, Christian, Muslim, Greek, Armenian, and Jewish students who, by their example of creating harmony together, could serve as a model for broader Arab and Jewish reconciliation.

Joseph and Dinah were primarily united by their shared love

Joseph and Dinah Yarmus Abileah.

of music because there was little else in Joseph's way of looking at the world that appealed to Dinah. Her father had been a strong nationalist and a personal friend of Ze'ev Jabotinsky, the leader of the World Union of Zionist Revisionists. She could not understand Joseph's feeling for the Arabs and was upset by his oft-stated conviction that the establishment of the Jewish state would be a disaster for Palestine. It took her a great while to accommodate herself to Joseph's way of looking at the world, but after two years of courtship, she agreed to marry him. Joseph's colleagues at the bank had warned him that she was getting serious when she decided to buy a secondhand piano, but he could scarcely believe his good fortune when she agreed to marry him. In the middle of an air raid, they were married on July 8, 1941.

When Joseph moved out of his parents' home, he moved into his father's business. To care for his new household, which also included his mother-in-law and her son, Joseph had to find a better position than the one afforded by the Holland Bank Union. Therefore, while Dinah continued her work with the Manufacturers' Association, Joseph formed a partnership with his father—teaching violin and selling music and instruments in the store. His pupils, as always, included many Arabs. It was at first difficult for Dinah to get used to social interaction with the Arab citizens of Haifa. When Joseph and she spent their first seder (Passover meal) with his parents, she was surprised to find that an Arab Anglican pastor and his wife had been invited. It had always been a custom in the cosmopolitan Abileah household to welcome at Passover guests from other faiths. Ephraim had put the Passover Haggadah to music, but there was one traditional phrase he would neither read nor put to music: "Pour out thy wrath upon the gentiles." Dinah not only became accustomed to having social intercourse with those of different faiths, she also became fast friends with the couple she met at that first Passover meal: Reverend and Mrs. Farah. Her warm and generous personality could never harbor prejudice for very long.

From 1941 to 1944, Joseph worked with his father, but the tension in Haifa, caused by the frequent air raids, the news of the Holocaust in Europe, and the growing military preparation of the Jewish population of Palestine, put strains on all phases of life, including business and family. Soon after his marriage, Joseph was visited by about ten young Jewish militants who ordered him to enlist in the Jewish Brigade or face a possible beating. Joseph asked for some time to think over their "offer" and left the next day for Jerusalem, where he hid with his uncle for about three weeks. Many people had moved to Jerusalem from Haifa during the war, and as Joseph began to look for work in Jerusalem, he found that no one would hire him because he had not done army service. It is important to note that under the British Mandate Administration there was no draft for the British army. Nevertheless, the Jewish Voluntary Enlistment offices were very busy. Only the most extreme right-wing followers of Jabotinsky (and later Menachem Begin) felt that they should not serve with the British. There was considerable Jewish resentment at the British White Paper of 1939, which severely limited Jewish immigration to Palestine when Jews were desperate to leave Europe, but most Jews heeded David Ben-Gurion's advice to fight the war "as if there were no White Paper, and to fight the White Paper as if there were no war."

The Jewish Defense Force, which now included Rudi, was very active in Haifa. Under the British, Haifa had become a major port. All through the war, efforts were made to smuggle in illegal refugees, especially when all the major allied powers closed their doors to Jews. This situation led to incidents like the May 1940 sinking of the *Patria*, a ship in the Haifa harbor. The *Patria* had arrived with hundreds of refugees aboard and had been ordered to turn back by the British. To keep the boat in the harbor and to prevent the forced return of hundreds of Jewish refugees to Europe, the Haganah (Jewish Defense Army) had sought to disable the engines. In a tragic miscalculation, the boat itself was sunk and 260 lives were lost as hundreds of spectators lining the slopes of Mount Carmel watched helplessly.

The desperate plight of European Jewry almost silenced debate in Zionist circles about the advisability of a Jewish, as opposed to a binational, state. Then when the World Zionist Organization met at the Biltmore Hotel in New York City in 1942, there was near unanimity expressed for the creation of a Jewish state. The adoption of the Biltmore program, which made statism the only acceptable form of Zionism, left people like Joseph in a real dilemma. Members of organizations like the Ihud, which had evolved from Brit Shalom in the early forties and had worked for Arab-Jewish cooperation, were effectively silenced. Joseph joined the Ihud at the time of the Biltmore program, his first significant membership in such an organization, but it was a Jerusalem-based organization and Joseph felt always a bit intimidated by towering figures like Martin Buber and Judah Magnes. The group in Haifa took some time to gain strength and were fairly quiet during World War II.

When a Jew was beaten to death in Haifa by persons who

unsuccessfully pressured him to join the Jewish Brigade, the British closed down the recruiting offices. Joseph returned from Jerusalem, yet with a heavy heart because he felt that his own life was now spared only because of the death of another. He was concerned about the atmosphere of hatred in Haifa and saw an impending disaster unless something were done quickly.

In 1944, he quarreled with his father because his father had asked him to sign some income-tax forms that did not accurately report their full income. Joseph had always been particular about the truth, and in a world of chaos, when one had to find stability somewhere, he had sworn to find his by never compromising the truth. Rather than sign the forms, he resigned from the family business and broke with his father. He did not speak to him for months and was only reconciled to him during the seder.

It was precisely at this time that Dinah and Joseph's first child, Adiel (Adi) was born (March 18, 1944). The responsibilities of fatherhood made Joseph even more desperate about the world his son would inherit. Dinah and his mother were much more concerned with short-term security, for the loss of income from the music business was a severe blow. But Joseph threw himself into political activity, seeking ways to hold Arabs and Jews together while begging the British to take a more constructive role. In November 1944, Lord Walter Moyne was assassinated in Cairo, allegedly by one of the persons who had watched the sinking of the *Patria* in the Haifa harbor. The murder of Lord Moyne, who was perceived as being sympathetic to the Arab plight and whose murder would thus inflame the tensions, almost drove Joseph mad.

In September of that year, his family talked him into taking a rest and going to Beit Daniel, a retreat center in Zichron Ya'acov for artists, endowed by the Bentwich family. His uncle Leo (Arie) had made the arrangements, but despite the beautiful and restful surroundings and the availability of good and nourishing food (a rarity during wartime rationing), his spirit was not at rest. His letters to Dinah reveal that he was still angry and disappointed with his father over the tax matter and that he desperately wanted her to be with him. Her letters to him urged him to "put on weight and don't think too much," and she put off his requests for her to visit him by writing about how busy she was with her work and with the baby. The rest at Beit Daniel did not cool the fires in his brain as his quarrel with his father gave way to attempts to counteract the nationalistic direction Zionism was taking. Judah Magnes had written, "The Jews have more than a claim upon the world for justice. But as far as I am concerned, I am not ready to achieve justice to the Jew through injustice to the Arab. I would regard it as an injustice to the Arab to put them under Jewish rule without their consent. If I am not for a Jewish State, it is solely for the reason I have stated: I do not want war with the Arab world." Like Magnes, Joseph felt that this war was coming.

In November, Joseph left his family and went to Jerusalem. While staying at the YMCA, he began a document on November 11, Armistice Day, which he delivered to the British high commissioner. Bishop Stewart of St. George's Church helped him with his English. He probably also should have edited the document, which was a rambling and intemperate excoriation of the Jewish Agency, political Zionism, nationalism in general, and contained accounts of his trips to Jordan. He pleaded with the British to unite all of Mandated Palestine under King Abdullah before a civil war would tear it apart. From the notes the British commissioner wrote in the margins of the document that was returned to Joseph, it was clear that the British dismissed him as a crank, although they did acknowledge the accuracy of some of his observations and did express interest in some of his proposals, especially the one to dissolve the Jewish Agency. Joseph now wishes he had not written such a negative document, but it mirrors well the despair he must have felt as his dreams of a Zionist homeland that could be a light of justice and equality for all nations were being shattered.

His sole source of optimism during this period seems to have been derived from his contact with Arabs, who, he was sure, did not want war and who could be persuaded to govern jointly with Jews once Mandated Palestine was finished. Given his antipathy to all forms of nationalism, it is a bit strange that he tends to discount strong Arab nationalism as merely the influence from other countries in the East. His own experiences in these troubled years had sustained his faith in the Arabs' instinctive generosity and warmth. He was convinced that it was still not too late for Jews to come to the Arabs as brothers, asking for a common home where both had roots and where both could jointly govern.

To those who are skeptical that such cooperation was still possible at this time, Joseph offers the following story. Shortly after a terrorist bomb had gone off in the Haifa railway station, Joseph went for a hike on Mount Carmel with his brother Benjamin and some music pupils. On the way, they encountered a young Arab boy who greeted them and, according to custom, asked them back to his father's tent. Although he invited them, he also warned them that his father was very sick. When the bomb went off, his father had feared for the life of his brother, who was employed at the station. When the news of the explosion hit the village, he had run down the mountain in a state of panic to look for his brother. On the way to the station, he collapsed and had to be taken to the hospital. Since that time, he had been paralyzed, unable to move from his tent. With the knowledge of this story, Joseph entered the tent and said in Arabic, "Please, my brother, don't stand up and please remain comfortable." To his amazement, the man stood up and returned his greeting and later even posed for a photograph with Joseph and his group. To Joseph, it was clear that fear had caused the paralysis but that the man had been liberated from his sickness by his joy at being able to receive a visitor in his tent. Joseph remained convinced that, if the causes of fear and hatred could be lessened, the latent good instincts in all human beings could come to the surface and prevail.

From 1945 to 1947, life was taking a violent turn in Haifa even though the world war had ended. Joseph continued to give music lessons and Dinah continued with her job while her mother took care of Adi. Streams of illegal aliens poured into Haifa. Joseph had always argued for unlimited immigration for

Joseph, his brother Benjamin, and the "paralyzed man" of Mount Carmel.

Jews but never at the expense of the Arab inhabitants. It was for this reason that the idea of a Palestine including Transjordan appealed to him, because there would then be ample room for everyone. Even in the forties, he thought of opening a music store in Amman, and his 1936 view from the Jordan Mountains looking westward from Ajlun was now a vision of an undivided land stretching from the sea past Amman to the desert. He had read Walter Lowdermilk's *Palestine: Land of Promise* and was a disciple of his plan. Lowdermilk had been the man behind the Tennessee Valley Authority in the United States, and his 1939 visit to Palestine convinced him that a similar "Jordan Valley Authority" could reclaim the land for the benefit of all the inhabitants. Lowdermilk proposed channeling water from the Mediterranean to the Dead Sea and sharing the freshwater resources of the Sea of Galilee, which would be diverted for agricultural purposes. Though Lowdermilk himself did not propose it, Joseph saw in his plan the geopolitical logic for an undivided nation. Throughout the forties he tried to convince people of his plan and goal.

He also tried to convince people to use nonviolent means to attain that goal. On the occasion of Albert Schweitzer's seventieth birthday in 1945, Joseph sent the famous doctor birthday greetings in Lambaréné, western Africa, inviting Schweitzer to the Holy Land, thanking him for his writings and marking the birthday by his own decision to become a vegetarian. Joseph was beginning to feel that he was not alone in his way of looking at the world, and he not only read more of Schweitzer but began a serious study of Gandhi. His first book on Gandhi had been a 1945 birthday present from his mother-in-law! However, he still drew most of the material for his philosophy of life not from books, not from the examples of others, but from his own life. He wore himself down in his efforts to keep Jews and Arabs from fighting one another and made many journeys throughout the land, often when giving music lessons to Arab families, who sometimes told him of being forced to supply food, money, and support to secret fighting groups. The penalty for noncompliance would have been to have their houses burned. Joseph himself knew of the pressures on the Jews. He was confronted with a situation in which no one really wanted to fight the other, but all were being drawn toward a conflict. He was convinced that the British were continuing to play a duplicitous role. They pretended to be concerned, as they had in 1936–39 with the buildup of arms, but secretly they helped both sides. In a report he made in 1947 to the Special Committee on Palestine (UNSCOP), set up by the United Nations, Joseph tells the story of how the British were dealing with illegal arms. It is worth quoting in full because it reveals his anger and anguish.

> The following happened to me in March of this year (1947) and will help illustrate the conditions of illegal armament in this country.
> After a visit to the infant welfare centres of the Government Hospital at which I was accompanied by a doctoress of the Mos-

lem community, we had a conversation about the most deplorable conditions in Palestine and I wanted to prove to her that the illegal armament is not severely suppressed by the Government. We went together to a Military Post and I reported to the first man I met an address of an illegal Tommy-gun hidden in a well in a Jewish quarter. The man instead of taking immediate action remitted the plan to another soldier and the latter to a third one, who in turn went away to report the matter to the Officer in Charge of the area. After half an hour, which was sufficient time to remove the arm in case information had reached the responsible persons that it had been reported to the authorities, the man came back to call me to his O/i.C. The latter started asking my about my personal data and about the reason for reporting the address to him. I replied that it is my moral duty to report a Tommy-gun with which ten people can be killed at one shot and asked him to take action at once so that there would not be time to remove the weapon. Worried about my personal safety, the O/i.C. gave orders to dress me in a soldier's uniform and took me in a Jeep with three other men to collect the firearm. But instead of going to the place indicated, he went to another camp and from there to a third one, in order to add to the party five more soldiers. Afterwards, he drove over to the Police Station and at last, back to the first camp. It took four and a half hours, sufficient time to transfer a whole magazine of illegal arms and bring the responsible persons to safety. While arriving back to the office, the following conversation took place between the O/i.C. and myself.

THE O/I.C.: It is not the matter of the army to collect illegal arms, but the matter of the police. The police know the address you indicated to us and we have further found ten other plans in their files, but they do not think it necessary and prudent to collect the arms just now at the present situation.

ME: I insist upon this firearm to be immediately collected. It had perhaps been used against our Arab brothers, now it can be used against you and tomorrow it may be used against Jews if quarrels occur between the different parties. You are responsible for the order and safety in Palestine. It is an illegal arm and has to be forthwith transferred to safe hands.

THE O/I.C.: We have also to consider your personal safety.

ME: I sacrifice my life if it is to save some of your soldiers' lives. You are not my enemies. I consider every man as a human being like me.

(Indeed, thinking about the lovely boys who were killed some days before just around the corner of the street I am living on and giving my lessons, I cannot but feel with their mothers and sisters abroad and join in our common mourning for the precious lives lost. In a country where our greatest moral teacher of all times lived and preached love for the enemy and forgiveness, I cannot consider the English my enemies even if they killed my countrymen some time ago at Tel Aviv.)

THE O/I.C.: Wherefrom do you know the address of the firearm?
ME: I was myself using it illegally for exercises at the "Hagana" in the days of the disturbances.

Then we had some further talk of a more friendly character and I was released and seen home.

Some days later I called to the police and reported the address. The police inspector told me that he has no special orders from higher places to collect the arm. Who is going to give an order to collect the firearm? The police inspector will ask it from a higher ranked officer who will ask it from the High Commissioner. His Excellency will ask for instructions from Mr. Bevin and Mr. Bevin will never give such an order. We do not want to be armed with semi-legal arms which are obviously also found within the Arab sector and use these arms against each other for the interest of a third party. We must of course understand and support the needs of the English as regards the Oil and the Port which is a vital necessity for them and not menace them that they will be sent away from the country, thereby forcing them to take such means as dissociating us in order to maintain their position in the Middle East.

As is clear from the quoted passage, Joseph felt that only by binding together could Arab and Jew survive the intentions of both the West and the reactionary regimes of the East. As a protest against the British desire to divide Arab from Jew, he

Joseph's altered identity card. Courtesy of Yossi Yarmus.

took his identity card in 1946 and crossed out the word *Jew* under *Race* and wrote in *Semitic*. He convinced a few others to do the same thing, although it must be said that more Arabs responded to his suggestion than did Jews. The British chastised him for tampering with his identification but tolerated his idiosyncrasies because they did not appear to draw much of a following. The man who had a desire to redeem the land, but not "in the Joshua way," was left to his ramblings through the land. His family, as they had done in 1936, worried much for his safety and for his sanity. They might have done well to heed the words of Rabbi Benjamin (Yehoshua Radler-Feldman): "If a man doesn't lose his mind these days, it's a sign that he has nothing to lose."

4

Fanatic for Truth
1947–1950

> Truth has no special time of its own. Its hour is now—always, and indeed then most truly when it seems most unsuitable to actual circumstances.
> —Albert Schweitzer

> But he who knows the truth, the truth that alone can help us, is compelled to speak out, no matter whether a whole people is listening or only a few individuals.
> —Martin Buber

> Insanity is a rare thing in individuals, but habitual to groups, parties and ages.
> —Friedrich Nietzsche

❧ THE CHAOS AND CRAZINESS of the decade of the forties in Haifa and elsewhere throughout Palestine are certainly mirrored in Joseph's personal life. There were times when he appeared on the edge of a nervous breakdown, such as in 1944, and his memories of the period lack the clarity necessary to work out an orderly chronology of events; but it is doubtful that his aberrations ever matched the madness that gripped the entire world during this period. Indeed, when viewed against the background of the Holocaust, the terror and bloodshed attendant upon the partition of Palestine, and the fear-inspired hardening of lines drawn in the cold war, his life has a consistency and sanity and logic that are remarkable—at least when viewed in retrospect.

Establishing rights on "the point of a bayonet" had suddenly become the only option open to those wishing national liberation, despite the agonies endured during the long world war. Great Britain had no stomach for further military conflict and was anxious to give up its mandate in Palestine. The Haganah and the Irgun sabotaged the railways, killed British soldiers, and destroyed British ships. In late June 1946, the British tried to suppress all illegal Jewish activity, activity that was generated largely by their unwillingness to open up the gates of Palestine to unlimited Jewish immigration. In July, Begin's terrorist organization, the Irgun, blew up the King David Hotel in Jerusalem, the headquarters of the British Mandate. Scores of Arabs, Jews, and British were killed. The British looked for a way to withdraw that would not bring total chaos to the region, but perhaps by 1947 it was already too late.

Great Britain welcomed the establishment of the United Nations Special Committee on Palestine (UNSCOP), which was assembled to determine the fate of the region. When he heard that the committee would be conducting open hearings in Jerusalem, Joseph threw himself into political action as never before. The threat of partition meant that his longed-for united Palestine would be broken up. This potential breakup was accompanied by the near breakup of his own family, his career, and his own sanity. Nevertheless, as the clouds of war loomed on the horizon, he still caught glimpses of the sun of reconciliation and peace.

One group that had never been reconciled to the Biltmore program was the Ihud, centered in Jerusalem under the leadership of Martin Buber and Judah Magnes. Joseph attended their strategy meetings as they planned their presentation to UNSCOP. The group as a whole was convinced that the binational solution, a state of both Arabs and Jews ruling jointly, was the only way that bloodshed and chaos could be averted. Magnes was selected as the spokesman. Joseph attended most of the meetings without speaking anything, but when the Ihud's program excluded any mention of the fate of Transjordan, he raised an objection. From his experience, he said, he did not see that binationalism was comprehensive enough, because

Transjordan needed access to the sea, and Zionism would one day need further space for immigrants. Then too, the development of the Jordan Valley, the key to the future development of the country, required the cooperation of the peoples living on both sides of the Jordan. While there were those in the Ihud who agreed with him, the majority felt that introducing Transjordan into the deliberations would only complicate matters. The important thing in their eyes was to avoid the tragedy of partition. When Joseph refused to withdraw his objection to the Ihud proposal, the other members urged him to submit his own plan to the committee.

With characteristic single-mindedness, Joseph set to work to update his 1944 memorandum to the British high commissioner. While his proposals did not vary greatly from that earlier document, he tried to tone down its negative character and to stress positive reasons for a united Palestine and Transjordan. The Nassar family of Haifa, owners of the largest hotel in the city, gave him a room for four days where he could isolate himself from everyone, including Dinah, who had just given birth in May to a second son, Daniel (Dani). As was the case with Adi, this new responsibility in the family made him more determined than ever to secure a peaceful future for his family and country. If it appeared (as it did to some members of his family) that his activities caused him to abandon Dinah and her babies at a time when he was most needed, he remained convinced that all his actions were taken for them. He submitted his memo on June 11, 1947.

It was a surprise to a great many people when he was informed on June 28 that his memo had been read with interest and that he had been chosen as one of only three individuals to appear before the committee. The other invitees were official organizations. The *Palestine Post* of June 29 contained the following notice:

UNSCOP DECIDES ON TESTIMONY

After a private meeting on Friday, it was officially announced that the organizations and individuals to be heard will include the Agency, Sec. Chaim Weizmann, the Vaad Leumi, the General Federation of Jewish Labour, the Agudath Israel, the Ashkenazic Jewish Community of Jerusalem, the Central Committee of the Communist Party of Palestine, the Ihud (Union) Association), and Mr. J. W. Abileah, of Haifa, a teacher of violin.

Requests from other individuals and organizations to appear before the Committee will be considered at another meeting.

Josef Wilhelm Abileah has submitted three points in his memorandum to the Committee—Arab-Jewish collaboration; a united Palestine and Trans-Jordan under King Abdullah; and free immigration. Mr. Abileah, who is 32, was for two years an official in the Government Survey Department and submitted a similar memorandum to the Chief Secretary in 1944. The burden of his submission is that the Arabs can be educated to work in cooperation with the Jews.

Victor Hoo, the personal representative of the secretary general before UNSCOP, had written Joseph on June 28 asking him for thirty copies of the memorandum he was preparing and also inviting him to make an oral supplement to the memorandum before the committee. On July 15, Joseph wrote the following letter:

c/o Y.M.C.A.
Jerusalem   Jerusalem, 15th July 1947

Dr. Victor Hoo
c/o U.N.S.C.O.P.
Y.M.C.A. Bldg.
Jerusalem.

Dear Sir,

    re: my memorandum of the 11.6.47.

I thank you for your letter of the 28th June inviting me to make an oral statement before the Committee with regard to my above memorandum and beg to apologize for the delay in my answer.

The detailed memorandum you requested me to submit in thirty copies is not ready as yet for technical reasons which I have explained in my letter addressed to the Chairman on the 11th instant. I have already remitted three chapters thereof to Mr. Stavropoulous and the remainder is ready, partly in draft and partly in conception. It is supposed to contain the following chapters:

1) Constitution.
2) Conditions of illegal armament and means to fight against.—Abolition of Jewish Agency.
3) Differences in standard of living and social relations between the Arabs and Jews in Palestine to be considered as the main reason for struggles.
4) My first visit to the King's palace at Amman.
5) How my confidence in King Abdullah's personality is based.
6) Information on present conditions in various government departments and hints for re-organization.
7) Education.

My relative speech will start with a few introductory words on Schweitzer's Philosophy of Civilization [sic] and his principle of reverence for life which is the basis of my world-view. Thereupon I will show in the darkest colours the political and economical danger of the partition plan pointing out the principal aims of Abdullah's politics in the M.E. The Arab Legion whose force is growing from day to day is making its manoeuvres now at the Syrian boundary. King Abdullah is fighting for the formation of Grand Syria and will succeed by convincing the governments concerned of the economical advantages to form this federation together with the Arab part of Palestine which will comprise the hills in the Eastern part of the country. Haifa will be an international port for the English, the Arabs and the Jews. King Abdullah will ask for a corridor through the plain of Esdralon to connect Grand Syria with the port by a great commercial road along which strategical points will be situated to guard also the pipe-line for the English with whom he is in very good relation. This will devide [sic] the Jewish settlements and take the possibility of a united military power. Even if the Negev will be added to the Jewish State it will not be possible to populate it at a large scale because no central irrigation work could be carried out, the Jordan being part of the Arab State. Thereupon, the Arab Legion will start its manoeuvres in the Palestinian hills near Nablus and Hebron. The army will be enlarged by recruits from Syria and Lebanon. The slightest provocation of a man killed in Jaffa or something else will be reason for an ultimatum by the Arab state to join Grand Syria or they will start coming down from the hills and finish once for ever the Zionists' aspirations for a Jewish State in Palestine. King Abdullah being a great hearted man will have a terrible fight with his concious [sic] to exterminate a nation which has suffered so much up till now. But if King Abdullah will not do it, some of his followers may do it and there is a constant danger for the future peace of the Holy Country. Thereagainst I will show the economic and cultural advantages a co-operation with Grand-Syria can give.

Regarding the abolition of the Jewish Agency, I ask only to take its power as a political representation and it will continue to exist as a welfare institution as proposed by Mr. Ben-Gurion in his evidence. At the same time it will be necessary to suppress the political representation of the Arab Higher Committee and the Moslem Supreme Council who are using their religious authority to stir up the people to kill non-Moslems. I myself ought to [had] be[en] killed in the year 1936 under this influence and was only saved by a wonder. The English government could not suppress such an authority as it would make a noise in the whole Moslem world and endanger their position in the Middle East. But King Abdullah who is himself a religious authority being a Hashimite will send these people to the mosque and ask them to comment [on] the Kor'an: Din Mohamed b'ilikna'a and not Din Mohamed b'isseif (which means: the religon of Mohamed by conviction and not by the sword) as it was originally conceived. The Jihad was already a danger during the war 1914–1918 and can only be avoided for future generations by a great hearted man like King Abdullah who is himself a poet and an artist with a human feeling heart and there is hope that during the period of his reign such basic comments on the Kor'an will be done.

Commenting [on] the third chapter, I will give striking examples from daily life and show that the Arabs in this country have been treated by the Jews as a despised race throughout the period of the Mandate and they have no confidence that they will enjoy equal rights should they come under Jewish rulership as a minority.

In completion of Chapter four, I will relate some stories of my trips in Trans-Jordan and Palestine, how I was treated and what I spoke with the people. I will draw therefrom the proofs for my unlimited confidence in the loyalty and high moral standing of King Abdullah who will protect the Jewish as well as the other minorities better than any European ruler has done up till now. Passing to the 10th point of my memorandum I will try to prove that there is no religion whatsoever in the world which has not got social elements in itself. Socialistic and Communistic governments having failed, we must try to take a religious socialism as the basis for a future legislation. This paragraph has been dealt with in the Bishop's evidence last week.

The information on conditions of Government departments and hints for re-organization will mainly be taken from my memorandum of the year 1944 omitting chapters which had relation to war-conditions.

A great part of the speech will be devoted to the problem of education. I will speak about my experience as a teacher for both Arabs and Jews, about my common orchestras, the common excursions made and other opportunities of educating the children together. Anything proposed will be based on facts out of my experience as a teacher in this country.

Replying to the last paragraph of your letter, I think that one morning session of 4 hours will be amply sufficient to give you the required information. A good deal of this time should be devoted to questions. I could however also summerize [sic] and contract my speech to a shorter duration should your time table not provide a full morning session.

With further reference to the fourth paragraph of my letter addressed to the Chairman, I hereby irrevocably declare that I agree to appear before the Committee in republic [sic] session.

I am looking forward to your communication with regard to the date and time of the hearing which communication can reach me at the Y.M.C.A. or St. Julian's Hotel, Jerusalem, and beg to remain, Dear Sir,

Yours faithfully,
[signed] J. W. Abileah

This letter was preceded by a shorter one on July 11, whose interest lies in its revelation that Joseph was now operating under a threat to his life and under very straitened circumstances. He later learned from his brothers, who were in the Haganah, that his name was near the top of an assassination list compiled by the Irgun; so the threat mentioned in the following letter was not an idle one.

The Chairman of the United Nations
Special Committee on Palestine
c/o the Secretariat
Y.M.C.A. Building
JERUSALEM

Dear Sir:

re: My memorandum of 11.6.47

Enclosed I beg to hand you a copy of my letter addressed to Hani Bey Hashem, Master of Ceremonies, Amman, on the 22.6.47 for your perusal.

I have received in the meantime a communication from Dr. Victor Hoo informing me that you have honoured me with an oral statement and have taken up matters with the departments concerned to prepare everything for my relative speech.

Being aware that it is of the utmost importance that the Boycott of our Arab brothers be stopped before you leave the country, I am doing my utmost to bring about a relative decision by visiting my friends in the Arab towns, handing them copies of my memorandum and calling at every opportunity for cooperation. I have also handed a copy to the Arab Higher Committee at Jerusalem and intend to ask for an interview with Jamal Bey Hussein to whom I will be introduced by his cousin who was my colleague in the Survey Department many years ago. My former school fellows of Jaffa, most of whom are now people of influence in the town, are delighted at the solution submitted by me and are ready to support same in order to have at last peace in the country.

Thereagainst, I have received a letter from an unknown man of Tel-Aviv advising me that my life is in danger should I not withdraw the decision to appear before the Committee. I have not withdrawn this decision as I hope to have the public opinion on my side until then. Anyhow, I will be obliged not to do it in the last minute if I still see that there is any danger. In this case you will have to be satisfied with my detailed memorandum of about 25 pages and written comments thereon.

As regards the detailed memorandum at which I am working now, I must inform you that the work is progressing very slowly owing to financial difficulties which I have been entrained owing to the fact that I was obliged to take unpaid leave from my students for several months. I have already sacrificed my own little fortune and cannot accept financial support as people already expressed the opinion that Arab or English money is working in the matter. I must be very careful in such delicate things to be free from accusations. I have, therefore, applied for a job as interpreter and guide in your Committee, which, up till now, was not granted to me. Anyhow, any support you could give me in form of office work to be done by your staff or a car put at my disposal would facilitate my work considerabl[y].

Another most important thing would be to grant me an immediate interview to explain to you the various points of my memorandum verbally prior to my speech so that you will have the full information in case something happens to me and this information will go with me to the grave.

Looking forward to your early news, I beg to remain, Sir,
Yours faithfully,
[Signed] J. W. Abileah.

A preliminary interview was in fact granted to Joseph, and he talked with one C. Stavropoulous in private at the UNSCOP office in Jerusalem about his memorandum. After Stavropoulous made a report to the committee, Joseph was told on July 17 that his testimony would no longer be needed.

It is impossible to know what was in the Stavropoulous report, but it is not hard to guess that Joseph's agitated state of mind was clear to this UN functionary. Perhaps the committee was trying to guard his personal safety, but it is more likely that they had already decided against giving serious consideration to his proposal. In any case, Joseph was not in the best of shape to make the public presentation. One day in June, after the memorandum had been completed at the Nassar Hotel, Joseph went for a walk, but he was suddenly seized by two men, who took him to Dr. Blumenthal's sanatorium (where he had also been kept for observation in 1936). Joseph was furious to be held in the sanatorium against his will, especially when he thought he would be testifying in Jerusalem. He blamed his family for doing this to him, though he later discovered that his doctors, consulting with Dinah's obstetrician, had ordered it. In the end, the enforced two weeks' rest did him a great deal of good, and he felt vindicated when the chief doctor's diagnosis was that there was nothing mentally or physically wrong with him except that he was, in the doctor's words, "a fanatic for truth." This phrase was a particularly apt one, especially if one remembers Joseph's quarrels with his father over the 1944 tax returns or those with his mother-in-law, who once had deceived him about the wages she was paying an Arab servant girl. She knew that Joseph insisted on paying Arabs wages that were equal to those of Jews, and she told him when she hired the young Arab girl that she was following his instructions. When he discovered that Mrs. Yarmus had not told him the truth, he moved out of the house for three weeks.

In the hospital, feeling betrayed by his family and fearing that his vision of a united Palestine would be shattered by the obvious preparations for civil war, he was lifted from his own problems by his attentiveness to the problems of others. The problem of one particular patient is worth mentioning because it reminds us that music continued to be a powerful, peaceful force in his life at this time. A young woman had entered the hospital and had not spoken a word for more than a month. Doctors feared that her condition might become permanent. Her doctor told Joseph that she had loved music but that her parents had kept her from it. She especially loved to play the violin, and when her father in a fit of rage had broken her violin before her eyes, something in her snapped as well. Knowing that Joseph was a musician, her doctor asked Joseph to talk to the girl. Joseph entered her room with his violin under his arm and placed it between them on the table. As she looked at it, her eyes lit up, much as the eyes of the shepherd on the top of Mount Carmel had done. When Joseph held out the violin to her and asked if she would like to play it, she said, "Yes," the first word she had spoken. This one word of affirmation seemed to unlock a torrent of other words, and they spoke together for more than three hours. Thereafter Joseph gave her lessons every day until she was released. Soon after he received word from UNSCOP that his oral testimony would not be required, he received a letter from her, dated July 21, stating that her father was very angry with Joseph's meddling and forbade any further communication. Her heartfelt thanks to him for understanding how important music was to her was further proof to Joseph that there must be a link between music and the human heart. He wrote back to her on July 30 and told her, "a hurt heart can feel your heart," but this letter was intercepted by her father, who wrote a sharp response to Joseph, with a thinly veiled threat to his family if he persisted in communicating with his daughter. Joseph realized that his intercession on her behalf had strengthened him in dealing with his own troubles and disappointments. Further, her appreciation for his act of kindness balanced his outrage at having been committed against his will.

The threat made by the girl's father was an unnecessary complication to the very real threat already present. Joseph was not the only one to suffer during these months. Dinah had had a rough time giving birth to Dani and felt deserted by Joseph when she needed him most. It was cold comfort to her that he was working on his memorandum to UNSCOP while she was so weak that she could not care for her own child. She had to leave him in the care of a nurse to go to a rest home in Ramat Gan. From there she wrote Joseph, confessing that his activities had taken a great toll on her emotional and physical resources. She wrote of the need to rest "in body and in spirit," and longed for the time when Joseph would cease his mad activities and return to build a life for his family. Plaintively she ended her letter with concern about when she could be a real mother to Dani and when she would regain strength from the blood she lost "for him and for" Joseph.

When Joseph was released from Dr. Blumenthal's sanatorium and went to Jerusalem instead of returning directly to Haifa, Dinah wrote to Joseph on July 23, in a weary tone, that she was not strong enough to accompany him to Jerusalem; she needed rest before returning to work on August 1. On top of her physical problems, she now had to worry about how to feed her children since Joseph had suspended all his music lessons and had used up his little savings so that he could devote himself to gathering information for his UNSCOP presentation. While she sensed a real crisis in their marriage and urged Joseph to contact Bishop Stewart to be a sort of intermediary between them, Dinah had little energy for confronting the problem directly. She ended her letter by wishing Joseph success in his work, stating that she was taking up the piano again, and finally reminding Joseph that he had not yet arranged for Dani's birth certificate. Joseph was not unaffected by the sorrow that was transparent in the letter, but he stayed in Jerusalem, doggedly pursuing his activity.

Everyone in his family criticized him for his neglect of Dinah and the two boys. He wrote angry, often-defiant replies to them. One to his sister Julia reveals his passionate hatred of all forms of nationalism, a hatred that led him to commit himself to political activity. Joseph told Julia in this letter that he was about to become more public and vocal in his criticism of the form of nationalism espoused by both Arab and Jew. He went on to say, "A prominent doctor of Haifa called me a fanatic for truth. This I am and shall remain all my life even for the price of my head, fortune and family. I will not change and will fight my work of peace with the fanaticism of a semitic person.

I have much to report [to] you on my private life too, but there is no time now for such things. We have to avoid the partition plan at any rate, otherwise the country will be in fire very soon and no future for our children here."

On October 28, 1947, Joseph expanded on the remarks in

the August letter, referring to his relatives now as "dear opponents." His anguish had not in any way diminished.

You asked me if I have ever stopped to think whether I have the right to devote my life to my ideas. Has any man of my age stopped to think about his family when he enrolled in any of the different armies which fought during the war? He was sent to Egypt, embarked for different countries of the continent to carry a rifle and kill other fathers of families or to lose his own life for the sake of imperialistic interests of some great powers and for the prosperity of the war industry. As time has shown, these "Idealists" of our country have not even fought for their own nation. Nationalism as a whole is an idea of egoism enlarged to a great scale and I would never agree to educate my children as Jews in the sense of Judaism as it is understood in our generation *viz* a national unit. A religion must not be confounded and mixed with national ideas as it has always been done, bringing with it so much suffering to the people who belonged to this community. Our greatest true Jew, Jesus of Nazareth, was the highest ethical genius who ever lived and he preached against the national religion. I am very much in his line and nevertheless not a Christian, as the European churches failed to accomplish the spirit of his high ideals to influence the ways of living and politics effectively. We must try in this country to revive his true spirit and so live according to a complete and developed religion and not transplant the spirit of Hitler to this country. A man who has much influence on my thought and conception of matters is the great living musician and philosopher, Dr. Albert Schweitzer, of Lambaréné (Gaboun [sic], Equatorial Africa), previously of Alsace. I range among his numerous disciples and admirers. Occasionally I will send you his Philosophy of Civilization [sic] and if I will have more leisure to write, I will also send you an essay on my religious philosophy.

You can easily understand that with the above convictions I have difficulties with my wife, who is of a nationalistic family who previously belonged to the Revisionist party. I have been away from home for the last few months in order to be able to work. In the meantime I have lost a number of my students and am in a worse financial position now. I want to find a new job but am pending the decision of my physician regarding an operation on my appendix which worried me several times this year. I am back at home now but despite the kind treatment and love I enjoy am not feeling well in the atmosphere and therefore accepted some students at Jerusalem in order to respire from time to time and keep up my connections in the capital. . . .

As regards my personal safety I emphasize again that all what I am doing is not more dangerous than to enroll in an army or participate in the Haganah or be stabbed down or bombed unconsciously as a civilian. The partition plan is good for you Americans who are safe in your country and will not be present at the terrible bloodshed and/or economical depression which will follow its realization. I will write more about it to Rudi [Joseph's brother-in-law].

I thank you for the congratulations for the birth of Daniel. He is not brought up at home because his mother is obliged to continue to work until I find a proper job. But if I will see him grow up as a good Jew in your nationalistic sense I would rather never see him at home at all.

I am annexing some parts of my detailed memorandum to the UNSCOP and will send you further stuff later. I am doing almost all the typing work by myself in the houses of my Arab friends and other persons who encourage me in my work.

I hope to hear from you soon so that our correspondence will be maintained and remain with all my love

Your
[signed] Willi

The month of August was spent in continued activity in and around Jerusalem. Almost in desperation, he wrote the following letter to King Abdullah. As was the fate of all his letters sent to Jordan, this one received no answer. It it worth including here for what it reveals about his frame of mind as he made a somewhat-exaggerated appeal to the King's emotions—an appeal that reveals Joseph's conviction that people of the Orient are best appealed to through their hearts and instincts.

To His Majesty
King Abdullah I of Trans-Jordan
Royal Palace
Amman, Trans-Jordan.

Haifa, 16th August 1947.

Your Majesty,

At the occasion of the blessed Feast please accept, Majesty, my hearty wishes to you and to my dear brothers, your esteemed subjects.

I had the opportunity to visit your palace in the year 1936 and to present my wishes personally for the Great Feast. Your first vezir, Ibrahim Pasha Hashem, then told me after a short conversation: Are you a Jew? I answered: Yes, Sir. Then he made reply: You are a hundred times welcome, please enter. These words and the extraordinary kind treatment I enjoyed from the part of your subjects the following days, inspired to me the idea that your people might be ready for a co-operation with your Palestinian neighbours should the approach be gentle and made with mutual understanding.

With this conviction I have been working now since at the idea of uniting Palestine and Trans-Jordan under your most esteemed leadership.

We have seen in the course of this time the disturbances of the years 1936–1939, then came the war and we also took a small share in the sufferings of the world. We are not yet cured from the great wounds these hard years inflicted to us and the country is again in fire.

Please accept this letter as a cry from your neighbours. Come to our help and restore peace in the country. Please help us to fight the undesirable institutions as the Zionist movement and the like.

It will not be necessary to pour the blood of your men. The fear your well trained army will inspire to the people will make them stop instantly the hostilities started.

We will then form a Palestinian government under your most distinguished rulership, a government based on religious principles.

The trust and confidence many people have in your loyalty and democracy which you have shown so many times during the period of your reign will help to bring about the so long awaited peace to the Holy Country.

The present Mandatory government will withdraw its intern[al] administration as soon as the Haifa port and the Oil concessions are assured to them. In this respect they only trust your Majesty as you have shown to them your faithfulness in their hardest days of wartime.

You are the only king at present in the Middle East who is able to save the situation and help [in] founding a great and prosperous kingdom based on the wisdom of the prophets.

Dear King Abdullah, hear our cry for help. Save us in this difficult situation and God will reward you and your people. You are the man chosen by God to accomplish this hard task. Follow the cry of a sinking people and help to bring them back to their God whom they have left and who has left them.

At least allow me to mention a phrase said by the late King Feissal to Samy Shawa, the famous musician: The language of the violin is the language which all people understand.

Being myself a musician, I hope one day to visit you again in your palace and if I will not be able to speak to you in Arabic, I will communicate you in sounds the immense sufferings of our people and pray you to save us. Your heart of a poet will hear this language in which we speak from heart to heart and will induce you to listen to its commands which is the order of God to us.

May God give you many years of good health, to you and to all those who will accomplish the task of bringing peace to the Middle East and give an example to the fighting nations of the world to solve their problems in peace.

Your great admirer in Palestine
[signed] J. W. Abileah

Although he returned to Haifa in August, he was uncomfortable at home and spent a great deal of time traveling to propagate his ideas. In September, on the eve of Yom Kippur, he decided to make another trip to what is now known as the West Bank. He began his trip with a visit to Mrs. Arafat of

Nablus, a woman he had met in the hospital in Haifa. While in her home, he asked about the possibility of visiting the hot salt springs at Wadi Maleh, a spa going back to Roman times, which lay almost in the Jordan Valley, some fourteen kilometers east of the small town of Tubas. He had no other reason for his visit than curiosity stemming from an insatiable thirst for sight-seeing. His friends were horrified. Nablus was not on the best of terms with the Jewish population, but the villages and countryside were very hostile indeed, especially since recent clashes between Arabs and Jews in Jaffa and Tel Aviv. When it became clear to the Arafat family that Joseph could not be dissuaded from his journey, they told him that they knew a certain Abu Hashem in Tubas who would guarantee Joseph's personal safety. Joseph believed that he was perfectly safe under the Arab code of safety for guests and had no hesitation in immediately setting out for Tubas. By chance, he and his host met Abu Hashem in a café in Nablus. Mr. Arafat explained Joseph's desire to visit the springs, and Abu Hashem rather reluctantly offered to take him to Tubas.

When they arrived at Tubas, Abu Hashem took Joseph to his home, but when they sat down, Joseph noted that he was offered neither coffee nor tea. For the first time, he began to feel uneasy; such a breach in the rules of hospitality could only mean that he was not fully accepted as a guest. His apprehension increased when Abu Hashem advised against the excursion to the springs because four people from his village had just been killed in Jaffa. When he went on to say that one of the men killed was his own cousin, Joseph became truly worried, knowing that the responsibilities of hospitality were in conflict with those of revenge. Furthermore, as a leading citizen of Tubas, Abu Hashem was closely observed by the villagers, who by now must have been aware that the stranger in his home might be Jewish. In spite of his apprehensions, Joseph drew himself together and accepted calmly, as he had done at the well in 1936, whatever fate awaited him. It crossed his mind that, in some ways, his death might atone for the murders caused by his Jewish brothers. He reached this sense of calm while resting alone in a room in which he had been put. But the fragile nature of this calm was made clear to him when he jumped as the wind banged a door shut. Thinking it might have been a shot, he was startled when his host entered the room immediately after the sound. However, when he was simply asked to join Abu Hashem for a cup of coffee, his fears began to dissipate. These fears were aroused again toward evening when several merchants from Transjordan arrived, each accompanied by two Bedouin guards who were heavily armed. The guards kept their hands on their daggers and stared at Joseph, who by now was sure he should never have left Haifa. With the approach of night, and with only one flickering kerosene lamp to light the room, huge shadows ran up the walls and gripped Joseph's imagination as tightly as the Bedouin had their daggers.

Joseph knew he was in no imminent danger when his host asked him to break bread with all those assembled in his house. Sharing bread and salt traditionally indicated acceptance of the code of hospitality, and Joseph began to relax and enjoy his food as Abu Hashem proposed to drive him to the spring that night and to leave him with a guide while he himself transacted some business with the men from Transjordan. When Joseph boarded the truck that was to take him down into the valley, his guide told him to tell anyone who asked that he was Armenian. For once, Joseph's fanaticism for truth did not keep him from telling a lie. Joseph suspected that the men were going to collect an arms shipment in preparation for their war with the Jews, but all they told him was that they were "doing some work against the government." Joseph tried to make light conversation and told his host that this was the first time he had ever taken a desert bath at midnight. His host turned to him sharply and asked if he were afraid. Joseph replied without hesitation that he put his complete trust in his host's protection. The host looked away, staring in silence into the night.

The road from Tubas to Wadi Maleh drops about twelve hundred feet, and after they passed the small village of Tayassir, the barren land stretched out before them in the bright moonlight. Joseph's mind wandered back to the Roman times when the bath was built in Wadi Maleh, and the ruined terraces he passed reminded him that there was a time in the past when men had carved an existence out of hostile terrain. If they had done so, he mused, could not this same land support a more dense population in the future?

Joseph and his guide were dropped off, and the truck, with its smugglers aboard, rattled off towards the Jordan River. It occurred to Joseph that perhaps he knew too much about the village's activities, but he joined his guide as they followed the light of a small kerosene lamp and approached a modern concrete structure built over the Roman site. Before entering the water, the guide boasted to Joseph that he was a great user of hashish then burst out in a song in honor of his guest. When he finished, Joseph said, "*Salem tummak*" (blessed be your mouth), which pleased the man so much that he sang the song again as Joseph let himself down into the Roman basin. The harmony of the song, echoing in the concrete shelter, made Joseph once again aware not only of his affinity with the Arab people but of his affinity with all men and women once differences in religious, national, and social backgrounds could be stripped away. His nakedness did not make him feel defenseless but, in fact, more at one with all living things. He felt separated from the other man only by skin color, a color that his own forefathers must have shared before their diaspora in the cold and sunless countries of the north.

Thus, when the man broke off his singing and unexpectedly asked Joseph to dive underwater, Joseph did not hesitate for a moment or show any fear at the strange command. If it had been a test of trust, he must have passed it, for his guide asked him to get dressed to meet the truck. When the truck did not appear, Joseph curled up in his towel and *khaffieh* (Arab head cloth) and slept, confident that he would be safe and at one both with his guide and with the land that stretched to the hills of Gil'ad, where more than a decade before he had experienced a similar feeling of union. The turmoil of the previous months seemed far removed, and the dark rumblings of the coming months seemed not quite so ominous.

The truck came at dawn and took them back to the village. His host still seemed uneasy and asked Joseph if he would mind having his breakfast in the village square. Joseph agreed and proceeded to share his meal with any who passed by. There were many passers-by since the whole village seemed curious about the stranger. His time there was marred by a man who approached him with a rope in his hands. It was clear that his intention was to harm Joseph, perhaps even to hang him, but when Joseph looked into his eyes and welcomed him as a brother to share his bread, the man dropped the rope and disappeared. Thereafter, Joseph entertained the villagers by reading his August letter to King Abdullah, which was greeted with great enthusiasm by the villagers, who by now knew they had an unarmed and solitary Jew in their midst. When Joseph left the village with his host, he felt he had made many friends. As he walked the road from Nablus to Jenin, he was happy that, in the midst of such upheaval as the end of the mandate was causing, he had once again tapped the roots of hospitality, friendship, and brotherhood and that he had found that the nonviolent ways of love were the means by which these roots could grow.

This feeling was deeply religious for him, as if he had discovered the flame of God burning within the hearts of those who knew what it was to be fortunate to live in a holy land. This spiritual experience sustained him in the weeks and months ahead and became a strong foundation for the sort of religious socialism and spiritual Zionism he later espoused so wholeheartedly. His brand of socialism was a simple sharing of the more fortunate with the less so, not a socialism in which the less fortunate sought to expropriate the position of those who were better off. As before, what struck him most from this experience was not the goal so much as the importance of the way to that goal.

Hans Kohn, one of Martin Buber's closest friends and his

biographer, had left Palestine in 1929, after the riots in Hebron, because he felt that Zionism as a spiritual movement was dying. He had come to the conviction that Zionism no longer believed that a good and just end required good and just means. It is worth quoting some of his letter of farewell to Zionism, because he articulates well Joseph's own belief both in 1947 and now. The crucial difference is that Joseph stayed to fight for another way, truer to the goals of spiritual Zionism.

> The means determine the goal. If lies and violence are the means, the results cannot be good. . . . We have been in Palestine for twelve years without having even once made a serious attempt at seeking through negotiations the consent of the indigenous people. . . . I believe that it will be possible for us to hold Palestine and continue to grow for a long time. This will be done first with British aid and then later with the help of our own bayonets—shamefully called Haganah—clearly because we have no faith in our own policy. But by that time we will not be able to do without the bayonets. The means will have determined the goal. Jewish Palestine will no longer have anything of that Zion for which I once put myself on the line.

Almost twenty years later, Joseph Abileah was fighting to convince those already sharpening their bayonets that it was not too late to renounce the means of violence. When he suffered appendicitis later that November, right before the fateful UN decision to partition Palestine, he had time to reflect on all his experiences and began an autobiography, which he called "My Faith in the Human Heart." The autobiography was never completed, but his faith in the human heart continued to give direction to his life. His journal entry of November 15 and 16, 1947, has a quality that is as true for him today as it was forty years ago. That the hope expressed there has not been fulfilled reflects more the nature of the world than the quality of the vision itself. Like Beethoven's music, Joseph had faced the sadness and chaos of the world directly. This period in his life was like the early part of a Beethoven symphony, when the conflict is articulated but not yet resolved. He ended his hospital reflections in the following way:

> What is the use of arms nowadays when one atomic bomb can destroy a whole well-fitted army? Is it not time to turn to spiritual powers which are stronger than arms? We are competing in a senseless armament, killing from time to time people in order to test arms and keep them working. The end will be that we shall send all our money to the arms factories of Europe and America, kill one another and be defenseless as soon as the great powers see *we* are too strongly armed and disarm us by using an atomic bomb. What is that hatred preached throughout the country to two peoples of the same race? One group of people must put down their arms first. Let us be heroic in this. If we have the power to forgive and forget everything and stretch our hands for peace, we shall have given an example to the world which might lead to disarmament and world peace. We can then say that the people of Israel are people chosen by God to save the world by their example of love and forgiveness, as one of us had done—over 1900 years ago.

The conditions of November 1947 made the fulfillment of this hope seem very distant indeed. On November 29, the United Nations accepted the UNSCOP recommendation to partition Palestine. Thirty nations had been represented on the committee. Of these thirty nations, eleven were commissioned to formulate the proposal to be put forth to the UN General Assembly. One of the eleven, Australia, withdrew, and of the remaining ten, three commissioned Dr. Ralph Bunche, secretary of UNSCOP, to draft an alternative to the partition plan. This proposal, the Minority Report, called for a confederation plan. The Minority Report lost November approval, and partition was accepted by the UN. Joseph greeted the news not with surprise but with sadness. All his frantic activity had failed to prevent what he foresaw would be a tragedy. Still, he did not stop his struggle against the partition, hoping that somehow it might not be implemented.

Within his family, Joseph's father too feared the outbreak of war and hoped it could be averted; but unlike his son, he welcomed the partition. Not unlike Joseph, Ephraim was fond of constructing detailed plans on how states might function in an era of peace, and in his unpublished writings, he makes it clear that the utopia he devised in the Mödling forests in World War I could be applied to the Middle East as well. Though he held a patronizing attitude towards the Arabs, who he felt stood in great need of the benefits of the "higher" Hebrew culture, Ephraim was generally interested in reconciliation, certainly on a person-to-person level, especially as it might be achieved through the activities of the Freemasons.

Ephraim expressed this opinion in a piece he wrote in September 1947, perhaps as an address to his lodge, in which he was a master. In this short prose work, he describes a vision he said he experienced on the balcony of the home of one of his piano students, an Arab woman named Mrs. Tumah. Looking from her balcony, Ephraim saw a great light, like that from the atomic bomb, appear over Haifa Bay. In that light, he saw the figures of Jesus, Moses, and Mohammed coming towards him. Jesus spoke to him first and urged him to be active in the formation of the new nations, because he had much to offer them. Jesus reminded him that three major events in his life had prepared him to strive for cooperation now between the new Jewish and Arab states. The first was his writing of "The Power of Love." There he had learned of the unity of all human beings, and that lesson should enable him now to see that Arabs and Jews, people of the same race, should be able to cooperate with one another. The second event was the visit in 1921 that Ephraim made at the age of forty to his father's grave. This visit occurred before Ephraim left for Palestine in 1923, and at the graveside, Ephraim had promised his father that he would act in his spirit once he had arrived in the Holy Land. The third event of which Jesus spoke was Ephraim's composition of three songs—"You Love Your Neighbor as Yourself," "God Will Be King of the Whole World and His Name Will Be Love," and "Love of the World, the House of Israel." Because of these three experiences, Jesus said that he had chosen Ephraim to act in the language of love. He approached Ephraim as a master in the Freemason's lodge and gave him the craft's traditional kiss. After Jesus spoke, Moses and Mohammed approached Ephraim and affirmed the words of Jesus. Moses stated his intentions of working with the Jews and Mohammed his of working with the Arabs.

This "vision," probably a metaphorical one only, was intended to encourage the Arab and Jewish members of all the lodges in Palestine to work in a common effort. The ideas informing this vision are very much Joseph's own, but Joseph saw the partition plan as the gravest danger to the sort of union the vision talked about bringing into being. Instead of a place of refuge and light, Joseph's fear was that the creation of two states would make Palestine a place of enmity and fire. In the end, he was more right than his father, though he took no pride or joy in the accuracy of his predictions.

Even though the partition plan was passed, Joseph worked for its repeal, especially when the violence he so clearly saw coming began in earnest and when the clandestine arms he had urged the British to control were brought out of hiding. Though his brothers had joined military units, including seventeen-year-old Benjamin, Joseph steadfastly refused to take up arms. At the end of December, he issued "A Call," in which some of his longings are set forth. In it can be seen the strands of a spiritual Zionism that link him clearly with Ahad Ha'am, Judah Magnes, and Martin Buber. What cannot be seen in this call is the torment he was undergoing. With this call, the year of madness, 1947, came to an end; but the madness remained.

A Call
Written in Haifa on the 31st of December 1947

A well-known German writer living in Haifa once told me: "Why, when speaking of Arabs, you say "cousins" and not "brothers"? Investigations made by scientists have aroused the supposition that the Palestinian Arab population is in the main part composed of remnants of the ten tribes of Israel lost and scattered many centuries ago."

I have always felt such an inclination towards the Arabs which cannot be explained but by blood relation. And so are many like me who are only ashamed to confess because of the nationalism taught to them from early youth which stops and kills all natural feeling.

If the case stands so, let us not hesitate to embrace them, kiss them and cry aloud: "Oh, our dear brothers and sisters, now we have found you, those tribes we are longing to meet for 2500 years. When we came to Palestine, 30 years ago, we did not recognize you. You were so poor, so neglected. How is it that we did not know you? Oh, dear brothers, take what we have of money and education. We will teach you technics and arts, languages and sciences. Your forefathers brought them to Europe through Spain some centuries ago and we have brought them back to you, farther developed and more advanced. Europe is not able to develop them any more. It is too poor now. Let us stick to the common inheritance and continue to build the civilization with our semitic energy and revive it by the spirit of the prophets who lived centuries ago in this country. Let us start the common work and look forward to a prosperous future when we will be able to feed Europe also with our surplus."

The reply of the Arabs to our call will be:

"Oh, dear brothers and sisters! Yes, we recognize you now. But how did you change while you were away! Your skin is white and your languages are different from our language. We did not know that you were our brothers as your manners were so strange to us. We welcome you now. Please sit down and have a coffee with us. We will then teach you to live according to the law of our common forefathers, to eat and dress according to the climate and economical possibilities of the country. There is no question of buying land. There is plenty for all of us; it must only be watered properly. Let us make a common irrigation system with the money with which you intended to nationalize areas of the Holy Country and we will be able to settle the Bedouins and the needy immigrants alike. Take off your hats. Cover your heads with "Hatta wa'agal" and let your thoughts be directed by hearts warmed in the Eastern sun.

> "PALESTINE IS THE PROMISED LAND FOR HUMANITY AND NOT FOR THE PEOPLE OF ISRAEL ALONE. IT IS THE PARADISE LOST BY THE SINFALL OF ADAM AND EVE, AND WILL BE REGAINED BY OUR COMMON WORK OF SOIL RECLAMATION AND RECONSTRUCTION, SACRIFICING OUR EFFORTS AS PENITENCE FOR THE REDEMPTION OF THE SINS OF THE WORLD!"
>
> Joseph W. Abileah

By February 1948, Haifa and all of Palestine were being ripped apart, far in advance of the May 15 target date for the end of the British Mandate. The British forces were caught in the middle as Arabs and Jews battled for strategic positions that would give them some advantage when what appeared to be inevitable and full-scale war took place. Joseph continued to try to draw the attention of the United Nations to the mistake it had made on November 29. There were in fact many nations who were having second thoughts, but the letter Joseph sent the secretary general on February 4, containing the following twelve points, did not have much effect.

J. W. Abileah
1, Herzlia St.
Haifa (Palestine)

Haifa, the 4th of February 1948

To the
Secretary General
U.N.O.
Lake Success, N.Y.

Re: *Palestine Problem*

Dear Sir,

With a view to the present dangerous situation in this country aroused by the decision in favour of the partition plan I beg to draw your kind attention to the memorandum submitted by me to the UNSCOP at the sojourn in Palestine and which met their consideration.

I have now amended my suggestions to read as follows:
1) Re-consideration of UNO decision and rejection of partition plan.
2) International and interconfessional immigration according to economic capacity.
3) Union of Palestine and Transjordan in one area under rulership of King Abdullah in order to enable the immigration.
4) If percentage of Jewish immigration will be too high, military precautions are to be taken in order to avoid possibility of proclamation of a Jewish State in the future.
5) King Abdullah may accept members of any community in his advisory council in which an adviser of international reknown appointed by the UNO will participate for control of external politics.
6) Complete disarmament of local population including discharge of Palestinians serving at present in police and military units, operations to be carried out solely by military units actually stationed in the country and/or international reinforcements from abroad in cooperation with the Arab Legion.
7) Execution of great soil conservation and irrigation works (Lowdermilk scheme) which may serve as example for other countries in the M.E. as for Iraq in diverting the Euphrates to the Syrian desert.
8) Present and future interests of foreign nations in Palestine to be secured by concessions as regards exploitation of natural resources and building of factories.
9) Representatives of all religious communities in governmental body.
10) Abolition of Jewish Agency as political representation of the members of the Jewish community as well as restrictions of Moslem Supreme Council to religious duties.
11) Large scale educational scheme having for aim a common education to all Palestinians with full consideration of the religious peculiarities of each community. Such education should begin with common art lessons, common sports, common Scout movement, playgrounds for children and common Kindergartens. Further common agricultural schools.

12) Health department and social welfare to be put entirely under Government control.

I hereby, beg you to re-consider the above in the light of the present situation.

Upon your request I shall be glad to furnish you with further details and documents as well as information regarding my activity in connection therewith.

Looking forward to the honour of your reply I beg to remain, Dear Sir,

Yours very respectfully,
[signed] J. W. Abileah

Copy to:—
The Chief Secretary
Government of Palestine
Jerusalem.

A reading of these twelve points shows how Joseph thought not just in terms of stopping war—what one might call a negative approach to peace—but also how he looked towards the future, especially in his irrigation schemes and in his desire for a common education, one stressing mutual respect for religious differences.

Joseph wrote letters in a much sharper tone to his own family. One written on February 8 gives a good idea of the situation in Haifa. It is also remarkable in that it reveals the only time when Joseph seriously thought about leaving the country. He soon gave up thoughts of emigrating and resolutely decided to stay to fight for his ideals and for what he in "A Call" termed "the redemption of the sins of the world."

Haifa, February 8th, 1948

My dear folks,

I have not yet received your answers but am nevertheless writing you again as events in Palestine have justified the views expressed in my previous letters.

Where are the Americans who wish to avoid the bloodshed of "Jewish Blood" as Rudi says? Is it a consolation for us that also Arab citizens are killed and their families destroyed?

The situation is horrible. People are killed every day in every part of the town and the country. We are living in a Ghetto in order not to expose ourselves to danger but are neither safe here. Papa and Mama keep their shop closed since the beginning of December 1947 (and so many other business men). They have lost 20 students and I myself have less than half of my previous income. I am earning approximately the cost of living for one of my children. For the other four heads of the family Dinah must provide with her salary. To earn this she exposes herself every day to danger going down town to the office. A bomb exploded some weeks ago near her office at the bus station where she is waiting for the bus and several people were killed—one hour after she left the station. Rudi lives at Neve Shaanan quarter and the convoy going there was attacked and several people killed some days ago just one hour before he had to go home. So Clara was in a bus which was attacked by a bomb and she was saved by a wonder. We are living by chance and do not know what will happen tomorrow—and with all this Ultra-Nationalistic aspirations are enhanced by the UNO and the U.S.A. in order to aggravate the situation and have a chance to sell more arms.

Regarding myself you can imagine that I am in a terrible situation. I cannot co-operate in the up-building of a national state as it is entirely contrary to my convictions. So I am fighting against it—on the paper. I have written a number of letters and essays and will send you by ordinary mail a copy of the fifth part and closing chapter of my "Call for Arab-Jewish Collaboration" which I intend to publish in three languages. I urgently ask Rudi to offer the travelling stories to some paper if it is only for a few dollars. It will be some help for me in my difficult financial situation.

Now regarding my future in this country, it is obvious that I have nothing to do here if—God beware—the Jewish State becomes a reality. The Nationalist groups will try to put to trial and condemn persons who publicly fought against the National State. So I must escape from here as soon as possible. I am trying to have a job with the International Red Cross Society as interpreter but am not sure to be accepted there. Could you take me over to the U.S. to try my luck there as clerk or—musician? There, of course, I think I will stop my political activity as nobody will oblige me to participate in the up-building of a nation-state. Think it over please and send me your opinion as soon as possible. I could take over my family later if I am successful until I will have the opportunity to immigrate to Transjordan where I am sure to find good jobs as teacher for languages or something else.

I am awaiting your early reply which I hope will still reach me at home and remain with all my love

Your
[signed] Willi

As Joseph points out, the turmoil in Haifa had left him almost without pupils. Because of his bookkeeping skills, he was able to get a job in the early spring of 1948 with the railways, figuring out pensions for employees who would be paid by the British once the mandate had ended. The dangers of getting to work, mentioned in the February 8 letter, were multiplied now because his office was in the Arab section of town. As he had done in 1936–39, Joseph had to crawl across dangerous street intersections to get to work. So did his Arab coworkers, who explained to him that much of the firing came from Arab irregulars who had slipped into Haifa from villages in the Galilee and, in some cases, from other Arab countries.

The eighty thousand Arab citizens of Haifa had had a harmonious relationship, by and large, with their Jewish fellow citizens, and the Sephardic mayor of Haifa, Shabetay Levy, spent a great deal of time and energy urging both sides to remain at peace. Since Haifa was, even at this time, being "liberated" by Jewish forces, even before the official beginning of the Jewish state, it was difficult for the Arab residents to stay as calm and steadfast as Mayor Levy had requested. Most feared for the safety of their families and left the city, hoping to return when the troubles were over. In the end, only five to ten thousand stayed, and the houses of those who fled were savagely plundered and then confiscated. Families like the Farsoons, the Nassars, the Jabers—the parents of more than half of Joseph's pupils—left Haifa with little more than they could carry. When visiting a Baha'i house in Acre, Joseph found that even the copper tubing in the walls had been ripped out.

Of course the robbery and looting were not one-sided. When Joseph was shifted from the accounting office to the railway stores, soon after independence, he discovered while taking inventory that Arab workers had stolen as much as they could before leaving the stores. As he inventoried what was left with other Jewish workers, he saw the robbery continue. War seemed to be breaking down all the civilized restraints under which society normally operated. For example, if there were three hammers in stock, one would be taken and two would be officially listed as inventory. One day his colleagues came up with two whistles and told Joseph to take them to his sons. Joseph said that, if he wanted whistles, he would stop at a toy store. This made him the butt of many jokes at work—the man who would not even take whistles for his children. Those at work did not seem to realize that Joseph's honesty, his commitment to truth, gave him stability, an anchor in a world that seemed to be slipping towards chaos. Ironically, this story of the whistles was responsible for him being offered the position of first deputy in the stores' management: the Israeli chief storekeeper said that Joseph was the only one whose honesty was unquestionable.

This same officer came to Joseph one day in June to tell him that he had received orders to list all men working for him who had not yet done military service. The new state of Israel was now at war with the surrounding Arab nations and needed to mobilize all men. Even though a law had just been passed on conscription, the officer offered to lie for Joseph because he knew that, if he wrote Joseph's name down, it would cost Joseph his job and possibly lead to a term in jail. Joseph refused to have anyone lie for him and prepared himself for what he knew was coming—his confrontation as a pacifist with the state whose existence he had so long opposed. It did not occur to him that there were others in his situation, and he later learned that most pacifists had either left the country or had had quiet trials. One of his former students was being tried for resistance to war, and Joseph was asked to appear as a witness. The lawyers warned Joseph that, if he expressed his own views in court, he could expect immediate arrest. As one would expect, Joseph insisted on testifying. In court, the defense lawyer told the judges he had warned Joseph not to appear, but that, since he had known the risk and yet appeared, the court would have to admit that his evidence was credible. The young man, Eric Schiffman, was found guilty and sentenced to an indefinite period of hard labor—until the end of the war.*

Just as he was warned, Joseph's arrest followed on the heels of the Schiffman trial. Joseph's reaction to his arrest is revealing. He was taken to a small police station on Khoury Street and was told he would be spending the night. He did not argue or resist arrest but only asked the guard for a blanket and asked him if he "would be so kind to call my wife." The guards were moved by his gentleness and ended up bringing him seven blankets, which he shared with others in his cell. The quality of meekness, which seems to strike Joseph's opponents in almost every situation of potential conflict with him, has often disarmed his most angry critics. But it must be said, also, that his meekness is not submissiveness but rather the quality described by Aristotle as *proates*, the mean between excessive anger and submission, a quality that allows one, as St. Paul put it, to waive one's rights but to hold on to principles. Moses, in Numbers 12:3, was called the meekest man on earth, and

---

*Actually, Schiffman's case was very interesting. He had maintained his Austrian passport and asked to be repatriated rather than serve his prison term. The court granted him his request, but when he returned to Austria, he discovered that anti-Semitism had not died. In a despairing mood, he went to Switzerland and got a job instructing young European Jews about to make *aliyah*. After a few years, he changed his name and returned to Israel as a new immigrant. He performed military service and now lives in a kibbutz in the Galilee. Like many Israelis, he honors Joseph without necessarily believing in his ideas any longer.

it is in that tradition of meekness that Joseph must be placed. If meekness is the mean between hot temper and submission, then it is also true that Joseph is the mean between the temperament of his father and of his mother.

Schiffman had been an obscure waiter, whose sentence probably reflected his having gone into hiding to avoid conscription. Joseph's views were widely known, and his family was a prominent one in Haifa. The authorities decided to publicize his trial to show everyone that even the most privileged persons could not avoid the draft. Many lawyers came to Joseph's house to ask to handle his defense. His reply to each of them was, "If I plan to tell the truth, why do I need my own lawyer?" On August 30, 1948, before a tribunal of five judges, in a hot room packed with spectators, Joseph's trial took place. No one from his family attended the trial, except for a cousin of Dinah's. As he had done so many times in the past, Ephraim tried to protect Joseph by contacting a doctor who worked at the recruiting office and who then offered to declare Joseph medically unfit. Joseph indignantly refused this offer and, in fact, revealed that it had been made to him (without mentioning the doctor's name) in his opening statement in court.

He went to court fully expecting to go from there to prison. When he met Dinah's cousin in the corridor outside the courtroom, he was carrying a small bag. In response to the cousin's query about its contents, Joseph replied that he was taking his pajamas with him to jail. What he did not tell the cousin was that he had also packed several books on Hebrew grammar and on music theory. For a long time, Joseph had been trying to develop a theory regarding the connection between the laws of spoken language and the laws of harmony—perhaps building on what Dr. Schweitzer had done with the connection between words and music in Bach chorales. It says much of Joseph's calmness, determination, and sense of priority that he was almost looking forward to prison so that he could devote more time to his music. In an almost metaphorical fashion, he was also trying to find a harmony in the act of oral communication and self-expression that he knew existed in music.

On that sweltering August day, Joseph began his defense by noting that he was being accused of not serving in the Haganah even before there was a state of Israel and before Israeli law was in force. By not joining a clandestine military organization, he was merely obeying British law. Further, there was a municipal law in Haifa that he also would have broken had he participated in an armed struggle. Nevertheless, he agreed that after May 15, the birthdate of the nation-state of Israel, he had refused to appear at the recruiting office. He pointed out that he was not basing his defense on his compliance with British law, he just wanted to make the court aware of that fact. He continued by stating that, because of his work in Haifa, his appearance in 1947 before UNSCOP, and his refusal to help construct defense fortifications around Haifa, his pacifist position was well known. Having established that he had made no effort to conceal his objection to what he called the "unhappy war of brother against brother," Joseph went on to confront what he thought was a more serious, if unspecified, accusation than the one of merely avoiding service in the military. In anticipation of a line that the prosecutor would take later in the trial, Joseph rhetorically asked himself how he could stand by while the nation itself was imperiled, even at the moment of its birth, and while others were dying so that he could live in safety.

His answer to the accusation he made to himself involved establishing for the court how he came to his own worldview, a view he described as "Gandhism without the nationalistic component." Before a now-hushed court, Joseph recounted those experiences of his life that brought him to where he was in 1948. He began by mentioning Dr. Albert Schweitzer, whose philosophy of reverence for life had struck such a deep chord in him. When he read Schweitzer for the first time, he noted, he found expression for all the feelings that had been fostered in him by music and the natural world. As he explained it, Schweitzer had touched something hidden in his soul, put there by the experiences of his life in this holiest of all lands. Espousing a sort of universalism, at one with the kind of religious socialism in which he had always believed, Joseph went on to explain that his belief was consistent with what he saw to be the line of development in Jewish ethics from Moses through Jesus. He made it clear that he responded to the ethics of the Jesus of Nazareth not to the divinity of the Jesus of the Catholic church. Furthermore, he was especially drawn to the nonviolent personality of Jesus as it was manifested in the modern personalities of Schweitzer and Gandhi.

As he attempted to show for the court how the power of nonviolence had been revealed to him, Joseph drew upon his experience with the savage dog in the Jordan Valley, went on to the story at the well near Ben Shemen and at the springs of Wadi Maleh, and ended with a story of a recent episode near Um el Fahm, where he was stopped by a man as he walked with his brother Benjamin. This Arab, who had approached Joseph with a wrench raised in his hand, feared that Joseph had a bomb in his knapsack. Knowing that he was in some danger, yet not fearful of the man, Joseph reached into his pack and drew out some chocolate, which he offered to the menacing figure. "Please, my brother, help yourself," had been Joseph's first words. Immediately, the wrench had been lowered when the Arab sensed that he was neither in danger himself nor in the presence of an enemy. From this experience, Joseph told the court, he was confirmed in his belief that everyone possesses both a "good and a bad heart," that is, is capable of responding either to the good or to the bad. He was convinced that those who trust their instincts and feelings are more likely to respond to the good than are those who make decisions based solely on their intellect. Although some might find his Rousseauism sorely strained by modern history, he still feels that civilization, especially the sort that produces structures like the nation-state and exalts the life of the theorizing intellect and science, is more likely to stifle the spark in the human heart than to help make it glow. This belief is why he felt at home in the desert with the Bedouin and why he talked so animatedly about the Arab's ability to sense the truth intuitively, much as the desert watchdog sensed that he had nothing to fear from the man who sat down quietly before him.

Joseph's passionate defense of nonviolence and the obvious sincerity of his beliefs made an impression on the judges. Nonetheless, as the following verdict, presented in its entirety, reveals, they were not persuaded that there was much hope that his worldview could prevail in a world still numbed by the horrors of the Holocaust. Joseph had tried to explain that those who were fighting for the nation were not fighting on his behalf; rather, they were fighting for the benefit of some abstraction called *the state*. But the judges saw the case differently and ordered him to report for national service, though in a noncombatant capacity.

File No. 8/48

In the Supreme Court of the Recruiting Centre, Haifa.

SENTENCE

given at the session of the Supreme Court on the 25th Av 5709 (30.8.48)

The Judges: Adv. J. Klebanoff (Chairman), Dr. B. Avniel, Sh. Goldberg, J. Aharoni & Dr. S. Greenwald.

Public Prosecutor: Adv. J. Halevi.

THE PROSECUTOR AGAINST JOSEPH W. ABILEAH.

a) The Court after hearing the accusation and the defence of the defendant decided that the way of the defendant is erroneous and could, beware God, bring a disaster to the population if his way would have been followed. The defendant was also obliged to agree in reply to the questions of the judges that in our situation and special circumstances the population cannot take this way. However, as the whole nation, except of some outsiders, realize the situation, we can indulge ourselves to treat with utmost tolerance single cases of these erring people.

b) The Court disapprove the behavior of the defendant who up to today, over half a year, has found the courage not to participate in any form in the nation's struggle to stand for their life even in a form which is not opposed to his "conscientious" views of not using force. It is only by the great bravery of our fighters and soldiers that the defendant, his wife and his children could remain alive and that he could continue his regular way of living here in this situation.

1.—In view of the above we fix that the defendant is to be punished for his evading up till now to participate in a vital service in favour of the nation even not as a fighter. Therefore, the Court fine the defendant with LP.50. (Fifty Pal. Pounds) to the treasurer of the state. However, considering the special circumstances of the case, we postpone the execution of this judgment until he will have fulfilled his duty of national service and we allow in case of good behavior whilst in the service, according to our following sentence, to forgive this punishment.

2.—The defendant has to enter in the course of one week from today the recruiting centre and present himself for full service in a non-combatant charge as first aid, essential auxiliary service, etc.

3.—We fix that no use of arms and force has to be imposed upon him and he has to be released from any military training.

4.—If the defendant will not fulfil this judgement the Court order hereby to treat him as it is used to treat any shirker or deserter whose fault has been proved.

Sgd. [the above judges]

30.8.48

After the judgment was read, Joseph was given the opportunity to comment. He stated in clear tones that he did not accept the verdict. He could not accept noncombatant service, which he likened to the case of a thief who watched for the police while another thief performed the actual robbery. He then warned the court that, if he had to be on telephone duty as a noncombatant in the military and had to pass on a message that would involve him in the possibility of creating violence, he would not transmit the message. The judges, one of whom had been with Joseph's uncle in Russia, another of whom had been Dinah's employer, and a third of whom was later to serve on the governing board of the Haifa Symphony Orchestra, were unmoved by his response. They had already been as lenient as they felt they could and had disregarded the prosecutor's demand for a heavy sentence to discourage others from taking such a stand. When Joseph had finished his response, the judges ordered him to report for a medical examination.

Within a short period of time, Joseph was examined in a room of specialists, each of whom wrote a report on some aspect of his physical health. When he approached the final desk, reports in hand, the doctor in charge looked at him and said, "Oh, you're Abileah?" and without looking at the reports, stamped "unfit" on his health form. Joseph took this exemption and, a few days later, threw it in the wastepaper basket. He was not bothered again by the military until 1956, when he was once more examined by a panel. He agreed to this later appearance after the authorities had agreed that they would allow him to do civilian service and would give him a serious and objective physical examination. The second examination found him fit but deferred him for one year. At the end of this year, he received another deferment, and this series of deferrals continued until he was past the age of military service.

There had been several reporters at Joseph's trial, and most of the newspaper accounts were highly sarcastic, perhaps reflecting the fact that, in August 1948, Israel was still fighting for its right to exist as an independent state and did not want to give serious attention to dissidents. The August 31 edition of *Ha'Aretz* ran a story with the headline "A Jew, an admirer of Abdullah, refuses to register for reasons of conscience." Other papers referred to Joseph as one who talked about dogs and Gandhi. Several persons, not reporters, had followed the trial a little more attentively. One such person, Nathan Chofshi, the famous Tolstoyan pacifist from Nahallal, wrote Joseph to tell him of a group of people like himself who were members of the War Resisters International. He invited him to learn more about their group. On April 29, 1949, after meeting with Chofshi and beginning a friendship that was to last more than thirty years, Joseph wrote to the War Resisters International in England to apply for membership.

As 1949 drew to a close, Israel had established itself as a

state. The costs had been great. More than six thousand Jews had lost their lives, and more than seven hundred thousand Arabs had become refugees. The cosmopolitan world of Haifa no longer existed. Though the binational dreams of the Ihud had been shattered, there was still work to be done. This work could be done neither alone nor outside a political frame. It was time for the fanatic for truth to join forces with like-minded men and women.

5
A Task Worthy of Jews
1950–1967

> But the time has come for the Jews to take into account the Arab factor as the most important facing us. If we have a just cause, so have they. If promises were made to us, so were they to the Arabs. If we love the land and have a historical connection with it, so too the Arabs. Even more realistic than the ugly realities of imperialism is the fact that the Arabs live here and in this part of the world, and will probably be here long after the collapse of one imperialism and the rise of another. If we too wish to live in this living space, we must live with the Arabs, try to make peace with them. I do not know if this is possible. But this is a task worthy of Jews.
> —Judah Magnes, 1939

THE YEAR 1949 MARKED A CHANGE in Joseph's life. From the obscure violin teacher who pursued his quest for peace in a solitary fashion, unsupported by friends or family, he became one who sought the fellowship of like-minded thinkers and activists. Having been sought out by Nathan Chofshi and his small coterie of pacifists, Joseph soon assumed responsible positions in many organizations. He describes the years from 1950 to 1967 as being full of peace activities, not of political ones. By that he means that, during this period, he worked for reconciliation between individuals and small groups and not for a change in the political system.

For sixteen years, he was secretary to Nathan Chofshi, going to his home once a week to handle his English correspondence or accompanying him on trips to Arab villages as his translator. That Nathan Chofshi, a great man of peace, had come in the early part of the century to Palestine with other "vision-ridden" (Uri Davis's term) members of the Second Aliyah and had never learned Arabic reveals much about the development of the country. It might have been true that Chofshi's heart went out to all the oppressed, but he never learned how to communicate with them in their own language.

There is a beautiful story that illustrates the sad history of Arab-Jewish relations. Shortly after Joseph met Nathan Chofshi, Chofshi asked him to accompany him to Nazareth, where some Arab families had been sent after their village was taken over by new Jewish immigrants, who flooded the country after 1949. The inhabitants of this village had, in 1910, taken into their homes for a whole year the Jewish pioneers who were struggling to establish the settlement later known as Nahallal, when the pioneers were devastated by an epidemic of malaria. Chofshi never forgot this act of kindness and was full of remorse and guilt when the new Jewish state forced the inhabitants of this small village in the Galilee to leave their homes after the War of Independence. No one in Nahallal had spoken up for these villagers. For that matter, few Israelis spoke up for any of the villagers of the more than 390 Arab villages within the borders of the new state that were destroyed in these years. Joseph, the translator, had to be the one to find the language to express the remorse and to ask for the forgiveness. He was happy in this role, though not in his task, because he liked the idea of bringing two peoples together. This role of mediator, reconciler, and translator became one he assumed more and more in the following years.

It was also in 1949 that Joseph first learned about the Quakers from meeting Quaker volunteers who had come as relief workers to Acre ('Akko) soon after the cease-fire. The more he learned, the more he was drawn to the Quakers, especially to their commitment to nonviolence and constructive social action. As the following letter states, he also interested Chofshi in the Quaker movement, and in 1950, they both decided to join the Wider Quaker Fellowship.

1, Herzliah St.

April 8th, 1950

Wider Quaker Fellowship
20 South 12th Street,
Philadelphia 7, Pa.

Dear Friends,

Your papers about the Wider Quaker Fellowship have been handed to me by Eng. E. A. Glueckauf of Tel-Aviv.

In the sheet about Purpose, Membership and Program you say that many members have enrolled desiring to have the spiritual foundation of their Peace Testimony strengthened. Others because of the manner in which Friends express their religious faith in a program of social action. Still others to whom the Quaker mystical approach to God appealed. I should say that I [would] like to join the fellowship for all the three reasons which are in conformity with my philosophy and ways of life.

I am in close contact with the unit of the American Friends Service Committee working at Acre since over a year and although the people are exchanged there from time to time, I have had the opportunity to make good friendship with a number of Friends and their co-operators at the unit. I have further been acquainted with the Quaker principles through the reading of literature received from the Friends' Home Service Committee, Friends' House, London.

Mr. Nathan Chofshi of Nahallal Nr. Haifa (Israel) who desires also to enrol in the Wider Quaker Fellowship asks if you could send to him some literature in German language as he does not read English. Have you possibly some information in Hebrew language for Hebrew speaking applicants?

Regarding my share in bearing expenses, I regret to inform you that at the present moment I will not be able to contribute anything because of the foreign exchange restrictions ruling in this country. I hope, however, to cover at least your postage expenses by International Postage Coupons as soon as these will be available at the local post offices.

I wish to add that I am an active member of the Israel branch of the War Resisters' International. Apart from the Quaker Peace Testimony it is their adherence to truth which appeals to me so much and which makes this Religious Society so attractive to me.

I am looking forward to your news and remain with many thanks in advance and the best greetings of peace,

Yours cordially,
[signed] J. W. Abileah

When reading through the Quaker literature, which was sent to him in German translation, Nathan Chofshi was excited to read about how William Penn approached the matter of colonization when he settled in what was to become the state of Pennsylvania. When Penn and his fellow refugees from European religious persecution approached the Indian inhabitants, they asked their permission to settle and to live in peace. They asked permission, even though the king of England had granted them deed to the land. Furthermore, they came without a single gun. Chofshi and Joseph were struck by how similar this situation was to the coming of Jews to Palestine after the Balfour Declaration, and yet how different had been the consequences when the argument for legal and historic rights had been substituted for the permission of the native inhabitants. Both Chofshi and Joseph believed that it was not too late to learn from the example of Penn, and Chofshi fulfilled a long-held dream when he translated, in 1968, these Quaker documents into Hebrew. The following introduction to this translation is an important example of the kind of thinking that kept both Joseph and Chofshi active in international peace movements. In this introduction, translated into English by Joseph, is to be found reference to the "divine sparkle" that lies at the center of Joseph's continuing faith in the power of the human heart.

The State of Peace, Justice and Truth Which Was Founded by the English Quakers in North America in the 17th Century

Translated from German sources and provided with an introduction by Nathan Chofshi (By the Translator)

Is there in our generation, filled with reciprocal mistrust between men and nations, a generation torn by bloody world wars and hate, fear from the approaching most terrible of world wars, a war of total destruction for all inhabitants of this planet—is there still a hope, a possibility, that man will return to an inner repentance, to an increasing faith in a flame of the brotherhood of man created in the image of God? Will man devote himself to a life of justice, compassion, love and goodness to everything? Has mankind this inner power, or is it, God beware, doomed to final destruction by its own hands without a saviour?

These are the doubts and questions which befall in our days anyone who looks at the happenings of our wonderful and deplorable world and does not see a salvation from the general folly which has attained and hurts everything.

However, there is a strong basis for faith and hope. There are still people who, despite powers of hell, fears of destruction which the inhabitants of this globe draw upon themselves by order of Satan—have not darkened and extinguished in their hearts the ray of faith and hope that not everything is lost. They believe that the divine sparkle is still alive deep in the heart of each man, conscious or unconscious. It is still whispering and quivering and sometimes it awakens and takes shape of a flame and accomplishes great things, so that the people who were in the darkness see a great light.

The facts related in this small booklet give an encouraging, positive and soothing answer to all these questions and doubts.

A terrible situation ravaged in the 17th century in the "New World" of America, in wars of blood and fire and reciprocal destruction between the white race which came there from Europe and Indians, the redskins, who were the inhabitants of the country. These latters waged terrible wars of revenge against their white conquerers and destroyers. In all this confusion, the community of the "Religious Society of the Friends" or with their abbreviated name "Quakers" appeared without weapons, great or small, and with their strong religious conviction in the sanctity of the life of every man. They refused to use any violence and had a strong faith in the divine sparkle which whispers and lights in the heart of every human being, without exception. They established friendly relations with the Indian tribes who lived in the area called today Pennsylvania and there founded a State of peace, justice and brotherhood which became exemplary.

The story of the foundation of this State, its functioning for a period of over 70 years, all this is related in this little book according to sources of old, reliable Quaker books, founded on the faith and way of life of the members of this religious movement since three hundred years and until our days.

I have translated its contents from the following books in German language: 1. Die Weise Feder—Verlag, Neu-Sonnenfelder Jugend—Collection of Quaker stories, 1930; 2. Die Weise der Quaker, by A. Ruth Fry—2 Auflage 1946, Verlag Leonard Friedrich, Bad Pyrmont; 3. Unter Freunden, by William Wistar Comfort—Christlicher Zeitschriftenverlag, Berlin 1950.

The history which is told here is a living testimony for the force of the goodness, truth and righteousness, and it constitutes an encouragement and strengthening for every man and nation which accepts the divine destination, the calling of which is the driving force of all their deeds in this world. With the conviction and inner force and faith they walk and swim against the gray stream, without fear of failures, difficulties or dangers, for a new world of true peace, true brotherhood of man, for the life of man created in the image of God.

Nathan Chofshi

For Joseph, Nathan Chofshi was more a support than an influence. It became clear to Joseph that his experiences up to 1945 had formed his way of looking at the world and that later contacts and friends merely confirmed and strengthened what he already believed to be true. Thus, he is fond of saying that he was a Quaker fourteen years before he even knew the Quakers existed. Likewise, he never read the Sermon on the Mount until 1963, when at a Baptist convention he played a chamber-music concert outside the Church of the Beatitudes, which overlooks the Sea of Galilee. On the wall of the church are inscribed the key words of Jesus's sermon, and Joseph listened in stunned admiration as one of the Baptists recited them. For years, he had believed in these words without ever having heard or read them. He had exalted Jesus as the man of ethics, but now he saw the precise language in which that ethic had presented itself to the world. Of the Sermon on the Mount, Joseph was later to say, "In the ethical relations toward our fellowmen we must not be short of what is required in the Sermon of the Mount. It is only by taking the way of most radical love, up to love of our enemy, that we can expect the same attitude from the other side. The strongest hate splits and melts in a sincere sun of love. We can walk along this path more than we believe to be possible. The Sermon of the Mount was not written for angels but for humans."

One important idea that Nathan and Joseph came to share was the belief that the Zionist dream had not been a wrong one. There was a time in 1944 and 1947 when Joseph took a very anti-Zionist posture, especially when he saw the coming of the nation-state. In some of his letters, he even mentions a "blue-white Nazism." But in the company of Chofshi, and aided no doubt by a more settled family and professional life, Joseph came to see that there are many Zionisms and that one could be comfortable in calling oneself a Zionist if one linked oneself to the fulfillment of the Second Aliyah's vision of a just and peaceful society. From the time of his contact with Chofshi, Joseph has felt a sense of discomfort at being dragged into an alliance with those whose only interest appears to be the destruction of the state of Israel.

The focus of Joseph's activity in Israel in 1950 was working for minority rights within the state of Israel, hoping that, through cultural transformation, there might be a change in the structure and purpose of the government. He is often a reflection of the change that took place within the Ihud, which, after the binational idea was defeated in 1947, continued to exist in order to press for equality for all Israeli citizens. Such pressure was extremely important because the lot of those Arabs remaining in Israel after 1949 was not a happy one, though their condition was not widely known and at times was deliberately misrepresented.

One clear example of this misrepresentation occurred in 1950 in an article written for *The Jerusalem Post* about Arabs leaving the town of Majdal (later called Migdal Gad by the Israelis), on the southern coast of Israel near the Gaza Strip. Judging from the article, it would seem that the inhabitants were happy about being relocated in Gaza refugee camps, and in general, this picture was the one the world chose to accept, just as they had accepted the now-discredited contention that three hundred thousand Arabs living in what the UN partitioned as the Jewish state left it of their own free will between November 1947 and May 1948. There were those in Israel who knew otherwise and dared to speak out. One of these, Yehoshua Radler-Feldman, better known as Rabbi Benjamin, was the editor of the Ihud paper, *Ner*. Even before the story of Migdal Gad came out in *The Jerusalem Post*, Radler-Feldman had asked Joseph to investigate Migdal Gad (Majdal) on his own. It is interesting to juxtapose the article in the *Post*, written on October 25, 1950, with Joseph's letter of December 1, 1950, which was based on his visit to Majdal on October 8. The *Post* did not print Joseph's report, but *Ner* published a version of it on January 6, 1951.

"Arabs Leave Migdal Gad with Cheerful Goodwill"
by H. Ben Adi

Despite claims made by Egypt in the United Nations regarding the eviction of Palestine Arabs from Israel into Egyptian territory, the recent evacuation of the final group of Migdal Gad's Arab population to the Gaza Strip was carried out in an atmosphere of order and general cheerfulness.

The group, which expressed anxiety only as it moved into the alien territory, bore with it a total of IL22,000 [in the old Palestine bank notes] which had been exchanged for Israel currency.

A total of LP.170,000 was taken out of the country altogether by the transfer of the Migdal Gad families which was undertaken at their request. During the noon hours I watched the evacuees, who had been transported in the 45 minute journey from Migdal Gad to the boundary post in 17 trucks piled high with household goods, being transferred across the border with a minimum of formality. Baggage was not inspected, and papers had been ordered beforehand.

Transport Shortage

The main difficulty confronted during the transfer was one of transportation. The large convoy bearing the Israel expatriates was met at the border by four small Egyptian army vehicles. The lack of adequate transport was explained by an Egyptian army officer with the words, "It will do for them."

The Israel truck drivers, many of them immigrants from Poland and Rumania, expressed surprise at the simplicity and order of the procedure. Their exit from the countries of their origin was not so easily effected, they said.

Most of the evacuees planned to join their families in Gaza. Arabs who remained in Migdal Gad, whose Arab quarter had a deserted look after the series of evacuations, explained that hardships in the town, and desire to reunite families which had broken up during the war had motivated those who left.

If there were complaints about the circumstances of the transfer or the economic conditions which led to the request for evacuation, none were made during the operation. Good cheer reigned till the last minute, and a number of the departing Arabs shook hands with the Military Governor before leaving and thanked him.

And Joseph's reply:

To some they may have appeared leaving with cheerful goodwill, those late Arabs of Migdal Gad, just as people do who, having no choice, put a good face on the matter. To me who has spoken to them and seen them in their distress, they were embittered, pitiable people. A Jewish immigrant living in Migdal for eighteen months knew to relate that it was the "Sochnuth" who sent them away and that against their own free will they left the Ghetto into which they had been penned. The houses of the Ghetto were already being allotted to new immigrants while the last inhabitants left. I saw them busy in the Ghetto setting, ready for the exodus. In the street one sells a writing desk, another various other belongings: Tomorrow they have to go, there is no point in taking with you all that belongs to you. Soldiers patrol the streets. They keep order. In one solitary weaving workshop two workers keep the shuttles running until the last minute and in the small coffeehouses a few guests sit idle in their doom just as some believers who squat motionless at the gate of the mosque.

The remarkable number of 12,000 Arab inhabitants had dwindled down to 2,700 after the Arab-Jewish war. Of these 2,700, a great number had been promised Israel citizenship with full civil rights. Instead they were now served with notices to leave Migdal. This was done diplomatically. Every citizen was requested to fill in a questionnaire and state whether he wants to leave for Egypt or Jordan or for another place in Israel where he would have to live as a refugee. Almost all of them chose Egypt or Jordan and consequently were urged to sign an application, addressed to the military governor, for permission to leave Israel. Thereupon they were allowed to take their belongings and money and also given transport to the frontier.

Their immovable property, put in the custody of the Custodian of Abandoned Property, they could not sell, but on application they could take title deeds with them. The income from these and other sources would be placed to their credit—but this will be counterbalanced by the dues for the administration of the properties and taxes.

To end the preliminary formalities they had to sign a declaration that they do not intend to return to Israel.

The role of the military governor in this foul play was to "advise" everybody to sign, for after October 15th, 1950, the remaining inhabitants would be removed by force and driven out of the country in destitution, and then, of course, "he would be unable to help them." So in the first days of the action when their consternation was great, they sold their belongings with great loss; now, with government assistance, they get reasonable prices.

Within 3½ months this episode had been brought to an end.

Migdal is now "araberrein." We shall not forget the "cheerful goodwill" with which these unfortunate people bade farewell to their town, the town of their fathers and forefathers, where they were to become Israel citizens with full civil rights.

Joseph Abileah
Haifa 1.12.50.
(based on a visit made 8.10.50)

To the student of history, such a juxtaposition of reports is an important microcosm of the whole problem of equal rights for Arab citizens in the construction of a Jewish state. It raises the question of whether what Joseph calls "full civil rights" can ever be truly possible for non-Jews. For example, Joseph's report mentions the "Custodian of Abandoned Property." This custodian, more properly called *custodian of absentee property*, was a position created by the Absentee Property Law passed in March 1950, before the exodus from Migdal Gad. Under this law, more than 70 percent (estimates range as high as 88 percent) of the territory of pre-1967 Israel was classified as absentee property. At the time of the partition plan, Jews owned about 7 percent of the land granted them as a Jewish state and perhaps as much as 10 percent of the land they added as a result of the War of Independence. The property of those Arabs who became refugees passed to the care of the custodian of absentee property in 1950. By law, it was to remain in his hands until the state of emergency was declared to be over. (As of 1987, this state of emergency was still in effect.) Those who were classified as absentees were excluded from citizenship.

In 1950, there were still villages like Majdal that were predominantly Arab. When their lands were given over to the custodian, the inhabitants became absentees. Those who remained within the borders of Israel were called *present absentees* because, while they were absent from their land, they were still within the borders of the country. Many Arabs living in Israel in 1987 could be said to fall into this present absentee category. Joseph and others like him fought during these years for the rights of these people who chose to remain in Israel. It was an uphill fight for equal rights because their land was effectively lost. Don Peretz states that, between 1948 and 1953, of the 370 new settlements built in Israel, 350 were established with the permission of the custodian on absentee property. Many of those settling there came to Israel under the provision of the Law of Return, passed in July 1950, *after* the Absentee Property Law was enacted. The Law of Return gave any Jew anywhere in the world the right to immigrate to Israel — but it did not include in its definition of *return* the seven hundred thousand Arabs who had become refugees in 1947–49. Later, the Israeli Lands Law of 1960 apparently sealed the fate of the refugees, as far as a return to their homes was concerned, by excluding non-Jews from ownership of about 92 percent of pre-1967 Israel.

The case of Majdal (Migdal Gad) is not as well known as that of the villages of Bir'am and Ikrit, whose Christian inhabitants did not fight against Jews in the War of Independence but whose lands were taken for security purposes in 1950. Ever since that time, the inhabitants have been given assurances that they could return (chronicled in *Blood Brothers*, the autobiography of Bir'am's most famous son, Father Elias Chacour), but as of 1987, the promise had yet to be fulfilled. In the summer of 1986, Father Chacour organized a work camp in the now-ruined village of Bir'am. Those who participated were the children and grandchildren of those evicted in 1950. Two hundred four of these youngsters pitched their tents on the places where their houses once were. "You would think the authorities' hearts would melt," said Father Chacour, "but it has produced no change. Still we do not hate them, because when we hate we lose our dignity."

Joseph approached both Migdal Gad and other subsequent alleged human rights violations, not with the view of using them to condemn the government, but with positive feelings for those being oppressed. He has never allowed his love for his fellow human beings to be contaminated with hatred for what human beings are sometimes capable of doing to one another. "Why waste time in condemning, when what is important is to create for the future?" is his reply to those who have asked him why he does not express more righteous indignation at flagrant human rights abuses.

This outlook is the reason that during these years he spent less time investigating abuses than he did in building bridges between the Arab and Jewish communities. He enjoyed his work with the Quakers in Acre, where he came to know Frank and Pat ("she was part angel") Hunt. With the Hunt's help, he planned and participated in the first international work camp in Israel, held at Kfar Vitkin in 1952. The choice of Kfar Vitkin as the site for the construction of the first youth hostel in Israel, built by and open to young persons of all nationalities, was a significant one—Kfar Vitkin has an interesting place in Israeli history. On June 11, 1948, the day the UN achieved a temporary cease-fire in the War of Independence, a ship, the *Altalena*, left the port of Marseilles loaded with weapons and with almost a thousand volunteers who were coming to aid the Irgun, the terrorist military organization headed by Menachem Begin. The regular Israeli army, the Haganah, feared that these weapons and men might be used by Begin to take over the provisionary government, so they laid a trap for them. David Ben-Gurion arranged for the ship to land on the beach at Kfar Vitkin, a *moshav* (agricultural settlement with private ownership of property) south of Haifa. When the Irgun began to unload the ship, regular Haganah units surrounded them and asked them to surrender. Begin and some others escaped to the ship and sailed for Tel Aviv. In the Tel Aviv harbor, Ben-Gurion demanded that the *Altalena* surrender. When it refused, the Haganah opened fire and sank the ship, killing at least sixteen members of the Irgun. Begin escaped by swimming ashore. While this incident meant that the Irgun would no longer exist as an independent fighting force, the defeat was never forgotten—especially by Begin. Kfar Vitkin stands for a deep division among the founding fathers—a split that is still present today.

By erecting a youth hostel at the *moshav,* Joseph and his friends were able to participate in an activity that united, not divided, people. Jews, Arabs, foreign volunteers worked side by side, creating something for the future, hoping to overcome the divisions of the past. From 1952 to 1960, Joseph participated in fifteen work camps, eleven in Israel and four abroad, and for some years he served as secretary to the work-camp movement. Many of his friends in the War Resisters International were also active in the work-camp movement. One of the chief forces behind the movement was another pacifist from Haifa, Meir Rubinstein, who with his wife, Hannah, gave to the movement the sort of dedication that Joseph was later to bring to the Society for Middle East Confederation. The Rubinsteins worked out a system whereby the work camps would alternate between Jewish and Arab villages. A loyal core of Jewish and Arab volunteers was supplemented by young people from abroad, and the work camps became linked with the Service Civil International (SCI), which had been, with the American Friends Service Committee, instrumental in organizing the camp at Kfar Vitkin.

While the international work camps were a successful venture for more than thirteen years, not enough of the participants were brought to them who shared the same commitment to the ideals of those who began them in 1952. Then, the main purpose had been to help overcome prejudice and to make friends of enemies. Joseph threw himself into the movement because it was a perfect example of the practical idealism he espoused. By cutting across national lines, especially in the SCI, who went wherever they were needed, the work camps made those who participated in them feel like world citizens. There was another reason, however, for Joseph's participation. Because his country had denied him service outside the military, he settled with his own conscience by looking at the time he spent in the camps as his form of national reserve duty. Thus he laid the groundwork for one of his life's guidelines—"True defense of one's country lies in winning the trust of one's neighbors." In the genuine Arab-Jewish rapprochement that grew from the work-camp experiences, Joseph hoped to be preparing for an Israel its founders had dreamed of, an Israel that, in Joseph's eyes, had suffered a terrific setback by the partition plan and the subsequent War of Independence. He often remembered Schweitzer's dictum that "nationalism is an ignoble patriotism" and was convinced that movements like the work camps could be a more inclusive and creative expression of one's patriotism than could service in the military.

A good example of what the work camps could accomplish can be seen in the work camp of 1955, held in Rame, a small Arab town in the Galilee. Here, young Jews and Arabs worked alongside international volunteers, and a frail but genuine harmony began to develop. This harmony was broken when the work-camp director announced one day that the military governor would like to come to visit the group. One must remember that all Arab towns in Israel were under military law until 1966, and so the military represented to them not so much defense as oppression. One fiery young Arab stood up and demanded that the invitation be withdrawn or else the Arabs would leave the camp. What happened next shows the good such work camps were capable of achieving.

The young Arab expected to be confronted with angry objections from the Jewish volunteers. He was convinced that the work camp itself was an unreal interlude, almost a subterfuge, in a long history of enmity and oppression and that his objection would reveal how this romantic notion of cooperation could not stand the test of reality. Instead of the argument he anticipated, he found that a man rose on his left to support his view and then another did the same on his right. Turning to see who they were, he found that one was a Jew, Joseph, and the other was an Englishman. As he describes it today, more than thirty years later, he is still amazed that the two bitter enemies of all Palestinians should be the ones supporting him. From that day on, the young man's life was changed. Today, Elias Jabbour of Shefa Amr (Shefr-Am) operates a community center, the House of Hope, and he has dedicated his life to reconciliation and justice. He is absolutely convinced that, if he had not experienced that moment when human beings reached over national and religious boundaries, over barricades erected and maintained by the forces of hatred, to embrace the humanity of another of God's creatures, he would have been shaped by his own bitterness and, in the end, would have been destroyed by it. It is not without reason that, when Joseph Abileah visits the house of Jabbour, he is always given the seat of honor. Elias Jabbour has never recovered the lands taken from his father in 1949, and every day he must pass the kibbutz that was built there. But his heart, though saddened by the injustice of the world, is not full of hate. Elias Jabbour feels that he has been able to fulfill the biblical injunction to choose life, not death, which is why, in 1987, he still remained one of the centers of hope for those who desired peace in the Middle East.

Almost all the work camps experienced moments of tension. One in 1954, at Ein Tsurim in the northern Negev, had to build a regional school for thirteen new immigrant settlements. Here, the Arab participants were troubled about building a home for people newly come to the country, when hundreds of thousands of refugees enjoyed no similar right of return. That the work-camp committee was committed to alternating sites between Jewish and Arab communities eased the situation, as did the presence of compassionate persons who listened sympathetically. In the end, the Arabs were able to reconcile themselves to working to help fellow human beings, and many of them participated in later work camps.

While Joseph had received little support from his family in most of his other peace work, he found that Dinah and his sons were enthusiastic about the work camps, especially because they could be with him in his activities. The bar mitzvah celebrations for Adi and Dani culminated in the experience of a European work camp run by the SCI. Even though Adi had the misfortune of having a grandfather clock fall on him in Stewart Castle in Cove, Scotland, he still remembers the work camp with great fondness; and Dani, whose views on the Arab question are now diametrically opposed to those of his father, clearly values the time spent working in the Arab village of Sha'ab, as well as the summer he spent in Santa Maria, Switzerland, where in 1959 the SCI constructed a road to the mountain village.

Joseph at an international work camp in Israel. Joseph in back row, far right.

Dinah, in particular, saw work camps as constructive. Having worried over Joseph's peregrinations and having never been completely in sympathy with his political views, she valued the first family work camp held in Nazareth in 1958, where the campers constructed the foundation for Dr. Bernath's outpatient clinic. Dr. Bernath of the Edinburgh Mission Hospital (now called the English Hospital) is a legendary figure in Nazareth, and this work camp began his long friendship with the Abileah family. It was he who came to Dinah's rescue in 1973 when she suffered intense pain from a nail that had been inserted into her leg to help it heal after she was struck by a car in late 1972. Although the country was in a state of upheaval over the October War with Egypt, Dr. Bernath dropped everything he was doing to remove the nail from her leg—after which Dinah's health improved greatly.

It was at the Nazareth work camp that Joseph had the pleasure of giving a farewell concert with his son Adi, by now a gifted fourteen-year-old horn player, and with Meir Rubinstein, who in addition to being a fine painter was a gifted amateur pianist. Whenever possible, Joseph liked to inject music into the work-camp activities since he saw both the music and the work as accomplishing the same human purpose.

Music remained Joseph's vocation. In 1949, he became a founding member of the Haifa Symphony Orchestra, where he headed the viola section. In the same year, he also joined the staff of the Haifa Conservatory of Music, teaching violin, viola, chamber music, and theory. In each group, he also undertook some administrative duties, including bookkeeping and, for a while, keeping program notes for the symphony. Among the musicians themselves, he was recognized as a peacemaker, often soothing bruised egos and settling quarrels. One such incident is revealing. A string player had broken his bow and asked to borrow another while his was being repaired. When he returned the borrowed bow, its owner found it had been cracked and accused the borrower of causing the crack. The borrower replied that anyone could see the bow had been cracked in the past as it still retained traces of old glue. Joseph was asked to mediate and, after some discussion, suggested that each player pay half the cost of the repair. This was not satisfactory to either party, each of whom felt he was completely innocent. Joseph then suggested that he himself pay one-third (a substantial sum for a professional bow), and the two parties were shocked that one who had had nothing to do with the bow would actually pay one-third. This offer made them ashamed of their own selfishness, and they accepted the original compromise. Further, they forgave one another for the heated words and remained good colleagues in the orchestra. This habit of not giving way to blame and recrimination is a fundamental part of Joseph's strength as a peacemaker. The incident with the musicians also indicates that this strength has a suggestive force in others, just as it did with the startled Arab near Um el Fahm who, in the shadow of impending war, was offered a piece of chocolate.

When asked why he moved in his adult life from the violin to the viola, Joseph explained that he did not like to be in the limelight, carrying the melody, but preferred to provide the harmony.

As Joseph felt more financially secure because he was teaching and performing in the orchestra, he sought the means to leave the crowded apartment at 1 Herzlia Street, which had been rented to his mother-in-law and where he had lived since his marriage. It had three rooms. In the early days of the marriage, when Joseph's differences with his father meant he had to rely on Dinah's job with the Manufacturers' Association and on his own lessons, one room had been let out to supplement the family's meager income. Later, his researches in the mid and late forties, as he scrambled frantically to find a way to avoid the coming bloodshed, meant that he was on the move all the time and could not teach as much as he would have liked. When the two boys were born, they took over the third room (though the renter left only after a court case over his tenant rights). The cramped space made for family tension, and Mrs. Yarmus, a nationalistic and religious woman who kept a kosher kitchen, had a hard time tolerating Joseph's eccentric behavior. Nevertheless, she was a source of support for Dinah during the years of upheaval and helped care for the children when Dinah went back to work. The flat itself was owned by a Mr. Halaby, an Arab from Jaffa. Right after the war, Joseph was asked if he wanted to buy the flat at a very low price. When he asked, "From whom?" he was told, "The Custodian of Absentee Property." He replied that he would only buy the flat from its rightful owner and continued to rent at a time when ownership would have eased his financial situation considerably.

In 1956, a third child, Efrat (Effie), the daughter Dinah had prayed for, was born, which meant that the family had outgrown their living quarters. Joseph and Dinah looked for months for a home, and after rejecting a large flat on the top of Mount Carmel because it would be too far from his pupils, they found 55A Rehov Hillel. They decided to buy it outright. Dinah, who felt that Joseph was at last secure in his profession, quit her job to raise Effie and took her compensation from twenty-two hard years of work to buy the apartment. This sum was supplemented by the sale of a piano and of Joseph's expensive viola. Selling the viola was a sacrifice but a sacrifice that turned out well for them because it made it easy to live when they had no rent to pay. Joseph often jokes about his simple life by saying it never matters how much you make, only how much you spend. Dinah had learned to be an economical housekeeper. The excitement of moving into the flat (which has remained the family home to this day and in which statesmen and kings have been entertained) was marred by the death of Dinah's mother just a short while before the move. What was to be her room was turned into a room for Effie; Joseph and Dinah's bedroom was not only their sleeping room but also their living room and the room in which Joseph taught and played quartets with many different Haifa musicians, professional and amateur. Here, Adi played the horn and Dani the bassoon. When the boys were older and left the room they shared, Joseph transferred his files and office from a tiny pantry off the kitchen into the boys' former room.

This domestic order and stability—with the boys in school and with Dinah a full-time mother for Effie—freed Joseph (not always to the delight of Dinah) for more and more travels. His extensive involvement with international work camps has already been discussed. A related activity was his growing responsibilities in the War Resisters International (WRI). In 1957, he was elected to the International Council of the WRI. While on this council, he attended all the triennial meetings. In 1957, they were held in Roehampton, England; in 1960, Gandhigram, India; in 1963, Stavanger, Norway; in 1966, Rome, Italy; and in 1969, Haverford, Pennsylvania, United States. Though somewhat removed from the central activities of the WRI in London, Joseph diligently tried to keep up with their activities. Reading twelve years' worth of minutes of the Executive Committee of the International Council of the WRI is a mixed experience. While the idealism that created this group remained intact, the group itself has been torn from within. This same pattern is repeated in almost every group Joseph joined in these years, including the work-camp movement, though it must be said that he was never one to contribute to the groups' tensions. One of the retiring members of the WRI Executive Committee claimed that no one could be an effective peace worker for more than five years because of the frustrations created by an unresponsive world and the subsequent tensions these frustrations produced in the small band of men and women who faced a battle that yielded few victories. A great many men and women gave up the struggle when the world and their expectations did not correspond. Joseph had no illusions about the ethical nature of the world. In this view, he was like Dr. Schweitzer, who in the epilogue to *My Life and Thought* stated,

> I am pessimistic in that I experience in its full weight what we conceive to be the absence of purpose in the course of world happenings. Only at quite rare moments have I felt really glad to be alive. I could not but feel with a sympathy full of regret all the pain that I saw around me, not only that of men but that of the whole creation. From this community of suffering I have never tried to withdraw myself. It seemed to me a matter of course that we should all take our share of the burden of pain which lies upon the world. Even when I was a boy at school it was clear to me that no explanation of the evil in the world could ever satisfy me: all explanations, I felt, ended in sophistries, and at bottom had no other object than to make it possible for me to share in the misery around them, with less keen feelings. That a thinker like Leibnitz could reach the miserable conclusion that though this world is, indeed, not good, it is the best that was possible, I have never been able to understand.

Schweitzer still did not give up the struggle. It is a tribute to Joseph's quiet heroism that he, too, though people have called him a dreamer, harbors no illusions about the world. Like Schweitzer, he accepts that the world is not what we would dream it to be, yet he does not give up in his efforts to change it. His efforts for peace did not die out after five years but have been sustained for more than fifty. He knows that peace is not the result of a single action, which is why he avoids most demonstrations like those called for by *Shalom Achshav* (Peace Now) in Israel. Instead, he has settled in for the campaign.

In this campaign, lonely as it has been for him, he has been sustained by many of those he has met in the WRI. Three of the most important of these men have been Abbé Pierre, the resourceful creator of the idea of the working priest; Vinova Bhave, the disciple of Gandhi; and Danilo Dolci, the man who brought dignity back to the peasants of Sicily. All three labored for peace in their attempts to create a practical idealism, working on everyday problems like housing for the homeless, land distribution for the poor, or land reclamation for farmers.

The trips connected with Joseph's work for the WRI have also appealed to his sense of adventure and love of sight-seeing. He sees the world with all the wonder of a child and remembers what he sees in Baedeker-like detail. He crisscrossed Europe twice on his motor scooter, once with Adi and once in 1959 with both Dinah and Dani. When Joseph first bought his scooter in 1952, there were only three people in Haifa who owned them. For thirty years, he was linked in many people's minds with his scooter, and his adventures through torrential rains in Switzerland and England still bring smiles at family gatherings. He proudly boasts of having traveled four thousand kilometers in Europe one summer with only one map-reading mistake.

One part of his sons' European experience was a visit to Dr. Schweitzer's home in Gunsbach, France, tucked into the foothills of the Vosges Mountains. A visit to Gunsbach today reveals great similarities between the Schweitzer and Abileah homes. Not only are there letters from thousands of correspondents in neatly ordered files, but one is also struck by the similar commitment to living simply. Joseph's and Schweitzer's luggage are almost interchangeable, and Schweitzer's habit of carrying money in a plain cotton bag is similar to Joseph's bag of scraps of bread, which he saves from one meal and consumes at the next. In each home, the most spartan of furnishings

Joseph, Dinah, Adi, and Dani on the family scooter.

contains one group of items on which no expense is spared—musical instruments. So important are musical instruments to Joseph that, while he never gave his sons pocket money for candy or other treats, he would go fourth-class deck passage to Europe to buy the right instrument for them, or he would go without luxuries to provide them with the best instruction. Schweitzer would use packing crates as writing tables, but his organ, lead lined to prevent jungle rot, was carefully boxed and lovingly transported to Lambaréné. It might be said that, for each man, music was never seen as a luxury but as the necessary foundation on which all social action and concern for peace was based.

Many of the pacifists in the WRI were also musicians, and Joseph's later friendship with Yehudi Menuhin brought together two musicians who from their music learned to dream of a world suffused with harmony. Each man acknowledges the dream and challenges those who claim that dreams can never be realized. Once, when Menuhin was defending Joseph against charges of being a dreamer, he pointed out that Israel itself was created by those persons the world regarded as ineffectual dreamers. If their dreams could one day have substance, was there not a chance for his?

Joseph's dream in the power of the human heart was put to the test during his WRI visit to India in 1960. After completing an especially difficult work camp in the village of Sha'ab, Israel, where the workers were not able to handle the strains of very hard physical labor and the villagers themselves failed to enter into the work, Joseph was a bit discouraged. He remembers having to carry away heavy poles and support scaffolding used for roofing a community center, while people in the village looked on. After this experience he was anxious to go to India, though he knew that the 120 dollars of foreign currency he could take outside Israel would make it difficult for him to travel for a whole month. To economize, he went third class on Indian trains. Traveling third class on Indian trains is an experience virtually unknown to foreigners, yet he traveled this way for eight days and covered eight thousand kilometers. He was awestruck by the unbelievably crowded conditions on the trains. Getting a seat was impossible. Eight to ten men would be found standing together in the men's toilet. He sat on his suitcase in the corridor much of the time. The people he met on the train were also those whom most foreigners successfully avoid. Huddled together were to be found the poor of India, their faces marked by generations of hunger; their bodies, scarred by skin diseases, leprosy and other ailments, were barely covered and foul smelling. And yet Joseph drew strength from being with them. To his incredulous listeners, he has explained that he survived this trip by looking into the eyes of these destitute Indians. There he found the "divine sparkle," their souls shining through their dark pupils as bright as the soul shining in the eyes of the priest in *Les Misérables*. Their eyes made him forget all his discomfort as he came to realize the definitive difference between the world of the spirit and the world of the flesh. Though he was overwhelmed at the sight of the Taj Mahal, nothing matched the beauty of the light in those eyes.

A memory from this time that ranks next in importance was Joseph's walk with Vinova Bhave. Bhave, it will be remembered, walked all over India, asking for the rich to redistribute their lands among the poor. Disciples and foreigners drawn to this nonviolent approach to social change would join him for portions of these walks. After inquiring where he could be found, Joseph joined Bhave at Bihar. He was content to fade into the crowd of about two hundred but was surprised to be summoned by one of Bhave's assistants. "The master [*acharia*] would like to talk to the man from Israel." Joseph joined Bhave at the head of the procession, and as was Bhave's custom, he took Joseph's hand and held it as they walked. Bhave asked him many questions for more than two hours, though he revealed that he had little knowledge of the complexities of the Middle East situation. For example, at one point he said, "Why can't you settle your differences peacefully?" As they approached a village, children brought out flowers to welcome the *acharia*. Bhave asked Joseph to remain with him, but Joseph asked to be allowed to go back into the crowd, saying that the honor was for Bhave, not him. As he has done so often, Joseph left center stage to walk just as happily with the masses in the audience.

He performed much the same role at the WRI Triennial Meeting at Gandhigram, India. There, although he was a member of the executive committee, he worked as a translator, using both his considerable language skills and his ability to communicate with all sorts of people. He spent much of his time helping others learn what was going on during the proceedings. Still, he found time to spend with other delegates, and it was here that he began his friendship with Danilo Dolci. To find out more about Dolci's work, he made a special trip to visit him in Sicily in 1961, when the International Council of the WRI met in executive session there.

It is hard to find two men so physically dissimilar yet so alike in spirit. Joseph is about five feet, eight inches tall and has always been very slight. Dolci is a comparative giant, well over six feet tall and weighing close to 250 pounds. One of the great untaken photographs of all time is that of Dolci perched on the back of Joseph's scooter in 1962, driving from Ben-Gurion airport to Tel Aviv, where visits had been arranged for him with Israeli experts on soil conservation and reclamation. Dolci appealed to Joseph immediately because Dolci was a man who would not let an idea remain a dream. Setting himself up in Sicily, Dolci probed the roots of corruption and Mafia dominance. After generations of neglect by absentee landowners anxious for a quick return, the land had lost its sustaining power. Dolci had to win over the peasants by making them believe both in themselves and in the land's ability to sustain them. He created a dam, and with the water he conserved, he began irrigating fields that were fertile but neglected and unproductive. The fields represented the state of the peasants themselves. Dolci worked patiently and hard convincing the peasants that they had within them both intelligence and a grasp of the truth and that these needed only nourishment to spring to life. Dolci called his educational philosophy a sort of midwifery—helping to bring to birth the life that each person, however ignorant she or he might be of it, contained within. When the peasants believed this, they would be freed from the power of the Mafia. This shared belief in the innate power of the human spirit established a great bond between Joseph and Dolci, as did their desire to find a practical means for giving it expression. When Abraham Lotan, an Israeli soil expert, arrived in Sicily to spend his three-week vacation helping Dolci, he was greeted in the following fashion: "You are three times welcome—first as my guest; second because you come from Israel to help Sicily; and third because you are the friend of Abileah." Dolci's success in giving the people of Sicily courage to face the Mafia, when everyone else in the world thought the Mafia's grip was so strong that no one could dare break the code of silence and speak out against it, gave Joseph courage to continue his work in Israel, where he confronted the same sort of skepticism that Arab-Jewish enmity could ever be overcome and a common community be established.

Joseph had received similar inspiration from Abbé Pierre, whom he met in 1953. Abbé Pierre had struggled for the homeless who had to sleep beneath the bridges of Paris. He achieved amnesty for them from petty offenses and found places for them to live, yet he was threatened with excommunication from his order because he had left the walls of the monastery. In a similar fashion, Danilo Dolci and Joseph himself had been threatened for daring to challenge the mores of their own, more secular, society. Yet the pope himself said that, while Pierre had transgressed the rules of his order, he had remained true to the religion that lay behind that order. Many in Israel regarded Joseph as disloyal to the security of the state, but he hoped one day to be judged as one who, despite attack and ridicule, remained true to the ideals that gave justification for that state's existence. "A traitor," he claimed, "is one who is disloyal to his ideals."

Joseph's efforts in the WRI were not limited to attending international conferences. Indeed they are characterized by his careful records as secretary of the Israeli branch and by his patient work with young conscientious objectors who sought the WRI's support and advice. Connected with this work was his participation in the League for Human and Civil Rights (LHCR), which he joined in 1950. Though his most notable work with the league took place in 1970 and will be discussed later, between 1950 and 1967 he went wherever he was needed in Israel. One such trip, to Migdal Gad, has been discussed. He was also an active participant in the Karmiel affair of 1964. Karmiel is a large development town that was constructed in the Galilee for new Jewish immigrants, largely coming from Muslim countries. While Joseph had always been in favor of enlarging the absorptive capacity of the country and was not in principle against the idea of development towns, he was not in favor of confiscating Arab land to build these centers. He accepted the Balfour Declaration's desire for creating a home for the Jews in Palestine, but he also accepted the often-forgotten second part of that declaration, which protected the civil rights of the non-Jewish inhabitants. It was clear that Karmiel might easily have been built one or two kilometers away from the chosen site and would not have then involved expropriation of land belonging to nearby Arab villages. But it was also clear to Joseph and others that the choice of that particular site was a deliberate attempt to drive a wedge between Jews and Arab villagers and to encroach on the livelihood of the Arab towns by constructing the town on olive groves and on a productive stone quarry. When a small group of protesters began a protest walk from 'Akko (Acre) to Karmiel, they were set upon and severely beaten. Joseph had started off with the group but had left it to give a music lesson just before the arrest took place. He later rejoined them, bringing them replacements for their banners and signs that had been ripped savagely from them outside 'Akko. The young leader of that group, Uri Davis, was placed in jail. Joseph then joined four hundred other artists and public figures in a demonstration against the arrest and against the construction of the town. They deliberately sought arrest, but their numbers were too great to be rounded up for the small prison available. While they were not successful in stopping construction, they achieved some success in alerting Israeli public opinion to the long-term dangers of land expropriation. How could these new immigrants hope to live in peace with their neighbors when the houses they built rested on terraces that had been tilled for generations by the Arab inhabitants? The problem of Karmiel was the problem of Israel, and it was one Joseph had been struggling with his whole life.

During the period of 1963–66, Joseph worked with others to abolish the reign of military law in the Arab towns within Israel. Because the Arabs were under military law, they lacked fundamental civil rights guaranteed to every other Israeli citizen. These rights included freedom of assembly, of movement, and so on. In 1966, military law was lifted. Joseph joined less successful fights against other laws he found discriminatory, such as the Law of Citizenship (1952) and the Absentee Property Law (1950). As we have seen, the latter law created people like those he had found at the Sha'ab work camp in 1960. It was not simply that the village had not shared in the work. More than two-thirds of the village did not really feel that Sha'ab was their home. This group were present absentees, Bedouin who had been displaced from the Huleh area north of the Sea of Galilee or groups from other villages who had left their homes in 1948 but had stayed within the 1948 borders of the state. Sha'ab had been a village of two thousand before the war, and only 10 percent of the original inhabitants had stayed. The town of six hundred that Joseph worked for in 1960 was more a group living in what they hoped were temporary quarters than a village with its own pride in its identity. It is not difficult to see why it was an uphill struggle to get them to participate in the completion of a road that would link them to the main road and thus to other villages and towns.

The path to reconciliation was a rocky one during this period. People have difficulty remembering the small forward steps taken when incidents like the massacre at Kfar Qasim take place. Kfar Qasim was especially painful because it so easily could have been avoided. Kfar Qasim is a small Arab-Israeli town near the green line, a line drawn in 1949 to separate Israel from the land controlled by Jordan. In the early days of the Suez War of 1956, Israelis were uneasy about the loyalties of their own Arab population and declared a state of emergency in Arab areas. This declaration led to the imposition of a strict curfew in Arab border villages. The curfew imposed stated that, between five in the afternoon and six in the morning, all the inhabitants had to be in their homes or else they would be shot. Having decided on the curfew, it took some time for word of it to get to the many villages. The *mukhtar* (head man) in Kfar Qasim was informed of the five o'clock curfew just thirty minutes before it was to go into effect. He informed the authorities that more than four hundred villagers were at work in the fields, that they were ignorant that such a curfew had been imposed. They assured him that those working would be permitted to return in safety, but when they came back to the village, forty-nine were taken off their bicycles, trucks, or carts and shot at close range between the hours of five and six that afternoon. Orders were then given to stop the shooting. To those who had been struggling for Arab-Jewish reconciliation, this massacre was a severe setback, but almost equally depressing was that, within three years, all those found guilty had been pardoned, and the man who initiated the order to shoot everyone not in his or her home at five in the afternoon, Brigadier Shadnir, was found guilty of "a technical error" and fined one pound. The one glimmer of light to be seen in the incident was that it had been Israelis who forced the news of the massacre into the open, thus bringing about the trial of those who otherwise might not even have been prosecuted.

The period 1950–67, which saw Joseph's emergence as a pacifist dedicated to concrete action in solidarity with such groups as the WRI, the SCI, the American Friends Service Committee (AFSC), and the Israeli League for Human and Civil Rights (ILHCR), also reveals that Joseph was thinking of himself more and more as a world citizen. In 1961, he joined Dr. Hugh Schonfield's Mondcivitan Republic, a group promoting world citizenship, and he has been an important Middle Eastern link with them since that time. He also decided to learn Esperanto, a world language, and joined several groups and societies promoting its use. Finally, he is proud of his membership and work in the International Vegetarian Society. It is hard to believe that he found time for all these activities and also for his work with the conservatory and with the orchestra. His energies were, however, enormous, and the strength he drew from his music always seemed to give him the ability to hold his life together.

Before ending this chapter, it is important to turn to his family. The years 1950 through 1967 were those in which his children grew to become adults, his own parents died, and his own marriage held together after the crisis in 1947. A simple description of the family's life is impossible, yet some idea of the complicated relationships (and in this respect, Joseph's family is no different from any other family) is important.

Two things are often true for peacemakers who are also parents. First, persons who are successful as public peacemakers are often less so within the structure of the family itself, despite their own recognition that true peacemaking should begin at home. Erik H. Erikson's disturbing study of Gandhi (*Gandhi's Truth*, 1969) reveals a man who was successful as a proponent of nonviolence on the public front but who was guilty of severe psychological violence with his own family. Erikson traces this to Gandhi's belief that he alone possessed the truth, and perhaps without knowing it, he imposed his idea of truth on those near to him without paying full respect to the truth that they might possess in themselves, thereby committing an action of psychological violence against the integrity of people for whom he genuinely cared.

Second, because relations between parents and children are extremely complex and at times irrational, we often interact with our children in ways we vowed we never would after our experiences with our own parents. Within the family, we often face our most difficult task in reconciling our intentions with our deeds. For peacemakers in particular, it seems to be difficult to make the move from public to private success. They are often like physicians who, after being treated in their clinics and hospitals as gods, come home to families wanting them to be merely fathers or mothers, not wanting to be healed but only to be loved. It is indeed more ambitious to be an ordinary, whole, human being than to be a saint, as Camus pointed out in *The Plague*. Joseph's human and fallible qualities, which he shares with numerous other husbands and fathers, are revealed in his interactions with his wife and children.

After 1950 and especially after the move to 55A Rehov Hillel in 1957, Joseph's extended family life went more smoothly. After being reconciled at the 1944 Passover seder with his father, he continued on good terms with him until Ephraim's death in 1953. In 1950, much to his father's delight, Joseph became a Freemason, and they worked together to use the lodge as a place where barriers of religion and race could be dismantled. Ephraim had taken a partner in the music business, Arthur Sawady, but Joseph continued to do the bookkeeping, and after his father's death, worked with his brothers on the board of directors of the firm. He found at times that he had to function as a peacemaker when arguments about the business came up, but generally the brothers worked well together, even when they had to split up the fifty-seven pianos they inherited. Joseph's mother continued to live in the flat above the music store until her death in 1960 and had a warm relationship with Joseph and her grandchildren. Dinah's mother died in 1957, and at her grave, Joseph acknowledged that he had not been easy to live with, but he expressed great appreciation for all she had done for him and his family during the sixteen years they lived together.

Joseph had done his best to fulfill Dinah's request for a happy home, though he had trouble convincing her that all his trips abroad were necessary. He tried to tell her that he spent no more time away from his family than other Israeli men who had to perform reserve duty every year, but she remained skeptical and often complained that he should include the family in more of his travels. At the same time, she continued to worry a great deal about their financial security, even when he explained that one of the reasons he made so many solitary trips abroad was that there was no money for more than one of them to go. These trips abroad did seem to have some adverse effects on the children as they were growing up. It may have been true that his own father's absence in the formative years of 1923–26 did not have a bad effect on Joseph, but Adi, in particular, suffered much from his father's absences from home and, for that reason, treasured the times (like 1957 in Europe and the family work camps in Israel) when he could be with his father.

As a child, Joseph had watched with discomfort as his father's explosive temper often erupted within the family, usually to be absorbed by his mother, who most often suffered in silence. Not unlike Gandhi, perhaps, Ephraim Abileah had been a man of peace who ruled his house with an iron will. While Joseph's manner was neither explosive nor violent, he did seem to inherit from his father a tendency to make unilateral, nondiscussable decisions for the whole family. The boys often felt they were hearing lectures not being invited into conversations where their views might be respected. Joseph freely admits deciding what was best for his children while they were growing up, but he is perhaps unaware of how that affected them.

For example, Joseph decided that neither of his boys should have military training while in school, which meant that the boys would be excused during certain periods of the day when military exercises took place. But it also meant that they would not go to summer camps with their friends, since all the camps involved some sort of military training. The Leo Baeck School, where Adi was enrolled, complied with Joseph's request, but Dani's school, a vocational training center, refused. Adi felt singled out during this time, and it was doubly hard on him because nonparticipation in military training was not something he freely chose to do. This lack of choice probably accounts for why Adi had no compunction about joining the army when he became eighteen. Likewise, neither Dani nor Effie chose Joseph's path of conscientious objection, which was a disappointment to him. He seemed particularly upset with Adi's decision. During Adi's first months in the army, Joseph would not even read the letters he sent home. Joseph told Dinah, who begged him to read them, that the letters had been screened by a military censor and hence would not be truthful accounts of army life, but this reason thinly masks the disappointment he felt.

Dinah did not disapprove of her children's military service, though she was constantly concerned for their safety. She strove to mediate between her children and their father, just as Joseph's own mother had done, and in the end, family harmony was established. One of the components of this harmony was music. Adi was a skilled horn player and once played the horn solo in Joseph's beloved Sixth Symphony by Beethoven. Dani was a bassoonist, who still plays in a wind chamber group and at times plays with the Haifa Symphony Orchestra.

The children had parted company with their father's politics and pacifist philosophy by 1967, but they respected his commitment to his ideals and were beginning to understand the sacrifices he was willing to make for them. Nevertheless, it had not always been easy for them to reach that understanding while they were still children and wanted their father to spend more time with them and less with his peace work.

When Dr. Magnes in 1939 talked of peacemaking between Jews and Arabs as a "task worthy of Jews," he was well aware of how difficult this task would be. But neither he nor Joseph felt it was impossible. The years 1949–67 are marked by Joseph's tireless efforts as a peacemaker but often with such activities as work camps, which were far from the public eye. In Uri Davis's *Dissent and Ideology in Israel,* a study of conscientious objectors in Israel from 1948 to 1973, we learn that many pacifists of Joseph's generation are now severely criticized by those on the left, as well as by those who support the military establishment. Davis charges these pacifists with too often making a separate peace with the state, of being passivistic, not pacifistic. This description would be unfair to Joseph's efforts during this period, as we have seen, because he worked for peace in an active manner and in all phases of his life.

At the same time, it is true that he did not fully plunge into the political arena, though plans for a political resolution to the conflict were much on his mind. When the June 1967 War took place, the situations of Arabs and Jews drastically changed. An opportunity was then presented for those who would turn from private to public peacemaking. The opportunity had to be seized, even if it meant a disruption of the fragile stability Joseph had worked so hard to achieve in his private and domestic life. Joseph did not enjoy being thrust into the role of prophet. Still less did he enjoy the many consequences he warned of in 1944 and 1947 that had in fact taken place as a result of partition. But the truths he encountered in 1936 kept their grip on him. Time and time again he had fulfilled Ahad Ha'am's definition of a prophet: "He tells the truth not because he wishes, but because he is forced to do so. It is a trait characteristic of his nature, from which he could not liberate himself, even if he would. The prophet is an extremist. He concentrates his mind and heart upon the idea in which he finds the purpose of life. He would subjugate life to this ideal."

6

Isaiah's Teaching
1967–1972

> Will the Jews here, in their efforts to create a political organism, become devotees of brute force and militarism, as were some of the late Hasmoneans, and will they, like the Edomite Herod become the obedient servants of economic and militaristic imperialism? It is among the possibilities that some day it may become political treason for someone sincerely to repeat in the streets of Jerusalem Isaiah's teaching that swords are to be beaten into ploughshares, and men are to learn war no more.
> —Judah Magnes, 1923

LIKE MANY ISRAELIS who were struck by the suddenness and completeness of their nation's victory in the June 1967 War, Joseph was filled with optimism that peace was closer. The dramatic shift in configuration of the map of the Middle East opened up new possibilities for peace, and Joseph felt that his own dream of uniting Jordan with Mandated Palestine had moved one step closer to being realized. Israel found itself with over one million more Arabs within the borders of the new cease-fire. The country was genuinely puzzled about what to do with the West Bank and Gaza and seemed open to discussing a wide range of options. While Joseph saw clearly the danger posed by a heady and victorious nationalism that wanted all the conquered territories, including the Sinai, he felt some hope that his own plan of twenty years might be given a chance. For the first time, he found himself in demand as a speaker. The year 1967 was to be a turning point for him as a public figure.

It was a turning point in other ways as well. The history of his life showed remarkable points of intersection with the history of his country. We have seen how in 1936, at the beginning of the Arab Revolt, he discovered his belief in the power of nonviolence and in the idea of a land that could be holy for both Arab and Jew. Likewise, the assassination of Lord Walter Moyne in 1944 coincided with the birth of his first son. We have seen how these new responsibilities as a father led Joseph to want to see a land where his son could be raised in peace. His frantic activity and the UNSCOP appearance in 1947 were triggered by the birth of his second son, and Effie's birth in 1956 coincided with the Suez War. The 1967 war was immediately followed in August by the sudden death of Joseph's older brother Hans. Although Joseph did not agree with the political views of Hans, his brother's death at the early age of fifty-five inspired Joseph to make a vow that whatever years were left to him would be spent in the pursuit of peace. He made this vow at the graveside of his brother, in a manner reminiscent of the vow Ephraim had made in 1921 at his own father's grave. This graveside pledge had momentous consequences.

Despite his great love of music and despite his being the sole means of support for the family since Dinah's 1957 decision to leave her job, Joseph determined to leave the Haifa Symphony Orchestra and the conservatory and to cut back gradually on his private lessons. Dinah was in a state of panic about how her family would survive, especially when Joseph announced that 1968 would be a sabbatical year for him. After seventeen years of relative stability, the family was, in her opinion, being returned to the chaos and uncertainties of the 1940s.

It was then that Joseph felt what he has termed the "finger of God" on his fortunes. Within a week after having made the pledge to his brother, Joseph received two gifts of substantial amounts of money. The first came from Yehudi Menuhin, who had met Joseph and was so moved by Joseph's peace efforts that he placed a substantial sum at his disposal to use as he saw fit. Almost on the same day that Joseph received the money, he received notice from the lawyer of Fred Steingardt that proceeds from the sale of a tractor were to be given to Joseph for his peace work.

Fred Steingardt had come to Palestine from Turkey. He was a brilliant engineer who helped lay plans for the National Water Carrier, a major engineering achievement that took waters from the Sea of Galilee and pumped them into the arid regions of the south. Steingardt was also an ardent pacifist, and when the government attempted to force him into the army, he left the country. He left behind some property, including a tractor that was on loan to a *moshav*. After years of not receiving rent for the tractor's use, Steingardt decided to sell it. He instructed his lawyer to give some of the proceeds from the sale to Joseph. Steingardt also made Joseph his agent for supporting his nephew in Israel, on the condition that his nephew adopt a pacifist position with respect to military service. When the nephew, as Joseph's own sons had done, went into the army, his allowance was withdrawn. Steingardt's commitment to his principles later caused him to resign from a prestigious position with the Port Authority in New York: he discovered that some of his fellow engineers were skimming money from an important project by shaving on specifications in the building plans. He felt that weakening the strength of the construction was endangering human lives, and he wanted nothing to do with it.

The gift from this friend who shared his uncompromising attitude towards the truth almost equaled the amount of Menuhin's contribution, and Joseph approached his new peace activity with confidence. He cited these gifts to the doubting Dinah as examples of how they would be taken care of in the years ahead. The first thing he did with some of the money was to rent a truck and collect furniture, clothes, and tools for Palestinians along the green line who had lost their homes and possessions in the June 1967 War. But where should he deliver the goods? He contacted the UN relief team, who advised him to contact their local center in Qalqilya. When the UN official there did not show up for their scheduled interview, Joseph struck up a conversation with a young Palestinian working in the office, who said, "Why bother going through the UN and their bureaucracy? My village, Habla, is just a few kilometers away and desperately needs help."

The small village of Habla lay almost directly on the border. For security reasons, twenty-two houses in the village were demolished, and others severely damaged soon after the war, in an effort to make it impossible for the villagers to return, since their presence might one day pose a threat to Israel. It seemed as if Habla would be like 390 other Arab villages that were destroyed after the founding of the state of Israel, although this time the village was located in land on the other side of the green line. Habla was like the villages of Amwas, Yalu, and Beit Nuba, which were located near Latrun near the Tel Aviv–Jerusalem road and which in 1967 were totally destroyed and replaced with a park. However, the inhabitants of Habla had no intention of becoming refugees, or even present absentees, and remained in the hills surrounding their village. After a month in the hills, they returned to the ruined village and stayed among the rubble, even though the military denied them permission to repair or rebuild their homes. The military had also denied the villagers permission to go out to find work.

When Joseph reached the village in late 1967, just as winter was setting in, the village was at a low point and desperate. Joseph drove the hired truck, full of goods collected from sympathetic Jewish citizens of Haifa, into the middle of the town square and began to distribute its contents. As might be expected, people began to fight over the few bits of furniture, despite Joseph's pleas for them to be considerate of one another. He told them how people in India had taken land given to Bhave, but when one man arrived too late to get any, another had asked that half his portion be shared with the latecomer since he needed it so badly. But India was not the Palestine of 1967, and the arguments continued. Two men began to fight over a bed, and one raised a rock to hit the other. Joseph interposed and was ready to take the blow. The man did not strike, but Joseph said he would not leave the village until the two men had made peace. Although they agreed to make peace, Joseph left the village with a still-heavy heart, knowing that one truckload of goods did little to solve the problems of Habla, though it did strengthen the will of the inhabitants to remain in their homes.

Joseph was determined to see the village rebuilt and went to the military governor to get permission to hold an international work camp there. The military governor told him it was against military law for the homes to be rebuilt, and Joseph acknowledged that this law made strategic sense. But Joseph told him that his own purpose was strictly humanitarian and stressed that he regarded it as a duty to help his fellow human beings, especially since the 1967 war had left him with a roof over his own house. Because the governor felt that Joseph was not criticizing him and had acknowledged the strategic need for the law, since Habla was just a few meters from the border and a few kilometers from heavily populated Jewish areas, he could respond more generously to Joseph's humanitarian appeal. He said he could not break the law but that, since the law said that only destroyed houses could not be rebuilt, Joseph could repair the ones that had not been destroyed. Joseph was convinced that once again his thesis about the human heart's ability to respond with goodness was confirmed in the governor's decision, and he rushed back to the village to tell them the news.

When he arrived at the village, however, he saw that they had an even more urgent need for funds to purchase tools and seeds, since without crops and without permission to leave the village to look for work, the village was doomed. He took more of the Menuhin-Steingardt money and bought tools and seeds and then left on a summer 1968 lecture tour of Europe to see if he could raise more money. On his return, he saw that the village, unlike Sha'ab, had taken the situation into its own hands and was helping itself. The military governor had seen that the villagers were not going to leave. Rather than let them starve, he had given permission for 10 percent of them to leave the village to work. Further, he granted the village permission to use the Jordanian pumping station to bring water for their crops. With these concessions, the village was slowly able to reestablish itself.

When Joseph took to the *mukhtar* of the village a check he

had received from the Mennonite Central Committee for his peace work, he was told that, rather than distribute the money, he should give it for the construction of a school for girls in the village. After eight or nine months of petitioning, Joseph got the village permission to build their school. Not only that, but the Israeli government agreed to bear half the cost of its construction.

Jospeh looks upon this incident as an example of what is possible between people of good will who develop a small amount of trust in one another. For example, the day he received permission to go ahead with the school, he telephoned the village *mukhtar*, Abu Hashem, to say that the Mennonite funds were now at his disposal. The *mukhtar's* son was sent to Haifa to get money. Joseph went with him to the bank, counted out the money for him, asked for no receipt, and told him to take it to his father. Later in the year when Joseph visited Habla, Abu Hashem asked what he could do to repay Joseph for all he had done for the village. Joseph mentioned that he was making a trip to Europe that summer but would not have money for the boat fare until he received the honoraria connected with his speaking engagements. Abu Hashem went to his own home, gathered up his money, which he gave to Joseph, and never asked him when or how he would be paid back. "When you treat your enemies like brothers," Joseph asserts, "they become your brothers," which is why he always replies to questions concerning the issue of secure borders for Israel with the words, "the friendship of my neighbor is the only true security border."

From being a witness at Migdal Gad, Joseph had become an active participant at Habla. After seventeen years of fighting for equal civil rights within the state of Israel, he was now ready to launch his greatest project, the uniting of both banks of the Jordan. It was time once again to try to make an impact at the UN, although his faith in that organization was considerably less than total.

In the summer of 1967, while vacationing at the family house on Mount Kena'an, Joseph made the acquaintance of Anwar El-

Khatib. El-Khatib had been the governor of the Jerusalem district, and after the June war, he had been exiled to the city of Safad where he was placed under town arrest. While he had to report three times daily to the police station, El-Khatib's movements in Safad were not otherwise restricted, and after being introduced to Joseph through a letter from Joseph's friend, Wajdi-Farid Tabari, the two often met together in El-Khatib's hotel. They discovered that they had much in common, and as Joseph unfolded his dream to El-Khatib, the latter encouraged him to make a presentation of his ideas to the UN once again. It was with El-Khatib's encouragement and approval that Joseph drew up the following ten-point solution to the conflict:

Points for a Solution of the Arab-Jewish Problem

1. Union of both banks of the Jordan (the original mandatory area) under one common government. (*)
2. Central irrigation scheme (Lowdermilk or any other plan) and soil reclamation for immediate settlement of all refugees.
3. Representation in parliament without distinction of national, religious, racial or ethnical affiliation, preferably on personal merit but, if not feasible, in party system.
4. Second house of a religious council in which all monotheistic religious communities are represented to deal with holy places and matters arising in legislation on ethical principles.
5. Another house of specialised scientists in various fields where bills dealing with economics have to be sanctioned before becoming law.
6. The personality of H. M. King Hussein of Jordan to be safeguarded by preserving his title, with powers limited by parliament, or by allowing him to head a list in democratic elections.
7. The sovereignty of the state of Israel and of Jordan being automatically cancelled and the refugee problem settled, the Arab population will demand the neighbouring countries to stop their belligerent attitude and invite any state to enter into federation.

8. After success of the irrigation scheme, steps should be taken to irrigate the Syrian desert with the Euphrates and Tigris. Enjoying prosperity while neighbours are poor is not ethical and not practical in the long run. The same with Egypt, offering our help in building dams. This will avoid interference of far away powers in the region and our obligation to serve their interests when occasion arises.
9. Special emphasis on common education of the next generation, pointing out affinities of semitic languages.
10. Encouragement of tourism with other countries.

Joseph W. Abileah
(55A Hillel Str., Haifa)

Mt. Canaan (Safed), 10,8.1967

(*) After the conversation with Mr. Yofe suggesting a Federation as a first step, this point would read as follows:—"Federation of three states, viz. Jordan, Arab Palestine (West Bank) and Israel with respective capitals in Amman, Nablus and Tel-Aviv, and with Jerusalem as the Federal Capital."

As is clear, these points differ very little from those Joseph had presented to UNSCOP in 1947, but having reformulated them, Joseph was buoyed by the support of such an important political figure as El-Khatib. Six months later, he wrote to King Hussein and asked for his opinion of the ten points. In this January 4 letter, Joseph recounted his visit to Hussein's grandfather back in 1936. The letter closes in the following fashion:

Dear Brother Hussein, may the bitter tears I wept in compassion with the refugees and the warm tears of love and reconciliation which I poured on the manuscript of this letter move your great heart inherited from your forefathers of Mecca and our common father Abraham.

I am enclosing the 10 Points of my plan and a call which I wrote in the year 1947 and which constitutes its spiritual foundation.

The words of Ibrahim Basha at the palace are still ringing in my ears and I pray to God that I may live to say to Your Majesty in my little home at Haifa: "Welcome a hundred thousand times."

I await your encouraging reply and remain,
>Your faithful and devoted,
>[signed] Joseph W. Abileah

In December 1968, Joseph followed up his earlier letter with the following letter, written in his role as "Special Commissioner of the Mondcivitan Republic for Middle East Mediation."

>Joseph W. Abileah
>Special Commissioner of the Mondcivitan
>Republic for Middle East Mediation
>55a Hillel St.—Tel.521794—Haifa
>4th of December, 1968

To His Majesty King Hussein,
Hashemite Kingdom of Jordan
Royal Palace
Amman

Your Royal Majesty,

On the 4th of January, 1968, I have ventured to address a letter to Your Majesty and, in absence of regular mail service to Amman, have sent same by various ways. It eventually became an open letter, as it had been printed abroad and in summary also in the local press.

Assuming that contents of the said letter have come to your knowledge, I now avail myself to the kindness of Dr. Schonfield, President of the Mondcivitan Republic (Commonwealth of World Citizens) of which I am also a member, who offered to personally transmit another letter to Your Majesty.

Since January I have been active in propagating the idea of a Confederation of Jordan, Arab Palestine (West Bank) and Israel, with a federal capital in the Old City of Jerusalem. This I have done within the country, amongst Arabs and Jews, and by a lecture-tour in European countries. Being a musician by profession, I have taken a sabbatical year in order to be able to devote my whole time to the implementation of the project. Here are some points which emerged from numerous discussions in Israel, in the West Bank and abroad and which I wish to submit to Your Majesty's consideration:

1) The federal government should deal for the time being, only with foreign policy and economic integration.
2) The economic integration will enable us to solve the refugee problem almost without the help of foreign nations.
3) The help of the UNO is required for an immediate irrigation system in the Syrian desert with the waters of the Euphrates and Tigris, in order to put irrigated land at the disposal of Iraqi and Syrian soldiers, so that they can leave your country and return to their families.
4) The pressure put on your country by the Egyptian government can be lessened by a scheme of economic recovery in which we will share and which will enable the Egyptians to shake off their obligations towards the Russians.
5) A religious council, which will form a second house in the federal parliament, should be composed of representatives of all faiths and religious communities in the area. The ethic principles contained in the code of each religion which have so many points in common, will eventually form a basis for a constitution.
6) The Federation should be open for any other country in the Middle East to join and is formed with a view to create a United States of the M.E. which, though welcoming trade with other countries, will be able to refuse serving political ends of the power blocks.

These constructive proposals have been submitted to many groups, have appeared in the press and were broadcast over the Israeli Radio. They have met no opposition and many members of Your Majesty's government living in the West Bank have personally given their full agreement. In my representations to the Prime Minister's and Israeli Foreign Office I have received "green light" for action and I have the feeling that in a debate it will be accepted in the Kneseth.

The question of the many doubters whom I encounter is always: Where is the other side? This is the reason why I am applying today to Your Majesty and beseech you to give serious consideration to this exceptional opportunity. Please help me in breaking the ice, and brotherly love will warm the waters underneath. We all together, repentant sons of Abraham, will fulfill our mission in giving an example to humanity and create a beginning for a wave which will bring about world federation and world peace. Your Majesty's favourable reply will be a great encouragement and set a possibility for me and my co-workers to form the necessary public opinion in Israel and abroad which will lead to success.

I remain, Royal Majesty, respectfully

Your devoted and grateful
[signed] Joseph W. Abileah

It is a good thing that Joseph did not wait for the king to reply before continuing with his own activities because, more than twenty years later, he still has not received an answer. In the letter of January 4 he proposed a trip to Dr. Gunnar Jarring in Cyprus, and after his work with Habla had been completed, this trip took place.

Dr. Jarring had been proposed by the United Nations as a mediator in the Arab-Israeli conflict, and for almost two years, he shuttled back and forth from country to country looking for a solution to the new problems created in the aftermath of the June 1967 War. As he stated in his letter to Hussein, Joseph decided to take his plan directly to Jarring's headquarters rather than work through intermediaries. Dinah was delighted when he suggested that she and Effie accompany him for a small holiday. Before he left for Cyprus in the spring, he spent time reflecting on his past life and took up again his projected autobiography, "My Faith in the Human Heart," which unfortunately had to be set aside in the flurry of activity created by his determination to work for a political solution to the Arab-Jewish problem. He realized that Israel was sensitive to world opinion and perhaps would take ideas from abroad more seriously than those proposed by some of its own citizens, so he decided to try to get support for his ideas there. He began the lecture tours, which were to gain him worldwide attention, with 1968 visits to Switzerland and Germany, immediately following the spring visit to Cyprus.

One would have to say that the visits to Europe were more successful than the one to Dr. Jarring. While he was treated cordially when he showed up at the UN's door in Nicosia, Cyprus, he was also told that no private individuals could see Dr. Jarring. Indeed, only those officially appointed by their governments could meet with him. Some of Jarring's assistants met with Joseph and took careful notes on his plans. When Joseph took a look at the bureaucratic machinery in place, he despaired of his ideas ever filtering through to Jarring himself. Moreover, this man who shared Schweitzer's belief in material simplicity was repelled by the lush arrangements for the UN staff and with how they seemed more concerned with having the best hotel accommodations in Nicosia than they were with the task confronting them. The contrast between the two men of Habla, who struggled over a used bed, and the UN diplomats, who each had a private limousine and chauffeur, offended Joseph, but it also showed him what he would be up against once he dared to take his ideas into the public arena. Joseph might have wasted precious personal funds on his trip to Cyprus, but this waste did not begin to compare with the amount wasted by Jarring's fruitless mission.

The encouragement Joseph felt in Europe, as a result of his forty speaking engagements, caused him to plan an even larger lecture tour for the following year in Europe and America. People seeking solutions for what appeared to be an intractable dilemma were impressed by his simple and logical approach, the strength of his own convictions, and his way of remaining optimistic about what could be achieved. Viewing a person who so obviously believed in the oneness of the human community appeared to make his audiences sense that peace and reconciliation in the Middle East might one day be possible. Excerpts from some of the press reviews of his speaking tour of 1969 give a good indication of the effect he produced.

> KUNSELSAU: 'Israel and the problems of the Middle East' are treated very often in the mass-media but there is seldom an opportunity to hear on these matters an objective picture, free from

emotions. A few days ago, Joseph W. Abileah, member of the War Resisters International Int. Council and Israeli citizen gave us such a description at a short visit in Kunselsau. . . . At this junction, the discussion necessarily turned to his basic world-view which is non-violence. Abileah, who has the title of "Mediator of the Commonwealth of World Citizens" considers his task to bring the message to people that no problem of our time can be solved with violence. In his conversation with Arab refugees, who, in the fatalism of their faith, accept everything as predestined by fate, he said the following: "War is not an unavoidable natural phenomenon. It is made by man and man has the mental power to prevent it if he wants to." His challenge to mankind is again and again not to preach love to fellowmen but to practice it daily. His motto is: In order to prevent violence, we must awake the good sparkle which exists permanently in every human being.

J. W. Abileah tries hard in travelling all over the world to find adherers for his idea. Now he is again on a lecture tour which brings him through Germany, Holland and England to the USA. On his journeys he makes contacts in order to obtain financial support for his plans. He shows his principles in practice by small services, as the reconstruction of an Arab village destroyed during the war.

He is not in agreement with the deeds of his government and hopes to induce the leaders to a new policy by intensive work at grass-roots level within the population.

In conclusion, one must say that Jos. W. Abileah devotes all his powers to promote peace in the world. Some may admire him and many smile at him—as a Utopist. However, his leading principle to devote his forces and mental power to reconstruction and reconciliation should be preferred to serving destruction of man through man.

—*Hohenlocher Zeitung*, July 12, 1969

Abileah, a convinced and convincing disciple of nonviolence, is proposing a federation plan for Israel, Jordan, and a still-to-be-formed Arab state for the West Bank of the Jordan.

Paraphrasing a Quaker aphorism, Abileah says, "Many good things have not been done in the world because people thought there was not time enough."

Many people feel that the plan to reconcile the Jews and the

Joseph lecturing the War Resisters International.

Arabs in the Middle East is too idealistic and will take too much time to accomplish. So military solutions are followed.

But this has been going on for forty years, observes Abileah, because most people feel there is not enough time. Efforts for reconciliation must begin now.

—*The Mennonite,* August 15, 1969

On the local Israeli level he has been propagating his ideas through the press, radio, public interviews, and lectures. He is frequently called on to participate in symposiums and discussions. He has made numerous lecture tours through Europe, England and North America.

"I cannot say that public opinion has been changed," Abileah

says, "but at least a public discussion is taking place. Arabs on the West Bank are still reluctant to join, lacking the conviction of nonviolence and fearing pressure from their surroundings. However, a recent five-day inquiry in towns and villages of the West Bank revealed full consent and even enthusiasm for a solution according to the principles I have outlined."
—*Lancaster Independent Press*, August 16, 1969

The lecture tour to the United States enabled Joseph to attend two Quaker conferences as well as the War Resisters International (WRI) triennial conference in Haverford, Pennsylvania. The first of these Quaker conferences was held at Grindstone Island, on the St. Lawrence River. This was to be an Institute on Nonviolence to which Joseph, accompanied by Dinah and Effie, had been invited as a resource person. Although the location was lovely and the chance for recreation and good family time was much appreciated, Joseph was disappointed with the conference as a whole. It was his first encounter with peace researchers, and as we might expect, he found their theoretical approach to nonviolence far too abstract for his tastes. Many of the participants had never really practiced nonviolence, instead they argued in a lofty manner about its merits and shortcomings. When he wrote a report to the American Friends Service Committee (AFSC), who had sponsored him at Grindstone Island, he gently criticized the academic approach the institute took, saying, "Scholars used statistics, diagrams, and other scientific devices to explain theories, tactics, and systems to follow in nonviolent group action. I wonder if this branch of science will not develop to end in scientific research like philosophy and theology, detached from everyday life. It must remain the concern of the man in the street."

Joseph's approach was not so much anti-intellectual as it was pragmatic. He, like Gandhi, knew the urgency of the situation in his country. In 1969, with the chance for a permanent and genuine peace slipping through the hands of recalcitrant Israeli and Arab governments, it was difficult to get too excited about complex theories and diagrams. Joseph's approach, directed toward what was possible for the man or woman of the street to do or understand, ran the risk of appearing simplistic. As Joseph himself acknowledges, it is difficult to be simple without sounding simplistic. Yet the simple truths are the most complex. Reducing complex issues to their basic components is one of Joseph's gifts, though it has been one that has often been misperceived and undervalued.

What was not misperceived or undervalued by audiences who heard him on this and subsequent lecture tours was that he was a man who narrowed the gap between his words and his actions. As he calmed down often-hostile audiences, as he did a group of Arabs and Palestinians at Columbia University in 1969, one could sense that nonviolence was truly a way of life for him. He not only believed in harmony but was able to produce it.

When a lecturer at an AFSC family camp in Colorado later in the summer of 1969 failed to show up, Joseph gave an impromptu talk on the connection between aesthetics and ethics. Using Bach and Beethoven as his examples, he stressed the idea that music was made more deeply meaningful by the worldviews of the composers, and he reflected that the creation of musical harmony was a way of restoring the dominance of love in the world. He told his audience that, while he loved Bach, he preferred Beethoven because the latter's music came more seriously to grips with the notion of evil in the world and yet, in the end, was able to assert the supremacy of love. Joseph might well have been talking about his own music and life. That he was able to project his own music, his own harmony, made skeptics take his viewpoints more seriously, and even those who rejected his idea as utopian had respect for the passion and obvious sincerity with which he put these ideas forward. Even to seasoned peace workers, it must have been thrilling to hear someone who believed there was a dynamic connection between beauty and peace.

At the WRI conference at Haverford, Joseph declined to accept a fifth term on the council. He felt that it was time for younger people like his nominee, Uri Davis, to be involved in the central committee, but he also felt that he needed to cut down on his involvement with any group whose main purpose was not Middle East peace. Just as he had done with the SCI and other groups in the past, he gave up leadership positions but continued to support local activities in any way he could.

Having now tried out his ideas on a wide variety of audiences at home and abroad, Joseph was determined to found a society to promote his ideas and to work for their implementation. In 1970, the groundwork was laid for what in 1971 was to become the Society for Middle East Confederation. Joseph cut back even further on his concert and teaching activities, and Dinah, who had always had to run an economical household, was asked to be even more creative with the meager funds now placed at her disposal. Joseph continued to be absent from home, gathering support for his ideas throughout the country and in the Occupied Territories. Some of the initial 1967 interest among the Israeli population was diminishing as occupation became more and more accepted, and the status quo appeared to be stable. As the occupation hardened, so did the treatment of those occupied. Joseph's plans for the confederation were postponed for a while in 1970, when he was asked by the Israeli League for Human and Civil Rights (ILHCR) to represent them at the special hearing of the United Nations, set up to examine alleged Israeli violations of human rights in the Occupied Territories of the West Bank and Gaza.

On December 19, 1968, the United Nations General Assembly, through Resolution 2443 [XXIII], established the Special Committee to Investigate Israeli Practices Affecting the Human Rights of the Population of the Occupied Territories. The actual appointment of the members of this committee did not take place until September 12, 1969, when Ceylon, Somalia, and Yugoslavia were asked to send representatives to the committee. Part of the reason for this delay was the death of Dr. Emilio Arenales, the president of the twenty-third session of the UN General Assembly; but part also was caused by the delay tactics of those who did not want to see the committee created in the first place. On January 6, 1970, Israel replied to the request to cooperate with the committee first by referring to its original rejection of Resolution 2443, then by objecting to the way the process was taken over by the secretary general, and finally by protesting the composition of the committee itself, which included one state, Somalia, that refused to recognize the state of Israel, another, Yugoslavia, that broke off diplomatic ties with Israel after the June 1967 War, and a third, Ceylon, that Israel accused of "generally" voting in favor of Arab resolutions at the UN.

The committee thus worked under the cloud of Israeli allegations of bias and of Israeli determination not to cooperate in any way with a committee it feared had already prejudged the outcome of its hearings. Israel has always believed that UN resolutions have been extremely one-sided, and Israeli hostility to the idea of the hearings made it particularly difficult for Israeli peace and civil rights groups to think about submitting evidence, either as individuals or as organizations. Nevertheless, after a great deal of internal debate, the Israeli League for Human and Civil Rights responded to the UN's invitation to submit evidence and on April 24, 1970, sent a memorandum to the committee. They were then invited to appear in person during the June 10 to June 15 hearings at the UN headquarters in New York City.

How it happened that Joseph represented the league in New York is an interesting story, surprising in one way because he had not been involved in drafting the April memorandum nor even in the league's recent activity. The league itself, which had suspended its work for three years after the June 1967 War, had recently been revived under the controversial but dynamic joint leadership of Israel Shahak and Uri Davis. The pressures, on these two men in particular and on the league in general, *not* to appear were immense. The debate within the league itself was made public on May 7, 1970, in an article in the influential *Ha'Aretz* paper, which showed that much of the league's membership was against the direction Shahak was taking them.

One gathers that it was out of a desire to have someone represent the league who was not connected with the infighting or connected with any political party that Shahak and Davis turned to Joseph, a man whose integrity would not be questioned. The first problem to be confronted was that Joseph felt uncomfortable with the April 24 memorandum, which was largely based on newspaper evidence as was the later, fuller June 8 memorandum that he eventually took with him to New York. Joseph informed Shahak and Davis that he would testify about human rights abuses, but he would do it only on the basis of what he himself saw and knew. His lifelong distrust of the news media made him skeptical about any evidence based upon newspapers, and his unwillingness to compromise with truth made him hesitant about committing himself to evidence presented by those he did not know. As he told Davis, "The press is never a serious matter in any country. You can never take a press report as evidence." Finally, his lack of recent active participation in the league itself made him uncomfortable about being its representative. When Shahak and Davis agreed to let him speak as an individual as well as their representative, he agreed to go, though it left him with less than a month in which to gather his own evidence.

Joseph's reluctance to represent the league should not be interpreted to mean that he was in any way skeptical about alleged abuses. He knew that human rights were being violated in Israel and in the Occupied Territories. In 1968, his had been the first signature affixed to a public petition calling for an end to these abuses. The strong tone it adopted shows how serious those who signed it thought the situation was.

End the Violations of Human Rights in Israel and the Administered Territories

The papers have published details concerning events taking place in Israel and the occupied territories; orders of confinement, limitation of travel and arrests without trial have been issued recently against Israeli citizens, Arabs and Jews.

Collective punishments of curfew and blowing up houses in towns and villages in the occupied territories continue at a disquieting rate. Families of workers and peasants, children, women and aged are left without shelter and without means of subsistence. The stream of refugees and escapees from the Gaza Strip and the West Bank continues incessantly. The number of Arabs expelled from the West Bank by order of the Israeli Military regime is increasing. In a petition of protest published in the West Bank it is noted that this policy contradicts international norms (and violates) the fundamental rights of a resident to live on his land and in his home. The expulsion of a resident against his expressed wish and on political grounds brings to mind the days of the British colonial regime.

Where does this policy lead to other than an abyss of hostility? These acts will strengthen the resistance and rebellion movement, will increase the casualties of both parties and will lead to the eruption of another war. And who knows who will be its victims? The domination of one people over another will of necessity lead to moral degeneration and to the undermining of democracy in the ruling people as well. A people oppressing another must end in losing its own freedom and the freedom of its citizens.

Jew! Remember the righteous among the nations who stood at our side in times of disaster. When disaster meets a neighbouring people—will you stand aside and remain silent?

Raise your voice and act against violations of human rights!

This petition had received wide circulation in Israel and abroad. When *Pravda* published it, the petition became known as the *Pravda* Letter, a description intended to discredit it in Israel and in the West. The USSR's role in the 1967 war had created a strong anti-Soviet bias in Israel, and rather than deal with the substance of the letter, people tended to pass it off as the work of communists and to regard those who signed it as traitors. Lines were being drawn in Israel, and those seeking reconciliation ran a great risk of being thought disloyal to the state. Because Joseph's name headed the alphabetically arranged list of signatures, he perhaps received more notoriety than others who signed the letter, who included some of his old friends like Meir Rubinstein, Yeshayahu Toma Shik, Uri Davis, and Edith Wolff.

Threats were made to Joseph, telling him not to go to New York, once his representative status and time of departure were made public; and while he was gone, Dinah received many crank calls. Still, he never hesitated about where his duty lay. We should remember that in agreeing to go, he was making it hard for the Society for Middle East Confederation to get the initial Israeli support it needed. He could have been political and kept in mind his larger objective, but he did not. In his marvelously simple and clear-sighted way, he told the UN committee on June 12 what it was that ultimately caused him to make the trip. "The very first thing is to protect human rights, and this thing I put in the first place, even if my loyalty to my Government will be disturbed or infringed by this. I think this is the most important thing. The loyalty to humanity is the first thing and your loyalty to your nation the second thing."

Joseph was no fool; he knew the risk he was running in making his appearance. Because of this risk, he was scrupulous when gathering information. If he were to suffer from his testimony, he wanted to make sure that he would at least be suffering for what he believed to be the truth. Collecting the relevant information was difficult. Members of the league were banned from prisons, where they had hoped to collect evidence regarding alleged acts of torture and brutality towards political prisoners, so they had had to rely on newspapers. No Israeli officials in the Occupied Territories were allowed to cooperate with them at all. Then, as was mentioned, the league's general reputation in Israel was not good, which restricted more unofficial contacts. As he had done so often in the past, Joseph dropped everything he was doing and made daily trips to the West Bank and Gaza, building on trips and contacts he had made before, talking to trusted Arab friends, and using them to make contacts with alleged victims and their families. He himself talked to attorneys and inspected housing demolitions, attended military court hearings, and once even used his Masonic connections to talk with a member of his lodge who was also a military judge.

Joseph testified at both a morning and an afternoon hearing

Joseph interviewing an inhabitant of the occupied West Bank.

on June 12. From the transcript of the hearings, it is clear that the members of the committee were no more used to dealing with someone like Joseph than many Israeli governmental figures were. They chafed at his unwillingness to say more than he saw or to corroborate evidence of those he personally did not know. At one point, the chairman, H. S. Amerisinghe of Ceylon, had the following interchange with Joseph in the afternoon session:

> JA—On a personal basis, not as a member of the League, I myself would not like to testify to something which I have not seen myself.
> CHAIRMAN—With respect to the position of this special Committee, if we were to rely merely on newspaper reports, then we would not have any need to get a member of the League to come and speak to us.
> JA—I am very sorry I disappoint you in this part of my mission.
> CHAIRMAN—Yes, I must confess that some things are a disappointment in this respect. I will not conceal that.

ISAIAH'S TEACHING

Joseph's fact-finding mission during the occupation.

The transcript from these sessions reveals Joseph as he always presents himself—simple, direct, modest, yet ready to launch off on favorite topics of nonviolence, the evils of the nation-state, the need for a federal political solution to the Arab-Israeli problem, and the testimony to the goodness of the human heart. There are times in the testimony when one gets the sense that he was, at best, merely tolerated by an increasingly frustrated committee, anxious to wrap up its 1970 hearings, at which he was the one hundred forty-sixth and last witness. Yet in the end, his manner prevailed, so much so that in its final report to the twenty-fifth session of the UN General Assembly in 1971, the committee singled out his evidence as being particularly effective. Perhaps remembering the Israeli UN delegate's January 6 charge that the committee could not render an impartial report, the committee said,

> There were other witnesses from Israel who corroborated the general evidence of systematic violations of human rights. The special Committee would refer in particular to the evidence given

by a representative of the Israeli League for Human and Civil Rights on behalf of that organization, Mr. Joseph Abileah, an executive member of the League who was authorized by the League's executive to testify before the special Committee. He presented on behalf of the League a memorandum dated June 8, 1970, which forms part of the records of the Special Committee. In this memorandum the Israeli League for Human and Civil Rights refers to alleged instances of breaches of human rights, such as collective punishment, blowing up of houses, administrative detention, expulsions and torture, killing during curfew, and supports these allegations with statistics and names of persons affected. Mr. Abileah supplemented the memorandum with oral evidence.

In an effort to eliminate any possibility of political prejudice or any other form of bias on the part of Mr. Abileah and the organization he represents, namely the Israeli League for Human and Civil Rights, against the Government of Israel, the members of the Special Committee subjected Mr. Abileah to a thorough and exhaustive cross-examination. Mr. Abileah withstood this cross-examination without faltering, and left no doubt in the minds of the members of the Committee as to his credibility.

What was the importance of the picture of the occupation from 1967 to 1970 that one gets from reading Joseph's testimony? By discounting exaggerations and hearsay, by refusing to use loaded language like *terrorist* or *racist*, he was able to make a statement that was at once accurate and, as the Israeli newspapers later acknowledged, true. He may not have pleased those anxious to make Israel appear the arch-criminal of the world, but he made it clear that the occupation was far from benign and that its abuses, if not as flagrant as many Arab witnesses had claimed, were nonetheless serious and clear violations of the Geneva Accords of 1949. When presenting his evidence, he often first gave the rationale of the occupying forces for the acts of violence, such as the explanation that house demolition was preferable to killing the house's inhabitants, but then quietly said, "This is a justification which I don't accept, but it is their justification." In his testimony, he never pictured his fellow countrymen as brutal monsters but regarded them as potentially good men and women held hostage to a worldview and a political structure that made brutal actions unavoidable. He never lost his ability to separate the actors from the actions, whether they were Palestinians or Israelis. He described his interview with Arkin, the military governor of the West Bank, as an interview with a man who was "kind and helpful," though the actions for which he was responsible Joseph found reprehensible. He maintained his commitment to the humanity of both the oppressed and the oppressor all through the hearings.

Perhaps this commitment to humanity is why his evidence was so convincing. No one could avoid coming to terms with his charges by dismissing his evidence as obviously biased—a technique most of us use when confronted with unpleasant truths about ourselves. Note the disarmingly simple and direct way he refers to the death of an old woman in the demolition of Habla, a statement which is also a powerful testimony against the horrors of war.

> I made some distribution of clothing and all these kind of things to keep the people on the place, to help them in their first difficult situation. Then I went around the village with all the people. They showed me the destroyed houses, because I had promised to help them. So everyone said, "This is my house; this is my house." And the whole village was around me, and once we came to a heap of stones where there was a big hole in this, and you could see a part of the pavement of the house. I asked the Arab man "Why did you do this? Why did you make a hole here to clear this pavement?" He said, "This is the place where my mother died under the rubble." You see, he said this in a way, not that he accused me of something, he had a look, you know, that he was not complaining anything against me. He said, "I have to keep this place, just to remember my mother." The case happened that they had to leave very quickly and this woman was sick. They could not take her along. They didn't know what would happen to their village. They thought they would be able to come back very soon. So they gave her food and they gave

her everything she needed for a number of days and left her in her bed. But when the shooting and the destroying started, and the bombing and the exploding of everything, the Israeli Government was sure that all the people had left.

Joseph was careful in telling his stories. He had read earlier evidence presented to the committee and was anxious to strip his own testimony of excessive rhetoric and emotion. "I tell you all these things because the report which you receive[d] from Arab evidence might be true things—I don't want to say that their reports were not true—but it has an undertone of hate, propaganda and some political opinions. It is mentioned, but it has that undertone. In reading this I felt that the emphasis is always put only on the negative and not on the positive." Some Palestinians, hearing these words, might wonder where the positive elements in their situation were to be found, but the words are proof of Joseph's commitment to a humanity that knows no national boundaries, one that stresses links, not differences. Later in his testimony, Joseph explained his method of getting information. "If I go, I go and drink coffee in this restaurant and then I go and visit a friend, who gives me some information. You know, I don't go even with the purpose of investigating. But, of course, I hear many things and I am very concerned about them. I am less concerned about criticizing and finding out injustices than in putting right injustices—that's what I am most concerned about . . . and that was the reason I went to the village, to the rehabilitation village."

Israelis who followed his testimony closely or who might have feared that his participation would condemn Israel even more in the eyes of the world were reasonably satisfied that, on the whole, Joseph's testimony had been temperate. U.S. Jewry were less sympathetic and tried to discredit the league itself. Thus, while *Ha'Aretz* conducted a lengthy, fairly positive interview with Joseph on his return, an anonymous "analyst" investigated the league and sent a damning report of its activities to all the league's European affiliates. Mordechay Avi-Shaul, vice-chairman of the league, sent an angry December 1971 reply to the director of the International League for the Rights of Man, quoting from this secret analysis. "The present status of the Israeli League is in some doubt. It is not clear whether the present Executive Committee was properly elected in accordance with the by-laws of the Israeli League and there is some information to the effect that the election is being contested. We understand that some individual members of the Israeli League had advocated activities of violence, but to our knowledge the Israeli League has not done so." Avi-Shaul could not let such slurs and innuendos pass, especially when they appeared to challenge the accuracy of the league's findings. His long, angry letter ends in the following manner:

> While analysing the "Blowing up of Houses" Mr. Analyst does not understand the chart that shows the number of the destructed [sic] houses, because some of them were blown up as *"part of a military operation."* He singles out the destruction perpetrated in Qalqilya—a nice "military operation," after the cease fire: And what about the obliteration of the villages of Imwas, Beit Nuba, Yalu, the stigma written on our face? What about the barbaric revenge in Halhul? Study, study Mr. Analyst, what "neighborhood punishment" means in practice:
>
> And what about the refugee camps in the Gaza Strip, where 6360 dwellings of human beings have been demolished and tens of thousands [of] inhabitants uprooted? Will he argue against the "chart" of Sir John Rennie, Commissioner General of UNRRA, because of lack of "supporting data"?
>
> Army units (of a Military Governor) laid siege to two villages, Beit Iqsa and Nebi Samwil. Very few of the inhabitants of Nebi Samwil remained in their home after June 1967. They were now driven out. Those of Beit Iqsa were kept in quarantine. The two villages were surrounded—the siege lasted 5 days. At the end of 5 days the siege was raised and 30 houses on the top of the hill had been razed, i.e. made level with the ground. It happened in March 1971. Why? The greater part of the land of the fellahin was long ago "taken over" by the Jewish National Fund.
>
> Can you explain such bloodless, but bloody, robbery? Almost idyllic. . . . Very simple. The land is needed for sight-seeing and

... building villas. . . . It is very easy to understand—naturally. The villas will be built for my Jewish brethren, whereas the demolished houses were "taken over" from only Arab fallahin. What do they know about the beauty of the Biblical landscape . . . !

Now, is it my patriotic duty to remain silent?

There has been in Israel and in the Occupied Territories political oppression; there have been collective punishments on a grand scale, blowing up houses of *suspects* and of parents, brothers and other relatives of *suspects*—I don't remember whether a single house was ever destroyed on strength of a verdict of a court of law. There have been administrative detentions, expulsion of individuals and masses; there have been torture during interrogation and killing during curfew and in broad daylight. Just, while I began the writing of this letter (on the 15th of December, 1600 o'clock) I hear on the Israeli Broadcasting: A Beduin boy was killed in the North-Sinai; an army patrol perceived at 11.30 o'clock a *suspect figure,* which started to run away when called by the patrol. He was fired at, and died before he could have been taken to a hospital.—Yesterday and to-morrow—the same, or a similar, story. No advocate can quibble away the horrors of Gaza and of the rest of the Occupied Territories.

I am reading the threats of the Gentleman "Analyst": "Serious consideration (of the International League) should be given to whether there should be a continued affiliation with any body which has not demonstrated its willingness to act in a studied and reasoned manner. The current record of the Israeli League leads one to believe that it is more interested in serving as an organ of political propaganda on behalf of the interests of some of its members than in ascertaining the facts"—etc.

"Of course," says the analyst-moralist, "If endorsement of violence were an official position of the Israeli League, a re-examination of the affiliate status of the Israeli League certainly would be in order."

Poor analyst: "Certainly."

No threats will silence us:

On the strength of my recommendation the Committee of the Israeli League for Human and Civil Rights authorizes our chairman Dr. Israel Shahak—at present a visitor lecturer in the Imperial College, London—who prepares for a trip in the U.S.A., to represent there our cause, the cause of Human and

Civil Rights, vis-à-vis any forum, in any form he considers necessary.

Despite the angry rejoinder, the league lost its international affiliation a short while later—the reason given being that they had ceased to be objective and were using their investigations for political not humanitarian aims. Like the labeling of the *Pravda* Letter, this charge of lack of objectivity had the effect of obfuscating the issues and perhaps was intended to silence the league.

While Joseph's reconciling manner might have been useful to all parties during this angry interchange, his own involvement with the league was diminishing. It was not that he objected to the nature of its activities, but rather that his activities on behalf of the Society for Middle East Confederation were now becoming all consuming. These activities allowed him a role he always found more natural to his temperament because they involved building something positive rather than tearing down or criticizing. For this reason, Joseph valued his meeting with Dr. Ralph Bunche at the United Nations the day after he gave his testimony. Dr. Bunche, who had taken over from the assassinated Count Bernadotte in 1948, remembered Joseph's 1947 proposals and now encouraged him to go ahead with his work, even as Anwar El-Khatib had done in 1967. Bunche told Joseph that he regretted the partition plan and revealed to Joseph that he had been the author of the Minority Report of UNSCOP, which argued in favor of the confederative solution.

The conversation with Dr. Bunche meant a great deal to Joseph. He felt he had done his duty to the league and to truth by his appearance at the UN, but what was needed was not only an exposition of the problems in Israel and the West Bank and Gaza but also a plan for remedying them. Dr. Bunche had strengthened Joseph's resolve that the plan he had in mind for twenty-five years could solve the dilemma of two peoples with two senses of justice and rights who wanted the same piece of land. Joseph was willing to run the risk about which Judah

Magnes had warned in 1923 when he said that it might one day become political treason for "someone in the streets of Jerusalem" to repeat "Isaiah's teaching that swords are to be beaten into ploughshares, and men are to learn war no more." Joseph had, in fact, been accused of political treason for his pacifist ideas, but his actions in 1967–70 echoed Isaiah's words 62:1. "For Zion's sake will I not hold my peace and for Jerusalem's sake I will not rest until the righteousness thereof go forth as brightness, and the salvation thereof as a lamp that burneth."

7

Society for Middle East Confederation 1972–1987

> Today it appears absurd to many—especially in the present intra-Arab situation—to think now about Israel's participation in a Near East federation. Tomorrow with an alteration in certain world-political situations independent of us, this possibility may arise in a highly positive sense. Insofar as it depends on us, we must prepare the ground for it. There can be no peace between Jews and Arabs that is only a cessation of war; there can only be a peace of genuine cooperation. Today, under such manifoldly aggravated circumstances, the command of the spirit is still to prepare the way for the cooperation of peoples.
> —Martin Buber, 1958

⇥ THE FINAL PHASE of Joseph's peace activity has found him more convinced than ever that the structure of society is largely responsible for determining its response to conflict. His ideas about the potential goodness of the human heart have not changed, but his conviction that political structures can often keep that goodness from finding expression has led him to pursue single-mindedly a new political configuration for the Middle East. He looks at most of the wars since 1948 as having been inevitable once Israel opted for the structure of the nation-state and bought into the notion of right of conquest. There is a calmness in his voice that belies his sadness when he notes that the doctrine of might makes right has won over Israel as it has all other nation-states. Often in his correspondence, one comes across the following description of his addresses to audiences in Israel and abroad: "I said to these people that the structure of the nation state will not survive the 21st Century. It is obsolete for our lives. We must plan new ways for relating. When will it happen? It could happen tomorrow or in the future, generally. But the alternative is mutual annihilation."

Joseph knows the uphill fight his plan for confederation has before it. It challenges not only the present political structure but, in some ways, five thousand years of human history, which claim that winners are the ones to determine the definition of what are rights. As he ruefully observes, Israel won its historical rights to the land with the conquest of Joshua; the Muslims with the seventh-century conquest of Jerusalem; the Christians with the Crusades of the Middle Ages; the Ottomans with the military conquest of their empire; and the British with the victory over Germany in World War I. If might makes right, how is a confederation possible, where winners would be asked to share with losers? Joseph's answer is that a political superstructure need not be built over a base of the violence of conquest. If one changes the base, certain political structures seem more natural than others. The base of nonviolence makes logical a system of government that stresses cooperation, the sort of cooperation mentioned by Martin Buber in the epigraph to this chapter. For Joseph, the most logical choice of system is the one of confederation.

Buoyed by his lectures abroad and *still* convinced that the June 1967 War presented a unique opportunity for putting forth creative long-term solutions, Joseph realized part of his dream by forming on May 26, 1971, at the Pension Wohlman in Haifa, the Society for Middle East Confederation. Present at the meeting were longtime friends Edith Wolff, Wajdi-Farid Tabari, Reverend K. Musallem, and about forty others. The American, Landrum Bolling, then president of Earlham College in Richmond, Indiana; Yehudi Menuhin; Dr. Hugh Schonfield, founder of the Commonwealth of World Citizens; and Hein van Wijk, a member of the senate of the Netherlands, agreed to be international sponsors. By August, fifty members had enrolled, and the first governing body was elected. Wajdi-Farid Tabari, a well-known Haifa lawyer and later a *Qadi* (judge) in the Islamic courts of Jaffa and Jerusalem, agreed to be the first chairman. Joseph assumed the post he has now held for more than fifteen years, that of secretary. Edith Wolff is a good example of the people who were early drawn to this new society. She was a German, who during World War II, wanted to show her solidarity with the oppressed by publicly converting to Judaism. During the war, she served as a member of the German underground, hiding many Jews in her Berlin flat. She was arrested and spent time in ten different concentration camps. Like so many other unconquerable spirits, she had survived to come to Israel after the war, and there she continued her work for the oppressed of the world. She was drawn to Joseph and his work because she saw in him her own commitment to a humanity that knew no national borders nor acknowledged any religious barriers.

Joseph's plans for the confederation have changed little since 1972. He has been a strong advocate of a particular goal. He has been equally strong as an advocate of a certain means to that goal. The means involve a definition of the worldview he has held for such a long time. Before seeing it in its most complete form, we should examine in more detail the plan for confederation, and there is no better way to do so than to reproduce a 1977 interview Joseph had with Dr. Jeffrey M. Elliot, an award-winning scholar and journalist. This interview has been published by the society and is sent out regularly to those wanting to know more about its aims. In it are to be found themes that have been part of Joseph's political thinking for a long time—his distrust of the nation-state, his disappointment with the UN and the role of the superpowers, his belief in learning from geophysical realities, his compassion for Arabs, the pragmatism of his idealism, and his unfailing optimism.

ELLIOT: What is the Society for Middle East Confederation?
ABILEAH: The Society was conceived as a forum for the discus-

sion of constructive ideas which aim at solving the Middle East conflict by cooperation of Arabs and Jews on the economic and political level. These range from a BENELUX pattern (economic cooperation) to a full confederation of states, providing equal status and representation to each of the member-components.

ELLIOT: When did the group first come into being?

ABILEAH: The founders' meeting took place on May 26, 1971, at Pension Wohlman, Haifa. It was called by two Arab citizens (a Moslem advocate and a Lutheran pastor) and two Jewish citizens (an immigrant from Germany and myself, who was locally educated). In a second general meeting, the rules were established and the official registration with the District Commissioner of Haifa was confirmed on January 9, 1972, by a notice in the press.

ELLIOT: Who comprises the membership of the Society?

ABILEAH: The Society consists of both registered members as well as sympathizers. The total of registered members exceeds 150, including Israelis, Jews, Arabs, and nationals of other countries. The sympathizers, mostly abroad, number between 400–500. All professions and walks of life are represented. The international sponsors include: Dr. Landrum Bolling (United States), Yehudi Menuhin (England), Dr. Martin Niemöller (West Germany), Dr. Hugh Schonfield (England), and Adv. Hein van Wijk (Netherlands).

ELLIOT: What is the thrust of the Society's peace initiative?

ABILEAH: Having lived in the region for almost 50 years, I have become very concerned about its future. As a convinced pacifist, I have always advocated peaceful solutions based upon a common homeland for Jews, Arabs, and other people who would like to share our fate. The Society has not adopted a definite plan. My own program includes six points: (1) A confederation composed of three states, viz. Jordan, Arab Palestine (West Bank), and Israel, with a federal capitol in Jerusalem. (2) The federal government should deal, at least in the beginning, with foreign policy and economic integration. (3) Economic integration would enable the confederation to solve the refugee problem without massive foreign aid. (4) The help of the United Nations is required for an enlargement of the irrigation scheme in the Syrian desert with the waters of the Tigris and Euphrates. This would provide the Iraqis and the Syrians with irrigated land. (5) A religious council, which would form a second house in the federal parliament, should be composed of representatives of all faiths and religious communities in the area. This council would be entrusted with the creation of a federal constitution based on ethical principles. (6) The confederation would be open to any country in the Middle East to join. It should be formed with the idea of creating a United States of the Middle East in the future.

ELLIOT: Why should Israel, under your proposal, give up its status as a sovereign nation?

ABILEAH: Like the other member-states, Israel must be willing to limit its absolute sovereignty if we are to become a tripartite confederation or even a binational constellation. We cannot expect our neighbor to do something which we are not prepared to do ourselves. Besides, this fact only reflects the realities of the situation, as Israel has become entirely dependent on the United States. In this regard, it lost its independence and sovereignty some time ago. It is important to challenge the notion of national sovereignty as such. In our century, with the advancement of technology, improved living standards, and mass communications, this political term has lost its meaning in a practical sense. It has become an anachronism, one which has encouraged the outbreak of war owing to the semantic weight of the word as myth. Similarly as Israel has lost her sovereignty, so will a sovereign Palestinian state lose her independence as one of the super-powers or an Arab state in the area. It cannot hope to survive with limited natural resources and lack of access to the major seaports. The establishment of an Arab-Palestinian state without close ties to Israel or Jordan or both is precarious at best. Add to this the law of return for refugees, and you further increase the risk of war. It is clear that Israel will do her utmost to remain in a position of readiness and will escalate an endless arms race with the result of economic decline for herself and the whole region.

ELLIOT: At the heart of your proposal is the concept of confederation. What kind of confederation do you envision?

ABILEAH: The answer is to create a confederation, very loose in the beginning, of perhaps two or three states which would depend on each other in a geo-political way. This would encompass the areas on both banks of the Jordan, the present state of

Israel, the Hashemite Kingdom of Jordan, the creation of a new member-state on the West Bank and the Gaza area reserved for the Palestinians. Each state would establish a local government as well as send representatives to the confederative government on a parity basis. The central government would deal with common concerns, chief of which should be the rehabilitation of refugees. This task must be viewed as a shared burden and responsibility.

ELLIOT: What do you see as the geographic boundaries of a Middle East Confederation?

ABILEAH: The smallest Middle East Confederation which could meet the present needs would comprise the territory on both banks of the River Jordan. This would provide the Hashemite Kingdom and the new Palestinian state with access to the seaports of the eastern Mediterranean, vital to their respective economies. The state boundaries would be roughly those of June, 1967, it being understood that these would constitute ethnic-cultural divisions and not strategic frontiers to be defended. There exists the possibility of a division into smaller states according to the majority of inhabitants of one ethnic group or another. This approach resembles a plan proposed by Yitzhak Hayutman in 1975, which would establish three types of sub-states based on ethnicity: Arab, Jewish, and mixed. There could be as many as twelve or more of these states, each of which would be represented in the confederative government. A similar approach was advanced by Professor Johan Galtung, Oslo, and would address the problem of the large minorities in preponderantly Jewish or Arab states.

ELLIOT: In what ways will a confederation turn enmity into friendship in the Middle East?

ABILEAH: Enmity and hate are created by fear. At present, the Arabs are as much afraid of being pushed into the desert as the Jews are afraid of being thrown into the sea. The Jewish immigration is opposed by the Arabs for fear of being outnumbered. The return of the refugees is opposed by the Israelis for fear of the Arab majority. If we could agree on the principle of parity-representation in the constitution, this mutual fear would be eliminated and a new bond of trust created in its place. This is the difference between a confederation which is merely a military alliance and one which has a common constructive purpose.

ELLIOT: How will a confederation improve the economic posture of the area?

ABILEAH: Under a confederation, the present population of 500,000 unemployed people who live in the camps would be made productive, which would substantially benefit the economy of the new confederation. I do not envision one industrialized member-state, with the other member-states providing the manpower. Each member-state should make use, as much as possible, of local natural treasures and available potential in agriculture, crafts, and industry. Israel has utilized, to a great extent, her various natural resources, employing reclamation, irrigation, and other methods to improve her yield. The other two member-states could likewise be developed and their resources increased. Stone cutting is a specialty of the east. There are quarries of many different kinds of stones and marble available in the West Bank and Jordan. The existence of one or two family houses in the area with ornaments of differently colored stone is very attractive. An industry of stone buildings of diverse architectural designs with ready stones to be assembled could be a valuable source of income for the local artisans. It is also an excellent way of providing decent housing for newly settled refugees who, with their unique brand of individuality, would not be happy living in big apartment buildings without aesthetic appeal. Numerous olive trees provide the raw materials for the soap industry which has an old tradition in Nablus. The vineyards of Judea and Gilead provide the material for outstanding wines. The chemical treasures of the Dead Sea have supplied the Israeli as well as the Jordanian potash works. Spa springs abound in the valley of the Jordan and the eastern parts of the Dead Sea. Add to these the agricultural products which a developed West Bank could yield, as well as the advantages of a coordinated tourist trade, and it would be quite possible to eliminate the present negative trade balance. With all of these possibilities, I would not be so eager to accept the achievements of western technology en bloc, as have many people in the world without regard for the environment or future growth.

ELLIOT: What are the basic advantages of a confederation?

ABILEAH: A confederation is a partnership, a safeguard of common interests. The existing state boundaries cease to be strategic "security borders" and become merely ethnic cultural frontiers designed to keep various groups apart. All military fortifications and armaments could be gradually reduced and eventually abolished, and the resources used instead for the rehabilitation of refugees, creation of infrastructure, and improvement of social welfare. The greatest advantage of a confederation is a geopolitical one. The distance from the sea to the edge of the desert is less than 100 miles. It is inconceivable that in this narrow stretch of land, where geographically one region complements another, there should be three national sovereign states with separate, competing economies.

ELLIOT: What common Arab-Israeli interests make a confederation possible?

ABILEAH: In addition to what I have already mentioned, a confederation would enable us to shake off our present dependence on foreign aid and the political strings connected therewith. A well-knitted partnership would encourage the super-powers to maintain a hands-off policy and no longer view us as a pawn in their rivalry for spheres of influence. It is vital that we do everything possible to avoid a confrontation between the United States and the Soviet Union. A confederation would help make that possible.

ELLIOT: How would you deal with the problem of the Palestinian Arabs?

ABILEAH: According to our proposal, the Arabs would have their own member-state within the confederation. If Jordan became a constitutional monarchy, it might be possible that the Palestinians would form a common Arab member-state on both banks of the River Jordan. This would be an important step forward in terms of parity-representation in the federal government. The law of return must be extended to include the Arabs, and the returning refugees should be permitted to settle in a member-state of their choice. Family affiliations, cultural surroundings, economic opportunities, and nostalgia for the past would be the determining factors in such a decision. Based upon these considerations, we could expect as many as 250,000 returnees to each of the three territories (Jordan, West-Bank, and Israel). These would be people who still reside in the refugee camps. The remaining 650,000 people with refugee status, who have been able to rehabilitate themselves in the United States, Canada, various European countries, or the neighboring Arab states should be given the option of leaving their present positions and returning to one of the territories. In the event that they opt to stay in their host countries, they should be fully compensated for their property as were the Jewish immigrants who came from various Arab countries in the past decades. If the Jewish inhabitants of the new settlements in occupied territories wish to stay (provided that these settlements were not built on confiscated land) or if religious zealots wish to live in Hebron or other places connected with Jewish history, they should be allowed to stay, but they must be aware that they will have to respect the civil laws of the respective Arab member-states the same as we expect Israeli Arabs to abide by Israeli civil law. I believe that the present attitude towards the Arab minorities in Israel, which has often been discriminatory because of our nation-state structure, will be ameliorated and levelled out the moment the Palestinians secure their homeland.

ELLIOT: What do you see as the basic foreign policy of a Middle East Confederation?

ABILEAH: The cornerstone of a confederative foreign policy should reflect the common welfare of the region. This is idealistically expressed. However, in practical terms, it should include trade agreements with Egypt, Syria, and Lebanon. We might begin with an irrigation scheme in the Syrian desert. As I indicated earlier, this is a very fertile region. Adding to it the area between the Rivers Euphrates and Tigris, which might require agricultural development projects, Syria and Iraq will achieve a stable economic position. They will no longer take part in bitter political rivalries. This is what occurred in Jordan, in 1970, as well as in Lebanon for the last two years. Indeed, conflict has been an unhappy part of our region for the last 29 years.

ELLIOT: How will the confederation be governed?

ABILEAH: The responsibility for administration and decision-making in the various member-states must be left to the local governments. The confederative government should deal, at least in the beginning, with common regional concerns. These might include a coordinated foreign policy and the rehabilitation of refugees. Once we have made progress in these areas, we will find ourselves cooperating in such areas as health services, road building, meteorological services, port authorities, and many others. A president should be elected on a rotating basis, similar to the system in Switzerland, when seven members of the cabinet hold office as chairman for a period of one-year in rotation. The concept of parity representation in the confederative government is essential, especially since every sector is afraid of being outnumbered.

ELLIOT: Do you envision the United Nations playing a role in maintaining peace in the area while the confederation is taking hold?

ABILEAH: The answer is no. When partition was decided by the United Nations General Assembly, it was implemented by Israelis fighting the Arab opposition without the participation of a single United Nations soldier. Later, when United Nations soldiers were posted at the Israeli-Egyptain frontier, they were unable to prevent infiltration and conflict during the entire period, 1957–1967, and left altogether when the war broke out. The weakness of the United Nations in such cases is well-documented by Michael Mekory in his book, *The Peace Scroll: The Way to Universal Peace*. What we need are peace-makers, not peace-keepers. I applaud the United Nations in those areas in which they are best suited: health, technical assistance, human rights, world traffic, environmental pollution, etc. However, in the areas of peace-making and peace-keeping, the United Nations will always fail because of structural shortcomings. We must discover better ways to involve our citizens in the solutions to their own problems.

ELLIOT: How would a confederation deal with the problem of social, political, and economic integration?

ABILEAH: The problems which exist today are the result of the fact that the new State of Israel consists of citizens who brought with them the cultures and habits of 80 different countries. The main differences appear in the clash between east and west. We have a majority of eastern Jews (whom the Palestinians call the Arab Jews) and a minority of immigrants from the west. Nevertheless, an attempt has been made to impose western values on the whole society, with the result that we are becoming more and more "Levantinized." On the other hand, the Arabs are shaking off more and more of their traditions in favor of western ways of life (one of them being nationalism). It remains to be seen how the confederation will influence the integration of the two cultures, and how we will incorporate the desirable parts of each to the needs of the area. Economic integration should include development projects for the rehabilitation of the returning refugees. There should be a common budget in which we pool our available resources. With the advancement of living standards in the member-states, the economic situation will level out in the future. With regard to political integration, we must allow each member-state to follow along its own lines. For example, Israel comprises all forms of political structure: extreme communism in the Kibbutz to trade union-owned agriculture and industry to capitalist private enterprise. It is inevitable that the Palestinian state will experience a class struggle until it finds a suitable structure. It is also clear that Jordan will gradually become a constitutional monarchy, with the pressure from below growing stronger.

ELLIOT: What role would the super-powers play in a Middle East Confederation?

ABILEAH: The super-powers are not interested at the present time in the outbreak of peace in the Middle East because they are afraid of losing their foothold in their respective spheres of influence in the region. Oil interests and weapons markets are also involved. As far back as 1969, I argued that we should ask for help from the nations of the world in irrigating the Syrian desert, but at the same time guarantee the oil interests for these nations. This induced Mr. Maynard Shelly, the former editor of *The Mennonite*, to write an article entitled, "Take Your Oil. Give Us Water." The super-powers are not interested in a big fire which would mean a direct confrontation, but they do not mind if a few thousand Arabs and Jews are killed from time to time. The situation demands that we no longer kill or be killed to protect foreign interests. Our conscientious objectors have made an important start in this direction. This is a first step, but a passive one. We must become more active in peace-making by awakening our citizens to the true facts of the situation. Even for the super-powers the present policies are short-sighted. The arms supplied to the Middle East are paid for in cash only by rich countries. Those supplied to Israel are mostly in the form of loans, few of which will ever be paid back. This fact does not worry the United States as long as we remain their serfs. Arms do not produce anything; they can only be used for destructive purposes. On the other hand, if credit was granted in the form of tractors and other agricultural machinery, new skills could be developed, and in time, all loans repaid with interest. In a confederation comprising all countries of the Middle East or even a common market constellation, regular commercial relations on equal standing could be established with western as well as eastern nations, including the super-powers.

ELLIOT: How has the Israeli public reacted to your proposals?

ABILEAH: The reaction of the Israeli public can best be described as skeptical. This fact is changing, however, as the idea of confederation is being advanced by many political leaders, as well as discussed in the news media. We rarely encounter direct opposition, although doubters are still abundant.

ELLIOT: Does your plan have support in the Arab community?

ABILEAH: In the Arab community, we find a better reaction, although seldom in public statements. The further the individual who is approached lives from the scene of the conflict, the more nationalistic and uncompromising he seems to be. Peoples in the West-Bank realize that they must eventually unite with Jordan or Israel in order to survive. In a union with Israel, they fear being labeled as traitors to the Arab cause. When a tripartite confederation is proposed to them, they see a basis on which to agree; more than that, they welcome such a plan as a possible solution to the problem. The fact that Arabs were among the founders of our Society, and continue to demonstrate great cooperation, indicates that they are as eager as the Israelis to assure the future of their children. Indeed, the chairman of our Society, Mr. Ibrahim Sima'an, is himself an Arab.

ELLIOT: Have the Palestinian national movements evidenced a willingness to support your plan?

ABILEAH: Yes. I have talked with several members of the political committees of the Palestine Liberation Organization and also with members of the so-called "rejectionists." Without daring to commit themselves, they expressed the view that the confederation idea might constitute a positive first step towards the realization of a democratic state in Palestine. Moreover, they indicated that if the proposed confederation resembled the system in Switzerland, they could accept it without losing face. They realize that such a confederation would entail compromise, that they would have to abandon many of the declared aims of their movement. However, they also realize that Israel would have to make similar concessions, which would satisfy their sense of justice.

ELLIOT: Are you optimistic over the prospects of Arab-Israeli co-existence?

ABILEAH: I am optimistic in terms of peaceful co-existence provided that we can work out a suitable political framework. This cannot be the same pattern which was invented in the nineteenth century and which precipitated two world wars. We cannot turn the wheels back. We must look ahead to a new world order. We must be prepared to adapt our policies to the realities of the twenty-first century. If, however, we continue to accept the idea of the nation-state, then I see a bleak future ahead.

Before discussing how the plans for this confederation have been publicized in Israel and abroad for the past seventeen years and what the reception has been, it is good to pause to consider the worldview that is implicitly present in the interview, because without knowing Joseph's religious and philosophical base, one cannot hope to get a full picture of him as a peacemaker. As in all things, there is a connection between the goal and the means of attaining that goal. As stated earlier, Joseph believes that a new structure can be based on nonviolence, peace, and social justice. After a long struggle, he has reconciled these principles with his religious beliefs.

One way of examining these difficulties is to see how the universal humanism characteristic of Joseph's Judaism came to be at odds with what happened to Judaism under the impact of the nation-state structure of Israel. His desperate struggle against the partition plan is part of a struggle to hold on to his own beliefs in Zionism and Judaism, even as it was a struggle against what he correctly saw as a guarantee of endless strife between Arab and Jew. Recent historians of Zionism like Bernard Avishai have observed that Zionism, as it moved towards the nation-state, became less universal. Avishai, in *The Tragedy of Zionism*, sees the loss of ideals of labor Zionism (a secular, classless, propertyless society informed by social justice for all its members) replaced by values of statism (xenophobic exaltation of the military achievement, pride in lack of cultural diversity, etc.). Joseph sensed this change in the late 1940s, and his abhorrence of a nationalistic socialism led him to such verbal excess that at times he sounded almost anti-Zionist.

But there are many Zionisms, and while he rejected the new definitions of Zionism, which sounded more and more like those espoused by Ze'ev Jabotinsky and his followers, he tried to remain true to the spiritual and cultural Zionism of the Second Aliyah. As he grew older and felt the need to define for his audiences the spiritual base from which he operated, he came to believe that his religion was a Judaism practiced by the early Christians. His long conversations with Nathan Chofshi, who was a true biblical scholar, helped Joseph realize that the sort of brotherhood he felt, experienced, and worked for had deep Jewish roots. Christianity had no exclusive right to speak of the radical path of love because, after all, Jesus was a Jew. His Sermon on the Mount is seen by Christians as a radical break with the past, but for Joseph, it was the logical extension of post-Babylonian Jewish thought. The messianism present in that line of thought has always inspired Joseph and has made him feel that he was and is a genuine Zionist, though one who has learned from the inspiration of the men and women of other religions.

In an effort to explain his kind of Judaism and Zionism and how his own pacifism could not only be reconciled with it but also be seen to grow out of it, Joseph wrote "Le Judaisme et la Non-violence" for a French Fellowship of Reconciliation (FOR) publication in 1981. This brief essay, in which he seeks Jewish roots for nonviolence, reminds one of Arie Eliav's *Shalom: Peace in the Jewish Tradition* and represents a good statement of Joseph's own credo.

He begins the essay by noting that, while the Jewish religion is not "a pacifist philosophy," nonetheless there is from the beginning a desire for peace and a desire to avoid violent conflict. Abraham, Genesis 13:8-9, tries to avoid a conflict with his nephew Lot, and Jacob tries to be reconciled with Esau. Yet most of the desire for peace was accompanied by fear. The fear usually meant that one hand offered peace while the other rested on the sword, Nehemiah 4:17. Genuine peace can come only if it is offered with both hands, and the precondition for this step would be the loss of fear. Because even the word *peace* means many things to many persons, Joseph goes on to explain the many meanings of the word *shalom*—peace, as it is used in the early Hebrew scriptures. The word often referred to a completed state—being at peace—which also sometimes meant being secure. This kind of peace could be attained by violence, since what was important was the end, the state of security, and not the means. Because there was no necessary connection between means and ends, there was no necessary connection between peace and nonviolence. Modern slogans, such as "There is no way to Peace; Peace is the way," meant little to those in the Hebrew scriptures who, in their longing for security, did not renounce the sword.

According to Joseph's reading of the Hebrew scriptures, it was only in the period of the Babylonian exile that Jews, perhaps under the influence of Zoroastrianism (which in turn had been influenced by other eastern religions), came to the realization that an eye for an eye, a tooth for a tooth, could be tempered by mercy. At the same time, Jewish thought embraced the notion of love and forgiveness that went beyond family, tribe, and nation. In this period, until the destruction of the Second Temple, "the great prophets preached forgiveness rather than reprisal, love for one's enemy and a God of all nations and not just the exclusive God of Israel." These five hundred years represent the period in which Joseph finds the roots of his universal, messianic Judaism.

He believes that Jesus had his roots there as well. The Talmud commentators on the Bible were also rooted here. Thus, in their commentary, Aaron becomes a model of a man of peace. He reconciles enemies by going to each separately to tell each what the other had said in praise of him. Yet the Talmudic writers were convinced that true peace would come only with the Messiah, and hence they could justify war in certain situations, even though they did not glorify it. For Joseph, such glorification came about only with the birth of the nation-state. For Joseph, the beautiful prayer of Reform Judaism—"Give us peace, your most precious gift, O eternal source of peace. Let Israel be a messenger to all the people of the world. Bless our nation so that it may always be a fortress of peace and an intercessor in the council of nations"—has been undercut by the structure of the nation-state. Too much emphasis had been placed on the fortress, on the notion of peace as security, and not enough on peace as a transforming power that melts hostility. Only those who have faith in the human heart can realize that to make peace one needs to offer both hands, not keep one resting on the sword. In Joseph's lifetime, peace on the part of both Jews and Arabs had been at best a one-handed gesture.

The essay continues with a description of his own two-handed gestures in 1936 and 1947 (the well near Ben Shemen and the bath at Wadi Maleh). Only at such a time, when gestures like these spread, will we "be able to say that we were people chosen by God to set such an example, as one of our own (Jesus) did more than 1900 years ago." The true hero, according to Rabbi Nathan, is he who converts his enemy to a friend. As Jesus proclaimed in the Sermon on the Mount, "If you love only those who love you, what reward do you deserve?" Joseph ends the essay and this belief description of his belief in love and nonviolence, a belief that has informed his whole life and work, by quoting a letter he received from Nathan Chofshi in 1969, soon after Joseph had dedicated whatever life was left to him to the search for a political structure for peace.

> You read me yesterday a letter from a stranger in which he said that the Bible tells us various things and according to the correspondent's interpretation, it leans towards violence. You replied that it contains everything. As you were in a hurry, I left my reply until today. Those who say the Bible establishes this or that don't know their scripture, or else they are demagogues. The Bible is neither a legislator nor a pedagogue. It is divided into two parts: the Laws, which the Talmud has fundamentally changed by adding humanitarian elements, and there is not a

Rabbi in the world who is going to judge according to the Laws of the Bible, but only according to the Talmud, which interprets the Bible in its own fashion. Only the Samaritans and Karaites held exclusively to the Bible. The rest of the Bible in its first part is composed of the history of people and events, with high and low points, and the atmosphere is still primitive—idolatrous. Violence there is dominant. One finds sparks of goodness, but one could not judge according to this part and say "The Bible tells us thus and so." The one who has read deeply sees morality there, an allusion against violence, and he who understands it feels it.

But in the part of the Bible we call the late prophets, one finds a true world of purity, and it is there that there is an ethical Judaism at once Jewish and universal, not one or the other. I will never say "The Bible says that," but it is our prophets who have made prophecies for us and for all peoples. Among the prophets there is no deviation from the eternal truths from their time to ours, and there we hear time and again the vision of peace between individuals, between one nation and another, between men and woman and every thing that lives. This is my summary, albeit a brief one, on this delicate subject.

Joseph has always responded to the words of late prophets like Jeremiah and Isaiah, who offer peace through love and reconciliation as the supreme good. He treasures the words of Hillel, who defined the essence of the Torah itself as "Thou shalt love thy neighbor as thyself." Shalom for Joseph has never meant a state but a process, a power of transformation, whereby enemies become friends, swords are beaten into ploughshares, and men study war no more. Thus, it seems logical to him that the confederation he has proposed is built upon the friendship of one's neighbors, a structure that discourages xenophobic possessiveness and fear and encourages the cooperation that lies within the grasp of every person who would live according to his or her heart.

Having discussed the ideas and beliefs that inform the proposal for the Society for Middle East Confederation, it is now time for us to turn to the activities through which the society hoped to spread its ideas. Between the years 1971 and 1987, Joseph made thirteen lecture tours abroad. He also worked among Arabs and Jews in Israel and the West Bank and Gaza, speaking wherever he was invited. There are certain characteristics that all the trips abroad seem to share, as do some of the activities at home. When on his trips to Europe and America, Joseph undertook a lecture schedule that would do in the ordinary traveler. Traveling with just a small suitcase, he rushed at an unbelievably hectic pace from city to city. Overbooked, he was extremely thankful for the few times when lectures were canceled, yet he was also pleased that most of the tours were extremely well planned in advance. Because he did not like the idea of spending money on travel and lodging, he took the cheapest transportation and stayed in hostels or with friends. The chronicle of each year, meticulously kept in extensive travel diaries, reveals his delight at meeting new people, seeing new places, and establishing his own personal peace network around the world. The experiences he had on his travels confirmed him in the road he had taken and deepened his commitment to nonviolence. Just as importantly, the persons he met convinced him that he was not alone.

The solidarity with peacemakers abroad was extremely important to Joseph because he had trouble receiving an enthusiastic reception for his ideas in Israel. Many friends criticize him for not working harder with Israeli groups, but he spoke wherever and whenever he was asked; and while he might have pushed harder to talk with hard-line groups in the Israeli right, he did his best. The reception that audiences gave him tended to vary according to the political climate within a given year. This variance had always been true of his reception in Israel. In 1955, for example, he was asked by the municipality of Haifa to give a series of lectures commemorating the eightieth birthday of Dr. Albert Schweitzer. Joseph seized the opportunity to talk about Schweitzer's ethics and how his universalism challenged both the notion of right by conquest and the structure of the nation-state. The lecture series was quickly canceled after Joseph had delivered just the first two. Israel, on the eve of the expansionist Suez War for the Sinai, was not ready to hear about Schweitzer's politics, though they were quite open to learning more about his music and humanitarian activities in Africa. Joseph could not separate Schweitzer's music from his pacifism any more than he could separate the two in his own life.

When, as we have seen, Israel acquired through war vast amounts of new territory in 1967, people seemed open to new ways of achieving peace. Similarly, for a brief period of time after the 1973 war, when Israel felt that it might be more vulnerable militarily than it had previously thought, there was some receptivity to the idea of confederation. In 1977, when Sadat made his dramatic visit to Jerusalem, things looked up for the society, and there was some interest after the Lebanese War of 1982. On the whole, however, the idea of a confederation has never been able to overcome the skeptical response of groups whose fears have led them to maintain known strategies for survival rather than embrace those that involve a great deal of risk.

These years convinced Joseph that at home he had to become part of a peace network to gain wider acceptance, and so he established links with many of the new peace groups springing up in Israel, especially those that stressed Arab and Jewish reconciliation at the grass-roots level. Among these groups he has had the satisfaction of seeing his ideas discussed, and several public figures have talked of confederation, from Shimon Peres to the editor of the Arabic newspaper *Al-Fajr*, Hanna Siniora. Still, no young person has come along to whom Joseph could leave the work of the society. Aaron Kamis, who for a while looked as if he would be Joseph's successor, has moved to Switzerland; and though he is secretary of the Friends of the Society for Middle East Confederation, he is removed from the part of the world where he would do the most good. Similarly Saba Shami, who was sent with Joseph's help to study in the United States, decided to stay and become a U.S. citizen. Arie Hess, a Jerusalemite very active in the Labour party, remains the best hope for carrying on the fight within Israel itself, though his commitment to the political solution does not appear to have the same philosophical foundation as Joseph's own, despite the similarity in confederal plans.

After the August 1971 meeting, Joseph undertook a four-month tour abroad, propagating the new society and gathering support through membership and funding. It was at this time, for example, that Dr. Martin Niemöller agreed to become an international sponsor. Dinah was with Joseph as he began his trip in London with an address to the Commonwealth of World Citizens conference. After addresses arranged by various English peace groups, including the Fellowship of the Friends of Truth, headed by Ruth Richardson of Birmingham, who was to remain a friend and supporter in the following years, Joseph visited the Hesbjerg Peace Research College in Denmark and the International Peace Research Institute in Oslo. It was in Oslo that his old WRI friend, Johan Galtung, arranged a seminar on Middle East peace possibilities. Galtung, one of the famous international names in the field of peace research, was later to embrace a Middle East peace plan that was similar to Joseph's own.

One incident during the European trip is worth describing in detail to throw light on the kind of impact Joseph could make on an audience. He had gone to a Quaker quarterly meeting in Langenburg, Germany, and was asked if he would visit the youth prison at Schwäbisch Hall. He was asked to give a short talk on the subject of fear, and he cited his own experiences in the thirties and forties of how fear could be overcome with friendship and love. After he talked, he heard music whose power has remained a vivid memory with him ever since. Two of the prisoners played with such conviction and passion that Joseph was reminded, as he was when performing Beethoven, that true and great art always arises from suffering. What Joseph did not realize was that he was in part responsible for the power of that music. He denies that his talk had anything to do with the way the two musicians performed, but others in attendance have a different version of what happened. Rosalie

Regen, writing in the *Friends Journal* of April 1972, described Joseph's impact when he finished his speech by telling the prisoners how the power of nonviolence lay within anyone's grasp, as did the power to overcome fear,

> Suddenly great waves of sound washed over us. The prisoners responded to Joseph's message with a powerful pounding of feet and arms against floor and benches. It was an ecstatic roar of approval and affirmation. They had been moved deeply; I felt lifted up as if to heaven's gates in a great surge of joy.
>
> In this highly charged atmosphere, two prisoners, Martin Hetz and Gerhard Wissman, played their guitars and sang, "I Like How You Look, I Don't Want to Leave You Now," and "Hush, Little Baby" from *Porgy and Bess*, with their own variations, which seemed to us more poignant than the original. They screwed up their faces in emotion. Blond Bob moaned; dark, intense Gerhard, his guitar held in front of him, played grace notes as a counterpoint to Bob's intent singing.
>
> The response was deafening, until the pastor reminded us that we should not applaud—this was a church. One encore was allowed, and then a group of us Quakers sang "We Shall Overcome."

On his trip to the United States, Joseph was delighted to meet peace workers like Viktor Pashkis, of Fellowship Farm; Thalia Stern, AFSC Middle East peace worker in Miami; and Jeanne Gevaert, a talented sculptress and world citizen from Atlanta. But he spent a great deal of time trying to establish political contacts. In Washington, D.C., he spoke with members of the state department and to the aides and offices of Senators George McGovern and Mark Hatfield. Senator McGovern, in spite of his own busy schedule, had a private meeting with Joseph and expressed interest in his ideas. In Washington, D.C., he had a productive meeting with the famous journalist I. F. Stone and met with Dr. John Davis, who had been the head of United Nations Works and Relief Agency (UNWRA). Many of his lectures were arranged by the Hillel Foundation on university campuses.

Some of the Hillel groups had received pressure not to invite him as a speaker, but almost all the rabbis in charge of them felt that his message should be heard, if for no other reason than that Jewish students needed to hear minority as well as mainstream Israeli ideas. After speaking at the Massachusetts Institute of Technology and at Brandeis University, the major Jewish university in the United States, Joseph was asked by the prestigious *Christian Science Monitor* to write an article explaining his plans for a confederation. The article appeared in March 1972.

In general, American and European audiences were receptive to his views, especially because they were delivered in a gentle manner and with great personal conviction. He never responded defensively or angrily to attacks, and by thus disarming his critics, he won respect for the integrity of his nonviolent life if not for the details of his peace plan. One Arab student did say to his companions, "We did not know of such moderate views in the Israeli sector. Should we not tell our countrymen about these minority groups and embark ourselves on a similar course?" Rarely did people leave the talks in protest, a notable exception being in Basel, Switzerland, where after Joseph had explained the four pillars of his faith, on which the bridge to peace are supported (brotherhood and sisterhood of all humanity; sanctity of human life; nonviolence and truth; good means required for good ends), he was asked by someone if that meant that Egyptians were his brothers. When Joseph replied without hesitation, "Of course, they are my brothers," his questioner left the gathering.

There were others who left the society. During the early stages of the society's meetings, more than twelve Arab members of the Israeli Communist party expressed interest in the plan of confederation. When Joseph and others made it clear that the society required a commitment to nonviolence in the implementation of its goals, all the communists, with the exception of Assam Abassi, a personal friend to Joseph, stopped coming to the meetings. Even Abassi, editor of *Ittihad*, the communist newspaper, left the group one year later. Although the society was officially founded on January 9, 1972, Israeli public interest in Joseph's proposals was already on the wane. Over the years, the society lost about as many members as it gained and now numbers only about two hundred.

Joseph did his best to fight this general drift towards indifference. In 1972, the society presented a biweekly forum in Haifa's Baptist Center for discussion of various confederative solutions. The results of these discussions were published in a small pamphlet in 1973. Because the society was not committed to a single political plan, eight different approaches were put forth. One of these, which had earlier appeared in a truncated form in *The Jerusalem Post*, was by Naftali Bein.

Bein was a well-known political figure in the Independent Liberal party who had, in 1933, traveled with a delegation of Palestinian Jews to Transjordan in an effort to buy land for Jewish settlement. His travels took him the length and breadth of the country; and while they produced no tangible results, they left him with a conviction that, from a geopolitical perspective, Transjordan and Palestine should be united as one country. Like Joseph, Bein believed that the Jordan River was not a natural border but a vein running through the heart of the country. Also like Joseph, Bein advocated a Middle East federation as an example for other nations to follow. "The writer is convinced that the peace of the world can be ultimately secured only through a system of voluntary federations of free nations, culminating finally in a federal world government, which should hold, in its hands, by proxy, the ultimate military power of the world." Bein is unambiguous in this article in his belief that confederation is the only way to peace. "If we genuinely want peace, security and the integrity of the character of our own state within the wholeness of the Holy Land, within its historical borders on both sides of the Jordan—as we do—and if the Arabs demand a similar status for themselves—as they do—then both parties can have that only in the form of an economic and political federation of two independent states, Israel on the one hand, and an Arab-Palestinian-Jordan state on both sides of the Jordan, on the other."

Bein, who had political influence within his party, managed to convince the Liberal leadership, which in 1976 had four members in the Knesset, to include a federal solution in its party platform. At the last moment before the 1977 election, fearing a negative reaction from voters who were obviously swinging to the right, the Independent Liberal party withdrew the proposal from its platform. Ironically, their representation after the election was reduced from four to one. Joseph, who normally does not engage in wistful "what-might-have-beens," wonders what might have been the situation if the proposal had been left in and if the Liberal seats had been increased from four to five. At the very least, the issue would have had a serious airing and debate.

With the formal beginnings of the society in 1972, Joseph felt he needed more time for his political work than the extended holiday he took every year from the symphony and conservatory. In 1972, he made his final break from teaching and performing, yet it would be incorrect to say he ever broke with music. His evenings were filled with chamber music, and music continued to nourish other phases of his life. For example, he often began political lectures with a short musical piece. Once, when someone was trying to assess the language in which Joseph was most comfortable, Joseph replied that his mother tongue was German, his formal education was in French, and the languages of his daily life were Hebrew and, to a lesser degree, Arabic. The frustrated interviewer asked, "But what is the language of your prayers?" To this Joseph replied, "Music." Music remains the inspirational force behind his work as he attempts to translate harmony from the musical score to the living world.

In the first months of 1972, Joseph met with many young people in Israel, including students from universities in Jerusalem and Haifa. He took some of them into the West Bank to meet with Arab leaders and promoted Arab-Israeli dialogue whenever he could. It was in 1972 that he first visited Neve Shalom, the only intentional living community in Israel set up by Muslims, Christians, and Jews. Foreign groups of students, especially from Germany, sought Joseph as a guide, a translator, and a contact with Arabs and with those in the Israeli peace movement. One group was the Aktion Sühnezeichen-Friedendienste, a group of young Germans who volunteered for two years' service in countries affected by the terrible years of Nazi power. He has maintained close ties with them and was a special guest at the 1986 reception that marked the completion of twenty-five years of service in Israel.

After completing a short trip to Germany in September 1972, where he had been invited back to the International Friendship House in Bückeburg to mediate an Israeli-Arab-German encounter, Joseph returned to plan for a more extensive tour abroad in 1973. Late in the year, Dinah suffered an accident that changed his plans. That year Effie had been an exchange student in the United States, but while she studied in America, she also had to keep up with her work in Israel. To help her do so, Dinah used to go over to her classmates' homes each day to take their lecture notes back to be copied. One day, her copying kept her so late that she had to rush to the railway station to catch a train to Tel Aviv, where she was to join Joseph at a family wedding. In the rush to make the train connection, she slipped from the pavement into the path of an automobile. She suffered a serious fracture of the leg, which took more than one and one-half years to heal. Joseph was her nurse during the whole period of her immobility.

Even though his movements were restricted, he still managed to participate in peace activities that were important to him. He went to Europe in 1973 for thirty-three lectures and again in 1974 for sixty-five. During these trips, he tried to deepen support for his ideas abroad, even though he was somewhat discouraged about his lack of progress at home. He counted on these tours not only to put the pressure of world opinion on the Israeli government but also to produce some revenue for his activities at home. While his lecture fees were always modest and his mode of travel just a cut above his travels in India, he had to count on gifts, membership fees, and honoraria to keep both the society and his own family going. Every trip more than met his expenses and usually produced later funding. By 1976, he was receiving annual contributions from Swiss, Dutch, and German Quaker groups as well as from the American Friends Service Committee, the Mennonite Central Committee, and, since 1977, the Brethren Service Commission. By 1983, more than 90 percent of his budget came from abroad, which meant that staying in touch with these groups was essential, though keeping up with the correspondence was increasingly difficult. He did not get rich from these ventures. He charged the society only seventeen dollars a month for his office and not more than one hundred dollars a month for his services as secretary. While he could have used the additional income from music during this period, he also could not possibly have nursed Dinah and kept up with his work for the society had he also had to give lessons and perform with the Haifa Symphony Orchestra. Guests continued to stream through the front door, but they probably never suspected what a toll their presence was taking on their hosts' meager resources.

On the Israeli front, Joseph spent 1973 working for the rights of citizens of Ikrit and Bir'am and, in the summer, helped to organize a successful work camp at Jdeide, an Arab town in the western Galilee. The work camp constructed a playground for the town and was one of the first successful undertakings of Father Elias Chacour. The interfaith cooperation in planning and running the camp brought back memories of the successful work-camp activities of the fifties, and this camp, as well as the one the next summer for the Arab inhabitants of Lod, received support from the Israeli branch of the WRI and financial backing from private individuals and from groups like the German Quakers. When the Jdeide project was finished, the group realized that it needed a fence around the playground to keep it safe for the very young and to discourage using it as a place to dump rubbish. An appeal to Yehudi Menuhin for help brought the funds needed for the fencing material.

It is important to remember that these camps represented constructive reconciling activity that "sandwiched" the 1973 October War. In the years 1973 and 1974 there was more interest within Israel for the society's proposals because of the sudden and almost catastrophic war with Egypt. The myth of Israeli military invincibility was severely shaken; and when Arie Eliav, former secretary of the Histadrut and an influential Knesset member, told Joseph that his name could be used as one who in the Knesset favored the proposal for confederation, it seemed that at last a public debate might take place. But although the society received a small increase in membership, the Israeli public as a whole swung in the direction of strengthening Israel's defenses so that they would never be surprised as they were on October 6, 1973. Few seemed interested in the long-term goal of creating conditions of a positive peace, and Joseph's plans were thwarted by a decided shift to support for right-wing opinions. Sometimes it was hard to think of going against the tide, but incidents occurred that gave him strength to continue.

One such incident was a meeting in 1974 in Switzerland with Lore Steinestel Abbady. Joseph had first met Lore Steinestel, a young German from Stuttgart, when he received her in his home in Haifa in 1971. She subsequently married an Egyptian, Sayed Abbady, and moved to Port Said. During the October War, she was evacuated from Port Said and sent to Switzerland. There she went to hear Joseph lecture. After the meeting, she went up to him and told him how desperate she was both for reunification with her husband, who had stayed behind in Port Said, and for reassurance that one day these wars would end. Still hanging on his words of hope, she accompanied Joseph to the train station. As he looked out from the window of the train, his last sight was of her beseeching eyes. Loyalty to those eyes—as to the eyes of Mrs. Jaber, who on her death bed asked Joseph to continue to work so that mothers would not be separated from their children as she had been from hers; and to the eyes of the young mother in Tel Aviv, who tearfully thanked Joseph for giving words to her deepest hopes for a peaceful country, where Israeli mothers would not have to wonder which of their sons would survive the war—all these eyes made Joseph feel he had the obligation to pursue his work. He realized as he lectured at home and abroad that, while parties and governments and even organizations rejected his ideas, these same ideas were held by the ordinary people of the world. His dream was not a solitary one, and when dreams are not solitary, they have a chance of becoming real.

Joseph's second lecture tour to the United States in 1975 brought him audiences that, in many ways, were more receptive than they had been in 1971, even when Israeli audiences were becoming less so. He had received backing from the Mennonites for this trip, especially because his plans were to be on the same lecture platform with Ibrahim Sima'an, who had replaced Wajdi-Farid Tabari as chairman of the society. The Mennonite Central Committee (MCC) had hoped to show the American public living proof that Arab-Jewish cooperation was possible, and when at the last minute Ibrahim had to cancel the trip because of his wife's illness, the MCC cut down on some of their responsibilities for organizing the tour as a whole. Other groups took up the slack, and Joseph gave seventy lectures in a thirty-nine-day period. Highlights were talks in California and Florida, where his constructive approach to the future seemed to instill a new spirit into Jewish and Arab groups that had been sharply at odds with one another. One California spectator wrote to a friend, "The power of nonviolent reason was proven. Joseph Abileah played God's servant as Martin Luther King, Albert Schweitzer and Gandhi had. I place Joseph in that group as I hope I can you and myself and many others when we allow the power of truth and love to express itself."

In Washington, D.C., Joseph made his second visit to Congress, this time in the company of George Assousa, a Palestinian, and Yossi Ben-Dak, an Israeli, who were coleaders of a new association, the Foundation for Arab-Israeli Reconciliation (FAIR), which promoted a tripartite confederation scheme. This initial contact with FAIR was encouraging to Joseph, but the organization lasted only a short while as its leaders adopted different stances. Unfortunately, such setbacks were not new to Joseph, but he carried on. When organizations let him down, there always seemed to be people who picked him up again.

One such person was Joe Maizlish, who lived in a small one- to two-room apartment and drove around in a car that seemed destined to fail any automobile inspection. Joe had a consuming passion for justice and was active in West Coast peace groups. One day in 1981, he discovered that he had inherited part interest in an orange grove in Israel. When he checked on this land, Joe Maizlish discovered that it had been confiscated from Arabs in 1948. Although he was a man of modest means, Maizlish decided he could not keep money earned on land he did not genuinely believe was his own. Consequently, he turned over his share of the profits every year to Joseph and the society to use as they saw fit for building bridges between Arabs and Jews. A notable use of one year's proceeds was to begin a school building for the Ein Hilweh camp in Lebanon, a refugee camp that had been almost destroyed during the 1982 war in Lebanon. Joseph and Ibrahim Sima'an took the money and purchased a module for one room. Then they used that one room to attract support for the construction of the whole school. Private individuals in Israel and the government itself, along with the UN, contributed enough to build a school. The most important of these individuals was Dov Yermiya, author of *My War Diary*, a moving account of an Israeli's moral struggle with the 1982 invasion of Lebanon. Yermiya, a lieutenant colonel in the Israeli Defense Forces, was assigned to civilian relief during the war. As part of his activities, he rasied funds for nine classrooms. The Israeli government eventually stepped in with funding for three more rooms and the UNO provided funds for furniture and salaries for the teaching staff.

Maizlish did not at the time want his name made public, but it is important to name him because he is one of many individuals who form a network with Joseph and who, like Joseph, are peace workers unknown to the public but honored by those who come within the orbit of their lives. In a part of the world where so much destruction occurs, it is important to memorialize those whose lives have been dedicated to creation, not only for what they themselves have done but because they suggest that perhaps there are many more who may be working in the same way.

Joseph believes that there are others and keenly feels his fellowship with workers for peace whom he has never met, as well as with countless numbers who are now his friends. The list of people he encountered in these years includes famous figures in the peace movement like Joan Baez, Scott Kennedy, Martin Niemöller, John Davis, Jim Forest, Allan Solomonow, I. F. Stone, Johan Galtung; but it includes others whose names are not as well known but whose lives have touched those who have felt the warm light of their spirit. People like Reverend Martin England, a Baptist minister from South Carolina; Willi and Margreth Halli and Liesel and Joseph Mertens from Germany; Ida and Abe Kaufman and Thalia Stern (Broudy) from Florida; Alan Carnoy of California; Rabbi Michael Robinson of Croton-on-Hudson, New York; and Ruth Richardson of Birmingham, England. To each of these names belongs a story, but we must be content to name them as one names the precious threads that weave the fabric of peace. And in doing so, we must not forget the threads contributed by people living in the Middle East: Sister Marie Goldstein, Elias Jabbour, Kamil Shehadeh, Aaron Kamis, Amos Gvirtz, Mubarak Awad, and others already mentioned. And to these persons should be added the names of organizations that form a part of Joseph's peace network: the Quakers, the Mennonites, the FOR and IFOR, and the WRI and ILHCR have been discussed; but there are many other groups like Viktor Pashkis's Fellowship Farm, Ned Hanauer's Search for Justice and Equality in the Middle East, the Women's International League for Peace and Freedom, the Committee to Bridge the Gap, Alan Carnoy's Association for Peace in the Middle East, the Communauté de l'Arche, the Peace Village of Ste. Dorothéa in Switzerland, the Meditran, the International Vegetarian Society; also Neve Shalom and Shutafut (Partnership) whose work has intersected with Joseph's own and who have given him important encouragement to carry on.

There are many times when he needed this strength. On April 26, 1978, he took a group of young Germans working in Israel to visit the West Bank. They hired a bus from an Arab company that had bought an old Israeli bus and had repainted it. Some of the Hebrew letters showed through the paint, and when the bus got to Nablus, people became suspicious of it. Thinking that it was full of Israelis, someone threw a bomb through a window. Two young people, Suzanne Zahn and Christoph Gaede, were killed, and Christoph's brother, Dietrich, lost the sight of one eye and suffered damage to the other. Fortunately, Joseph had left the bus minutes before the blast to get transportation back to Haifa. He heard nothing of the attack until he got home, where a frantic Dinah, not knowing if he had still been on the bus, met him with the news of the tragedy. In a part of the world that never ceases to surprise one with its cruel ironies, the fact that this group of young Germans, who in their efforts to promote healing and to atone for the crimes of their own country through their work with Aktion Sühnezeichen-Friedendienste, had come to the West Bank to hear the Palestinian point of view and had been mistaken for Israelis seemed a cruel blow to those who believed in the possibility of peace. It appeared to confirm the worst fears of those who thought Arab-Jewish reconciliation was a dangerous and fruitless undertaking. Joseph was devastated by the event and vowed never to arrange a trip for any foreigners again to the West Bank. Dietrich Gaede, the remarkable young survivor, refused to blame Joseph or anyone else for the tragedy. Quick action by the Israeli army had saved the sight of one of his eyes, and the Israeli government has given him a pension to help compensate for the loss he suffered; but when he was asked to make a public statement about the incident, he asked for attention to be paid to the conditions that made such terrorism possible. Though almost blind, he courageously held to a vision that sought to "take away the occasion of all wars," and as Joseph played the viola at a memorial service for the victims, his own eyes could barely see the score, blinded as they were by tears caused by guilt, regret, and, curiously, hope. The example of Dietrich impressed upon him once again that, at the moment of darkest tragedy and cruelest irony, the light of hope, the "divine sparkle" in the human heart, manifested in Dietrich's ability to forgive, could continue to assert itself.

Later in 1979, Joseph made another trip to America and Europe, his second in two years. In fifty-one lectures and fourteen interviews he reached more than thirty-four hundred listeners. After the Nablus tragedy, it was good to find audiences receptive to his ideas who also encouraged him to continue his work. A significant event was his participation in a meeting held by the Committee for a Just Peace in the Middle East, where Allan Solomonow of the Middle East Peace Project was debating Mr. Zuhdi Terazi, the PLO ambassador to the United Nations. Joseph was asked from the floor to address the meeting, and many in the audience came away with the conviction that the federal solution was the only way out of the Middle East dilemma. He met a similar response at the Resource Center for Nonviolence in California, where he met with Scott Kennedy, from whom he received one thousand dollars to help with his work.

In the following year, Joseph was able to continue his dialogue with officials of the PLO when, on a trip limited to Europe, he spoke with Daoud Barakat, the PLO representative in Geneva. Before a large audience, they had a frank exchange of ideas. Barakat did not rule out the idea of a confederation, but he insisted that it could come about only after the creation of a Palestinian sovereign state. Barakat's point of view is the one shared by most Palestinians who listen to Joseph. His notion of a confederation is possibly reconcilable with the goal of a secular democratic state, but after forty years of stateless existence, few Palestinians are willing to give up the idea that establishing a sovereign state in the West Bank and Gaza is the first step toward an eventual peace.

Joseph spoke to large audiences, especially after he appeared at the German Book Trade Peace Prize ceremony, which that year was given to Yehudi Menuhin. When Joseph had told Menuhin that he would like to be present at the award, he was sent an invitation. When he arrived at the large hall, Joseph was surprised to find himself escorted to a seat near the platform. In the course of his acceptance of the award, Yehudi Menuhin, with characteristic modesty and humility, told of Joseph and his work, and the television cameras zoomed in on the embarrassed Joseph, who suddenly realized why Menuhin had secured such a good seat for him. Menuhin arranged for Joseph to be seated with the Israeli ambassador later at the awards dinner, so that he could tell him more about his work and ideas.

It was greatly frustrating to be received so well abroad and yet have so much trouble getting a speaking engagement in Israel. In 1981, on the one trip he made to America with Ibrahim Sima'an, he was asked to have a radio discussion with Mohammed Milhem, the deposed mayor of the Palestinian town of Halhul. At the end of the discussion, Joseph was asked to sum up and to give his hopes for the future. When he finished, the interviewer turned to Milhem to ask him for his own concluding remarks. Milhem replied, "I have nothing to add. What this gentleman says comes straight from my heart." In 1982, he was similarly welcomed by Dr. Boutros Ghali, minister for foreign affairs of Egypt. Joseph had heard from his friends Ida and Abe Kaufman that Dr. Ghali appeared to be a believer in a federal solution to the conflict. After trying for several years to arrange a meeting, Joseph, accompanied by Dinah and Jehudith and Meir Sarid, friends from Haifa, met with Ghali on March 28, some two months before the Israeli invasion of Lebanon. Dr. Ghali told Joseph that he had dreamed of a federated Middle East for more than thirty years and that, after a period of normal relations between Egypt and Israel, who had just recently signed the Camp David Accord (1978), he hoped to work for a peace that meant more than just the absence of war between the two countries. More importantly, he confirmed Joseph's belief that it would be the grass-roots organizations like the Society for Middle East Confederation, working amongst the people and not cloistered in academic think tanks, who would be instrumental in creating this peace. Joseph gave Dr. Ghali a selection from the transcript of his dialogue with Daoud Barakat, and Ghali assured him that the Voice of Cairo would report on their meeting with him. The war in June 1982 erased any good that broadcast might have done.

Through the years, Joseph has become an effective public

speaker. The format of his lectures usually divides the time equally between lecture and discussion. His success has often been linked to the manner of his presentation. Though he speaks with conviction, he never gives way to emotions. More importantly, he never reacts to emotional comments and questions in a defensive manner. To veterans of debates on the Middle East, where each side is determined to blame the other as much as possible, it has been refreshing to hear someone who is not so much interested in finding fault as in planning ahead. It is not that he thinks the past is unimportant, for he acknowledges the claim of both Jews and Arabs to the same piece of land, but since each claim is based on historical conquest, he does not find it profitable to spend too much time deciding who has the most rights. Thus in 1971, he wrote to Thalia Stern, who had written him to say how disappointed she had been in a meeting with a Palestinian Quaker who did nothing but dispute the numbers killed in the Holocaust:

> And here we come to the conversation you had with Dr. Mansour at Ramallah. I myself never experienced such unpleasant talk with him. This owing to the fact that I never bring up the negative side and wrong-doings of other people, but always turn to positive, constructive matters. I thereby create a dialogue on what has to be done in the future in order to reach peace. To cut it short: it is not relevant to inquire who first started the dispute, but it is very important to know who will stop first. For me it is not important to fix exactly the correct number of Nazi victims or the number of synagogues destroyed, but to find a way that such things do not happen again.

During one of his lectures in California, he was challenged by a young Palestinian who, not untypically at these occasions, gave a speech under the guise of asking a question. In his diatribe, he mentioned that there were six million Palestinian refugees. It would have been easy for Joseph to correct his figure and perhaps to humiliate him for his lack of accurate historical knowledge. But Joseph has never called anyone a liar during his lectures. Instead, he simply said that he would not get involved in a debate on blame because "there had not been one thing that the Jews experienced from Arabs that we did not do to them.... We want no balance sheet, but only to stop the chain reaction. It may be that many Jews abroad did not know about the massacre of 254 Palestinians in the village of Deir Yssin in 1948, but there are also many Palestinians who did not know about the massacre of 77 Jewish doctors and nurses a few days later on the road leading to the Hadassah Hospital in Jerusalem." It might be argued that this approach at times minimizes the impact of past sufferings, but few can argue that it clears the way for thinking of the future without being chained to the past.

Joseph begs his audiences not to revert to the use of loaded words that can mean many things to different people. He asks each member of his audience to refrain from using slogans and to be logical and clear as they listen to his own simple and pragmatic position. To those people who are able to respond to requests to avoid such words as *terrorism, racism, Zionism*—almost any "ism" as a matter of fact—the effect has been remarkable. Time and time again, people respond both to his simple logic and to the authenticity of its presentation. There is no gap between the moral base from which he speaks and its political projection. The world has grown a bit weary of public figures whose personal lives are often deeply at odds with their public rhetoric, and Joseph awakens the belief that this need not be the case. Though many peace leaders have had feet of clay, the following review of a speech he made on May 23, 1985, in Germany is typical of those listeners who are struck by his integrity. "He is not a bitter prophet of peace nor is he a lone dissenter in his homeland, but young and old who came, invited by Pax Christi, met a man with passion but also with gentleness, a witness of the happenings of the Middle East. And in a humane, convincing way, he strives for reconciliation between Jews and Arabs. He is far from an airy idealist, because he puts analytically the situation by knowing exactly all the historical facts and differences of the mentalities."

The continuing and expanding support from abroad has somewhat offset the frustration of not having his ideas take deeper root in Israel. Arab and Jewish friends who believed in the confederation urged Joseph to spend more time talking with Israelis and less time abroad. Among Israeli Arabs and, to a lesser degree, West Bank Palestinians, his ideas have received a positive hearing, partly because they have answered a deep Palestinian longing for self-determination, an end to discrimination, and the assertion of individual dignity. Anwar El-Khatib wrote to *Qadi* Wajdi-Farid Tabari after Joseph met him in 1967, "I enjoyed meeting Abileah. He is a great man and I would like to see him again."

Such positive words have not come from the mouths of many Israelis. While there are those like Arie Eliav, who shares his dream, or those like Professor Daniel Elazar, who believes in a federal solution to the problem, most Israelis are unwilling to give up the hard-won national sovereignty for something as risky as a confederation. With most Israelis, he has been more interested in his ideas getting a hearing than in having his name associated with them. He possesses the rare gift of absorbing the criticism of his fellow citizens without being too discouraged or personally crushed. He has been able to absorb abuse because he has questioned neither the truth of his own commitment to all his fellow creatures nor the belief that his own plan was one that would one day prevail.

One important convert to his ideas was his wife, Dinah. As we have seen, the early years of their marriage were difficult for her. Because she did not share his ideas, his frequent absences and his disregard for the financial security of his family weighed heavily on her. She never understood his frantic activity at the time of the partition, and she grieved when he refused to read Adi's letters after he had joined the army. There were times when she wondered how long they could live together, though she always loved him deeply. While she did not accept his ideas in the early days of their marriage, she did her best to give him the sort of stable home he needed for his ac-

Joseph and Dinah.

tivities. She even became used to cooking vegetarian meals for him and separate ones for the children and herself.

After 1967, especially after Effie was grown, Dinah became more and more involved with the society. Her participation in work camps had convinced her that one could work for and create peace; and on her trips abroad with Joseph, she became more and more willing to believe that his dreams might one day be realizable. While never totally or enthusiastically in agreement with the aims of the society, she served many hours as its corresponding secretary and helped Joseph keep up with the files of hundreds of correspondents that began to fill the office, which had been the bedroom of her sons. When she broke her leg in 1972 and Joseph attended to her, he realized how much he counted on her and needed her steadiness to keep him going. She had several other serious illnesses during this period, but in 1983, doctors discovered that she had bone cancer. She bore this extremely painful illness with great patience and watched with some amusement as Joseph learned to drive a car to help her get around. The veteran scooter driver required almost three hundred hours of instruction before passing his test. It seems he was too cautious and too willing to waive his rights when on the highway; in this, like everything else in his life, he is consistent. The same man who is willing to waive his national rights in exchange for peace is the one who would waive his driving rights at intersections. Israel has had as much trouble accommodating his driving style as it has his politics.

On May 9, 1986, Dinah died. Though her death was expected, Joseph was shattered by it. She seemed to take much of his strength with her, and friends have been alarmed that perhaps something had broken in Joseph with her death. His old friend *Qadi* Tabari visited him the day after the funeral. He found Joseph on the floor of his bedroom, polishing Dinah's shoes. He had spent all day at it—to give them away. Emptiness and despair came upon him whenever he was alone. Letters from friends all over the world remained unanswered on his desk. He began to wonder if he would ever get back to his work.

In the end, the dream reasserted itself. As he remembered

Joseph Abileah, musician of Haifa. Courtesy of Yossi Yarmus.

the pledge he had made at his brother's grave in 1967, he pledged himself again to the task of peace. In the spring of 1987, he rose above his despair and undertook a strenuous two-month lecture tour of Europe and the United States. While it was painful to visit old friends, he appreciated their efforts to comfort him and turn him to the future. It was also heartening to rediscover that there was an audience for his ideas and an urgency that they be implemented before the state of affairs in the Middle East grew worse. He faces the future still holding fast to his vision and to his faith in the human heart, but he is apprehensive about who will accompany him on his journey or take over from him when he is gone. Dinah's death appears to have impressed him with how solitary he can be, even at a time when the greatest solidarity imaginable is needed. His work is not yet done.

8
The True Victories

> To believe in God is easy. But to believe that one day this world will be God's world; to believe this in a faith so firm and resolute as to mold one's life according to it—this requires faithfulness until death.
> —Leonard Ragaz

> If we keep our eyes fixed on the foreground, the true victories, won in secret, sometimes look like defeats. True victories happen slowly and imperceptibly, but they have far-reaching effects.
> —Martin Buber

How DO YOU MEASURE the value of a life? Do you assess the efforts of a peacemaker only by whether peace is achieved in his or her lifetime? If so, Joseph Abileah's lack of success in winning peace in a land he loves so much would seem to cast a shadow over his life and permit the comparison of his activities to those of Don Quixote, tilting at windmills, hopelessly out of touch in a world that has moved beyond magic, knighthood, and ladies in distress. Indeed, the history of Israel might be written without Joseph Abileah appearing even in a footnote. So many things he has worked for have never been realized. Arabs have still not come back to Bir'am, despite a 1952 court ruling that favored their right to return, subject only to the permission of the minister of defense; houses continue to be expropriated and destroyed, even though in 1987 Joseph drove his car through fields of mud to try to stop the demolition of Bedouin homes on Mount Carmel; olive trees continue to be uprooted, despite Joseph's participation in marches designed to insure the protection of the green line, and Jews are stabbed in Gaza markets and in the streets of Jerusalem, despite Joseph's pleading for the use of nonviolence. Each day seems to create more enmity between Arab and Jew. A 1987 poll found that 60 percent of the Israeli Jewish teenagers would refuse to live in the same apartment building as an Arab and that 40 percent would not want to work with an Arab. If the same poll had been taken among Israeli Arabs or Palestinians on the West Bank and Gaza, the percentages would have been even higher. Real peace in the spring of 1987 seemed even farther away than it did in 1947, the year Joseph began in earnest his peacemaking efforts.

The face of the Middle East changed, perhaps forever, on December 9, 1987. The beginning of the Palestinian *intifada* (uprising) occurred when Joseph was in Germany, recovering from a slight stroke he suffered while on a speaking tour. The *intifada*, like many other crises in the state of Israel, appears to offer an opportunity to break out of stale ways of thinking. Somewhat surprisingly, an amazing number of voices have now been heard who advocate confederation between Israel, Jordan, and Palestine as the only viable long-range solution to the conflict. People as diverse as Samuel Lewis, a former United States ambassador to Israel; Hanna Siniora, the Palestinian editor of the Arabic newspaper, *Al-Fajr*; Shlomo El Baz, the head of the Sephardic peace group, East for Peace; and Abba Eban, former Israeli ambassador to the United Nations have all spoken in favor of confederation. The *intifada* has made abundantly clear three important situations: (1) the steadfastness of the Palestinian people's desire to achieve national self-determination; (2) the lack of support for the so-called Jordanian option—a plan to absorb Palestinians into the kingdom of Jordan; and (3) the impossibility of either expelling or absorbing the Palestinians of the West Bank and Gaza into Israel. With a December 1988 decision on the part of the United States to begin talks with the Palestine Liberation Organization, even United States newspapers are printing articles arguing for a confederation.

No one seems to have recognized that the father of the confederation of three states is neither Martin Buber nor Judah

Magnes; it is Joseph Abileah. Joseph continues his long convalescence in Germany while the ideas he fought to realize his whole adult life are no longer regarded as mere pipe dreams; they are being seriously debated as viable political solutions to a seemingly intractable problem. It may be that these ideas, which he despaired of seeing implemented in 1987, will yet bear fruit in his lifetime. If so, the results will be highly gratifying both to him and to others who have shared his dream.

But while results are important, especially because they are quantifiable, they are not the true measure of a human life. When one thinks of Joseph Abileah, one thinks not of shadows but of light. He has not wasted his life in pursuit of an unrealizable dream. His dream has given his life a meaning, and the consistency of his witness has made of his life a thing of beauty. "How beautiful upon the mountains are the feet of him that bringeth good tidings; that publisheth peace," Isaiah 52:7. No one should dismiss Joseph's single-minded pursuit of his truth as grotesque and foolish without looking at that truth itself and how its power has transformed those who observe in Joseph its embodiment. In Joseph's life, the way of achieving the goal is as important as the goal itself. In some respects, the way *is* the goal—the means are the ends.

One can see this tenet by examining one last time the most important pillar of Joseph's faith—the brotherhood and sisterhood of all humankind. He is not unique in his belief nor is he alone in Israel in asserting the common humanity of Arab and Jew. But he has lived his ideal as few have done and has exhibited great staying power. Examine the following passages: "We are not transient wayfarers here. We have come to strike roots in this land, and as we meet its Arab cultivators, who are rooted in it, the roots we are sending down into the ground meet their roots in the depth of the soil, and they cling together and draw nourishment from one source. We, the Jewish and the Arab workers, are sons of one land, and our way of life is intertwined forever." And, "Every person has the right for a homeland and every person must have his roots somewhere. If I feel my roots at the same place as my Arab brother feels his roots, we must find a common way in this common homeland." The metaphor used is the same in each passage, as is the underlying idea. The first passage is more poetic, and its rhetorical beauty makes it sound more persuasive. The first is from the mouth of David Ben-Gurion, speaking at a labor convention in 1924. The second is by Joseph Abileah, conversing with PLO member Daoud Barakat at a debate in Switzerland in 1979. By the time he became the first prime minister of Israel, Ben-Gurion had sunk his roots and had stood by and watched as the Arabs he once claimed as brothers were uprooted, including three hundred thousand in what was determined by the UN partition plan to be the Jewish state in Palestine. The 1979 statement made by Joseph represents a commitment he had held onto and lived by since arriving in Palestine in 1926, and his roots have been forever intertwined with those of his Arab brothers.

In the fall of 1986, Joseph and I were sitting in the restaurant of a petrol station outside the Israeli Arab town of Shefa Amr. We had arrived early for an appointment with Elias Jabbour, and to avoid disturbing him at lunchtime, we decided to eat at the station. As we took our salad plates to the table, I noticed two men eyeing us closely. We had been served with polite coldness by the Arab waiters, and I was beginning to feel uncomfortable and out of place. At last, one of the two men came over to our table and stopped in front of us. "Abileah?" he asked. Joseph replied affirmatively in Arabic, though it was clear from his face that he did not recognize the man. The man broke into a grin and hugged Joseph, who had tentatively risen from his seat. The man insisted that we join him for the rest of our lunch and explained that he had last seen Joseph in 1947, in Haifa. He, Josef Khoury, had been employed by the British, and one day while on his way to work in the midst of heavy fighting between Arabs and Jews, he had been stopped in the street by Joseph, who asked for directions to the Muslim head of the Arab Défense Force. Khoury, who had never met Joseph but had heard of him and had recognized this skinny and bespectacled Jew wearing a white *khaffieh,* had been afraid to accompany Joseph. He gave him directions and hurried away, but he had always remembered him and had followed accounts of his trial and of his peace work in the newspapers. Khoury himself is resigned to second-class citizenship and thinks that his situation will never change, but he expressed admiration and affection for the man who had clung to his own ideals. The other Arab at the table was from the village of Sahnin, where Joseph had gone to comfort victims after the violence of Land Day in 1976. He, too, had heard of Abileah, the "good Jew."

Joseph has earned his status as persona grata in the Palestinian community by his unwavering commitment to brotherhood. A Mennonite minister once met in Beirut a prominent member of the PLO who had come from Haifa. He asked him what life had been like before the partition. The PLO official, Nabil Shaath, said that he left when he was only ten and had few memories, but one memory he had was of a Jewish neighbor, Joseph Abileah, whose example of genuine and peaceful coexistence and manner of treating all Arabs with respect had stayed with him and had led him to believe that, in spite of all the hatred, it might be true that Jews and Arabs could one day live in peace.

What is important about these tributes is not that they speak of Joseph's plan for confederation, which may or may not be realized, but that they bear witness to his person. Many nationalistic Israelis who think his ideas are dangerous for the state still honor him as a person, as a man too good for a brutal world. Israelis on the left end of the political spectrum who have themselves left their country respect his tenacity in pursuing what, to them, is not so much a dangerous as an unfortunately unattainable ideal. His sister-in-law, Miriam, who lives in Canada, wrote, "Pack up dear fellow, your life's work wasn't worth a sou. This is the age of brutality triumphant." Yet Joseph alone, of all those she left behind, commands her affection. It is difficult to know if the seeds he plants will grow in the uncertain soil of Israel/Palestine. But people will remember the sower. *Vebaharta betov,* says the Hebrew—you are able to choose the good.

Joseph is the man of peace who has chosen goodness. He has chosen it from a purity of heart that sparkles in its clarity. John Woolman, an American Quaker, wrote, "There is a Principle which is pure, placed in the human mind, which in different places and ages hath had different names; it is, however, pure, and proceeds from God. It is deep, and inward, confined to no forms of religion, nor excluded from any, where the heart stands in perfect sincerity. In whomsoever this takes root and grows, of what nation soever, they become brethren." This extraordinary purity of heart and clarity of vision suggest affinity not only with Magnes and Buber but also with early Hebrew prophets. But while he shares this vision, which involves the defense of the weak against the mighty and the obligation to work for a society characterized by justice and mercy, he would not want to be remembered as a prophet but as a worker—as one who could not wait until the world was ready, as one who with every ounce of his strength and determination worked for the final triumph of the good. What he learned from Beethoven's symphonies and quartets was that the good will prevail but that one has to work for it. What he learned from his religion, which is at one with his music, is that "the final outcome of the messianic age is not in our hands, but if we work for it, it will come."

Qadi Tabari said of Joseph, "He is a rare Jew of our times. He is a real human being; a true citizen of the world with a heart for everyone. I would love to see one Arab like him who would speak as openly and bravely about relations with the Jews as he does about the Arabs."

In a land created from a dream, Joseph is one of the few remaining dreamers. His mentor, Albert Schweitzer, once said, "One belief of my childhood I have preserved with the certainty that I can never lose it: belief in truth. I am confident that the spirit generated by truth is stronger than the force of circumstances. In my view no other destiny awaits mankind than that which, through its mental and spiritual disposition, it prepares for itself. Therefore I do not believe that it will have to tread the road to ruin right to the end." Like Dr. Schweitzer, Joseph remains an optimist. His life may be proof that humankind has a future. At times when we seem destined to "tread the road to ruin right to the end," it is important to recall that there are those whose lives reveal a different, better way. One can only wish him well as he continues on his journey, sharing his dream with others, moving his dream a few steps closer to reality. His example is enough to suggest that it may one day be possible for men and women to achieve the "true victory"—a life of peace, shalom. Abileah, shalom.

ISRAELI PACIFIST

was composed in 10 on 12½ Trump Medieval on Digital Compugraphic equipment
by Metricomp;
printed by sheet-fed offset on 50-pound, acid-free Glatfelter Natural Hi Bulk
and Smyth sewn and bound over binder's boards in Holliston Roxite B
by Braun-Brumfield, Inc.;
with dust jackets printed in 2 colors
by Braun-Brumfield, Inc.;
and published by
SYRACUSE UNIVERSITY PRESS
SYRACUSE, NEW YORK 13244-5160

WITHDRAWN